STATUTORY SUPPLEMENT

to

FEDERAL PUBLIC LAND

AND

RESOURCES LAW

SIXTH EDITION

By

GEORGE CAMERON COGGINS
Frank Edwards Tyler Professor of Law
University of Kansas

CHARLES F. WILKINSON
Moses Lasky Professor of Law
University of Colorado

JOHN D. LESHY
Harry D. Sunderland Distinguished Professor of Law
University of California
Hastings College of the Law

ROBERT L. FISCHMAN
Professor of Law and Harry T. Ice Faculty Fellow
Indiana University—Bloomington

FOUNDATION PRESS
2007

 *TEXT IS PRINTED ON 10% POST CONSUMER RECYCLED PAPER*

INTRODUCTION

This volume consists of selected and edited provisions of the United States Code which govern the allocation and management of public natural resources. It is designed as a companion to Coggins, Wilkinson, Leshy & Fischman Federal Public Land and Resources Law (6th ed. 2007).

The selection is of statutes we judge of most general significance to students. Many of the laws in the United States Code are applicable to individual tracts or units of federal lands, or deal with narrow or peripheral subjects. Almost without exception, these have not been included.

We have, furthermore, usually edited the included statutes, sometimes ruthlessly, to excise such things as personnel rules, sections containing platitudes urging consultation, advisory committees, detailed enforcement rules, and the like. Excisions within a statute are marked by * * *.

While the gist of the statutes remains, we caution that particular provisions which may be of interest to a researcher or practitioner faced with a specific problem may not be included. Therefore, although this volume can serve as a convenient desk reference for practicing lawyers, we make no pretense that it is comprehensive.

In a few cases, where a statute has well-known sections (e.g., section 7 of the Endangered Species Act) which do not correspond to how it is codified, we have indicated the common section number in brackets preceding the section.

Likewise in a few cases, the codified versions of statutes have footnotes to call out what appear to be typographical or related errors in the text as enacted by Congress. We have included these footnotes.

The Supplement is generally current through Mar. 1, 2007.

Because the field of federal public lands and resources law is heavily informed by history, we have included in an Historical Appendix several important acts of Congress, now repealed, which have had major impact on the evolution of public land law and policy—such as the 1862 Homestead Act, R.S. 2477, and the Pickett Act.

INTRODUCTION

We thank Michael Lynes, Kristin Howse, Scott Miller, Roger Flynn, and Etta Walker for their help in earlier editions.

G.C.C.
C.F.W.
J.D.L.
R.L.F.

Mar. 2007

TABLE OF CONTENTS

TABLE OF CONTENTS

STATUTORY SUPPLEMENT

to

FEDERAL PUBLIC LAND

AND

RESOURCES LAW

*

UNITED STATES CODE

TITLE 5 GOVERNMENT ORGANIZATION AND EMPLOYEES

THE ADMINISTRATIVE PROCEDURE ACT

(5 U.S.C.A. §§ 551–559, 701–706)

* * *

§ 701. Application; definitions

(a) This chapter applies, according to the provisions thereof, except to the extent that—

(1) statutes preclude judicial review; or

(2) agency action is committed to agency discretion by law.

(b) For the purpose of this chapter—

(1) "agency" means each authority of the Government of the United States, whether or not it is within or subject to review by another agency, but does not include—

(A) the Congress;

(B) the courts of the United States;

(C) the governments of the territories or possessions of the United States;

(D) the government of the District of Columbia;

(E) agencies composed of representatives of the parties or of representatives of organizations of the parties to the disputes determined by them;

(F) courts martial and military commissions;

(G) military authority exercised in the field in time of war or in occupied territory; or

(H) functions conferred by sections 1738, 1739, 1743, and 1744 of title 12; chapter 2 of title 41; subchapter II of chapter 471 of title 49; or sections 1884, 1891–1902, and former section 1641(b)(2), of title 50, appendix; and

(2) "person", "rule", "order", "license", "sanction", "relief", and "agency action" have the meanings given them by section 551 of this title.

Pub.L. 89–554, Sept. 6, 1966, 80 Stat. 392; Pub.L. 103–272, § 5(a), July 5, 1994, 108 Stat. 1373.

§ 702. Right of review

A person suffering legal wrong because of agency action, or adversely affected or aggrieved by agency action within the meaning of a relevant statute, is entitled to judicial review thereof. An action in a court of the United States seeking relief other than money damages and stating a claim that an agency or an officer or employee thereof acted or failed to act in an official capacity or under color of legal authority shall not be dismissed nor relief therein be denied on the ground that it is against the United States or that the United States is an indispensable party. The United States may be named as a defendant in any such action, and a judgment or decree may be entered against the United States: Provided, That any mandatory or injunctive decree shall specify the Federal officer or officers (by name or by title), and their successors in office, personally responsible for compliance. Nothing herein (1) affects other limitations on judicial review or the power or duty of the court to dismiss any action or deny relief on any other appropriate legal or equitable ground; or (2) confers authority to grant relief if any other statute that grants consent to suit expressly or impliedly forbids the relief which is sought.

Pub.L. 89–554, Sept. 6, 1966, 80 Stat. 392; Pub.L. 94–574, § 1, Oct. 21, 1976, 90 Stat. 2721.

* * *

§ 704. Actions reviewable

Agency action made reviewable by statute and final agency action for which there is no other adequate remedy in a court are subject to judicial review. A preliminary, procedural, or intermediate agency action or ruling not directly reviewable is subject to review on the review of the final agency action. Except as otherwise expressly required by statute, agency action otherwise final is final for the purposes of this section whether or not there has been presented or determined an application for a declaratory order, for any form of reconsideration, or, unless the agency otherwise requires by rule and provides that the action meanwhile is inoperative, for an appeal to superior agency authority.

Pub.L. 89–554, Sept. 6, 1966, 80 Stat. 392.

§ 705. Relief pending review

When an agency finds that justice so requires, it may postpone the effective date of action taken by it, pending judicial review. On such conditions as may be required and to the extent necessary to prevent irreparable injury, the reviewing court, including the court to which a case may be taken on appeal from or on application for certiorari or other writ to a reviewing court, may issue all necessary and appropriate process to postpone the effective date of an agency action or to preserve status or rights pending conclusion of the review proceedings.

Pub.L. 89–554, Sept. 6, 1966, 80 Stat. 393.

§ 706. Scope of review

To the extent necessary to decision and when presented, the reviewing court shall decide all relevant questions of law, interpret constitutional and statutory provisions, and determine the meaning or applicability of the terms of an agency action. The reviewing court shall—

(1) compel agency action unlawfully withheld or unreasonably delayed; and

(2) hold unlawful and set aside agency action, findings, and conclusions found to be—

(A) arbitrary, capricious, an abuse of discretion, or otherwise not in accordance with law;

(B) contrary to constitutional right, power, privilege, or immunity;

(C) in excess of statutory jurisdiction, authority, or limitations, or short of statutory right;

(D) without observance of procedure required by law;

(E) unsupported by substantial evidence in a case subject to sections 556 and 557 of this title or otherwise reviewed on the record of an agency hearing provided by statute; or

(F) unwarranted by the facts to the extent that the facts are subject to trial de novo by the reviewing court.

In making the foregoing determinations, the court shall review the whole record or those parts of it cited by a party, and due account shall be taken of the rule of prejudicial error.

Pub.L. 89–554, Sept. 6, 1966, 80 Stat. 393.

UNITED STATES CODE

TITLE 16 CONSERVATION

NATIONAL PARK SERVICE ORGANIC
ACT OF 1916 (as amended)

(16 U.S.C.A. §§ 1–18f)

§ 1. Service created; director; other employees

There is created in the Department of the Interior a service to be called the National Park Service, which shall be under the charge of a director who shall be appointed by the President, by and with the advice and consent of the Senate. The Director shall have substantial experience and demonstrated competence in land management and natural or cultural resource conservation. The Director shall select two Deputy Directors. The first Deputy Director shall have responsibility for National Park Service operations, and the second Deputy Direct shall have responsibility for other programs assigned to the National Park Service. The service thus established shall promote and regulate the use of the Federal areas known as national parks, monuments, and reservations hereinafter specified, except such as are under the jurisdiction of the Secretary of the Army, as provided by law, by such means and measures as conform to the fundamental purpose of the said parks, monuments, and reservations, which purpose is to conserve the scenery and the natural and historic objects and the wild life therein and to provide for the enjoyment of the same in such manner and by such means as will leave them unimpaired for the enjoyment of future generations.

Aug. 25, 1916, c. 408, § 1, 39 Stat. 535; Mar. 4, 1923, c. 265, 42 Stat. 1488; Mar. 3, 1925, c. 462, 43 Stat. 1176; Ex.Ord. No. 6166, § 2, June 10, 1933; Mar. 2, 1934, c. 38, § 1, 48 Stat. 389; Nov. 12, 1996, Pub.L. 104–333, Div. I, Title VIII, § 814(e)(1), 110 Stat. 4197.

§ 1a–1. National Park System: administration; declaration of findings and purpose

Congress declares that the national park system, which began with establishment of Yellowstone National Park in 1872, has since grown to include superlative natural, historic, and recreation areas in every major region of the United States, its territories and island possessions; that these areas, though distinct in character, are united through their interrelated purposes and resources into one national park system as cumulative expressions of a single national heritage; that, individually and collectively, these areas derive increased national dignity and recognition of their superb environmental quality through their inclusion jointly with each other in one national park system preserved and managed for the benefit and inspiration of all the people of the United States; and that it is the purpose of this Act to include all such areas in the System and to clarify the authorities applicable to the system. Congress further reaffirms, declares, and directs that the promotion and regulation of the various areas of the National Park System, as defined in section 1c of this title, shall be consistent with and founded in the purpose established by section i of this title, to the common benefit of all the people of the United States. The authorization of activities shall be construed and the protection, management, and administration of these areas shall be conducted in light of the high public value and integrity of the National Park System and shall not be exercised in derogation of the values and purposes for which these various areas have been established, except as may have been or shall be directly and specifically provided by Congress.

Pub.L. 91–383, § 1, Aug. 18, 1970, 84 Stat. 825, as amended Pub.L. 95–250, Title I, § 101(b), Mar. 27, 1978, 92 Stat. 166.

§ 1a–2. Same; Secretary of Interior's authorization of activities

In order to facilitate the administration of the national park system, the Secretary of the Interior is authorized, under such terms and conditions as he may deem advisable, to carry out the following activities:

* * *

Advisory committees; compensation and travel expenses

(c) appoint and establish such advisory committees in regard to the functions of the National Park Service as he may deem advisable, * * *

* * *

Services, resources, or water contracts

(e) enter into contracts which provide for the sale or lease to persons, States, or their political subdivisions, of services, resources, or water available within an area of the national park system, as long as such activity does not jeopardize or unduly interfere with the primary natural or historic resource of the area involved, if such person, State, or its political subdivision—

(1) provides public accommodations or services within the immediate vicinity of an area of the national park system to persons visiting the area; and

(2) has demonstrated to the Secretary that there are no reasonable alternatives by which to acquire or perform the necessary services, resources, or water;

* * *

Regulations; promulgation and enforcement

(h) promulgate and enforce regulations concerning boating and other activities on or relating to waters located within areas of the National Park

System, including waters subject to the jurisdiction of the United States:
* * *

* * *

Cooperative management agreements

(*l*)(1) In general

Where a unit of the National Park System is located adjacent to or near a State or local park area, and cooperative management between the National Park Service and a State or local government agency of a portion of either park will allow for more effective and efficient management of the parks, the Secretary may enter into an agreement with a State or local government agency to provide for the cooperative management of the Federal and State or local park areas. The Secretary may not transfer administration responsibilities for any unit of the National Park System under this paragraph.

* * *

Pub.L. 91–383, § 3, Aug. 18, 1970, 84 Stat. 826; Pub.L. 94–458, § 1, Oct. 7, 1976, 90 Stat. 1939; Pub.L. 104–333, Div. I, Title VII, § 703, Title VIII, § 818, Nov. 12, 1996, 110 Stat. 4185, 4201; Pub.L. 105–391, Title VIII, § 802(a), Nov. 13, 1998, 112 Stat. 3522; Pub.L. 106–176, Title I, §§ 118, Mar. 10, 2000, 114 Stat. 28.

§ 1a–3. Legislative jurisdiction; relinquishment by Secretary; submittal of proposed agreement to congressional committees; concurrent legislative jurisdiction

Notwithstanding any other provision of law, the Secretary of the Interior may relinquish to a State, or to a Commonwealth, territory, or possession of the United States, part of the legislative jurisdiction of the United States over National Park System lands or interests therein in that State, Commonwealth, territory, or possession: *Provided,* That prior to consummating any such relinquishment, the Secretary shall submit the proposed agreement to the Committee on Energy and Natural Resources of the Senate and the Committee on Natural Resources of the House of Representatives, and shall not finalize such agreement until sixty calendar days after such submission shall have elapsed. Relinquishment of legislative jurisdiction under this section may be accomplished (1) by filing with the Governor (or, if none exists, with the chief executive officer) of the State, Commonwealth, territory, or possession concerned a notice of relinquishment to take effect upon acceptance thereof, or (2) as the laws of the State, Commonwealth, territory, or possession may otherwise provide. The Secretary shall diligently pursue the consummation of arrangements with each State, Commonwealth, territory, or possession within which a unit of the National Park System is located to the end that insofar as practicable the United States shall exercise concurrent legislative jurisdiction within units of the National Park System.

Pub.L. 91–383, § 6 as added Pub.L. 94–458, § 2, Oct. 7, 1976, 90 Stat. 1939, as amended Pub.L. 103–437, § 6(a)(1), Nov. 2, 1994, 108 Stat. 4583.

* * *

§ 1a–5. Additional areas for National Park System

Areas of national significance for potential inclusion; investigation and study; transmittal to Congress of report and annual listing of areas, included on Registry of Natural Landmarks and National Register of Historic places, subject to threat of damage; printing as House document; authorization of appropriations

(a) The Secretary of the Interior is directed to investigate, study, and continually monitor the welfare of areas whose resources exhibit qualities of national significance and which may have potential for inclusion in the National Park System. At the beginning of each fiscal year, the Secretary shall transmit to the Speaker of the House of Representatives and to the President of the Senate, comprehensive reports on each of those areas upon which studies have been completed. Each such report shall indicate and elaborate on the theme(s) which the area represents as indicated in the National Park System Plan. On this same date, and accompanying such reports, the Secretary shall transmit a listing, in generally descending order of importance or merit, of not less than twelve such areas which appear to be of national significance and which may have potential for inclusion in the National Park System. Threats to resource values, and cost escalation factors shall be considered in listing the order of importance or merit. Such listing may be comprised of any areas heretofore submitted under terms of this section, and which at the time of listing are not included in the National Park System. Accompanying the annual listing of areas shall be a synopsis, for each report previously submitted, of the current and changed condition of the resource integrity of the area and other relevant factors, compiled as a result of continual periodic monitoring and embracing the period since the previous such submission or initial report submission one year earlier. The Secretary is also directed to transmit annually to the Speaker of the House of Representatives and to the President of the Senate, at the beginning of each fiscal year, a complete and current list of all areas included on the Registry of Natural Landmarks and those areas of national significance listed on the National Register of Historic places which areas exhibit known or anticipated damage or threats to the integrity of their resources, along with notations as to the nature and severity of such damage or threats. * * *

Pub.L. 91–383, § 8, as added Pub.L. 94–458, § 2, Oct. 7, 1976, 90 Stat. 1940, and amended Pub.L. 95–625, Title VI, § 604(1), Nov. 10, 1978, 92 Stat. 3518; Pub.L. 96–199, Title I, § 104, Mar. 5, 1980, 94 Stat. 68; Pub.L. 96–344, § 8, Sept. 8, 1980, 94 Stat. 1135; as amended Pub.L. 103–437, § 6(b), Nov. 2, 1994, 108 Stat. 4583; Pub.L. 104–333, Div. I, Title VIII, § 814(d)(1)(I), Nov. 12, 1996, 110 Stat. 4196.

§ 1a–6. Law enforcement personnel within National Park System

Designation authority of Secretary; powers and duties of designees

(a) In addition to any other authority conferred by law, the Secretary of the Interior is authorized to designate, pursuant to standards prescribed in regulations by the Secretary, certain officers or employees of the Department of the Interior who shall maintain law and order and protect persons and property within areas of the National Park System. In the performance of such duties, the officers or employees, so designated, may—

(1) carry firearms and make arrests without warrant for any offense against the United States committed in his presence, or for any felony cognizable under the laws of the United States if he has reasonable grounds to believe that the person to be arrested has committed or is committing such felony, provided such arrests occur within that system or the person to be arrested is fleeing therefrom to avoid arrest;

(2) execute any warrant or other process issued by a court or officer of competent jurisdiction for the enforcement of the provisions of any Federal law or regulation issued pursuant to law arising out of an offense committed in that system or, where the person subject to the warrant or process is in that system, in connection with any Federal offense; and

(3) conduct investigations of offenses against the United States committed in that system in the absence of investigation thereof by any other Federal law enforcement agency having investigative jurisdiction over the offense committed or with the concurrence of such other agency.

* * *

Federal investigative jurisdiction and State civil and criminal jurisdiction not preempted within National Park System

(d) Nothing contained in this Act shall be construed or applied to limit or restrict the investigative jurisdiction of any Federal law enforcement agency other than the National Park Service, and nothing shall be construed or applied to affect any right of a State or a political subdivision thereof to exercise civil and criminal jurisdiction within the National Park System.

Pub.L. 91–383, § 10(b)–(e), as added Pub.L. 94–458, § 2, Oct. 7, 1976, 90 Stat. 1941.

§ 1a–7. National Park System development program

Transmittal to Congressional committees

(a) Not later than January 15 of each calendar year, the Secretary of the Interior shall transmit to the Committee on Energy and Natural

Resources of the Senate and the Committee on Natural Resources of the House of Representatives a detailed program for the development of facilities, structures, or buildings for each unit of the National Park System consistent with the general management plans required in subsection (b) of this section.

General management plans; preparation and revision by Director of National Park Service; list to Congress; contents

(b) General management plans for the preservation and use of each unit of the National Park System, including areas within the national capital area, shall be prepared and revised in a timely manner by the Director of the National Park Service. On January 1 of each year, the Secretary shall submit to the Congress a list indicating the current status of completion or revision of general management plans for each unit of the National Park System. General management plans for each unit shall include, but not be limited to:

(1) measures for the preservation of the area's resources;

(2) indications of types and general intensities of development (including visitor circulation and transportation patterns, systems and modes) associated with public enjoyment and use of the area, including general locations, timing of implementation, and anticipated costs;

(3) identification of and implementation commitments for visitor carrying capacities for all areas of the unit; and

(4) indications of potential modifications to the external boundaries of the unit, and the reasons therefor.

Pub.L. 91–383, § 12, as added Pub.L. 94–458, § 2, Oct. 7, 1976, 90 Stat. 1942, and amended Pub.L. 95–625, Title VI, § 604(3), (4), Nov. 10, 1978, 92 Stat. 3518, 3519, as amended Pub.L. 103–437, § 6(c), Nov. 2, 1994, 108 Stat. 4583.

* * *

§ 1a–9. Periodic review of National Park System

The Secretary of the Interior (hereafter in sections 1a–9 to 1a–13 of this title referred to as the "Secretary") is authorized and directed to conduct a systematic and comprehensive review of certain aspects of the National Park System and to submit on a periodic basis but not later than every 3 years a report to the Committee on Natural Resources and the Committee on Appropriations of the United States House of Representatives and the Committee on Energy and Natural Resources and the Committee on Appropriations of the United States Senate on the findings of such review, together with such recommendations as the Secretary determines necessary. The first report shall be submitted no later than 3 years after November 28, 1990.

Pub.L. 101–628, title XII, § 1213, Nov. 28, 1990, 104 Stat. 4507, as amended Pub.L. 103–437, § 6(d)(2), Nov. 2, 1994, 108 Stat. 4583.

§ 1b. Secretary of Interior's authorization of additional activities; administration of National Park System

In order to facilitate the administration of the National Park System, the Secretary of the Interior is authorized to carry out the following activities, and he may use applicable appropriations for the aforesaid system for the following purposes:

Emergency assistance

1. Rendering of emergency rescue, fire fighting, and cooperative assistance to nearby law enforcement and fire prevention agencies and for related purposes outside of the National Park System.

Utility facilities; erection and maintenance

2. The erection and maintenance of fire protection facilities, water lines, telephone lines, electric lines, and other utility facilities adjacent to any area of the said National Park System, where necessary, to provide service in such area.

* * *

Contracts for utility facilities

6. Contracting, under such terms and conditions as the said Secretary considers to be in the interest of the Federal Government, for the sale, operation, maintenance, repair, or relocation of Government-owned electric and telephone lines and other utility facilities used for the administration and protection of the National Park System, regardless of whether such lines and facilities are located within or outside said system and areas.

Rights-of-way

7. Acquiring such rights-of-way as may be necessary to construct, improve, and maintain roads within the authorized boundaries of any area of the said National Park System, and the acquisition also of land and interests in land adjacent to such rights-of-way, when deemed necessary by the Secretary, to provide adequate protection of natural features or to avoid traffic and other hazards resulting from private road access connections, or when the acquisition of adjacent residual tracts, which otherwise would remain after acquiring such rights-of-way, would be in the public interest.

* * *

§ 1c. Same; general provisions—Definition

(a) The "national park system" shall include any area of land and water now or hereafter administered by the Secretary of the Interior through the National Park Service for park, monument, historic, parkway, recreational, or other purposes.

Specific provisions applicable to area; uniform application of sections 1b to 1d and other provisions of this title to all areas when not in conflict with specific provisions; references in other provisions to national parks, monuments, recreation areas, historic monuments, or parkways not limitation of such other provisions to those areas

(b) Each area within the national park system shall be administered in accordance with the provisions of any statute made specifically applicable to that area. In addition, the provisions of sections 1b to 1d of this title, and the various authorities relating to the administration and protection of areas under the administration of the Secretary of the Interior through the National Park Service, including but not limited to the Act of August 25, 1916 (39 Stat. 535), as amended (sections 1 and 2 to 4 of this title), the Act of March 4, 1911 (36 Stat. 1253), as amended (section 5 of this title) relating to rights-of-way, the Act of June 5, 1920 (41 Stat. 917), as amended (section 6 of this title), relating to donation of land and money, sections 1, 4, 5, and 6 of the Act of April 9, 1924 (43 Stat. 90), as amended (sections 8 and 8a to 8c of this title), relating to roads and trails, the Act of March 4, 1931 (46 Stat. 1570; section 8d of this title) relating to approach roads to national monuments, the Act of June 3, 1948 (62 Stat. 334), as amended (sections 8e to 8f of this title), relating to conveyance of roads to States, the Act of August 31, 1954 (68 Stat. 1037), as amended (section 452a of this title), relating to acquisitions of inholdings, section I of the Act of July 3, 1926 (44 Stat. 900), as amended (section 12 of this title), relating to aid to visitors in emergencies, the Act of March 3, 1905 (33 Stat. 873; section 10 of this title), relating to arrests, sections 3, 4, 5, and 6 of the Act of May 26, 1930 (46 Stat. 381), as amended (sections 17b, 17c, 17d, and 17e of this title), relating to services or other accommodations for the public, emergency supplies and services to concessioners, acceptability of travelers checks, care and removal of indigents, the Act of October 9, 1965 (79 Stat. 696; sections 20 to 20g of this title), relating to concessions, the Land and Water Conservation Fund Act of 1965, as amended [16 U.S.C. 460l–4 et seq.], and the Act of July 15, 1968 (82 Stat. 355), shall, to the extent such provisions are not in conflict with any such specific provision, be applicable to all areas within the national park system and any reference in such Act to national parks, monuments, recreation areas, historic monuments, or parkways shall hereinafter not be construed as limiting such Acts to those areas.

Aug. 8, 1953, c. 384, § 2, 67 Stat. 496; Aug. 18, 1970, Pub.L. 91–383, § 2(b), 84 Stat. 826.

* * *

§ 1g. Transfer of National Park Service funds; cooperative agreements

The National Park Service may in fiscal year 1997 and thereafter enter into cooperative agreements that involve the transfer of National Park Service appropriated funds to State, local and tribal governments, other public entities, educational institutions, and private nonprofit organizations for the public purpose of carrying out National Park Service programs pursuant to section 6305 of Title 31 to carry out public purposes of National Park Service programs.

Pub.L. 104–208, Div. A, Title I, § 101(d) [Title I], Sept. 30, 1996, 110 Stat. 3009.

§ 2. National parks, reservations, and monuments; supervision

The director shall, under the direction of the Secretary of the Interior, have the supervision, management, and control of the several national parks and national monuments which on August 25, 1916, were under the jurisdiction of the Department of the Interior, and of the Hot Springs National Park in the State of Arkansas, and of such other national parks and reservations of like character as may be created by Congress. In the supervision, management, and control of national monuments contiguous to national forests the Secretary of Agriculture may cooperate with said National Park Service to such extent as may be requested by the Secretary of the Interior.

Aug. 25, 1916, c. 408, § 2, 39 Stat. 535; Mar. 4, 1921, c. 161, § 1, 41 Stat. 1407.

§ 3. Same; rules and regulations; timber; leases

The Secretary of the Interior shall make and publish such rules and regulations as he may deem necessary or proper for the use and management of the parks, monuments, and reservations under the jurisdiction of the National Park Service, and any violation of any of the rules and regulations authorized by this section and sections 1, 2 and 4 of this title shall be punished by a fine of not more than $500 or imprisonment for not exceeding six months or both, and be adjudged to pay all costs of the proceedings. He may also, upon terms and conditions to be fixed by him, sell or dispose of timber in those cases where in his judgment the cutting of such timber is required in order to control the attacks of insects or diseases or otherwise conserve the scenery or the natural or historic objects in any such park, monument, or reservation. He may also provide in his discretion for the destruction of such animals and of such plant life as may be detrimental to the use of any of said parks, monuments, or reservations. He may also grant privileges, leases, and permits for the use of land for the accommodation of visitors in the various parks, monuments, or other reservations provided for under section 2 of this title, but for periods not exceeding thirty years; and no natural curiosities, wonders, or objects of interest shall be leased, rented, or granted to anyone on such terms as to interfere with free access to them by the public: *Provided, however,* That the Secretary of the Interior may, under such rules and regulations and on such terms as he may prescribe, grant the privilege to graze livestock within any national park, monument, or reservation referred to in this section and sections 1, 2 and 4 of this title when in his judgment such use is not detrimental to the primary purpose for which such park, monument, or reservation was created, except that this provision shall not apply to the Yellowstone National Park: *And provided further,* That the Secretary of the Interior may grant said privileges, leases, and permits and enter into contracts relating to the same with responsible persons, firms, or corporations without advertising and without securing competitive bids: *And provided further,* That no contract, lease, permit, or privilege granted shall be assigned or transferred by such grantees, permittees, or licensees without the approval of the Secretary of the Interior first obtained in writing: *And provided further,* That the Secretary may, in his discretion, authorize such grantees, permittees, or licensees to execute mortgages and issue bonds, shares of stock, and other evidences of interest in or indebtedness upon their rights, properties, and franchises, for the purposes of installing, enlarging, or improving plant and equipment and extending facilities for the accommodation of the public within such national parks and monuments.

Aug. 25, 1916, c. 408, § 3, 39 Stat. 535; June 2, 1920, c. 218, § 5, 41 Stat. 732; Mar. 7, 1928, c. 137, § 1, 45 Stat. 235; May 29, 1958, Pub.L. 85–434, 72 Stat. 152.

§ 4.   Rights-of-way through public lands

Nothing contained in sections 1, 2 and 3 of this title shall affect or modify the provisions of sections 79 and 522 of this title, and section 959 of Title 43.

Aug. 25, 1916, c. 408, § 4, 39 Stat. 536.

§ 5.   Rights-of-way through parks or reservations for power and communications facilities

The head of the department having jurisdiction over the lands is authorized and empowered, under general regulations to be fixed by him, to grant an easement for rights-of-way, for a period not exceeding fifty years from the date of the issuance of such grant, over, across, and upon the public lands and reservations of the United States for electrical poles and lines for the transmission and distribution of electrical power, and for poles and lines for communication purposes, and for radio, television, and other forms of communication transmitting, relay and receiving structures and facilities, to the extent of two hundred feet on each side of the center line of such lines and poles and not to exceed four hundred feet by four hundred feet for radio, television, and other forms of communication transmitting, relay, and receiving structures and facilities, to any citizen, association, or corporation of the United States, where it is intended by such to exercise the right-of-way herein granted for any one or more of the purposes herein named: *Provided,* That such right-of-way shall be allowed within or through any national park or any other reservation only upon the approval of the chief officer of the department under whose supervision or control such reservation falls, and upon a finding by him that the same is not incompatible with the public interest: *Provided further,* That all or any part of such right-of-way may be forfeited and annulled by declaration of the head of the department having jurisdiction over the lands for nonuse for a period of two years or for abandonment.

* * *

Mar. 4, 1911, c. 238, 36 Stat. 1253; May 27, 1952, c. 338, 66 Stat. 95.

Repeals

Section repealed by Pub.L. 94–579, Title VII, § 706(a), Oct. 21, 1976, 90 Stat. 2793, effective on and after Oct. 21, 1976, insofar as applicable to the issuance of rights-of-way over, upon, under, and through the public lands and lands in the National Forest System.

§ 6. Donations of lands within national parks and monuments and moneys

The Secretary of the Interior in his administration of the National Park Service is authorized, in his discretion, to accept patented lands, rights-of-way over patented lands or other lands, buildings, or other property within the various national parks and national monuments, and moneys which may be donated for the purposes of the national park and monument system.

June 5, 1920, c. 235, § 1, 41 Stat. 917.

§ 7a. Airports in national parks, monuments and recreation areas; construction, etc.

The Secretary of the Interior (hereinafter called the "Secretary") is authorized to plan, acquire, establish, construct, enlarge, improve, maintain, equip, operate, regulate, and protect airports in the continental United States in, or in close proximity to, national parks, national monuments, and national recreation areas, when such airports are determined by him to be necessary to the proper performance of the functions of the Department of the Interior: *Provided,* That no such airport shall be acquired, established, or constructed by the Secretary unless such airport is included in the then current revision of the national airport plan formulated by the Secretary of Transportation pursuant to the provisions of the Federal Airport Act: *Provided further,* That the operation and maintenance of such airports shall be in accordance with the standards, rules, or regulations prescribed by the Secretary of Transportation.

Mar. 18, 1950, c. 72, § 1, 64 Stat. 28; Aug. 23, 1958, Pub.L. 85–726, Title XIV, § 1402(e), 72 Stat. 807; May 21, 1970, Pub.L. 91–258, Title I, § 52(b)(1), 64 Stat. 235.

* * *

§ 8. Roads and trails in national parks and monuments; construction, etc.

The Secretary of the Interior, in his administration of the National Park Service, is authorized to construct, reconstruct, and improve roads and trails, inclusive of necessary bridges, in the national parks and monuments under the jurisdiction of the Department of the Interior.

Apr. 9, 1924, c. 86, § 1, 43 Stat. 90.

* * *

§ 9a. Government of parks, etc.; violation of regulations as misdemeanor

The Secretary of the Army is authorized to prescribe and publish such regulations as he deems necessary for the proper government and protection of, and maintenance of good order in, national military parks, national parks, battlefield sites, national monuments, and miscellaneous memorials as are now or hereafter may be under the control of the Department of the Army; and any person who knowingly and willfully violates any such regulation shall be deemed guilty of a misdemeanor and punishable by a fine of not more than $100 or by imprisonment for not more than three months, or by both such fine and imprisonment.

Mar. 2, 1933, c. 180, § 1, 47 Stat. 1420.

* * *

§ 17k. Park, parkway and recreational-area programs; study by National Park Service; consent of States; purpose; cooperation of government agencies

The Secretary of the Interior (hereinafter referred to as the "Secretary") is authorized and directed to cause the National Park Service to make a comprehensive study, other than on lands under the jurisdiction of the Department of Agriculture, of the public park, parkway, and recreational-area programs of the United States, and of the several States and political subdivisions thereof, and of the lands throughout the United States which are or may be chiefly valuable as such areas, but no such study shall be made in any State without the consent and approval of the State officials, boards, or departments having jurisdiction over such lands and park areas. The said study shall be such as, in the judgment of the Secretary, will provide data helpful in developing a plan for coordinated and adequate public park, parkway, and recreational-area facilities for the people of the United States. In making the said study and in accomplishing any of the purposes of this section and sections 17l and 17m of this title, the Secretary is authorized and directed, through the National Park Service, to seek and accept the cooperation and assistance of Federal departments or agencies having jurisdiction of lands belonging to the United States, and may cooperate and make agreements with and seek and accept the assistance of other Federal agencies and instrumentalities, and of States and political subdivisions thereof and the agencies and instrumentalities of either of them.

June 23, 1936, c. 735, § 1, 49 Stat. 1894.

§ 17l. Same; coordination; planning by States with aid of National Park Service

For the purpose of developing coordinated and adequate public park, parkway, and recreational-area facilities for the people of the United States, the Secretary is authorized to aid the several States and political subdivisions thereof in planning such areas therein, and in cooperating

15

with one another to accomplish these ends. Such aid shall be made available through the National Park Service acting in cooperation with such State agencies or agencies of political subdivisions of States as the Secretary deems best.

June 23, 1936, c. 735, § 2, 49 Stat. 1894.

§ 17m.   Same; consent of Congress to agreements between States; when agreements effective

The consent of Congress is given to any two or more States to negotiate and enter into compacts or agreements with one another with reference to planning, establishing, developing, improving, and maintaining any park, parkway, or recreational area. No such compact or agreement shall be effective until approved by the legislatures of the several States which are parties thereto and by the Congress of the United States.

June 23, 1936, c. 735, § 3, 49 Stat. 1895.

§ 17n.   Same; "State" defined

As used in sections 17k and 17l of this title the term "State" shall be deemed to include Hawaii, Alaska, Puerto Rico, Guam, the Virgin Islands, and the District of Columbia.

June 23, 1936, c. 735, § 4, 49 Stat. 1895; Aug. 1, 1956, c. 852, § 6, 70 Stat. 908.

§ 18.   Promotion of tourist travel

The Secretary of Commerce shall encourage, promote, and develop travel within the United States, including any Commonwealth, territory, and possession thereof, through activities which are in the public interest and which do not compete with activities of any State, city, or private agency.

July 19, 1940, ch. 642, § 1, 54 Stat. 773; Dec. 19, 1973, Pub.L. 93–193, § 2, 87 Stat. 765; as amended July 9, 1975, Pub.L. 94–55, § 2(b), 89 Stat. 262.

§ 18a.   Same; cooperation with travel agencies; publicity abroad; printing and sale of publications

In carrying out the purposes of sections 18 to 18d of this title, the Secretary is authorized to cooperate with public and private tourist, travel, and other agencies in the display of exhibits, and in the collection, publication, and dissemination of information with respect to places of interest, routes, transportation facilities, accommodations, and such other matters as he deems advisable and advantageous for the purpose of encouraging, promoting, or developing such travel. Nothing in said sections shall prohibit the preparation of graphic materials in foreign languages, designed to call attention to the attractions and places of interest in the United States and to encourage the use of American registered ships and planes. The existing facilities of the United States Government in foreign countries are authorized to assist in the distribution of this material. The Secretary may enter into contracts with private publishers for such printing and binding as he may deem advisable in carrying out the purposes of said sections. The Secretary is also authorized to make charges for any publications made available to the public pursuant to said sections; and any proceeds from the sale of publications produced by the expenditure of contributed funds shall continue to be available for printing and binding as aforesaid.

July 19, 1940, c. 642, § 2, 54 Stat. 773.

* * *

§ 18f. Management of museum properties

The purpose of this section and sections 18f–2 and 18f–3 of this title shall be to increase the public benefits from museums established within the individual areas administered by the Secretary of the Interior through the National Park Service as a means of informing the public concerning the areas and preserving valuable objects and relics relating thereto. The Secretary of the Interior, notwithstanding other provisions or limitations of law, may perform the following functions in such manner as he shall consider to be in the public interest:

Donations and bequests

(a) Accept donations and bequests of money or other personal property, and hold, use, expend, and administer the same for purposes of this section and sections 18f–2 and 18f–3 of this title;

Use of donations

(b) Purchase museum objects, museum collections, and other personal properties at prices he considers to be reasonable;

Exchanges

(c) Make exchanges by accepting museum objects, museum collections, and other personal properties, and by granting in exchange therefor museum property under the administrative jurisdiction of the Secretary which is no longer needed or which may be held in duplicate among the museum properties administered by the Secretary, such exchanges to be consummated on a basis which the Secretary considers to be equitable and in the public interest;

Accepting loans of museum objects

(d) Accept the loan of museum objects, museum collections, and other personal properties and pay transportation costs incidental thereto, such loans to be accepted upon terms and conditions which he shall consider necessary; and

Making loans of museum objects

(e) Loan to responsible public or private organizations, institutions, or agencies, without cost to the United States, such museum objects, museum collections, and other personal property as he shall consider advisable, such loans to be made upon terms and conditions which he shall consider necessary to protect the public interest in such properties.

July 1, 1955, c. 259, 69 Stat. 242; Nov. 12, 1996, Pub.L. 104–333, Div. I, Title VIII, § 804(a)(1), 110 Stat. 4187.

ANTIQUITIES ACT OF 1906 (as amended)

(16 U.S.C. §§ 431–33)

§ 431. National monuments; reservation of land; relinquishment of private claims

The President of the United States is authorized, in his discretion, to declare by public proclamation historic landmarks, historic and prehistoric structures, and other objects of historic or scientific interest that are situated upon the lands owned or controlled by the Government of the United States to be national monuments, and may reserve as a part thereof parcels of land, the limits of which in all cases shall be confined to the smallest area compatible with the proper care and management of the objects to be protected. When such objects are situated upon a tract covered by a bona fide unperfected claim or held in private ownership, the tract, or so much thereof as may be necessary for the proper care and management of the object, may be relinquished to the Government, and the Secretary of the Interior is authorized to accept the relinquishment of such tracts in behalf of the Government of the United States.

June 8, 1906, c. 3060, § 2, 34 Stat. 225.

§ 431a. Limitation on further extension or establishment of national monuments in Wyoming

No further extension or establishment of national monuments in Wyoming may be undertaken except by express authorization of Congress.

Sept. 14, 1950, c. 950, § 1, 64 Stat. 849.

§ 432. Permits to examine ruins, excavations, and gathering of objects; regulations

Permits for the examination of ruins, the excavation of archaeological sites, and the gathering of objects of antiquity upon the lands under their respective jurisdictions may be granted by the Secretaries of the Interior, Agriculture, and Army to institutions which they may deem properly qualified to conduct such examination, excavation, or gathering, subject to such rules and regulations as they may prescribe: *Provided,* That the examinations, excavations, and gatherings are undertaken for the benefit of reputable museums, universities, colleges, or other recognized scientific or educational institutions, with a view to increasing the knowledge of such objects, and that the gatherings shall be made for permanent preservation in public museums. The Secretaries of the departments aforesaid shall make and publish from time to time uniform rules and regulations for the purpose of carrying out the provisions of this section and sections 431 and 433 of this title.

June 8, 1906, c. 3060, §§ 3, 4, 34 Stat. 225.

§ 433. American antiquities

Any person who shall appropriate, excavate, injure, or destroy any historic or prehistoric ruin or monument, or any object of antiquity, situate on lands owned or controlled by the Government of the United States, without the permission of the Secretary of the Department of the Government having jurisdiction over the lands on which said antiquities are situated, shall, upon conviction, be fined in a sum of not more than $500 or be imprisoned for a period of not more than ninety days, or shall suffer both fine and imprisonment, in the discretion of the court.

June 8, 1906, c. 3060, § 1, 34 Stat. 225.

REFUGE RECREATION ACT OF 1962 (as amended)

(16 U.S.C.A. §§ 460k–460k–4)

§ 460k. Public recreation use of fish and wildlife conservation areas; compatibility with conservation purposes; appropriate incidental or secondary use; consistency with other Federal operations and primary objectives of particular areas; curtailment; forms of recreation not directly related to primary purposes of individual areas; repeal or amendment of provisions for particular areas

In recognition of mounting public demands for recreational opportunities on areas within the National Wildlife Refuge System, national fish hatcheries, and other conservation areas administered by the Secretary of the Interior for fish and wildlife purposes; and in recognition also of the resulting imperative need, if such recreational opportunities are provided, to assure that any present or future recreational use will be compatible with, and will not prevent accomplishment of, the primary purposes for which the said conservation areas were acquired or established, the Secretary of the Interior is authorized, as an appropriate incidental or secondary use, to administer such areas or parts thereof for public recreation when in his judgment public recreation can be an appropriate incidental or secondary use: *Provided,* That such public recreation use shall be permitted only to the extent that is practicable and not inconsistent with other previously authorized Federal operations or with the primary objectives for which each particular area is established: *Provided further,* That in order to insure accomplishment of such primary objectives, the Secretary, after consideration of all authorized uses, purposes, and other pertinent factors relating to individual areas, shall curtail public recreation use generally or certain types of public recreation use within individual areas or in portions thereof whenever he considers such action to be necessary: *And provided further,* That none of the aforesaid refuges, hatcheries, game ranges, and other conservation areas shall be used during any fiscal year for those forms of recreation that are not directly related to the primary purposes

19

and functions of the individual areas until the Secretary shall have determined—

> (a) that such recreational use will not interfere with the primary purposes for which the areas were established, and

> (b) that funds are available for the development, operation, and maintenance of these permitted forms of recreation. This section shall not be construed to repeal or amend previous enactments relating to particular areas.

Pub.L. 87–714, § 1, Sept. 28, 1962, 76 Stat. 653; Pub.L. 89–669, § 9, Oct. 15, 1966, 80 Stat. 930.

§ 460k–1. Acquisition of lands for recreational development; funds

The Secretary is authorized to acquire areas of land, or interests therein, which are suitable for—

> (1) incidental fish and wildlife-oriented recreational development,

> (2) the protection of natural resources,

> (3) the conservation of endangered species or threatened species listed by the Secretary pursuant to section 1533 of this title, or

> (4) carrying out two or more of the purposes set forth in paragraphs (1) through (3) of this section, and are adjacent to, or within, the said conservation areas, except that the acquisition of any land or interest therein pursuant to this section shall be accomplished only with such funds as may be appropriated therefor by the Congress or donated for such purposes, but such property shall not be acquired with funds obtained from the sale of Federal migratory bird hunting stamps. Lands acquired pursuant to this section shall become a part of the particular conservation area to which they are adjacent.

Pub.L. 87–714, § 2, Sept. 28, 1962, 76 Stat. 653; Pub.L. 92–534, Oct. 23, 1972, 86 Stat. 1063; Pub.L. 93–205, § 13(d), Dec. 28, 1973, 87 Stat. 902.

§ 460k–2. Cooperation with agencies, organizations and individuals; acceptance of donations; restrictive covenants

In furtherance of the purposes of sections 460k to 460k–4 of this title, the Secretary is authorized to cooperate with public and private agencies, organizations, and individuals, and he may accept and use, without further authorization, donations of funds and real and personal property. Such acceptance may be accomplished under the terms and conditions of restrictive covenants imposed by donors when such covenants are deemed by the Secretary to be compatible with the purposes of the wildlife refuges, game ranges, fish hatcheries, and other fish and wildlife conservation areas.

Pub.L. 87–714, § 3, Sept. 28, 1962, 76 Stat. 653.

§ 460k–3. Charges and fees; permits; regulations; penalties; enforcement

The Secretary may establish reasonable charges and fees and issue permits for public use of national wildlife refuges, game ranges, national fish hatcheries, and other conservation areas administered by the Department of the Interior for fish and wildlife purposes. The Secretary may issue regulations to carry out the purposes of sections 460k to 460k–4 of this title. A violation of such regulations shall be a misdemeanor with maximum penalties of imprisonment for not more than six months, or a fine of not more than $500, or both, The provisions of sections 460k to 460k–4 of this title and any such regulation shall be enforced by any officer or employee of the United States Fish and Wildlife Service designated by the Secretary of the Interior.

Pub.L. 87–714, § 4, Sept. 28, 1962; 76 Stat. 654; as amended Pub.L. 95–616, § 3(e), Nov. 8, 1978, 92 Stat. 3111; Pub.L. 98–473, Title II, § 221, Oct. 12, 1984, 98 Stat. 2028.

* * *

OUTDOOR RECREATION COORDINATION ACT OF 1963 (as amended)

(16 U.S.C.A. §§ 460l–460l–2)

§ 460l. Congressional declaration of policy

The Congress finds and declares it to be desirable that all American people of present and future generations be assured adequate outdoor recreation resources, and that it is desirable for all levels of government and private interests to take prompt and coordinated action to the extent practicable without diminishing or affecting their respective powers and functions to conserve, develop, and utilize such resources for the benefit and enjoyment of the American people.

Pub.L. 88–29, § 1, May 28, 1963, 77 Stat. 49.

§ 460l–1. Powers and duties of Secretary of Interior

In order to carry out the purposes of sections 460l to 460l–3 of this title, the Secretary of the Interior is authorized to perform the following functions and activities:

Inventory and evaluation of needs and resources

(a) Prepare and maintain a continuing inventory and evaluation of outdoor recreation needs and resources to the United States.

Classification of resources

(b) Prepare a system for classification of outdoor recreation resources to assist in the effective and beneficial use and management of such resources.

Nationwide plan; contents; problems, solutions and actions; initial plan; revisions of plan; transmittal to Congress and Governors

(c) Formulate and maintain a comprehensive nationwide outdoor recreation plan, taking into consideration the plans of the various Federal agencies, States, and their political subdivisions. The plan shall set forth the needs and demands of the public for outdoor recreation and the current and foreseeable availability in the future of outdoor recreation resources to meet those needs. The plan shall identify critical outdoor recreation problems, recommend solutions, and recommend desirable actions to be taken at each level of government and by private interests. The Secretary shall transmit the initial plan, which shall be prepared as soon as practicable within five years on and after May 28, 1963, to the President for transmittal to the Congress. Future revisions of the plan shall be similarly transmitted at succeeding five-year intervals. When a plan or revision is transmitted to the Congress, the Secretary shall transmit copies to the Governors of the several States.

Technical assistance and advice; cooperation with States and private interests

(d) Provide technical assistance and advice to and cooperate with States, political subdivisions, and private interests, including nonprofit organizations, with respect to outdoor recreation.

Interstate and regional cooperation

(e) Encourage interstate and regional cooperation in the planning, acquisition, and development of outdoor recreation resources.

Research and education

(f)(1) Sponsor, engage in, and assist in research relating to outdoor recreation, directly or by contract or cooperative agreements, and make payments for such purposes without regard to the limitations of section 3324(a) and (b) of Title 31 concerning advances of funds when he considers such action in the public interest, (2) undertake studies and assemble information concerning outdoor recreation, directly or by contract or cooperative agreement, and disseminate such information without regard to the provisions of section 3204 of Title 39, and (3) cooperate with educational institutions and others in order to assist in establishing education programs and activities and to encourage public use and benefits from outdoor recreation.

Federal interdepartmental cooperation; coordination of Federal plans and activities; expenditures; reimbursement

(g)(1) Cooperate with and provide technical assistance to Federal departments and agencies and obtain from them information, data, reports, advice, and assistance that are needed and can reasonably be furnished in carrying out the purposes of sections 460l to 460l–3 of this title, and (2) promote coordination of Federal plans and activities generally relating to outdoor recreation. Any department or agency furnishing advice or assistance hereunder may expend its own funds for such purposes, with or without reimbursement, as may be agreed to by that agency.

Donations

(h) Accept and use donations of money, property, personal services, or facilities for the purposes of sections 4601 to 4601–3 of this title.

Pub.L. 88–29, § 2, May 28, 1963, 77 Stat. 49; Pub.L. 91–375, § 6(h), Aug. 12, 1970, 84 Stat. 776; as amended Pub.L. 97–258, § 4(b), Sept. 13, 1982, 96 Stat. 1067.

§ 4601–2. Consultations of Secretary of Interior with administrative officers; execution of administrative responsibilities in conformity with nationwide plan

In order further to carry out the policy declared in section 4601 of this title, the heads of Federal departments and independent agencies having administrative responsibility over activities or resources the conduct or use of which is pertinent to fulfillment of that policy shall, either individually or as a group, (a) consult with and be consulted by the Secretary from time to time both with respect to their conduct of those activities and their use of those resources and with respect to the activities which the Secretary of the Interior carries on under authority of sections 4601 to 4601–3 of this title which are pertinent to their work, and (b) carry out such responsibilities in general conformance with the nationwide plan authorized under section 4601–1(c) of this title.

Pub.L. 88–29, § 3, May 28, 1963, 77 Stat. 50.

* * *

LAND AND WATER CONSERVATION ACT OF 1964 (as amended)

(16 U.S.C.A. §§ 4601–4–4601–11)

§ 4601–4. Land and water conservation provisions; statement of purposes

The purposes of sections 4601–4 to 4601–11 of this title are to assist in preserving, developing, and assuring accessibility to all citizens of the United States of America of present and future generations and visitors who are lawfully present within the boundaries of the United States of America such quality and quantity of outdoor recreation resources as may be available and are necessary and desirable for individual active participation in such recreation and to strengthen the health and vitality of the citizens of the United States by (1) providing funds for and authorizing Federal assistance to the States in planning, acquisition, and development of needed land and water areas and facilities and (2) providing funds for the Federal acquisition and development of certain lands and other areas.

Pub.L. 88–578, Title I, § 1(b), Sept. 3, 1964, 78 Stat. 897.

§ 4601–5. Land and water conservation fund; establishment; covering certain revenues and collections into fund

During the period ending September 30, 2015, there shall be covered into the land and water conservation fund in the Treasury of the United States, which fund is hereby established and is hereinafter referred to as the "fund", the following revenues and collections:

Surplus property sales

(a) All proceeds (except so much thereof as may be otherwise obligated, credited, or paid under authority of those provisions of law set forth in section 485(b)(e) of Title 40, or the Independent Offices Appropriation Act, 1963 (76 Stat. 725) or in any later appropriation Act) hereafter received from any disposal of surplus real property and related personal property under the Federal Property and Administrative Services Act of 1949, as amended [40 U.S.C.A. § 471 et seq.], notwithstanding any provision of law that such proceeds shall be credited to miscellaneous receipts of the Treasury. Nothing in sections 4601–4 to 4601–11 of this title shall affect existing laws or regulations concerning disposal of real or personal surplus property to schools, hospitals, and States and their political subdivisions.

Motorboat fuels tax

(b) The amounts provided for in section 4601–11 of this title.

Other revenues

(c)(1) In addition to the sum of the revenues and collections estimated by the Secretary of the Interior to be covered into the fund pursuant to this section, as amended, there are authorized to be appropriated annually to the fund out of any money in the Treasury not otherwise appropriated such amounts as are necessary to make the income of the fund not less than $300,000,000 for fiscal year 1977, and $900,000,000 for fiscal year 1978 and for each fiscal year thereafter through September 30, 2015.

(c)(2) To the extent that any such sums so appropriated are not sufficient to make the total annual income of the fund equivalent to the amounts provided in clause (1), an amount sufficient to cover the remainder thereof shall be credited to the fund from revenues due and payable to the United States for deposit in the Treasury as miscellaneous receipts under the Outer Continental Shelf Lands Act, as amended (43 U.S.C. 1331 et seq.): *Provided,* That notwithstanding the provisions of section 4601–6 of this title, moneys covered into the fund under this paragraph shall remain in the fund until appropriated by the Congress to carry out the purpose of sections 4601–4 to 4601–11 of this title.

Pub.L. 88–578, Title I, § 2, Sept. 3, 1964, 78 Stat. 897; Pub.L. 89–72, § 11, July 9, 1965, 79 Stat. 218; Pub.L. 90–401, §§ 1(a), 2, July 15, 1968, 82 Stat. 354, 355; Pub.L. 91–308, § 2, July 7, 1970, 84 Stat. 410; Pub.L. 91–485, § 1, Oct. 22, 1970, 84 Stat. 1084; as amended Pub.L. 94–273, § 2(7), Apr. 21, 1976, 90 Stat. 375; Pub.L. 94–422, Title I, § 101(1), Sept. 28, 1976, 90 Stat. 1313; Pub.L. 95–42, § 1(1), June 10, 1977, 91 Stat. 210. As amended Pub.L. 94–273, § 2(7), Apr. 21, 1976, 90 Stat. 375; Pub.L. 94–422, Title I,

§ 101(1), Sept. 28, 1976, 90 Stat. 1313; Pub.L. 95–42, § 1(1), June 10, 1977, 91 Stat. 210; Pub.L. 100–203, Title V, § 5201(f)(1), Dec. 22, 1987, 101 Stat. 1330–267.

§ 4601–6. Obligation or expenditure of land and water conservation fund or special account moneys

Moneys made available for obligation or expenditure from the fund or from the special account established under section 4601–6a(i)(1) of this title may be obligated or expended only as provided in section 4601–4 to 4601–11 of this title.

Pub.L. 88–578, Title I, § 3, Sept. 3, 1964, 78 Stat. 899. As amended Pub.L. 100–203, Title V, § 5201(f)(2), Dec. 22, 1987, 101 Stat. 1330–267.

§ 4601–6a. Admission and special recreation use fees

Admission fees at designated areas; "Golden Eagle Passport" annual admission permit; single-visit fees; fee-free travel areas; "Golden Age Passport" annual entrance permit; lifetime admission permit

(a) Entrance or admission fees shall be charged only at designated units of the National Park System or National Conservation Areas administered by the Department of the Interior and National Recreation Areas, National Monuments, National Volcanic Monuments, National Scenic Areas and no more than 21 areas of concentrated public use administered by the Department of Agriculture. For the purposes of this subsection, the term "area of concentrated public use" means an area that is managed primarily for outdoor recreation purposes, contains at least one major recreation attraction, where facilities and services necessary to accommodate heavy public use are provided, and public access to the area is provided in such a manner that admission fees can be efficiently collected at one or more centralized locations. No admission fees of any kind shall be charged or imposed for entrance into any other federally owned areas which are operated and maintained by a Federal agency and used for outdoor recreation purposes.

* * *

Contracts with public or private entities for visitor reservation services

(f) The head of any Federal agency, under such terms and conditions as he deems appropriate, may contract with any public or private entity to provide visitor reservation services. Any such contract may provide that the contractor shall be permitted to deduct a commission to be fixed by the agency head from the amount charged the public for providing such services and to remit the net proceeds therefrom to the contracting agency.

Federal and State laws unaffected

(g) Nothing in this part shall authorize Federal hunting or fishing licenses or fees or charges for commercial or other activities not related to recreation, nor shall it affect any rights or authority of the States with respect to fish and wildlife, nor shall it repeal or modify any provision of law that permits States or political subdivisions to share in the revenues from Federal lands or any provision of law that provides that any fees or charges collected at particular Federal areas shall be used for or credited to specific purposes or special funds as authorized by that provision of law.

Pub.L. 88–578, Title I, § 4, as added Pub.L. 92–347, § 2, July 11, 1972, 86 Stat. 459, and amended Pub.L. 93–81, §§ 1,2, Aug. 1, 1973, 87 Stat. 178, 179; Pub.L. 93–303, § 1, June 7, 1974, 88 Stat. 192; Pub.L. 96–344, § 9, Sept. 8, 1980, 94 Stat. 1135; Pub.L. 100–203, Title V, § 5201(a) to (c), Dec. 22, 1987, 101 Stat. 1330–263, 1330–264; Pub.L. 101–650, Title III, § 321, Dec. 1, 1990, 104 Stat. 5117; as amended Pub.L. 103–66, Title V, § 5001(b), Title X, §§ 10001, 10002, Aug. 10, 1993, 107 Stat. 379, 402, 403; Pub.L. 103–437, § 6(p)(1), Nov. 2, 1994, 108 Stat. 4586; Pub.L. 104–66, Title I, § 1081(f), Dec. 21, 1995, 109 Stat. 721; Pub.L. 105–327, § 1, Oct. 30, 1998, 112 Stat. 3055.

* * *

§ 4601–6d. Commercial filming

Commercial filming fee

(a) The Secretary of the Interior and the Secretary of Agriculture (hereafter individually referred to as the ''Secretary'' with respect to lands under their respective jurisdiction) shall require a permit and shall establish a reasonable fee for commercial filming activities or similar projects on Federal lands administered by the Secretary. Such fee shall provide a fair return to the United States and shall be based upon the following criteria:

(a)(1) The number of days the filming activity or similar project takes place on Federal land under the Secretary's jurisdiction.

(a)(2) The size of the film crew present on Federal land under the Secretary's jurisdiction.

(a)(3) The amount and type of equipment present.

The Secretary may include other factors in determining an appropriate fee as the Secretary deems necessary.

Recovery of costs

(b) The Secretary shall also collect any costs incurred as a result of filming activities or similar project, including but not limited to administrative and personnel costs. All costs recovered shall be in addition to the fee assessed in subsection (a).

Still photography

(c)(1) Except as provided in paragraph (2), the Secretary shall not require a permit nor assess a fee for still photography on lands administered by the Secretary if such photography takes place where members of the public are generally allowed. The Secretary may require a permit, fee, or both, if such photography takes place at other locations where members of the public are generally not allowed, or where additional administrative costs are likely.

(c)(2) The Secretary shall require and shall establish a reasonable fee for still photography that uses models or props which are not a part of the site's natural or cultural resources or administrative facilities.

Protection of resources

(d) The Secretary shall not permit any filming, still photography or other related activity if the Secretary determines—

(d)(1) there is a likelihood of resource damage;

(d)(2) there would be an unreasonable disruption of the public's use and enjoyment of the site; or

(d)(3) that the activity poses health or safety risks to the public.

Use of proceeds

(e)(1) All fees collected under this section shall be available for expenditure by the Secretary, without further appropriation, in accordance with the formula and purposes established for the Recreational Fee Demonstration Program (Public Law 104–134). All fees collected shall remain available until expended.

(e)(2) All costs recovered under this section shall be available for expenditure by the Secretary, without further appropriation, at the site where collected. All costs recovered shall remain available until expended.

Processing of permit applications

(f) The Secretary shall establish a process to ensure that permit applicants for commercial filming, still photography, or other activity are responded to in a timely manner.

Pub.L. 106–206, § 1, May 26, 2000, 114 Stat. 314.

§ 4601–7. Allocation of land and water conservation fund for State and Federal purposes

There shall be submitted with the annual budget of the United States a comprehensive statement of estimated requirements during the ensuing fiscal year for appropriations from the fund. Not less than 40 per centum of such appropriations shall be available for Federal purposes. Those appropriations from the fund up to and including $600,000,000 in fiscal year 1978 and up to and including $750,000,000 in fiscal year 1979 shall continue to be allocated in accordance with this section. There shall be credited to a special account within the fund $300,000,000 in fiscal year 1978 and $150,000,000 in fiscal year 1979 from the amounts authorized by section 4601–5 of this title. Amounts credited to this account shall remain in the account until appropriated. Appropriations from the special account shall be available only with respect to areas existing and authorizations enacted prior to the convening of the Ninety-fifth Congress, for acquisition of lands, waters, or interests in lands or waters within the exterior boundaries, as aforesaid, of—

    (1) the national park system;

    (2) national scenic trails;

    (3) the national wilderness preservation system;

    (4) federally administered components of the National Wild and Scenic Rivers System; and

    (5) national recreation areas administered by the Secretary of Agriculture.

Pub.L. 88–578, Title I, § 5, formerly § 4, Sept. 3, 1964, 78 Stat. 900; Pub.L. 90–401, § 3, July 15, 1968, 82 Stat. 355, renumbered Pub.L. 92–347, § 2, July 11, 1972, 86 Stat. 459, and amended Pub.L. 94–273, § 3(4), Apr. 21, 1976, 90 Stat. 376; Pub.L. 94–422, Title I, § 101(2), Sept. 28, 1976, 90 Stat. 1314; Pub.L. 95–42, § 1(2), June 10, 1977, 91 Stat. 210.

§ 4601–8. Financial assistance to States

Authority of Secretary of Interior; payments to carry out purposes of land and water conservation provisions

(a) The Secretary of the Interior (hereinafter referred to as the "Secretary") is authorized to provide financial assistance to the States from moneys available for State purposes. Payments may be made to the States by the Secretary as hereafter provided, subject to such terms and conditions as he considers appropriate and in the public interest to carry out the purposes of this part for outdoor recreation: (1) planning, (2) acquisition of land, waters, or interests in land or waters, or (3) development.

Apportionment among States; finality of administrative determination; formula; notification; reapportionment of unobligated amounts; definition of State

(b) Sums appropriated and available for State purposes for each fiscal year shall be apportioned among the several States by the Secretary, whose determination shall be final, in accordance with the following formula:

    (1) Forty per centum of the first $225,000,000; thirty per centum of the next $275,000,000; and twenty per centum of all additional appropriations shall be apportioned equally among the several States; and

    (2) At any time, the remaining appropriation shall be apportioned on the basis of need to individual States by the Secretary in such amounts as in his judgment will best accomplish the purposes this part. The determination of need shall include among other things a consideration of the proportion which the population of each State bears to the total population of the United States and of the use of outdoor recreation resources of individual States by persons from outside the State as well as a consideration of the Federal resources and programs in the particular States.

(3) The total allocation to an individual State under paragraphs (1) and (2) of this subsection shall not exceed 10 per centum of the total amount allocated to the several States in any one year.

(4) The Secretary shall notify each State of its apportionments; and the amounts thereof shall be available thereafter for payment to such State for planning, acquisition, or development projects as hereafter prescribed. Any amount of any apportionment that has not been paid or obligated by the Secretary during the fiscal year in which such notification is given and for two fiscal years thereafter shall be reapportioned by the Secretary in accordance with paragraph (2) of this subsection, without regard to the 10 per centum limitation to an individual State specified in this subsection.

(5) For the purposes of paragraph (1) of this subsection, the District of Columbia, Puerto Rico, the Virgin Islands, Guam, American Samoa, and the Commonwealth of the Northern Mariana Islands (when such islands achieve Commonwealth status) shall be treated collectively as one State, and shall receive shares of such apportionment in proportion to their populations. The above listed areas shall be treated as States for all other purposes of this title.

Matching requirements

(c) Payments to any State shall cover not more than 50 per centum of the cost of planning, acquisition, or development projects that are undertaken by the State. The remaining share of the cost shall be borne by the State in a manner and with such funds or services as shall be satisfactory to the Secretary. No payment may be made to any State for or on account of any cost or obligation incurred or any service rendered prior to September 3, 1964.

Comprehensive State plan; necessity; adequacy; contents; correlation with other plans; factors for formulation of Housing and Home Finance Agency financed plans; planning projects; wetlands consideration; wetlands priority plan

(d) A comprehensive statewide outdoor recreation plan shall be required prior to the consideration by the Secretary of financial assistance for acquisition or development projects. The plan shall be adequate if, in the judgment of the Secretary, it encompasses and will promote the purposes of this part: *Provided,* That no plan shall be approved unless the Governor of the respective State certifies that ample opportunity for public participation in plan development and revision has been accorded. The Secretary shall develop, in consultation with others, criteria for public participation, which criteria shall constitute the basis for the certification by the Governor. The plan shall contain—

(1) the name of the State agency that will have authority to represent and act for the State in dealing with the Secretary for purposes of this part;

(2) an evaluation of the demand for and supply of outdoor recreation resources and facilities in the State;

(3) a program for the implementation of the plan; and

(4) other necessary information, as may be determined by the Secretary.

The plan shall take into account relevant Federal resources and programs and shall be correlated so far as practicable with other State, regional, and local plans. Where there exists or is in preparation for any particular State a comprehensive plan financed in part with funds supplied by the Housing and Home Finance Agency, any statewide outdoor recreation plan prepared for purposes of this part shall be based upon the same population, growth, and other pertinent factors as are used in formulating the Housing and Home Finance Agency financed plans.

The Secretary may provide financial assistance to any State for projects for the preparation of a comprehensive statewide outdoor recreation plan when such plan is not otherwise available or for the maintenance of such plan.

For fiscal year 1988 and thereafter each comprehensive statewide outdoor recreation plan shall specifically address wetlands within that State as an important outdoor recreation resource as a prerequisite to approval, except that a revised comprehensive statewide outdoor recreation plan shall not be required by the Secretary, if a State submits, and the Secretary, acting through the Director of the National Park Service, approves, as a part of and as an addendum to the existing comprehensive statewide outdoor recreation plan, a wetlands priority plan developed in consultation with the State agency with responsibility for fish and wildlife resources and consistent with the national wetlands priority conservation plan developed under section 3921 of this title or, if such national plan has not been completed, consistent with the provisions of that section.

Projects for land and water acquisition; development

(e) In addition to assistance for planning projects, the Secretary may provide financial assistance to any State for the following types of projects or combinations thereof if they are in accordance with the State comprehensive plan:

(1) For the acquisition of land, waters, or interests in land or waters, or wetland areas and interests therein as identified in the wetlands provisions of the comprehensive plan (other than land, waters, or interests in land or waters acquired from the United States for less than fair market value), but not including incidental costs relating to acquisition.

Whenever a State provides that the owner of a single-family residence may, at his option, elect to retain a right of use and occupancy for not less than six months from the date of acquisition of such residence and such owner elects to retain such a right, such owner shall be deemed to have waived any benefits under sections 4623, 4624, 4625, and 4626 of Title 42 and for the purposes of those sections such owner shall not be considered a displaced person as defined in section 4601(6) of Title 42.

(2) For development of basic outdoor recreation facilities to serve the general public, including the development of Federal lands under lease to States for terms of twenty-five years or more: *Provided*, That no assistance shall be available under this part to enclose or shelter facilities normally used for outdoor recreation activities, but the Secretary may permit local funding, and after September 28, 1976, not to exceed 10 per centum of the total amount allocated to a State in any one year to be used for sheltered facilities for swimming pools and ice skating rinks in areas where the Secretary determines that the severity of climatic conditions and the increased public use thereby made possible justifies the construction of such facilities.

Requirements for project approval; conditions; progress payments; payments to Governors or State officials or agencies; State transfer of funds to public agencies; conversion of property to other uses; reports to Secretary; accounting; records; audit; discrimination prohibited

(f)(1) Payments may be made to States by the Secretary only for those planning, acquisition, or development projects that are approved by him. No payment may be made by the Secretary for or on account of any project with respect to which financial assistance has been given or promised under any other Federal program or activity, and no financial assistance may be given under any other Federal program or activity for or on account of any project with respect to which such assistance has been given or promised under this part. The Secretary may make payments from time to time in keeping with the rate of progress toward the satisfactory completion of individual protects: *Provided*, That the approval of all projects and all payments, or any commitments relating thereto, shall be withheld until the Secretary receives appropriate written assurance from the State that the State has the ability and intention to finance its share of the cost of the particular project, and to operate and maintain by acceptable standards, at State expense, the particular properties or facilities acquired or developed for public outdoor recreation use.

(f)(2) Payments for all projects shall be made by the Secretary to the Governor of the State or to a State official or agency designated by the Governor or by State law having authority and responsibility to accept and to administer funds paid hereunder for approved projects. If consistent with an approved project, funds may be transferred by the State to a political subdivision or other appropriate public agency.

(f)(3) No property acquired or developed with assistance under this section shall, without the approval of the Secretary, be converted to other than public outdoor recreation uses. The Secretary shall approve such conversion only if he finds it to be in accord with the then existing comprehensive statewide outdoor recreation plan and only upon such conditions as he deems necessary to assure the substitution of other recreation properties of at least equal fair market value and of reasonably equivalent usefulness and location: *Provided*, That wetland areas and interests therein as identified in the wetlands provisions of the comprehensive plan and proposed to be acquired as suitable replacement property within that same State that is otherwise acceptable to the Secretary, acting through the Director of the National Park Service, shall be considered to be of reasonably equivalent usefulness with the property proposed for conversion.

(f)(4) No payment shall be made to any State until the State has agreed to (1) provide such reports to the Secretary, in such form and containing such information, as may be reasonably necessary to enable the Secretary to perform his duties under this part, and (2) provide such fiscal control and fund accounting procedures as may be necessary to assure proper disbursement and accounting for Federal funds paid to the State under this part.

(f)(5) Each recipient of assistance under this part shall keep such records as the Secretary shall prescribe, including records which fully disclose the amount and the disposition by such recipient of the proceeds of such assistance, the total cost of the project or undertaking in connection with which such assistance is given or used, and the amount and nature of that portion of the cost of the project or undertaking supplied by other sources, and such other records as will facilitate an effective audit.

(f)(6) The Secretary, and the Comptroller General of the United States, or any of their duly authorized representatives, shall have access for the purpose of audit and examination to any books, documents, papers, and records of the recipient that are pertinent to assistance received under this part.

(f)(7) [Repealed. Pub.L. 104–333, Div. I, Title VIII, § 814(d)(1)(H), Nov. 12, 1996, 110 Stat. 4196]

(f)(8) With respect to property acquired or developed with assistance from the fund, discrimination on the basis of residence, including preferential reservation or membership systems, is prohibited except to the extent that reasonable differences in admission and other fees may be maintained on the basis of residence.

Coordination with Federal agencies

(g) In order to assure consistency in policies and actions under this part, with other related Federal programs and activities (including those conducted pursuant to Title VII of the Housing Act of 1961 [42 U.S.C.A. § 1500 et seq.] and section 701 of the Housing Act of 1954 [40 U.S.C.A. § 461]) and to assure coordination of the planning, acquisition, and development assistance to States under this section with other related Federal programs and activities, the President may issue such regulations with respect thereto as he deems desirable and such assistance may be provided only in accordance with such regulations.

Pub.L. 88–578, title I, § 6, formerly § 5, Sept. 3, 1964, 78 Stat. 900, renumbered Pub.L. 92–347, § 2, July 11, 1972, 86 Stat. 459, and amended Pub.L. 93–303, § 2, June 7, 1974, 88 Stat. 194, as amended Pub.L. 94–422, Title I, § 101(3), Sept. 28, 1976, 90 Stat. 1314; Pub.L. 95–625, Title VI, § 606, Nov. 10, 1978, 92 Stat. 3519. As amended Pub.L. 94–422, Title I, § 101(3), Sept. 28, 1976, 90 Stat. 1314; Pub.L. 95–625, Title VI, § 606, Nov. 10, 1978, 92 Stat. 3519; Pub.L. 99–645, Title III, § 303, Nov. 10, 1986, 100 Stat. 3587, as amended Pub.L. 103–322, Title IV, § 40133, Sept. 13,

1994, 108 Stat. 1918; Pub.L. 103–437, § 6(p)(2), Nov. 2, 1994, 108 Stat. 4586; Pub.L. 104–333, Div. I, Title VIII, § 814(d)(1)(H), Nov. 12, 1996, 110 Stat. 4196.

§ 4601–9. Allocation of land and water conservation fund moneys for Federal purposes

Allowable purposes and subpurposes; acquisition of land and waters and interests therein; offset for specified capital costs

(a) Moneys appropriated from the fund for Federal purposes shall, unless otherwise allotted in the appropriation Act making them available, be allotted by the President to the following purposes and subpurposes:

(1) For the acquisition of land, waters, or interests in land or waters as follows:

National Park System; recreation areas—Within the exterior boundaries of areas of the National Park System now or hereafter authorized or established and of areas now or hereafter authorized to be administered by the Secretary of the Interior for outdoor recreation purposes.

National Forest System—Inholdings within (a) wilderness areas of the National Forest System, and (b) other areas of national forests as the boundaries of those forests exist on the effective date of this Act, or purchase units approved by the National Forest Reservation Commission subsequent to the date of this Act, all of which other areas are primarily of value for outdoor recreation purposes: *Provided*, That lands outside of but adjacent to an existing national forest boundary, not to exceed three thousand acres in the case of any one forest, which would comprise an integral part of a forest recreational management area may also be acquired with moneys appropriated from this fund: *Provided* further, That except for areas specifically authorized by Act of Congress, not more than 15 per centum of the acreage added to the National Forest System pursuant to this section shall be west of the 100th meridian.

National Wildlife Refuge System—Acquisition for (a) endangered species and threatened species authorized under section 1534(a) of this title; (b) areas authorized by section 460k–1 of this title; (c) national wildlife refuge areas under section 742f(a)(4) of this title and wetlands acquired under section 3922 of this title; (d) any areas authorized for the National Wildlife Refuge System by specific Acts.

(2) For payment into miscellaneous receipts of the Treasury as a partial offset for those capital costs, if any, of Federal water development projects hereafter authorized to be constructed by or pursuant to an Act of Congress which are allocated to public recreation and the

33

enhancement of fish and wildlife values and financed through appropriations to water resource agencies.

* * *

Acquisition restrictions

(b) Appropriations from the fund pursuant to this section shall not be used for acquisition unless such acquisition is otherwise authorized by law: *Provided, however*, That appropriations from the fund may be used for preacquisition work in instances where authorization is imminent and where substantial monetary savings could be realized.

* * *

Pub.L. 88–578, title I, § 7, formerly § 6, Sept. 3, 1964, 78 Stat. 903; Pub.L. 90–401, § 1(c), July 15, 1968, 82 Stat. 355; renumbered Pub.L. 92–347, § 2, July 11, 1972, 86 Stat. 459, and amended Pub.L. 93–205, § 13(c), Dec. 28, 1973, 87 Stat. 902, as amended Pub.L. 94–422, Title I, § 101(4), Sept. 28, 1976, 90 Stat. 1317; Pub.L. 95–42, § 1(3)–(5), June 10, 1977, 91 Stat. 210, 211; Pub.L. 96–203, § 2, Mar. 10, 1980, 94 Stat. 81. As amended Pub.L. 94–422, Title I, § 101(4), Sept. 28, 1976, 90 Stat. 1317; Pub.L. 95–42, § 1(3)–(5), June 10, 1977, 91 Stat. 210, 211; Pub.L. 96–203, § 2, Mar. 10, 1980, 94 Stat. 81; Pub.L. 99–645, Title III, § 302, Nov. 10, 1986, 100 Stat. 3587, as amended Pub.L. 103–437, § 6(p)(3), Nov. 2, 1994, 108 Stat. 4586; Pub.L. 104–333, Div. I, Title VIII, § 814(b), (d)(2)(C), Nov. 12, 1996, 110 Stat. 4194, 4196; Pub.L. 106–176, Title I, §§ 120(b), 129, Mar. 10, 2000, 114 Stat. 28, 30.

§ 4601–10. Availability of land and water conservation fund for publicity purposes; standardized temporary signing; standards and guidelines

Moneys derived from the sources listed in section 4601–5 of this title shall not be available for publicity purposes: *Provided, however,* That in each case where significant acquisition or development is initiated, appropriate standardized temporary signing shall be located on or near the affected site, to the extent feasible, so as to indicate the action taken is a product of funding made available through the Land and Water Conservation Fund. Such signing may indicate the per centum and dollar amounts financed by Federal and non-Federal funds, and that the source of the funding includes moneys derived from Outer Continental Shelf receipts. The Secretary shall prescribe standards and guidelines for the usage of such signing to assure consistency of design and application.

Pub.L. 88–578, title I, § 8, formerly § 7, Sept. 3, 1964, 78 Stat. 903; renumbered Pub.L. 92–347, § 2, July 11, 1972, 86 Stat. 459, as amended Pub.L. 94–422, Title I, § 101(5), Sept. 28, 1976, 90 Stat. 1318.

* * *

§ 460l–10b. Contracts for options to acquire lands and waters in national park system

The Secretary of the Interior may enter into contracts for options to acquire lands, waters, or interests therein within the exterior boundaries of any area the acquisition of which is authorized by law for inclusion in the national park system. The minimum period of any such option shall be two years, and any sums expended for the purchase thereof shall be credited to the purchase price of said area. Not to exceed $500,000 of the sum authorized to be appropriated from the fund by section 460l–6 of this title may be expended by the Secretary in any one fiscal year for such options.

Pub.L. 88–578, Title I, § 10, formerly 9, as added Pub.L. 90–401, § 4, July 15, 1968, 82 Stat. 355, and renumbered Pub.L. 92–347, § 2, July 11, 1972, 86 Stat. 459.

§ 460l–10c. Repeal of provisions prohibiting collection of recreation fees or user charges

All provisions of law that prohibit the collection of entrance, admission, or other recreation user fees or charges authorized by sections 460l–4 to 460l–11 of this title or that restrict the expenditure of funds if such fees or charges are collected are hereby repealed: *Provided,* That no provision of any law or treaty which extends to any person or class of persons a right of free access to the shoreline of any reservoir or other body of water, or to hunting and fishing along or on such shoreline, shall be affected by this repealer.

Pub.L. 88–578, Title I, § 11, formerly 10, as added Pub.L. 90–401, § 1(a), July 15, 1968, 82 Stat. 354, and renumbered Pub.L. 92–347, § 2, July 11, 1972, 86 Stat. 459.

* * *

HELLS CANYON NATIONAL RECREATION AREA

(16 U.S.C.A. §§ 460gg through 460gg–13)

§ 460gg. Establishment

In general

(a) To assure that the natural beauty, and historical and archeological values of the Hells Canyon area and the seventy-one-mile segment of the Snake River between Hells Canyon Dam and the Oregon–Washington border, together with portions of certain of its tributaries and adjacent lands, are preserved for this and future generations, and that the recreational and ecologic values and public enjoyment of the area are thereby enhanced, there is hereby established the Hells Canyon National Recreation Area.

Boundaries; publication in Federal Register

(b) The Hells Canyon National Recreation Area (hereinafter referred to as the "recreation area"), which includes the Hells Canyon Wilderness (hereinafter referred to as the "wilderness"), the components of the Wild and Scenic Rivers System designated in section 3 of this Act, and the wilderness study areas designated in section 460gg–5(d) of this title, shall comprise the lands and waters generally depicted on the map entitled "Hells Canyon National Recreation Area" dated May 1978, which shall be on file and available for public inspection in the office of the Chief, Forest Service, United States Department of Agriculture. The Secretary of Agriculture (hereinafter referred to as "the Secretary"), shall, as soon as practicable, but no later than eighteen months after December 31, 1975, publish a detailed boundary description of the recreation area, the wilderness study areas designated in section 460gg–5(d) of this title, and the wilderness established in section 460gg–1 of this title in the Federal Register.

Pub.L. 94–199, § 1, Dec. 31, 1975, 89 Stat. 1117; Pub.L. 95–625, Title VI, § 607, Nov. 10, 1978, 92 Stat. 3520.

* * *

§ 460gg–2. Federal power and water resources projects

Licenses by Federal Energy Regulatory Commission

(a) Notwithstanding any other provision of law, or any authorization heretofore given pursuant to law, the Federal Energy Regulatory Commission may not license the construction of any dam, water conduit, reservoir, powerhouse, transmission line, or other project work under the Federal Power Act (41 Stat. 1063), as amended (16 U.S.C. 791a et seq.), within the recreation area: *Provided,* That the provisions of the Federal Power Act (41 Stat. 1063) shall continue to apply to any project (as defined in such Act), and all of the facilities and improvements required or used in connection with the operation and maintenance of said project, in existence within the recreation area which project is already constructed or under construction on December 31, 1975.

Assistance detrimental to protected waters

(b) No department or agency of the United States may assist by loan, grant, license, or otherwise the construction of any water resource facility within the recreation area which the Secretary determines would have a direct and adverse effect on the values for which the waters of the area are protected.

Pub.L. 94–199, § 4, Dec. 31, 1975, 89 Stat. 1118; Pub.L. 95–91, Title IV, § 402(a)(1)(A), Aug. 4, 1977, 91 Stat. 583.

§ 460gg–3. Present and future use of Snake River

Waters upstream from boundaries of area

(a) No provision of the Wild and Scenic Rivers Act [16 U.S.C.A. § 1271 et seq.], nor of this subchapter, nor any guidelines, rules, or regulations issued hereunder, shall in any way limit, restrict, or conflict with present and future use of the waters of the Snake River and its tributaries upstream from the boundaries of the Hells Canyon National Recreation Area created hereby, for beneficial uses, whether consumptive or nonconsumptive, now or hereafter existing, including, but not limited to, domestic, municipal, stockwater, irrigation, mining, power, or industrial uses.

Flow requirements

(b) No flow requirements of any kind may be imposed on the waters of the Snake River below Hells Canyon Dam under the provisions of the Wild and Scenic Rivers Act [16 U.S.C.A. § 1271 et seq.], of this subchapter, or any guidelines, rules, or regulations adopted pursuant thereto.

Pub.L. 94–199, § 6, Dec. 31, 1975, 89 Stat. 1118.

§ 460gg–4. Administration, protection, and development

Except as otherwise provided in section 460gg–1 of this title and section 3 of this Act, and subject to the provisions of section 460gg–7 of this title, the Secretary shall administer the recreation area in accordance with the laws, rules, and regulations applicable to the national forests for public outdoor recreation in a manner compatible with the following objectives:

(1) the maintenance and protection of the freeflowing nature of the rivers within the recreation area;

(2) conservation of scenic, wilderness, cultural, scientific, and other values contributing to the public benefit;

(3) preservation, especially in the area generally known as Hells Canyon, of all features and peculiarities believed to be biologically unique including, but not limited to, rare and endemic plant species, rare combinations of aquatic, terrestrial, and atmospheric habitats, and the rare combinations of outstanding and diverse ecosystems and parts of ecosystems associated therewith;

(4) protection and maintenance of fish and wildlife habitat;

(5) protection of archeological and paleontologic sites and interpretation of these sites for the public benefit and knowledge insofar as it is compatible with protection;

(6) preservation and restoration of historic sites associated with and typifying the economic and social history of the region and the American West; and

(7) such management, utilization, and disposal of natural resources on federally owned lands, including, but not limited to, timber harvesting by selective cutting, mining, and grazing and the continuation of such existing uses and developments as are compatible with the provisions of this subchapter.

Pub.L. 94–199, § 7, Dec. 31, 1975, 89 Stat. 1118.

§ 460gg–5. Management plan for recreation area

Development and submission

(a) Within five years from December 31, 1975 the Secretary shall develop and submit to the Committees on Interior and Insular Affairs of the United States Senate and House of Representatives a comprehensive management plan for the recreation area which shall provide for a broad range of land uses and recreation opportunities.

Consideration of historic, archeological and paleontological resources; inventory; recommendation of areas for listing in National Register of Historic Places; recommendation for protection and research of resources

(b) In the development of such plan, the Secretary shall consider the historic, archeological, and paleontological resources within the recreation area which offer significant opportunities for anthropological research. The Secretary shall inventory such resources and may recommend such areas as he deems suitable for listing in the National Register of Historic Places. The Secretary's comprehensive plan shall include recommendations for future protection and controlled research use of all such resources.

Scenic roads and other means of transit

(c) The Secretary shall, as a part of his comprehensive planning process, conduct a detailed study of the need for, and alternative routes of, scenic roads and other means of transit to and within the recreation area. In conducting such study the Secretary shall consider the alternative for upgrading existing roads and shall, in particular, study the need for and alternative routes of roads or other means of transit providing access to scenic views of and from the Western rim of Hells Canyon.

Wilderness areas; review by Secretary; recommendations of President to Congress; notice of hearings and meetings

(d) The Secretary shall review, as to their suitability or nonsuitability for preservation as wilderness, the areas generally depicted on the map referred to in section 460gg of this title as the "Lord Flat–Somers Point Plateau Wilderness Study Area", and the "West Side Reservoir Face Wilderness Study Area", and the "Mountain Sheep Wilderness Study Area" and report his findings to the President. The Secretary shall complete his review and the President shall, within five years from December 31, 1975, advise the United States Senate and House of Representatives of his recommendations with respect to the designation of lands within such area as wilderness. In conducting his review the Secretary shall comply with the provisions of section 1132(d) of this title and shall give public notice at least sixty days in advance of any hearing or other public meeting concerning the wilderness study area. The Secretary shall administer all Federal lands within the study areas so as not to preclude their possible future designation by the Congress as wilderness. Nothing contained herein shall limit the President in proposing, as part of this recommendation to Congress, the designation as wilderness of any additional area within the recreation area which is predominately of wilderness value.

Public participation in reviews and preparation of plan; cooperation of other Federal agencies

(e) In conducting the reviews and preparing the comprehensive management plan required by this section, the Secretary shall provide for full public participation and shall consider the views of all interested agencies, organizations, and individuals including but not limited to, the Nez Perce Tribe of Indians, and the States of Idaho, Oregon, and Washington. The Secretaries or Directors of all Federal departments, agencies, and commissions having a relevant expertise are hereby authorized and directed to cooperate with the Secretary in his review and to make such studies as the Secretary may request on a cost reimbursable basis.

Continuation of ongoing activities

(f) Such activities as are as [sic] compatible with the provisions of this subchapter, but not limited to, timber harvesting by selective cutting, mining, and grazing may continue during development of the comprehensive management plan, at current levels of activity and in areas of such activity on December 31, 1975. Further, in development of the management plan, the Secretary shall give full consideration to continuation of these ongoing activities in their respective areas.

Pub.L. 94–199, § 8, Dec. 31, 1975, 89 Stat. 1119.

* * *

§ **460gg-7.** Rules and regulations

The Secretary shall promulgate, and may amend, such rules and regulations as he deems necessary to accomplish the purposes of this subchapter. Such rules and regulations shall include, but are not limited to—

(a) standards for the use and development of privately owned property within the recreation area, which rules or regulations the Secretary may, to the extent he deems advisable, implement with the authorities delegated to him in section 460gg-6 of this title, and which may differ among the various parcels of land within the recreation area;

(b) standards and guidelines to insure the full protection and preservation of the historic, archeological, and paleontological resources in the recreation area;

(c) provision for the control of the use of motorized and mechanical equipment for transportation over, or alteration of, the surface of any Federal land within the recreation area;

(d) provision for the control of the use and number of motorized and nonmotorized river craft: *Provided*, That the use of such craft is hereby recognized as a valid use of the Snake River within the recreation area; and

(e) standards for such management, utilization, and disposal of natural resources on federally owned lands, including but not limited to, timber harvesting by selective cutting, mining, and grazing and the continuation of such existing uses and developments as are compatible with the provisions of this subchapter.

Pub.L. 94–199, § 10, Dec. 31, 1975, 89 Stat. 1121.

§ 460gg–8. Lands withdrawn from location, entry, and patent under United States mining laws

Notwithstanding the provisions of section 1133(d)(2) of this title and subject to valid existing rights, all Federal lands located in the recreation area are hereby withdrawn from all forms of location, entry, and patent under the mining laws of the United States, and from disposition under all laws pertaining to mineral leasing and all amendments thereto.

Pub.L. 94–199, § 11, Dec. 31, 1975, 89 Stat. 1122.

§ 460gg–9. Hunting and fishing

The Secretary shall permit hunting and fishing on lands and waters under his jurisdiction within the boundaries of the recreation area in accordance with applicable laws of the United States and the States wherein the lands and waters are located except that the Secretary may designate zones where, and establish periods when, no hunting or fishing shall be permitted for reasons for public safety, administration, or public use and enjoyment. Except in emergencies, any regulations of the Secretary pursuant to this section shall be put into effect only after consultation with the appropriate State fish and game department.

Pub.L. 94–199, § 12, Dec. 31, 1975, 89 Stat. 1122.

§ 460gg–10. Ranching, grazing, etc., as valid uses of area

Ranching, grazing, farming, timber harvesting, and the occupation of homes and lands associated therewith, as they exist on December 31, 1975, are recognized as traditional and valid uses of the recreation area.

Pub.L. 94–199, § 13, Dec. 31, 1975, 89 Stat. 1122.

* * *

HISTORIC SITES, BUILDINGS AND ANTIQUITIES ACT OF 1935

(16 U.S.C.A. §§ 461–467)

§ 461. Declaration of national policy

It is declared that it is a national policy to preserve for public use historic sites, buildings, and objects of national significance for the inspiration and benefit of the people of the United States.

Aug. 21, 1935, c. 593, § 1, 49 Stat. 666.

§ 462. Administration by Secretary of the Interior; powers and duties enumerated

The Secretary of the Interior (hereinafter in sections 461 to 467 of this title referred to as the Secretary), through the National Park Service, for the purpose of effectuating the policy expressed in section 461 of this title, shall have the following powers and perform the following duties and functions:

(a) Secure, collate, and preserve drawings, plans, photographs, and other data of historic and archaeologic sites, buildings, and objects.

(b) Make a survey of historic and archaeologic sites, buildings, and objects for the purpose of determining which possess exceptional value as commemorating or illustrating the history of the United States.

(c) Make necessary investigations and researches in the United States relating to particular sites, buildings, or objects to obtain true and accurate historical and archaeological facts and information concerning the same.

(d) For the purpose of sections 461 to 467 of this title, acquire in the name of the United States by gift, purchase, or otherwise any property, personal or real, or any interest or estate therein, title to any real property to be satisfactory to the Secretary: *Provided,* That no such property which is owned by any religious or educational institution, or which is owned or administered for the benefit of the public shall be so acquired without the consent of the owner: *Provided further,* That no such property shall be acquired or contract or agreement for the acquisition thereof made which will obligate the general fund of the Treasury for the payment of such property, unless or until Congress has appropriated money which is available for that purpose.

(e) Contract and make cooperative agreements with States, municipal subdivisions, corporations, associations, or individuals, with proper bond where deemed advisable, to protect, preserve, maintain, or operate any historic or archaeologic building, site, object, or property used in connection therewith for public use, regardless as to whether the title thereto is in the United States: *Provided,* That no contract or cooperative agreement shall be made or entered into which will obligate the general fund of the Treasury unless or until Congress has appropriated money for such purpose.

(f) Restore, reconstruct, rehabilitate, preserve, and maintain historic or prehistoric sites, buildings, objects, and properties of national historical or archaeological significance and where deemed desirable establish and maintain museums in connection therewith.

(g) Erect and maintain tablets to mark or commemorate historic or prehistoric places and events of national historical or archaeological significance.

(h) Operate and manage historic and archaeologic sites, buildings, and properties acquired under the provisions of sections 461 to 467 of this title together with lands and subordinate buildings for the benefit of the public, such authority to include the power to charge reasonable visitation fees and grant concessions, leases, or permits for the use of land, building space, roads, or trails when necessary or desirable either to accommodate the public or to facilitate administration: *Provided,* That the Secretary may grant such concessions, leases, or permits and enter into contracts relating to the same with responsible persons, firms, or corporations without advertising and without securing competitive bids.

(i) When the Secretary determines that it would be administratively burdensome to restore, reconstruct, operate, or maintain any particular historic or archaeologic site, building, or property donated to the United States through the National Park Service, he may cause the same to be done by organizing a corporation for that purpose under the laws of the District of Columbia or any State.

(j) Develop an educational program and service for the purpose of making available to the public facts and information pertaining to American historic and archaeologic sites, buildings, and properties of national significance. Reasonable charges may be made for the dissemination of any such facts or information.

(k) Perform any and all acts, and make such rules and regulations not inconsistent with sections 461 to 467 of this title as may be necessary and proper to carry out the provisions thereof. Any person violating any of the rules and regulations authorized by said sections shall be punished by a fine of not more than $500 and be adjudged to pay all cost of the proceedings.

Aug. 21, 1935, c. 593, § 2, 49 Stat. 666; Oct. 9, 1965, Pub.L. 89–249, § 8, 79 Stat. 971; Nov. 13, 1998, Pub.L. 105–391, Title IV, § 415(a), 112 Stat. 3515.

* * *

NATIONAL HISTORIC PRESERVATION ACT

(16 U.S.C.A. §§ 470 through 470w–6)

§ 470. Short title; Congressional finding and declaration of policy

(a) This subchapter may be cited as the "National Historic Preservation Act".

(b) The Congress finds and declares that—

(1) the spirit and direction of the Nation are founded upon and reflected in its historic heritage;

(2) the historical and cultural foundations of the Nation should be preserved as a living part of our community life and development in order to give a sense of orientation to the American people;

(3) historic properties significant to the Nation's heritage are being lost or substantially altered, often inadvertently, with increasing frequency;

(4) the preservation of this irreplaceable heritage is in the public interest so that its vital legacy of cultural, educational, aesthetic,

inspirational, economic, and energy benefits will be maintained and enriched for future generations of Americans;

(5) in the face of ever-increasing extensions of urban centers, highways, and residential, commercial, and industrial developments, the present governmental and nongovernmental historic preservation programs and activities are inadequate to insure future generations a genuine opportunity to appreciate and enjoy the rich heritage of our Nation;

(6) the increased knowledge of our historic resources, the establishment of better means of identifying and administering them, and the encouragement of their preservation will improve the planning and execution of Federal and federally assisted projects and will assist economic growth and development; and

(7) although the major burdens of historic preservation have been borne and major efforts initiated by private agencies and individuals, and both should continue to play a vital role, it is nevertheless necessary and appropriate for the Federal Government to accelerate its historic preservation programs and activities, to give maximum encouragement to agencies and individuals undertaking preservation by private means, and to assist State and local governments and the National Trust for Historic Preservation in the United States to expand and accelerate their historic preservation programs and activities.

Pub.L. 89–665, § 1, Oct. 15, 1966, 80 Stat. 915; Pub.L. 96–515, Title I, § 101(a), Dec. 12, 1980, 94 Stat. 2987.

* * *

§ **470a.** Historic preservation program

National Register of Historic Places; designation of properties as historic landmarks; properties deemed included; criteria; nomination of properties by States, local governments or individuals; regulations; review of threats to properties

(a)(1)(A) The Secretary of the Interior is authorized to expand and maintain a National Register of Historic Places composed of districts, sites, buildings, structures, and objects significant in American history, architecture, archeology, engineering, and culture. Notwithstanding section 1125(c) of Title 15, buildings and structures on or eligible for inclusion on the National Register of Historic Places (either individually or as part of a historic district), or designated as an individual landmark or as a contributing building in a historic district by a unit of State or local government, may retain the name historically associated with the building or structure.

(B) Properties meeting the criteria for National Historic Landmarks established pursuant to paragraph (2) shall be designated as "National Historic Landmarks" and included on the National Register, subject to the requirements of paragraph (6). All historic properties included on the National Register on December 12, 1980, shall be deemed to be included on the National Register as of their initial listing for purposes of this subchapter. All historic properties listed in the Federal Register of February 6, 1979, as "National Historic Landmarks" or thereafter prior to the effective date of this Act are declared by Congress to be National Historic Landmarks of national historic significance as of their initial listing as such in the Federal Register for purposes of this subchapter and sections 461 to 467 of this title; except that in cases of National Historic Landmark districts for which no boundaries have been established, boundaries must first be published in the Federal Register.

(2) The Secretary in consultation with national historical and archaeological associations, shall establish or revise criteria for properties to be included on the National Register and criteria for National Historic Landmarks, and shall also promulgate or revise regulations as may be necessary for—

(A) nominating properties for inclusion in, and removal from, the National Register and the recommendation of properties by certified local governments;

(B) designating properties as National Historic Landmarks and removing such designation;

(C) considering appeals from such recommendations, nominations, removals, and designations (or any failure or refusal by a nominating authority to nominate or designate);

(D) nominating historic properties for inclusion in the World Heritage List in accordance with the terms of the Convention concerning the Protection of the World Cultural and Natural Heritage;

(E) making determinations of eligibility of properties for inclusion on the National Register; and

(F) notifying the owner of a property, any appropriate local governments, and the general public, when the property is being considered for inclusion on the National Register, for designation as a National Historic Landmark or for nomination to the World Heritage List.

(3) Subject to the requirements of paragraph (6), any State which is carrying out a program approved under subsection (b) of this section, shall nominate to the Secretary properties which meet the criteria promulgated under subsection (a) of this section for inclusion on the National Register. Subject to paragraph (6), any property nominated under this paragraph or under section 470h–2(a)(2) of this title shall be included on the National Register on the date forty-five days after receipt by the Secretary of the nomination and the necessary documentation, unless the Secretary disapproves such nomination within such forty-five day period or unless an appeal is filed under paragraph (5).

(4) Subject to the requirements of paragraph (6) the Secretary may accept a nomination directly from any person or local government for inclusion of a property on the National Register only if such property is located in a State where there is no program approved under subsection (b) of this section. The Secretary may include on the National Register any property for which such a nomination is made if he determines that such property is eligible in accordance with the regulations promulgated under

paragraph (2). Such determination shall be made within ninety days from the date of the nomination unless the nomination is appealed under paragraph (5).

(5) Any person or local government may appeal to the Secretary a nomination of any historic property for inclusion on the National Register and may appeal to the Secretary the failure or refusal of a nominating authority to nominate a property in accordance with this subsection.

(6) The Secretary shall promulgate regulations requiring that before any property or district may be included on the National Register or designated as a National Historic Landmark, the owner or owners of such property, or a majority of the owners of the properties within the district in the case of an historic district, shall be given the opportunity (including a reasonable period of time) to concur in, or object to, the nomination of the property or district for such inclusion or designation. If the owner or owners of any privately owned property, or a majority of the owners of such properties within the district in the case of an historic district, object to such inclusion or designation, such property shall not be included on the National Register or designated as a National Historic Landmark until such objection is withdrawn. The Secretary shall review the nomination of the property or district where any such objection has been made and shall determine whether or not the property or district is eligible for such inclusion or designation, and if the Secretary determines that such property or district is eligible for such inclusion or designation, he shall inform the Advisory Council on Historic Preservation, the appropriate State Historic Preservation Officer, the appropriate chief elected local official and the owner or owners of such property, of his determination. The regulations under this paragraph shall include provisions to carry out the purposes of this paragraph in the case of multiple ownership of a single property.

(7) The Secretary shall promulgate, or revise, regulations—

(A) ensuring that significant prehistoric and historic artifacts, and associated records, subject to section 470h–2 of this title, the Act of June 27, 1960 (16 U.S.C. 469c [16 U.S.C.A. § 469 et seq.]), and the Archaeological Resources Protection Act of 1979 (16 U.S.C. 470aa and following [16 U.S.C.A. § 470aa et seq.]) are deposited in an institution with adequate long-term curatorial capabilities;

(B) establishing a uniform process and standards for documenting historic properties by public agencies and private parties for purposes of incorporation into, or complementing, the national historical architectural and engineering records within the Library of Congress; and

(C) certifying local governments, in accordance with subsection (c)(1) of this section and for the allocation of funds pursuant to section 470c(c) of this title.

(8) The Secretary shall, at least once every 4 years, in consultation with the Council and with State Historic Preservation Officers, review significant threats to properties included in, or eligible for inclusion on, the National Register, in order to—

(A) determine the kinds of properties that may be threatened;

(B) ascertain the causes of the threats; and

(C) develop and submit to the President and Congress recommendations for appropriate action.

Regulations for State Historic Preservation Programs; periodic evaluations and fiscal audits of State programs; administration of State programs; contracts and cooperative agreements with nonprofit or educational institutions and State Historic Preservation Officers; treatment of State programs as approved programs

(b)(1) The Secretary, in consultation with the National Conference of State Historic Preservation Officers and the National Trust for Historic Preservation, shall promulgate or revise regulations for State Historic Preservation Programs. Such regulations shall provide that a State program submitted to the Secretary under this section shall be approved by the Secretary if he determines that the program—

(A) provides for the designation and appointment by the Governor of a "State Historic Preservation Officer" to administer such program in accordance with paragraph (3) and for the employment or appointment by such officer of such professionally qualified staff as may be necessary for such purposes;

(B) provides for an adequate and qualified State historic preservation review board designated by the State Historic Preservation Officer unless otherwise provided for by State law; and

(C) provides for adequate public participation in the State Historic Preservation Program, including the process of recommending properties for nomination to the National Register.

(2)(A) Periodically, but not less than every 4 years after the approval of any State program under this subsection, the Secretary, in consultation with the Council on the appropriate provisions of this subchapter, and in cooperation with the State Historic Preservation Officer, shall evaluate the program to determine whether it is consistent with this subchapter.

(B) If, at any time, the Secretary determines that a major aspect of a State program is not consistent with this subchapter, the Secretary shall disapprove the program and suspend in whole or in part any contracts or cooperative agreements with the State and the State Historic Preservation Officer under this subchapter, until the program is consistent with this subchapter, unless the Secretary determines that the program will be made consistent with this subchapter within a reasonable period of time.

(C) The Secretary, in consultation with State Historic Preservation Officers, shall establish oversight methods to ensure State program consistency and quality without imposing undue review burdens on State Historic Preservation Officers.

(D) At the discretion of the Secretary, a State system of fiscal audit and management may be substituted for comparable Federal systems so long as the State system—

(i) establishes and maintains substantially similar accountability standards; and

(ii) provides for independent professional peer review.

The Secretary may also conduct periodic fiscal audits of State programs approved under this section as needed and shall ensure that such programs meet applicable accountability standards.

(3) It shall be the responsibility of the State Historic Preservation Officer to administer the State Historic Preservation Program and to—

(A) in cooperation with Federal and State agencies, local governments, and private organizations and individuals, direct and conduct a comprehensive statewide survey of historic properties and maintain inventories of such properties;

(B) identify and nominate eligible properties to the National Register and otherwise administer applications for listing historic properties on the National Register;

(C) prepare and implement a comprehensive statewide historic preservation plan;

(D) administer the State program of Federal assistance for historic preservation within the State;

(E) advise and assist, as appropriate, Federal and State agencies and local governments in carrying out their historic preservation responsibilities;

(F) cooperate with the Secretary, the Advisory Council on Historic Preservation, and other Federal and State agencies, local governments, and organizations and individuals to ensure that historic properties are taken into consideration at all levels of planning and development;

(G) provide public information, education, and training and technical assistance in historic preservation;

(H) cooperate with local governments in the development of local historic preservation programs and assist local governments in becoming certified pursuant to subsection (c) of this section;

(I) consult with appropriate Federal agencies in accordance with this subchapter on—

(i) Federal undertakings that may affect historic properties; and

(ii) the content and sufficiency of any plans developed to protect, manage, or reduce or mitigate harm to such properties; and

(J) advise and assist in the evaluation of proposals for rehabilitation projects that may qualify for Federal assistance.

(4) Any State may carry out all or any part of its responsibilities under this subsection by contract or cooperative agreement with any qualified nonprofit organization or educational institution.

(5) Any State historic preservation program in effect under prior authority of law may be treated as an approved program for purposes of this subsection until the earlier of—

(A) the date on which the Secretary approves a program submitted by the State under this subsection, or

(B) three years after December 12, 1992.

(6)(A) Subject to subparagraphs (C) and (D), the Secretary may enter into contracts or cooperative agreements with a State Historic Preservation Officer for any State authorizing such Officer to assist the Secretary in carrying out one or more of the following responsibilities within that State—

(i) Identification and preservation of historic properties.

(ii) Determination of the eligibility of properties for listing on the National Register.

(iii) Preparation of nominations for inclusion on the National Register.

(iv) Maintenance of historical and archaeological data bases.

(v) Evaluation of eligibility for Federal preservation incentives.

Nothing in this paragraph shall be construed to provide that any State Historic Preservation Officer or any other person other than the Secretary shall have the authority to maintain the National Register for properties in any State.

(B) The Secretary may enter into a contract or cooperative agreement under subparagraph (A) only if—

(i) the State Historic Preservation Officer has requested the additional responsibility;

(ii) the Secretary has approved the State historic preservation program pursuant to subsection (b)(1) and (2) of this section;

(iii) the State Historic Preservation Officer agrees to carry out the additional responsibility in a timely and efficient manner acceptable to the Secretary and the Secretary determines that such Officer is fully capable of carrying out such responsibility in such manner;

(iv) the State Historic Preservation Officer agrees to permit the Secretary to review and revise, as appropriate in the discretion of the Secretary, decisions made by the Officer pursuant to such contract or cooperative agreement; and

(v) the Secretary and the State Historic Preservation Officer agree on the terms of additional financial assistance to the State, if there is to be any, for the costs of carrying out such responsibility.

(C) For each significant program area under the Secretary's authority, the Secretary shall establish specific conditions and criteria essential for the assumption by State Historic Preservation Officers of the Secretary's duties in each such program.

(D) Nothing in this subsection shall have the effect of diminishing the preservation programs and activities of the National Park Service.

Certification of local governments by State Historic Preservation Officer; transfer of portion of grants; certification by Secretary; nomination of properties by local governments for inclusion on National Register

(c)(1) Any State program approved under this section shall provide a mechanism for the certification by the State Historic Preservation Officer of local governments to carry out the purposes of this subchapter and provide for the transfer, in accordance with section 470c(c) of this title, of a portion of the grants received by the States under this subchapter, to such local governments. Any local government shall be certified to participate under the provisions of this section if the applicable State Historic Preservation Officer, and the Secretary, certifies that the local government—

(A) enforces appropriate State or local legislation for the designation and protection of historic properties;

(B) has established an adequate and qualified historic preservation review commission by State or local legislation;

(C) maintains a system for the survey and inventory of historic properties that furthers the purposes of subsection (b) of this section;

(D) provides for adequate public participation in the local historic preservation program, including the process of recommending properties for nomination to the National Register; and

(E) satisfactorily performs the responsibilities delegated to it under this subchapter.

Where there is no approved State program, a local government may be certified by the Secretary if he determines that such local government meets the requirements of subparagraphs (A) through (E); and in any such case the Secretary may make grants-in-aid to the local government for purposes of this section.

(2)(A) Before a property within the jurisdiction of the certified local government may be considered by the State to be nominated to the Secretary for inclusion on the National Register, the State Historic Preservation Officer shall notify the owner, the applicable chief local elected official, and the local historic preservation commission. The commission, after reasonable opportunity for public comment, shall prepare a report as to whether or not such property, in its opinion, meets the criteria of the National Register. Within sixty days of notice from the State Historic Preservation Officer, the chief local elected official shall transmit the report of the commission and his recommendation to the State Historic Preservation Officer. Except as provided in subparagraph (B), after receipt of such report and recommendation, or if no such report and recommendation are received within sixty days, the State shall make the nomination pursuant to subsection (a) of this section. The State may expedite such process with the concurrence of the certified local government.

(B) If both the commission and the chief local elected official recommend that a property not be nominated to the National Register, the State Historic Preservation Officer shall take no further action, unless within thirty days of the receipt of such recommendation by the State Historic Preservation Officer an appeal is filed with the State. If such an appeal is filed, the State shall follow the procedures for making a nomination pursuant to subsection (a) of this section. Any report and recommendations made under this section shall be included with any nomination submitted by the State to the Secretary.

(3) Any local government certified under this section or which is making efforts to become so certified shall be eligible for funds under the provisions of section 470c(c) of this title, and shall carry out any responsibilities delegated to it in accordance with such terms and conditions as the Secretary deems necessary or advisable.

(4) For the purposes of this section the term—

(A) "designation" means the identification and registration of properties for protection that meet criteria established by the State or the locality for significant historic and prehistoric resources within the jurisdiction of a local government; and

(B) "protection" means a local review process under State or local law for proposed demolition of, changes to, or other action that may affect historic properties designated pursuant to this subsection.

Historic properties of Indian tribes

(d)(1)(A) The Secretary shall establish a program and promulgate regulations to assist Indian tribes in preserving their particular historic properties. The Secretary shall foster communication and cooperation between Indian tribes and State Historic Preservation Officers in the administration of the national historic preservation program to ensure that all types of historic properties and all public interests in such properties are given due consideration, and to encourage coordination among Indian tribes, State Historic Preservation Officers, and Federal agencies in historic preservation planning and in the identification, evaluation, protection, and interpretation of historic properties.

(B) The program under subparagraph (A) shall be developed in such a manner as to ensure that tribal values are taken into account to the extent feasible. The Secretary may waive or modify requirements of this section to conform to the cultural setting of tribal heritage preservation goals and objectives. The tribal programs implemented by specific tribal organizations may vary in scope, as determined by each tribe's chief governing authority.

(C) The Secretary shall consult with Indian tribes, other Federal agencies, State Historic Preservation Officers, and other interested parties and initiate the program under subparagraph (A) by not later than October 1, 1994.

(2) A tribe may assume all or any part of the functions of a State Historic Preservation Officer in accordance with subsections (b)(2) and (b)(3) of this section, with respect to tribal lands, as such responsibilities may be modified for tribal programs through regulations issued by the Secretary, if—

(A) the tribe's chief governing authority so requests;

(B) the tribe designates a tribal preservation official to administer the tribal historic preservation program, through appointment by the tribe's chief governing authority or as a tribal ordinance may otherwise provide;

(C) the tribal preservation official provides the Secretary with a plan describing how the functions the tribal preservation official proposes to assume will be carried out;

(D) the Secretary determines, after consulting with the tribe, the appropriate State Historic Preservation Officer, the Council (if the tribe proposes to assume the functions of the State Historic Preservation Officer with respect to review of undertakings under section 470f of this title), and other tribes, if any, whose tribal or aboriginal lands may be affected by conduct of the tribal preservation program—

(i) that the tribal preservation program is fully capable of carrying out the functions specified in the plan provided under subparagraph (C);

(ii) that the plan defines the remaining responsibilities of the Secretary and the State Historic Preservation Officer; and

(iii) that the plan provides, with respect to properties neither owned by a member of the tribe nor held in trust by the Secretary for the benefit of the tribe, at the request of the owner thereof, the State Historic Preservation Officer, in addition to the tribal preservation official, may exercise the historic preservation responsibilities in accordance with subsections (b)(2) and (b)(3) of this section; and

(E) based on satisfaction of the conditions stated in subparagraphs (A), (B), (C), and (D), the Secretary approves the plan.

(3) In consultation with interested Indian tribes, other Native American organizations and affected State Historic Preservation Officers, the Secretary shall establish and implement procedures for carrying out section 470c(a) of this title with respect to tribal programs that assume responsibilities under paragraph (2).

(4) At the request of a tribe whose preservation program has been approved to assume functions and responsibilities pursuant to paragraph (2), the Secretary shall enter into contracts or cooperative agreements with such tribe permitting the assumption by the tribe of any part of the responsibilities referred to in subsection (b)(6) of this section on tribal land, if—

(A) the Secretary and the tribe agree on additional financial assistance, if any, to the tribe for the costs of carrying out such authorities;

(B) the Secretary finds that the tribal historic preservation program has been demonstrated to be sufficient to carry out the contract or cooperative agreement and this subchapter; and

(C) the contract or cooperative agreement specifies the continuing responsibilities of the Secretary or of the appropriate State Historic Preservation Officers and provides for appropriate participation by—

(i) the tribe's traditional cultural authorities;

(ii) representatives of other tribes whose traditional lands are under the jurisdiction of the tribe assuming responsibilities; and

(iii) the interested public.

(5) The Council may enter into an agreement with an Indian tribe to permit undertakings on tribal land to be reviewed under tribal historic preservation regulations in place of review under regulations promulgated by the Council to govern compliance with section 470f of this title, if the Council, after consultation with the tribe and appropriate State Historic Preservation Officers, determines that the tribal preservation regulations will afford historic properties consideration equivalent to those afforded by the Council's regulations.

(6)(A) Properties of traditional religious and cultural importance to an Indian tribe or Native Hawaiian organization may be determined to be eligible for inclusion on the National Register.

(B) In carrying out its responsibilities under section 470f of this title, a Federal agency shall consult with any Indian tribe or Native Hawaiian organization that attaches religious and cultural significance to properties described in subparagraph (A).

(C) In carrying out his or her responsibilities under subsection (b)(3) of this section, the State Historic Preservation Officer for the State of Hawaii shall—

(i) consult with Native Hawaiian organizations in assessing the cultural significance of any property in determining whether to nominate such property to the National Register;

(ii) consult with Native Hawaiian organizations in developing the cultural component of a preservation program or plan for such property; and

(iii) enter into a memorandum of understanding or agreement with Native Hawaiian organizations for the assessment of the cultural significance of a property in determining whether to nominate such property to the National Register and to carry out the cultural component of such preservation program or plan.

Matching grants to States; grants to National Trust for Historic Preservation in the United States; program of direct grants for preservation of properties included on National Register; grants or loans to Indian tribes and ethnic or minority groups for preservation of cultural heritage; grants for religious properties; direct grants to Indian tribes, Native Hawaiian organizations, and Micronesian States

(e)(1) The Secretary shall administer a program of matching grants to the States for the purposes of carrying out this subchapter.

(2) The Secretary may administer grants to the National Trust for Historic Preservation in the United States, chartered by sections 468 to 468d of this title consistent with the purposes of its charter and this subchapter.

(3)(A) In addition to the programs under paragraphs (1) and (2), the Secretary shall administer a program of direct grants for the preservation of properties included on the National Register. Funds to support such program annually shall not exceed 10 per centum of the amount appropriated annually for the fund established under section 470h of this title. These grants may be made by the Secretary, in consultation with the appropriate State Historic Preservation Officer—

(i) for the preservation of National Historic Landmarks which are threatened with demolition or impairment and for the preservation of historic properties of World Heritage significance,

(ii) for demonstration projects which will provide information concerning professional methods and techniques having application to historic properties,

(iii) for the training and development of skilled labor in trades and crafts, and in analysis and curation, relating to historic preservation, and

(iv) to assist persons or small businesses within any historic district included in the National Register to remain within the district.

(B) The Secretary may also, in consultation with the appropriate State Historic Preservation Officer, make grants or loans or both under this section to Indian tribes and to nonprofit organizations representing ethnic or minority groups for the preservation of their cultural heritage.

(C) Grants may be made under subparagraph (A)(i) and (iv) only to the extent that the project cannot be carried out in as effective a manner through the use of an insured loan under section 470d of this title.

(4) Grants may be made under this subsection for the preservation, stabilization, restoration, or rehabilitation of religious properties listed in the National Register of Historic Places, provided that the purpose of the grant is secular, does not promote religion, and seeks to protect those qualities that are historically significant. Nothing in this paragraph shall be construed to authorize the use of any funds made available under this section for the acquisition of any property referred to in the preceding sentence.

(5) The Secretary shall administer a program of direct grants to Indian tribes and Native Hawaiian organizations for the purpose of carrying out this subchapter as it pertains to Indian tribes and Native Hawaiian organizations. Matching fund requirements may be modified. Federal funds available to a tribe or Native Hawaiian organization may be used as matching funds for the purposes of the tribe's or organization's conducting its responsibilities pursuant to this section.

(6)(A) As part of the program of matching grant assistance from the Historic Preservation Fund to States, the Secretary shall administer a program of direct grants to the Federated States of Micronesia, the Republic of the Marshall Islands, the Trust Territory of the Pacific Islands, and upon termination of the Trusteeship Agreement for the Trust Territory of the Pacific Islands, the Republic of Palau (referred to as the Micronesian States) in furtherance of the Compact of Free Association between the United States and the Federated States of Micronesia and the Marshall

Islands, approved by the Compact of Free Association Act of 1985 (48 U.S.C. 1681 note), the Trusteeship Agreement for the Trust Territory of the Pacific Islands, and the Compact of Free Association between the United States and Palau, approved by the Joint Resolution entitled "Joint Resolution to approve the 'Compact of Free Association' between the United States and Government of Palau, and for other purposes" (48 U.S.C. 1681 note). The goal of the program shall be to establish historic and cultural preservation programs that meet the unique needs of each Micronesian State so that at the termination of the compacts the programs shall be firmly established. The Secretary may waive or modify the requirements of this section to conform to the cultural setting of those nations.

(B) The amounts to be made available to the Micronesian States shall be allocated by the Secretary on the basis of needs as determined by the Secretary. Matching funds may be waived or modified.

Prohibition of use of funds for compensation of intervenors in preservation program

(f) No part of any grant made under this section may be used to compensate any person intervening in any proceeding under this subchapter.

Guidelines for Federal agency responsibility for agency-owned historic properties

(g) In consultation with the Advisory Council on Historic Preservation, the Secretary shall promulgate guidelines for Federal agency responsibilities under section 470h–2 of this title.

Professional standards for preservation of federally owned or controlled historic properties

(h) Within one year after December 12, 1980, the Secretary shall establish, in consultation with the Secretaries of Agriculture and Defense, the Smithsonian Institution, and the Administrator of the General Services Administration, professional standards for the preservation of historic properties in Federal ownership or control.

Dissemination of information concerning professional methods and techniques for preservation of historic properties

(i) The Secretary shall develop and make available to Federal agencies, State and local governments, private organizations and individuals, and other nations and international organizations pursuant to the World Heritage Convention, training in, and information concerning, professional methods and techniques for the preservation of historic properties and for the administration of the historic preservation program at the Federal, State, and local level. The Secretary shall also develop mechanisms to provide information concerning historic preservation to the general public including students.

Preservation education and training program

(j)(1) The Secretary shall, in consultation with the Council and other appropriate Federal, tribal, Native Hawaiian, and non-Federal organizations, develop and implement a comprehensive preservation education and training program.

(2) The education and training program described in paragraph (1) shall include—

(A) new standards and increased preservation training opportunities for Federal workers involved in preservation-related functions;

(B) increased preservation training opportunities for other Federal, State, tribal and local government workers, and students;

(C) technical or financial assistance, or both, to historically black colleges and universities, to tribal colleges, and to colleges with a high enrollment of Native Americans or Native Hawaiians, to establish preservation training and degree programs; and

(D) coordination of the following activities, where appropriate, with the National Center for Preservation Technology and Training—

(i) distribution of information on preservation technologies;

(ii) provision of training and skill development in trades, crafts, and disciplines related to historic preservation in Federal training and development programs; and

(iii) support for research, analysis, conservation, curation, interpretation, and display related to preservation.

Pub.L. 89–665, Title I, § 101, Oct. 15, 1966, 80 Stat. 915; Pub.L. 93–54, § 1(d), July 1, 1973, 87 Stat. 139; Pub.L. 91–383, § 11, as added Pub.L. 94–458, § 2, Oct. 7, 1976, 90 Stat. 1942; Pub.L. 96–205, Title VI, § 608(a)(1), (2), Mar. 12, 1980, 94 Stat. 92; Pub.L. 96–515, Title II, § 201(a), Dec. 12, 1980, 94 Stat. 2988, and amended Pub.L. 102–575, Title XL, §§ 4003 to 4005, 4006(a), 4007, 4008, Oct. 30, 1992, 106 Stat. 4753 to 4755, 4758; Pub.L. 103–437, § 6(d)(29), Nov. 2, 1994, 108 Stat. 4584; Pub.L. 104–333, Div. I, Title VIII, § 814(d)(2)(F), Nov. 12, 1996, 110 Stat. 4196; Pub.L. 106–113, Div. B, § 1000(a)(9) [Title III, § 3007], Nov. 29, 1999, 113 Stat. 1536, 1501A–551; Pub.L. 106–208, § 5(a)(1) to (4), May 26, 2000, 114 Stat. 318.

* * *

§ 470f. Effect of Federal undertakings upon property listed in National Register; comment by Advisory Council on Historic Preservation

The head of any Federal agency having direct or indirect jurisdiction over a proposed Federal or federally assisted undertaking in any State and the head of any Federal department or independent agency having authority to license any undertaking shall, prior to the approval of the expenditure of any Federal funds on the undertaking or prior to the issuance of any license, as the case may be, take into account the effect of the undertaking on any district, site, building, structure, or object that is included in or eligible for inclusion in the National Register. The head of any such Federal agency shall afford the Advisory Council on Historic Preservation established under part B of this subchapter a reasonable opportunity to comment with regard to such undertaking.

Pub.L. 89–665, Title I, § 106, Oct. 15, 1966, 80 Stat. 917; Pub.L. 94–422, Title II, § 201(3), Sept. 28, 1976, 90 Stat. 1320.

* * *

§ 470h–2. Historic properties owned or controlled by Federal agencies

Responsibilities of Federal agencies; program for identification, evaluation, nomination, and protection

(a)(1) The heads of all Federal agencies shall assume responsibility for the preservation of historic properties which are owned or controlled by such agency. Prior to acquiring, constructing, or leasing buildings for purposes of carrying out agency responsibilities, each Federal agency shall use, to the maximum extent feasible, historic properties available to the agency, in accordance with Executive Order No. 13006, issued May 21, 1996 (61 Fed. Reg. 26071). Each agency shall undertake, consistent with the preservation of such properties and the mission of the agency and the professional standards established pursuant to section 470a(g) of this title, any preservation, as may be necessary to carry out this section.

(2) Each Federal agency shall establish (unless exempted pursuant to section 470v of this title), in consultation with the Secretary, a preservation program for the identification, evaluation, and nomination to the National Register of Historic Places, and protection of historic properties. Such program shall ensure—

  (A) that historic properties under the jurisdiction or control of the agency, are identified, evaluated, and nominated to the National Register;

  (B) that such properties under the jurisdiction or control of the agency as are listed in or may be eligible for the National Register are managed and maintained in a way that considers the preservation of their historic, archaeological, architectural, and cultural values in compliance with section 470f of this title and gives special consideration to the preservation of such values in the case of properties designated as having National significance;

  (C) that the preservation of properties not under the jurisdiction or control of the agency, but subject to be potentially affected by agency actions are given full consideration in planning;

  (D) that the agency's preservation-related activities are carried out in consultation with other Federal, State, and local agencies, Indian tribes, Native Hawaiian organizations carrying out historic preservation planning activities, and with the private sector; and

  (E) that the agency's procedures for compliance with section 470f of this title—

(i) are consistent with regulations issued by the Council pursuant to section 470s of this title;

(ii) provide a process for the identification and evaluation of historic properties for listing in the National Register and the development and implementation of agreements, in consultation with State Historic Preservation Officers, local governments, Indian tribes, Native Hawaiian organizations, and the interested public, as appropriate, regarding the means by which adverse effects on such properties will be considered; and

(iii) provide for the disposition of Native American cultural items from Federal or tribal land in a manner consistent with section 3002(c) of Title 25.

Records on historic properties to be altered or demolished; deposit in Library of Congress or other appropriate agency

(b) Each Federal agency shall initiate measures to assure that where, as a result of Federal action or assistance carried out by such agency, an historic property is to be substantially altered or demolished, timely steps are taken to make or have made appropriate records, and that such records then be deposited, in accordance with section 470a(a) of this title, in the Library of Congress or with such other appropriate agency as may be designated by the Secretary, for future use and reference.

Agency Preservation Officer; responsibilities; qualifications

(c) The head of each Federal agency shall, unless exempted under section 470v of this title, designate a qualified official to be known as the agency's "preservation officer" who shall be responsible for coordinating that agency's activities under this subchapter. Each Preservation Officer may, in order to be considered qualified, satisfactorily complete an appropriate training program established by the Secretary under section 470a(h) of this title.

Agency programs and projects

(d) Consistent with the agency's missions and mandates, all Federal agencies shall carry out agency programs and projects (including those under which any Federal assistance is provided or any Federal license, permit, or other approval is required) in accordance with the purposes of this subchapter and, give consideration to programs and projects which will further the purposes of this subchapter.

Review of plans of transferees of surplus federally owned historic properties

(e) The Secretary shall review and approve the plans of transferees of surplus federally owned historic properties not later than ninety days after his receipt of such plans to ensure that the prehistorical, historical, architectural, or culturally significant values will be preserved or enhanced.

Planning and actions to minimize harm to National Historic Landmarks

(f) Prior to the approval of any Federal undertaking which may directly and adversely affect any National Historic Landmark, the head of the responsible Federal agency shall, to the maximum extent possible, undertake such planning and actions as may be necessary to minimize harm to such landmark, and shall afford the Advisory Council on Historic Preservation a reasonable opportunity to comment on the undertaking.

Costs of preservation as eligible project costs

(g) Each Federal agency may include the costs of preservation activities of such agency under this subchapter as eligible project costs in all undertakings of such agency or assisted by such agency. The eligible project costs may also include amounts paid by a Federal agency to any State to be used in carrying out such preservation responsibilities of the Federal agency under this subchapter, and reasonable costs may be charged to Federal licensees and permittees as a condition to the issuance of such license or permit.

Annual preservation awards program

(h) The Secretary shall establish an annual preservation awards program under which he may make monetary awards in amounts of not to exceed $1,000 and provide citations for special achievement to officers and employees of Federal, State, and certified local governments in recognition of their outstanding contributions to the preservation of historic resources. Such program may include the issuance of annual awards by the President of the United States to any citizen of the United States recommended for such award by the Secretary.

Environmental impact statement

(i) Nothing in this subchapter shall be construed to require the preparation of an environmental impact statement where such a statement would not otherwise be required under the National Environmental Policy Act of 1969 [42 U.S.C.A. § 4321 et seq.], and nothing in this subchapter shall be construed to provide any exemption from any requirement respecting the preparation of such a statement under such Act.

Waiver of provisions in event of natural disaster or imminent threat to national security

(j) The Secretary shall promulgate regulations under which the requirements of this section may be waived in whole or in part in the event of a major natural disaster or an imminent threat to the national security.

Assistance for adversely affected historic property

(k) Each Federal agency shall ensure that the agency will not grant a loan, loan guarantee, permit, license, or other assistance to an applicant who, with intent to avoid the requirements of section 470f of this title, has intentionally significantly adversely affected a historic property to which the grant would relate, or having legal power to prevent it, allowed such significant adverse effect to occur, unless the agency, after consultation with the Council, determines that circumstances justify granting such assistance despite the adverse effect created or permitted by the applicant.

Documentation of decisions respecting undertakings

(*l*) With respect to any undertaking subject to section 470f of this title which adversely affects any property included in or eligible for inclusion in the National Register, and for which a Federal agency has not entered into an agreement pursuant to regulations issued by the Council, the head of such agency shall document any decision made pursuant to section 470f of this title. The head of such agency may not delegate his or her responsibilities pursuant to such section. Where a section 470f of this title memorandum of agreement has been executed with respect to an undertaking, such memorandum shall govern the undertaking and all of its parts.

Pub.L. 89–665, Title I, § 110, as added Pub.L. 96–515, Title II, § 206, Dec. 12, 1980, 94 Stat. 2996, and amended Pub.L. 102–575, Title XL, §§ 4006(b), 4012, Oct. 30, 1992, 106 Stat. 4757, 4760; Pub.L. 106–208, §§ 4, 5(a)(8), May 26, 2000, 114 Stat. 318, 319; Pub.L. 108–352, § 13, Oct. 21, 2004, 118 Stat. 1397.

* * *

ARCHAEOLOGICAL RESOURCES PROTECTION ACT OF 1979

(16 U.S.C.A. §§ 470aa–470ll)

§ 470aa. Congressional findings and declaration of purpose

(a) The Congress finds that—

(1) archaeological resources on public lands and Indian lands are an accessible and irreplaceable part of the Nation's heritage;

(2) these resources are increasingly endangered because of their commercial attractiveness;

(3) existing Federal laws do not provide adequate protection to prevent the loss and destruction of these archaeological resources and sites resulting from uncontrolled excavations and pillage; and

(4) there is a wealth of archaeological information which has been legally obtained by private individuals for noncommercial purposes and which could voluntarily be made available to professional archaeologists and institutions.

(b) The purpose of this chapter is to secure, for the present and future benefit of the American people, the protection of archaeological resources and sites which are on public lands and Indian lands, and to foster increased cooperation and exchange of information between governmental authorities, the professional archaeological community, and private individuals having collections of archaeological resources and data which were obtained before October 31, 1979.

Pub.L. 96–95, § 2, Oct. 31, 1979, 93 Stat. 721.

§ 470bb. Definitions

As used in this chapter—

(1) The term "archaeological resource" means any material remains of past human life or activities which are of archaeological interest, as determined under uniform regulations promulgated pursuant to this chapter. Such regulations containing such determination shall include, but not be limited to: pottery, basketry, bottles, weapons, weapon projectiles, tools, structures or portions of structures, pit houses, rock paintings, rock carvings, intaglios, graves, human skeletal materials, or any portion or piece of any of the foregoing items. Nonfossilized and fossilized paleontological specimens, or any portion or piece thereof, shall not be considered archaeological resources, under the regulations under this paragraph, unless found in an archaeological context. No item shall be treated as an archaeological resource under regulations under this paragraph unless such item is at least 100 years of age.

(2) The term "Federal land manager" means, with respect to any public lands, the Secretary of the department, or the head of any other agency or instrumentality of the United States, having primary management authority over such lands. In the case of any public lands or Indian lands with respect to which no department, agency, or instrumentality has primary management authority, such term means the Secretary of the Interior. If the Secretary of the Interior consents, the responsibilities (in whole or in part) under this chapter of the Secretary of any department (other than the Department of the Interior) or the head of any other agency or instrumentality may be delegated to the Secretary of the Interior with respect to any land managed by such other Secretary or agency head, and in any such case, the term "Federal land manager" means the Secretary of the Interior.

(3) The term "public lands" means—

(A) lands which are owned and administered by the United States as part of—

(i) the national park system,

(ii) the national wildlife refuge system, or

(iii) the national forest system; and

(B) all other lands the fee title to which is held by the United States, other than lands on the Outer Continental Shelf and lands which are under the jurisdiction of the Smithsonian Institution.

(4) The term "Indian lands" means lands of Indian tribes, or Indian individuals, which are either held in trust by the United States or subject to a restriction against alienation imposed by the United States, except for any subsurface interests in lands not owned or controlled by an Indian tribe or an Indian individual.

(5) The term "Indian tribe" means any Indian tribe, band, nation, or other organized group or community, including any Alaska Native

village or regional or village corporation as defined in, or established pursuant to, the Alaska Native Claims Settlement Act (85 Stat. 688) [43 U.S.C.A. § 1601 et seq.].

(6) The term "person" means an individual, corporation, partnership, trust, institution, association, or any other private entity or any officer, employee, agent, department, or instrumentality of the United States, of any Indian tribe, or of any State or political subdivision thereof.

(7) The term "State" means any of the fifty States, the District of Columbia, Puerto Rico, Guam, and the Virgin Islands.

Pub.L. 96–95, § 3, Oct. 31, 1979, 93 Stat. 721, as amended Pub.L. 100–588, § 1(a), Nov. 3, 1988, 102 Stat. 2983.

§ 470cc. Excavation and removal

Application for permit

(a) Any person may apply to the Federal land manager for a permit to excavate or remove any archaeological resource located on public lands or Indian lands and to carry out activities associated with such excavation or removal. The application shall be required, under uniform regulations under this chapter, to contain such information as the Federal land manager deems necessary, including information concerning the time, scope, and location and specific purpose of the proposed work.

Determinations by Federal land manager prerequisite to issuance of permit

(b) A permit may be issued pursuant to an application under subsection (a) of this section if the Federal land manager determines, pursuant to uniform regulations under this chapter, that—

(1) the applicant is qualified, to carry out the permitted activity,

(2) the activity is undertaken for the purpose of furthering archaeological knowledge in the public interest,

(3) the archaeological resources which are excavated or removed from public lands will remain the property of the United States, and such resources and copies of associated archaeological records and data will be preserved by a suitable university, museum, or other scientific or educational institution, and

(4) the activity pursuant to such permit is not inconsistent with any management plan applicable to the public lands concerned.

Notification to Indian tribes of possible harm to or destruction of sites having religious or cultural importance

(c) If a permit issued under this section may result in harm to, or destruction of, any religious or cultural site, as determined by the Federal land manager, before issuing such permit, the Federal land manager shall notify any Indian tribe which may consider the site as having religious or cultural importance. Such notice shall not be deemed a disclosure to the public for purposes of section 470hh of this title.

Terms and conditions of permit

(d) Any permit under this section shall contain such terms and conditions, pursuant to uniform regulations promulgated under this chapter, as the Federal land manager concerned deems necessary to carry out the purposes of this chapter.

Identification of individuals responsible for complying with permit terms and conditions and other applicable laws

(e) Each permit under this section shall identify the individual who shall be responsible for carrying out the terms and conditions of the permit and for otherwise complying with this chapter and other law applicable to the permitted activity.

Suspension or revocation of permits; grounds

(f) Any permit issued under this section may be suspended by the Federal land manager upon his determination that the permittee has violated any provision of subsection (a), (b), or (c) of section 470ee of this title. Any such permit may be revoked by such Federal land manager upon assessment of a civil penalty under section 470ff of this title against the permittee or upon the permittee's conviction under section 470ee of this title.

Excavation or removal by Indian tribes or tribe members; excavation or removal of resources located on Indian lands

(g)(1) No permit shall be required under this section or under the Act of June 8, 1906 (16 U.S.C. 431), for the excavation or removal by any Indian tribe or member thereof of any archaeological resources located on Indian lands of such Indian tribe, except that in the absence of tribal law regulating the excavation or removal of archaeological resources located on Indian lands, an individual tribal member shall be required to obtain a permit under this section.

(g)(2) In the case of any permits for the excavation or removal of any archaeological resource located on Indian lands, the permit may be granted only after obtaining the consent of the Indian or Indian tribe owning or having jurisdiction over such lands. The permit shall include such terms and conditions as may be requested by such Indian or Indian tribe.

Permits issued under Antiquities Act of 1906

(h)(1) No permit or other permission shall be required under the Act of June 8, 1906 (16 U.S.C. 431–433), for any activity for which a permit is issued under this section.

(h)(2) Any permit issued under the Act of June 8, 1906 [16 U.S.C.A. 431–433], shall remain in effect according to its terms and conditions following the enactment of this chapter. No permit under this chapter shall be required to carry out any activity under a permit issued under the Act of

June 8, 1906, before October 31, 1979, which remains in effect as provided in this paragraph, and nothing in this chapter shall modify or affect any such permit.

Compliance with provisions relating to undertakings on property listed in the National Register not required

(i) Issuance of a permit in accordance with this section and applicable regulations shall not require compliance with section 470f of this title.

Issuance of permits to State Governors for archaeological activities on behalf of States or their educational institutions

(j) Upon the written request of the Governor of any State, the Federal land manager shall issue a permit, subject to the provisions of subsections (b)(3), (b)(4), (c), (e), (f), (g), (h), and (i) of this section for the purpose of conducting archaeological research, excavation, removal, and curation, on behalf of the State or its educational institutions, to such Governor or to such designee as the Governor deems qualified to carry out the intent of this chapter.

Pub.L. 96–95, § 4, Oct. 31, 1979, 93 Stat. 722.

§ **470dd.** Custody of archaeological resources

The Secretary of the Interior may promulgate regulations providing for—

(1) the exchange, where appropriate, between suitable universities, museums, or other scientific or educational institutions, of archaeological resources removed from public lands and Indian lands pursuant to this chapter, and

(2) the ultimate disposition of such resources and other resources removed pursuant to the Act of June 27, 1960 (16 U.S.C. 469–469c) [16 U.S.C.A. §§ 469 to 469c–1] or the Act of June 8, 1906 (16 U.S.C. 431–433).

Any exchange or ultimate disposition under such regulation of archaeological resources excavated or removed from Indian lands shall be subject to the consent of the Indian or Indian tribe which owns or has jurisdiction over such lands. Following promulgation of regulations under this section, notwithstanding any other provision of law, such regulations shall govern the disposition of archaeological resources removed from public lands and Indian lands pursuant to this chapter.

Pub.L. 96–95, § 5, Oct. 31, 1979, 93 Stat. 724.

§ **470ee.** Prohibited acts and criminal penalties

Unauthorized excavation, removal, damage, alteration, or defacement of archaeological resources

(a) No person may excavate, remove, damage, or otherwise alter or deface, or attempt to excavate, remove, damage, or otherwise alter or deface any archaeological resource located on public lands or Indian lands unless such activity is pursuant to a permit issued under section 470cc of this title, a permit referred to in section 470cc(h)(2) of this title, or the exemption contained in section 470cc(g)(1) of this title.

Trafficking in archaeological resources the excavation or removal of which was wrongful under Federal law

(b) No person may sell, purchase, exchange, transport, receive, or offer to sell, purchase, or exchange any archaeological resource if such resource was excavated or removed from public lands or Indian lands in violation of—

(1) the prohibition contained in subsection (a) of this section, or

(2) any provision, rule, regulation, ordinance, or permit in effect under any other provision of Federal law.

Trafficking in interstate or foreign commerce in archaeological resources the excavation, removal, sale, purchase, exchange, transportation or receipt of which was wrongful under State or local law

(c) No person may sell, purchase, exchange, transport, receive, or offer to sell, purchase, or exchange, in interstate or foreign commerce, any archaeological resource excavated, removed, sold, purchased, exchanged, transported, or received in violation of any provision, rule, regulation, ordinance, or permit in effect under State or local law.

Penalties

(d) Any person who knowingly violates, or counsels, procures, solicits, or employs any other person to violate, any prohibition contained in subsection (a), (b), or (c) of this section shall, upon conviction, be fined not more than $10,000 or imprisoned not more than one year, or both: *Provided, however,* That if the commercial or archaeological value of the archaeological resources involved and the cost of restoration and repair of such resources exceeds the sum of $5,000, such person shall be fined not more than $20,000 or imprisoned not more than two years, or both. In the case of a second or subsequent such violation upon conviction such person shall be fined not more than $100,000, or imprisoned not more than five years, or both.

Effective date

(e) The prohibitions contained in this section shall take effect on October 31, 1979.

Prospective application

(f) Nothing in subsection (b)(1) of this section shall be deemed applicable to any person with respect to an archaeological resource which was in the lawful possession of such person prior to October 31, 1979.

Removal of arrowheads located on ground surface

(g) Nothing in subsection (d) of this section shall be deemed applicable to any person with respect to the removal of arrowheads located on the surface of the ground.

Pub.L. 96–95, § 6, Oct. 31, 1979, 93 Stat. 724. As amended Pub.L. 100–588, § 1(b), (c), Nov. 3, 1988, 102 Stat. 2983.

§ 470ff.   Civil penalties

Assessment by Federal land manager

(a)(1) Any person who violates any prohibition contained in an applicable regulation or permit issued under this chapter may be assessed a civil penalty by the Federal land manager concerned. No penalty may be assessed under this subsection unless such person is given notice and opportunity for a hearing with respect to such violation. Each violation shall be a separate offense. Any such civil penalty may be remitted or mitigated by the Federal land manager concerned.

(a)(2) The amount of such penalty shall be determined under regulations promulgated pursuant to this chapter, taking into account, in addition to other factors—

    (A) the archaeological or commercial value of the archaeological resource involved, and

    (B) the cost of restoration and repair of the resource and the archaeological site involved.

Such regulations shall provide that, in the case of a second or subsequent violation by any person, the amount of such civil penalty may be double the amount which would have been assessed if such violation were the first violation by such person. The amount of any penalty assessed under this subsection for any violation shall not exceed an amount equal to double the cost of restoration and repair of resources and archaeological sites damaged and double the fair market value of resources destroyed or not recovered.

(a)(3) No penalty shall be assessed under this section for the removal of arrowheads located on the surface of the ground.

Judicial review of assessed penalties; collection of unpaid assessments

(b)(1) Any person aggrieved by an order assessing a civil penalty under subsection (a) of this section may file a petition for judicial review of such order with the United States District Court for the District of Columbia or for any other district in which such a person resides or transacts business. Such a petition may only be filed within the 30–day period beginning on the date the order making such assessment was issued. The court shall hear such action on the record made before the Federal land manager and shall sustain his action if it is supported by substantial evidence on the record considered as a whole.

(2) If any person fails to pay an assessment of a civil penalty—

(A) after the order making the assessment has become a final order and such person has not filed a petition for judicial review of the order in accordance with paragraph (1), or

(B) after a court in an action brought under paragraph (1) has entered a final judgment upholding the assessment of a civil penalty,

the Federal land managers may request the Attorney General to institute a civil action in a district court of the United States for any district in which such person is found, resides, or transacts business to collect the penalty and such court shall have jurisdiction to hear and decide any such action. In such action, the validity and amount of such penalty shall not be subject to review.

* * *

Pub.L. 96–95, § 7, Oct. 31, 1979, 93 Stat. 725.

* * *

§ 470hh. Confidentiality of information concerning nature and location of archaeological resources

(a) Information concerning the nature and location of any archaeological resource for which the excavation or removal requires a permit or other permission under this chapter or under any other provision of Federal law may not be made available to the public under subchapter II of chapter 5 of Title 5 or under any other provision of law unless the Federal land manager concerned determines that such disclosure would—

(1) further the purposes of this chapter or the Act of June 27, 1960 (16 U.S.C. 469–469c) [16 U.S.C.A. 469 to 469c–1], and

(2) not create a risk of harm to such resources or to the site at which such resources are located.

(b) Notwithstanding the provisions of subsection (a) of this section, upon the written request of the Governor of any State, which request shall state—

(1) the specific site or area for which information is sought,

(2) the purpose for which such information is sought,

(3) a commitment by the Governor to adequately protect the confidentiality of such information to protect the resource from commercial exploitation,

the Federal land manager concerned shall provide to the Governor information concerning the nature and location of archaeological resources within the State of the requesting Governor.

Pub.L. 96–95, § 9, Oct. 31, 1979, 93 Stat. 727.

§ 470ii. Rules and regulations; intergovernmental coordination

Promulgation; effective date

(a) The Secretaries of the Interior, Agriculture and Defense and the Chairman of the Board of the Tennessee Valley Authority, after consultation with other Federal land managers, Indian tribes, representatives of concerned State agencies, and after public notice and hearing, shall promulgate such uniform rules and regulations as may be appropriate to carry out the purposes of this chapter. Such rules and regulations may be promulgated only after consideration of the provisions of the American Indian Religious Freedom Act (92 Stat. 469; 42 U.S.C. 1996). Each uniform rule or regulation promulgated under this chapter shall be submitted on the same calendar day to the Committee on Energy and Natural Resources of the United States Senate and to the Committee on Natural Resources of the United States House of Representatives, and no such uniform rule or regulation may take effect before the expiration of a period of ninety calendar days following the date of its submission to such Committees.

Federal land managers' rules

(b) Each Federal land manager shall promulgate such rules and regulations, consistent with the uniform rules and regulations under subsection (a) of this section, as may be appropriate for the carrying out of his functions and authorities under this chapter.

Pub.L. 96–95, § 10, Oct. 31, 1979, 93 Stat. 727, as amended Pub.L. 100–588, § 1(d), Nov. 3, 1988, 102 Stat. 2983; Pub.L. 103–437, § 6(d)(30), Nov. 2, 1994, 108 Stat. 4584; Pub.L. 104–333, Div. I, Title VIII, § 814(d)(2)(A), Nov. 12, 1996, 110 Stat. 4196.

* * *

§ 470kk. Savings provisions

(a) Nothing in this chapter shall be construed to repeal, modify, or impose additional restrictions on the activities permitted under existing laws and authorities relating to mining, mineral leasing, reclamation, and other multiple uses of the public lands.

(b) Nothing in this chapter applies to, or requires a permit for, the collection for private purposes of any rock, coin, bullet, or mineral which is not an archaeological resource, as determined under uniform regulations promulgated under section 470bb(1) of this title.

(c) Nothing in this chapter shall be construed to affect any land other than public land or Indian land or to affect the lawful recovery, collection, or sale of archaeological resources from land other than public land or Indian land.

Pub.L. 96–95, § 12, Oct. 31, 1979, 93 Stat. 728.

* * *

FOREST SERVICE—GENERAL PROVISIONS

§ 471. National Forests; establishment; limitations on additions in certain states; lands suitable for production of timber

Repeal

Section repealed by Pub.L. 94–579, Title VII, § 704(a), Oct. 21, 1976, 90 Stat. 2792. See the History Supplement, below.

§ 472. Laws affecting national forest lands

The Secretary of the Department of Agriculture shall execute or cause to be executed all laws affecting public lands reserved under the provisions of section 471 of this title [repealed in 1976], or sections supplemental to and amendatory thereof, subject to the provisions for national forests established under subdivision (b) of section 471 of this title [repealed in 1976], after such lands have been so reserved, excepting such laws as affect the surveying, prospecting, locating, appropriating, entering, relinquishing, reconveying, certifying, or patenting of any of such lands.

Feb. 1, 1905, c. 288, § 1, 33 Stat. 628.

§ 472a. Timber sales on National Forest System lands

Authorization; rules and regulations; appraised value as minimum sale price

(a) For the purpose of achieving the policies set forth in the Multiple–Use Sustained–Yield Act of 1960 (74 Stat. 215; 16 U.S.C. 528–531) and the Forest and Rangeland Renewable Resources Planning Act of 1974 (88 Stat. 476) [16 U.S.C.A. § 1600 et seq.], the Secretary of Agriculture, under such rules and regulations as he may prescribe, may sell, at not less than appraised value, trees, portions of trees, or forest products located on National Forest System lands.

Designation on map; prospectus

(b) All advertised timber sales shall be designated on maps, and a prospectus shall be available to the public and interested potential bidders.

Terms and conditions of contract

(c) The length and other terms of the contract shall be designed to promote orderly harvesting consistent with the principles set out in section 6 of the Forest and Rangeland Renewable Resources Planning Act of 1974, as amended [16 U.S.C.A. § 1604]. Unless there is a finding by the Secretary of Agriculture that better utilization of the various forest resources (consistent with the provisions of the Multiple–Use Sustained–Yield Act of 1960 [16 U.S.C.A. §§ 528 to 531]) will result, sales contracts shall be for a period not to exceed ten years: *Provided,* That such period may be adjusted at the discretion of the Secretary to provide additional time due to time delays caused by an act of an agent of the United States or by other circumstances beyond the control of the purchaser. The Secretary shall require the purchaser to file as soon as practicable after execution of a contract for any advertised sale with a term of two years or more, a plan of operation, which shall be subject to concurrence by the Secretary. The Secretary shall not extend any contract period with an original term of two years or more unless he finds (A) that the purchaser has diligently performed in accordance with an approved plan of operation or (B) that the substantial overriding public interest justifies the extension.

Advertisement of sales; exceptions

(d) The Secretary of Agriculture shall advertise all sales unless he determines that extraordinary conditions exist, as defined by regulation, or that the appraised value of the sale is less than $10,000. If, upon proper offering, no satisfactory bid is received for a sale, or the bidder fails to complete the purchase, the sale may be offered and sold without further advertisement.

Bidding methods; purposes; oral auction procedures; monitoring and enforcement for prevention of collusive practices

(e)(1) In the sale of trees, portions of trees, or forest products from National Forest System lands (hereinafter referred to in this subsection as "national forest materials"), the Secretary of Agriculture shall select the bidding method or methods which—

(A) insure open and fair competition;

(B) insure that the Federal Government receive not less than the appraised value as required by subsection (a) of this section;

(C) consider the economic stability of communities whose economies are dependent on such national forest materials, or achieve such other objectives as the Secretary deems necessary; and

(D) are consistent with the objectives of this Act and other Federal statutes.

The Secretary shall select or alter the bidding method or methods as he determined necessary to achieve the objectives stated in clauses (A), (B), (C), and (D) of this paragraph.

(e)(2) In those instances when the Secretary selects oral auction as the bidding method for the sale of any national forest materials, he shall require that all prospective purchasers submit written sealed qualifying bids. Only prospective purchasers whose written sealed qualifying bids are equal to or in excess of the appraised value of such national forest materials may participate in the oral bidding process.

(e)(3) The Secretary shall monitor bidding patterns involved in the sale of national forest materials. If the Secretary has a reasonable belief that collusive bidding practices may be occurring, then—

(A) he shall report any such instances of possible collusive bidding or suspected collusive bidding practices to the Attorney General of the United States with any and all supporting data;

(B) he may alter the bidding methods used within the affected area; and

(C) he shall take such other action as he deems necessary to eliminate such practices within the affected area.

* * *

Designation, marking, and supervision of harvesting; personnel

(g) Designation, marking when necessary, and supervision of harvesting of trees, portions of trees, or forest products shall be conducted by persons employed by the Secretary of Agriculture. Such persons shall have no personal interest in the purchase or harvest of such products and shall not be directly or indirectly in the employment of the purchaser thereof.

Utilization standards, methods of measurement, and harvesting practices; monetary deposits by purchasers of salvage harvests; nature, purposes and availability of designated fund; return of surplus to Treasury

(h) The Secretary of Agriculture shall develop utilization standards, methods of measurement, and harvesting practices for the removal of trees, portions of trees, or forest products to provide for the optimum practical use of the wood material. Such standards, methods, and practices shall reflect consideration of opportunities to promote more effective wood utilization, regional conditions, and species characteristics and shall be compatible with multiple use resource management objectives in the affected area. To accomplish the purpose of this subsection in situations involving salvage of insect-infested, dead, damaged, or down timber, and to remove associated trees for stand improvement, the Secretary is authorized to require the purchasers of such timber to make monetary deposits, as a part of the payment for the timber, to be deposited in a designated fund from which sums are to be used, to cover the cost to the United States for design, engineering, and supervision of the construction of needed roads and the cost for Forest Service sale preparation and supervision of the harvesting of such timber. Deposits of money pursuant to this subsection are to be available until expended to cover the cost to the United States of accomplishing the purposes for which deposited: *Provided,* That such deposits shall not be considered as moneys received from the national forests within the meaning of sections 500 and 501 of this title: *And provided further,* That sums found to be in excess of the cost of accomplishing the purposes for which deposited on any national forest shall be transferred to miscellaneous receipts in the Treasury of the United States.

Purchaser credit for permanent road construction; right of election of small business concerns; estimated cost; date of completion; use of funds for construction; effective date

(i)(1) For sales of timber which include a provision for purchaser credit for construction of permanent roads with an estimated cost in excess of $20,000, the Secretary of Agriculture shall promulgate regulations requiring that the notice of sale afford timber purchasers qualifying as "small business concerns" under the Small Business Act, as amended [15

U.S.C.A. § 631 et seq.], and the regulations issued thereunder, an estimate of the cost and the right, when submitting a bid, to elect that the Secretary build the proposed road.

(i)(2) If the purchaser makes such an election, the price subsequently paid for the timber shall include all of the estimated cost of the road. In the notice of sale, the Secretary of Agriculture shall set a date when such road shall be completed which shall be applicable to either construction by the purchaser or the Secretary, depending on the election. To accomplish requested work, the Secretary is authorized to use from any receipts from the sale of timber a sum equal to the estimate for timber purchaser credits, and such additional sums as may be appropriated for the construction of roads, such funds to be available until expended, to construct a road that meets the standards specified in the notice of sale.

(i)(3) The provisions of this subsection shall become effective on October 1, 1976.

Pub.L. 94–568, § 14, Oct. 22, 1976, 90 Stat. 2958, amended Pub.L. 95–233, Feb. 20, 1978, 92 Stat. 32, Pub.L. 95–233, Feb. 20, 1978, 92 Stat. 32; Pub.L. 101–626, Title I, § 105(a), Nov. 28, 1990, 104 Stat. 4427.

§ 473. Revocation, modification, or vacation of orders or proclamations establishing national forests

The President of the United States is authorized and empowered to revoke, modify, or suspend any and all Executive orders and proclamations or any part thereof issued under section 471 of this title, from time to time as he shall deem best for the public interests. By such modification he may reduce the area or change the boundary lines or may vacate altogether any order creating a national forest.

June 4, 1897, c. 2, § 1, 30 Stat. 34, 36.

§ 474. Surveys; plats and field notes; maps; effect under Act June 4, 1897

Surveys, field notes, and plats returned from the survey of public lands designated as national forests undertaken under the supervision of the Director of the United States Geological Survey in accordance with the provisions of Act June 4, 1897, chapter 2, section 1, Thirtieth Statutes, pages 34, shall have the same legal force and effect as surveys, field notes, and plats returned through the Field Surveying Service; and such surveys, which include subdivision surveys under the rectangular system, shall be approved by the Secretary of the Interior or such officer as he may designate as in other cases, and properly certified copies thereof shall be filed in the respective land offices of the districts in which such lands are situated, as in other cases. All laws inconsistent with the provisions hereof are hereby declared inoperative as respects such survey. A copy of every topographic map and other maps showing the distribution of the forests, together with such field notes as may be taken relating thereto, shall be certified thereto by the Director of the Survey and filed in the Bureau of Land Management.

June 4, 1897, c. 2, § 1, 30 Stat. 34; Mar. 3, 1925, ch. 462, 43 Stat. 1144; 1946 Reorg. Plan No. 3, § 403, eft. July 16, 1946, 11 F.R. 7876, 60 Stat. 1100, as amended Nov. 13, 1991, Pub.L. 102–154, Title I, 105 Stat. 1000; May 18, 1992, Pub.L. 102–285, § 10(a), 106 Stat. 171.

§ 475. Purposes for which national forests may be established and administered

All public lands designated and reserved prior to June 4, 1897, by the President of the United States under the provisions of section 471 of this title, the orders for which shall be and remain in full force and effect, unsuspended and unrevoked, and all public lands that may hereafter be set aside and reserved as national forests under said section, shall be as far as practicable controlled and administered in accordance with the following provisions. No national forest shall be established, except to improve and protect the forest within the boundaries, or for the purpose of securing favorable conditions of water flows, and to furnish a continuous supply of timber for the use and necessities of citizens of the United States; but it is not the purpose or intent of these provisions, or of said section, to authorize the inclusion therein of lands more valuable for the mineral therein, or for agricultural purposes, than for forest purposes.

June 4, 1897, c. 2, § 1, 30 Stat. 34.

* * *

§ 477. Use of timber and stone by settlers

The Secretary of Agriculture may permit, under regulations to be prescribed by him, the use of timber and stone found upon national forests, free of charge, by bona fide settlers, miners, residents, and prospectors for minerals, for firewood, fencing, buildings, mining, prospecting, and other domestic purposes, as may be needed by such persons for such purposes; such timber to be used within the State or Territory, respectively, where such national forests may be located.

June 4, 1897, c. 2, § 1, 30 Stat. 35; Feb. 1, 1905, ch. 288, § 1, 33 Stat. 628.

§ 478. Egress or ingress of actual settlers; prospecting

Nothing in sections 473 to 478, 479 to 482 and 551 of this title shall be construed as prohibiting the egress or ingress of actual settlers residing within the boundaries of national forests, or from crossing the same to and from their property or homes; and such wagon roads and other improvements may be constructed thereon as may be necessary to reach their homes and to utilize their property under such rules and regulations as may be prescribed by the Secretary of Agriculture. Nor shall anything herein prohibit any person from entering upon such national forests for all proper and lawful purposes, including that of prospecting, locating, and developing the mineral resources thereof. Such persons must comply with the rules and regulations covering such national forests.

June 4, 1897, c. 2, § 1, 30 Stat. 36; Feb. 1, 1905, ch. 288, § 1, 33 Stat. 628.

§ 478a. Townsites

When the Secretary of Agriculture determines that a tract of National Forest System land in Alaska or in the eleven contiguous Western States is located adjacent to or contiguous to an established community, and that transfer of such land would serve indigenous community objectives that outweigh the public objectives and values which would be served by maintaining such tract in Federal ownership, he may, upon application, set aside and designate as a townsite an area of not to exceed six hundred and forty acres of National Forest System land for any one application. After public notice, and satisfactory showing of need therefor by any county, city, or other local governmental subdivision, the Secretary may offer such area for sale to a governmental subdivision at a price not less than the fair market value thereof: *Provided, however,* That the Secretary may condition conveyances of townsites upon the enactment, maintenance, and enforcement of a valid ordinance which assures any land so conveyed will be controlled by the governmental subdivision so that use of the area will not interfere with the protection, management, and development of adjacent or contiguous National Forest System lands.

Pub.L. 85–569, July 31, 1958, 72 Stat. 438; as amended Pub.L. 94–579, Title II, § 213, Oct. 21, 1976, 90 Stat. 2760.

§ 479. Sites for schools and churches

The settlers residing within the exterior boundaries of national forests, or in the vicinity thereof, may maintain schools and churches within such national forest, and for that purpose may occupy any part of the said national forest, not exceeding two acres for each schoolhouse and one acre for a church.

June 4, 1897, c. 2, § 1, 30 Stat. 36.

§ 480. Civil and criminal jurisdiction

The jurisdiction, both civil and criminal, over persons within national forests shall not be affected or changed by reason of their existence, except so far as the punishment of offenses against the United States therein is concerned; the intent and meaning of this provision being that the State wherein any such national forest is situated shall not, by reason of the establishment thereof, lose its jurisdiction, nor the inhabitants thereof their rights and privileges as citizens, or be absolved from their duties as citizens of the State.

June 4, 1897, c. 2, § 1, 30 Stat. 36; Mar. 1, 1911, c. 186, § 12, 36 Stat. 963.

§ 481. Use of waters

All waters within the boundaries of national forests may be used for domestic, mining, milling, or irrigation purposes, under the laws of the State wherein such national forests are situated, or under the laws of the United States and the rules and regulations established thereunder.

June 4, 1897, c. 2, § 1, 30 Stat. 36.

§ 482. Mineral lands; restoration to public domain; location and entry

Upon the recommendation of the Secretary of the Interior, with the approval of the President, after sixty days' notice thereof, published in two papers of general circulation in the State or Territory wherein any national forest is situated, and near the said national forest, any public lands embraced within the limits of any such forest which, after due examination by personal inspection of a competent person appointed for that purpose by the Secretary of the Interior, shall be found better adapted for mining or for agricultural purposes than for forest usage, may be restored to the public domain. And any mineral lands in any national forest which have been or which may be shown to be such, and subject to entry under the existing mining laws of the United States and the rules and regulations applying thereto, shall continue to be subject to such location and entry, notwithstanding any provisions contained in sections 473 to 478, 479 to 482 and 551 of this title.

June 4, 1897, c. 2, § 1, 30 Stat. 36.

§ 497. Use and occupation of lands for hotels, resorts, summer homes, stores, and facilities for industrial, commercial, educational or public uses

The Secretary of Agriculture is authorized, under such regulations as he may make and upon such terms and conditions as he may deem proper, (a) to permit the use and occupancy of suitable areas of land within the national forests, not exceeding eighty acres and for periods not exceeding thirty years, for the purpose of constructing or maintaining hotels, resorts, and any other structures or facilities necessary or desirable for recreation, public convenience, or safety; (b) to permit the use and occupancy of suitable areas of land within the national forests, not exceeding five acres and for periods not exceeding thirty years, for the purpose of constructing or maintaining summer homes and stores; (c) to permit the use and occupancy of suitable areas of land within the national forest, not exceeding eighty acres and for periods not exceeding thirty years, for the purpose of constructing or maintaining buildings, structures, and facilities for industrial or commercial purposes whenever such use is related to or consistent with other uses on the national forests; (d) to permit any State or political subdivision thereof, or any public or nonprofit agency, to use and occupy suitable areas of land within the national forests not exceeding eighty acres and for periods not exceeding thirty years, for the purpose of constructing or maintaining any buildings, structures, or facilities necessary or desirable for education or for any public use or in connection with any public activity. The authority provided by this section shall be exercised in such manner as not to preclude the general public from full enjoyment of the natural, scenic, recreational, and other aspects of the national forests.

Mar. 4, 1915, c. 144, 38 Stat. 1101; July 28, 1956, c. 771, 70 Stat. 708.

NATIONAL FOREST SKI AREA PERMIT ACT OF 1986

(16 U.S.C.A. § 497)

§ 497b. Ski area permits

Law applicable to permits

(a) The provisions of section 497 of this title notwithstanding, the term and acreage of permits for the operation of nordic and alpine ski areas and facilities on National Forest System lands shall henceforth be governed by this Act and other applicable law.

Authority of Secretary of Agriculture

(b) The Secretary of Agriculture (hereinafter referred to as "the Secretary") is authorized to issue permits (hereinafter referred to as "ski area permits") for the use and occupancy of suitable lands within the National Forest System for nordic and alpine skiing operations and purposes. A ski area permit—

(1) may be issued for a term not to exceed 40 years;

(2) shall ordinarily be issued for a term of 40 years (unless the Secretary determines that the facilities or operations are of a scale or nature as are not likely to require long-term financing or operation), or that there are public policy reasons specific to a particular permit for a shorter term;

(3) shall encompass such acreage as the Secretary determines sufficient and appropriate to accommodate the permittee's needs for ski operations and appropriate ancillary facilities;

(4) may be renewed at the discretion of the Secretary;

(5) may be cancelled by the Secretary in whole or in part for any violation of the permit terms or conditions, for nonpayment of permit fees, or upon the determination by the Secretary in his planning for the uses of the national forests that the permitted area is needed for higher public purposes;

(6) may be modified from time to time by the Secretary to accommodate changes in plans or operations in accordance with the provisions of applicable law;

(7) shall be subject to such reasonable terms and conditions as the Secretary deems appropriate; and

(8) shall be subject to a permit fee based on fair market value in accordance with applicable law.

Rules and regulations

(c) Within one year after October 22, 1986, the Secretary shall promulgate rules and regulations to implement the provisions of this Act, and shall, to the extent practicable and with the consent of existing permit holders, convert all existing ski area permits or leases on National Forest

System lands into ski area permits which conform to the provisions of this Act within 3 years of October 22, 1986.

Construction with Secretary's duties under other laws

(d) Nothing in this Act shall be deemed to amend, modify or otherwise affect the Secretary's duties under the National Environmental Policy Act [42 U.S.C.A. § 4321 et seq.], or the Forest and Rangelands Renewable Resources Planning Act as amended by the National Forest Management Act [16 U.S.C.A. § 1600 et seq.] including his duties to involve the public in his decisionmaking and planning for the national forests.

Pub.L. 99–522, § 3, Oct. 22, 1986, 100 Stat. 3000.

* * *

FOREST SERVICE, MORE GENERAL PROVISIONS

(16 U.S.C.A. § 515–525)

§ 515. Examination, location, and purchase of forested, cut-over, or denuded lands; consent of State legislature to acquisition of land by the United States

The Secretary of Agriculture is hereby authorized and directed to examine, locate, and purchase such forested, cut-over, or denuded lands within the watersheds of navigable streams as in his judgment may be necessary to the regulation of the flow of navigable streams or for the production of timber. No deed or other instrument of conveyance of lands referred to herein shall be accepted or approved by the Secretary of Agriculture under this Act until the legislature of the State in which the land lies shall have consented to the acquisition of such land by the United States for the purpose of preserving the navigability of navigable streams.

Mar. 1, 1911, ch. 186, § 6, 36 Stat. 962; June 7, 1924, ch. 348, § 6, 43 Stat. 654; as amended Oct. 22, 1976, Pub.L. 94–588, § 17(a)(3), 90 Stat. 2961.

§ 516. Exchange of lands in the public interest; equal value; cutting and removing timber; publication of contemplated exchange

When the public interests will be benefited thereby, the Secretary of Agriculture is hereby authorized, in his discretion, to accept on behalf of the United States title to any lands within the exterior boundaries of national forests which, in his opinion, are chiefly valuable for the purposes of this Act, and in exchange therefor to convey by deed not to exceed an equal value of such national forest land in the same State, or he may authorize the grantor to cut and remove an equal value of timber within such national forests in the same State, the values in each case to be determined by him: *Provided,* That before any such exchange is effected notice of the contemplated exchange reciting the lands involved shall be published once each week for four successive weeks in some newspaper of general circulation in the county or counties in which may be situated the lands to be accepted, and in some like newspaper published in any county in which may be situated any lands or timber to be given in such exchange. Timber given in such exchanges shall be cut and removed under the laws and regulations relating to such national forests, and under the direction and supervision and in accordance with the requirements of the Secretary of Agriculture. Lands so accepted by the Secretary of Agriculture shall, upon acceptance, become parts of the national forests within whose exterior boundaries they are located, and be subjected to all provisions of this Act.

Mar. 1, 1911, ch. 186, § 7, 36 Stat. 962; Mar. 3, 1925, ch. 473, 43 Stat. 1215; as amended Oct. 22, 1976, Pub.L. 94–588, § 17(a)(4), 90 Stat. 2961.

* * *

§ 519. Agricultural lands included in tracts acquired; sale for homesteads

Inasmuch as small areas of land chiefly valuable for agriculture may of necessity or by inadvertence be included in tracts acquired under sections 513 to 519 and 521 of this title, the Secretary of Agriculture may, in his discretion, and he is authorized, upon application or otherwise, to examine and ascertain the location and extent of such areas as in his opinion may be occupied for agricultural purposes without injury to the forests or to stream flow and which are not needed for public purposes, and may list and describe the same by metes and bounds, or otherwise, and offer them for sale as homesteads at their true value, to be fixed by him, to actual settlers, in tracts not exceeding eighty acres, in area, under such rules and regulations as he may prescribe; and in case of such sale the jurisdiction over the lands sold shall, ipso facto, revert to the State in which the lands sold lie. And no right, title, interest, or claim in or to any lands acquired under said sections, or the waters thereon, or the products, resources, or use thereof after such lands shall have been so acquired, shall be initiated or perfected, except as in this section provided.

Mar. 1, 1911, c. 186, § 10, 36 Stat. 962; June 11, 1960, Pub.L. 86–509, § 1(k), 74 Stat. 205.

* * *

§ 520. Regulations as to mineral resources

The Secretary of Agriculture is authorized, under general regulations to be prescribed by him, to permit the prospecting, development, and utilization of the mineral resources of the lands acquired under sections 513 to 519 and 521 of this title, upon such terms and for specified periods or otherwise, as he may deem to be for the best interests of the United States; and all moneys received on account of charges, if any, made under this section shall be disposed of as is provided by existing law for the disposition of receipts from national forests.

Mar. 4, 1917, c. 179, 39 Stat. 1150; 1946 Reorg. Plan No. 3, § 402, eff. July 16, 1946, 11 F.R. 7876, 60 Stat. 1099; June 11, 1960, Pub.L. 86–509, § 1(1), 74 Stat. 205.

§ 521. Lands acquired to be reserved, held, and administered as national forest lands; designation

Subject to the provisions of section 519 of this title the lands acquired under sections 513 to 519 and 521 of this title shall be permanently reserved, held, and administered as national forest lands under the provisions of section 471 of this title and Acts supplemental to and amendatory thereof. And the Secretary of Agriculture may from time to time divide the lands acquired under the aforesaid sections into such specific national forests and so designate the same as he may deem best for administrative purposes.

Mar. 1, 1911, c. 186, § 11, 36 Stat. 963.

§ 521a. Administration, management and consolidation of certain lands

In order to facilitate the administration, management, and consolidation of the national forests, all lands of the United States within the exterior boundaries of national forests which were or hereafter are acquired for or in connection with the national forests or transferred to the Forest Service, Department of Agriculture, for administration and protection substantially in accordance with national forest regulations, policies, and procedures, excepting (a) lands reserved from the public domain or acquired pursuant to laws authorizing the exchange of land or timber reserved from or part of the public domain, and (b) lands within the official limits of towns or cities, notwithstanding the provisions of any other Act, are made subject to the Weeks Act, as amended, and to all laws, rules, and regulations applicable to national forest lands acquired thereunder: *Provided,* That nothing in this section shall be construed as (1) affecting the status of lands administered by the Secretary of Agriculture under sections 1181f to 1181j of Title 43, and which are revested Oregon and California Railroad grant lands, administered as national forest lands, or (2) changing the disposition of revenues from or authorizing the exchange of the lands, or the timber thereon, described in the Act of February 11, 1920 (ch. 69, 41 Stat. 405), the Act of September 22, 1922 (ch. 407, 42 Stat. 1019), and the Act of June 4, 1936 (ch. 494, 49 Stat. 1460).

Pub.L. 85–862, Sept. 2, 1958, 72 Stat. 1571.

§ 521b. Report of Secretary of Agriculture prior to purchase or exchange of land; contents; waiting period

For purposes of providing information that will aid the Congress in its oversight responsibilities and improve the accountability of expenditures for the acquisition of forest land, the Secretary of Agriculture may not hereafter enter into any land purchase or exchange relating to the National Forest System of $150,000 or more for the types of lands which have been heretofore approved by the National Forest Reservation Commission until after 30 days from the date upon which a detailed report of the facts concerning such proposed purchase or transfer is submitted to the Committee on Agriculture of the House of Representatives and the Committee on

Agriculture, Nutrition, and Forestry of the Senate or such earlier time as may be approved by both such committees. Such report shall contain at least the following:

(1) guidelines utilized by the Secretary in determining that the land should be acquired;

(2) the location and size of the land;

(3) the purchase price of the land and the criteria used by the Secretary in determining such price;

(4) the person from whom the land is being acquired; and

(5) any adjustment made by the Secretary of relative value pursuant to section 1716(f)(2)(B)(ii) of Title 43.

Pub.L. 94–588, § 17(b), Oct. 22, 1976, 90 Stat. 2962; S.Res. 4, Feb. 4, 1977. As amended Pub.L. 100–409, § 6, Aug. 20, 1988, 102 Stat. 1090, Pub.L. 103–437, § 6(r), Nov. 2, 1994, 108 Stat. 4587.

§ 521c. Definitions

For purposes of sections 521c to 521i of this title—

(1) the term "person" includes any State or any political subdivision or entity thereof;

(2) the term "interchange" means a land transfer in which the Secretary and another person exchange titles to lands or interests in lands of approximately equal value where the Secretary finds that such a value determination can be made without a formal appraisal and under such regulations as the Secretary may prescribe; and

(3) the term "Secretary" means the Secretary of Agriculture of the United States.

Pub.L. 97–465, § 1, Jan. 12, 1983, 96 Stat. 2535.

§ 521d. Sale, exchange, or interchange of National Forest System land

The Secretary is authorized, when the Secretary determines it to be in the public interest—

(1) to sell, exchange, or interchange by quitclaim deed, all right, title, and interest, including the mineral estate, of the United States in and to National Forest System lands described in section 521e of this title; and

(2) to accept as consideration for the lands sold, exchanged, or interchanged other lands, interests in lands, or cash payment, or any combination of such forms of consideration, which, in the case of conveyance by sale or exchange, is at least equal in value, including the mineral estate, or, in the case of conveyance by interchange, is of approximately equal value, including the mineral estate, to the lands being conveyed by the Secretary. The Secretary shall insert in any such quitclaim deed such terms, covenants, conditions, and reservations as the Secretary deems necessary to ensure protection of the

public interest, including protection of the scenic, wildlife, and recreation values of the National Forest System and provision for appropriate public access to and use of lands within the System. The preceding sentence shall not be applicable to deeds issued by the Secretary to lands outside the boundary of units of the National Forest System.

Pub.L. 97–465, § 2, Jan. 12, 1983, 96 Stat. 2535.

§ 521e. Small parcels and road rights-of-way

The National Forest System lands which may be sold, exchanged, or interchanged under sections 521c to 521i of this title are those the sale or exchange of which is not practicable under any other authority of the Secretary, which have a value as determined by the Secretary of not more than $150,000, and which are—

(1) parcels of forty acres or less which are interspersed with or adjacent to lands which have been transferred out of Federal ownership under the mining laws and which are determined by the Secretary, because of location or size, not to be subject to efficient administration;

(2) parcels of ten acres or less which are encroached upon by improvements occupied or used under claim or color of title by persons to whom no advance notice was given that the improvements encroached or would encroach upon such parcels, and who in good faith relied upon an erroneous survey, title search, or other land description indicating that there was not such encroachment; or

(3) road rights-of-way, reserved or acquired, which are substantially surrounded by lands not owned by the United States and which are no longer needed by the United States, subject to the first right of abutting landowners to acquire such rights-of-way.

Pub.L. 97–465, § 3, Jan. 12, 1983, 96 Stat. 2535.

§ 521f. Costs of conveyance and value of improvements

Any person to whom lands are conveyed under sections 521c to 521i of this title shall bear all reasonable costs of administration, survey, and appraisal incidental to such conveyance, as determined by the Secretary. In determining the value of any lands or interest in lands to be conveyed under sections 521c to 521i of this title, the Secretary may, in those cases in which the Secretary determines it would be in the public interest, exclude from such determination the value of any improvements to the lands made by any person other than the Government. In the case of road rights-of-way conveyed under sections 521c to 521i of this title, the person to whom the right-of-way is conveyed shall reimburse the United States for the value of any improvements to such right-of-way which may have been made by the United States. The Secretary may, in those cases in which the Secretary determines that it would be in the public interest, waive payment by any person of costs incidental to any conveyance authorized by sections 521c to 521i of this title or reimbursement by any person for the value of improvements to rights-of-way otherwise required by this section.

Pub.L. 97–465, § 4, Jan. 12, 1983, 96 Stat. 2536.

§ 521g. Road rights-of-way subject to State or local law

Conveyance of any road rights-of-way under sections 521c to 521i of this title shall not be construed as permitting any designation, maintenance, or use of such rights-of-way for road or other purposes except to the extent permitted by State or local law and under conditions imposed by such law.

Pub.L. 97–465, § 5, Jan. 12, 1983, 96 Stat. 2536.

§ 521h. Regulations; contents

The Secretary shall issue regulations to carry out the provisions of sections 521c to 521i of this title, including specification of—

(1) criteria which shall be used in making the determination as to what constitutes the public interest;

(2) the definition of and the procedure for determining "approximately equal value"; and

(3) factors relating to location or size which shall be considered in connection with determining the lands to be sold, exchanged, or interchanged under clause (1) of section 521e of this title.

Pub.L. 97–465, § 6, Jan. 12, 1983, 96 Stat. 2536.

§ 521i. Unaffected lands

Nothing in sections 521c to 521i of this title shall authorize conveyance of Federal lands within the National Wilderness Preservation System, National Wild and Scenic Rivers System, National Trails System, or National Monuments. Nothing in this Act shall authorize sale of Federal lands, within National Recreation Areas.

Pub.L. 97–465, § 7, Jan. 12, 1983, 96 Stat. 2536.

§ 522. Rights-of-way for electrical plants

The Secretary of Agriculture is authorized and empowered, under general regulations to be fixed by him, to permit the use of rights of way through the national forests for electrical plants, poles, and lines for the generation and distribution of electrical power, and for telephone and telegraph purposes, and for canals, ditches, pipes and pipe lines, flumes, tunnels, or other water conduits, and for water plants, dams, and reservoirs used to promote irrigation or mining or quarrying, or the manufacturing or cutting of timber or lumber, or the supplying of water for domestic, public, or any other beneficial uses to the extent of the ground occupied by such canals, ditches, flumes, tunnels, reservoirs, or other water conduits or water plants, or electrical or other works permitted hereunder, and not to exceed fifty feet on each side of the marginal limits thereof, or not to exceed fifty feet on each side of the center line of such pipes and pipe lines, electrical, telegraph, and telephone lines and poles, by any citizen, association, or corporation of the United States, where it is intended by such to exercise the use permitted hereunder for any one or more of the purposes herein named. Such permits shall be allowed within or through any national forest, only upon the approval of the chief officer of the

81

department under whose supervision such national forest falls and upon a finding by him that the same is not incompatible with the public interest. All permits given hereunder for telegraph and telephone purposes shall be subject to the provision of sections I to 6 and 8 of Title 47 regulating rights of way for telegraph companies over the public domain. Any permission given by the Secretary of Agriculture under the provisions of this section may be revoked by him or his successor in his discretion, and shall not be held to confer any right, or easement, or interest in, to, or over any national forest.

Feb. 15, 1901, c. 372, 31 Stat. 790; Feb. 1, 1905, ch. 288, § 1, 33 Stat. 628.

§§ 522 to 525.

Repeals

Sections repealed by Pub.L. 94–579, Title VII, § 706(a), Oct. 21, 1976, 90 Stat. 2793, effective on and after Oct. 21, 1976, insofar as applicable to the issuance of rights-of-way over, upon, under, and through the public lands and lands in the National Forest System.

§ 523. Rights-of-way through national forests for power and communications facilities

The head of the department having jurisdiction over the lands is authorized and empowered, under general regulations to be fixed by him, to grant an easement for rights-of-way, for a period not exceeding fifty years from the date of the issuance of such grant, over, across, and upon the national forests of the United States for electrical poles and lines for the transmission and distribution of electrical power, and for poles and lines for communication purposes, and for radio, television, and other forms of communication transmitting, relay, and receiving structures and facilities, to the extent of two hundred feet on each side of the center line of such lines and poles and not to exceed four hundred feet by four hundred feet for radio, television, and other forms of communication transmitting, relay, and receiving structures and facilities, to any citizen, association, or corporation of the United States, where it is intended by such to exercise the right-of-way herein granted for any one or more of the purposes herein named: *Provided,* That such right-of-way shall be allowed within or through any national forest only upon the approval of the chief officer of the department under whose supervision or control such national forest falls, and upon a finding by him that the same is not incompatible with the public interest: *Provided further,* That all or any part of such right-of-way may be forfeited and annulled by declaration of the head of the department having jurisdiction over the lands for nonuse for a period of two years or for abandonment.

Any citizen, association, or corporation of the United States to whom there has been issued a permit prior to March 4, 1911, for any of the purposes specified herein under any law existing at that date, may obtain the benefit of this section upon the same terms and conditions as shall be required of citizens, associations, or corporations making application under the provisions of this section subsequent to said date.

Mar. 4, 1911, c. 238, 36 Stat. 1253; May 27, 1952, c. 338, 66 Stat. 95.

§ 524. Rights-of-way for dams, reservoirs, or water plants for municipal, mining, and milling purposes

Rights of way for the construction and maintenance of dams, reservoirs, water plants, ditches, flumes, pipes, tunnels, and canals, within and across the national forests of the United States, are granted to citizens and corporations of the United States for municipal or mining purposes, and for the purposes of the milling and reduction of ores, during the period of their beneficial use, under such rules and regulations as may be prescribed by the Secretary of the Interior, and subject to the laws of the State or Territory in which said forests are respectively situated.

Feb. 1, 1905, c. 288, § 4, 33 Stat. 628.

§ 525. Rights-of-way for wagon roads or railroads

In the form provided by existing law the Secretary of the Interior may file and approve surveys and plats of any right of way for a wagon road, railroad, or other highway over and across any national forest when in his judgment the public interests will not be injuriously affected thereby.

Mar. 3, 1899, c. 427, § 1, 30 Stat. 1233.

MULTIPLE–USE, SUSTAINED–YIELD ACT OF 1960

(16 U.S.C.A. §§ 528–31)

§ 528. Development and administration of renewable surface resources for multiple use and sustained yield of products and services; Congressional declaration of policy and purpose

It is the policy of the Congress that the national forests are established and shall be administered for outdoor recreation, range, timber, watershed, and wildlife and fish purposes. The purposes of sections 528 to 531 of this title are declared to be supplemental to, but not in derogation of, the purposes for which the national forests were established as set forth in section 475 of this title. Nothing herein shall be construed as affecting the jurisdiction or responsibilities of the several States with respect to wildlife and fish in the national forests. Nothing herein shall be construed so as to affect the use or administration of the mineral resources of national forest lands or to affect the use or administration of Federal lands not within national forests.

Pub.L. 86–517, § 1, June 12, 1960, 74 Stat. 215.

§ 529. Same; authorization; consideration to relative values of resources; areas of wilderness

The Secretary of Agriculture is authorized and directed to develop and administer the renewable surface resources of the national forests for multiple use and sustained yield of the several products and services obtained therefrom. In the administration of the national forests due consideration shall be given to the relative values of the various resources in particular areas. The establishment and maintenance of areas of wilderness are consistent with the purposes and provisions of sections 528 to 531 of this title.

Pub.L. 86–517, § 2, June 12, 1960, 74 Stat. 215.

§ 530. Same; cooperation with State and local governmental agencies and others

In the effectuation of sections 528 to 531 of this title the Secretary of Agriculture is authorized to cooperate with interested State and local governmental agencies and others in the development and management of the national forests.

Pub.L. 86–517, § 3, June 12, 1960, 74 Stat. 215.

§ 531. Same; definitions

As used in sections 528 to 531 of this title, the following terms shall have the following meanings:

(a) "Multiple use" means: The management of all the various renewable surface resources of the national forests so that they are utilized in the combination that will best meet the needs of the American people; making the most judicious use of the land for some or all of these resources or related services over areas large enough to provide sufficient latitude for periodic adjustments in use to conform to changing needs and conditions; that some land will be used for less than all of the resources; and harmonious and coordinated management of the various resources, each with the other, without impairment of the productivity of the land, with consideration being given to the relative values of the various resources, and not necessarily the combination of uses that will give the greatest dollar return or the greatest unit output.

(b) "Sustained yield of the several products and services" means the achievement and maintenance in perpetuity of a high-level annual or regular periodic output of the various renewable resources of the national forests without impairment of the productivity of the land.

Pub.L. 86–517, § 4, June 12, 1960, 74 Stat. 215.

FEDERAL ROADS AND TRAILS ACT OF 1964

(16 U.S.C.A. §§ 532–38)

§ 532. Roads and trails system; Congressional findings and declaration of policy

The Congress hereby finds and declares that the construction and maintenance of an adequate system of roads and trails within and near the national forests and other lands administered by the Forest Service is essential if increasing demands for timber, recreation, and other uses of such lands are to be met; that the existence of such a system would have the effect, among other things, of increasing the value of timber and other resources tributary to such roads; and that such a system is essential to enable the Secretary of Agriculture (hereinafter called the Secretary) to provide for intensive use, protection, development, and management of these lands under principles of multiple use and sustained yield of products and services.

Pub.L. 88–657, § 1, Oct. 13, 1964, 78 Stat. 1089.

§ 533. Same; grant of easements; authority of Secretary of Agriculture; regulations

The Secretary is authorized, under such regulations as he may prescribe, subject to the provisions of sections 532 to 538 of this title, to grant permanent or temporary easements for specified periods or other-wise for road rights-of-way (1) over national forest lands and other lands administered by the Forest Service, and (2) over any other related lands with respect to which the Department of Agriculture has rights under the terms of the grant to it.

Pub.L. 88–657, § 2, Oct. 13, 1964, 78 Stat. 1089.

§ 534. Same; termination and cancellation of easements; notice; hearing

An easement granted under sections 532 to 538 of this title may be terminated by consent of the owner of the easement, by condemnation, or after a five-year period of nonuse the Secretary may, if he finds the owner has abandoned the easement, make a determination to cancel it. Before the Secretary may cancel an easement for nonuse the owner of such easement must be notified of the determination to cancel and be given, upon his request made within sixty days after receipt of the notice, a hearing in accordance with such rules and regulations as may be issued by the Secretary.

Pub.L. 88–657, § 3, Oct. 13, 1964, 78 Stat. 1089.

§ 535. Same; forest development roads; acquisition, construction, and maintenance; maximum economy; methods of financing; cost arrangements for construction standards; transfer of unused effective purchaser credit for road construction

The Secretary is authorized to provide for the acquisition, construction, and maintenance of forest development roads within and near the national forests and other lands administered by the Forest Service in locations and according to specifications which will permit maximum economy in harvesting timber from such lands tributary to such roads and at the same time meet the requirements for protection, development, and management thereof, and for utilization of the other resources thereof. Financing of such roads may be accomplished (1) by the Secretary utilizing appropriated funds, (2) by requirements on purchasers of national forest timber and other products, including provisions for amortization of road costs in contracts, (3) by cooperative financing with other public agencies and with private agencies or persons, or (4) by a combination of these methods: *Provided,* That where roads of a higher standard than that needed in the harvesting and removal of the timber and other products covered by the particular sale are to be constructed, the purchaser of the national forest timber and other products shall not be required to bear that part of the costs necessary to meet such higher standard, and the Secretary is authorized to make such arrangements to this end as may be appropriate. The Secretary is authorized, under such rules and regulations as he shall prescribe, to permit the transfer of unused effective purchaser credit for road construction earned after December 16, 1975, from one timber sale to a purchaser to another timber sale to the same purchaser within the same National Forest.

Pub.L. 88–657, § 4, Oct. 13, 1964, 78 Stat. 1089; as amended Pub.L. 94–154, Dec. 16, 1975, 89 Stat. 823.

* * *

§ 537. Same; maintenance and reconstruction by road users; funds for maintenance and reconstruction: availability of deposits until expended, transfer of funds, and refunds

The Secretary may require the user or users of a road under the control of the Forest Service, including purchasers of Government timber and other products, to maintain such roads in a satisfactory condition commensurate with the particular use requirements of each. Such maintenance to be borne by each user shall be proportionate to total use. The Secretary may also require the user or users of such a road to reconstruct the same when such reconstruction is determined to be necessary to accommodate such use. If such maintenance or reconstruction cannot be so provided or if the Secretary determines that maintenance or reconstruction by a user would not be practical, then the Secretary may require that sufficient funds be deposited by the user to provide his portion of such total maintenance or reconstruction. Deposits made to cover the maintenance or reconstruction of roads are hereby made available until expended to cover the cost to the United States of accomplishing the purposes for which deposited: *Provided,* That deposits received for work on adjacent and overlapping areas may be combined when it is the most practicable and efficient manner of performing the work, and cost thereof may be determined by estimates: *And provided further,* That unexpended balances upon accomplishment of the purpose for which deposited shall be transferred to miscellaneous receipts or refunded.

Pub.L. 88–657, § 6, Oct. 13, 1964, 78 Stat. 1090.

§ 538. Same; user fees fund for delayed payments to grantors

Whenever the agreement under which the United States has obtained for the use of, or in connection with, the national forests and other lands administered by the Forest Service a right-of-way or easement for a road or an existing road or the right to use an existing road provides for delayed payments to the Government's grantor, any fees or other collections received by the Secretary for the use of the road may be placed in a fund to be available for making payments to the grantor.

Pub.L. 88–657, § 7, Oct. 13, 1964, 78 Stat. 1090.

FOREST SERVICE—MORE GENERAL PROVISIONS

§ 551. Protection of national forests; rules and regulations

The Secretary of Agriculture shall make provisions for the protection against destruction by fire and depredations upon the public forests and national forests which may have been set aside or which may be hereafter set aside under the provisions of section 471 of this title, and which may be continued; and he may make such rules and regulations and establish such service as will insure the objects of such reservations, namely, to regulate their occupancy and use and to preserve the forests thereon from destruction; and any violation of the provisions of sections 473 to 478 and 479 to 482 of this title or such rules and regulations shall be punished by a fine of not more than $500 or imprisonment for not more than six months, or both. Any person charged with the violation of such rules and regulations may be tried and sentenced by any United States magistrate specially designated for that purpose by the court by which he was appointed, in the same manner and subject to the same conditions as provided for in section 3401(b) to (e) of Title 18.

June 4, 1897, c. 2, § 1, 30 Stat. 35; Feb. 1, 1905, c. 288, § 1, 33 Stat. 628; Oct. 23, 1962, Pub.L. 87–869, § 6, 76 Stat. 1157; Aug. 31, 1964, Pub.L. 88–537, 78 Stat. 745; Oct. 17, 1968, Pub.L. 90–578, Title IV, § 402, 82 Stat. 1118. As amended Dec. 1, 1990, Pub.L. 101–650, Title III, § 321, 104 Stat. 5117.

Repeals

Section repealed by Pub.L. 94–579, Title VII, § 706(a), Oct. 21, 1976, 90 Stat. 2793, effective on and after Oct. 21, 1976, insofar as applicable to the issuance of rights-of-way over, upon, under, and through the public lands and lands in the National Forest System.

§ 551a. Cooperation by Secretary of Agriculture with states and political subdivisions in law enforcement

The Secretary of Agriculture, in connection with the administration and regulation of the use and occupancy of the national forests and national grasslands, is authorized to cooperate with any State or political subdivision thereof, on lands which are within or part of any unit of the national forest system, in the enforcement or supervision of the laws or ordinances of a State or subdivision thereof. Such cooperation may include the reimbursement of a State or its subdivision for expenditures incurred in connection with activities on national forest system lands. This section shall not deprive any State or political subdivision thereof of its right to exercise civil and criminal jurisdiction, within or on lands which are a part of the national forest system.

Pub.L. 92–82, Aug. 10, 1971, 85 Stat. 303.

* * *

§ 552. Consent to agreement by States for conservation of forests and water supply

Consent of the Congress of the United States is given to each of the several States of the Union to enter into any agreement or compact, not in conflict with any law of the United States, with any other State or States for the purpose of conserving the forests and the water supply of the States entering into such agreement or compact.

Mar. 1, 1911, c. 186, § 1, 36 Stat. 961.

§ 552a. Restoration of withdrawn national forest lands to appropriation

The President, upon recommendation of the Secretaries of the Interior and Agriculture, may, by Executive order, when in his judgment the public interest would best be served thereby and after reasonable notice has been given through the Department of the Interior, restore any reserved national-forest lands covered by a cooperative agreement with the Secretary of Agriculture for the protection of a watershed within a national forest from which water is secured, to appropriation under any applicable public-lands law.

May 28, 1940, ch. 220, § 1, 54 Stat. 224; Oct. 21, 1976, Pub.L. 94–579, Title VII, § 704(a), 90 Stat. 2792.

TIMBER CONTRACT MODIFICATION ACT OF 1984

(16 U.S.C.A. § 618)

§ 618. Timber contract payment modification

* * *

Monitoring of bidding patterns on timber sale contracts; discouragement of bids; reporting requirements

(c) The Secretary of Agriculture and the Secretary of the Interior shall monitor bidding patterns on timber sale contracts and take action to discourage bidding at such a rate as would indicate that the bidder, if awarded the contract, would be unable to perform the obligations as required, or that the bid is otherwise for the purpose of speculation. Each Secretary shall include in the annual report to Congress information concerning actions taken under this paragraph.

Cash down-payment and periodic payments for contracts; effective date

(d) Effective January 1, 1985, in any contract for the sale of timber from the National Forests, the Secretary of Agriculture shall require a cash downpayment at the time the contract is executed and periodic payments to be made over the remaining period of the contract.

Pub.L. 98–478, § 2, Oct. 16, 1984, 98 Stat. 2213.

FISH AND WILDLIFE COORDINATION ACT OF 1934

(16 U.S.C.A. §§ 661–67)

§ 661. Declaration of purpose; cooperation of agencies; surveys and investigations; donations

For the purpose of recognizing the vital contribution of our wildlife resources to the Nation, the increasing public interest and significance thereof due to expansion of our national economy and other factors, and to provide that wildlife conservation shall receive equal consideration and be coordinated with other features of water-resource development programs through the effectual and harmonious planning, development, maintenance, and coordination of wildlife conservation and rehabilitation for the purposes of sections 661 to 666c of this title in the United States, its Territories and possessions, the Secretary of the Interior is authorized (1) to provide assistance to, and cooperate with, Federal, State, and public or private agencies and organizations in the development, protection, rearing, and stocking of all species of wildlife, resources thereof, and their habitat, in controlling losses of the same from disease or other causes, in minimizing damages from overabundant species, in providing public shooting and fishing areas, including easements across public lands for access thereto, and in carrying out other measures necessary to effectuate the purposes of said sections; (2) to make surveys and investigations of the wildlife of the public domain, including lands and waters or interests therein acquired or controlled by any agency of the United States; and (3) to accept donations of land and contributions of funds in furtherance of the purposes of said sections.

Mar. 10, 1934, c. 55, § 1, 48 Stat. 401; 1939 Reorg. Plan No. II, § 4(e), (f), eff. July 1, 1939, 4 F.R. 2731, 53 Stat. 1433; Aug. 14, 1946, c. 965, 60 Stat. 1080; Aug. 12, 1958, Pub.L. 85–624, § 2, 72 Stat. 563.

§ 662. Impounding, diverting, or controlling of waters—Consultations between agencies

(a) Except as hereafter stated in subsection (h) of this section, whenever the waters of any stream or other body of water are proposed or authorized to be impounded, diverted, the channel deepened, or the stream or other body of water otherwise controlled or modified for any purpose whatever, including navigation and drainage, by any department or agency of the United States, or by any public or private agency under Federal permit or license, such department or agency first shall consult with the United States Fish and Wildlife Service, Department of the Interior, and with the head of the agency exercising administration over the wildlife resources of the particular State wherein the impoundment, diversion, or other control facility is to be constructed, with a view to the conservation of wildlife resources by preventing loss of and damage to such resources as well as providing for the development and improvement thereof in connection with such water-resource development.

Reports and recommendations; consideration

(b) In furtherance of such purposes, the reports and recommendations of the Secretary of the Interior on the wildlife aspects of such projects, and any report of the head of the State agency exercising administration over the wildlife resources of the State, based on surveys and investigations conducted by the United States Fish and Wildlife Service and such State agency for the purpose of determining the possible damage to wildlife resources and for the purpose of determining means and measures that should be adopted to prevent the loss of or damage to such wildlife resources, as well as to provide concurrently for the development and improvement of such resources, shall be made an integral part of any report prepared or submitted by any agency of the Federal Government responsible for engineering surveys and construction of such projects when such reports are presented to the Congress or to any agency or person having the authority or the power, by administrative action or otherwise, (1) to authorize the construction of water-resource development projects or (2) to approve a report on the modification or supplementation of plans for previously authorized projects, to which sections 661 to 666c of this title apply. Recommendations of the Secretary of the Interior shall be as specific as is practicable with respect to features recommended for wildlife conservation and development, lands to be utilized or acquired for such purposes, the results expected, and shall describe the damage to wildlife attributable to the project and the measures proposed for mitigating or compensating for these damages. The reporting officers in project reports of the Federal agencies shall give full consideration to the report and recommendations of the Secretary of the Interior and to any report of the State agency on the wildlife aspects of such projects, and the project plan shall include such justifiable means and measures for wildlife purposes as the reporting agency finds should be adopted to obtain maximum overall project benefits.

Modification of projects; acquisition of lands

(c) Federal agencies authorized to construct or operate water-control projects are authorized to modify or add to the structures and operations of such projects, the construction of which has not been substantially completed on the date of enactment of the Fish and Wildlife Coordination Act, and to acquire lands in accordance with section 663 of this title, in order to accommodate the means and measures for such conservation of wildlife resources as an integral part of such projects: * * *

Project costs

(d) The cost of planning for and the construction or installation and maintenance of such means and measures adopted to carry out the conservation purposes of this section shall constitute an integral part of the cost of such projects: *Provided,* That such cost attributable to the development and improvement of wildlife shall not extend beyond that necessary for (1) land acquisition, (2) facilities as specifically recommended in water resource project reports, (3) modification of the project, and (4) modification of project operations, but shall not include the operation of wildlife facilities.

* * *

Estimation of wildlife benefits or losses

(f) In addition to other requirements, there shall be included in any report submitted to Congress supporting a recommendation for authorization of any new project for the control or use of water as described herein (including any new division of such project or new supplemental works on such project) an estimation of the wildlife benefits or losses to be derived therefrom including benefits to be derived from measures recommended specifically for the development and improvement of wildlife resources, the cost of providing wildlife benefits (including the cost of additional facilities to be installed or lands to be acquired specifically for that particular phase of wildlife conservation relating to the development and improvement of wildlife), the part of the cost of joint-use facilities allocated to wildlife, and the part of such costs, if any, to be reimbursed by non-Federal interests.

* * *

Exempt projects and activities

(h) The provisions of sections 661 to 666c of this title shall not be applicable to those projects for the impoundment of water where the maximum surface area of such impoundments is less than ten acres, nor to activities for or in connection with programs primarily for land management and use carried out by Federal agencies with respect to Federal lands under their jurisdiction.

Mar. 10, 1934, c. 55, § 2, 48 Stat. 401; 1939 Reorg. Plan No. II, § 4(e), (f), eff. July 1, 1939, 4 F.R. 2731, 53 Stat. 1433; Aug. 14, 1946, ch. 965, 60 Stat. 1080; Aug. 12, 1958, Pub.L. 85–624, § 2, 72 Stat. 564; July 9, 1965, Pub.L. 89–72, § 6(b), 79 Stat. 216.

* * *

§ 664. Administration; rules and regulations; availability of lands to State agencies

Such areas as are made available to the Secretary of the Interior for the purposes of sections 661 to 666c of this title, pursuant to sections 661 and 663 of this title or pursuant to any other authorization, shall be administered by him directly or in accordance with cooperative agreements entered into pursuant to the provisions of section 661 of this title and in accordance with such rules and regulations for the conservation, maintenance, and management of wildlife, resources thereof, and its habitat thereon, as may be adopted by the Secretary in accordance with general plans approved jointly by the Secretary of the Interior and the head of the department or agency exercising primary administration of such areas: *Provided,* That such rules and regulations shall not be inconsistent with the laws for the protection of fish and game of the States in which such area is situated: *Provided further,* That lands having value to the National Migratory Bird Management Program may, pursuant to general plans, be made available without cost directly to the State agency having control over wildlife resources, if it is jointly determined by the Secretary of the Interior and such State agency that this would be in the public interest: *And provided further,* That the Secretary of the Interior shall have the right to assume the management and administration of such lands in behalf of the National Migratory Bird Management Program if the Secretary finds that the State agency has withdrawn from or otherwise relinquished such management and administration.

Mar. 10, 1934, c. 55, § 4, 48 Stat. 402; 1939 Reorg. Plan No. II, § 4(e), (f), eff. July 1, 1939, 4 F.R. 2731, 53 Stat. 1433; 1940 Reorg. Plan No. III, § 3, eff. June 30, 1940, 5 F.R. 2108, 54 Stat. 1232; Aug. 14, 1946, c. 965, 60 Stat. 1080; Aug. 12, 1958, Pub.L. 85–624, § 2, 72 Stat. 567.

* * *

§ 666b. Definitions

The terms "wildlife" and "wildlife resources" as used in sections 661 to 666c of this title include birds, fishes, mammals, and all other classes of wild animals and all types of aquatic and land vegetation upon which wildlife is dependent.

Mar. 10, 1934, c. 55, § 8, as added Aug. 14, 1946, c. 965, 60 Stat. 1080.

* * *

BALD AND GOLDEN EAGLE PROTECTION ACT OF 1940 (as amended)

(16 U.S.C.A. §§ 668–668d)

§ 668. Bald and golden eagles—Prohibited acts; criminal penalties

(a) Whoever, within the United States or any place subject to the jurisdiction thereof, without being permitted to do so as provided in sections 668 to 668d of this title, shall knowingly, or with wanton disregard for the consequences of his act take, possess, sell, purchase, barter, offer to sell, purchase or barter, transport, export or import, at any time or in any manner, any bald eagle commonly known as the American eagle, or any golden eagle, alive or dead, or any part, nest, or egg thereof of the foregoing eagles, or whoever violates any permit or regulation issued pursuant to sections 668 to 668d of this title, shall be fined not more than $5,000 or imprisoned not more than one year or both: *Provided,* That in the case of a second or subsequent conviction for a violation of this section committed after October 23, 1972, such person shall be fined not more than $10,000 or imprisoned not more than two years, or both: *Provided further,* That the commission of each taking or other act prohibited by this section with respect to a bald or golden eagle shall constitute a separate violation of this section: *Provided further,* That one-half of any such fine, but not to exceed $2,500, shall be paid to the person or persons giving information which leads to conviction: *Provided further,* That nothing in said sections shall be construed to prohibit possession or transportation of any bald eagle, alive or dead, or any part, nest, or egg thereof, lawfully taken prior to June 8, 1940, and that nothing in said sections shall be construed to prohibit possession or transportation of any golden eagle, alive or dead, or any part, nest, or egg thereof, lawfully taken prior to the addition to said sections of the provisions relating to preservation of the golden eagle.

Civil penalties

(b) Whoever, within the United States or any place subject to the jurisdiction thereof, without being permitted to do so as provided in sections 668 to 668d of this title, shall take, possess, sell, purchase, barter, offer to sell, purchase or barter, transport, export or import, at any time or in any manner, any bald eagle, commonly known as the American eagle, or any golden eagle, alive or dead, or any part, nest, or egg thereof of the foregoing eagles, or whoever violates any permit or regulation issued pursuant to sections 668 to 668d of this title, may be assessed a civil penalty by the Secretary of not more than $5,000 for each such violation. Each violation shall be a separate offense. No penalty shall be assessed unless such person is given notice and opportunity for a hearing with respect to such violation. In determining the amount of the penalty, the gravity of the violation, and the demonstrated good faith of the person charged shall be considered by the Secretary. For good cause shown, the Secretary may remit or mitigate any such penalty. Upon any failure to pay the penalty assessed under this section, the Secretary may request the

Attorney General to institute a civil action in a district court of the United States for any district in which such person is found or resides or transacts business to collect the penalty and such court shall have jurisdiction to hear and decide any such action. In hearing any such action, the court must sustain the Secretary's action if supported by substantial evidence.

Cancellation of grazing agreements

(c) The head of any Federal agency who has issued a lease, license, permit, or other agreement authorizing the grazing of domestic livestock on Federal lands to any person who is convicted of a violation of sections 668 to 668d of this title or of any permit or regulation issued hereunder may immediately cancel each such lease, license, permit, or other agreement. The United States shall not be liable for the payment of any compensation, reimbursement, or damages in connection with the cancellation of any lease, license, permit, or other agreement pursuant to this section.

June 8, 1940, c. 278, § 1, 54 Stat. 250; June 25, 1959, Pub.L. 86–70, § 14, 73 Stat. 143; Oct. 24, 1962, Pub.L. 87–884, 76 Stat. 1246; Oct. 23, 1972, Pub.L. 92–535, § 1, 86 Stat. 1064.

§ 668a. Taking and using of the bald and golden eagle for scientific, exhibition and religious purposes

Whenever, after investigation, the Secretary of the Interior shall determine that it is compatible with the preservation of the bald eagle or the golden eagle to permit the taking, possession, and transportation of specimens thereof for the scientific or exhibition purposes of public museums, scientific societies, and zoological parks, or for the religious purposes of Indian tribes, or that it is necessary to permit the taking of such eagles for the protection of wildlife or of agricultural or other interests in any particular locality, he may authorize the taking of such eagles pursuant to regulations which he is hereby authorized to prescribe: *Provided,* That on request of the Governor of any State, the Secretary of the Interior shall authorize the taking of golden eagles for the purpose of seasonally protecting domesticated flocks and herds in such State, in accordance with regulations established under the provisions of this section, in such part or parts of such State and for such periods as the Secretary determines to be necessary to protect such interests: *Provided further,* That bald eagles may not be taken for any purpose unless, prior to such taking, a permit to do so is procured from the Secretary of the Interior: *Provided further,* That the Secretary of the Interior, pursuant to such regulations as he may prescribe, may permit the taking, possession, and transportation of golden eagles for the purposes of falconry, except that only golden eagles which would be taken because of depredations on livestock or wildlife may be taken for purposes of falconry: *Provided further,* That the Secretary of the Interior, pursuant to such regulations as he may prescribe, may permit the taking of golden eagle nests which interfere with resource development or recovery operations.

June 8, 1940, ch. 278, § 2, 54 Stat. 251; Oct. 24, 1962, Pub.L. 87–884, 76 Stat. 1246; Oct. 23, 1972, Pub.L. 92–535, § 2, 86 star. 1065; Nov. 8, 1978, Pub.L. 95–616, § 9, 92 Stat. 3114.

* * *

§ 668c. Same; definitions

As used in sections 668 to 668d of this title "whoever" includes also associations, partnerships, and corporations; "take" includes also pursue, shoot, shoot at, poison, wound, kill, capture, trap, collect, or molest or disturb; "transport" includes also ship, convey, carry, or transport by any means whatever, and deliver or receive or cause to be delivered or received for such shipment, conveyance, carriage, or transportation.

June 8, 1940, c. 278, § 4, 54 Stat. 251; Oct. 23, 1972, Pub.L. 92–535, § 4, 86 Stat. 1065.

* * *

NATIONAL WILDLIFE REFUGE ADMINISTRATION ACT OF 1966 (as amended)

(16 U.S.C.A. §§ 668dd–668ee)

§ 668dd. National Wildlife Refuge System

Designation; administration; continuance of resources-management-programs for refuge lands in Alaska; disposal of acquired lands; proceeds

(a)(1) For the purpose of consolidating the authorities relating to the various categories of areas that are administered by the Secretary for the conservation of fish and wildlife, including species that are threatened with extinction, all lands, waters, and interests therein administered by the Secretary as wildlife refuges, areas for the protection and conservation of fish and wildlife that are threatened with extinction, wildlife ranges, game ranges, wildlife management areas, or waterfowl production areas are hereby designated as the "National Wildlife Refuge System" (referred to herein as the "System"), which shall be subject to the provisions of this section, and shall be administered by the Secretary through the United States Fish and Wildlife Service. With respect to refuge lands in the State of Alaska, those programs relating to the management of resources for which any other agency of the Federal Government exercises administrative responsibility through cooperative agreement shall remain in effect, subject to the direct supervision of the United States Fish and Wildlife Service, as long as such agency agrees to exercise such responsibility.

(a)(2) The mission of the System is to administer a national network of lands and waters for the conservation, management, and where appropriate, restoration of the fish, wildlife, and plant resources and their habitats within the United States for the benefit of present and future generations of Americans.

(a)(3) With respect to the System, it is the policy of the United States that—

(A) each refuge shall be managed to fulfill the mission of the System, as well as the specific purposes for which that refuge was established;

(B) compatible wildlife-dependent recreation is a legitimate and appropriate general public use of the System, directly related to the mission of the System and the purposes of many refuges, and which generally fosters refuge management and through which the American public can develop an appreciation for fish and wildlife;

(C) compatible wildlife-dependent recreational uses are the priority general public uses of the System and shall receive priority consideration in refuge planning and management; and

(D) when the Secretary determines that a proposed wildlife-dependent recreational use is a compatible use within a refuge, that activity should be facilitated, subject to such restrictions or regulations as may be necessary, reasonable, and appropriate.

(a)(4) In administering the System, the Secretary shall—

(A) provide for the conservation of fish, wildlife, and plants, and their habitats within the System;

(B) ensure that the biological integrity, diversity, and environmental health of the System are maintained for the benefit of present and future generations of Americans;

(C) plan and direct the continued growth of the System in a manner that is best designed to accomplish the mission of the System, to contribute to the conservation of the ecosystems of the United States, to complement efforts of States and other Federal agencies to conserve fish and wildlife and their habitats, and to increase support for the System and participation from conservation partners and the public;

(D) ensure that the mission of the System described in paragraph (2) and the purposes of each refuge are carried out, except that if a conflict exists between the purposes of a refuge and the mission of the System, the conflict shall be resolved in a manner that first protects the purposes of the refuge, and, to the extent practicable, that also achieves the mission of the System;

(E) ensure effective coordination, interaction, and cooperation with owners of land adjoining refuges and the fish and wildlife agency of the States in which the units of the System are located;

(F) assist in the maintenance of adequate water quantity and water quality to fulfill the mission of the System and the purposes of each refuge;

(G) acquire, under State law, water rights that are needed for refuge purposes;

(H) recognize compatible wildlife-dependent recreational uses as the priority general public uses of the System through which the American public can develop an appreciation for fish and wildlife;

(I) ensure that opportunities are provided within the System for compatible wildlife-dependent recreational uses;

(J) ensure that priority general public uses of the System receive enhanced consideration over other general public uses in planning and management within the System;

(K) provide increased opportunities for families to experience compatible wildlife-dependent recreation, particularly opportunities for parents and their children to safely engage in traditional outdoor activities, such as fishing and hunting;

(L) continue, consistent with existing laws and interagency agreements, authorized or permitted uses of units of the System by other Federal agencies, including those necessary to facilitate military preparedness;

(M) ensure timely and effective cooperation and collaboration with Federal agencies and State fish and wildlife agencies during the course of acquiring and managing refuges; and

(N) monitor the status and trends of fish, wildlife, and plants in each refuge.

(a)(5) No acquired lands which are or become a part of the System may be transferred or otherwise disposed of under any provision of law (except by exchange pursuant to subsection (b)(3) of this section) unless—

(A) the Secretary determines with the approval of the Migratory Bird Conservation Commission that such lands are no longer needed for the purposes for which the System was established; and

(B) such lands are transferred or otherwise disposed of for an amount not less than—

(i) the acquisition costs of such lands, in the case of lands of the System which were purchased by the United States with funds from the migratory bird conservation fund, or fair market value, whichever is greater; or

(ii) the fair market value of such lands (as determined by the Secretary as of the date of the transfer or disposal), in the case of lands of the System which were donated to the System.

The Secretary shall pay into the migratory bird conservation fund the aggregate amount of the proceeds of any transfer or disposal referred to in the preceding sentence.

(a)(6) Each area which is included within the System on January 1, 1975, or thereafter, and which was or is—

(A) designated as an area within such System by law, Executive order, or secretarial order; or

(B) so included by public land withdrawal, donation, purchase, exchange, or pursuant to a cooperative agreement with any State or local government, any Federal department or agency, or any other governmental entity,

shall continue to be a part of the System until otherwise specified by Act of Congress, except that nothing in this paragraph shall be construed as precluding—

(i) the transfer or disposal of acquired lands within any such area pursuant to paragraph (5) of this subsection;

(ii) the exchange of lands within any such area pursuant to subsection (b)(3) of this section; or

(iii) the disposal of any lands within any such area pursuant to the terms of any cooperative agreement referred to in subparagraph (B) of this paragraph.

Administration; public accommodations contracts; acceptance and use of funds; exchange of properties; cash equalization payments

(b) In administering the System, the Secretary is authorized to take the following actions:

(1) Enter into contracts with any person or public or private agency through negotiation for the provision of public accommodations when, and in such locations, and to the extent that the Secretary determines will not be inconsistent with the primary purpose for which the affected area was established.

(2) Accept donations of funds and to use such funds to acquire or manage lands or interests therein.

(3) Acquire lands or interests therein by exchange (A) for acquired lands or public lands, or for interests in acquired or public lands, under his jurisdiction which he finds to be suitable for disposition, or (B) for the right to remove, in accordance with such terms and conditions as he may prescribe, products from the acquired or public lands within the System. The values of the properties so exchanged either shall be approximately equal, or if they are not approximately equal the values shall be equalized by the payment of cash to the grantor or to the Secretary as the circumstances require.

(4) Subject to standards established by and the overall management oversight of the Director, and consistent with standards established by this Act, to enter into cooperative agreements with State fish and wildlife agencies for the management of programs on a refuge.

(5) Issue regulations to carry out this Act.

Prohibited and permitted activities; application of mining and mineral leasing laws, hunting or fishing regulations, and State laws or regulations

(c) No person shall disturb, injure, cut, burn, remove, destroy, or possess any real or personal property of the United States, including natural growth, in any area of the System; or take or possess any fish, bird, mammal, or other wild vertebrate or invertebrate animals or part or nest or egg thereof within any such area; or enter, use, or otherwise occupy any such area for any purpose; unless such activities are performed by persons authorized to manage such area, or unless such activities are permitted either under subsection (d) of this section or by express provision of the law, proclamation, Executive order, or public land order establishing the area, or amendment thereof: *Provided,* That the United States mining and mineral leasing laws shall continue to apply to any lands within the System to the same extent they apply prior to October 15, 1966, unless subsequently withdrawn under other authority of law. With the exception of endangered species and threatened species listed by the Secretary pursuant to section 1533 of this title in States wherein a cooperative agreement does not exist pursuant to section 1535(c) of this title, nothing in this Act shall be construed to authorize the Secretary to control or regulate hunting or fishing of resident fish and wildlife on lands not within the system. The regulations permitting hunting and fishing of resident fish and wildlife within the System shall be, to the extent practicable, consistent with State fish and wildlife laws and regulations.

Use of areas; administration of migratory bird sanctuaries as game taking areas; rights of way, easements, and reservations; payment of fair market value

(d)(1) The Secretary is authorized, under such regulations as he may prescribe, to—

(A) permit the use of any area within the System for any purpose, including but not limited to hunting, fishing, public recreation and accommodations, and access whenever he determines that such uses are compatible with the major purposes for which such areas were established: *Provided,* That not to exceed 40 per centum at any one time of any area that has been, or hereafter may be acquired, reserved, or set apart as an inviolate sanctuary for migratory birds, under any law, proclamation, Executive order, or public land order may be administered by the Secretary as an area within which the taking of migratory game birds may be permitted under such regulations as he may prescribe unless the Secretary finds that the taking of any species of migratory game birds in more than 40 percent of such area would be beneficial to the species; and

(B) permit the use of, or grant easements in, over, across, upon, through, or under any areas within the System for purposes such as but not necessarily limited to, powerlines, telephone lines, canals, ditches, pipelines, and roads, including the construction, operation, and maintenance thereof, whenever he determines that such uses are compatible with the purposes for which these areas are established.

(d)(2) Notwithstanding any other provision of law, the Secretary may not grant to any Federal, State, or local agency or to any private individual or organization any right-of-way, easement, or reservation in, over, across, through, or under any area within the system in connection with any use permitted by him under paragraph (1)(B) of this subsection unless the grantee pays to the Secretary, at the option of the Secretary, either (A) in lump sum the fair market value (determined by the Secretary as of the date of conveyance to the grantee) of the right-of-way, easement, or reservation; or (B) annually in advance the fair market rental value (determined by the Secretary) of the right-of-way, easement, or reservation. If any Federal, State, or local agency is exempted from such payment by any other provision of Federal law, such agency shall otherwise compensate the Secretary by any other means agreeable to the Secretary, including, but not limited to, making other land available or the loan of equipment or personnel; except that (A) any such compensation shall relate to, and be consistent with, the objectives of the National Wildlife Refuge System, and (B) the Secretary may waive such requirement for compensation if he finds such requirement impracticable or unnecessary. All sums received by the Secretary of the Interior pursuant to this paragraph shall, after payment of any necessary expenses incurred by him in administering this paragraph, be deposited into the Migratory Bird Conservation Fund and shall be available to carry out the provisions for land acquisition of the Migratory Bird Conservation Act (16 U.S.C. 715 et seq.) and the Migratory Bird Hunting Stamp Act (16 U.S.C. 718 et seq.).

(d)(3)(A)(i) Except as provided in clause (iv), the Secretary shall not initiate or permit a new use of a refuge or expand, renew, or extend an existing use of a refuge, unless the Secretary has determined that the use is a compatible use and that the use is not inconsistent with public safety. The Secretary may make the determinations referred to in this paragraph for a refuge concurrently with development of a conservation plan under subsection (e).

(A)(ii) On lands added to the System after March 25, 1996, the Secretary shall identify, prior to acquisition, withdrawal, transfer, reclassification, or donation of any such lands, existing compatible wildlife-dependent recreational uses that the Secretary determines shall be permitted to continue on an interim basis pending completion of the comprehensive conservation plan for the refuge.

(A)(iii) Wildlife-dependent recreational uses may be authorized on a refuge when they are compatible and not inconsistent with public safety. Except for consideration of consistency with State laws and regulations as provided for in subsection (m), no other determinations or findings are required to be made by the refuge official under this Act or the Refuge Recreation Act for wildlife-dependent recreation to occur.

(A)(iv) Compatibility determinations in existence on October 9, 1997 shall remain in effect until and unless modified.

(d)(3)(B) Not later than 24 months after October 9, 1997, the Secretary shall issue final regulations establishing the process for determining under subparagraph (A) whether a use of a refuge is a compatible use. These regulations shall—

(i) designate the refuge official responsible for making initial compatibility determinations;

(ii) require an estimate of the timeframe, location, manner, and purpose of each use;

(iii) identify the effects of each use on refuge resources and purposes of each refuge;

(iv) require that compatibility determinations be made in writing;

(v) provide for the expedited consideration of uses that will likely have no detrimental effect on the fulfillment of the purposes of a refuge or the mission of the System;

(vi) provide for the elimination or modification of any use as expeditiously as practicable after a determination is made that the use is not a compatible use;

(vii) require, after an opportunity for public comment, reevaluation of each existing use, other than those uses specified in clause (viii), if conditions under which the use is permitted change significantly or if there is significant new information regarding the effects of the use, but not less frequently than once every 10 years, to ensure that the use remains a compatible use, except that, in the case of any use authorized for a period longer than 10 years (such as an electric utility right-of-way), the reevaluation required by this clause shall examine compliance with the terms and conditions of the authorization, not examine the authorization itself;

(viii) require, after an opportunity for public comment, reevaluation of each compatible wildlife-dependent recreational use when conditions under which the use is permitted change significantly or if there is significant new information regarding the effects of the use, but not less frequently than in conjunction with each preparation or revision of a conservation plan under subsection (e) of this section or at least every 15 years, whichever is earlier; and

(ix) provide an opportunity for public review and comment on each evaluation of a use, unless an opportunity for public review and comment on the evaluation of the use has already been provided during the development or revision of a conservation plan for the refuge under subsection (e) of this section or has otherwise been provided during routine, periodic determinations of compatibility for wildlife-dependent recreational uses.

(d)(4) The provisions of this Act relating to determinations of the compatibility of a use shall not apply to—

(A) overflights above a refuge; and

(B) activities authorized, funded, or conducted by a Federal agency (other than the United States Fish and Wildlife Service) which has primary jurisdiction over a refuge or a portion of a refuge, if the management of those activities is in accordance with a memorandum of understanding between the Secretary or the Director and the head of the Federal agency with primary jurisdiction over the refuge governing the use of the refuge.

Refuge conservation planning program for non-Alaskan refuge lands

(e)(1)(A) Except with respect to refuge lands in Alaska (which shall be governed by the refuge planning provisions of the Alaska National Interest Lands Conservation Act (16 U.S.C. 3101 et seq.)), the Secretary shall—

(i) propose a comprehensive conservation plan for each refuge or related complex of refuges (referred to in this subsection as a "planning unit") in the System;

(ii) publish a notice of opportunity for public comment in the Federal Register on each proposed conservation plan;

(iii) issue a final conservation plan for each planning unit consistent with the provisions of this Act and, to the extent practicable, consistent with fish and wildlife conservation plans of the State in which the refuge is located; and

(iv) not less frequently than 15 years after the date of issuance of a conservation plan under clause (iii) and every 15 years thereafter, revise the conservation plan as may be necessary.

(B) The Secretary shall prepare a comprehensive conservation plan under this subsection for each refuge within 15 years after October 9, 1997.

(C) The Secretary shall manage each refuge or planning unit under plans in effect on October 9, 1997, to the extent such plans are consistent with this Act, until such plans are revised or superseded by new comprehensive conservation plans issued under this subsection.

(D) Uses or activities consistent with this Act may occur on any refuge or planning unit before existing plans are revised or new comprehensive conservation plans are issued under this subsection.

(E) Upon completion of a comprehensive conservation plan under this subsection for a refuge or planning unit, the Secretary shall manage the refuge or planning unit in a manner consistent with the plan and shall revise the plan at any time if the Secretary determines that conditions that affect the refuge or planning unit have changed significantly.

(e)(2) In developing each comprehensive conservation plan under this subsection for a planning unit, the Secretary, acting through the Director, shall identify and describe—

(A) the purposes of each refuge comprising the planning unit;

(B) the distribution, migration patterns, and abundance of fish, wildlife, and plant populations and related habitats within the planning unit;

(C) the archaeological and cultural values of the planning unit;

(D) such areas within the planning unit that are suitable for use as administrative sites or visitor facilities;

(E) significant problems that may adversely affect the populations and habitats of fish, wildlife, and plants within the planning unit and the actions necessary to correct or mitigate such problems; and

(F) opportunities for compatible wildlife-dependent recreational uses.

(e)(3) In preparing each comprehensive conservation plan under this subsection, and any revision to such a plan, the Secretary, acting through the Director, shall, to the maximum extent practicable and consistent with this Act—

(A) consult with adjoining Federal, State, local, and private landowners and affected State conservation agencies; and

(B) coordinate the development of the conservation plan or revision with relevant State conservation plans for fish and wildlife and their habitats.

(e)(4)(A) In accordance with subparagraph (B), the Secretary shall develop and implement a process to ensure an opportunity for active public involvement in the preparation and revision of comprehensive conservation plans under this subsection. At a minimum, the Secretary shall require that publication of any final plan shall include a summary of the comments made by States, owners of adjacent or potentially affected land, local governments, and any other affected persons, and a statement of the disposition of concerns expressed in those comments.

(B) Prior to the adoption of each comprehensive conservation plan under this subsection, the Secretary shall issue public notice of the draft proposed plan, make copies of the plan available at the affected field and regional offices of the United States Fish and Wildlife Service, and provide opportunity for public comment.

Penalties

(f)(1) Knowing violations

Any person who knowingly violates or fails to comply with any of the provisions of this Act or any regulations issued thereunder shall be fined under Title 18 or imprisoned for not more than 1 year, or both.

(f)(2) Other violations

Any person who otherwise violates or fails to comply with any of the provisions of this Act (including a regulation issued under this Act) shall be fined under Title 18 or imprisoned not more than 180 days, or both.

Enforcement provisions; arrests, searches, and seizures; custody of property; forfeiture; disposition

(g) Any person authorized by the Secretary to enforce the provisions of this Act or any regulations issued thereunder, may, without a warrant, arrest any person violating this Act or regulations in his presence or view, and may execute any warrant or other process issued by an officer or court of competent jurisdiction to enforce the provisions of this Act or regulations, and may with a search warrant search for and seize any property, fish, bird, mammal, or other wild vertebrate or invertebrate animals or part or nest or egg thereof, taken or possessed in violation of this Act or the regulations issued thereunder. Any property, fish, bird, mammal, or other wild vertebrate or invertebrate animals or part or egg thereof seized with or without a search warrant shall be held by such person or by a United States marshal, and upon conviction, shall be forfeited to the United States and disposed of by the Secretary, in accordance with law. The Director of the United States Fish and Wildlife Service is authorized to utilize by agreement, with or without reimbursement, the personnel and services of any other Federal or State agency for purposes of enhancing the enforcement of this Act.

Regulations; continuation, modification, or rescission

(h) Regulations applicable to areas of the System that are in effect on October 15, 1966, shall continue in effect until modified or rescinded.

National conservation recreational area provisions; amendment, repeal, or modification

(i) Nothing in this section shall be construed to amend, repeal, or otherwise modify the provision of the Act of September 28, 1962 (76 Stat. 653; 16 U.S.C. 460k to 460k–4) which authorizes the Secretary to administer the areas within the System for public recreation. The provisions of this section relating to recreation shall be administered in accordance with the provisions of said sections.

Exemption from State water laws

(j) Nothing in this Act shall constitute an express or implied claim or denial on the part of the Federal Government as to exemption from State water laws.

Emergency power

(k) Notwithstanding any other provision of this Act, the Secretary may temporarily suspend, allow, or initiate any activity in a refuge in the System if the Secretary determines it is necessary to protect the health and safety of the public or any fish or wildlife population.

Hunting and fishing on lands and waters not within the System

(*l*) Nothing in this Act shall be construed to authorize the Secretary to control or regulate hunting or fishing of fish and resident wildlife on lands or waters that are not within the System.

State authority

(m) Nothing in this Act shall be construed as affecting the authority, jurisdiction, or responsibility of the several States to manage, control, or regulate fish and resident wildlife under State law or regulations in any area within the System. Regulations permitting hunting or fishing of fish and resident wildlife within the System shall be, to the extent practicable, consistent with State fish and wildlife laws, regulations, and management plans.

Water rights

(n)(1) Nothing in this Act shall—

(A) create a reserved water right, express or implied, in the United States for any purpose;

(B) affect any water right in existence on October 9, 1997; or

(C) affect any Federal or State law in existence on October 9, 1997, regarding water quality or water quantity.

(n)(2) Nothing in this Act shall diminish or affect the ability to join the United States in the adjudication of rights to the use of water pursuant to section 666 of Title 43.

Coordination with State agencies

(o) Coordination with State fish and wildlife agency personnel or with personnel of other affected State agencies pursuant to this Act shall not be subject to the Federal Advisory Committee Act (5 U.S.C.App.).

Pub.L. 89–669, § 4, Oct. 15, 1966, 80 Stat. 927; Pub.L. 90–404, § 1, July 18, 1968, 82 Stat. 359; Pub.L. 93–205, § 13(a), Dec. 28, 1973, 87 Stat. 902; Pub.L. 93–509, § 2, Dec. 3, 1974, 88 Stat. 1603; Pub.L. 94–215, § 5, Feb. 17, 1976, 90 Stat. 190; Pub.L. 94–223, Feb. 27, 1976, 90 Stat. 199; Pub.L. 95–616, §§ 3(f), 6, Nov. 8, 1978, 92 Stat. 3111, 3114; Pub.L. 100–226, § 4, Dec. 31, 1987, 101 Stat. 1551; Pub.L. 100–653, Title IX, § 904, Nov. 14, 1988, 102 Stat. 3834; Pub.L. 105–57, §§ 3(b) to 8, Oct. 9, 1997, 111 Stat. 1254; Pub.L. 105–312, Title II, § 206, Oct. 30, 1998, 112 Stat. 2958.

§ 668ee. Definitions

For purposes of this Act:

(1) The term "compatible use" means a wildlife-dependent recreational use or any other use of a refuge that, in the sound professional judgment of the Director, will not materially interfere with or detract from the fulfillment of the mission of the System or the purposes of the refuge.

(2) The terms "wildlife-dependent recreation" and "wildlife-dependent recreational use" mean a use of a refuge involving hunting, fishing, wildlife observation and photography, or environmental education and interpretation.

(3) The term "sound professional judgment" means a finding, determination, or decision that is consistent with principles of sound fish and wildlife management and administration, available science and resources, and adherence to the requirements of this Act and other applicable laws.

(4) The terms "conserving", "conservation", "manage", "managing", and "management", mean to sustain and, where appropriate, restore and enhance, healthy populations of fish, wildlife, and plants utilizing, in accordance with applicable Federal and State laws, methods and procedures associated with modern scientific resource programs. Such methods and procedures include, consistent with the provisions of this Act, protection, research, census, law enforcement, habitat management, propagation, live trapping and transplantation, and regulated taking.

(5) The term "Coordination Area" means a wildlife management area that is made available to a State—

(A) by cooperative agreement between the United States Fish and Wildlife Service and a State agency having control over wildlife resources pursuant to section 664 of this title; or

(B) by long-term leases or agreements pursuant to title III of the Bankhead-Jones Farm Tenant Act (50 Stat. 525; 7 U.S.C. 1010 et seq.).

(6) The term "Director" means the Director of the United States Fish and Wildlife Service or a designee of that Director.

(7) The terms "fish", "wildlife", and "fish and wildlife" mean any wild member of the animal kingdom whether alive or dead, and regardless of whether the member was bred, hatched, or born in captivity, including a part, product, egg, or offspring of the member.

(8) The term "person" means any individual, partnership, corporation, or association.

(9) The term "plant" means any member of the plant kingdom in a wild, unconfined state, including any plant community, seed, root, or other part of a plant.

(10) The terms "purposes of the refuge" and "purposes of each refuge" mean the purposes specified in or derived from the law, proclamation, executive order, agreement, public land order, donation document, or administrative memorandum establishing, authorizing, or expanding a refuge, refuge unit, or refuge subunit.

(11) The term "refuge" means a designated area of land, water, or an interest in land or water within the System, but does not include Coordination Areas.

(12) The term "Secretary" means the Secretary of the Interior.

(13) The terms "State" and "United States" mean the several States of the United States, Puerto Rico, American Samoa, the Virgin Islands, Guam, and the territories and possessions of the United States.

(14) The term "System" means the National Wildlife Refuge System designated under section 668dd(a)(1) of this title.

(15) The terms "take", "taking", and "taken" mean to pursue, hunt, shoot, capture, collect, or kill, or to attempt to pursue, hunt, shoot, capture, collect, or kill.

Pub.L. 89–669, § 5, Oct. 15, 1966, 80 Stat. 929; Pub.L. 105–57, § 3(a), Oct. 9, 1997, 111 Stat. 1253.

PROTECTION OF MIGRATORY GAME AND INSECTIVOROUS BIRDS

(16 U.S.C.A. §§ 701–718)

§ 701. Game and wild birds; preservation

The duties and powers of the Department of the Interior include the preservation, distribution, introduction, and restoration of game birds and other wild birds. The Secretary of the Interior is authorized to adopt such measures as may be necessary to carry out the purposes of this Act, and to purchase such game birds and other wild birds as may be required therefor, subject, however, to the laws of the various States and Territories. The object and purpose of this Act is to aid in the restoration of such birds in those parts of the United States adapted thereto where the same have become scarce or extinct, and also to regulate the introduction of American or foreign birds or animals in localities where they have not heretofore existed.

The Secretary of the Interior shall from time to time collect and publish useful information as to the propagation, uses, and preservation of such birds.

And the Secretary of the Interior shall make and publish all needful rules and regulations for carrying out the purposes of this Act, and shall expend for said purposes such sums as Congress may appropriate therefor.

May 25, 1900, c. 553, § 1, 31 Stat. 187; 1939 Reorg. Plan No. II, § 4(f), eft. July 1, 1939, 4 F.R. 2731, 53 Stat. 1433.

§ 702. Importation of eggs of game birds for propagation

The Secretary of the Interior shall have the power to authorize the importation of eggs of game birds for purposes of propagation, and he shall prescribe all necessary rules and regulations governing the importation of eggs of said birds for such purposes.

June 3, 1902, c. 983, 32 Stat. 285; 1939 Reorg. Plan No. II, § 4(f), eft. July 1, 1939, 4 F.R. 2731, 53 Stat. 1433.

MIGRATORY BIRD TREATY ACT OF 1918

(16 U.S.C.A. §§ 703–712)

§ 703. Taking, killing, or possessing migratory birds unlawful

Unless and except as permitted by regulations made as hereinafter provided in this subchapter, it shall be unlawful at any time, by any means or in any manner, to pursue, hunt, take, capture, kill, attempt to take, capture, or kill, possess, offer for sale, sell, offer to barter, barter, offer to purchase, purchase, deliver for shipment, ship, export, import, cause to be shipped, exported, or imported, deliver for transportation, transport or cause to be transported, carry or cause to be carried, or receive for shipment, transportation, carriage, or export, any migratory bird, any part, nest, or egg of any such bird, or any product, whether or not manufactured, which consists, or is composed in whole or in part, of any such bird or any part, nest, or egg thereof, included in the terms of the conventions between the United States and Great Britain for the protection of migratory birds concluded August 16, 1916 (39 Stat. 1702), the United States and the United Mexican States for the protection of migratory birds and game mammals concluded February 7, 1936, the United States and the Government of Japan for the protection of migratory birds and birds in danger of extinction, and their environment concluded March 4, 1972 and the convention between the United States and the Union of Soviet Socialist Republics for the conservation of migratory birds and their environments concluded November 19, 1976.

July 3, 1918, c. 128, § 2, 40 Stat. 755; June 20, 1936, c. 634, § 3, 49 Stat. 1556; June 1, 1974, Pub.L. 93–300, § 1, §§ Stat. 190, Dec. 13, 1989, Pub.L. 101–233, § 15, 103 Stat. 1977.

§ 704. Determination as to when and how migratory birds may be taken, killed, or possessed

(a) Subject to the provisions and in order to carry out the purposes of the conventions, referred to in section 703 of this title, the Secretary of the Interior is authorized and directed, from time to time, having due regard to the zones of temperature and to the distribution, abundance, economic value, breeding habits, and times and lines of migratory flight of such birds, to determine when, to what extent, if at all, and by what means, it is compatible with the terms of the conventions to allow hunting, taking, capture, killing, possession, sale, purchase, shipment, transportation, carriage, or export of any such bird, or any part, nest, or egg thereof, and to adopt suitable regulations permitting and governing the same, in accordance with such determinations, which regulations shall become effective when approved by the President.

(b) It shall be unlawful for any person to—

(1) take any migratory game bird by the aid of baiting, or on or over any baited area, if the person knows or reasonably should know that the area is a baited area; or

(2) place or direct the placement of bait on or adjacent to an area for the purpose of causing, inducing, or allowing any person to take or attempt to take any migratory game bird by the aid of baiting on or over the baited area.

July 3, 1918, c. 128, § 3, 40 Stat. 755; June 20, 1936, c. 634, § 2, 49 Stat. 1556; 1939 Reorg. Plan No. II, § 4(f), eff. July 1, 1939, 4 F.R. 2731, 53 Stat. 1433; Oct. 30, 1998, Pub.L. 105–312, Title I, § 102, 112 Stat. 2956.

§ 705. Transportation or importation of migratory birds; when unlawful

It shall be unlawful to ship, transport, or carry, by any means whatever, from one State, Territory, or district to or through another State, Territory, or district, or to or through a foreign country, any bird, or any part, nest, or egg thereof, captured, killed, taken, shipped, transported, or carried at any time contrary to the laws of the State, Territory, or district in which it was captured, killed, or taken, or from which it was shipped, transported, or carried. It shall be unlawful to import any bird, or any part, nest, or egg thereof, captured, killed, taken, shipped, transported, or carried contrary to the laws of any Province of the Dominion of Canada in which the same was captured, killed, or taken, or from which it was shipped, transported, or carried.

July 3, 1918, c. 128, § 4, 40 Stat. 755; June 20, 1936, c. 634, § 4, 49 Stat. 1556; 1939 Reorg. Plan No. II, § 4(f), eff. July 1, 1939, 4 F.R. 2731, 53 Stat. 1433; Dec. 5, 1969, Pub.L. 91–135, § 10, 83 Stat. 282.

* * *

§ 707. Violations and penalties; forfeitures

(a) Except as otherwise provided in this section, any person, association, partnership, or corporation who shall violate any provisions of said conventions or of this subchapter, or who shall violate or fail to comply with any regulation made pursuant to this subchapter shall be deemed guilty of a misdemeanor and upon conviction thereof shall be fined not more than $15,000 or be imprisoned not more than six months, or both.

(b) Whoever, in violation of this subchapter, shall knowingly—

(1) take by any manner whatsoever any migratory bird with intent to sell, offer to sell, barter or offer to barter such bird, or

(2) sell, offer for sale, barter or offer to barter, any migratory bird shall be guilty of a felony and shall be fined not more than $2,000 or imprisoned not more than two years, or both.

(c) Whoever violates section 704(b)(2) of this title shall be fined under Title 18, imprisoned not more than 1 year, or both.

(d) All guns, traps, nets and other equipment, vessels, vehicles, and other means of transportation used by any person when engaged in pursuing, hunting, taking, trapping, ensnaring, capturing, killing, or attempting to take, capture, or kill any migratory bird in violation of this subchapter with the intent to offer for sale, or sell, or offer for barter, or barter such bird in violation of this subchapter shall be forfeited to the United States and may be seized and held pending the prosecution of any person arrested for violating this subchapter and upon conviction for such violation, such forfeiture shall be adjudicated as a penalty in addition to any other provided for violation of this subchapter. Such forfeited property shall be disposed of and accounted for by, and under the authority of, the Secretary of the Interior.

(July 3, 1918, c. 128, § 6, 40 Stat. 756; June 20, 1936, c. 634, § 2, 49 Stat. 1556; Sept. 8, 1960, Pub.L. 86–732, 74 Stat. 866; Pub.L. 99–645, Title V, § 501, Nov. 10, 1986, 100 Stat. 3590; Pub.L. 105–312, Title I, § 103, Oct. 30, 1998, 112 Stat. 2956.)

§ 708. State or Territorial laws or regulations

Nothing in this subchapter shall be construed to prevent the several States and Territories from making or enforcing laws or regulations not inconsistent with the provisions of said conventions or of this subchapter, or from making or enforcing laws or regulations which shall give further protection to migratory birds, their nests, and eggs, if such laws or regulations do not extend the open seasons for such birds beyond the dates approved by the President in accordance with section 704 of this title.

July 3, 1918, c. 128, § 7, 40 Stat. 756; June 20, 1936, c. 634, § 2, 49 Stat. 1556.

* * *

WILDERNESS ACT OF 1964 (as amended)

(16 U.S.C.A. §§ 1131–36)

§ **1131.** National Wilderness Preservation System—Establishment; Congressional declaration of policy; wilderness areas; administration for public use and enjoyment, protection, preservation, and gathering and dissemination of information; provisions for designation as wilderness areas

(a) In order to assure that an increasing population, accompanied by expanding settlement and growing mechanization, does not occupy and modify all areas within the United States and its possessions, leaving no lands designated for preservation and protection in their natural condition, it is hereby declared to be the policy of the Congress to secure for the American people of present and future generations the benefits of an enduring resource of wilderness. For this purpose there is hereby established a National Wilderness Preservation System to be composed of federally owned areas designated by Congress as "wilderness areas", and these shall be administered for the use and enjoyment of the American people in such manner as will leave them unimpaired for future use and enjoyment as wilderness, and so as to provide for the protection of these areas, the preservation of their wilderness character, and for the gathering and dissemination of information regarding their use and enjoyment as wilderness; and no Federal lands shall be designated as "wilderness areas" except as provided for in this chapter or by a subsequent Act.

Management of area included in System; appropriations

(b) The inclusion of an area in the National Wilderness Preservation System notwithstanding, the area shall continue to be managed by the Department and agency having jurisdiction thereover immediately before its inclusion in the National Wilderness Preservation System unless otherwise provided by Act of Congress. No appropriation shall be available for the payment of expenses or salaries for the administration of the National Wilderness Preservation System as a separate unit nor shall any appropriations be available for additional personnel stated as being required solely for the purpose of managing or administering areas solely because they are included within the National Wilderness Preservation System.

Definition of wilderness

(c) A wilderness, in contrast with those areas where man and his own works dominate the landscape, is hereby recognized as an area where the earth and its community of life are untrammeled by man, where man himself is a visitor who does not remain. An area of wilderness is further defined to mean in this chapter an area of undeveloped Federal land retaining its primeval character and influence, without permanent improvements or human habitation, which is protected and managed so as to preserve its natural conditions and which (1) generally appears to have been affected primarily by the forces of nature, with the imprint of man's work substantially unnoticeable; (2) has outstanding opportunities for solitude or a primitive and unconfined type of recreation; (3) has at least five thousand acres of land or is of sufficient size as to make practicable its preservation and use in an unimpaired condition; and (4) may also contain ecological, geological, or other features of scientific, educational, scenic, or historical value.

Pub.L. 88–577, § 2, Sept. 3, 1964, 78 Stat. 890.

§ 1132. Extent of System—Designation of wilderness areas; filing of maps and descriptions with congressional committees; correction of errors; public records; availability of records in regional offices

(a) All areas within the national forests classified at least 30 days before September 3, 1964 by the Secretary of Agriculture or the Chief of the Forest Service as "wilderness", "wild", or "canoe" are hereby designated as wilderness areas. The Secretary of Agriculture shall—

(1) Within one year after September 3, 1964, file a map and legal description of each wilderness area with the Interior and Insular Affairs Committees of the United States Senate and the House of Representatives, and such descriptions shall have the same force and effect as if included in this chapter: *Provided, however,* That correction of clerical and typographical errors in such legal descriptions and maps may be made.

(2) Maintain, available to the public, records pertaining to said wilderness areas, including maps and legal descriptions, copies of regulations governing them, copies of public notices of, and reports submitted to Congress regarding pending additions, eliminations, or modifications. Maps, legal descriptions, and regulations pertaining to wilderness areas within their respective jurisdictions also shall be available to the public in the offices of regional foresters, national forest supervisors, and forest rangers.

Review by Secretary of Agriculture of classifications as primitive areas; Presidential recommendations to Congress; approval of Congress; size of primitive areas; Gore Range–Eagles Nest Primitive Area, Colorado

(b) The Secretary of Agriculture shall, within ten years after September 3, 1964, review, as to its suitability or nonsuitability for preservation as wilderness, each area in the national forests classified on September 3, 1964 by the Secretary of Agriculture or the Chief of the Forest Service as "primitive" and report his findings to the President. The President shall advise the United States Senate and House of Representatives of his recommendations with respect to the designation as "wilderness" or other reclassification of each area on which review has been completed, together with maps and a definition of boundaries. Such advice shall be given with respect to not less than one-third of all the areas now classified as

111

"primitive" within three years after September 3, 1964, not less than two-thirds within seven years after September 3, 1964, and the remaining areas within ten years after September 3, 1964. Each recommendation of the President for designation as "wilderness" shall become effective only if so provided by an Act of Congress. Areas classified as "primitive" on September 3, 1964 shall continue to be administered under the rules and regulations affecting such areas on September 3, 1964 until Congress has determined otherwise. Any such area may be increased in size by the President at the time he submits his recommendations to the Congress by not more than five thousand acres with no more than one thousand two hundred and eighty acres of such increase in any one compact unit; if it is proposed to increase the size of any such area by more than five thousand acres or by more than one thousand two hundred and eighty acres in any one compact unit the increase in size shall not become effective until acted upon by Congress. Nothing herein contained shall limit the President in proposing, as part of his recommendations to Congress, the alteration of existing boundaries of primitive areas or recommending the addition of any contiguous area of national forest lands predominantly of wilderness value. Notwithstanding any other provisions of this chapter, the Secretary of Agriculture may complete his review and delete such area as may be necessary, but not to exceed seven thousand acres, from the southern tip of the Gore Range–Eagles Nest Primitive Area, Colorado, if the Secretary determines that such action is in the public interest.

Review by Secretary of Interior of roadless areas of national park system and national wildlife refuges and game ranges and suitability of areas for preservation as wilderness; authority of Secretary of Interior to maintain roadless areas in national park system unaffected

(c) Within ten years after September 3, 1964 the Secretary of the Interior shall review every roadless area of five thousand contiguous acres or more in the national parks, monuments and other units of the national park system and every such area of, and every roadless island within, the national wildlife refuges and game ranges, under his jurisdiction on September 3, 1964 and shall report to the President his recommendation as to the suitability or nonsuitability of each such area or island for preservation as wilderness. The President shall advise the President of the Senate and the Speaker of the House of Representatives of his recommendation with respect to the designation as wilderness of each such area or island on which review has been completed, together with a map thereof and a definition of its boundaries. Such advice shall be given with respect to not less than one-third of the areas and islands to be reviewed under this subsection within three years after September 3, 1964, not less than two-thirds within seven years of September 3, 1964, and the remainder within ten years of September 3, 1964. A recommendation of the President for designation as wilderness shall become effective only if so provided by an Act of Congress. Nothing contained herein shall, by implication or otherwise, be construed to lessen the present statutory authority of the Secretary of the Interior with respect to the maintenance of roadless areas within units of the national park system.

Conditions precedent to administrative recommendations of suitability of areas for preservation as wilderness; publication in Federal Register; public hearings; views of State, county, and Federal officials; submission of views to Congress

(d)(1) The Secretary of Agriculture and the Secretary of the Interior shall, prior to submitting any recommendations to the President with respect to the suitability of any area for preservation as wilderness—

(A) give such public notice of the proposed action as they deem appropriate, including publication in the Federal Register and in a newspaper having general circulation in the area or areas in the vicinity of the affected land;

(B) hold a public hearing or hearings at a location or locations convenient to the area affected. The hearings shall be announced through such means as the respective Secretaries involved deem appropriate, including notices in the Federal Register and in newspapers of general circulation in the area: *Provided,* That if the lands involved are located in more than one State, at least one hearing shall be held in each State in which a portion of the land lies;

(C) at least thirty days before the date of a hearing advise the Governor of each State and the governing beard of each county, or in Alaska the borough, in which the lands are located, and Federal departments and agencies concerned, and invite such officials and Federal agencies to submit their views on the proposed action at the hearing or by no later than thirty days following the date of the hearing.

(d)(2) Any views submitted to the appropriate Secretary under the provisions of (1) of this subsection with respect to any area shall be included with any recommendations to the President and to Congress with respect to such area.

Modification or adjustment of boundaries; public notice and hearings; administrative and executive recommendations to Congress; approval of Congress

(e) Any modification or adjustment of boundaries of any wilderness area shall be recommended by the appropriate Secretary after public notice of such proposal and public hearing or hearings as provided in subsection (d) of this section. The proposed modification or adjustment shall then be recommended with map and description thereof to the President. The President shall advise the United States Senate and the House of Representatives of his recommendations with respect to such modification or adjustment and such recommendations shall become effective only in the same manner as provided for in subsections (b) and (c) of this section.

Pub.L. 88–577, § 3, Sept. 3, 1964, 78 Stat. 891.

§ 1133. Use of wilderness areas-Purposes of national forests, national park system, and national wildlife refuge system; other provisions applicable to national forests, Superior National Forest, and national park system

Agency responsibility for preservation and administration to preserve wilderness character; public purposes of wilderness areas

(a) The purposes of this chapter are hereby declared to be within and supplemental to the purposes for which national forests and units of the national park and national wildlife refuge systems are established and administered and—

(1) Nothing in this chapter shall be deemed to be in interference with the purpose for which national forests are established as set forth in the Act of June 4, 1897 (30 Stat. 11), and the Multiple–Use Sustained–Yield Act of June 12, 1960 (74 Stat. 215) [16 U.S.C.A. §§ 528–531].

(2) Nothing in this chapter shall modify the restrictions and provisions of the Shipstead–Nolan Act (Public Law 539, Seventy-first Congress, July 10, 1930; 46 Stat. 1020), the Thye–Blatnik Act (Public Law 733, Eightieth Congress, June 22, 1948; 62 Stat. 568), and the Humphrey–Thye–Blatnik–Andresen Act (Public Law 607, Eighty-fourth Congress, June 22, 1956; 70 Stat. 326), as applying to the Superior National Forest or the regulations of the Secretary of Agriculture.

(3) Nothing in this chapter shall modify the statutory authority under which units of the national park system are created. Further, the designation of any area of any park, monument, or other unit of the national park system as a wilderness area pursuant to this chapter shall in no manner lower the standards evolved for the use and preservation of such park, monument, or other unit of the national park system in accordance with sections 1 and 2 to 4 of this title, the statutory authority under which the area was created, or any other Act of Congress which might pertain to or affect such area, including, but not limited to, the Act of June 8, 1906 (34 Stat. 225; 16 U.S.C. 432 et seq.); section 3(2) of the Federal Power Act (16 U.S.C. 796(2)); and the Act of August 21, 1935 (49 Stat. 666; 16 U.S.C. 461 et seq.).

Agency responsibility for preservation and administration to preserve wilderness character; public purposes of wilderness areas

(b) Except as otherwise provided in this chapter, each agency administering any area designated as wilderness shall be responsible for preserving the wilderness character of the area and shall so administer such area for such other purposes for which it may have been established as also to preserve its wilderness character. Except as otherwise provided in this chapter, wilderness areas shall be devoted to the public purposes of recreational, scenic, scientific, educational, conservation, and historical use.

Prohibition provisions: commercial enterprise, permanent or temporary roads, mechanical transports, and structures or installations; exceptions: area administration and personal health and safety emergencies

(c) Except as specifically provided for in this chapter, and subject to existing private rights, there shall be no commercial enterprise and no permanent road within any wilderness area designated by this chapter and, except as necessary to meet minimum requirements for the administration of the area for the purpose of this chapter (including measures required in emergencies involving the health and safety of persons within the area), there shall be no temporary road, no use of motor vehicles, motorized equipment or motorboats, no landing of aircraft, no other form of mechanical transport, and no structure or installation within any such area.

Special provisions

(d) The following special provisions are hereby made:

Aircraft or motorboats; fire, insects, and diseases

(1) Within wilderness areas designated by this chapter the use of aircraft or motorboats, where these uses have already become established, may be permitted to continue subject to such restrictions as the Secretary of Agriculture deems desirable. In addition, such measures may be taken as may be necessary in the control of fire, insects, and diseases, subject to such conditions as the Secretary deems desirable.

Mineral activities, surveys for mineral value

(2) Nothing in this chapter shall prevent within national forest wilderness areas any activity, including prospecting, for the purpose of gathering information about mineral or other resources, if such activity is carried on in a manner compatible with the preservation of the wilderness environment. Furthermore, in accordance with such program as the Secretary of the Interior shall develop and conduct in consultation with the Secretary of Agriculture, such areas shall be surveyed on a planned, recurring basis consistent with the concept of wilderness preservation by the United States Geological Survey and the United States Bureau of Mines to determine the mineral values, if any, that may be present; and the results of such surveys shall be made available to the public and submitted to the President and Congress.

Mining and mineral leasing laws; leases, permits, and licenses; withdrawal of minerals from appropriation and disposition

(3) Notwithstanding any other provisions of this chapter, until midnight December 31, 1983, the United States mining laws and all laws pertaining to mineral leasing shall, to the same extent as applicable prior to September 3, 1964, extend to those national forest lands designated by this chapter as "wilderness areas"; subject, however, to such reasonable regulations governing ingress and egress as may be prescribed by the Secretary of Agriculture consistent with the use of the land for mineral

location and development and exploration, drilling, and production, and use of land for transmission lines, waterlines, telephone lines, or facilities necessary in exploring, drilling, producing, mining, and processing operations, including where essential the use of mechanized ground or air equipment and restoration as near as practicable of the surface of the land disturbed in performing prospecting, location, and, in oil and gas leasing, discovery work, exploration, drilling, and production, as soon as they have served their purpose. Mining locations lying within the boundaries of said wilderness areas shall be held and used solely for mining or processing operations and uses reasonably incident thereto; and hereafter, subject to valid existing rights, all patents issued under the mining laws of the United States affecting national forest lands designated by this chapter as wilderness areas shall convey title to the mineral deposits within the claim, together with the right to cut and use so much of the mature timber therefrom as may be needed in the extraction, removal, and beneficiation of the mineral deposits, if needed timber is not otherwise reasonably available, and if the timber is cut under sound principles of forest management as defined by the national forest rules and regulations, but each such patent shall reserve to the United States all title in or to the surface of the lands and products thereof, and no use of the surface of the claim or the resources therefrom not reasonably required for carrying on mining or prospecting shall be allowed except as otherwise expressly provided in this chapter: *Provided*, That, unless hereafter specifically authorized, no patent within wilderness areas designated by this chapter shall issue after December 31, 1983, except for the valid claims existing on or before December 31, 1983. Mining claims located after September 3, 1964 within the boundaries of wilderness areas designated by this chapter shall create no rights in excess of those rights which may be patented under the provisions of this subsection. Mineral leases, permits, and licenses covering lands within national forest wilderness areas designated by this chapter shall contain such reasonable stipulations as may be prescribed by the Secretary of Agriculture for the protection of the wilderness character of the land consistent with the use of the land for the purposes for which they are leased, permitted, or licensed. Subject to valid rights then existing, effective January 1, 1984, the minerals in lands designated by this chapter as wilderness areas are withdrawn from all forms of appropriation under the mining laws and from disposition under all laws pertaining to mineral leasing and all amendments thereto.

Water resources, reservoirs, and other facilities; grazing

(4) Within wilderness areas in the national forests designated by this chapter, (1) the President may, within a specific area and in accordance with such regulations as he may deem desirable, authorize prospecting for water resources, the establishment and maintenance of reservoirs, water-conservation works, power projects, transmission lines, and other facilities needed in the public interest, including the road construction and maintenance essential to development and use thereof, upon his determination that such use or uses in the specific area will better serve the interests of the United States and the people thereof than will its denial; and (2) the grazing of livestock, where established prior to September 3, 1964, shall be

permitted to continue subject to such reasonable regulations as are deemed necessary by the Secretary of Agriculture.

Commercial services

(5) Commercial services may be performed within the wilderness areas designated by this chapter to the extent necessary for activities which are proper for realizing the recreational or other wilderness purposes of the areas.

State water laws exemption

(6) Nothing in this chapter shall constitute an express or implied claim or denial on the part of the Federal Government as to exemption from State water laws.

State jurisdiction of wildlife and fish in national forests

(7) Nothing in this chapter shall be construed as affecting the jurisdiction or responsibilities of the several States with respect to wildlife and fish in the national forests.

Pub.L. 88–577, § 5, Sept. 3, 1964, 78 Stat. 893; Pub.L. 95–495, § 4(b), Oct. 21, 1978, 92 Stat. 1650, as amended Pub.L. 102–154, Title I, Nov. 13, 1991, 105 Stat. 1000; Pub.L. 102–285, § 10, May 18, 1992, 106 Stat. 171.

NOTE

Livestock Grazing in National Forest Wilderness Areas

Pub.L. 96–560, Title I, § 108, Dec. 22, 1980, 94 Stat. 3271, provided that:

"The Congress hereby declares that, without amending the Wilderness Act of 1964 [this chapter], with respect to livestock grazing in National Forest wilderness areas, the provisions of the Wilderness Act relating to grazing shall be interpreted and administered in accordance with the guidelines contained under the heading 'Grazing in National Forest Wilderness' in the House Committee Report (H. Report 96–617) accompanying this Act [Pub.L. 96–560]."

§ 1134. State and private lands within wilderness areas

Access; exchange of lands; mineral interests restriction

(a) In any case where State-owned or privately owned land is completely surrounded by national forest lands within areas designated by this chapter as wilderness, such State or private owner shall be given such rights as may be necessary to assure adequate access to such State-owned or privately owned land by such State or private owner and their successors in interest, or the State-owned land or privately owned land shall be exchanged for federally owned land in the same State of approximately equal value under authorities available to the Secretary of Agriculture: *Provided, however,* That the United States shall not transfer to a State or private owner any mineral interests unless the State or private owner relinquishes or causes to be relinquished to the United States the mineral interest in the surrounded land.

Customary means for ingress and egress to wilderness areas subject to mining claims or other occupancies

(b) In any case where valid mining claims or other valid occupancies are wholly within a designated national forest wilderness area, the Secretary of Agriculture shall, by reasonable regulations consistent with the preservation of the area as wilderness, permit ingress and egress to such surrounded areas by means which have been or are being customarily enjoyed with respect to other such areas similarly situated.

Acquisition of lands

(c) Subject to the appropriation of funds by Congress, the Secretary of Agriculture is authorized to acquire privately owned land within the perimeter of any area designated by this chapter as wilderness if (1) the owner concurs in such acquisition or (2) the acquisition is specifically authorized by Congress.

Pub.L. 88–577, § 5, Sept. 3, 1964, 78 Stat. 896.

* * *

NATIONAL TRAILS SYSTEM ACT OF 1968 (as amended)

(16 U.S.C.A. §§ 1241–49)

§ 1241.   Congressional statement of policy and declaration of purpose

Considerations determining establishment of trails

(a) In order to provide for the ever-increasing outdoor recreation needs of an expanding population and in order to promote the preservation of, public access to, travel within, and enjoyment and appreciation of the open-air, outdoor areas and historic resources of the Nation, trails should be established (i) primarily, near the urban areas of the Nation, and (ii) secondarily, within scenic areas and along historic travel routes of the Nation, which are often more remotely located.

Initial components

(b) The purpose of this chapter is to provide the means for attaining these objectives by instituting a national system of recreation, scenic and historic trails, by designating the Appalachian Trail and the Pacific Crest Trail as the initial components of that system, and by prescribing the methods by which, and standards according to which, additional components may be added to the system.

Volunteer citizen involvement

(c) The Congress recognizes the valuable contributions that volunteers and private, nonprofit trail groups have made to the development and maintenance of the Nation's trails. In recognition of these contributions, it is further the purpose of this chapter to encourage and assist volunteer citizen involvement in the planning, development, maintenance, and management, where appropriate, of trails.

Pub.L. 90–543, § 2, Oct. 2, 1968, 82 Stat. 919; as amended Pub.L. 95–625, Title V, § 551(1)–(3), Nov. 10, 1978, 92 Stat. 3511; Pub.L. 98–11, Title II, § 202, Mar. 28, 1983, 97 Stat. 42.

§ 1242. National trails system

Composition: Recreation trails; scenic trails; historic trails; connecting or side trails; uniform markers

(a) The national system of trails shall be composed of the following:

(1) National recreation trails, established as provided in section 1243 of this title, which will provide a variety of outdoor recreation uses in or reasonably accessible to urban areas.

(2) National scenic trails, established as provided in section 1244 of this title, which will be extended trails so located as to provide for maximum outdoor recreation potential and for the conservation and enjoyment of the nationally significant scenic, historic, natural, or cultural qualities of the areas through which such trails may pass. National scenic trails may be located so as to represent desert, marsh, grassland, mountain, canyon, river, forest, and other areas, as well as landforms which exhibit significant characteristics of the physiographic regions of the Nation.

(3) National historic trails, established as provided in section 1244 of this title, which will be extended trails which follow as closely as possible and practicable the original trails or routes of travel of national historical significance. Designation of such trails or routes shall be continuous, but the established or developed trail, and the acquisition thereof, need not be continuous onsite. National historic trails shall have as their purpose the identification and protection of the historic route and its historic remnants and artifacts for public use and enjoyment. Only those selected land and water based components of an historic trail which are on federally owned lands and which meet the national historic trail criteria established in this chapter are included as Federal protection components of a national historic trail. The appropriate Secretary may certify other lands as protected segments of an historic trail upon application from State or local governmental agencies or private interests involved if such segments meet the national historic trail criteria established in this chapter and such criteria supplementary thereto as the appropriate Secretary may prescribe, and are administered by such agencies or interests without expense to the United States.

(4) Connecting or side trails, established as provided in section 1245 of this title, which will provide additional points of public access

to national recreation, national scenic or national historic trails or which will provide connections between such trails.

The Secretary of the Interior and the Secretary of Agriculture, in consultation with appropriate governmental agencies and public and private organizations, shall establish a uniform marker for the national trails system.

Pub.L. 90–543, § 3, Oct. 2, 1968, 82 Stat. 919; as amended Pub.L. 95–625, Title V, § 551(4), (5), Nov. 10, 1978, 92 Stat. 3511, 3512; Pub.L. 98–11, Title II, § 203, Mar. 28, 1983, 97 Stat. 42, as amended Pub.L. 104–333, Div. I, Title VIII, § 814(d)(1)(E), Nov. 12, 1996, 110 Stat. 4196.

§ 1243. National recreation trails; establishment and designation; prerequisites

Consent of political entities having jurisdiction over land involved; criteria for designation

(a) The Secretary of the Interior, or the Secretary of Agriculture where lands administered by him are involved, may establish and designate national recreation trails, with the consent of the Federal agency, State, or political subdivision having jurisdiction over the lands involved, upon finding that—

(i) such trails are reasonably accessible to urban areas, and, or

(ii) such trails meet the criteria established in this chapter and such supplementary criteria as he may prescribe.

Trails within federally administered areas; trails when no Federal land acquisition is involved

(b) As provided in this section, trails within park, forest, and other recreation areas administered by the Secretary of the Interior or the Secretary of Agriculture or in other federally administered areas may be established and designated as "National Recreation Trails" by the appropriate Secretary and, when no Federal land acquisition is involved—

(i) trails in or reasonably accessible to urban areas may be designated as "National Recreation Trails" by the appropriate Secretary with the consent of the States, their political subdivisions, or other appropriate administering agencies;

(ii) trails within park, forest, and other recreation areas owned or administered by States may be designated as "National Recreation Trails" by the appropriate Secretary with the consent of the State; and

(iii) trails on privately owned lands may be designated "National Recreation Trails" by the appropriate Secretary with the written consent of the owner of the property involved.

Pub.L. 90–543, § 4, Oct. 2, 1968, 82 Stat. 919; as amended Pub.L. 98–11, Title II, § 204, Mar. 28, 1983, 97 Stat. 43.

§ 1244. National scenic and national historic trails Establishment and designation; administration

(a) National scenic and national historic trails shall be authorized and designated only by Act of Congress. There are hereby established the following National Scenic and National Historic Trails:

* * *

Pub.L. 90–543, § 5, Oct. 2, 1968, 82 Stat. 920; Pub.L. 94–527, Oct. 17, 1976, 90 Stat. 2481; Pub.L. 95–248, § 1(1), (2), Mar. 21, 1978, 92 Stat. 159; Pub.L. 95–625, Title V, § 551(7)–(15), Nov. 10, 1978, 92 Stat. 3512–3515; Pub.L. 96–87, Title IV, § 401(m)(1), Oct. 12, 1979, 93 Stat. 666; Pub.L. 96–199, Title I, § 101(b)(1)–(3), Mar. 5, 1980, 94 Stat. 67, 68; Pub.L. 96–344, § 14, Sept. 8, 1980, 94 Stat. 1136; Pub.L. 96–370, § 1(a), Oct. 3, 1980, 94 Stat. 1360; Pub.L. 98–11, Title II, § 205, Mar. 28, 1983, 97 Stat. 43; Pub.L. 98–405, § 1, Aug. 28, 1984, 98 Stat. 1483; as amended Pub.L. 99–445, § 1, Oct. 6, 1986, 100 Stat. 1122; Pub.L. 100–35, § 1(a), May 8, 1987, 101 Stat. 302; Pub.L. 100–187, § 3, Dec. 11, 1987, 101 Stat. 1287; Pub.L. 100–192, § 1, Dec. 16, 1987, 101 Stat. 1309; Pub.L. 100–470, § 4, Oct. 4, 1988, 102 Stat. 2283; Pub.L. 100–559, Title II, § 203, Oct. 28, 1988, 102 Stat. 2797; Pub.L. 101–321, § 3, July 3, 1990, 104 Stat. 293; Pub.L. 101–365, § 2(a), Aug. 15, 1990, 104 Stat. 429; Pub.L. 102–328, § 1, Aug. 3, 1992, 106 Stat. 845; Pub.L. 102–461, Oct. 23, 1992, 106 Stat. 2273; Pub.L. 103–144, § 3, Nov. 17, 1993, 107 Stat. 1494; Pub.L. 103–145, § 3, Nov. 17, 1993, 107 Stat. 1497; Pub.L. 103–437, § 6(d)(38), Nov. 2, 1994, 108 Stat. 4585; Pub.L. 104–333, Div. I, Title IV, §§ 402, 403, Title V, § 501, Nov. 12, 1996, 110 Stat. 4148, 4153; Pub.L. 106–135, § 3, Dec. 7, 1999, 113 Stat. 1686. As amended Pub.L. 106–307, § 3, Oct. 13, 2000, 114 Stat. 1075; Pub.L. 106–509, § 3, Nov. 13, 2000, 114 Stat. 2361; Pub.L. 107–214, § 3, Aug. 21, 2002, 116 Stat. 1053; Pub.L. 107–325, § 2, Dec. 4, 2002, 116 Stat. 2790; Pub.L. 107–338, § 2, Dec. 16, 2002, 116 Stat. 2886.

* * *

§ 1246. Administration and development of national trails system

Consultation of Secretary with other agencies; transfer of management responsibilities; selection of rights-of-way; criteria for selection; notice; impact upon established uses

(a)(1)(A) The Secretary charged with the overall administration of a trail pursuant to section 1244(a) of this title shall, in administering and managing the trail, consult with the heads of all other affected State and Federal agencies. Nothing contained in this chapter shall be deemed to transfer among Federal agencies any management responsibilities established under any other law for federally administered lands which are components of the National Trails System. Any transfer of management responsibilities may be carried out between the Secretary of the Interior and the Secretary of Agriculture only as provided under subparagraph (B).

(a)(1)(B) The Secretary charged with the overall administration of any trail pursuant to section 1244(a) of this title may transfer management of any specified trail segment of such trail to the other appropriate Secretary pursuant to a joint memorandum of agreement containing such terms and conditions as the Secretaries consider most appropriate to accomplish the purposes of the chapter. During any period in which management responsibilities for any trail segment are transferred under such an agreement, the management of any such segment shall be subject to the laws, rules, and regulations of the Secretary provided with the management authority under the agreement, except to such extent as the agreement may otherwise expressly provide.

(a)(2) Pursuant to section 1244(a) of this title, the appropriate Secretary shall select the rights-of-way for national scenic and national historic trails and shall publish notice of the availability of appropriate maps or descriptions in the Federal Register: *Provided,* That in selecting the rights-of-way full consideration shall be given to minimizing the adverse effects upon the adjacent landowner or user and his operation. Development and management of each segment of the National Trails System shall be designed to harmonize with and complement any established multiple-use plans for that specific area in order to insure continued maximum benefits from the land. The location and width of such rights-of-way across Federal lands under the jurisdiction of another Federal agency shall be by agreement between the head of that agency and the appropriate Secretary. In selecting rights-of-way for trail purposes, the Secretary shall obtain the advice and assistance of the States, local governments, private organizations, and landowners and land users concerned.

* * *

Facilities on national scenic or historic trails; permissible activities; use of motorized vehicles; trail markers; establishment of uniform marker; placement of uniform markers; trail interpretation sites

(c) National scenic or national historic trails may contain campsites, shelters, and related-public-use facilities. Other uses along the trail, which will not substantially interfere with the nature and purposes of the trail, may be permitted by the Secretary charged with the administration of the trail. Reasonable efforts shall be made to provide sufficient access opportunities to such trails and, to the extent practicable, efforts shall be made to avoid activities incompatible with the purposes for which such trails were established. The use of motorized vehicles by the general public along any national scenic trail shall be prohibited and nothing in this chapter shall be construed as authorizing the use of motorized vehicles within the natural and historical areas of the national park system, the national wildlife refuge system, the national wilderness preservation system where they are presently prohibited or on other Federal lands where trails are designated as being closed to such use by the appropriate Secretary: *Provided,* That the Secretary charged with the administration of such trail shall establish regulations which shall authorize the use of motorized vehicles when, in his judgment, such vehicles are necessary to meet emergencies or to enable adjacent landowners or land users to have reasonable access to their lands or timber rights: *Provided further,* That private lands included in the national recreation, national scenic, or national historic trails by cooperative agreement of a landowner shall not preclude such owner from using motorized vehicles on or across such trails or adjacent lands from time to time in accordance with regulations to be established by the appropriate Secretary. * * *

Use and acquisition of lands within exterior boundaries of areas included within right-of-way

(d) Within the exterior boundaries of areas under their administration that are included in the right-of-way selected for a national recreation, national scenic, or national historic trail, the heads of Federal agencies may use lands for trail purposes and may acquire lands or interests in lands by written cooperative agreement, donation, purchase with donated or appropriated funds or exchange.

Right-of-way lands outside exterior boundaries of federally administered areas; cooperative agreements or acquisition; failure to agree or acquire; agreement or acquisition by Secretary concerned; right of first refusal for original owner upon disposal

(e) Where the lands included in a national scenic or national historic trail right-of-way are outside of the exterior boundaries of federally administered areas, the Secretary charged with the administration of such trail shall encourage the States or local governments involved (1) to enter into written cooperative agreements with landowners, private organizations, and individuals to provide the necessary trail right-of-way, or (2) to acquire such lands or interests therein to be utilized as segments of the national scenic or national historic trail: *Provided,* That if the State or local governments fail to enter into such written cooperative agreements or to acquire such lands or interests therein after notice of the selection of the right-of-way is published, the appropriate Secretary may (i) enter into such agreements with landowners, States, local governments, private organizations, individuals for the use of lands for trail purposes, or (ii) acquire private lands or interests therein by donation, purchase with donated or appropriated funds or exchange in accordance with the provisions of subsection (f) of this section: *Provided further,* That the appropriate Secretary may acquire lands or interests therein from local governments or governmental corporations with the consent of such entities. The lands involved in such rights-of-way should be acquired in fee, if other methods of public control are not sufficient to assure their use for the purpose for which they are acquired: *Provided,* That if the Secretary charged with the administration of such trail permanently relocates the right-of-way and disposes of all title or interest in the land, the original owner, or his heirs or assigns, shall be offered, by notice given at the former owner's last known address, the right of first refusal at the fair market price.

Condemnation proceedings to acquire private lands; limitations; availability of funds for acquisition of lands or interests therein; acquisition of high potential, route segments or historic sites

(g) The appropriate Secretary may utilize condemnation proceedings without the consent of the owner to acquire private lands or interests therein pursuant to this section only in cases where, in his judgment, all reasonable efforts to acquire such lands or interests therein by negotiation have failed, and in such cases he shall acquire only such title as, in his judgment, is reasonably necessary to provide passage across such lands: *Provided,* That condemnation proceedings may not be utilized to acquire fee title or lesser interests to more than an average of one hundred and twenty-five acres per mile. * * *

Development and maintenance of national scenic or historic trails; cooperation with states over portions located outside of federally administered areas; cooperative agreements; participation of volunteers; reservation of right-of-way for trails in conveyances by Secretary of the Interior

(h)(1) The Secretary charged with the administration of a national recreation, national scenic, or national historic trail shall provide for the development and maintenance of such trails within federally administered areas and shall cooperate with and encourage the States to operate, develop, and maintain portions of such trails which are located outside the boundaries of federally administered areas. When deemed to be in the public interest, such Secretary may enter written cooperative agreements with the States or their political subdivisions, landowners, private organizations, or individuals to operate, develop, and maintain any portion of such a trail either within or outside a federally administered area. Such agreements may include provisions for limited financial assistance to encourage participation in the acquisition, protection, operation, development, or maintenance of such trails, provisions provided volunteer in the park or volunteer in the forest status (in accordance with the Volunteers in the Parks Act of 1969 [16 U.S.C.A. § 18g et seq.] and the Volunteers in the Forests Act of 1972 [16 U.S.C.A. § 558a et seq.]) to individuals, private organizations, or landowners participating in such activities, or provisions of both. types. The appropriate Secretary shall also initiate consultations with affected States and their political subdivisions to encourage—

(A) the development and implementation by such entities of appropriate measures to protect private landowners from trespass resulting from trail use and from unreasonable personal liability and property damage caused by trail use, and

(B) the development and implementation by such entities of provisions for land practices, compatible with the purposes of this chapter,

for property within or adjacent to trail rights-of-way. After consulting with States and their political subdivisions under the preceding sentence, the Secretary may provide assistance to such entities under appropriate cooperative agreements in the manner provided by this subsection.

(h)(2) Whenever the Secretary of the Interior makes any conveyance of land under any of the public land laws, he may reserve a right-of-way for trails to the extent he deems necessary to carry out the purposes of this chapter.

Regulations; issuance; concurrence and consultation; revision; publication; violations; penalties; utilization of national park or national forest authorities

(i) The appropriate Secretary, with the concurrence of the heads of any other Federal agencies administering lands through which a national recreation, national scenic, or national historic trail passes, and after consultation with the States, local governments, and organizations concerned, may issue regulations, which may be revised from time to time, governing the use, protection, management, development, and administration of trails of the national trails system. In order to maintain good conduct on and along the trails located within federally administered areas and to provide for the proper government and protection of such trails, the Secretary of the Interior and the Secretary of Agriculture shall prescribe and publish such uniform regulations as they deem necessary and any person who violates such regulations shall be guilty of a misdemeanor, and may be punished by a fine of not more than $500, or by imprisonment not exceeding six months, or by both such fine and imprisonment. The Secretary responsible for the administration of any segment of any component of the National Trails System (as determined in a manner consistent with subsection (a)(1) of this section) may also utilize authorities related to units of the national park system or the national forest system, as the case may be, in carrying out his administrative responsibilities for such component.

Types of trail use allowed

(j) Potential trail uses allowed on designated components of the national trails system may include, but are not limited to, the following; bicycling, cross-country skiing, day hiking, equestrian activities, jogging or similar fitness activities, trail biking, overnight and long-distance backpacking, snowmobiling, and surface water and underwater activities. Vehicles which may be permitted on certain trails may include, but need not be limited to, motorcycles, bicycles, four-wheel drive or all-terrain off-road vehicles. In addition, trail access for handicapped individuals may be provided. The provisions of this subsection shall not supersede any other provisions of this chapter or other Federal laws, or any State or local laws.

Donations or other conveyances of qualified real property interests

(k) For the conservation purpose of preserving or enhancing the recreational, scenic, natural, or historical values of components of the national trails system, and environs thereof as determined by the appropriate Secretary, landowners are authorized to donate or otherwise convey qualified real property interests to qualified organizations consistent with section 170(h)(3) of Title 26, including, but not limited to, right-of-way, open space, scenic, or conservation easements, without regard to any limitation on the nature of the estate or interest otherwise transferable within the jurisdiction where the land is located. The conveyance of any such interest in land in accordance with this subsection shall be deemed to further a Federal conservation policy and yield a significant public benefit for purposes of section 6 of Public Law 96–541.

Pub.L. 90–543, § 7, Oct. 2, 1968, 82 Stat. 922; as amended Pub.L. 95–248, § 1(3), (4), Mar. 21. 1978, 92 Stat. 160; Pub.L. 95–625, Title V, § 551(17)–(21), Nov. 10, 1978, 92 Stat. 3515, 3516; Pub.L. 96–87, Title IV, § 401(m)(2), (3), Oct. 12, 1979, 93 Stat. 666; Pub.L. 97–449, § 6(b), Jan. 12, 1983, 96 Stat. 2443; Pub.L. 98–11, Title II, § 207, Mar. 28, 1983, 97 Stat. 45.

* * *

§ 1248.   Easements and rights-of-way

(a) The Secretary of the Interior or the Secretary of Agriculture as the case may be, may grant easements and rights-of-way upon, over, under, across, or along any component of the national trails system in accordance with the laws applicable to the national park system and the national forest system, respectively: *Provided,* That any conditions contained in such easements and rights-of-way shall be related to the policy and purposes of this chapter.

* * *

Abandoned railroad grants; retention of rights

(c) Commencing upon October 4, 1988, any and all right, title, interest, and estate of the United States in all rights-of-way of the type described in the Act of March 8, 1922 (43 U.S.C. 912), shall remain in the United States upon the abandonment or forfeiture of such rights-of-way, or portions thereof, except to the extent that any such right-of-way, or portion thereof, is embraced within a public highway no later than one year after a determination of abandonment or forfeiture, as provided under such Act.

Location, incorporation, and management

(d)(1) All rights-of-way, or portions thereof, retained by the United States pursuant to subsection (c) of this section which are located within the boundaries of a conservation system unit or a National Forest shall be added to and incorporated within such unit or National Forest and managed in accordance with applicable provision of law, including this chapter.

(d)(2) All such retained rights-of-way, or portions thereof, which are located outside the boundaries of a conservation system unit or a National Forest but adjacent to or contiguous with any portion of the public lands shall be managed pursuant to the Federal Land Policy and Management Act of 1976 and other applicable law, including this section.

(d)(3) All such retained rights-of-way, or portions thereof, which are located outside the boundaries of a conservation system unit or National Forest which the Secretary of the Interior determines suitable for use as a public recreational trail or other recreational purposes shall be managed by the Secretary for such uses, as well as for such other uses as the Secretary determines to be appropriate pursuant to applicable laws, as long as such uses do not preclude trail use.

Release and quitclaim; conditions; sale; proceeds

(e)(1) The Secretary of the Interior is authorized where appropriate to release and quitclaim to a unit of government or to another entity meeting the requirements of this subsection any and all right, title, and interest in the surface estate of any portion of any right-of-way to the extent any such right, title, and interest was retained by the United States pursuant to subsection (c) of this section, if such portion is not located within the boundaries of any conservation system unit or National Forest. Such release and quitclaim shall be made only in response to an application therefor by a unit of State or local government or another entity which the Secretary of the Interior determines to be legally and financially qualified to manage the relevant portion for public recreational purposes. Upon receipt of such an application, the Secretary shall publish a notice concerning such application in a newspaper of general circulation in the area where the relevant portion is located. Such release and quitclaim shall be on the following conditions:

(A) If such unit or entity attempts to sell, convey, or otherwise transfer such right, title, or interest or attempts to permit the use of any part of such portion for any purpose incompatible with its use for public recreation, then any and all right, title, and interest released and quitclaimed by the Secretary pursuant to this subsection shall revert to the United States.

(B) Such unit or entity shall assume full responsibility and hold the United States harmless for any legal liability which might arise with respect to the transfer, possession, use, release, or quitclaim of such right-of-way.

(C) Notwithstanding any other provision of law, the United States shall be under no duty to inspect such portion prior to such release and quitclaim, and shall incur no legal liability with respect to any hazard or any unsafe condition existing on such portion at the time of such release and quitclaim.

(e)(2) The Secretary is authorized to sell any portion of a right-of-way retained by the United States pursuant to subsection (c) of this section located outside the boundaries of a conservation system unit or National Forest if any such portion is—

(A) not adjacent to or contiguous with any portion of the public lands; or

(B) determined by the Secretary, pursuant to the disposal criteria established by section 203 of the Federal Land Policy and Management Act of 1976, to be suitable for sale.

Prior to conducting any such sale, the Secretary shall take appropriate steps to afford a unit of State or local government or any other entity an opportunity to seek to obtain such portion pursuant to paragraph (1) of this subsection.

(e)(3) All proceeds from sales of such retained rights of way shall be deposited into the Treasury of the United States and credited to the Land and Water Conservation Fund as provided in section 2 of the Land and Water Conservation Fund Act of 1965.

(e)(4) The Secretary of the Interior shall annually report to the Congress the total proceeds from sales under paragraph (2) during the preceding fiscal year. Such report shall be included in the President's annual budget submitted to the Congress.

"Conservation system unit", "public lands" defined

(f) As used in this section—

(1) The term "conservation system unit" has the same meaning given such term in the Alaska National Interest Lands Conservation Act (Public Law 96–487; 94 Stat. 2371 et seq.), except that such term shall also include units outside Alaska.

(2) The term "public lands" has the same meaning given such term in the Federal Land Policy and Management Act of 1976.

Pub.L. 90–543, § 9, Oct. 2, 1968, 82 Stat. 925; Pub.L. 95–91, Title III, § 301(b), Aug. 4, 1977, 91 Stat. 577; As amended Pub.L. 100–470, § 3, Oct. 4, 1988, 102 Stat. 2281; Pub.L. 104–88, Title III, § 317(2), Dec. 29, 1995, 109 Stat. 949.

NATIONAL WILD AND SCENIC RIVERS ACT OF 1968 (as amended)

(16 U.S.C.A. §§ 1271–87)

§ 1271.   Congressional declaration of policy

It is hereby declared to be the policy of the United States that certain selected rivers of the Nation which, with their immediate environments, possess outstandingly remarkable scenic, recreational, geologic, fish and wildlife, historic, cultural, or other similar values, shall be preserved in free-flowing condition, and that they and their immediate environments shall be protected for the benefit and enjoyment of present and future generations. The Congress declares that the established national policy of dam and other construction at appropriate sections of the rivers of the United States needs to be complemented by a policy that would preserve other selected rivers or sections thereof in their free-flowing condition to protect the water quality of such rivers and to fulfill other vital national conservation purposes.

Pub.L. 90–542, § 1(b), Oct. 2, 1968, 82 Stat. 906.

§ 1272.   Congressional declaration of purpose

The purpose of this chapter is to implement the policy set out in section 1271 of this title by instituting a national wild and scenic rivers system, by designating the initial components of that system, and by prescribing the methods by which and standards according to which additional components may be added to the system from time to time.

Pub.L. 90–542, § 1(c), Oct. 2, 1968, 82 Stat. 906.

§ **1273.** **National wild and scenic rivers system; Congressional authorization for inclusion; designation by State legislatures; permanent administration by States; application for inclusion by Governors; satisfaction of criteria; eligibility for inclusion; notification of Federal Energy Regulatory Commission; publication in Federal Register; expense to the United States; federally owned lands within boundaries of State rivers**

(a) The national wild and scenic rivers system shall comprise rivers (i) that are authorized for inclusion therein by Act of Congress, or (ii) that are designated as wild, scenic or recreational rivers by or pursuant to an act of the legislature of the State or States through which they flow, that are to be permanently administered as wild, scenic or recreational rivers by an agency or political subdivision of the State or States concerned that are found by the Secretary of the Interior, upon application of the Governor of the State or the Governors of the States concerned, or a person or persons thereunto duly appointed by him or them, to meet the criteria established in this chapter and such criteria supplementary thereto as he may prescribe, and that are approved by him for inclusion in the system, including, upon application of the Governor of the State concerned, the Allagash Wilderness Waterway, Maine; that segment of the Wolf River, Wisconsin, which flows through Langlade County; and that segment of the New River in North Carolina extending from its confluence with Dog Creek downstream approximately 26.5 miles to the Virginia State line. Upon receipt of an application under clause (ii) of this subsection, the Secretary shall notify the Federal Energy Regulatory Commission and publish such application in the Federal Register. Each river designated under clause (ii) shall be administered by the State or political subdivision thereof without expense to the United States other than for administration and management of federally owned lands. For purposes of the preceding sentence, amounts made available to any State or political subdivision under the Land and Water Conservation Act of 1965 [16 U.S.C.A. § 460l–4 et seq.] or any other provision of law shall not be treated as an expense to the United States. Nothing in this subsection shall be construed to provide for the transfer to, or administration by, a State or local authority of any federally owned lands which are within the boundaries of any river included within the system under clause (ii).

(b) A wild, scenic or recreational river area eligible to be included in the system is a free-flowing stream and the related adjacent land area that possesses one or more of the values referred to in section 1271 of this title. Every wild, scenic or recreational river in its free-flowing condition, or upon restoration to this condition, shall be considered eligible for inclusion in the national wild and scenic rivers system and, if included, shall be classified, designated, and administered as one of the following:

(1) Wild river areas—Those rivers or sections of rivers that are free of impoundments and generally inaccessible except by trail, with

watersheds or shorelines essentially primitive and waters unpolluted. These represent vestiges of primitive America.

(2) Scenic river areas—Those rivers or sections of rivers that are free of impoundments, with shorelines or watersheds still largely primitive and shorelines largely undeveloped, but accessible in places by roads.

(3) Recreational river areas—Those rivers or sections of rivers that are readily accessible by road or railroad, that may have some development along their shorelines, and that may have undergone some impoundment or diversion in the past.

Pub.L. 90–542, § 2, Oct. 2, 1968, 82 Stat. 906; as amended Pub.L. 94–407, § 1(1), Sept. 11, 1976, 90 Stat. 1238; Pub.L. 95–625, Title VII, § 761, Nov. 10, 1978, 92 Stat. 3533.

§ 1274. Component rivers and adjacent lands; establishment of boundaries; classification; development plans designation

(a) The following rivers and the land adjacent thereto are hereby designated as components of the national wild and scenic rivers system: * * *

Establishment of boundaries; classification; development plans

(b) The agency charged with the administration of each component of the national wild and scenic rivers system designated by subsection (a) of this section shall, within one year from the date of designation of such component under subsection (a) of this section (except where a different date if provided in subsection (a) of this section), establish detailed boundaries therefor (which boundaries shall include an average of not more than 320 acres of land per mile measured from the ordinary high water mark on both sides of the river); and determine which of the classes outlined in section 1273(b) of this title best fit the river or its various segments.

Notice of the availability of the boundaries and classification, and of subsequent boundary amendments shall be published in the Federal Register and shall not become effective until ninety days after they have been forwarded to the President of the Senate and the Speaker of the House of Representatives.

Public inspection of maps and descriptions

(c) Maps of all boundaries and descriptions of the classifications of designated river segments, and subsequent amendments to such boundaries, shall be available for public inspection in the offices of the administering agency in the District of Columbia and in locations convenient to the designated river.

Comprehensive management plan for protection of river values; review of boundaries, classifications and plans

(d)(1) For rivers designated on or after January 1, 1986, the Federal agency charged with the administration of each component of the National

Wild and Scenic Rivers System shall prepare a comprehensive management plan for such river segment to provide for the protection of the river values. The plan shall address resource protection, development of lands and facilities, user capacities, and other management practices necessary or desirable to achieve the purposes of this chapter. The plan shall be coordinated with and may be incorporated into resource management planning for affected adjacent Federal lands. The plan shall be prepared, after consultation with State and local governments and the interested public within 3 full fiscal years after the date of designation. Notice of the completion and availability of such plans shall be published in the Federal Register.

(d)(2) For rivers designated before January 1, 1986, all boundaries, classifications, and plans shall be reviewed for conformity within the requirements of this subsection within 10 years through regular agency planning processes.

Pub.L. 90–542, § 3, Oct. 2, 1968, 82 Stat. 907; Pub.L. 92–560, § 2, Oct. 25, 1972, 86 Stat. 1174; Pub.L. 93–279, § 1(a), May 10, 1974, 88 Stat. 122; as amended Pub.L. 94–199, § 3(a), Dec. 31, 1975, 89 Stat. 1117; Pub.L. 94–486, Title I, § 101, Title II, § 201, Title III, § 301, Title VI, § 601, Oct. 12, 1976, 90 Stat. 2327, 2329, 2330; Pub.L. 95–625, Title VII, §§ 701–704(a), 705–708, 755, 763(a), Nov. 10, 1978, 92 Stat. 3521–3523, 3527–3529, 3533; Pub.L. 96–87, Title IV, § 401(p)(1), Oct. 12, 1979, 93 Stat. 666; Pub.L. 96–312, § 9(a), July 23, 1980, 94 Stat. 952; Pub.L. 96–344, § 16, Sept. 8, 1980, 94 Stat. 1137; Pub.L. 96–487, Title VI, §§ 601–603, Dec. 2, 1980, 94 Stat. 2412–2414; Pub.L. 96–580, Dec. 23, 1980, 94 Stat. 3370. As amended Pub.L. 99–530, § 1, Oct. 27, 1986, 100 Stat. 3021; Pub.L. 99–590, Title I, § 101, Title IV, § 401, Title V, § 501, Title VI, § 601, Oct. 30, 1986, 100 Stat. 3330, 3334, 3335, 3337; Pub.L. 99–663, § 13(c), Nov. 17, 1986, 100 Stat. 4294; Pub.L. 100–149, § 1, Nov. 2, 1987, 101 Stat. 879; Pub.L. 100–150, § 1, Nov. 3, 1987, 101 Stat. 881; Pub.L. 100–174, Nov. 24, 1987, 101 Stat. 924; Pub.L. 100–534, Title III, § 301, Title V, § 501, Oct. 26, 1988, 102 Stat. 2706, 2708; Pub.L. 100–547, Title I, § 101, Oct. 28, 1988, 102 Stat. 2736; Pub.L. 100–554, § 1, Oct. 28, 1988, 102 Stat. 2776; Pub.L. 100–557, Title I, § 102, Oct. 28, 1988, 102 Stat. 2782; Pub.L. 100–633, § 1, Nov. 7, 1988, 102 Stat. 3320; Pub.L. 100–668, Title V, § 501, Nov. 16, 1988, 102 Stat. 3967, Pub.L. 101–40, § 2(a), June 20, 1989, 103 Stat. 81; Pub.L. 101–306, § 2, June 6, 1990, 104 Stat. 260; Pub.L. 101–612, § 10(b), Nov. 16, 1990, 104 Stat. 3215; Pub.L. 101–628, Title XIII, § 1302, Nov. 28, 1990, 104 Stat. 4509; Pub.L. 102–50, § 2, May 24, 1991, 105 Stat. 254; Pub.L. 102–249, § 3, Mar. 3, 1992, 106 Stat. 45; Pub.L. 102–271, § 1, Apr. 20, 1992, 106 Stat. 108; Pub.L. 102–275, § 2, Apr. 22, 1992, 106 Stat. 123; Pub.L. 102–301, § 6, June 19, 1992, 106 Stat. 245; Pub.L. 102–432, § 1, Oct. 23, 1992, 106 Stat. 2212; Pub.L. 102–536, § 1, Oct. 27, 1992, 106 Stat. 3528; Pub.L. 103–162, § 2, Dec. 1, 1993, 107 Stat. 1969; Pub.L. 103–170, § 3, Dec. 2, 1993, 107 Stat. 1986; Pub.L. 103–242, § 2, May 4, 1994, 108 Stat. 611; Pub.L. 103–313, § 3, Aug. 26, 1994, 108 Stat. 1700; Pub.L. 103–437, § 6(d)(40), Nov. 2, 1994, 108 Stat. 4585; Pub.L. 104–208, Div. B, Title I, § 109, Sept. 30, 1996, 110 Stat. 3009–531; Pub.L. 104–314, Oct. 19, 1996, 110 Stat. 3823; Pub.L. 104–333, Div. I, Title IV, §§ 405(a), 406(d), 407(a), Title X, § 1023(h), Nov. 12, 1996, 110 Stat. 4149, 4151, 4223; Pub.L. 106–

20, § 2(b), (g), Apr. 9, 1999, 113 Stat. 31, 33; Pub.L. 106–176, Title I, § 106(a), Mar. 10, 2000, 114 Stat. 25; Pub.L. 106–192, § 2(a), May 2, 2000, 114 Stat. 233; Pub.L. 106–261, Aug. 18, 2000, 114 Stat. 735. As amended Pub.L. 106–299, § 3, Oct. 13, 2000, 114 Stat. 1051; Pub.L. 106–357, § 3, Oct. 24, 2000, 114 Stat. 1393; Pub.L. 106–418, § 3(5), Nov. 1, 2000, 114 Stat. 1817; Pub.L. 106–399, Title III, § 301(a), (b), Oct. 30, 2000, 114 Stat. 1667.

§ 1275. Additions to national wild and scenic rivers system

Reports by Secretaries of Interior and Agriculture; recommendations to Congress; contents of reports

(a) The Secretary of the Interior or, where national forest lands are involved, the Secretary of Agriculture or, in appropriate cases, the two Secretaries jointly shall study and submit to the President reports on the suitability or nonsuitability for addition to the national wild and scenic rivers system of rivers which are designated herein or hereafter by the Congress as potential additions to such system. The President shall report to the Congress his recommendations and proposals with respect to the designation of each such river or section thereof under this chapter. Such studies shall be completed and such reports shall be made to the Congress with respect to all rivers named in section 1276(a)(1) through (27) of this title no later than October 2, 1978. In conducting these studies the Secretary of the Interior and the Secretary of Agriculture shall give priority to those rivers (i) with respect to which there is the greatest likelihood of developments which, if undertaken, would render the rivers unsuitable for inclusion in the national wild and scenic rivers system, and (ii) which possess the greatest proportion of private lands within their areas. Every such study and plan shall be coordinated with any water resources planning involving the same river which is being conducted pursuant to the Water Resources Planning Act [42 U.S.C.A. § 1962 et seq.].

Each report, including maps and illustrations, shall show among other things the area included within the report; the characteristics which do or do not make the area a worthy addition to the system; the current status of land ownership and use in the area; the reasonably foreseeable potential uses of the land and water which would be enhanced, foreclosed, or curtailed if the area were included in the national wild and scenic rivers system; the Federal agency (which in the case of a river which is wholly or substantially within a national forest, shall be the Department of Agriculture) by which it is proposed the area, should it be added to the system, be administered; the extent to which it is proposed that such administration, including the costs thereof, be shared by State and local agencies; and the estimated cost to the United States of acquiring necessary lands and interests in land and of administering the area, should it be added to the system. Each such report shall be printed as a Senate or House document.

* * *

Pub.L. 90–542, § 4, Oct. 2, 1968, 82 Stat. 909; Pub.L. 93–279, § 1(b)(1), May 10, 1974, 88 Stat. 122; as amended Pub.L. 93–621, § 1(d), Jan. 3, 1975, 88 Stat. 2096; Pub.L. 94–486, Title V, § 501, Oct. 12, 1976, 90 Stat. 2330; Pub.L. 95–91, Title III,§ 301(b), Aug. 4, 1977, 91 Stat. 577, as amended Pub.L. 99–590, Title V, § 502, Oct. 30, 1986, 100 Stat. 3335.

§ 1276. Rivers constituting potential additions to national wild and scenic rivers system

* * *

Continuing consideration by Federal agencies to potential national, wild, scenic and recreational river areas

(d)(1) In all planning for the use and development of water and related land resources, consideration shall be given by all Federal agencies involved to potential national wild, scenic and recreational river areas, and all river basin and project plan reports submitted to the Congress shall consider and discuss any such potentials. The Secretary of the Interior and the Secretary of Agriculture shall make specific studies and investigations to determine which additional wild, scenic and recreational river areas within the United States shall be evaluated in planning reports by all Federal agencies as potential alternative uses of the water and related land resources involved.

(d)(2) The Congress finds that the Secretary of the Interior, in preparing the Nationwide Rivers Inventory as a specific study for possible additions to the National Wild and Scenic Rivers System, identified the Upper Klamath River from below the John Boyle Dam to the Oregon?California State line. The Secretary, acting through the Bureau of Land Management, is authorized under this subsection to complete a study of the eligibility and suitability of such segment for potential addition to the National Wild and Scenic Rivers System. Such study shall be completed, and a report containing the results of the study shall be submitted to Congress by April 1, 1990. Nothing in this paragraph shall affect the authority or responsibilities of any other Federal agency with respect to activities or actions on this segment and its immediate environment.

Pub.L. 90–542, § 5, Oct. 2, 1968, 82 Stat. 910; Pub.L. 93–279, § 1(b)(2), May 10, 1974, 88 Stat. 123; as amended Pub.L. 93–621, § 1(a), (b), Jan. 3, 1975, 88 Stat. 2094, 2095; Pub.L. 94–199, § 5(a), Dec. 31, 1975, 89 Stat. 1118; Pub.L. 94–486, Title IV, § 401, Title VII, § 701, Oct. 12, 1976, 90 Stat. 2330; Pub.L. 95–625, Title VII, § 8 721–736, Title XI, § 1108, Nov. 10, 1978, 92 Stat. 3530–3532, 3547; Pub.L. 96–87, Title IV, § 404, Oct. 12, 1979, 93 Stat. 667; Pub.L. 96–199, Title I, § 102, Mar. 5, 1980, 94 Stat. 68; Pub.L. 96–487, Title VI, § 604, Dec. 2, 1980, 94 Stat. 2415; Pub.L. 98–323, Title II, § 201, June 19, 1984, 98 Stat. 261; Pub.L. 98–484, § 5, Oct. 17, 1984, 98 Stat. 2259; Pub.L. 98–494, § 2, Oct. 19, 1984, 98 Stat. 2274; as amended Pub.L. 99–590, Title II, § 202(b), (c), Title III, § 301(a), (b), Title V, § 503, Oct. 30, 1986, 100 Stat. 3332 to 3336; Pub.L. 99–663, § 13(d), Nov. 17, 1986, 100 Stat. 4294; Pub.L. 100–33, § 1, May 7, 1987, 101 Stat. 299; Pub.L. 100–149, § 2, Nov. 2, 1987, 101 Stat. 880; Pub.L. 100–557, Title I, §§ 103, 104, Oct. 28, 1988, 102 Stat. 2790; Pub.L. 101–40, § 2(b), June 20, 1989, 103 Stat. 82; Pub.L. 101–356, §§ 2, 3, Aug. 10, 1990, 104 Stat. 417; Pub.L. 101–357, §§ 2, 3, Aug. 10, 1990, 104 Stat. 418; Pub.L.

101–364, § 1, Aug. 15, 1990, 104 Stat. 428; Pub.L. 101–538, § 1, Nov. 8, 1990, 104 Stat. 2376; Pub.L. 101–628, Title VII, § 703, Nov. 28, 1990, 104 Stat. 4497; Pub.L. 102–50, § 3(a), May 24, 1991, 105 Stat. 254; Pub.L. 102–214, §§ 2, 3, Dec. 11, 1991, 105 Stat. 1663; Pub.L. 102–215, §§ 3, 4, Dec. 11, 1991, 105 Stat. 1664; Pub.L. 102–249, § 4, Mar. 3, 1992, 106 Stat. 48; Pub.L. 102–271, § 5(a), Apr. 20, 1992, 106 Stat. 110; Pub.L. 102–301, § 7(a), June 19, 1992, 106 Stat. 245; Pub.L. 102–432, § 2, Oct. 23, 1992, 106 Stat. 2213; Pub.L. 102–460, § 1(a), (b), Oct. 23, 1992, 106 Stat. 2270; Pub.L. 102–525, Title IV, § 401, Oct. 26, 1992, 106 Stat. 3441; Pub.L. 103–242, § 3, May 4, 1994, 108 Stat. 611; Pub.L. 104–311, Oct. 19, 1996, 110 Stat. 3818; Pub.L. 104–333, Div. I, Title IV, § 407(b), Nov. 12, 1996, 110 Stat. 4152; As amended Pub.L. 106–318, §§ 3, 4, Oct. 19, 2000, 114 Stat. 1278; Pub.L. 107–65, §§ 3, 4, Nov. 6, 2001, 115 Stat. 484.

§ 1277. Land acquisition

Grant of authority to acquire; State and Indian lands; use of appropriated funds; acquisition of tracts partially outside component boundaries; disposition of lands

(a)(1) The Secretary of the Interior and the Secretary of Agriculture are each authorized to acquire lands and interest in land within the authorized boundaries of any component of the national wild and scenic rivers system designated in section 1274 of this title, or hereafter designated for inclusion in the system by Act of Congress, which is administered by him, but he shall not acquire fee title to an average of more than 100 acres per mile on both sides of the river. Lands owned by a State may be acquired only by donation or by exchange in accordance with subsection (d) of this section. Lands owned by an Indian tribe or a political subdivision of a State may not be acquired without the consent of the appropriate governing body thereof as long as the Indian tribe or political subdivision is following a plan for management and protection of the lands which the Secretary finds protects the land and assures its use for purposes consistent with this chapter. Money appropriated for Federal purposes from the land and water conservation fund shall, without prejudice to the use of appropriations from other sources, be available to Federal departments and agencies for the acquisition of property for the purposes of this chapter.

(a)(2) When a tract of land lies partially within and partially outside the boundaries of a component of the National Wild and Scenic Rivers System, the appropriate Secretary may, with the consent of the landowners for the portion outside the boundaries, acquire the entire tract. The land or interest therein so acquired outside the boundaries shall not be counted against the average one-hundred-acre-per-mile fee title limitation of subsection (a)(1) of this section. The lands or interests therein outside such boundaries, shall be disposed of, consistent with existing authorities of law, by sale, lease, or exchange.

Curtailment of condemnation power in area 50 per centum or more of which is owned in fee title by Federal or State government

(b) If 50 per centum or more of the entire acreage outside the ordinary high water mark on both sides of the river within a federally administered wild, scenic or recreational river area is owned in fee title by the United States, by the State or States within which it lies, or by political subdivisions of those States, neither Secretary shall acquire fee title to any lands by condemnation under authority of this chapter. Nothing contained in this section, however, shall preclude the use of condemnation when necessary to clear title or to acquire scenic easements or such other easements as are reasonably necessary to give the public access to the river and to permit its members to traverse the length of the area or of selected segments thereof.

Curtailment of condemnation power in urban areas covered by valid and satisfactory zoning ordinances

(c) Neither the Secretary of the Interior nor the Secretary of Agriculture may acquire lands by condemnation, for the purpose of including such lands in any national wild, scenic or recreational river area, if such lands are located within any incorporated city, village, or borough which has in force and applicable to such lands a duly adopted, valid zoning ordinance that conforms with the purposes of this chapter. In order to carry out the provisions of this subsection the appropriate Secretary shall issue guidelines, specifying standards for local zoning ordinances, which are consistent with the purposes of this chapter. The standards specified in such guidelines shall have the object of (A) prohibiting new commercial or industrial uses other than commercial or industrial uses which are consistent with the purposes of this chapter, and (B) the protection of the bank lands by means of acreage, frontage, and setback requirements on development.

* * *

Transfer of jurisdiction over federally owned property to appropriate Secretary

(e) The head of any Federal department or agency having administrative jurisdiction over any lands or interests in land within the authorized boundaries of any federally administered component of the national wild and scenic rivers system designated in section 1274 of this title or hereafter designated for inclusion in the system by Act of Congress is authorized to transfer to the appropriate secretary jurisdiction over such lands for administration in accordance with the provisions of this chapter. Lands acquired by or transferred to the Secretary of Agriculture for the purposes of this chapter within or adjacent to a national forest shall upon such acquisition or transfer become national forest lands.

* * *

Retained right of use and occupancy; termination; fair market value; improved property

(g)(1) Any owner or owners (hereinafter in this subsection referred to as "owner") of improved property on the date of its acquisition, may retain for themselves and their successors or assigns a right of use and occupancy of the improved property for noncommercial residential purposes for a definite term not to exceed twenty-five years or, in lieu thereof, for a term ending at the death of the owner, or the death of his spouse, or the death of either or both of them. The owner shall elect the term to be reserved. The appropriate Secretary shall pay to the owner the fair market value of the property on the date of such acquisition less the fair market value on such date of the right retained by the owner.

(g)(2) A right of use and occupancy retained pursuant to this subsection shall be subject to termination whenever the appropriate Secretary is given reasonable cause to find that such use and occupancy is being exercised in a manner which conflicts with the purposes of this chapter. In the event of such a finding, the Secretary shall tender to the holder of that right an amount equal to the fair market value of that portion of the right which remains unexpired on the date of termination. Such right of use or occupancy shall terminate by operation of law upon tender of the fair market price.

(g)(3) The term "improved property", as used in this chapter, means a detached, one-family dwelling (hereinafter referred to as "dwelling"), the construction of which was begun before January 1, 1967 (except where a different date is specifically provided by law with respect to any particular river) together with so much of the land on which the dwelling is situated, the said land being in the same ownership as the dwelling, as the appropriate Secretary shall designate to be reasonably necessary for the enjoyment of the dwelling for the sole purpose of noncommercial residential use, together with any structures accessory to the dwelling which are situated on the land so designated.

Pub.L. 90–542, § 6, Oct. 2, 1968, 82 Stat. 912; as amended Pub.L. 95–625, Title VII, § 763(b), Nov. 10, 1978, 92 Stat. 3533. As amended Pub.L. 99–590, Title V, § 504, Oct. 30, 1986, 100 Stat. 3336.

§ 1278. Restrictions on water resources projects

Construction projects licensed by Federal Energy Regulatory Commission

(a) The Federal Energy Regulatory Commission shall not license the construction of any dam, water conduit, reservoir, powerhouse, transmission line, or other project works under the Federal Power Act (41 Stat. 1063), as amended (16 U.S.C. 791a et seq.), on or directly affecting any river which is designated in section 1274 of this title as a component of the national wild and scenic rivers system or which is hereafter designated for inclusion in that system, and no department or agency of the United States shall assist by loan, grant, license, or otherwise in the construction of any water resources project that would have a direct and adverse effect on the values for which such river was established, as determined by the Secretary charged with its administration. Nothing contained in the foregoing sentence, however, shall preclude licensing of, or assistance to, developments below or above a wild, scenic or recreational river area or on any stream, tributary thereto which will not invade the area or unreasonably diminish the scenic, recreational, and fish and wildlife values present in the area on the date of designation of a river as a component of the National Wild and Scenic Rivers System. No department or agency of the United States shall recommend authorization of any water resources project that would have a direct and adverse effect on the values for which such river was established, as determined by the Secretary charged with its administration, or request appropriations to begin construction of any such project, whether heretofore or hereafter authorized, without advising the Secretary of the Interior or the Secretary of Agriculture, as the case may be, in writing of its intention so to do at least sixty days in advance, and without specifically reporting to the Congress in writing at the time it makes its recommendation or request in what respect construction of such project would be in conflict with the purposes of this chapter and would affect the component and the values to be protected by it under this chapter. Any license heretofore or hereafter issued by the Federal Energy Regulatory Commission affecting the New River of North Carolina shall continue to be effective only for that portion of the river which is not included in the National Wild and Scenic Rivers System pursuant to section 1273 of this title and no project or undertaking so licensed shall be permitted to invade, inundate or otherwise adversely affect such river segment.

Construction projects on rivers designated for potential addition to system

(b) The Federal Energy Regulatory Commission shall not license the construction of any dam, water conduit, reservoir, powerhouse, transmission line, or other project works under the Federal Power Act, as amended [16 U.S.C.A. § 791a et seq.], on or directly affecting any river which is listed in section 1276(a) of this title, and no department or agency of the United States shall assist by loan, grant, license, or otherwise in the construction of any water resources project that would have a direct and adverse effect on the values for which such river might be designated, as determined by the Secretary responsible for its study or approval—

(i) during the ten-year period following October 2, 1968 or for a three complete fiscal year period following any Act of Congress designating any river for potential addition to the national wild and scenic rivers system, whichever is later, unless, prior to the expiration of the relevant period, the Secretary of the Interior and, where national forest lands are involved, the Secretary of Agriculture, on the basis of study, determine that such river should not be included in the national wild and scenic rivers system and notify the Committee on Energy and Natural Resources of the Senate and the Committee on Natural Resources of the House of Representatives, in writing, including a copy of the study upon which the determination was made, at least one hundred and eighty days while Congress is in session prior to publishing notice to that effect in the Federal Register: *Provided,* That if any Act designating any river or rivers for potential addition to the national wild and scenic rivers system provides a period for the study or studies which exceeds such three complete fiscal year period the period provided for in such Act shall be substituted for the three complete fiscal year period in the provisions of this clause (i); and

(ii) during such interim period from the date a report is due and the time a report is actually submitted to the Congress; and

(iii) during such additional period thereafter as, in the case of any river the report for which is submitted to the President and the

Congress, is necessary for congressional consideration thereof or, in the case of any river recommended to the Secretary of the Interior for inclusion in the national wild and scenic rivers system under section 1273(a)(ii) of this title, is necessary for the Secretary's consideration thereof, which additional period, however, shall not exceed three years in the first case and one year in the second.

Nothing contained in the foregoing sentence, however, shall preclude licensing of, or assistance to, developments below or above a potential wild, scenic or recreational river area or on any stream tributary thereto which will not invade the area or diminish the scenic or recreational, and fish and wildlife values present in the potential wild, scenic or recreational river area on the date of designation of a river for study as provided for in section 1276 of this title. No department or agency of the United States shall, during the periods hereinbefore specified, recommend authorization of any water resources project on any such river or request appropriations to begin construction of any such project, whether heretofore or hereafter authorized, without advising the Secretary of the Interior and, where national forest lands are involved, the Secretary of Agriculture in writing of its intention so to do at least sixty days in advance of doing so and without specifically reporting to the Congress in writing at the time it makes its recommendation or request in what respect construction of such project would be in conflict with the purposes of this chapter and would affect the component and the values to be protected by it under this chapter.

* * *

Pub.L. 90–542, § 7, Oct. 2, 1968, 82 Stat. 913; Pub.L. 93–279, § 1(b)(3)(4), May 10, 1974, 88 Stat. 123; as amended Pub.L. 93–621, § 1(c), Jan. 3, 1975, 88 Stat. 2096; Pub.L. 94–407, § 1(2), Sept. 11, 1976, 90 Stat. 1238; Pub.L. 95–91, Title IV, § 402(a)(1)(A), Aug. 4, 1977, 91 Stat. 583. As amended Pub.L. 99–590, Title V, § 505, Oct. 30, 1986, 100 Stat. 3336, as amended Pub.L. 103–437, § 6(a)(7), Nov. 2, 1994, 108 Stat. 4583.

§ 1279. Withdrawal of public lands from entry, sale, or other disposition under public land laws

Lands within authorized boundaries of components of system

(a) All public lands within the authorized boundaries of any component of the national wild and scenic rivers system which is designated in section 1274 of this title or which is designated after October 2, 1968, for inclusion in that system are hereby withdrawn from entry, sale, or other disposition under the public land laws of the United States. This subsection shall not be construed to limit the authorities granted in section 1277(d) or 1285a of this title.

(b) All public lands which constitute the bed or bank, or are within one-quarter mile of the bank, of any river which is listed in section 1276(a) of this title are hereby withdrawn from entry, sale, or other disposition under the public land laws of the United States for the periods specified in section 1278(1) of this title. * * *

Pub.L. 90–542, § 8, Oct. 2, 1968, 82 Stat. 915; as amended Pub.L. 96–487, Title VI, § 606(c), Dec. 2, 1980, 94 Stat. 2417. As amended Pub.L. 99–590, Title V, § 506, Oct. 30, 1986, 100 Stat. 3336.

§ 1280. Federal mining and mineral leasing laws

Applicability to components of system

(a) Nothing in this chapter shall affect the applicability of the United States mining and mineral leasing laws within components of the national wild and scenic rivers system except that—

(i) all prospecting, mining operations, and other activities on mining claims which, in the case of a component of the system designated in section 1274 of this title, have not heretofore been perfected or which, in the case of a component hereafter designated pursuant to this chapter or any other Act of Congress, are not perfected before its inclusion in the system and all mining operations and other activities under a mineral lease, license, or permit issued or renewed after inclusion of a component in the system shall be subject to such regulations as the Secretary of the Interior or, in the case of national forest lands, the Secretary of Agriculture may prescribe to effectuate the purposes of this chapter;

(ii) subject to valid existing rights, the perfection of, or issuance of a patent to, any mining claim affecting lands within the system shall confer or convey a right or title only to the mineral deposits and such rights only to the use of the surface and the surface resources as are reasonably required to carrying on prospecting or mining operations and are consistent with such regulations as may be prescribed by the Secretary of the Interior or, in the case of national forest lands, by the Secretary of Agriculture; and

(iii) subject to valid existing rights, the minerals in Federal lands which are part of the system and constitute the bed or bank or are situated within one-quarter mile of the bank of any river designated a wild river under this chapter or any subsequent Act are hereby withdrawn from all forms of appropriation under the mining laws and from operation of the mineral leasing laws including, in both cases, amendments thereto.

Regulations issued pursuant to paragraphs (i) and (ii) of this subsection shall, among other things, provide safeguards against pollution of the river involved and unnecessary impairment of the scenery within the component in question.

Withdrawal from appropriation of minerals in Federal river beds or bank areas; prospecting, leases, licenses, and permits

(b) The minerals in any Federal lands which constitute the bed or bank or are situated within one-quarter mile of the bank of any river which is listed in section 1276(a) of this title are hereby withdrawn from all forms of appropriation under the mining laws during the periods specified in section 1278(b) of this title. Nothing contained in this subsection shall be construed to forbid prospecting or the issuance of leases, licenses, and permits under the mineral leasing laws subject to such conditions as the Secretary of the Interior and, in the case of national forest lands, the Secretary of Agriculture find appropriate to safeguard the area in the event it is subsequently included in the system. Notwithstanding the foregoing provisions of this subsection or any other provision of this chapter, all public lands which constitute the bed or bank, or are within an area extending two miles from the bank of the river channel on both sides of the river segments referred to in paragraphs (77) through (88) of section 1276(a) of this title, are hereby withdrawn, subject to valid existing rights, from all forms of appropriation under the mining laws and from operation of the mineral leasing laws including, in both cases, amendments thereto, during the periods specified in section 1278(b) of this title.

Pub.L. 90–542, § 9, Oct. 2, 1968, 82 Stat. 915; as amended Pub.L. 96–487, Title VI, § 606(b), Dec. 2, 1980, 94 Stat. 2416, as amended Pub.L. 99–590, Title V, § 507, Oct. 30, 1986, 100 Stat. 3336.

§ 1281. Administration—Public use and enjoyment of components; protection of features; management plans

(a) Each component of the national wild and scenic rivers system shall be administered in such manner as to protect and enhance the values which caused it to be included in said system without, insofar as is consistent therewith, limiting other uses that do not substantially interfere with public use and enjoyment of these values. In such administration primary emphasis shall be given to protecting its esthetic, scenic, historic, archeologic, and scientific features. Management plans for any such component may establish varying degrees of intensity for its protection and development, based on the special attributes of the area.

Wilderness areas

(b) Any portion of a component of the national wild and scenic rivers system that is within the national wilderness preservation system, as established by or pursuant to the Wilderness Act, shall be subject to the provisions of both the Wilderness Act and this chapter with respect to preservation of such river and its immediate environment, and in case of conflict between the provisions of the Wilderness Act and this chapter the more restrictive provisions shall apply.

Areas administered by National Park Service and Fish and Wildlife Service

(c) Any component of the national wild and scenic rivers system that is administered by the Secretary of the Interior through the National Park Service shall become a part of the national park system, and any such component that is administered by the Secretary through the Fish and Wildlife Service shall become a part of the national wildlife refuge system. The lands involved shall be subject to the provisions of this chapter and the Acts under which the national park system or national wildlife system, as the case may be, is administered, and in case of conflict between the provisions of this chapter and such Acts, the more restrictive provisions shall apply. The Secretary of the Interior, in his administration of any component of the national wild and scenic rivers system, may utilize such general statutory authorities relating to areas of the national park system and such general statutory authorities otherwise available to him for recreation and preservation purposes and for the conservation and management of natural resources as he deems appropriate to carry out the purposes of this chapter.

Statutory authorities relating to national forests

(d) The Secretary of Agriculture, in his administration of any component of the national wild and scenic rivers system area, may utilize the general statutory authorities relating to the national forests in such manner as he deems appropriate to carry out the purposes of this chapter.

Cooperative agreements with State and local governments

(e) The Federal agency charged with the administration of any component of the national wild and scenic rivers system may enter into written cooperative agreements with the Governor of a State, the head of any State agency, or the appropriate official of a political subdivision of a State for State or local governmental participation in the administration of the component. The States and their political subdivisions shall be encouraged to cooperate in the planning and administration of components of the system which include or adjoin State-or county-owned lands.

Pub.L. 90–542, § 10, Oct. 2, 1968, 82 Stat. 916.

* * *

§ 1283. Management policies

Action of Secretaries and heads of agencies; cooperative agreements

(a) The Secretary of the Interior, the Secretary of Agriculture, and the head of any other Federal department or agency having jurisdiction over any lands which include, border upon, or are adjacent to, any river included within the National Wild and Scenic Rivers System or under consideration for such inclusion, in accordance with section 1273(a)(ii), 1274(a), or 1276(a) of this title, shall take such action respecting management policies, regulations, contracts, plans, affecting such lands, following November 10, 1978, as may be necessary to protect such rivers in accordance with the purposes of this chapter. Such Secretary or other department or agency head shall, where appropriate, enter into written cooperative agreements with the appropriate State or local official for the planning, administration, and management of Federal lands which are within the boundaries of any rivers for which approval has been granted under section 1273(a)(ii) of this title. Particular attention shall be given to scheduled timber harvesting, road construction, and similar activities which might be contrary to the purposes of this chapter.

Existing rights, privileges, and contracts affecting Federal lands

(b) Nothing in this section shall be construed to abrogate any existing rights, privileges, or contracts affecting Federal lands held by any private party without the consent of said party.

Water pollution

(c) The head of any agency administering a component of the national wild and scenic rivers system shall cooperate with the Administrator, Environmental Protection Agency and with the appropriate State water pollution control agencies for the purpose of eliminating or diminishing the pollution of waters of the river.

Pub.L. 90–542, § 12, Oct. 2, 1968, 82 Stat. 917; as amended Pub.L. 95–625, Title VII, § 762, Nov. 10, 1978, 92 Stat. 3533. As amended Pub.L. 99–590, Title V, § 509, Oct. 30, 1986, 100 Stat. 3337.

§ 1284. Existing State jurisdiction and responsibilities—Fish and wildlife

(a) Nothing in this chapter shall affect the jurisdiction or responsibilities of the States with respect to fish and wildlife. Hunting and fishing shall be permitted on lands and waters administered as parts of the system under applicable State and Federal laws and regulations unless, in the case of hunting, those lands or waters are within a national park or monument. The administering Secretary may, however, designate zones where, and establish periods when, no hunting is permitted for reasons of public safety, administration, or public use and enjoyment and shall issue appropriate regulations after consultation with the wildlife agency of the State or States affected.

Compensation for water rights

(b) The jurisdiction of the States and the United States over waters of any stream included in a national wild, scenic or recreational river area shall be determined by established principles of law. Under the provisions of this chapter, any taking by the United States of a water right which is vested under either State or Federal law at the time such river is included in the national wild and scenic rivers system shall entitle the owner thereof to just compensation. Nothing in this chapter shall constitute an express or implied claim or denial on the part of the Federal Government as to exemption from State water laws.

Reservation of waters for other purposes or in unnecessary quantities prohibited

(c) Designation of any stream or portion thereof as a national wild, scenic or recreational river area shall not be construed as a reservation of the waters of such streams for purposes other than those specified in this chapter, or in quantities greater than necessary to accomplish these purposes.

State jurisdiction over included streams

(d) The jurisdiction of the States over waters of any stream included in a national wild, scenic or recreational river area shall be unaffected by this chapter to the extent that such jurisdiction may be exercised without impairing the purposes of this chapter or its administration.

Interstate compacts

(e) Nothing contained in this chapter shall be construed to alter, amend, repeal, interpret, modify, or be in conflict with any interstate compact made by any States which contain any portion of the national wild and scenic rivers system.

Rights of access to streams

(f) Nothing in this chapter shall affect existing rights of any State, including the right of access, with respect to the beds of navigable streams, tributaries, or rivers (or segments thereof) located in a national wild, scenic or recreational river area.

Easements and rights-of-way

(g) The Secretary of the Interior or the Secretary of Agriculture, as the case may be, may grant easements and rights-of-way upon, over, under, across, or through any component of the national wild and scenic rivers system in accordance with the laws applicable to the national park system and the national forest system, respectively: *Provided,* That any conditions precedent to granting such easements and rights-of-way shall be related to the policy and purpose of this chapter.

Pub.L. 90–542, § 13, Oct. 2, 1968, 82 Stat. 917.

* * *

§ 1286. Definitions

As used in this chapter, the term—

(a) "River" means a flowing body of water or estuary or a section, portion, or tributary thereof, including rivers, streams, creeks, runs, kills, rills, and small lakes.

(b) "Free-flowing", as applied to any river or section of a river, means existing or flowing in natural condition without impoundment, diversion, straightening, rip-rapping, or other modification of the waterway. The existence, however, of low dams, diversion works, and other minor structures at the time any river is proposed for inclusion in the national wild and scenic rivers system shall not automatically bar its consideration for such inclusion: *Provided,* That this shall not be construed to authorize, intend, or encourage future construction of such structures within components of the national wild and scenic rivers system.

(c) "Scenic easement" means the right to control the use of land (including the air space above such land) within the authorized boundaries of a component of the wild and scenic rivers system, for the purpose of protecting the natural qualities of a designated wild, scenic or recreational river area, but such control shall not affect, without the owner's consent, any regular use exercised prior to the acquisition of the easement. For any designated wild and scenic river, the appropriate Secretary shall treat the acquisition of fee title with the reservation of regular existing uses to the owner as a scenic easement for purposes of this chapter. Such an acquisition shall not constitute fee title ownership for purposes of section 1277(b) of this title.

Pub.L. 90–542, § 15, Oct. 2, 1968,. 82 Stat. 918; Pub.L. 93–279, § 1(c), May 10, 1974, 88 Stat. 123; renumbered Pub.L. 96–487, Title VI, § 606(a), Dec. 2, 1980, 94 Stat. 2416. As amended Pub.L. 99–590, Title V, § 510, Oct. 30, 1986, 100 Stat. 3337.

* * *

WILD, FREE–ROAMING HORSES AND BURROS ACT OF 1971 (as amended)

(16 U.S.C.A. §§ 1331–40)

§ 1331. Congressional findings and declaration of policy

Congress finds and declares that wild free-roaming horses and burros are living symbols of the historic and pioneer spirit of the West; that they contribute to the diversity of life forms within the Nation and enrich the lives of the American people; and that these horses and burros are fast disappearing from the American scene. It is the policy of Congress that wild free-roaming horses and burros shall be protected from capture, branding, harassment, or death; and to accomplish this they are to be considered in the area where presently found, as an integral part of the natural system of the public lands.

Pub.L. 92–195, § 1, Dec. 15, 1971, 85 Stat. 649.

§ 1332. Definitions

As used in this chapter—

(a) "Secretary" means the Secretary of the Interior when used in connection with public lands administered by him through the Bureau of Land Management and the Secretary of Agriculture in connection with public lands administered by him through the Forest Service;

(b) "wild free-roaming horses and burros" means all unbranded and unclaimed horses and burros on public lands of the United States;

(c) "range" means the amount of land necessary to sustain an existing herd or herds of wild free-roaming horses and burros, which does not exceed their known territorial limits, and which is devoted principally but not necessarily exclusively to their welfare in keeping with the multiple-use management concept for the public lands;

(d) "herd" means one or more stallions and his mares;

(e) "public lands" means any lands administered by the Secretary of the Interior through the Bureau of Land Management or by the Secretary of Agriculture through the Forest Service; and

(f) "excess animals" means wild free-roaming horses or burros (1) which have been removed from an area by the Secretary pursuant to applicable law or, (2) which must be removed from an area in order to preserve and maintain a thriving natural ecological balance and multiple-use relationship in that area.

Pub.L. 92–125, § 2, Dec. 15, 1971, 85 Stat. 649; as amended Pub.L. 95–514, § 14(b), Oct. 25, 1978, 92 Stat. 1810.

§ **1333.** Powers and duties of Secretary

(a) All wild free-roaming horses and burros are hereby declared to be under the jurisdiction of the Secretary for the purpose of management and protection in accordance with the provisions of this chapter. The Secretary is authorized and directed to protect and manage wild free-roaming horses and burros as components of the public lands, and he may designate and maintain specific ranges on public lands as sanctuaries for their protection and preservation, where the Secretary after consultation with the wildlife agency of the State wherein any such range is proposed and with the Advisory Board established in section 1337 of this title deems such action desirable. The Secretary shall manage wild free-roaming horses and burros in a manner that is designed to achieve and maintain a thriving natural ecological balance on the public lands. He shall consider the recommendations of qualified scientists in the field of biology and ecology, some of whom shall be independent of both Federal and State agencies and may include members of the Advisory Board established in section 1337 of this title. All management activities shall be at the minimal feasible level and shall be carried out in consultation with the wildlife agency of the State wherein such lands are located in order to protect the natural ecological balance of all wildlife species which inhabit such lands, particularly endangered wildlife species. Any adjustments in forage allocations on any such lands shall take into consideration the needs of other wildlife species which inhabit such lands.

Inventory and determinations; consultation; overpopulation; research study; submittal to Congress

(b)(1) The Secretary shall maintain a current inventory of wild free-roaming horses and burros on given areas of the public lands. The purpose of such inventory shall be to: make determinations as to whether and where an overpopulation exists and whether action should be taken to remove excess animals; determine appropriate management levels of wild free-roaming horses and burros on these areas of the public lands; and determine whether appropriate management levels should be achieved by the removal or destruction of excess animals, or other options (such as sterilization, or natural controls on population levels). In making such determinations the Secretary shall consult with the United States Fish and Wildlife Service, wildlife agencies of the State or States wherein wild free-roaming horses and burros are located, such individuals independent of

Federal and State government as have been recommended by the National Academy of Sciences, and such other individuals whom he determines have scientific expertise and special knowledge of wild horse and burro protection, wildlife management and animal husbandry as related to rangeland management.

(b)(2) Where the Secretary determines on the basis of (i) the current inventory of lands within his jurisdiction; (ii) information contained in any land use planning completed pursuant to section 1712 of Title 43; (iii) information contained in court ordered environmental impact statements as defined in section 1902 of Title 43; and (iv) such additional information as becomes available to him from time to time, including that information developed in the research study mandated by this section, or in the absence of the information contained in (i–iv) above on the basis of all information currently available to him, that an overpopulation exists on a given area of the public lands and that action is necessary to remove excess animals, he shall immediately remove excess animals from the range so as to achieve appropriate management levels. Such action shall be taken, in the following order and priority, until all excess animals have been removed so as to restore a thriving natural ecological balance to the range, and protect the range from the deterioration associated with overpopulation:

(A) The Secretary shall order old, sick, or lame animals to be destroyed in the most humane manner possible;

(B) The Secretary shall cause such number of additional excess wild free-roaming horses and burros to be humanely captured and removed for private maintenance and care for which he determines an adoption demand exists by qualified individuals, and for which he determines he can assure humane treatment and care (including proper transportation, feeding, and handling): *Provided,* That, not more than four animals may be adopted per year by any individual unless the Secretary determines in writing that such individual is capable of humanely caring for more than four animals, including the transportation of such animals by the adopting party; and

(C) The Secretary shall cause additional excess wild free-roaming horses and burros for which an adoption demand by qualified individuals does not exist to be destroyed in the most humane and cost efficient manner possible.

(b)(3) For the purpose of furthering knowledge of wild horse and burro population dynamics and their interrelationship with wildlife, forage and water resources, and assisting him in making his determination as to what constitutes excess animals, the Secretary shall contract for a research study of such animals with such individuals independent of Federal and State government as may be recommended by the National Academy of Sciences for having scientific expertise and special knowledge of wild horse and burro protection, wildlife management and animal husbandry as related to rangeland management. The terms and outline of such research study shall be determined by a research design panel to be appointed by the President of the National Academy of Sciences. Such study shall be completed and submitted by the Secretary to the Senate and House of Representatives on or before January 1, 1983.

Title of transferee to limited number of excess animals adopted for requisite period

(c) Where excess animals have been transferred to a qualified individual for adoption and private maintenance pursuant to this chapter and the Secretary determines that such individual has provided humane conditions, treatment and care for such animal or animals for a period of one year, the Secretary is authorized upon application by the transferee to grant title to not more than four animals to the transferee at the end of the one-year period.

Loss of status as wild free-roaming horses and burros; exclusion from coverage

(d) Wild free-roaming horses and burros or their remains shall lose their status as wild free-roaming horses or burros and shall no longer be considered as falling within the purview of this chapter—

(1) upon passage of title pursuant to subsection (c) except for the limitation of subsection (c)(1) of this section; or

(2) if they have been transferred for private maintenance or adoption pursuant to this chapter and die of natural causes before passage of title; or

(3) upon destruction by the Secretary or his designee pursuant to subsection (b) of this section; or

(4) if they die of natural causes on the public lands or on private lands where maintained thereon pursuant to section 1334 of this title and disposal is authorized by the Secretary or his designee; or

(5) upon destruction or death for purposes of or incident to the program authorized in this section: *Provided,* That no wild free-roaming horse or burro or its remains may be sold or transferred for consideration for processing into commercial products.

Pub.L. 92–195, § 3, Dec. 15, 1971, 85 Stat. 649; as amended Pub.L. 95–514, § 14(a), Oct. 25, 1978, 92 Stat. 1808.

§ 1334. Private maintenance; numerical approximation; strays on private lands; removal; destruction by agents

If wild free-roaming horses or burros stray from public lands onto privately owned land, the owners of such land may inform the nearest Federal marshall or agent of the Secretary, who shall arrange to have the animals removed. In no event shall such wild free-roaming horses and burros be destroyed except by the agents of the Secretary. Nothing in this section shall be construed to prohibit a private landowner from maintaining wild free-roaming horses or burros on his private lands, or lands leased from the Government, if he does so in a manner that protects them from harassment, and if the animals were not willfully removed or enticed from the public lands. Any individuals who maintain such wild free-roaming horses or burros on their private lands or lands leased from the Government shall notify the appropriate agent of the Secretary and supply him with a reasonable approximation of the number of animals so maintained.

Pub.L. 92–195, § 4, Dec. 15, 1971, 85 Stat. 650.

§ 1335.   Recovery rights

A person claiming ownership of a horse or burro on the public lands shall be entitled to recover it only if recovery is permissible under the branding and estray laws of the State in which the animal is found.

Pub.L. 92–195, § 5, Dec. 15, 1971, 85 Stat. 650.

§ 1336.   Cooperative agreements; regulations

The Secretary is authorized to enter into cooperative agreements with other landowners and with the State and local governmental agencies and may issue such regulations as he deems necessary for the furtherance of the purposes of this chapter.

Pub.L. 92–195, § 6, Dec. 15, 1971, 85 Stat. 650.

* * *

§ 1338.   Criminal provisions-Violations; penalties; trial

(a) Any person who—

(1) willfully removes or attempts to remove a wild free-roaming horse or burro from the public lands, without authority from the Secretary, or

(2) converts a wild free-roaming horse or burro to private use, without authority from the Secretary, or

(3) maliciously causes the death or harassment of any wild free-roaming horse or burro, or

(4) processes or permits to be processed into commercial products the remains of a wild free-roaming horse or burro, or

(5) sells, directly or indirectly, a wild free-roaming horse or burro maintained on private or leased land pursuant to section 1334 of this title, or the remains thereof, or

(6) willfully violates a regulation issued pursuant to this chapter,

shall be subject to a fine of not more than $2,000, or imprisonment for not more than one year or both. Any person so charged with such violation by the Secretary may be tried and sentenced by any United States commissioner or magistrate designated for that purpose by the court by which he was appointed, in the same manner and subject to the same conditions as provided for in section 3401 of Title 18.

* * *

Pub.L. 92–195, § 8, Dec. 15, 1971, 85 Stat. 650.

* * *

§ 1339. Limitation of authority

Nothing in this chapter shall be construed to authorize the Secretary to relocate wild free-roaming horses or burros to areas of the public lands where they do not presently exist.

Pub.L. 92–195, § 10, formerly § 9, Dec. 15, 1971, 85 Stat. 651, renumbered Pub.L. 94–579, Title IV, § 404, Oct. 21, 1976, 90 Stat. 2775.

* * *

ENDANGERED SPECIES ACT OF 1973 (as amended)

(16 U.S.C.A. §§ 1531–43)

§ 1531. Congressional findings and declaration of purposes and policy

Findings

(a) The Congress finds and declares that—

(1) various species of fish, wildlife, and plants in the United States have been rendered extinct as a consequence of economic growth and development untempered by adequate concern and conservation;

(2) other species of fish, wildlife, and plants have been so depleted in numbers that they are in danger of or threatened with extinction;

(3) these species of fish, wildlife, and plants are of esthetic, ecological, educational, historical, recreational, and scientific value to the Nation and its people;

(4) the United States has pledged itself as a sovereign state in the international community to conserve to the extent practicable the various species of fish or wildlife and plants facing extinction, pursuant to—

(A) migratory bird treaties with Canada and Mexico;

(B) the Migratory and Endangered Bird Treaty with Japan;

(C) the Convention on Nature Protection and Wildlife Preservation in the Western Hemisphere;

(D) the International Convention for the Northwest Atlantic Fisheries;

(E) the International Convention for the High Seas Fisheries of the North Pacific Ocean;

(F) the Convention on International Trade in Endangered Species of Wild Fauna and Flora; and

(G) other international agreements; and

(5) encouraging the States and other interested parties, through Federal financial assistance and a system of incentives, to develop and maintain conservation programs which meet national and international standards is a key to meeting the Nation's international commit-

ments and to better safeguarding, for the benefit of all citizens, the Nation's heritage in fish, wildlife, and plants.

Purposes

(b) The purposes of this chapter are to provide a means whereby the ecosystems upon which endangered species and threatened species depend may be conserved, to provide a program for the conservation of such endangered species and threatened species, and to take such steps as may be appropriate to achieve the purposes of the treaties and conventions set forth in subsection (a) of this section.

Policy

(c)(1) It is further declared to be the policy of Congress that all Federal departments and agencies shall seek to conserve endangered species and threatened species and shall utilize their authorities in furtherance of the purposes of this chapter.

(c)(2) It is further declared to be the policy of Congress that Federal agencies shall cooperate with State and local agencies to resolve water resource issues in concert with conservation of endangered species.

Pub.L. 93–205, § 2, Dec. 28, 1973, 87 Stat. 884; as amended Pub.L. 96–159, § 1, Dec. 28, 1979, 93 Stat. 1225; Pub.L. 97–304, § 9(a), Oct. 13, 1982, 96 Stat. 1426, Pub.L. 100–478, Title I, § 1013(a), Oct. 7, 1988, 102 Stat. 2315.

§ **1532.** Definitions

For the purposes of this chapter—

(1) The term "alternative courses of action" means all alternatives and thus is not limited to original project objectives and agency jurisdiction.

(2) The term "commercial activity" means all activities of industry and trade, including, but not limited to, the buying or selling of commodities and activities conducted for the purpose of facilitating such buying and selling: *Provided, however,* That it does not include exhibition of commodities by museums or similar cultural or historical organizations.

(3) The terms "conserve", "conserving", and "conservation" mean to use and the use of all methods and procedures which are necessary to bring any endangered species or threatened species to the point at which the measures provided pursuant to this chapter are no longer necessary. Such methods and procedures include, but are not limited to, all activities associated with scientific resources management such as research, census, law enforcement, habitat acquisition and maintenance, propagation, live trapping, and transplantation, and, in the extraordinary case where population pressures within a given ecosystem cannot be otherwise relieved, may include regulated taking.

(4) The term "Convention" means the Convention on International Trade in Endangered Species of Wild Fauna and Flora, signed on March 3, 1973, and the appendices thereto.

(5)(A) The term "critical habitat" for a threatened or endangered species means—

(i) the specific areas within the geographical area occupied by the species, at the time it is listed in accordance with the provisions of section 1533 of this title, on which are found these physical or biological features (I) essential to the conservation of the species and (II) which may require special management considerations or protection; and

(ii) specific areas outside the geographical area occupied by the species at the time it is listed in accordance with the provisions of section 1533 of this title, upon a determination by the Secretary that such areas are essential for the conservation of the species.

(5)(B) Critical habitat may be established for those species now listed as threatened or endangered species for which no critical habitat has heretofore been established as set forth in subparagraph (A) of this paragraph.

(5)(C) Except in those circumstances determined by the Secretary, critical habitat shall not include the entire geographical area which can be occupied by the threatened or endangered species.

(6) The term "endangered species" means any species which is in danger of extinction throughout all or a significant portion of its range other than a species of the Class Insecta determined by the Secretary to constitute a pest whose protection under the provisions of this chapter would present an overwhelming and overriding risk to man.

(7) The term "Federal agency" means any department, agency, or instrumentality of the United States.

(8) The term "fish or wildlife" means any member of the animal kingdom, including without limitation any mammal, fish, bird (including any migratory, nonmigratory, or endangered bird for which protection is also afforded by treaty or other international agreement), amphibian, reptile, mollusk, crustacean, arthropod or other invertebrate, and includes any part, product, egg, or offspring thereof, or the dead body or parts thereof.

(9) The term "Foreign commerce" includes, among other things, any transaction—

(A) between persons within one foreign country;

(B) between persons in two or more foreign countries;

(C) between a person within the United States and a person in a foreign country; or

(D) between persons within the United States, where the fish and wildlife in question are moving in any country or countries outside the United States.

(10) The term "import" means to land on, bring into, or introduce into, or attempt to land on, bring into, or introduce into, any place subject to the jurisdiction of the United States, whether or not such

landing, bringing, or introduction constitutes an importation within the meaning of the customs laws of the United States.

(11) Repealed. Pub.L. 97–304, § 4(b), Oct. 13, 1982, 96 Stat. 1420.

(12) The term "permit or license applicant" means, when used with respect to an action of a Federal agency for which exemption is sought under section 1536 of this title, any person whose application to such agency for a permit or license has been denied primarily because of the application of section 1536(a) of this title to such agency action.

(13) The term "person" means an individual, corporation, partnership, trust, association, or any other private entity; or any officer, employee, agent, department, or instrumentality of the Federal Government, of any State, municipality, or political subdivision of a State, or of any foreign government; any State, municipality, or political subdivision of a State; or any other entity subject to the jurisdiction of the United States.

(14) The term "plant" means any member of the plant kingdom, including seeds, roots and other parts thereof.

(15) The term "Secretary" means, except as otherwise herein provided, the Secretary of the Interior or the Secretary of Commerce as program responsibilities are vested pursuant to the provisions of Reorganization Plan Numbered 4 of 1970; except that with respect to the enforcement of the provisions of this chapter and the Convention which pertain to the importation or exportation of terrestrial plants, the term also means the Secretary of Agriculture.

(16) The term "species" includes any subspecies of fish or wildlife or plants, and any distinct population segment of any species of vertebrate fish or wildlife which interbreeds when mature.

(17) The term "State" means any of the several States, the District of Columbia, the Commonwealth of Puerto Rico, American Samoa, the Virgin Islands, Guam, and the Trust Territory of the Pacific Islands.

(18) The term "State agency" means any State agency, department, board, commission, or other governmental entity which is responsible for the management and conservation of fish, plant, or wildlife resources within a State.

(19) The term "take" means to harass, harm, pursue, hunt, shoot, wound, kill, trap, capture, or collect, or to attempt to engage in any such conduct.

(20) The term "threatened species" means any species which is likely to become an endangered species within the foreseeable future throughout all or a significant portion of its range.

(21) The term "United States", when used in a geographical context, includes all States.

Pub.L. 93–205, § 3, Dec. 28, 1973, 87 Stat. 885; as amended Pub.L. 94–359, § 5, July 12, 1976, 90 Stat. 913; Pub.L. 95–632, § 2, Nov. 10, 1978, 92 Stat. 3751; Pub.L. 96–159, § 2, Dec. 28, 1979, 93 Stat. 1225; Pub.L. 97–304,

§ 4(b), Oct. 13, 1982, 96 Stat. 1420. As amended Pub.L. 100–478, Title I, § 1001, Oct. 7, 1988, 102 Stat. 2306.

§ **1533.** Determination of endangered species and threatened species [Popularly known as § 4]

Generally

(a)(1) The Secretary shall by regulation promulgated in accordance with subsection (b) of this section determine whether any species is an endangered species or a threatened species because of any of the following factors:

(A) the present or threatened destruction, modification, or curtailment of its habitat or range;

(B) overutilization for commercial, recreational, scientific, or educational purposes;

(C) disease or predation;

(D) the inadequacy of existing regulatory mechanism; or

(E) other natural or manmade factors affecting its continued existence.

* * *

(a)(3) The Secretary, by regulation promulgated in accordance with subsection (b) of this section and to the maximum extent prudent and determinable—

(A) shall, concurrently with making a determination under paragraph (1) that a species is an endangered species or a threatened species, designate any habitat of such species which is then considered to be critical habitat; and

(B) may, from time-to-time thereafter as appropriate, revise such designation.

Basis for determinations

(b)(1)(A) The Secretary shall make determinations required by subsection (a)(1) of this section solely on the basis of the best scientific and commercial data available to him after conducting a review of the status of the species and after taking into account those efforts, if any, being made by any State or foreign nation, or any political subdivision of a State or foreign nation, to protect such species, whether by predator control, protection of habitat and food supply, or other conservation practices, within any area under its jurisdiction, or on the high seas.

(B) In carrying out this section, the Secretary shall give consideration to species which have been—

(i) designated as requiring protection from unrestricted commerce by any foreign nation, or pursuant to any international agreement; or

(ii) identified as in danger of extinction, or likely to become so within the foreseeable future, by any State agency or by any agency of a foreign nation that is responsible for the conservation of fish or wildlife or plants.

(b)(2) The Secretary shall designate critical habitat, and make revisions thereto, under subsection (a)(3) of this section on the basis of the best scientific data available and after taking into consideration the economic impact, and any other relevant impact, of specifying any particular area as critical habitat. The Secretary may exclude any area from critical habitat if he determines that the benefits of such exclusion outweigh the benefits of specifying such area as part of the critical habitat, unless he determines, based on the best scientific and commercial data available, that the failure to designate such area as critical habitat will result in the extinction of the species concerned.

(b)(3)(A) To the maximum extent practicable, within 90 days after receiving the petition of an interested person under section 553(e) of Title 5 to add a species to, or to remove a species from, either of the lists published under subsection (c) of this section, the Secretary shall make a finding as to whether the petition presents substantial scientific or commercial information indicating that the petitioned action may be warranted. If such a petition is found to present such information, the Secretary shall promptly commence a review of the status of the species concerned. The Secretary shall promptly publish each finding made under this subparagraph in the Federal Register.

(b)(3)(B) Within 12 months after receiving a petition that is found under subparagraph (A) to present substantial information indicating that the petitioned action may be warranted, the Secretary shall make one of the following findings:

(i) The petitioned action is not warranted, in which case the Secretary shall promptly publish such finding in the Federal Register.

(ii) The petitioned action is warranted, in which case the Secretary shall promptly publish in the Federal Register a general notice and the complete text of a proposed regulation to implement such action in accordance with paragraph (5).

(iii) The petitioned action is warranted, but that—

(I) the immediate proposal and timely promulgation of a final regulation implementing the petitioned action in accordance with paragraphs (5) and (6) is precluded by pending proposals to determine whether any species is an endangered species or a threatened species, and

(II) expeditious progress is being made to add qualified species to either of the lists published under subsection (c) of this section and to remove from such lists species for which the protections of this chapter are no longer necessary,

in which case the Secretary shall promptly publish such finding in the Federal Register, together with a description and evaluation of the reasons and data on which the finding is based.

(b)(3)(C)(i) A petition with respect to which a finding is made under subparagraph (B)(iii) shall be treated as a petition that is resubmitted to the Secretary under subparagraph (A) on the date of such finding and that presents substantial scientific or commercial information that the petitioned action may be warranted.

(ii) Any negative finding described in subparagraph (A) and any finding described in subparagraph (B)(i) or (iii) shall be subject to judicial review.

(iii) The Secretary shall implement a system to monitor effectively the status of all species with respect to which a finding is made under subparagraph (B)(iii) and shall make prompt use of the authority under paragraph 7 to prevent a significant risk to the well being of any such species.

(b)(3)(D)(i) To the maximum extent practicable, within 90 days after receiving the petition of an interested person under section 553(e) of Title 5, to revise a critical habitat designation, the Secretary shall make a finding as to whether the petition presents substantial scientific information indicating that the revision may be warranted. The Secretary shall promptly publish such finding in the Federal Register.

(ii) Within 12 months after receiving a petition that is found under clause (i) to present substantial information indicating that the requested revision may be warranted, the Secretary shall determine how he intends to proceed with the requested revision, and shall promptly publish notice of such intention in the Federal Register.

(b)(4) Except as provided in paragraphs (5) and (6) of this subsection, the provisions of section 553 of Title 5 (relating to rulemaking procedures), shall apply to any regulation promulgated to carry out the purposes of this chapter.

(b)(5) With respect to any regulation proposed by the Secretary to implement a determination, designation, or revision referred to in subsection (a)(1) or (3) of this section, the Secretary shall—

(A) not less than 90 days before the effective date of the regulation—

(i) publish a general notice and the complete text of the proposed regulation in the Federal Register, and

(ii) give actual notice of the proposed regulation (including the complete text of the regulation) to the State agency in each State in which the species is believed to occur, and to each county or equivalent jurisdiction in which the species is believed to occur, and invite the comment of such agency, and each such jurisdiction, thereon;

(B) insofar as practical, and in cooperation with the Secretary of State, give notice of the proposed regulation to each foreign nation in which the species is believed to occur or whose citizens harvest the species on the high seas, and invite the comment of such nation thereon;

(C) give notice of the proposed regulation to such professional scientific organizations as he deems appropriate;

(D) publish a summary of the proposed regulation in a newspaper of general circulation in each area of the United States in which the species is believed to occur; and

(E) promptly hold one public hearing on the proposed regulation if any person files a request for such a hearing within 45 days after the date of publication of general notice.

(b)(6)(A) Within the one-year period beginning on the date on which general notice is published in accordance with paragraph (5)(A)(i) regarding a proposed regulation, the Secretary shall publish in the Federal Register—

(i) if a determination as to whether a species is an endangered species or a threatened species, or a revision of critical habitat, is involved, either—

(I) a final regulation to implement such determination,

(II) a final regulation to implement such revision or a finding that such revision should not be made,

(III) notice that such one-year period is being extended under subparagraph (B)(i), or

(IV) notice that the proposed regulation is being withdrawn under subparagraph (B)(ii), together with the finding on which such withdrawal is based; or

(ii) subject to subparagraph (C), if a designation of critical habitat is involved, either—

(I) a final regulation to implement such designation, or

(II) notice that such one-year period is being extended under such subparagraph.

(b)(6)(B)(i) If the Secretary finds with respect to a proposed regulation referred to in subparagraph (A)(i) that there is substantial disagreement regarding the sufficiency or accuracy of the available data relevant to the determination or revision concerned, the Secretary may extend the one-year period specified in subparagraph (A) for not more than six months for purposes of soliciting additional data.

(ii) If a proposed regulation referred to in subparagraph (A)(i) is not promulgated as a final regulation within such one-year period (or longer period if extension under clause (i) applies) because the Secretary finds that there is not sufficient evidence to justify the action proposed by the regulation, the Secretary shall immediately withdraw the regulation. The finding on which a withdrawal is based shall be subject to judicial review. The Secretary may not propose a regulation that has previously been withdrawn under this clause unless he determines that sufficient new information is available to warrant such proposal.

(iii) If the one-year period specified in subparagraph (A) is extended under clause (i) with respect to a proposed regulation, then before the close of such extended period the Secretary shall publish in the Federal Register either a final regulation to implement the determination or revision concerned, a finding that the revision should not be made, or a notice of withdrawal of the regulation under clause (ii), together with the finding on which the withdrawal is based.

(b)(6)(C) A final regulation designating critical habitat of an endangered species or a threatened species shall be published concurrently with the final regulation implementing the determination that such species is endangered or threatened, unless the Secretary deems that—

(i) it is essential to the conservation of such species that the regulation implementing such determination be promptly published; or

(ii) critical habitat of such species is not then determinable, in which case the Secretary, with respect to the proposed regulation to designate such habitat, may extend the one-year period specified in subparagraph (A) by not more than one additional year, but not later than the close of such additional year the Secretary must publish a final regulation, based on such data as may be available at that time, designating, to the maximum extent prudent, such habitat.

(b)(7) Neither paragraph (4), (5), or (6) of this subsection nor section 553 of Title 5 shall apply to any regulation issued by the Secretary in regard to any emergency posing a significant risk to the well-being of any species of fish or wildlife or plants, but only if—

(A) at the time of publication of the regulation in the Federal Register the Secretary publishes therein detailed reasons why such regulation is necessary; and

(B) in the case such regulation applies to resident species of fish or wildlife, or plants, the Secretary gives actual notice of such regulation to the State agency in each State in which such species is believed to occur.

Such regulation shall, at the discretion of the Secretary, take effect immediately upon the publication of the regulation in the Federal Register. Any regulation promulgated under the authority of this paragraph shall cease to have force and effect at the close of the 240–day period following the date of publication unless, during such 240–day period, the rulemaking procedures which would apply to such regulation without regard to this paragraph are complied with. If at any time after issuing an emergency regulation the Secretary determines, on the basis of the best appropriate data available to him, that substantial evidence does not exist to warrant such regulation, he shall withdraw it.

(b)(8) The publication in the Federal Register of any proposed or final regulation which is necessary or appropriate to carry out the purposes of this chapter shall include a summary by the Secretary of the data on which such regulation is based and shall show the relationship of such data to such regulation; and if such regulation designates or revises critical habitat, such summary shall, to the maximum extent practicable, also include a brief description and evaluation of those activities (whether public or private) which, in the opinion of the Secretary, if undertaken may adversely modify such habitat, or may be affected by such designation.

157

Lists

(c)(1) The Secretary of the Interior shall publish in the Federal Register a list of all species determined by him or the Secretary of Commerce to be endangered species and a list of all species determined by him or the Secretary of Commerce to be threatened species. Each list shall refer to the species contained therein by scientific and common name or names, if any, specify with respect to each such species over what portion of its range it is endangered or threatened, and specify any critical habitat within such range. The Secretary shall from time to time revise each list published under the authority of this subsection to reflect recent determinations, designations, and revisions made in accordance with subsections (a) and (b) of this section.

(c)(2) The Secretary shall—

(A) conduct, at least once every five years, a review of all species included in a list which is published pursuant to paragraph (1) and which is in effect at the time of such review; and

(B) determine on the basis of such review whether any such species should—

(i) be removed from such list;

(ii) be changed in status from an endangered species to a threatened species; or

(iii) be changed in status from a threatened species to an endangered species.

Each determination under subparagraph (B) shall be made in accordance with the provisions of subsections (a) and (b) of this section.

Protective regulations

(d) Whenever any species is listed as a threatened species pursuant to subsection (c) of this section, the Secretary shall issue such regulations as he deems necessary and advisable to provide for the conservation of such species. The Secretary may by regulation prohibit with respect to any threatened species any act prohibited under section 1538(a)(1) of this title, in the case of fish or wildlife, or section 1538(a)(2) of this title, in the case of plants, with respect to endangered species; except that with respect to the taking of resident species of fish or wildlife, such regulations shall apply in any State which has entered into a cooperative agreement pursuant to section 1535(c) of this title only to the extent that such regulations have also been adopted by such State.

Similarity of appearance cases

(e) The Secretary may, by regulation of commerce or taking, and to the extent he deems advisable, treat any species as an endangered species or threatened species even though it is not listed pursuant to this section if he finds that—

(A) such species so closely resembles in appearance, at the point in question, a species which has been listed pursuant to such section that enforcement personnel would have substantial difficulty in attempting to differentiate between the listed and unlisted species;

(B) the effect of this substantial difficulty is an additional threat to an endangered or threatened species; and

(C) such treatment of an unlisted species will substantially facilitate the enforcement and further the policy of this chapter.

Recovery plans

(f)(1) The Secretary shall develop and implement plans (hereinafter in this subsection referred to as "recovery plans") for the conservation and survival of endangered species and threatened species listed pursuant to this section, unless he finds that such a plan will not promote the conservation of the species. The Secretary, in developing and implementing recovery plans, shall, to the maximum extent practicable—

(A) give priority to those endangered species or threatened species, without regard to taxonomic classification, that are most likely to benefit from such plans, particularly those species that are, or may be, in conflict with construction or other development projects or other forms of economic activity;

(B) incorporate in each plan—

(i) a description of such site-specific management actions as may be necessary to achieve the plan's goal for the conservation and survival of the species;

(ii) objective, measurable criteria which, when met, would result in a determination, in accordance with the provisions of this section, that the species be removed from the list; and

(iii) estimates of the time required and the cost to carry out those measures needed to achieve the plan's goal and to achieve intermediate steps toward that goal.

(f)(2) The Secretary, in developing and implementing recovery plans, may procure the services of appropriate public and private agencies and institutions, and other qualified persons. Recovery teams appointed pursuant to this subsection shall not be subject to the Federal Advisory Committee Act.

(f)(3) The Secretary shall report every two years to the Committee on Environment and Public Works of the Senate and the Committee on Merchant Marine and Fisheries of the House of Representatives on the status of efforts to develop and implement recovery plans for all species listed pursuant to this section and on the status of all species for which such plans have been developed.

(f)(4) The Secretary shall, prior to final approval of a new or revised recovery plan, provide public notice and an opportunity for public review and comment on such plan. The Secretary shall consider all information presented during the public comment period prior to approval of the plan.

(f)(5) Each Federal agency shall, prior to implementation of a new or revised recovery plan, consider all information presented during the public comment period under paragraph (4).

Monitoring

(g)(1) The Secretary shall implement a system in cooperation with the States to monitor effectively for not less than five years the status of all species which have recovered to the point at which the measures provided pursuant to this chapter are no longer necessary and which, in accordance with the provisions of this section, have been removed from either of the lists published under subsection (c) of this section.

(g)(2) The Secretary shall make prompt use of the authority under paragraph 7 of subsection (b) of this section to prevent a significant risk to the well being of any such recovered species.

* * *

Pub.L. 93–205, § 4, Dec. 28, 1973, 87 Stat. 886; as amended Pub.L. 94–359, § 1, July 12, 1976, 90 Stat. 911; Pub.L. 95–632, §§ 11, 13, Nov. 10, 1978, 92 Stat. 3764, 3766; Pub.L. 96–159, § 3, Dec. 28, 1979, 93 Stat. 1225; Pub.L. 97–304, § 2(a), Oct. 13, 1982, 96 Stat. 1411. As amended Pub.L. 100–478, Title I, §§ 1002–1004, Oct. 7, 1988, 102 Stat. 2306.

* * *

§ 1535. Cooperation with States

(a) In carrying out the program authorized by this chapter, the Secretary shall cooperate to the maximum extent practicable with the States. Such cooperation shall include consultation with the States concerned before acquiring any land or water, or interest therein, for the purpose of conserving any endangered species or threatened species.

Management agreements

(b) The Secretary may enter into agreements with any State for the administration and management of any area established for the conservation of endangered species or threatened species. Any revenues derived from the administration of such areas under these agreements shall be subject to the provisions of section 715s of this title.

Cooperative agreements

(c)(1) In furtherance of the purposes of this chapter, the Secretary is authorized to enter into a cooperative agreement in accordance with this section with any State which establishes and maintains an adequate and active program for the conservation of endangered species and threatened species. * * *

Allocation of funds

(d)(1) The Secretary is authorized to provide financial assistance to any State, through its respective State agency, which has entered into a cooperative agreement pursuant to subsection (c) of this section to assist in development of programs for the conservation of endangered and threatened species or to assist in monitoring the status of candidate species pursuant to subparagraph (C) of section 1533(b)(3) of this title and recovered species pursuant to section 1533(g) of this title. The Secretary shall allocate each annual appropriation made in accordance with the provisions of subsection (i) of this section to such States based on consideration of—

(A) the international commitments of the United States to protect endangered species or threatened species;

(B) the readiness of a State to proceed with a conservation program consistent with the objectives and purposes of this chapter;

(C) the number of endangered species and threatened species within a State;

(D) the potential for restoring endangered species and threatened species within a State;

(E) the relative urgency to initiate a program to restore and protect an endangered species or threatened species in terms of survival of the species;

(F) the importance of monitoring the status of candidate species within a State to prevent a significant risk to the well being of any such species; and

(G) the importance of monitoring the status of recovered species within a State to assure that such species do not return to the point at which the measures provided pursuant to this chapter are again necessary.

Review of State programs

(e) Any action taken by the Secretary under this section shall be subject to his periodic review at no greater than annual intervals.

Conflicts between Federal and State laws

(f) Any State law or regulation which applies with respect to the importation or exportation of, or interstate or foreign commerce in, endangered species or threatened species is void to the extent that it may effectively (1) permit what is prohibited by this chapter or by any regulation which implements this chapter, or (2) prohibit what is authorized pursuant to an exemption or permit provided for in this chapter or in any regulation which implements this chapter. This chapter shall not otherwise be construed to void any State law or regulation which is intended to conserve migratory, resident, or introduced fish or wildlife, or to permit or prohibit sale of such fish or wildlife. Any State law or regulation respecting the taking of an endangered species or threatened species may be more restrictive than the exemptions or permits provided for in this chapter or in any regulation which implements this chapter but not less restrictive than the prohibitions so defined.

* * *

Regulations

(h) The Secretary is authorized to promulgate such regulations as may be appropriate to carry out the provisions of this section relating to financial assistance to States.

Appropriations

(i)(1) To carry out the provisions of this section for fiscal years after September 30, 1988, there shall be deposited into a special fund known as the cooperative endangered species conservation fund, to be administered by the Secretary, an amount equal to 5 percent of the combined amounts covered each fiscal year into the Federal aid to wildlife restoration fund under section 669b of this title, and paid, transferred, or otherwise credited each fiscal year to the Sport Fishing Restoration Account established under 1016 of the Act of July 18, 1984.

(2) Amounts deposited into the special fund are authorized to be appropriated annually and allocated in accordance with subsection (d) of this section.

Pub.L. 93–205, § 6, Dec. 28, 1973, 87 Stat. 889; as amended Pub.L. 95–212, Dec. 19, 1977, 91 Stat. 1493; Pub.L. 95–632, § 10, Nov. 10, 1978, 92 Stat. 3762; Pub.L. 96–246, May 23, 1980, 94 Stat. 348; Pub.L. 97–304, §§ 3, 8(b), Oct. 13, 1982, 96 Stat. 1416, 1426, Pub.L. 100–478, Title I, § 1005, Oct. 7, 1988, 102 Stat. 2307.

§ 1536. Interagency cooperation [popularly known as § 7]

Federal agency actions and consultations

(a)(1) The Secretary shall review other programs administered by him and utilize such programs in furtherance of the purposes of this chapter. All other Federal agencies shall, in consultation with and with the assistance of the Secretary, utilize their authorities in furtherance of the purposes of this chapter by carrying out programs for the conservation of endangered species and threatened species listed pursuant to section 1533 of this title.

(a)(2) Each Federal agency shall, in consultation with and with the assistance of the Secretary, insure that any action authorized, funded, or carried out by such agency (hereinafter in this section referred to as an "agency action") is not likely to jeopardize the continued existence of any endangered species or threatened species or result in the destruction or adverse modification of habitat of such species which is determined by the Secretary, after consultation as appropriate with affected States, to be critical, unless such agency has been granted an exemption for such action by the Committee pursuant to subsection (h) of this section. In fulfilling the requirements of this paragraph each agency shall use the best scientific and commercial data available.

(a)(3) Subject to such guidelines as the Secretary may establish, a Federal agency shall consult with the Secretary on any prospective agency action at the request of, and in cooperation with, the prospective permit or license applicant if the applicant has reason to believe that an endangered species or a threatened species may be present in the area affected by his project and that implementation of such action will likely affect such species.

(a)(4) Each Federal agency shall confer with the Secretary on any agency action which is likely to jeopardize the continued existence of any species proposed to be listed under section 1533 of this title or result in the destruction or adverse modification of critical habitat proposed to be designated for such species. This paragraph does not require a limitation on the commitment of resources as described in subsection (d) of this section.

Opinion of Secretary

(b)(1)(A) Consultation under subsection (a)(2) of this section with respect to any agency action shall be concluded within the 90–day period beginning on the date on which initiated or, subject to subparagraph (B), within such other period of time as is mutually agreeable to the Secretary and the Federal agency.

(B) In the case of an agency action involving a permit or license applicant, the Secretary and the Federal agency may not mutually agree to conclude consultation within a period exceeding 90 days unless the Secretary, before the close of the 90th day referred to in subparagraph (A)—

(i) if the consultation period proposed to be agreed to will end before the 150th day after the date on which consultation was initiated, submits to the applicant a written statement setting forth—

(I) the reasons why a longer period is required,

(II) the information that is required to complete the consultation, and

(III) the estimated date on which consultation will be completed; or

(ii) if the consultation period proposed to be agreed to will end 150 or more days after the date on which consultation was initiated, obtains the consent of the applicant to such period.

The Secretary and the Federal agency may mutually agree to extend a consultation period established under the preceding sentence if the Secretary, before the close of such period, obtains the consent of the applicant to the extension.

(b)(2) Consultation under subsection (a)(3) of this section shall be concluded within such period as is agreeable to the Secretary, the Federal agency, and the applicant concerned.

(b)(3)(A) Promptly after conclusion of consultation under paragraph (2) or (3) of subsection (a) of this section, the Secretary shall provide to the Federal agency and the applicant, if any, a written statement setting forth the Secretary's opinion, and a summary of the information on which the opinion is based, detailing how the agency action affects the species or its critical habitat. If jeopardy or adverse modification is found, the Secretary shall suggest those reasonable and prudent alternatives which he believes would not violate subsection (a)(2) of this section and can be taken by the Federal agency or applicant in implementing the agency action.

(B) Consultation under subsection (a)(3) of this section, and an opinion issued by the Secretary incident to such consultation, regarding an agency action shall be treated respectively as a consultation under subsection (a)(2) of this section, and as an opinion issued after consultation under such subsection, regarding that action if the Secretary reviews the action before it is commenced by the Federal agency and finds, and notifies such agency, that no significant changes have been made with respect to the action and that no significant change has occurred regarding the information used during the initial consultation.

(b)(4) If after consultation under subsection (a)(2) of this section, the Secretary concludes that—

(A) the agency action will not violate such subsection, or offers reasonable and prudent alternatives which the Secretary believes would not violate such subsection;

(B) the taking of an endangered species or a threatened species incidental to the agency action will not violate such subsection; and

(C) if an endangered species or threatened species of a marine mammal is involved, the taking is authorized pursuant to section 1371(a)(5) of this title;

the Secretary shall provide the Federal agency and the applicant concerned, if any, with a written statement that—

(i) specifies the impact of such incidental taking on the species,

(ii) specifies those reasonable and prudent measures that the Secretary considers necessary or appropriate to minimize such impact,

(iii) in the case of marine mammals, specifies those measures that are necessary to comply with section 1371(a)(5) of this title with regard to such taking, and

(iv) sets forth the terms and conditions (including, but not limited to, reporting requirements) that must be complied with by the Federal agency or applicant (if any), or both, to implement the measures specified under clauses (ii) and (iii).

Biological assessment

(c)(1) To facilitate compliance with the requirements of subsection (a)(2) of this section, each Federal agency shall, with respect to any agency action of such agency for which no contract for construction has been entered into and for which no construction has begun on November 10, 1978, request of the Secretary information whether any species which is listed or proposed to be listed may be present in the area of such proposed action. If the Secretary advises, based on the best scientific and commercial data available, that such species may be present, such agency shall conduct a biological assessment for the purpose of identifying any endangered species or threatened species which is likely to be affected by such action. Such assessment shall be completed within 180 days after the date on which initiated (or within such other period as is mutually agreed to by the Secretary and such agency, except that if a permit or license applicant is involved, the 180-day period may not be extended unless such agency provides the applicant, before the close of such period, with a written statement setting forth the estimated length of the proposed extension and the reasons therefor) and, before any contract for construction is entered into and before construction is begun with respect to such action. Such assessment may be undertaken as part of a Federal agency's compliance with the requirements of section 4332 of Title 42.

(c)(2) Any person who may wish to apply for an exemption under subsection (g) of this section for that action may conduct a biological assessment to identify any endangered species or threatened species which is likely to be affected by such action. Any such biological assessment must, however, be conducted in cooperation with the Secretary and under the supervision of the appropriate Federal agency.

Limitation on commitment of resources

(d) After initiation of consultation required under subsection (a)(2) of this section, the Federal agency and the permit or license applicant shall not make any irreversible or irretrievable commitment of resources with respect to the agency action which has the effect of foreclosing the formulation or implementation of any reasonable and prudent alternative measures which would not violate subsection (a)(2) of this section.

Endangered Species Committee

(e)(1) There is established a committee to be known as the Endangered Species Committee (hereinafter in this section referred to as the "Committee").

(e)(2) The Committee shall review any application submitted to it pursuant to this section and determine in accordance with subsection (h) of this section whether or not to grant an exemption from the requirements of subsection (a)(2) of this section for the action set forth in such application.

(e)(3) The Committee shall be composed of seven members as follows:

(A) The Secretary of Agriculture.

(B) The Secretary of the Army.

(C) The Chairman of the Council of Economic Advisors.

(D) The Administrator of the Environmental Protection Agency.

(E) The Secretary of the Interior.

(F) The Administrator of the National Oceanic and Atmospheric Administration.

(G) The President, after consideration of any recommendations received pursuant to subsection (g)(2)(B) of this section shall appoint one individual from each affected State, as determined by the Secretary, to be a member of the Committee for the consideration of the application for exemption for an agency action with respect to which such recommendations are made, no later than 30 days after an application is submitted pursuant to this section.

* * *

Application for exemption and report to the Committee

(g)(1) A Federal agency, the Governor of the State in which an agency action will occur, if any, or a permit or license applicant may apply to the Secretary for an exemption for an agency action of such agency if, after consultation under subsection (a)(2) of this section, the Secretary's opinion under subsection (b) of this section indicates that the agency action would violate subsection (a)(2) of this section. An application for an exemption shall be considered initially by the Secretary in the manner provided for in this subsection, and shall be considered by the Committee for a final determination under subsection (h) of this section after a report is made pursuant to paragraph (5). The applicant for an exemption shall be referred to as the "exemption applicant" in this section.

(g)(2)(A) An exemption applicant shall submit a written application to the Secretary, in a form prescribed under subsection (f) of this section, not later than 90 days after the completion of the consultation process; except that, in the case of any agency action involving a permit or license applicant, such application shall be submitted not later than 90 days after the date on which the Federal agency concerned takes final agency action with respect to the issuance of the permit or license. For purposes of the preceding sentence, the term "final agency action" means (i) a disposition by an agency with respect to the issuance of a permit or license that is subject to administrative review, whether or not such disposition is subject to judicial review; or (ii) if administrative review is sought with respect to such disposition, the decision resulting after such review. Such application shall set forth the reasons why the exemption applicant considers that the agency action meets the requirements for an exemption under this subsection.

* * *

(g)(3) The Secretary shall within 20 days after the receipt of an application for exemption, or within such other period of time as is mutually agreeable to the exemption applicant and the Secretary—

(A) determine that the Federal agency concerned and the exemption applicant have—

(i) carried out the consultation responsibilities described in subsection (a) of this section in good faith and made a reasonable and responsible effort to develop and fairly consider modifications or reasonable and prudent alternatives to the proposed agency action which would not violate subsection (a)(2) of this section;

(ii) conducted any biological assessment required by subsection (c) of this section; and

(iii) to the extent determinable within the time provided herein, refrained from making any irreversible or irretrievable

166

commitment of resources prohibited by subsection (d) of this section; or

(B) deny the application for exemption because the Federal agency concerned or the exemption applicant have not met the requirements set forth in subparagraph (A)(i), (ii), and (iii).

The denial of an application under subparagraph (B) shall be considered final agency action for purposes of chapter 7 of Title 5.

* * *

(g)(5) Within 140 days after making the determinations under paragraph (3) or within such other period of time as is mutually agreeable to the exemption applicant and the Secretary, the Secretary shall submit to the Committee a report discussing—

(A) the availability of reasonable and prudent alternatives to the agency action, and the nature and extent of the benefits of the agency action and of alternative courses of action consistent with conserving the species or the critical habitat;

(B) a summary of the evidence concerning whether or not the agency action is in the public interest and is of national or regional significance;

(C) appropriate reasonable mitigation and enhancement measures which should be considered by the Committee; and

(D) whether the Federal agency concerned and the exemption applicant refrained from making any irreversible or irretrievable commitment of resources prohibited by subsection (d) of this section.

* * *

Grant of exemption

(h)(1) The Committee shall make a final determination whether or not to grant an exemption within 30 days after receiving the report of the Secretary pursuant to subsection (g)(5) of this section. The Committee shall grant an exemption from the requirements of subsection (a)(2) of this section for an agency action if, by a vote of not less than five of its members voting in person—

(A) it determines on the record, based on the report of the Secretary, the record of the hearing held under subsection (g)(4) and on such other testimony or evidence as it may receive, that—

(i) there are no reasonable and prudent alternatives to the agency action;

(ii) the benefits of such action clearly outweigh the benefits of alternative courses of action consistent with conserving the species or its critical habitat, and such action is in the public interest;

(iii) the action is of regional or national significance; and

(iv) neither the Federal agency concerned nor the exemption applicant made any irreversible or irretrievable commitment of resources prohibited by subsection (d) of this section; and

(B) it establishes such reasonable mitigation and enhancement measures, including, but not limited to, live propagation, transplantation, and habitat acquisition and improvement, as are necessary and appropriate to minimize the adverse effects of the agency action upon the endangered species, threatened species, or critical habitat concerned.

Any final determination by the Committee under this subsection shall be considered final agency action for purposes of chapter 7 of Title 5.

(h)(2)(A) Except as provided in subparagraph (B), an exemption for an agency action granted under paragraph (1) shall constitute a permanent exemption with respect to all endangered or threatened species for the purposes of completing such agency action—

(i) regardless whether the species was identified in the biological assessment; and

(ii) only if a biological assessment has been conducted under subsection (c) of this section with respect to such agency action.

(B) An exemption shall be permanent under subparagraph (A) unless—

(i) the Secretary finds, based on the best scientific and commercial data available, that such exemption would result in the extinction of a species that was not the subject of consultation under subsection (a)(2) of this section or was not identified in any biological assessment conducted under subsection (c) of this section, and

(ii) the Committee determines within 60 days after the date of the Secretary's finding that the exemption should not be permanent.

If the Secretary makes a finding described in clause (i), the Committee shall meet with respect to the matter within 30 days after the date of the finding.

* * *

Exemption decision not considered major federal action; environmental impact statement

(k) An exemption decision by the Committee under this section shall not be a major Federal action for purposes of the National Environmental Policy Act of 1969: *Provided,* That an environmental impact statement which discusses the impacts upon endangered species or threatened species or their critical habitats shall have been previously prepared with respect to any agency action exempted by such order.

* * *

Judicial review

(n) Any person, as defined by section 1532(13) of this title, may obtain judicial review, under chapter 7 of Title 5, of any decision of the Endangered Species Committee under subsection (h) of this section in the United States Court of Appeals for (1) any circuit wherein the agency action concerned will be, or is being, carried out, or (2) in any case in which the agency action will be, or is being, carried out outside of any circuit, the District of Columbia, by filing in such court within 90 days after the date of issuance of the decision, a written petition for review. A copy of such petition shall be transmitted by the clerk of the court to the Committee and the Committee shall file in the court the record in the proceeding, as provided in section 2112, of Title 28. Attorneys designated by the Endangered Species Committee may appear for, and represent the Committee in any action for review under this subsection.

Exemption as providing exception on taking of endangered species

(*o*) Notwithstanding sections 1533(d) and 1538(a)(1)(B) and (C) of this title, sections 1371 and 1372 of this title, or any regulation promulgated to implement any such section—

(1) any action for which an exemption is granted under subsection (h) of this section shall not be considered to be a taking of any endangered species or threatened species with respect to any activity which is necessary to carry out such action; and

(2) any taking that is in compliance with the terms and conditions specified in a written statement provided under subsection (b)(4)(iv) of this section shall not be considered to be a prohibited taking of the species concerned.

* * *

Pub.L. 93–205, § 7, Dec. 28, 1973, 87 Stat. 892; as amended Pub.L. 95–632, § 3, Nov. 10, 1978, 92 Stat. 3752; Pub.L. 96–159, § 4, Dec. 28, 1979, 93 Stat. 1226; Pub.L. 97–304, §§ 4(a), 8(b), Oct. 13, 1982, 96 Stat. 1417, 1426. As amended Pub.L. 99–659, Title IV, § 411(b), (c), Nov. 14, 1986, 105 Stat. 3742; Pub.L. 100–707, Title I, § 109(g), Nov. 23, 1988, 102 Stat. 4709.

§ 1537. International cooperation

Financial assistance

(a) As a demonstration of the commitment of the United States to the worldwide protection of endangered species and threatened species, the President may, subject to the provisions of section 1306 of Title 31, use foreign currencies accruing to the United States Government under the Agricultural Trade Development and Assistance Act of 1954 [7 U.S.C.A. § 1691 et seq.] or any other law to provide to any foreign country (with its consent) assistance in the development and management of programs in that country which the Secretary determines to be necessary or useful for the conservation of any endangered species or threatened species listed by the Secretary pursuant to section 1533 of this title. The President shall provide assistance (which includes, but is not limited to, the acquisition, by lease or otherwise, of lands, waters, or interests therein) to foreign countries under this section under such terms and conditions as he deems appropriate. Whenever foreign currencies are available for the provision of assistance under this section, such currencies shall be used in preference to funds appropriated under the authority of section 1542 of this title.

Encouragement of foreign programs

(b) In order to carry out further the provisions of this chapter, the Secretary, through the Secretary of State, shall encourage—

(b)(1) foreign countries to provide for the conservation of fish or wildlife and plants including endangered species and threatened species listed pursuant to section 1533 of this title;

(b)(2) the entering into of bilateral or multilateral agreements with foreign countries to provide for such conservation; and

(b)(3) foreign persons who directly or indirectly take fish or wildlife or plants in foreign countries or on the high seas for importation into the United States for commercial or other purposes to develop and carry out with such assistance as he may provide, conservation practices designed to enhance such fish or wildlife or plants and their habitat.

* * *

Pub.L. 93–205, § 8, Dec. 28, 1973, 87 Stat. 892; Pub.L. 96–159, § 5, Dec. 28, 1979, 93 Stat. 1228.

* * *

§ 1537a. Convention implementation

Management Authority and Scientific Authority

(a) The Secretary of the Interior (hereinafter in this section referred to as the "Secretary") is designated as the Management Authority and the Scientific Authority for purposes of the Convention and the respective functions of each such Authority shall be carried out through the United States Fish and Wildlife Service.

Management Authority functions

(b) The Secretary shall do all things necessary and appropriate to carry out the functions of the Management Authority under the Convention.

Scientific Authority functions

(c)(1) The Secretary shall do all things necessary and appropriate to carry out the functions of the Scientific Authority under the Convention.

(2) The Secretary shall base the determinations and advice given by him under Article IV of the Convention with respect to wildlife upon the best available biological information derived from professionally accepted wildlife management practices; but is not required to make, or require any State to make, estimates of population size in making such determinations or giving such advice.

* * *

Wildlife Preservation in Western Hemisphere

(e)(1) The Secretary of the Interior (hereinafter in this subsection referred to as the "Secretary"), in cooperation with the Secretary of State, shall act on behalf of, and represent, the United States in all regards as required by the Convention on Nature Protection and Wildlife Preservation in the Western Hemisphere (56 Stat. 1354, T.S. 982, hereinafter in this subsection referred to as the "Western Convention"). In the discharge of these responsibilities, the Secretary and the Secretary of State shall consult with the Secretary of Agriculture, the Secretary of Commerce, and the heads of other agencies with respect to matters relating to or affecting their areas of responsibility.

(e)(2) The Secretary and the Secretary of State shall, in cooperation with the contracting parties to the Western Convention and, to the extent feasible and appropriate, with the participation of State agencies, take such steps as are necessary to implement the Western Convention. Such steps shall include, but not be limited to—

   (A) cooperation with contracting parties and international organizations for the purpose of developing personnel resources and programs that will facilitate implementation of the Western Convention;

   (B) identification of those species of birds that migrate between the United States and other contracting parties, and the habitats upon which those species depend, and the implementation of cooperative measures to ensure that such species will not become endangered or threatened; and

   (C) identification of measures that are necessary and appropriate to implement those provisions of the Western Convention which address the protection of wild plants.

(e)(3) No later than September 30, 1985, the Secretary and the Secretary of State shall submit a report to Congress describing those steps taken in accordance with the requirements of this subsection and identifying the principal remaining actions yet necessary for comprehensive and effective implementation of the Western Convention.

(e)(4) The provisions of this subsection shall not be construed as affecting the authority, jurisdiction, or responsibility of the several States to manage, control, or regulate resident fish or wildlife under State law or regulations.

Pub.L. 93–205, § 8A, as added Pub.L. 96–159, § 6(a)(1), Dec. 28, 1979, 93 Stat. 1228, and amended Pub.L. 97–304, § 5, Oct. 13, 1982, 96 Stat. 1421.

§ 1538.   Prohibited acts [popularly known as § 9]

Generally

(a)(1) Except as provided in sections 1535(g)(2) and 1539 of this title, with respect to any endangered species of fish or wildlife listed pursuant to section 1533 of this title it is unlawful for any person subject to the jurisdiction of the United States to—

(A) import any such species into, or export any such species from the United States;

(B) take any such species within the United States or the territorial sea of the United States;

(C) take any such species upon the high seas;

(D) possess, sell, deliver, carry, transport, or ship, by any means whatsoever, any such species taken in violation of subparagraphs (B) and (C);

(E) deliver, receive, carry, transport, or ship in interstate or foreign commerce, by any means whatsoever and in the course of a commercial activity, any such species;

(F) sell or offer for sale in interstate or foreign commerce any such species; or

(G) violate any regulation pertaining to such species or to any threatened species of fish or wildlife listed pursuant to section 1533 of this title and promulgated by the Secretary pursuant to authority provided by this chapter.

(a)(2) Except as provided in sections 1535(g)(2) and 1539 of this title, with respect to any endangered species of plants listed pursuant to section 1533 of this title, it is unlawful for any person subject to the jurisdiction of the United States to—

(A) import any such species into, or export any such species from, the United States;

(B) remove and reduce to possession any such species from areas under Federal jurisdiction; maliciously damage or destroy any such species on any such area; or remove, cut, dig up, or damage or destroy any such species on any other area in knowing violation of any law or regulation of any State or in the course of any violation of a State criminal trespass law;

(C) deliver, receive, carry, transport, or ship in interstate or foreign commerce, by any means whatsoever and in the course of a commercial activity, any such species;

(D) sell or offer for sale in interstate or foreign commerce any such species; or

(E) violate any regulation pertaining to such species or to any threatened species of plants listed pursuant to section 1533 of this title and promulgated by the Secretary pursuant to authority provided by this chapter.

* * *

Pub.L. 93–205, § 9, Dec. 28, 1973, 87 Stat. 893; as amended Pub.L. 95–632, § 4, Nov. 10, 1978, 92 Stat. 3760; Pub.L. 97–304, § 9(b), Oct. 13, 1982, 96 Stat. 1426. As amended Pub.L. 100–478, Title I, § 1006, Title II, § 2301, Oct. 7, 1988, 102 Stat. 2308, 2321; Pub.L. 100–653, Title IX, § 905, Nov. 14, 1988, 102 Stat. 3835.

§ 1539. Exceptions [popularly known as § 10]

Permits

(a)(1) The Secretary may permit, under such terms and conditions as he shall prescribe—

(A) any act otherwise prohibited by section 1538 of this title for scientific purposes or to enhance the propagation or survival of the affected species, including, but not limited to, acts necessary for the establishment and maintenance of experimental populations pursuant to subsection (j) of this section; or

(B) any taking otherwise prohibited by section 1538(a)(1)(B) of this title if such taking is incidental to, and not the purpose of, the carrying out of an otherwise lawful activity.

(a)(2)(A) No permit may be issued by the Secretary authorizing any taking referred to in paragraph (1)(B) unless the applicant therefor submits to the Secretary a conservation plan that specifies—

(i) the impact which will likely result from such taking;

(ii) what steps the applicant will take to minimize and mitigate such impacts, and the funding that will be available to implement such steps;

(iii) what alternative actions to such taking the applicant considered and the reasons why such alternatives are not being utilized; and

(iv) such other measures that the Secretary may require as being necessary or appropriate for purposes of the plan.

(a)(2)(B) If the Secretary finds, after opportunity for public comment, with respect to a permit application and the related conservation plan that—

(i) the taking will be incidental;

(ii) the applicant will, to the maximum extent practicable, minimize and mitigate the impacts of such taking;

(iii) the applicant will ensure that adequate funding for the plan will be provided;

(iv) the taking will not appreciably reduce the likelihood of the survival and recovery of the species in the wild; and

(v) the measures, if any, required under subparagraph (A)(iv) will be met;

and he has received such other assurances as he may require that the plan will be implemented, the Secretary shall issue the permit. The permit shall contain such terms and conditions as the Secretary deems necessary or appropriate to carry out the purposes of this paragraph, including, but not limited to, such reporting requirements as the Secretary deems necessary for determining whether such terms and conditions are being complied with.

(a)(2)(C) The Secretary shall revoke a permit issued under this paragraph if he finds that the permittee is not complying with the terms and conditions of the permit.

* * *

Permit and exemption policy

(d) The Secretary may grant exceptions under subsections (a)(1)(A) and (b) of this section only if he finds and publishes his finding in the Federal Register that (1) such exceptions were applied for in good faith, (2) if granted and exercised will not operate to the disadvantage of such endangered species, and (3) will be consistent with the purposes and policy set forth in section 1531 of this title.

Alaskan natives

(e)(1) Except as provided in paragraph (4) of this subsection the provisions of this chapter shall not apply with respect to the taking of any endangered species or threatened species, or the importation of any such species taken pursuant to this section, by—

(A) any Indian, Aleut, or Eskimo who is an Alaskan Native who resides in Alaska; or

(B) any non-native permanent resident of an Alaskan native village;

if such taking is primarily for subsistence purposes. Non-edible byproducts of species taken pursuant to this section may be sold in interstate commerce when made into authentic native articles of handicrafts and clothing; except that the provisions of this subsection shall not apply to any non-native resident of an Alaskan native village found by the Secretary to be not primarily dependent upon the taking of fish and wildlife for consumption or for the creation and sale of authentic native articles of handicrafts and clothing.

(e)(2) Any taking under this subsection may not be accomplished in a wasteful manner.

* * *

Experimental populations

(j)(1) For purposes of this subsection, the term "experimental population" means any population (including any offspring arising solely therefrom) authorized by the Secretary for release under paragraph (2), but only when, and at such times as, the population is wholly separate geographically from nonexperimental populations of the same species.

(j)(2)(A) The Secretary may authorize the release (and the related transportation) of any population (including eggs, propagules, or individuals) of an endangered species or a threatened species outside the current range of such species if the Secretary determines that such release will further the conservation of such species.

(j)(2)(B) Before authorizing the release of any population under subparagraph (A), the Secretary shall by regulation identify the population and determine, on the basis of the best available information, whether or not such population is essential to the continued existence of an endangered species or a threatened species.

(j)(2)(C) For the purposes of this chapter, each member of an experimental population shall be treated as a threatened species; except that—

(i) solely for purposes of section 1536 of this title (other than subsection (a)(1) thereof), an experimental population determined under subparagraph (B) to be not essential to the continued existence of a species shall be treated, except when it occurs in an area within the National Wildlife Refuge System or the National Park System, as a species proposed to be listed under section 1533 of this title; and

(ii) critical habitat shall not be designated under this chapter for any experimental population determined under subparagraph (B) to be not essential to the continued existence of a species.

(j)(3) The Secretary, with respect to populations of endangered species or threatened species that the Secretary authorized, before October 13, 1982, for release in geographical areas separate from the other populations of such species, shall determine by regulation which of such populations are an experimental population for the purposes of this subsection and whether or not each is essential to the continued existence of an endangered species or a threatened species.

* * *

Pub.L. 93–205, § 10, Dec. 28, 1973, 87 Stat. 896; as amended Pub.L. 94–359, §§ 2, 3, July 12, 1976, 90 Stat. 911, 912; Pub.L. 95–632, § 5, Nov. 10, 1978, 92 Stat. 3760; Pub.L. 96–159, § 7, Dec. 28, 1979, 93 Stat. 1230; Pub.L. 97–304, § 6, Oct. 13, 1982, 96 Stat. 1422 to 1424; as amended Pub.L. 100–478, Title I, §§ 1011, 1013(b), (c), Oct. 7, 1988, 102 Stat. 2314, 2315.

§ 1540. Penalties and enforcement

Civil penalties

(a)(1) Any person who knowingly violates, and any person engaged in business as an importer or exporter of fish, wildlife, or plants who violates, any provision of this chapter, or any provision of any permit or certificate issued hereunder, or of any regulation issued in order to implement subsection (a)(1)(A), (B), (C), (D), (E), or (F), (a)(2)(A), (B), (C), or (D), (c), (d) (other than regulation relating to recordkeeping or filing of reports), (f) or (g) of section 1538 of this title, may be assessed a civil penalty by the Secretary of not more than $25,000 for each violation. Any person who knowingly violates, and any person engaged in business as an importer or exporter of fish, wildlife, or plants who violates, any provision of any other regulation issued under this chapter may be assessed a civil penalty by the Secretary of not more than $12,000 for each such violation. Any person who otherwise violates any provision of this chapter, or any regulation, permit, or certificate issued hereunder, may be assessed a civil penalty by the Secretary of not more than $500 for each such violation. No penalty may be assessed under this subsection unless such person is given notice and opportunity for a hearing with respect to such violation. Each violation shall be a separate offense. Any such civil penalty may be remitted or mitigated by the Secretary. Upon any failure to pay a penalty assessed under this subsection, the Secretary may request the Attorney General to institute a civil action in a district court of the United States for any district in which such person is found, resides, or transacts business to collect the penalty and such court shall have jurisdiction to hear and decide any such action. The court shall hear such action on the record made before the Secretary and shall sustain his action if it is supported by substantial evidence on the record considered as a whole.

(a)(2) Hearings held during proceedings for the assessment of civil penalties authorized by paragraph (1) of this subsection shall be conducted in accordance with section 554 of Title 5. The Secretary may issue subpenas for the attendance and testimony of witnesses and the production of relevant papers, books, and documents, and administer oaths. Witnesses summoned shall be paid the same fees and mileage that are paid to witnesses in the courts of the United States. In case of contumacy or refusal to obey a subpena served upon any person pursuant to this paragraph, the district court of the United States for any district in which such person is found or resides or transacts business, upon application by the United States and after notice to such person, shall have jurisdiction to issue an order requiring such person to appear and give testimony before the Secretary or to appear and produce documents before the Secretary, or both, and any failure to obey such order of the court may be punished by such court as a contempt thereof.

(a)(3) Notwithstanding any other provision of this chapter, no civil penalty shall be imposed if it can be shown by a preponderance of the evidence that the defendant committed an act based on a good faith belief that he was acting to protect himself or herself, a member of his or her family, or any other individual from bodily harm, from any endangered or threatened species.

Criminal violations

(b)(1) Any person who knowingly violates any provision of this chapter, of any permit or certificate issued hereunder, or of any regulation issued in order to implement subsection (a)(1)(A), (B), (C), (D), (E), or (F); (a)(2)(A), (B), (C), or (D), (c), (d) (other than a regulation relating to recordkeeping, or filing of reports), (f), or (g) of section 1538 of this title shall, upon conviction, be fined not more than $50,000 or imprisoned for not more than one year, or both. Any person who knowingly violates any provision of any other regulation issued under this chapter shall, upon conviction, be fined not more than $25,000 or imprisoned for not more than six months, or both.

(b)(2) The head of any Federal agency which has issued a lease, license, permit, or other agreement authorizing a person to import or export fish, wildlife, or plants, or to operate a quarantine station for imported wildlife, or authorizing the use of Federal lands, including grazing of domestic livestock, to any person who is convicted of a criminal violation of this chapter or any regulation, permit, or certificate issued hereunder may immediately modify, suspend, or revoke each lease, license, permit or other agreement. The Secretary shall also suspend for a period of up to one year, or cancel, any Federal hunting or fishing permits or stamps issued to any person who is convicted of a criminal violation of any provision of this chapter or any regulation, permit, or certificate issued hereunder. The United States shall not be liable for the payments of any compensation, reimbursement, or damages in connection with the modification, suspension, or revocation of any leases, licenses, permits, stamps, or other agreements pursuant to this section.

(b)(3) Notwithstanding any other provision of this chapter, it shall be a defense to prosecution under this subsection if the defendant committed the offense based on a good faith belief that he was acting to protect himself or herself, a member of his or her family, or any other individual, from bodily harm from any endangered or threatened species.

District court jurisdiction

(c) The several district courts of the United States, including the courts enumerated in section 460 of Title 28, shall have jurisdiction over any actions arising under this chapter. For the purpose of this chapter, American Samoa shall be included within the judicial district of the District Court of the United States for the District of Hawaii.

Rewards and certain incidental expenses

(d) The Secretary or the Secretary of the Treasury shall pay, from sums received as penalties, fines, or forfeitures of property for any violation of this chapter or any regulation issued hereunder (1) a reward to any person who furnishes information which leads to an arrest, a criminal conviction, civil penalty assessment, or forfeiture of property for any violation of this chapter or any regulation issued hereunder, and (2) the reasonable and necessary costs incurred by any person in providing temporary care for any fish, wildlife, or plant pending the disposition of any civil or criminal proceeding alleging a violation of this chapter with respect to that fish, wildlife, or plant. The amount of the reward, if any, is to be designated by the Secretary or the Secretary of the Treasury, as appropriate. Any officer or employee of the United States or any State or local government who furnishes information or renders service in the performance of his official duties is ineligible for payment under this subsection. Whenever the balance of sums received under this section and section 3375(d) of this title, as penalties or fines, or from forfeitures of property, exceed $500,000, the Secretary of the Treasury shall deposit an amount equal to such excess balance in the cooperative endangered species conservation fund established under section 1535(i) of this title.

* * *

Citizen suits

(g)(1) Except as provided in paragraph (2) of this subsection any person may commence a civil suit on his own behalf—

(A) to enjoin any person, including the United States and any other governmental instrumentality or agency (to the extent permitted by the eleventh amendment to the Constitution), who is alleged to be in violation of any provision of this chapter or regulation issued under the authority thereof; or

(B) to compel the Secretary to apply, pursuant to section 1535(g)(2)(B)(ii) of this title, the prohibitions set forth in or authorized pursuant to section 1533(d) or 1538(a)(1)(B) of this title with respect to the taking of any resident endangered species or threatened species within any State; or

(C) against the Secretary where there is alleged a failure of the Secretary to perform any act or duty under section 1533 of this title which is not discretionary with the Secretary.

The district courts shall have jurisdiction, without regard to the amount in controversy or the citizenship of the parties, to enforce any such provision or regulation, or to order the Secretary to perform such act or duty, as the case may be. In any civil suit commenced under subparagraph (B) the district court shall compel the Secretary to apply the prohibition sought if the court finds that the allegation that an emergency exists is supported by substantial evidence.

(g)(2)(A) No action may be commenced under subparagraph (1)(A) of this section—

(i) prior to sixty days after written notice of the violation has been given to the Secretary, and to any alleged violator of any such provision or regulation;

(ii) if the Secretary has commenced action to impose a penalty pursuant to subsection (a) of this section; or

(iii) if the United States has commenced and is diligently prosecuting a criminal action in a court of the United States or a State to redress a violation of any such provision or regulation.

(g)(2)(B) No action may be commenced under subparagraph (1)(B) of this section—

(i) prior to sixty days after written notice has been given to the Secretary setting forth the reasons why an emergency is thought to exist with respect to an endangered species or a threatened species in the State concerned; or

(ii) if the Secretary has commenced and is diligently prosecuting action under section 1535(g)(2)(B)(ii) of this title to determine whether any such emergency exists.

(g)(2)(C) No action may be commenced under subparagraph (1)(C) of this section prior to sixty days after written notice has been given to the Secretary; except that such action may be brought immediately after such notification in the case of an action under this section respecting an emergency posing a significant risk to the well-being of any species of fish or wildlife or plants.

(g)(3)(A) Any suit under this subsection may be brought in the judicial district in which the violation occurs.

(g)(3)(B) In any such suit under this subsection in which the United States is not a party, the Attorney General, at the request of the Secretary, may intervene on behalf of the United States as a matter of right.

(g)(4) The court, in issuing any final order in any suit brought pursuant to paragraph (1) of this subsection, may award costs of litigation (including reasonable attorney and expert witness fees) to any party, whenever the court determines such award is appropriate.

(g)(5) The injunctive relief provided by this subsection shall not restrict any right which any person (or class of persons) may have under any statute or common law to seek enforcement of any standard or limitation or to seek any other relief (including relief against the Secretary or a State agency).

* * *

Pub.L. 93–205, § 11, Dec. 28, 1973, 87 Stat. 897; as amended Pub.L. 94–359, § 4, July 12, 1976, 90 Stat. 913; Pub.L. 95–632, §§ 6–8, Nov. 10, 1978, 92 Stat. 3761, 3762; Pub.L. 97–79, § 9(e), Nov. 16, 1981, 95 Stat. 1079; Pub.L. 97–304, §§ 7, 9(c), Oct. 13, 1982, 96 Stat. 1425, 1427; as amended Pub.L. 100–478, Title I, § 1007, Oct. 7, 1988, 102 Stat. 2309, Pub.L. 101–650, Title III, § 321, Dec. 1, 1990, 104 Stat. 5117; as amended Pub.L. 107–171, Title X, § 10418(b)(3), May 13, 2002, 116 Stat. 508.

§ **1541.** Endangered plants

The Secretary of the Smithsonian Institution, in conjunction with other affected agencies, is authorized and directed to review (1) species of plants which are now or may become endangered or threatened and (2) methods of adequately conserving such species, and to report to Congress, within one year after December 28, 1973, the results of such review including recommendations for new legislation or the amendment of existing legislation.

Pub.L. 93–205, § 12, Dec. 28, 1973, 87 Stat. 901.

NATIONAL FOREST MANAGEMENT ACT OF 1976
(amending the Forest and Rangeland Renewable Resources Planning Act of 1974)

(16 U.S.C.A. §§ 1600–14)

§ **1600.** Congressional findings

The Congress finds that—

(1) the management of the Nation's renewable resources is highly complex and the uses, demand for, and supply of the various resources are subject to change over time;

(2) the public interest is served by the Forest Service, Department of Agriculture, in cooperation with other agencies, assessing the Na-

tion's renewable resources, and developing and preparing a national renewable resource program, which is periodically reviewed and updated;

(3) to serve the national interest, the renewable resource program must be based on a comprehensive assessment of present and anticipated uses, demand for, and supply of renewable resources from the Nation's public and private forests and rangelands, through analysis of environmental and economic impacts, coordination of multiple use and sustained yield opportunities as provided in the Multiple–Use Sustained–Yield Act of 1960 (74 Stat. 215; 16 U.S.C. 528–531), and public participation in the development of the program;

(4) the new knowledge derived from coordinated public and private research programs will promote a sound technical and ecological base for effective management, use, and protection of the Nation's renewable resources;

(5) inasmuch as the majority of the Nation's forests and rangeland is under private, State, and local governmental management and the Nation's major capacity to produce goods and services is based on these nonfederally managed renewable resources, the Federal Government should be a catalyst to encourage and assist these owners in the efficient long-term use and improvement of these lands and their renewable resources consistent with the principles of sustained yield and multiple use;

(6) the Forest Service, by virtue of its statutory authority for management of the National Forest System, research and cooperative programs, and its role as an agency in the Department of Agriculture, has both a responsibility and an opportunity to be a leader in assuring that the Nation maintains a natural resource conservation posture that will meet the requirements of our people in perpetuity; and

(7) recycled timber product materials are as much a part of our renewable forest resources as are the trees from which they originally came, and in order to extend our timber and timber fiber resources and reduce pressures for timber production from Federal lands, the Forest Service should expand its research in the use of recycled and waste timber product materials, develop techniques for the substitution of these secondary materials for primary materials, and promote and encourage the use of recycled timber product materials.

Pub.L. 93–378, § 2, as added Pub.L. 94–588, § 2, Oct. 22, 1976, 90 Stat. 2949.

§ **1601.** Renewable Resource Assessment

Preparation by Secretary of Agriculture; time of preparation, updating and contents

(a) In recognition of the vital importance of America's renewable resources of the forest, range, and other associated lands to the Nation's social and economic well-being, and of the necessity for a long term perspective in planning and undertaking related national renewable resource programs administered by the Forest Service, the Secretary of Agriculture shall prepare a Renewable Resource Assessment (hereinafter called the "Assessment"). The Assessment shall be prepared not later than December 31, 1975, and shall be updated during 1979 and each tenth year thereafter, and shall include but not be limited to—

(1) an analysis of present and anticipated uses, demand for, and supply of the renewable resources, with consideration of the international resource situation, and an emphasis of pertinent supply and demand and price relationship trends;

(2) an inventory, based on information developed by the Forest Service and other Federal agencies, of present and potential renewable resources, and an evaluation of opportunities for improving their yield of tangible and intangible goods and services, together with estimates of investment costs and direct and indirect returns to the Federal Government;

(3) a description of Forest Service programs and responsibilities in research, cooperative programs and management of the National Forest System, their interrelationships, and the relationship of these programs and responsibilities to public and private activities; and

(4) a discussion of important policy considerations, laws, regulations, and other factors expected to influence and affect significantly the use, ownership, and management of forest, range, and other associated lands.

(5) an analysis of the potential effects of global climate change on the condition of renewable resources on the forests and rangelands of the United States; and

(6) an analysis of the rural and urban forestry opportunities to mitigate the buildup of atmospheric carbon dioxide and reduce the risk of global climate change.

Contents of Assessments

(b) The Secretary shall report in the 1979 and subsequent Assessments on:

(1) the additional fiber potential in the National Forest System including, but not restricted to, forest mortality, growth, salvage potential, potential increased forest products sales, economic constraints, alternate markets, contract considerations, and other multiple use considerations;

(2) the potential for increased utilization of forest and wood product wastes in the National Forest System and on other lands, and of urban wood wastes and wood product recycling, including recommendations to the Congress for actions which would lead to increased utilization of material now being wasted both in the forests and in manufactured products; and

(3) the milling and other wood fiber product fabrication facilities and their location in the United States, noting the public and private forested areas that supply such facilities, assessing the degree of

utilization into product form of harvested trees by such facilities, and setting forth the technology appropriate to the facilities to improve utilization either individually or in aggregate units of harvested trees and to reduce wasted wood fibers. The Secretary shall set forth a program to encourage the adoption by these facilities of these technologies for improving wood fiber utilization.

Public involvement; consultation with governmental departments and agencies

(c) In developing the reports required under subsection (b) of this section, the Secretary shall provide opportunity for public involvement and shall consult with other interested governmental departments and agencies.

Congressional policy of multiple use sustained yield management; examination and certification of lands; estimate of appropriations necessary for reforestation and other treatment; budget requirements; authorization of appropriations

(d)(1) It is the policy of the Congress that all forested lands in the National Forest System shall be maintained in appropriate forest cover with species of trees, degree of stocking, rate of growth, and conditions of stand designed to secure the maximum benefits of multiple use sustained yield management in accordance with land management plans. Accordingly, the Secretary is directed to identify and report to the Congress annually at the time of submission of the President's budget together with the annual report provided for under section 1606(c) of this title, beginning with submission of the President's budget for fiscal year 1978, the amount and location by forests and States and by productivity class, where practicable, of all lands in the National Forest System where objectives of land management plans indicate the need to reforest areas that have been cutover or otherwise denuded or deforested, and all lands with stands of trees that are not growing at their best potential rate of growth. All national forest lands treated from year to year shall be examined after the first and third growing seasons and certified by the Secretary in the report provided for under this subsection as to stocking rate, growth rate in relation to potential and other pertinent measures. Any lands not certified as satisfactory shall be returned to the backlog and scheduled for prompt treatment. The level and types of treatment shall be those which secure the most effective mix of multiple use benefits.

(d)(2) Notwithstanding the provisions of section 1607 of this title, the Secretary shall annually for eight years following October 22, 1976, transmit to the Congress in the manner provided in this subsection an estimate of the sums necessary to be appropriated, in addition to the funds available from other sources, to replant and otherwise treat an acreage equal to the acreage to be cut over that year, plus a sufficient portion of the backlog of lands found to be in need of treatment to eliminate the backlog within the eight-year period. After such eight-year period, the Secretary shall transmit annually to the Congress an estimate of the sums necessary to replant and otherwise treat all lands being cut over and maintain planned timber production on all other forested lands in the National Forest System so as to prevent the development of a backlog of needed work larger than the needed work at the beginning of the fiscal year. The Secretary's estimate of sums necessary, in addition to the sums available under other authorities, for accomplishment of the reforestation and other treatment of National Forest System lands under this section shall be provided annually for inclusion in the President's budget and shall also be transmitted to the Speaker of the House and the President of the Senate together with the annual report provided for under section 1606(c) of this title at the time of submission of the President's budget to the Congress beginning with the budget for fiscal year 1978. The sums estimated as necessary for reforestation and other treatment shall include moneys needed to secure seed, grow seedlings, prepare sites, plant trees, thin, remove deleterious growth and underbrush, build fence to exclude livestock and adverse wildlife from regeneration areas and otherwise establish and improve growing forests to secure planned production of trees and other multiple use values.

* * *

Report on herbicides and pesticides

(e) The Secretary shall submit an annual report to the Congress on the amounts, types, and uses of herbicides and pesticides used in the National Forest System, including the beneficial or adverse effects of such uses.

Pub.L. 93–378, § 3(a), (c)(e), formerly § 2(a), Aug. 17, 1974, 88 Stat. 476, renumbered and amended Pub.L. 94–588, §§ 2–4, Oct. 22, 1976, 90 Stat. 2949, 2950; Pub.L. 101–624, Title XXIV, § 2408(a), Nov. 28, 1990, 104 Stat. 4061.

§ 1602. Renewable Resource Program; preparation by Secretary of Agriculture and transmittal to President; purpose and development of program; time of preparation, updating and contents

In order to provide for periodic review of programs for management and administration of the National Forest System, for research, for cooperative State and private Forest Service programs, and for conduct of other Forest Service activities in relation to the findings of the Assessment, the Secretary of Agriculture, utilizing information available to the Forest Service and other agencies within the Department of Agriculture, including data prepared pursuant to section 1010a of Title 7, shall prepare and transmit to the President a recommended Renewable Resource Program (hereinafter called the "Program"). The Program transmitted to the President may include alternatives, and shall provide in appropriate detail for protection, management, and development of the National Forest System, including forest development roads and trails; for cooperative Forest Service programs; and for research. The Programs shall be developed in accordance with principles set forth in the Multiple–Use Sustained–Yield Act of June 12, 1960 (74 Stat. 215; 16 U.S.C. 528–531), and the National Environmental Policy Act of 1969 (83 Stat. 852) [42 U.S.C.A. § 4321 et seq.]. The Program shall be prepared not later than December 31, 1975, to cover the four-year period beginning October 1, 1976, and at least each of the four fiscal decades next following such period, and shall be updated no later than during the first half of the fiscal year ending September 30, 1980, and the first half of each fifth fiscal year thereafter to cover at least each of the four fiscal decades beginning next after such updating. The Program shall include, but not be limited to—

(1) an inventory of specific needs and opportunities for both public and private program investments. The inventory shall differentiate between activities which are of a capital nature and those which are of an operational nature;

(2) specific identification of Program outputs, results anticipated, and benefits associated with investments in such a manner that the anticipated costs can be directly compared with the total related benefits and direct and indirect returns to the Federal Government;

(3) a discussion of priorities for accomplishment of inventoried Program opportunities, with specified costs, outputs, results, and benefits;

(4) a detailed study of personnel requirements as needed to implement and monitor existing and ongoing programs; and

(5) Program recommendations which—

(A) evaluate objectives for the major Forest Service programs in order that multiple-use and sustained-yield relationships among and within the renewable resources can be determined;

(B) explain the opportunities for owners of forests and rangeland to participate in programs to improve and enhance the condition of the land and the renewable resource products therefrom;

(C) recognize the fundamental need to protect and, where appropriate, improve the quality of soil, water, and air resources;

(D) state national goals that recognize the interrelationships between and interdependence within the renewable resources;

(E) evaluate the impact of the export and import of raw logs upon domestic timber supplies and prices; and

(F) account for the effects of global climate change on forest and rangeland conditions, including potential effects on the geographic ranges of species, and on forest and rangeland products.

Pub.L. 93–378, § 4, formerly § 3, Aug. 17, 1974, 88 Stat. 477, renumbered and amended Pub.L. 94–588, §§ 2, 5, Oct. 22, 1976, 90 Stat. 2949, 2951; amended Pub.L. 101–624, Title XXIV, § 2408(b), Nov. 28, 1990, 104 Stat. 4061.

§ 1603. National Forest System resource inventories; development, maintenance, and updating by Secretary of Agriculture as part of Assessment

As a part of the Assessment, the Secretary of Agriculture shall develop and maintain on a continuing basis a comprehensive and appropriately detailed inventory of all National Forest System lands and renewable resources. This inventory shall be kept current so as to reflect changes in conditions and identify new and emerging resources and values.

Pub.L. 93–378, § 5, formerly § 4, Aug. 17, 1974, 88 Stat. 477, renumbered Pub.L. 94–588, § 2, Oct. 22, 1976, 90 Stat. 2949.

§ 1604. National Forest System land and resource management plans

Development, maintenance, and revision by Secretary of Agriculture as part of Program; coordination

(a) As a part of the Program provided for by section 1602 of this title, the Secretary of Agriculture shall develop, maintain, and, as appropriate, revise land and resource management plans for units of the National Forest System, coordinated with the land and resource management planning processes of State and local governments and other Federal agencies.

Criteria

(b) In the development and maintenance of land management plans for use on units of the National Forest System, the Secretary shall use a systematic interdisciplinary approach to achieve integrated consideration of physical, biological, economic, and other sciences.

Incorporation of standards and guidelines by Secretary; time of completion; progress reports; existing management plans

(c) The Secretary shall begin to incorporate the standards and guidelines required by this section in plans for units of the National Forest System as soon as practicable after October 22, 1976, and shall attempt to complete such incorporation for all such units by no later than September 30, 1985. The Secretary shall report to the Congress on the progress of such incorporation in the annual report required by section 1606(c) of this title. Until such time as a unit of the National Forest System is managed under plans developed in accordance with this subchapter, the management of such unit may continue under existing land and resource management plans.

Public participation in management plans; availability of plans; public meetings

(d) The Secretary shall provide for public participation in the development, review, and revision of land management plans including, but not limited to, making the plans or revisions available to the public at convenient locations in the vicinity of the affected unit for a period of at least three months before final adoption, during which period the Secretary shall publicize and hold public meetings or comparable processes at locations that foster public participation in the review of such plans or revisions.

Required assurances

(e) In developing, maintaining, and revising plans for units of the National Forest System pursuant to this section, the Secretary shall assure that such plans—

(1) provide for multiple use and sustained yield of the products and services obtained therefrom in accordance with the Multiple–Use Sustained–Yield Act of 1960 [16 U.S.C.A. §§ 528–531], and, in particular, include coordination of outdoor recreation, range, timber, watershed, wildlife and fish, and wilderness; and

(2) determine forest management systems, harvesting levels, and procedures in the light of all of the uses set forth in subsection (c)(1) of this section, the definition of the terms "multiple use" and "sustained yield" as provided in the Multiple–Use Sustained–Yield Act of 1960, and the availability of lands and their suitability for resource management.

Required provisions

(f) Plans developed in accordance with this section shall—

(1) form one integrated plan for each unit of the National Forest System, incorporating in one document or one set of documents, available to the public at convenient locations, all of the features required by this section;

(2) be embodied in appropriate written material, including maps and other descriptive documents, reflecting proposed and possible actions, including the planned timber sale program and the proportion of probable methods of timber harvest within the unit necessary to fulfill the plan;

(3) be prepared by an interdisciplinary team. Each team shall prepare its plan based on inventories of the applicable resources of the forest;

(4) be amended in any manner whatsoever after final adoption after public notice, and, if such amendment would result in a significant change in such plan, in accordance with the provisions of subsections (e) and (f) of this section and public involvement comparable to that required by subsection (d) of this section; and

(5) be revised (A) from time to time when the Secretary finds conditions in a unit have significantly changed, but at least every fifteen years, and (B) in accordance with the provisions of subsections (e) and (f) of this section and public involvement comparable to that required by subsection (d) of this section.

Promulgation of regulations for development and revision of plans; environmental considerations; resource management guidelines; guidelines for land management plans

(g) As soon as practicable, but not later than two years after October 22, 1976, the Secretary shall in accordance with the procedures set forth in section 553 of Title 5, promulgate regulations, under the principles of the Multiple–Use Sustained–Yield Act of 1960 [16 U.S.C.A. §§ 528–531], that set out the process for the development and revision of the land management plans, and the guidelines and standards prescribed by this subsection. The regulations shall include, but not be limited to—

186

(1) specifying procedures to insure that land management plans are prepared in accordance with the National Environmental Policy Act of 1969 [42 U.S.C.A. § 4321 et seq.], including, but not limited to, direction on when and for what plans an environmental impact statement required under section 102(2)(C) of that Act [42 U.S.C.A. § 4332(2)(C)] shall be prepared;

(2) specifying guidelines which—

(A) require the identification of the suitability of lands for resource management;

(B) provide for obtaining inventory data on the various renewable resources, and soil and water, including pertinent maps, graphic material, and explanatory aids; and

(C) provide for methods to identify special conditions or situations involving hazards to the various resources and their relationship to alternative activities;

(3) specifying guidelines for land management plans developed to achieve the goals of the Program which—

(A) insure consideration of the economic and environmental aspects of various systems of renewable resource management, including the related systems of silviculture and protection of forest resources, to provide for outdoor recreation (including wilderness), range, timber, watershed, wildlife, and fish;

(B) provide for diversity of plant and animal communities based on the suitability and capability of the specific land area in order to meet overall multiple-use objectives, and within the multiple-use objectives of a land management plan adopted pursuant to this section, provide, where appropriate, to the degree practicable, for steps to be taken to preserve the diversity of tree species similar to that existing in the region controlled by the plan;

(C) insure research on and (based on continuous monitoring and assessment in the field) evaluation of the effects of each management system to the end that it will not produce substantial and permanent impairment of the productivity of the land;

(D) permit increases in harvest levels based on intensified management practices, such as reforestation, thinning, and tree improvement if (i) such practices justify increasing the harvests in accordance with the Multiple–Use Sustained–Yield Act of 1960, and (ii) such harvest levels are decreased at the end of each planning period if such practices cannot be successfully implemented or funds are not received to permit such practices to continue substantially as planned;

(E) insure that timber will be harvested from National Forest System lands only where—

(i) soil, slope, or other watershed conditions will not be irreversibly damaged;

(ii) there is assurance that such lands can be adequately restocked within five years after harvest;

(iii) protection is provided for streams, streambanks, shorelines, lakes, wetlands, and other bodies of water from detrimental changes in water temperatures, blockages of water courses, and deposits of sediment, where harvests are likely to seriously and adversely affect water conditions or fish habitat; and

(iv) the harvesting system to be used is not selected primarily because it will give the greatest dollar return or the greatest unit output of timber; and

(F) insure that clearcutting, seed tree cutting, shelterwood cutting, and other cuts designed to regenerate an even-aged stand of timber will be used as a cutting method on National Forest System lands only where—

(i) for clearcutting, it is determined to be the optimum method, and for other such cuts it is determined to be appropriate, to meet the objectives and requirements of the relevant land management plan;

(ii) the interdisciplinary review as determined by the Secretary has been completed and the potential environmental, biological, esthetic, engineering, and economic impacts on each advertised sale area have been assessed, as well as the consistency of the sale with the multiple use of the general area;

(iii) cut blocks, patches, or strips are shaped and blended to the extent practicable with the natural terrain;

(iv) there are established according to geographic areas, forest types, or other suitable classifications the maximum size limits for areas to be cut in one harvest operation, including provision to exceed the established limits after appropriate public notice and review by the responsible Forest Service officer one level above the Forest Service officer who normally would approve the harvest proposal: *Provided,* That such limits shall not apply to the size of areas harvested as a result of natural catastrophic conditions such as fire, insect and disease attack, or windstorms; and

(v) such cuts are carried out in a manner consistent with the protection of soil, watershed, fish, wildlife, recreation, and esthetic resources, and the regeneration of the timber resource.

Scientific committee to aid in promulgation of regulations; termination; revision committees; clerical and technical assistance; compensation of committee members

(h)(1) In carrying out the purposes of subsection (g) of this section, the Secretary of Agriculture shall appoint a committee of scientists who are not officers or employees of the Forest Service. The committee shall provide scientific and technical advice and counsel on proposed guidelines and procedures to assure that an effective interdisciplinary approach is proposed and adopted. The committee shall terminate upon promulgation of the regulations, but the Secretary may, from time to time, appoint similar committees when considering revisions of the regulations. The views of the committees shall be included in the public information supplied when the regulations are proposed for adoption.

(h)(2) Clerical and technical assistance, as may be necessary to discharge the duties of the committee, shall be provided from the personnel of the Department of Agriculture.

* * *

Consistency of resource plans, permits, contracts, and other instruments with land management plans; revision

(i) Resource plans and permits, contracts, and other instruments for the use and occupancy of National Forest System lands shall be consistent with the land management plans. Those resource plans and permits, contracts, and other such instruments currently in existence shall be revised as soon as practicable to be made consistent with such plans. When land management plans are revised, resource plans and permits, contracts, and other instruments, when necessary, shall be revised as soon as practicable. Any revision in present or future permits, contracts, and other instruments made pursuant to this section shall be subject to valid existing rights.

Effective date of land management plans and revisions

(j) Land management plans and revisions shall become effective thirty days after completion of public participation and publication of notification by the Secretary as required under subsection (d) of this section.

Development of land management plans

(k) In developing land management plans pursuant to this subchapter, the Secretary shall identify lands within the management area which are not suited for timber production, considering physical, economic, and other pertinent factors to the extent feasible, as determined by the Secretary, and shall assure that, except for salvage sales or sales necessitated to protect other multiple-use values, no timber harvesting shall occur on such lands for a period of 10 years. Lands once identified as unsuitable for timber production shall continue to be treated for reforestation purposes, particularly with regard to the protection of other multiple-use values. The Secretary shall review his decision to classify these lands as not suited for timber production at least every 10 years and shall return these lands to timber production whenever he determines that conditions have changed so that they have become suitable for timber production.

Program evaluation; process for estimating long-term costs and benefits; summary of data included in annual report

(*l*) Program evaluation; process for estimating long-term costs and benefits; summary of data included in annual report

The Secretary shall—

(1) formulate and implement, as soon as practicable, a process for estimating long-terms costs and benefits to support the program evaluation requirements of this subchapter. This process shall include

requirements to provide information on a representative sample basis of estimated expenditures associated with the reforestation, timber stand improvement, and sale of timber from the National Forest System, and shall provide a comparison of these expenditures to the return to the Government resulting from the sale of timber; and

(2) include a summary of data and findings resulting from these estimates as a part of the annual report required pursuant to section 1606(c) of this title, including an identification on a representative sample basis of those advertised timber sales made below the estimated expenditures for such timber as determined by the above cost process; and [sic, in original. The "; and" probably should be a period.]

Establishment of standards to ensure culmination of mean annual increment of growth; silvicultural practices; salvage harvesting; exceptions

(m) The Secretary shall establish—

(1) standards to insure that, prior to harvest, stands of trees throughout the National Forest System shall generally have reached the culmination of mean annual increment of growth (calculated on the basis of cubic measurement or other methods of calculation at the discretion of the Secretary): *Provided,* That these standards shall not preclude the use of sound silvicultural practices, such as thinning or other stand improvement measures: *Provided further,* That these standards shall not preclude the Secretary from salvage or sanitation harvesting of timber stands which are substantially damaged by fire, windthrow or other catastrophe, or which are in imminent danger from insect or disease attack; and

(2) exceptions to these standards for the harvest of particular species of trees in management units after consideration has been given to the multiple uses of the forest including, but not limited to, recreation, wildlife habitat, and range and after completion of public participation processes utilizing the procedures of subsection (d) of this section.

Pub.L. 93–378, § 6, formerly § 5, Aug. 17, 1974, 88 Stat. 477, renumbered and amended Pub.L. 94–588, §§ 2, 6, 12(a), Oct. 22, 1976, 90 Stat. 2949, 2952, 2958.

* * *

§ 1606.   Budget requests by President for Forest Service activities

Transmittal to Speaker of House and President of Senate of Assessment, Program and Statement of Policy used in framing requests; time for transmittal; implementation by President of programs established under Statement of Policy unless Statement subsequently disapproved by Congress; time for disapproval

(a) On the date Congress first convenes in 1976 and thereafter following each updating of the Assessment and the Program, the President shall transmit to the Speaker of the House of Representatives and the President of the Senate, when Congress convenes, the Assessment as set forth in section 1601 of this title and the Program as set forth in section 1602 of this title, together with a detailed Statement of Policy intended to be used in framing budget requests by that Administration for Forest Service activities for the five-or ten-year program period beginning during the term of such Congress for such further action deemed appropriate by the Congress. Following the transmission of such Assessment, Program, and Statement of Policy, the President shall, subject to other actions of the Congress, carry out programs already established by law in accordance with such Statement of Policy or any subsequent amendment or modification thereof approved by the Congress, unless, before the end of the first period of ninety calendar days of continuous session of Congress after the date on which the President of the Senate and the Speaker of the House are recipients of the transmission of such Assessment, Program, and Statement of Policy, either House adopts a resolution reported by the appropriate committee of jurisdiction disapproving the Statement of Policy. For the purpose of this subsection, the continuity of a session shall be deemed to be broken only by an adjournment sine die, and the days on which either House is not in session because of an adjournment of more than three days to a day certain shall be excluded in the computation of the ninety-day period. Notwithstanding any other provision of this subchapter, Congress may revise or modify the Statement of Policy transmitted by the President, and the revised or modified Statement of Policy shall be used in framing budget requests.

Contents of requests to show extent of compliance of projected programs and policies with policies approved by Congress; requests not conforming to approved policies; expenditure of appropriations

(b) Commencing with the fiscal budget for the year ending September 30, 1977, requests presented by the President to the Congress governing Forest Service activities shall express in qualitative and quantitative terms the extent to which the programs and policies projected under the budget meet the policies approved by the Congress in accordance with subsection (a) of this section. In any case in which such budget so presented recommends a course which fails to meet the policies so established, the President shall specifically set forth the reason or reasons for requesting the Congress to approve the lesser programs or policies presented. Amounts appropriated to carry out the policies approved in accordance with subsection (a) of this section shall be expended in accordance with the Congressional Budget and Impoundment Control Act of 1974.

Annual evaluation report to Congress of Program components; time of submission; status of major research programs; application of findings; status, etc., of cooperative forestry assistance programs and activities

(c) For the purpose of providing information that will aid Congress in its oversight responsibilities and improve the accountability of agency expenditures and activities, the Secretary of Agriculture shall prepare an annual report which evaluates the component elements of the Program required to be prepared by section 1602 of this title which shall be furnished to the Congress at the time of submission of the annual fiscal budget commencing with the third fiscal year after August 17, 1974. With regard to the research component of the program, the report shall include, but not be limited to, a description of the status of major research programs, significant findings, and how these findings will be applied in National Forest System management and in cooperative State and private Forest Service programs. With regard to the cooperative forestry assistance part of the Program, the report shall include, but not be limited to, a description of the status, accomplishments, needs, and work backlogs for the programs and activities conducted under the Cooperative Forestry Assistance Act of 1978 [16 U.S.C.A. § 2101 et seq.].

Required contents of annual evaluation report

(d) These annual evaluation reports shall set forth progress in implementing the Program required to be prepared by section 1602 of this title, together with accomplishments of the Program as they relate to the objectives of the Assessment. Objectives should be set forth in qualitative and quantitative terms and accomplishments should be reported accordingly. The report shall contain appropriate measurements of pertinent costs and benefits. The evaluation shall assess the balance between economic factors and environmental quality factors. Program benefits shall include, but not be limited to, environmental quality factors such as esthetics, public access, wildlife habitat, recreational and wilderness use, and economic factors such as the excess of cost savings over the value of foregone benefits and the rate of return on renewable resources.

Additional required contents of annual evaluation report

(e) The reports shall indicate plans for implementing corrective action and recommendations for new legislation where warranted.

Form of annual evaluation report

(f) The reports shall be structured for Congress in concise summary form with necessary detailed data in appendices.

Pub.L. 93–378, § 8, formerly § 7, Aug. 17, 1974, 88 Stat. 478, renumbered and amended Pub.L. 94–588, §§ 2, 7, 12(b), Oct. 22, 1976, 90 Stat. 2949, 2956, 2958; Pub.L. 95–313, § 12, July 1, 1978, 92 Stat. 374, renumbered Pub.L. 101–624, Title XII, § 1215(1), Nov. 28, 1990, 104 Stat. 3525.

§ 1606a. Reforestation Trust Fund

Establishment; source of funds

(a) There is established in the Treasury of the United States a trust fund, to be known as the Reforestation Trust Fund (hereinafter in this section referred to as the "Trust Fund"), consisting of such amounts as are transferred to the Trust Fund under subsection (b)(1) of this section and any interest earned on investment of amounts in the Trust Fund under subsection (c)(2) of this section.

* * *

Pub.L. 96–451, Title Ill, § 303, Oct. 14, 1980, 94 Stat. 1991, amended Pub.L. 97–258, § 4(b), Sept. 13, 1982, 96 Stat. 1067; Pub.L. 97–424, Title IV, § 422, Jan. 6, 1983, 96 Stat. 2164, as amended, Pub.L. 99–190, § 101(d)[Title II, § 201], Dec. 19, 1985, 99 Stat. 1245; Pub.L. 100–418, Title I, § 1214(r), Aug. 23, 1988, 102 Stat. 1160; Pub.L. 105–83, Title III, § 322, Nov. 14, 1997, 111 Stat. 1596.

§ **1607.** National Forest System renewable resources; development and administration by Secretary of Agriculture in accordance with multiple use and sustained yield concepts for products and services; target year for operational posture of resources; budget requests

The Secretary of Agriculture shall take such action as will assure that the development and administration of the renewable resources of the National Forest System are in full accord with the concepts for multiple use and sustained yield of products and services as set forth in the Multiple–Use Sustained–Yield Act of 1960 [16 U.S.C.A. §§ 528–531]. To further these concepts, the Congress hereby sets the year 2000 as the target year when the renewable resources of the National Forest System shall be in an operating posture whereby all backlogs of needed treatment for their restoration shall be reduced to a current basis and the major portion of planned intensive multiple-use sustained-yield management procedures shall be installed and operating on an environmentally-sound basis. The annual budget shall contain requests for funds for an orderly program to eliminate such backlogs: *Provided,* That when the Secretary finds that (1) the backlog of areas that will benefit by such treatment has been eliminated, (2) the cost of treating the remainder of such area exceeds the economic and environmental benefits to be secured from their treatment, or (3) the total supplies of the renewable resources of the United States are adequate to meet the future needs of the American people, the budget request for these elements of restoration may be adjusted accordingly.

Pub.L. 93–378, § 9, formerly § 8, Aug. 17, 1974, 88 Stat. 479, renumbered Pub.L. 94–588, § 2, Oct. 22, 1976, 90 Stat. 2949.

§ **1608.** National Forest Transportation System

Congressional declaration of policy; time for development; method of financing; financing of forest development roads

(a) The Congress declares that the installation of a proper system of transportation to service the National Forest System, as is provided for in sections 532 to 538 of this title, shall be carried forward in time to meet anticipated needs on an economical and environmentally sound basis, and the method chosen for financing the construction and maintenance of the transportation system should be such as to enhance local, regional, and national benefits: *Provided,* That limitations on the level of obligations for construction of forest roads by timber purchasers shall be established in annual appropriation Acts.

Construction of temporary roadways in connection with timber contracts, and other permits or leases

(b) Unless the necessity for a permanent road is set forth in the forest development road system plan, any road constructed on land of the National Forest System in connection with a timber contract or other permit or lease shall be designed with the goal of reestablishing vegetative cover on the roadway and areas where the vegetative cover has been disturbed by the construction of the road, within ten years after the termination of the contract, permit, or lease either through artificial or natural means. Such action shall be taken unless it is later determined that the road is needed for use as a part of the National Forest Transportation System.

Standards of roadway construction

(c) Roads constructed on National Forest System lands shall be designed to standards appropriate for the intended uses, considering safety, cost of transportation, and impacts on land and resources.

Pub.L. 93–378, § 10, formerly § 9, Aug. 17, 1974, 88 Stat. 479; renumbered and amended Pub.L. 94–588, §§ 2, 8, Oct. 22, 1976, 90 Stat. 2949, 2956; Pub.L. 97–100, Title II, § 200, Dec. 23, 1981, 95 Stat. 1405.

§ 1609. National Forest System; Congressional declaration of constituent elements and purposes; lands etc., included within; return of lands to public domain; location of Forest Service offices

(a) Congress declares that the National Forest System consists of units of federally owned forest, range, and related lands throughout the United States and its territories, united into a nationally significant system dedicated to the long-term benefit for present and future generations, and that it is the purpose of this section to include all such areas into one integral system. The "National Forest System" shall include all national forest lands reserved or withdrawn from the public domain of the United States, all national forest lands acquired through purchase, exchange, donation, or other means, the national grasslands and land utilization projects administered under title III of the Bankhead–Jones Farm Tenant Act [7 U.S.C.A. § 1010 et seq.], and other lands, waters, or interests therein which are administered by the Forest Service or are designated for administration through the Forest Service as a part of the system. Notwithstanding the provisions of section 473 of this title, no land now or hereafter reserved or withdrawn from the public domain as national forests pursuant to section 471 of this title, or any act supplementary to and amendatory thereof, shall be returned to the public domain except by an act of Congress.

(b) The on-the-ground field offices, field supervisory offices, and regional offices of the Forest Service shall be so situated as to provide the optimum level of convenient, useful services to the public, giving priority to the maintenance and location of facilities in rural areas and towns near the national forest and Forest Service program locations in accordance with the standards in section 3122(b) of Title 42.

Pub.L. 93–378, § 11, formerly § 10, Aug. 17, 1974, 88 Stat. 480, renumbered and amended Pub.L. 94–588, §§ 2, 9, Oct. 22, 1976, 90 Stat. 2949, 2957.

§ 1610. Implementation of provisions by Secretary of Agriculture; utilization of information and data of other organizations; avoidance of duplication of planning, etc., definition of "renewable resource"

In carrying out this subchapter, the Secretary of Agriculture shall utilize information and data available from other Federal, State, and private organizations and shall avoid duplication and overlap of resource assessment and program planning efforts of other Federal agencies. The term "renewable resources" shall be construed to involve those matters within the scope of responsibilities and authorities of the Forest Service on August 17, 1974 and on the date of enactment of any legislation amendatory or supplementary thereto.

Pub.L. 93–378, § 12, formerly § 11, Aug. 17, 1974, 88 Stat. 480, renumbered and amended Pub.L. 94–588, §§ 2, 10, Oct. 22, 1976, 90 Stat. 2949, 2957.

§ 1611. Limitations on timber removal; variations in allow able sale quantity; public participation; salvage harvesting

(a) The Secretary of Agriculture shall limit the sale of timber from each national forest to a quantity equal to or less than a quantity which can be removed from such forest annually in perpetuity on a sustained-yield basis: *Provided,* That, in order to meet overall multiple-use objectives, the Secretary may establish an allowable sale quantity for any decade which departs from the projected long-term average sale quantity that would otherwise be established: *Provided further,* That any such planned departure must be consistent with the multiple-use management objectives of the land management plan. Plans for variations in the allowable sale quantity must be made with public participation as required by section 1604(d) of this title. In addition, within any decade, the Secretary may sell a quantity in excess of the annual allowable sale quantity established pursuant to this section in the case of any national forest so long as the average sale quantities of timber from such national forest over the decade covered by the plan do not exceed such quantity limitation. In those cases where a forest has less than two hundred thousand acres of commercial forest land, the Secretary may use two or more forests for purposes of determining the sustained yield.

(b) Nothing in subsection (a) of this section shall prohibit the Secretary from salvage or sanitation harvesting of timber stands which are substantially damaged by fire, windthrow, or other catastrophe, or which are in imminent danger from insect or disease attack. The Secretary may either substitute such timber for timber that would otherwise be sold under the plan or, if not feasible, sell such timber over and above the plan volume.

Pub.L. 93–378, § 13, as added Pub.L. 94–588, § 11, Oct. 22, 1976, 90 Stat. 2957.

§ 1612. Public participation and advisory boards; functions; membership

(a) In exercising his authorities under this subchapter and other laws applicable to the Forest Service, the Secretary, by regulation, shall establish procedures, including public hearings where appropriate, to give the Federal, State, and local governments and the public adequate notice and an opportunity to comment upon the formulation of standards, criteria, and guidelines applicable to Forest Service programs.

(b) In providing for public participation in the planning for and management of the National Forest System, the Secretary, pursuant to the Federal Advisory Committee Act (86 Stat. 770) and other applicable law, shall establish and consult such advisory boards as he deems necessary to secure full information and advice on the execution of his responsibilities. The membership of such beards shall be representative of a cross section of groups interested in the planning for and management of the National Forest System and the various types of use and enjoyment of the lands thereof.

Pub.L. 93–378, § 14, as added Pub.L. 94–588, § 11, Oct. 22, 1976, 90 Stat. 2958.

§ 1613. Promulgation of regulations

The Secretary of Agriculture shall prescribe such regulations as he determines necessary and desirable to carry out the provisions of this subchapter.

Pub.L. 93–378, § 15, as added Pub.L. 94–588, § 11, Oct. 22, 1976, 90 Stat. 2958.

§ 1614. Severability of provisions

If any provision of this subchapter or the application thereof to any person or circumstances is held invalid, the validity of the remainder of this subchapter and of the application of such provision to other persons and circumstances shall not be affected thereby.

Pub.L. 93–378, § 16, as added Pub.L. 94–588, § 11, Oct. 22, 1976, 90 Stat. 2958.

NATIONAL PARK MINING REGULATION ACT OF 1976

(16 U.S.C.A. §§ 1901–12)

§ 1901.   Congressional findings and declaration of policy

The Congress finds and declares that—

(a) the level of technology of mineral exploration and development has changed radically in recent years and continued application of the mining laws of the United States to those areas of the National Park System to which it applies, conflicts with the purposes for which they were established; and

(b) all mining operations in areas of the National Park System should be conducted so as to prevent or minimize damage to the environment and other resource values, and, in certain areas of the National Park System, surface disturbance from mineral development should be temporarily halted while Congress determines whether or not to acquire any valid mineral rights which may exist in such areas.

Pub.L. 94–429, § 1, Sept. 28, 1976, 90 Stat. 1342.

§ 1902.   Preservation and management of areas by Secretary of Interior; promulgation of regulations

In order to preserve for the benefit of present and future generations the pristine beauty of areas of the National Park System, and to further the purposes of sections 1, and 2 to 4 of this title, as amended, and the individual organic Acts for the various areas of the National Park System, all activities resulting from the exercise of valid existing mineral rights on patented or unpatented mining claims within any area of the National Park System shall be subject to such regulations prescribed by the Secretary of the Interior as he deems necessary or desirable for the preservation and management of those areas.

Pub.L. 94–429, § 2, Sept. 28, 1976, 90 Stat. 1342.

* * *

§ 1907.   Recordation of mining claims; publication of notice

All mining claims under the Mining Law of 1872, as amended and supplemented (30 U.S.C. chapters 2, 12A, and 16 and sections 161 and 162) which lie within the boundaries of units of the National Park System shall be recorded with the Secretary of the Interior within one year after September 28, 1976. Any mining claim not so recorded shall be conclusively presumed to be abandoned and shall be void. Such recordation will not render valid any claim which was not valid on September 28, 1976, or which becomes invalid thereafter. Within thirty days following September

28, 1976, the Secretary shall publish notice of the requirement for such recordation in the Federal Register. * * *

Pub.L. 94–429, § 8, Sept. 28, 1976, 90 Stat. 1343.

§ 1908. Damage to natural and historical landmarks; procedures for determination and enforcement of abatement of damaging activities

(a) Whenever the Secretary of the Interior finds on his own motion or upon being notified in writing by an appropriate scientific, historical, or archeological authority, that a district, site, building, structure, or object which has been found to be nationally significant in illustrating natural history or the history of the United States and which has been designated as a natural or historical landmark may be irreparably lost or destroyed in whole or in part by any surface mining activity, including exploration for or removal or production of minerals or materials, he shall notify the person conducting such activity and submit a report thereon, including the basis for his finding that such activity may cause irreparable loss or destruction of a national landmark, to the Advisory Council on Historic Preservation, with a request for advice of the Council as to alternative measures that may be taken by the United States to mitigate or abate such activity.

* * *

Pub.L. 94–429, § 9, Sept. 28, 1976, 90 Stat. 1343.

* * *

§ 1910. Civil actions for just compensation by mining claim holders

The holder of any patented or unpatented mining claim subject to this chapter who believes he has suffered a loss by operation of this chapter, or by orders or regulations issued pursuant thereto, may bring an action in a United States district court to recover just compensation, which shall be awarded if the court finds that such loss constitutes a taking of property compensable under the Constitution.

Pub.L. 94–429, § 11, Sept. 28, 1976, 90 Stat. 1344; Pub.L. 98–620, Title IV, § 402(21), Nov. 8, 1984, 98 Stat. 3358.

§ 1911. Acquisition of land by Secretary

Nothing in this chapter shall be construed to limit the authority of the Secretary to acquire lands and interests in lands within the boundaries of any unit of the National Park System. The Secretary is to give prompt and careful consideration to any offer made by the owner of any valid right or other property within the areas named in section 1905 of this title to sell such right or other property, if such owner notifies the Secretary that the continued ownership of such right or property is causing, or would result in, undue hardship.

Pub.L. 94–429, § 12, Sept. 28, 1976, 90 Stat. 1344.

* * *

ALASKA NATIONAL INTEREST LANDS CONSERVATION ACT OF 1980

(16 U.S.C.A. §§ 3101–3233)

SUBCHAPTER I—GENERAL PROVISIONS

§ 3101. Congressional statement of purpose

(a) In order to preserve for the benefit, use, education, and inspiration of present and future generations certain lands and waters in the State of Alaska that contain nationally significant natural, scenic, historic, archeological, geological, scientific, wilderness, cultural, recreational, and wildlife values, the units described in the following titles are hereby established.

(b) It is the intent of Congress in this Act to preserve unrivaled scenic and geological values associated with natural landscapes; to provide for the maintenance of sound populations of, and habitat for, wildlife species of inestimable value to the citizens of Alaska and the Nation, including those species dependent on vast relatively undeveloped areas; to preserve in their natural state extensive unaltered arctic tundra, boreal forest, and coastal rainforest ecosystems; to protect the resources related to subsistence needs; to protect and preserve historic and archeological sites, rivers, and lands, and to preserve wilderness resource values and related recreational opportunities including but not limited to hiking, canoeing, fishing, and sport hunting, within large arctic and subarctic wildlands and on freeflowing rivers; and to maintain opportunities for scientific research and undisturbed ecosystems.

(c) It is further the intent and purpose of this Act consistent with management of fish and wildlife in accordance with recognized scientific principles and the purposes for which each conservation system unit is established, designated, or expanded by or pursuant to this Act, to provide the opportunity for rural residents engaged in a subsistence way of life to continue to do so.

(d) This Act provides sufficient protection for the national interest in the scenic, natural, cultural and environmental values on the public lands in Alaska, and at the same time provides adequate opportunity for satisfaction of the economic and social needs of the State of Alaska and its people; accordingly, the designation and disposition of the public lands in Alaska pursuant to this Act are found to represent a proper balance between the reservation of national conservation system units and those public lands necessary and appropriate for more intensive use and disposition, and thus Congress believes that the need for future legislation designating new conservation system units, new national conservation areas, or new national recreation areas, has been obviated thereby.

Pub.L. 96–487, Title I, § 101, Dec. 2, 1980, 94 Stat. 2374.

§ 3102. Definitions

As used in this Act (except that in titles IX and XIV the following terms shall have the same meaning as they have in the Alaska Native Claims Settlement Act [43 U.S.C.A. § 1601 et seq.], and the Alaska Statehood Act)—

(1) The term "land" means lands, waters, and interests therein.

(2) The term "Federal land" means lands the title to which is in the United States after December 2, 1980. "Federal land" does not include lands the title to which is in the State, an Alaska Native corporation, or other private ownership.

(3) The term "public lands" means land situated in Alaska which, after December 2, 1980, are Federal lands, except—

(A) land selections of the State of Alaska which have been tentatively approved or validly selected under the Alaska Statehood Act and lands which have been confirmed to, validly selected by, or granted to the Territory of Alaska or the State under any other provision of Federal law;

(B) land selections of a Native Corporation made under the Alaska Native Claims Settlement Act [43 U.S.C.A. ? 1601 et seq.] which have not been conveyed to a Native Corporation, unless any such selection is determined to be invalid or is relinquished; and

(C) lands referred to in section 19(b) of the Alaska Native Claims Settlement Act [43 U.S.C.A. ? 1618(b)].

(4) The term "conservation system unit" means any unit in Alaska of the National Park System, National Wildlife Refuge System, National Wild and Scenic Rivers Systems, National Trails System, National Wilderness Preservation System, or a National Forest Monument including existing units, units established, designated, or expanded by or under the provisions of this Act, additions to such units, and any such unit established, designated, or expanded hereafter.

* * *

(6) The term "Native Corporation" means any Regional Corporation, any Village Corporation, any Urban Corporation, and any Native Group.

* * *

(11) The term "Native land" means land owned by a Native Corporation or any Native Group and includes land which, as of December 2, 1980, had been selected under the Alaska Native Claims Settlement Act [43 U.S.C.A. § 1601 et seq.] by a Native Corporation or Native Group and had not been conveyed by the Secretary (except to the extent such selection is determined to be invalid or has been relinquished) and land referred to in section 19(b) of the Alaska Native Claims Settlement Act [43 U.S.C.A. § 1618(b)].

* * *

(17) The term "fish and wildlife" means any member of the animal kingdom, including without limitation any mammal, fish, bird (including any migratory, nonmigratory or endangered bird for which protection is also afforded by treaty or other international agreement), amphibian, reptile, mollusk, crustacean, arthropod or other invertebrate, and includes any part, product, egg, or offspring thereof, or the dead body or part thereof.

(18) The term "take" or "taking" as used with respect to fish or wildlife, means to pursue, hunt, shoot, trap, net, capture, collect, kill, harm, or attempt to engage in any such conduct.

Pub.L. 96–487, Title I, ? 102, Dec. 2, 1980, 94 Stat. 2375; Pub.L. 105–83, Title III, § 316(b)(2), Nov. 14, 1997, 111 Stat. 1592.

§ 3103. Maps

* * *

Lands included within unit; acquisition of land by Secretary

(c) Only those lands within the boundaries of any conservation system unit which are public lands (as such term is defined in this Act) shall be deemed to be included as a portion of such unit. No lands which, before, on, or after December 2, 1980, are conveyed to the State, to any Native Corporation, or to any private party shall be subject to the regulations applicable solely to public lands within such units. If the State, a Native Corporation, or other owner desires to convey any such lands, the Secretary may acquire such lands in accordance with applicable law (including this Act), and any such lands shall become part of the unit, and be administered accordingly.

Pub.L. 96–487, Title I, § 103, Dec. 2, 1980, 94 Stat. 2376.

SUBCHAPTER II—SUBSISTENCE MANAGEMENT AND USE

§ 3111. Congressional declaration of findings

The Congress finds and declares that—

(1) the continuation of the opportunity for subsistence uses by rural residents of Alaska, including both Natives and non-Natives, on the public lands and by Alaska Natives on Native lands is essential to Native physical, economic, traditional, and cultural existence and to non-Native physical, economic, traditional, and social existence;

(2) the situation in Alaska is unique in that, in most cases, no practical alternative means are available to replace the food supplies and other items gathered from fish and wildlife which supply rural residents dependent on subsistence uses;

(3) continuation of the opportunity for subsistence uses of resources on public and other lands in Alaska is threatened by the increasing population of Alaska, with resultant pressure on subsistence resources, by sudden decline in the populations of some wildlife species which are crucial subsistence resources, by increased accessibility of

remote areas containing subsistence resources, and by taking of fish and wildlife in a manner inconsistent with recognized principles of fish and wildlife management;

(4) in order to fulfill the policies and purposes of the Alaska Native Claims Settlement Act [43 U.S.C.A. § 1601 et seq.] and as a matter of equity, it is necessary for the Congress to invoke its constitutional authority over Native affairs and its constitutional authority under the property clause and the commerce clause to protect and provide the opportunity for continued subsistence uses on the public lands by Native and non-Native rural residents; and

(5) the national interest in the proper regulation, protection, and conservation of fish and wildlife on the public lands in Alaska and the continuation of the opportunity for a subsistence way of life by residents of rural Alaska require that an administrative structure be established for the purpose of enabling rural residents who have personal knowledge of local conditions and requirements to have a meaningful role in the management of fish and wildlife and of subsistence uses on the public lands in Alaska.

Pub.L. 96–487, Title VIII, ? 801, Dec. 2, 1980, 94 Stat. 2422; Pub.L. 105–83, Title III, § 316(b)(3), Nov. 14, 1997, 111 Stat. 1592.

§ 3112. Congressional statement of policy

It is hereby declared to be the policy of Congress that—

(1) consistent with sound management principles, and the conservation of healthy populations of fish and wildlife, the utilization of the public lands in Alaska is to cause the least adverse impact possible on rural residents who depend upon subsistence uses of the resources of such lands; consistent with management of fish and wildlife in accordance with recognized scientific principles and the purposes for each unit established, designated, or expanded by or pursuant to titles II through VII of this Act, the purpose of this subchapter is to provide the opportunity for rural residents engaged in a subsistence way of life to do so;

(2) nonwasteful subsistence uses of fish and wildlife and other renewable resources shall be the priority consumptive uses of all such resources on the public lands of Alaska when it is necessary to restrict taking in order to assure the continued viability of a fish or wildlife population or the continuation of subsistence uses of such population, the taking of such population for nonwasteful subsistence uses shall be given preference on the public lands over other consumptive uses; and

(3) except as otherwise provided by this Act or other Federal laws, Federal and managing agencies, in managing subsistence activities on the public lands and in protecting the continued viability of all wild renewable resources in Alaska, shall cooperate with adjacent landowners and land managers, including Native Corporations, appropriate State and Federal agencies, and other nations.

Pub.L. 96–487, Title VIII, § 802, Dec. 2, 1980, 94 Stat. 2422.

§ 3113.   Definitions

As used in this Act, the term "subsistence uses" means the customary and traditional uses by rural Alaska residents of wild, renewable resources for direct personal or family consumption as food, shelter, fuel, clothing, tools, or transportation; for the making and selling of handicraft articles out of nonedible byproducts of fish and wildlife resources taken for personal or family consumption; for barter, or sharing for personal or family consumption; and for customary trade. For the purposes of this section, the term?

(1) "family" means all persons related by blood, marriage, or adoption, or any person living within the household on a permanent basis; and

(2) "barter" means the exchange of fish or wildlife or their parts, taken for subsistence uses—

(A) for other fish or game or their parts; or

(B) for other food or for nonedible items other than money if the exchange is of a limited and noncommercial nature.

Pub.L. 96–487, Title VIII, § 803, Dec. 2, 1980, 94 Stat. 2423; Pub.L. 105–83, Title III, § 316(b)(4), Nov. 14, 1997, 111 Stat. 1593.

§ 3114.   Preference for subsistence uses

Except as otherwise provided in this Act and other Federal laws, the taking on public lands of fish and wildlife for nonwasteful subsistence uses shall be accorded priority over the taking on such lands of fish and wildlife for other purposes. Whenever it is necessary to restrict the taking of populations of fish and wildlife on such lands for subsistence uses in order to protect the continued viability of such populations, or to continue such uses, such priority shall be implemented through appropriate limitations based on the application of the following criteria:

(1) customary and direct dependence upon the populations as the mainstay of livelihood;

(2) local residency; and

(3) the availability of alternative resources.

Pub.L. 96–487, Title VIII, § 804, Dec. 2, 1980, 94 Stat. 2423.

* * *

§ 3117.   Judicial enforcement

Exhaustion of administrative remedies; civil action; parties; preliminary injunctive relief; other relief; costs and attorney's fees

(a) Local residents and other persons and organizations aggrieved by a failure of the State or the Federal Government to provide for the priority for subsistence uses set forth in section 3114 of this title (or with respect to the State as set forth in a State law of general applicability if the State has fulfilled the requirements of section 3115(d) of this title) may, upon exhaustion of any State or Federal (as appropriate) administrative remedies which may be available, file a civil action in the United States District Court for the District of Alaska to require such actions to be taken as are necessary to provide for the priority. In a civil action filed against the State, the Secretary may be joined as a party to such action. The court may grant preliminary injunctive relief in any civil action if the granting of such relief is appropriate under the facts upon which the action is based. No order granting preliminary relief shall be issued until after an opportunity for hearing. In a civil action filed against the State, the court shall provide relief, other than preliminary relief, by directing the State to submit regulations which satisfy the requirements of section 3114 of this title; when approved by the court, such regulations shall be incorporated as part of the final judicial order, and such order shall be valid only for such period of time as normally provided by State law for the regulations at issue. Local residents and other persons and organizations who are prevailing parties in an action filed pursuant to this section shall be awarded their costs and attorney's fees.

* * *

Section as sole Federal judicial remedy

(c) This section is the sole Federal judicial remedy created by this subchapter for local residents and other residents who, and organizations which, are aggrieved by a failure of the State to provide for the priority of subsistence uses set forth in section 3114 of this title.

Pub.L. 96–487, Title VIII, § 807, Dec. 2, 1980, 94 Stat. 2426; Pub.L. 98–620, Title IV, § 402(22)(A). Nov. 8, 1984, 98 Stat. 3358; Pub.L. 105–83, Title III, § 316(b)(7), Nov. 14, 1997, 111 Stat. 1594.

* * *

§ 3120. Subsistence and land use decisions

Factors considered; requirements

(a) In determining whether to withdraw, reserve, lease, or otherwise permit the use, occupancy, or disposition of public lands under any provision of law authorizing such actions, the head of the Federal agency having primary jurisdiction over such lands or his designee shall evaluate the effect of such use, occupancy, or disposition on subsistence uses and needs, the availability of other lands for the purposes sought to be achieved, and other alternatives which would reduce or eliminate the use, occupancy, or disposition of public lands needed for subsistence purposes. No such withdrawal, reservation, lease, permit, or other use, occupancy or disposition of such lands which would significantly restrict subsistence uses shall be effected until the head of such Federal agency—

(1) gives notice to the appropriate State agency and the appropriate local committees and regional councils established pursuant to section 3115 of this title;

(2) gives notice of, and holds, a hearing in the vicinity of the area involved; and

(3) determines that (A) such a significant restriction of subsistence uses is necessary, consistent with sound management principles for the utilization of the public lands, (B) the proposed activity will involve the minimal amount of public lands necessary to accomplish the purposes of such use, occupancy, or other disposition, and (C) reasonable steps will be taken to minimize adverse impacts upon subsistence uses and resources resulting from such actions.

* * *

Management or disposal of lands

(d) After compliance with the procedural requirements of this section and other applicable law, the head of the appropriate Federal agency may manage or dispose of public lands under his primary jurisdiction for any of those uses or purposes authorized by this Act or other law.

Pub.L. 96–487, Title VIII, § 810, Dec. 2, 1980, 94 Stat. 2427.

§ 3121. Access to subsistence resources; use of snowmobiles, motorboats, or other means of surface transportation

(a) The Secretary shall insure that rural residents engaged in subsistence uses shall have reasonable access to subsistence resources on the public lands.

(b) Notwithstanding any other provision of this Act or other law, the Secretary shall permit on the public lands appropriate use for subsistence purposes of snowmobiles, motorboats, and other means of surface transportation traditionally employed for such purposes by local residents, subject to reasonable regulation.

Pub.L. 96–487, Title VIII, § 811, Dec. 2, 1980, 94 Stat. 2428.

* * *

§ 3124. Regulations

The Secretary shall prescribe such regulations as are necessary and appropriate to carry out his responsibilities under this subchapter.

Pub.L. 96–487, Title VIII, § 814, Dec. 2, 1980, 94 Stat. 2429; Pub.L. 105–83, Title III, § 316(b)(8), Nov. 14, 1997, 111 Stat. 1594.

§ 3125. Limitations and savings clauses

Nothing in this subchapter shall be construed as—

(1) granting any property right in any fish or wildlife or other resource of the public lands or as permitting the level of subsistence uses of fish and wildlife within a conservation system unit to be inconsistent with the conservation of healthy populations, and within a national park or monument to be inconsistent with the conservation of

natural and healthy populations, of fish and wildlife. No privilege which may be granted by the State to any individual with respect to subsistence uses may be assigned to any other individual;

(2) permitting any subsistence use of fish and wildlife on any portion of the public lands (whether or not within any conservation system unit) which was permanently closed to such uses on January 1, 1978, or enlarging or diminishing the Secretary's authority to manipulate habitat on any portion of the public lands;

(3) authorizing a restriction on the taking of fish and wildlife for nonsubsistence uses on the public lands (other than national parks and park monuments) unless necessary for the conservation of healthy populations of fish and wildlife, for the reasons set forth in section 3126 of this title, to continue subsistence uses of such populations, or pursuant to other applicable law; or

(4) modifying or repealing the provisions of any Federal law governing the conservation or protection of fish and wildlife, * * *

Pub.L. 96–487, Title VIII, § 815, Dec. 2, 1980, 94 Stat. 2429; Pub.L. 96–561, Title II, § 238(b), Dec. 22, 1980, 94 Stat. 3300, as amended Pub.L. 104–208, Div. A, Title I, § 101(a) [Title II, § 211(b)], Sept. 30, 1996, 110 Stat. 3009–41; Pub.L. 105–83, Title III, § 316(b)(9), Nov. 14, 1997, 111 Stat. 1594.

§ 3126.   Closure to subsistence uses

(a) All national parks and park monuments in Alaska shall be closed to the taking of wildlife except for subsistence uses to the extent specifically permitted by this Act. Subsistence uses and sport fishing shall be authorized in such areas by the Secretary and carried out in accordance with the requirements of this subchapter and other applicable laws of the United States and the State of Alaska.

(b) Except as specifically provided otherwise by this section, nothing in this subchapter is intended to enlarge or diminish the authority of the Secretary to designate areas where, and establish periods when, no taking of fish and wildlife shall be permitted on the public lands for reasons of public safety, administration, or to assure the continued viability of a particular fish or wildlife population. Notwithstanding any other provision of this Act or other law, the Secretary, after consultation with the State and adequate notice and public hearing, may temporarily close any public lands (including those within any conservation system unit), or any portion thereof, to subsistence uses of a particular fish or wildlife population only if necessary for reasons of public safety, administration, or to assure the continued viability of such population. If the Secretary determines that an emergency situation exists and that extraordinary measures must be taken for public safety or to assure the continued viability of a particular fish or wildlife population, the Secretary may immediately close the public lands, or any portion thereof, to the subsistence uses of such population and shall publish the reasons justifying the closure in the Federal Register. Such emergency closure shall be effective when made, shall not extend for a period exceeding sixty days, and may not subsequently be extended unless the Secretary affirmatively establishes, after notice and public hearing, that such closure should be extended.

Pub.L. 96–487, Title VIII, § 816, Dec. 2, 1980, 94 Stat. 2430.

SUBCHAPTER III—FEDERAL NORTH SLOPE LANDS STUDIES, OIL AND GAS LEASING PROGRAM AND MINERAL ASSESSMENTS

* * *

§ 3143. Production of oil and gas from Arctic National Wildlife Refuge prohibited

Production of oil and gas from the Arctic National Wildlife Refuge is prohibited and no leasing or other development leading to production of oil and gas from the range shall be undertaken until authorized by an Act of Congress.

Pub.L. 96–487, Title X, § 1003, Dec. 2, 1980, 94 Stat. 2452.

* * *

§ 3148. Oil and gas leasing program for non-North Slope Federal lands

Establishment; restrictions

(a) The Secretary shall establish, pursuant to the Mineral Leasing Act of 1920, as amended [30 U.S.C.A. § 181 et seq.], an oil and gas leasing program on the Federal lands of Alaska not subject to the study required by section 3141 of this title, other than lands included in the National Petroleum Reserve–Alaska. Such program shall not be undertaken by the Secretary on those lands where applicable law prohibits such leasing or on those units of the National Wildlife Refuge System where the Secretary determines, after having considered the national interest in producing oil and gas from such lands, that the exploration for and development of oil or gas would be incompatible with the purpose for which such unit was established.

Study of oil and gas potential and impact of development and production; permits; consultations; State studies; reports to Congress

(b)(1)(A) In such areas as the Secretary deems favorable for the discovery of oil or gas, he shall conduct a study, or studies, or collect and analyze information obtained by permittees authorized to conduct studies under this section, of the oil and gas potential of such lands and those environmental characteristics and wildlife resources which would be affected by the exploration for and development of such oil and gas.

(b)(1)(B) The Secretary is authorized to issue permits for study, including geological, geophysical, and other assessment activities, if such activities can be conducted in a manner which is consistent with the purposes for which each affected area is managed under applicable law.

(b)(2) The Secretary shall consult with the Secretary of Energy regarding the national interest involved in exploring for and developing oil and gas from such lands and shall seek the views of the Governor of the State of Alaska, Alaskan local governments, Native Regional and Village Corporations, the Alaska Land Use Council, representatives of the oil and gas industry, conservation groups, and other interested groups and individuals in determining which land should be studied and/or leased for the exploration and development of oil and gas.

(b)(3) The Secretary shall encourage the State to undertake similar studies on lands associated, either through geological or other land values or because of possible transportation needs, with Federal lands. The Secretary shall integrate these studies, to the maximum extent practicable, with studies on Federal lands so that needs for cooperation between the Federal Government and the State of Alaska in managing energy and other natural resources, including fish and wildlife, can be established early in the program.

(b)(4) The Secretary shall report to the Congress by October 1, 1981, and yearly thereafter, on his efforts pursuant to this Act regarding the leasing of, and exploration and development activities on, such lands. * * *

Issuance of leases; competitive bidding

(d) Pursuant to the Mineral Leasing Act of 1920, as amended [30 U.S.C.A. § 181 et seq.], the Secretary is authorized to issue leases, on the Federal lands described in this section, under such terms and conditions as he may, by regulation, prescribe.

Exploration plan

(f) Prior to any exploration activities on a lease issued pursuant to this section, the Secretary shall require the lessee to describe exploration activities in an exploration plan. He shall approve such plan if such activities can be conducted in conformity with such requirements as may be made by the Secretary for the protection and use of the land for the purpose for which it is managed under applicable law.

Development and production plan

(g) Subsequent to a discovery of oil or gas in paying quantities, and prior to developing and producing such oil and gas, the Secretary shall require the lessee to describe development and production activities in a development and production plan. He shall approve such plan if such activities may be conducted in conformity with such requirements as may be made by the Secretary for the protection and use of the land for the purpose for which it is managed under applicable law.

Revised development and production plan

(h) The Secretary shall monitor the performance of the lessee and, if he determines that due to significant changes in circumstances regarding that operation, including environmental or economic changes, new requirements are needed, he may require a revised development and production plan.

Suspension and cancellation of lease

(i) If the Secretary determines that immediate and irreparable damage will result from continuation in force of a lease, that the threat will not disappear and that the advantages of cancellation outweigh the advantages of continuation in force of a lease, he shall suspend operations for up to five years. If such a threat persists beyond such five-year suspension period, he shall cancel a lease and provide compensation to the lease under such terms as the Secretary establishes, by regulation, to be appropriate.

Pub.L. 96–487, Title X, § 1008, Dec. 2, 1980, 94 Stat. 2454. As amended Pub.L. 100–203, Title V, § 5105, Dec. 22, 1987, 101 Stat. 1330–259.

§ 3149.   Oil and gas lease applications

Lands within National Wildlife Refuge System but not part of National Wilderness Preservation System

(a) Notwithstanding any other provision of law or regulation, whenever the Secretary receives an application for an oil and gas lease pursuant to the Mineral Leasing Act of 1920 [30 U.S.C.A. § 181 et seq.] for lands in Alaska within a unit of the National Wildlife Refuge System which are not also part of the National Wilderness Preservation System he shall, in addition to any other requirements of applicable law, follow the procedures set forth in this section.

Statement of reasons for decision to issue or not to issue lease

(b) Any decision to issue or not to issue a lease shall be accompanied by a statement setting forth the reasons for the decision, including the reasons why oil and gas leasing would be compatible or incompatible with the purposes of the refuge.

Environmental impact statement

(c) If the Secretary determines that the requirements of section 4332(2)(C) of Title 42 do not apply to his decision, the Secretary shall render his decision within six months after receipt of a lease application. If such requirements are applicable to the Secretary's decision, he shall render his decision within three months after publication of the final environmental impact statement.

Pub.L. 96–487, Title X, § 1009, Dec. 2, 1980, 94 Stat. 2456.

§ 3150.   Alaska mineral resource assessment program

Mineral assessments

(a) The Secretary shall, to the full extent of his authority, assess the oil, gas, and other mineral potential on all public lands in the State of Alaska in order to expand the data base with respect to the mineral potential of such lands. The mineral assessment program may include, but shall not be limited to, techniques such as side-looking radar imagery and, on public lands other than such lands within the national park system, core and test drilling for geologic information, notwithstanding any restriction on such drilling under the Wilderness Act [16 U.S.C.A. § 1131 et seq.]. For purposes of this Act, core and test drilling means the extraction by drilling of subsurface geologic samples in order to assess the metalliferous or other mineral values of geologic terrain, but shall not be construed as including exploratory drilling of oil and gas test wells. To the maximum extent practicable, the Secretary shall consult and exchange information with the State of Alaska regarding the responsibilities of the Secretary under this section and similar programs undertaken by the State. In order to carry out mineral assessments authorized under this or any other law, including but not limited to the National Uranium Resource Evaluation program, the Secretary shall allow for access by air for assessment activities permitted in this subsection to all public lands involved in such study. He shall consult with the Secretary of Energy and heads of other Federal agencies carrying out such programs, to determine such reasonable requirements as may be necessary to protect the resources of such area, including fish and wildlife. Such requirements may provide that access will not occur during nesting, calving, spawning or such other times as fish and wildlife in the specific area may be especially vulnerable to such activities. The Secretary is authorized to enter into contracts with public or private entities to carry out all or any portion of the mineral assessment program. This section shall not apply to the lands described in section 3141 of this title.

Regulations

(b) Activities carried out in conservation system units under subsection (a) of this section shall be subject to regulations promulgated by the Secretary. Such regulations shall ensure that such activities are carried out in an environmentally sound manner—

(1) which does not result in lasting environmental impacts which appreciably alter the natural character of the units or biological or ecological systems in the units; and

(2) which is compatible with the purposes for which such units are established.

Pub.L. 96–487, Title X, § 1010, Dec. 2, 1980, 94 Stat. 2456.

* * *

SUBCHAPTER IV—TRANSPORTATION AND UTILITY SYSTEMS IN AND ACROSS, AND ACCESS INTO, CONSERVATION SYSTEM UNITS

§ 3161. Congressional declaration of findings

Congress finds that—

(a) Alaska's transportation and utility network is largely undeveloped and the future needs for transportation and utility systems in Alaska would best be identified and provided for through an orderly, continuous decisionmaking process involving the State and Federal Governments and the public;

(b) the existing authorities to approve or disapprove applications for transportation and utility systems through public lands in Alaska are diverse, dissimilar, and, in some cases, absent; and

(c) to minimize the adverse impacts of siting transportation and utility systems within units established or expanded by this Act and to insure the effectiveness of the decisionmaking process, a single comprehensive statutory authority for the approval or disapproval of applications for such systems must be provided in this Act.

Pub.L. 96–487, Title XI, § 1101, Dec. 2, 1980, 94 Stat. 2457.

* * *

§ 3164. Procedural requirements

In general

(a) Notwithstanding any provision of applicable law, no action by any Federal agency under applicable law with respect to the approval or disapproval of the authorization, in whole or in part, of any transportation or utility system shall have any force or effect unless the provisions of this section are complied with.

* * *

Filing

(c) Each applicant for the approval of any transportation or utility system shall file on the same day an application with each appropriate Federal agency. The applicant shall utilize the consolidated form prescribed under subsection (b) of this section for the type of transportation or utility system concerned.

* * *

Other views

(f) During both the nine-month period, and the succeeding three-month period plus any extension thereof provided for in subsection (e) of this section, the heads of the Federal agencies concerned shall solicit and consider the views of other Federal departments and agencies, the Alaska Land Use Council, the State, affected units of local government in the State, and affected corporations formed pursuant to the Alaska Native Claims Settlement Act [43 U.S.C.A. 1601 et seq.], and, after public notice, shall receive and consider statements and recommendations regarding the application submitted by interested individuals and organizations.

Agency decision

(g)(1) Within four months after the final environmental impact statement is published in accordance with subsection (e) of this section with respect to any transportation or utility system, each Federal agency shall make a decision to approve or disapprove, in accordance with applicable law, each authorization that applies with respect to the system and that is within the jurisdiction of that agency.

(g)(2) The head of each Federal agency, in making a decision referred to in paragraph (1), shall consider, and make detailed findings supported by substantial evidence, with respect to—

(A) the need for, and economic feasibility of, the transportation or utility system;

(B) alternative routes and modes of access, including a determination with respect to whether there is any economically feasible and prudent alternative to the routing of the system through or within a conservation system unit, national recreation area, or national conservation area and, if not, whether there are alternative routes or modes which would result in fewer or less severe adverse impacts upon the conservation system unit;

(C) the feasibility and impacts of including different transportation or utility systems in the same area;

(D) short-and long-term social, economic, and environmental impacts of national, State, or local significance, including impacts on fish and wildlife and their habitat, and on rural, traditional lifestyles;

(E) the impacts, if any, on the national security interests of the United States, that may result from approval or denial of the application for a transportation or utility system;

(F) any impacts that would affect the purposes for which the Federal unit or area concerned was established;

(G) measures which should be instituted to avoid or minimize negative impacts; and

(H) the short-and long-term public values which may be adversely affected by approval of the transportation or utility system versus the short-and long-term public benefits which may accrue from such approval.

Pub.L. 96–487, Title XI, § 1104, Dec. 2, 1980, 94 Stat. 2459.

* * *

§ 3166. Agency, Presidential, and Congressional actions

Agency action in cases other than those involving section 3165 or wilderness areas

(a)(1) In the case of any application for the approval of any transportation or utility system to which section 3165 of this title does not apply or that does not occupy, use, or traverse any area within the National Wilderness Preservation System, if, in compliance with section 3164 of this title—

(A) each Federal agency concerned decides to approve each authorization within its jurisdiction with respect to that system, then the system shall be deemed to be approved and each such agency shall promptly issue, in accordance with applicable law, such rights-of-way, permits, licenses, leases, certificates, or other authorizations as are necessary with respect to the establishment of the system; or

(B) one or more Federal agencies decide to disapprove any authorization within its jurisdiction with respect, to that system, then the system shall be deemed to be disapproved and the applicant for the system may appeal the disapproval to the President.

(a)(2) If an applicant appeals under paragraph (1)(B), the President, within four months after receiving the appeal, shall decide whether to approve or deny the application. The President shall approve the application if he finds, after consideration of the factors set forth in section 3164(g)(2) of this title, that such approval would be in the public interest and that (1) such system would be compatible with the purposes for which the unit was established; and (2) there is no economically feasible and prudent alternative route for the system. In making a decision, the President shall consider any environmental impact statement prepared pursuant to section 3164(e) of this title, comments of the public and Federal agencies received during the preparation of such statement, and the findings and recommendations, if any, of each Federal agency that rendered a decision with respect to the application. The President's decision to approve or deny the application shall be published in the Federal Register, together with a statement of the reasons for his determination.

(a)(3) If the President approves an application under paragraph (2), each Federal agency concerned shall promptly issue, in accordance with applicable law, such rights-of-way, permits, licenses, leases, certificates, or other authorizations as are necessary with respect to the establishment of the system.

(a)(4) If the President denies an application under paragraph (2), the applicant shall be deemed to have exhausted his administrative remedies and may file suit in any appropriate Federal court to challenge such decision.

Agency action in cases involving section 3165 or wilderness areas

(b)(1) In the case of any application for the approval of a transportation or utility system to which section 3165 of this title applies or that proposes to occupy, use, or traverse any area within the National Wilderness Preservation System, each Federal agency concerned shall promptly submit to the President notification whether the agency tentatively approved or disapproved each authorization within its jurisdiction that applies with respect to the system. Such notification shall be accompanied by a statement of the reasons and findings supporting the agency position.

(b)(2) Within four months after receiving all notification referred to in paragraph (1) and after considering such notifications, any environmental impact statement prepared pursuant to section 3164(e) of this title, and the comments of the public and Federal agencies received during the preparation of such statement, the President shall decide whether or not the application for the system concerned should be approved. If the President denies an application the applicant shall be deemed to have exhausted his administrative remedies, and may file suit in any appropriate Federal court to challenge such decision. If the President approves the application, he shall submit to Congress his recommendation for approval of the transportation or utility system covered, whereupon the Congress shall consider the application as provided in subsection (c) of this section. The President shall include with his recommendation to Congress—

    (A) the application which is the subject of his recommendation;

    (B) a report setting forth in detail the relevant factual background and the reasons for his findings and recommendation;

    (C) the joint environmental impact statement;

    (D) a statement of the conditions and stipulations which would govern the use of the system if approved by the Congress.

Congressional approval

    (c)(1) No application for any transportation or utility system with respect to which the President makes a recommendation for approval under subsection (b) of this section shall be approved unless the Senate and House of Representatives approve a resolution described in paragraph (4) within the first period of one hundred and twenty calendar days of continuous session of the Congress beginning on the date after the date of receipt by the Senate and House of Representatives of such recommendation.

    (c)(2) For purposes of this subsection—

    (A) continuity of session of the Congress is broken only by an adjournment sine die; and

    (B) the days on which either House is not in session because of an adjournment of more than three days to a day certain are excluded in the computation of the one-hundred-and-twenty-day calendar period.

    (c)(3) This subsection is enacted by the Congress—

    (A) as an exercise of the rulemaking power of each House of the Congress respectively, but applicable only with respect to the procedure to be followed in the House in the case of resolutions described by paragraph (6) of this subsection; and it supersedes other rules only to the extent that it is inconsistent therewith; and

    (B) with full recognition of the constitutional right of either House to change the rules (so far as those relate to the procedure of that House) at any time, in the same manner and to the same extent as in the case of any other rule of such House.

    (c)(4) For the purposes of this subsection, the term "resolution" means a joint resolution, the resolving clause of which is as follows: "That the House of Representatives and Senate approve the application for _____ under title XI of the Alaska National Interest Lands Conservation Act submitted by the President to the Congress on _____, 19__."; the first blank space therein to be filled in with the appropriate transportation or utility system and the second blank therein to be filled with the date on which the President submits the application to the House of Representatives and the Senate.

(c)(5) Except as otherwise provided in this subsection, the provisions of section 719f(d) of Title 15 shall apply to the consideration of the resolution.

(c)(6) After an application for a transportation or utility system has been approved under subsection (a) of this section, the appropriate Federal agencies shall issue appropriate authorizations in accordance with applicable law. In any case in which an application for a transportation or utility system has been approved pursuant to subsection (b) of this section, the appropriate Federal agencies shall issue appropriate authorizations in accordance with Title V of the Federal Lands Policy Management Act [43 U.S.C.A. § 1761 et seq.] or other applicable law. After issuance pursuant to this subsection, the appropriate land managing agency shall administer the right-of-way in accordance with relevant management authorities of the land managing agency and Title V of the Federal Lands Policy Management Act.

Pub.L. 96–487, Title XI, 1106, Dec. 2, 1980, 94 Stat. 2461.

§ **3167.** Rights-of-way terms and conditions

Terms and conditions

(a) The Secretary, or the Secretary of Agriculture where national forest wilderness is involved, shall include in any right-of-way issued pursuant to an application under this subchapter, terms and conditions which shall include, but not be limited to—

(1) requirements to insure that, to the maximum extent feasible, the right-of-way is used in a manner compatible with the purposes for which the affected conservation system unit, national recreation area, or national conservation area was established or is managed;

(2) requirements for restoration, revegetation, and curtailment of erosion of the surface of the land;

(3) requirements to insure that activities in connection with the right-of-way will not violate applicable air and water quality standards and related facility siting standards established pursuant to law;

(4) requirements, including the minimum necessary width, designed to control or prevent—

(A) damage to the environment (including damage to fish and wildlife habitat),

(B) damage to public or private property, and

(C) hazards to public health and safety;

(5) requirements to protect the interests of individuals living in the general area of the right-of-way who rely on the fish, wildlife, and biotic resources of the area for subsistence purposes; and

(6) requirements to employ measures to avoid or minimize adverse environmental, social or economic impacts.

Wild and Scenic Rivers System

(b) Any transportation or utility system approved pursuant to this subchapter which occupies, uses, or traverses any area within the boundaries of a unit of the National Wild and Scenic Rivers System shall be subject to such conditions as may be necessary to assure that the stream flow of, and transportation on, such river are not interfered with or impeded, and that the transportation or utility system is located and constructed in an environmentally sound manner.

Pipeline rights-of-way

(c) In the case of a pipeline described in section 185(a) of Title 30, a right-of-way issued pursuant to this subchapter shall be issued in the same manner as a right-of-way is granted under section 185 of Title 30, and the provisions of subsections (c) through (j), (1) through (q), and (u) through (y) of section 185 of Title 30 shall apply to rights-of-way issued pursuant to this subchapter.

Pub.L. 96–487, Title XI, § 1107, Dec. 2, 1980, 94 Stat. 2463.

§ 3168. Injunctive relief

No court shall have jurisdiction to grant any injunctive relief lasting longer than ninety days against any action pursuant to this subchapter except in conjunction with a final judgment entered in a case involving an action pursuant to this subchapter.

Pub.L. 96–487, Title XI, § 1108, Dec. 2, 1980, 94 Stat. 2464; Pub.L. 98–620, Title IV, § 402(22)(B) Nov. 8, 1984, 98 Stat. 3358.

§ 3169. Valid existing right of access

Nothing in this subchapter shall be construed to adversely affect any valid existing right of access.

Pub.L. 96–487, Title XI, § 1109, Dec. 2, 1980, 94 Stat. 2464.

§ 3170. Special access and access to inholdings

(a) Notwithstanding any other provision of this Act or other law, the Secretary shall permit, on conservation system units, national recreation areas, and national conservation areas, and those public lands designated as wilderness study, the use of snowmachines (during periods of adequate snow cover, or frozen river conditions in the case of wild and scenic rivers), motorboats, airplanes, and nonmotorized surface transportation methods for traditional activities (where such activities are permitted by this Act or other law) and for travel to and from villages and homesites. Such use shall be subject to reasonable regulations by the Secretary to protect the natural and other values of the conservation system units, national recreation areas, and national conservation areas, and shall not be prohibited unless, after notice and hearing in the vicinity of the affected unit or area, the Secretary finds that such use would be detrimental to the resource values of the unit or area. Nothing in this section shall be construed as prohibiting the use of other methods of transportation for such travel and activities on conservation system lands where such use is permitted by this Act or other law.

(b) Notwithstanding any other provisions of this Act or other law, in any case in which State owned or privately owned land, including subsurface rights of such owners underlying public lands, or a valid mining claim or other valid occupancy is within or is effectively surrounded by one or more conservation system units, national recreation areas, national conservation areas, or those public lands designated as wilderness study, the State or private owner or occupier shall be given by the Secretary such rights as may be necessary to assure adequate and feasible access for economic and other purposes to the concerned land by such State or private owner or occupier and their successors in interest. Such rights shall be subject to reasonable regulations issued by the Secretary to protect the natural and other values of such lands.

Pub.L. 96–487, Title XI, § 1110, Dec. 2, 1980, 94 Stat. 2464.

* * *

SUBCHAPTER V—FEDERAL–STATE COOPERATION
* * *

SUBCHAPTER VI—ADMINISTRATIVE PROVISIONS

§ 3191. Management plans

Development; transmittal to congressional committees

(a) Within five years from December 2, 1980, the Secretary shall develop and transmit to the appropriate Committees of the Congress a conservation and management plan for each of the units of the National Park System established or to which additions are made by this Act.

National Park service plan requirements

(b) Each plan for a unit established, redesignated, or expanded by sections 410hh to 410hh–5 of this title shall identify management practices which will carry out the policies of this Act and will accomplish the purposes for which the concerned National Park System unit was established or expanded and shall include at least the following:

(1) Maps indicating areas of particular importance as to wilderness, natural, historical, wildlife, cultural, archeological, paleontological, geological, recreational, and similar resources and also indicating the areas into which such unit will be divided for administrative purposes.

(2) A description of the programs and methods that will be employed to manage fish and wildlife resources and habitats, cultural, geological, recreational, and wilderness resources, and how each conservation system unit will contribute to overall resources management goals of that region. Such programs should include research, protection, restoration, development, and interpretation as appropriate.

(3) A description of any areas of potential or proposed development, indicating types of visitor services and facilities to be provided, the estimated costs of such services and facilities, and whether or not such services and facilities could and should be provided outside the boundaries of such unit.

(4) A plan for access to, and circulation within, such unit, indicating the type and location of transportation routes and facilities, if any.

(5) A description of the programs and methods which the Secretary plans to use for the purposes of (A) encouraging the recognition and protection of the culture and history of the individuals residing, on December 2, 1980, in such unit and areas in the vicinity of such unit, and (B) providing and encouraging employment of such individuals.

(6) A plan for acquiring land with respect to such unit, including proposed modifications in the boundaries of such unit.

(7) A description (A) of privately owned areas, if any, which are within such unit, (B) of activities carried out in, or proposed for, such areas, (C) of the present and potential effects of such activities on such unit, (D) of the purposes for which such areas are used, and (E) of methods (such as cooperative agreements and issuance or enforcement of regulations) of controlling the use of such activities to carry out the policies of this Act and the purposes for which such unit is established or expanded.

(8) A plan indicating the relationship between the management of such unit and activities being carried out in, or proposed for, surrounding areas and also indicating cooperative agreements which could and should be entered into for the purpose of improving such management.

Consideration of factors

(c) In developing, preparing, and revising a plan under this section the Secretary shall take into consideration at least the following factors:

(1) The specific purposes for which the concerned conservation system unit was established or expanded.

(2) Protection and preservation of the ecological, environmental, wildlife, cultural, historical, archeological, geological, recreational, wilderness, and scenic character of the concerned unit and of areas in the vicinity of such unit.

(3) Providing opportunities for Alaska Natives residing in the concerned unit and areas adjacent to such unit to continue performing in such unit activities which they have traditionally or historically performed in such unit.

(4) Activities being carried out in areas adjacent to, or surrounded by, the concerned unit.

Hearing and participation

(d) In developing, preparing, and revising a plan under this section the Secretary shall hold at least one public hearing in the vicinity of the concerned conservation unit, hold at least one public hearing in a metropolitan area of Alaska, and, to the extent practicable, permit the following persons to participate in the development, preparation, and revision of such plan:

(1) The Alaska Land Use Council and officials of Federal agencies whose activities will be significantly affected by implementation of such plan.

(2) Officials of the State and of political subdivisions of the State whose activities will be significantly affected by implementation of such plan.

(3) Officials of Native Corporations which will be significantly affected by implementation of such plan.

(4) Concerned local, State, and National organizations and interested individuals.

Pub.L. 96–487, Title XIII, § 1301, Dec. 2, 1980, 94 Stat. 2472.

§ 3192.   Land acquisition authority

General authority

(a) Except as provided in subsections (b) and (c) of this section, the Secretary is authorized, consistent with other applicable law in order to carry out the purposes of this Act, to acquire by purchase, donation, exchange, or otherwise any lands within the boundaries of any conservation system unit other than National Forest Wilderness.

Restrictions

(b) Lands located within the boundaries of a conservation system unit which are owned by—

(A) the State or a political subdivision of the State;

(B) a Native Corporation or Native Group which has Natives as a majority of its stockholders;

(C) the actual occupant of a tract, title to the surface estate of which was on, before, or after December 1, 1980, conveyed to such occupant pursuant to section 1613(c)(1) and (h)(5) of Title 43, unless the Secretary determines that the tract is no longer occupied for the purpose described in section 1613(c)(1) or (h)(5) of Title 43 for which the tract was conveyed and that activities on the tract are or will be detrimental to the purposes of the unit in which the tract is located; or

(D) a spouse or lineal descendant of the actual occupant of a tract described in subparagraph (C), unless the Secretary determines that activities on the tract are or will be detrimental to the purposes of the unit in which the tract is located—

may not be acquired by the Secretary without the consent of the owner.

Exchanges

(c) Lands located within the boundaries of a conservation system unit (other than National Forest Wilderness) which are owned by persons or entities other than those described in subsection (b) of this section shall not be acquired by the Secretary without the consent of the owner unless prior to final judgment on the value of the acquired land, the owner, after being offered appropriate land of similar characteristics and like value (if such land is available from public lands located outside the boundaries of any conservation system unit), chooses not to accept the exchange. In identifying public lands for exchange pursuant to this subsection, the Secretary shall consult with the Alaska Land Use Council.

Improved property

(d) No improved property shall be acquired under subsection (a) of this section without the consent of the owner unless the Secretary first determines that such acquisition is necessary to the fulfillment of the purposes of this Act or to the fulfillment of the purposes for which the concerned conservation system unit was established or expanded.

Retained rights

(e) The owner of an improved property on the date of its acquisition, as a condition of such acquisition, may retain for himself, his heirs and assigns, a right of use and occupancy of the improved property for noncommercial residential or recreational purposes, as the case may be, for a definite term of not more than twenty-five years, or in lieu thereof, for a term ending at the death of the owner or the death of his spouse, whichever is later. The owner shall elect the term to be reserved. Unless the property is wholly or partially donated, the Secretary shall pay to the owner the fair market value of the owner's interest in the property on the date of its acquisition, less the fair market value on that date of the right retained by the owner. A right retained by the owner pursuant to this section shall be subject to termination by the Secretary upon his determination that such right is being exercised in a manner inconsistent with the purposes of this Act, and it shall terminate by operation of law upon notification by the Secretary to the holder of the right of such determination and tendering to him the amount equal to the fair market value of that portion which remains unexpired.

* * *

Exchange authority

(h)(1) Notwithstanding any other provision of law, in acquiring lands for the purposes of this Act, the Secretary is authorized to exchange lands (including lands within conservation system units and within the National Forest System) or interests therein (including Native selection rights) with the corporations organized by the Native Groups, Village Corporations, Regional Corporations, and the Urban Corporations, and other municipalities and corporations or individuals, the State (acting free of the restrictions of section 6(i) of the Alaska Statehood Act), or any Federal agency. Exchanges shall be on the basis of equal value, and either party to the exchange may pay or accept cash in order to equalize the value of the property exchanged, except that if the parties agree to an exchange and the

Secretary determines it is in the public interest, such exchanges may be made for other than equal value.

(h)(2) Nothing in this Act or any other provision of law shall be construed as authorizing the Secretary to convey, by exchange or otherwise, lands or interest in lands within the coastal plain of the Arctic National Wildlife Refuge (other than land validly selected prior to July 28, 1987), without prior approval by Act of Congress.

Donation or exchange

(i)(1) The Secretary is authorized to acquire by donation or exchange, lands (A) which are contiguous to any conservation system unit established or expanded by this Act, and (B) which are owned or validly selected by the State of Alaska.

(i)(2) Any such lands so acquired shall become a part of such conservation system unit.

Pub.L. 96–487, Title XIII, § 1302, Dec. 2, 1980, 94 Stat. 2474. As amended Pub.L. 100–395, § 201, Aug. 16, 1988, 102 Stat. 981.

* * *

§ 3194. Archeological and paleontological sites

Notwithstanding any acreage or boundary limitations contained in this Act with respect to the Cape Krusenstern National Monument, the Bering Land Bridge National Preserve, the Yukon–Charley Rivers National Preserve, and the Kobuk Valley National Park, the Secretary may designate Federal lands or he may acquire by purchase with the consent of the owner, donation, or exchange any significant archeological or paleontological site in Alaska located outside of the boundaries of such areas and containing resources which are closely associated with any such area. If any such site is so designated or acquired, it shall be included in and managed as part of such area. Not more than seven thousand five hundred acres of land may be designated or acquired under this section for inclusion in any single area. Before designation or acquisition of any property in excess of one hundred acres under the provisions of this section, the Secretary shall—

(1) submit notice of such proposed designation or acquisition to the appropriate committees of the Congress; and

(2) publish notice of such proposed designation or acquisition in the Federal Register.

Pub.L. 96–487, Title XIII, § 1304, Dec. 2, 1980, 94 Stat. 2478.

* * *

§ 3197. Revenue-producing visitor services

Continuation of existing visitor services

(a) Notwithstanding any other provision of law, the Secretary, under such terms and conditions as he determines are reasonable, shall permit any persons who, on or before January 1, 1979, were engaged in adequately providing any type of visitor service within any area established as or added to a conservation system unit to continue providing such type of service and similar types of visitor services within such area if such service or services are consistent with the purposes for which such unit is established or expanded.

Preference

(b) Notwithstanding provisions of law other than those contained in subsection (a) of this section, in selecting persons to provide (and in contracting for the provision of) any type of visitor service for any conservation system unit, except sport fishing and hunting guiding activities, the Secretary—

(1) shall give preference to the Native Corporations which the Secretary determines are most directly affected by the establishment or expansion of such unit by or under the provisions of this Act;

(2) shall give preference to persons whom he determines, by rule, are local residents; and

(3) shall, consistent with the provisions of this section, offer to Cook Inlet Region, Incorporated, in cooperation with Village Corporations within the Cook Inlet Region when appropriate, the right of first refusal to provide new revenue producing visitor services within the Kenai National Moose Range or that portion of the Lake Clark National Park and Preserve within the boundaries of the Cook Inlet Region that right to remain open for a period of ninety days as agreed to in paragraph VIII of the document referred to in section 12 of the Act of January 2, 1976 (Public Law 94–204).

"Visitor service" defined

(c) As used in this section, the term "visitor service" means any service made available for a fee or charge to persons who visit a conservation system unit, including such services as providing food, accommodations, transportation, tours, and guides excepting the guiding of sport hunting and fishing. Nothing in this Act shall limit or affect the authority of the Federal Government or the State of Alaska to license and regulate transportation services.

Pub.L. 96–487, Title XIII, § 1307, Dec. 2, 1980, 94 Stat. 2479; Pub.L. 105–333, § 10, Oct. 31, 1998, 112 Stat. 3134.

§ 3198. Local hire

Program

(a) After consultation with the Office of Personnel Management, the Secretary shall establish a program under which any individual who, by reason of having lived or worked in or near public lands, has special knowledge or expertise concerning the natural or cultural resources of public lands and the management thereof (as determined by the Secretary) shall be considered for selection for any position within public lands without regard to—

(1) any provision of the civil service laws or regulations thereunder which require minimum periods of formal training or experience,

(2) any such provision which provides an employment preference to any other class of applicant in such selection, and

(3) any numerical limitation on personnel otherwise applicable.

Individuals appointed under this subsection shall not be taken into account in applying any personnel limitation described in paragraph (3).

Preference eligibles within local hire

(b) Notwithstanding the provisions of subsection (a) of this section, any individual who is eligible to be selected for a position under the provisions of subsection (a) and is a preference eligible as defined in section 2108(3) of Title 5, shall be given an employment preference, consistent with the preference in the competitive service as defined in section 2102 of such title for which such person is eligible under subchapter I of chapter 33 of such title, in selection to such position.

Reports

(c) The Secretary shall from time to time prepare and submit to the Congress reports indicating the actions taken in carrying out the provisions of subsection (a) of this section together with any recommendations for legislation in furtherance of the purposes of this section.

Pub.L. 96–487, Title XIII, § 1308, Dec. 2, 1980, 94 Stat. 2480. As amended Pub.L. 100–689, Title IV, § 401, Nov. 18, 1988, 102 Stat. 4177; Pub.L. 102–415, § 16, Oct. 14, 1992, 106 Stat. 2124; PL 105–333, Oct. 31, 1998, 112 Stat. 3129.

* * *

§ 3201. Administration of national preserves

A National Preserve in Alaska shall be administered and managed as a unit of the National Park System in the same manner as a national park except as otherwise provided in this Act and except that the taking of fish and wildlife for sport purposes and subsistence uses, and trapping shall be allowed in a national preserve under applicable State and Federal law and regulation. Consistent with the provisions of section 3126 of this title, within national preserves the Secretary may designate zones where and periods when no hunting, fishing, trapping, or entry may be permitted for reasons of public safety, administration, floral and faunal protection, or public use and enjoyment. Except in emergencies, any regulations prescribing such restrictions relating to hunting, fishing, or trapping shall be put into effect only after consultation with the appropriate State agency having responsibility over hunting, fishing, and trapping activities.

Pub.L. 96–487, Title XIII, § 1313, Dec. 2, 1980, 94 Stat. 2483.

§ 3202.   Taking of fish and wildlife

Responsibility and authority of State of Alaska

(a) Nothing in this Act is intended to enlarge or diminish the responsibility and authority of the State of Alaska for management of fish and wildlife on the public lands except as may be provided in subchapter II of this chapter, or to amend the Alaska constitution.

Responsibility and authority of Secretary

(b) Except as specifically provided otherwise by this Act, nothing in this Act is intended to enlarge or diminish the responsibility and authority of the Secretary over the management of the public lands.

Areas controlled; areas closed, exceptions

(c) The taking of fish and wildlife in all conservation system units, and in national conservation areas, national recreation areas, and national forests, shall be carried out in accordance with the provisions of this Act and other applicable State and Federal law. Those areas designated as national parks or national park system monuments in the State shall be closed to the taking of fish and wildlife, except that—

(1) notwithstanding any other provision of this Act, the Secretary shall administer those units of the National Park System, and those additions to existing units, established by this Act and which permit subsistence uses, to provide an opportunity for the continuance of such uses by local rural residents; and

(2) fishing shall be permitted by the Secretary in accordance with the provisions of this Act and other applicable State and Federal law.

Pub.L. 96–487, Title XIII, § 1314, Dec. 2, 1980, 94 Stat. 2484.

§ 3203.   Wilderness management

Application only to Alaska

(a) The provisions of this section are enacted in recognition of the unique conditions in Alaska. Nothing in this section shall be construed to expand, diminish, or modify the provisions of the Wilderness Act [16 U.S.C.A. § 1131 et seq.] or the application or interpretation of such provisions with respect to lands outside of Alaska.

Aquaculture

(b) In accordance with the goal of restoring and maintaining fish production in the State of Alaska to optimum sustained yield levels and in a manner which adequately assures protection, preservation, enhancement, and rehabilitation of the wilderness resource, the Secretary of Agriculture may permit fishery research, management, enhancement, and rehabilitation activities within national forest wilderness and national forest wilderness study areas designated by this Act. Subject to reasonable regulations, permanent improvements and facilities such as fishways, fish weirs, fish ladders, fish hatcheries, spawning channels, stream clearance, egg planting, and other accepted means of maintaining, enhancing, and rehabilitating fish stocks may be permitted by the Secretary to achieve this objective. Any fish hatchery, fishpass or other aquaculture facility authorized for any such area shall be constructed, managed, and operated in a manner that minimizes adverse impacts on the wilderness character of the area. Developments for any such activities shall involve those facilities essential to these operations and shall be constructed in such rustic manner as to blend into the natural character of the area. Reasonable access solely for the purposes of this subsection, including temporary use of motorized equipment, shall be permitted in furtherance of research, management, rehabilitation and enhancement activities subject to reasonable regulations as the Secretary deems desirable to maintain the wilderness character, water quality, and fish and wildlife values of the area.

Existing cabins

(c) Previously existing public use cabins within wilderness designated by this Act, may be permitted to continue and may be maintained or replaced subject to such restrictions as the Secretary deems necessary to preserve the wilderness character of the area.

New cabins

(d) Within wilderness areas designated by this Act, the Secretary or the Secretary of Agriculture as appropriate, is authorized to construct and maintain a limited number of new public use cabins and shelters if such cabins and shelters are necessary for the protection of the public health and safety. All such cabins or shelters shall be constructed of materials which blend and are compatible with the immediate and surrounding wilderness landscape. The Secretary or the Secretary of Agriculture, as appropriate, shall notify the House Committee on Natural Resources and the Senate Committee on Energy and Natural Resources of his intention to remove an existing or construct a new public use cabin or shelter.

Timber contracts

(e) The Secretary of Agriculture is hereby directed to modify any existing national forest timber sale contracts applying to lands designated by this Act as wilderness by substituting, to the extent practicable, timber on the other national forest lands approximately equal in volume, species, grade, and accessibility for timber or relevant lands within such units.

Beach log salvage

(f) Within National Forest wilderness and national forest monuments designated by this Act, the Secretary of Agriculture may permit or otherwise regulate the recovery and salvage of logs from coastlines.

Pub.L. 96–487, Title XIII, § 1315, Dec. 2, 1980, 94 Stat. 2484, as amended Pub.L. 103–437, § 6(d)(31), Nov. 2, 1994, 108 Stat. 4584.

§ 3204. Allowed uses; establishment of new facilities and use of equipment; denial of proposed use or establishment

(a) On all public lands where the taking of fish and wildlife is permitted in accordance with the provisions of this Act or other applicable State and Federal law the Secretary shall permit, subject to reasonable regulation to insure compatibility, the continuance of existing uses, and the future establishment, and use, of temporary campsites, tent platforms, shelters, and other temporary facilities and equipment directly and necessarily related to such activities. Such facilities and equipment shall be constructed, used, and maintained in a manner consistent with the protection of the area in which they are located. All new facilities shall be constructed of materials which blend with, and are compatible with, the immediately surrounding landscape. Upon termination of such activities and uses (but not upon regular or seasonal cessation), such structures or facilities shall, upon written request, be removed from the area by the permittee.

(b) Notwithstanding the foregoing provisions, the Secretary may determine, after adequate notice, that the establishment and use of such new facilities or equipment would constitute a significant expansion of existing facilities or uses which would be detrimental to the purposes for which the affected conservation system unit was established, including the wilderness character of any wilderness area within such unit, and may thereupon deny such proposed use or establishment.

Pub.L. 96–487, Title XIII, § 1316, Dec. 2, 1980, 94 Stat. 2485.

§ 3205. General wilderness review

Suitability of lands for preservation; report to President

(a) Within five years from December 2, 1980, the Secretary shall, in accordance with the provisions of section 1132(d) of this title relating to public notice, public hearings, and review by State and other agencies, review, as to their suitability or nonsuitability for preservation as wilderness, all lands within units of the National Park System and units of the National Wildlife Refuge System in Alaska not designated as wilderness by this Act and report his findings to the President.

Presidential recommendations to Congress

(b) The Secretary shall conduct his review, and the President shall advise the United States Senate and House of Representatives of his recommendations, in accordance with the provisions of sections 1132(c) and (d) of this title. The President shall advise the Congress of his recommendations with respect to such areas within seven years from December 2, 1980.

Administration of units unaffected pending Congressional action

(c) Nothing in this section shall be construed as affecting the administration of any unit of the National Park System or unit of National Wildlife Refuge System in accordance with this Act or other applicable provisions of law unless and until Congress provides otherwise by taking action on any Presidential recommendation made pursuant to subsection (b) of this section.

Pub.L. 96–487, Title XIII, § 1317, Dec. 2, 1980, 94 Stat. 2485.

* * *

§ 3207. Effect on existing rights; water resources

Nothing in this Act shall be construed as limiting or restricting the power and authority of the United States or—

(1) as affecting in any way any law governing appropriation or use of, or Federal right to, water on lands within the State of Alaska;

(2) as expanding or diminishing Federal or State jurisdiction, responsibility, interests, or rights in water resources development or control; or

(3) as superseding, modifying, or repealing, except as specifically set forth in this Act, existing laws applicable to the various Federal agencies which are authorized to develop or participate in the development of water resources or to exercise licensing or regulatory functions in relation thereto.

Pub.L. 96–487, Title XIII, § 1319, Dec. 2, 1980, 94 Stat. 2486.

* * *

§ 3209. Effect on prior withdrawals

(a) The withdrawals and reservations of the public lands made by Public Land Orders No. 5653 of November 16, 1978, 5654 of November 17, 1978, Public Land Orders numbered 5696 through 5711 inclusive of February 12, 1980, Federal Register Documents No. 34051, of December 5, 1978 and No. 79–17803 of June 8, 1979 and Proclamations No. 4611 through 4627, inclusive, of December 1, 1978, were promulgated to protect these lands from selection, appropriation, or disposition prior to December 2, 1980. As to all lands not within the boundaries established by this Act of any conservation system unit, national conservation area, national recreation area, or national forest addition, the aforesaid withdrawals and reservations are hereby rescinded on the effective date of this Act, and such lands shall be managed by the Secretary pursuant to the Federal Land Policy and Management Act of 1976 [43 U.S.C.A. § 1701 et seq.], or in the case of lands within a national forest, by the Secretary of Agriculture pursuant to the laws applicable to the national forests, unless otherwise specified by this Act. As to the Federal lands which are within the aforesaid boundaries, the aforesaid withdrawals and reservations are, on the effective date of this Act, hereby rescinded and superseded by the withdrawals and reservations made by this Act. Notwithstanding any provision to the contrary contained in any other law, the Federal lands within the aforesaid boundaries established by this Act shall not be deemed available for selection, appropriation, or disposition except as expressly provided by this Act.

(b) This section shall become effective upon the relinquishment by the State of Alaska of selections made on November 14, 1978, pursuant to the Alaska Statehood Act which are located within the boundaries of conservation system units, national conservation areas, national recreation areas, and forest additions, established, designated, or expanded by this Act.

Pub.L. 96–487, Title XIII, § 1322, Dec. 2, 1980, 94 Stat. 2487.

§ 3210.   Access to nonfederally owned land

(a) Notwithstanding any other provision of law, and subject to such terms and conditions as the Secretary of Agriculture may prescribe, the Secretary shall provide such access to nonfederally owned land within the boundaries of the National Forest System as the Secretary deems adequate to secure to the owner the reasonable use and enjoyment thereof: *Provided*, That such owner comply with rules and regulations applicable to ingress and egress to or from the National Forest System.

(b) Notwithstanding any other provision of law, and subject to such terms and conditions as the Secretary of the Interior may prescribe, the Secretary shall provide such access to nonfederally owned land surrounded by public lands managed by the Secretary under the Federal Land Policy and Management Act of 1976 (43 U.S.C. 1701–82) as the Secretary deems adequate to secure to the owner the reasonable use and enjoyment thereof: *Provided*, That such owner comply with rules and regulations applicable to access across public lands.

Pub.L. 96–487, Title XIII, § 1323, Dec. 2, 1980, 94 Stat. 2488.

* * *

§ 3213.   Future executive branch actions

(a) No future executive branch action which withdraws more than five thousand acres, in the aggregate, of public lands within the State of Alaska shall be effective except by compliance with this subsection. To the extent authorized by existing law, the President or the Secretary may withdraw public lands in the State of Alaska exceeding five thousand acres in the aggregate, which withdrawal shall not become effective until notice is provided in the Federal Register and to both Houses of Congress. Such withdrawal shall terminate unless Congress passes a joint resolution of approval within one year after the notice of such withdrawal has been submitted to Congress.

(b) No further studies of Federal lands in the State of Alaska for the single purpose of considering the establishment of a conservation system unit, national recreation area, national conservation area, or for related or similar purposes shall be conducted unless authorized by this Act or further Act of Congress.

Pub.L. 96–487, Title XIII, § 1326, Dec. 2, 1980, 94 Stat. 2488.

§ 3214.   Alaska gas pipeline

Nothing in this Act shall be construed as imposing any additional requirements in connection with the construction and operation of the transportation system designated by the President and approved by the Congress pursuant to the Alaska Natural Gas Transportation Act of 1976 (Public Law 94–586; 90 Stat. 2903) [15 U.S.C.A. § 719 et seq.], or as imposing any limitations upon the authority of the Secretary concerning such system.

Pub.L. 96–487, Title XIII, § 1327, Dec. 2, 1980, 94 Stat. 2489.

§ 3215.   Public land entries in Alaska

Application approval; adjudication; protests; voluntary relinquishment of application

(a)(1) Subject to valid existing rights, all applications made pursuant to the Acts of June 1, 1938 (52 Stat. 609) [43 U.S.C.A. § 682a], May 3, 1927 (44 Stat. 1364) [43 U.S.C.A. § 687a], May 14, 1898 (30 Stat. 413), and March 3, 1891 (26 Stat. 1097), which were filed with the Department of the Interior within the time provided by applicable law, and which describe land in Alaska that was available for entry under the aforementioned statutes when such entry occurred, are hereby approved on the one hundred and eightieth day following the effective date of this Act, except where provided otherwise by paragraph (3) or (4) of this subsection, or where the land description of the entry must be adjusted pursuant to subsection (b) of this section, in which cases approval pursuant to the terms of this subsection shall be effective at the time the adjustment becomes final.

(a)(2) Where an application describes land within the boundaries of a unit of the National Park System or a unit of the National Wildlife Refuge System, or a unit of the National Wilderness Preservation System in the Tongass or Chugach National Forests established before the effective date of this Act or by this Act, and the described land was not withdrawn pursuant to section 11(a)(1) of the Alaska Native Claims Settlement Act [43 U.S.C.A. § 1610(A)(1)], or where an application describes land which has been patented or deeded to the State of Alaska or which on or before the date of entry was validly selected by, tentatively approved, patented, deeded or confirmed to the State of Alaska pursuant to applicable law and was not withdrawn pursuant to section 11(a)(1)(A) of the Alaska Native Claims Settlement Act [43 U.S.C.A. § 1610(a)(1)(A)] from those lands made available for selection by section 11(a)(2) of the Act [43 U.S.C.A. § 1610(a)(2)] by any Native Village certified as eligible pursuant to section 11(b) of such Act [43 U.S.C.A. § 1610(b)], paragraph (1) of this subsection and subsection (c) of this section shall not apply and the application shall be adjudicated pursuant to the requirements of the Acts referred to in paragraph (1) of this subsection, the Alaska Native Claims Settlement Act [43 U.S.C.A. § 1601 et seq.], and other applicable law.

(a)(3) Paragraph (1) of this subsection and subsection (c) of this section shall not apply and the application shall be adjudicated pursuant to the requirements of the Acts referred to in paragraph (1) of this subsection, if on or before the one hundred and eightieth day following the effective date of the Act—

(A) a Native Corporation files a protest with the Secretary of the Interior (the Secretary) stating that the applicant is not entitled to the land described in the application, and said land is withdrawn for selection by the corporation pursuant to the Alaska Native Claims Settlement Act [43 U.S.C.A. § 1601 et seq.]; or

(B) the State of Alaska fries a protest with the Secretary stating that the land described in the application is necessary for access to lands owned by the United States, the State of Alaska, or a political subdivision of the State of Alaska, to resources located thereon, or to a public body of water regularly employed for transportation purposes, and the protest states with specificity the facts upon which the conclusions concerning access are based and that no reasonable alternatives for access exist; or

(C) a person or entity files a protest with the Secretary stating that the applicant is not entitled to the land described in the application and that said land is the situs of improvements claimed by the person or entity; or

(D) the State of Alaska files a protest with the Secretary respecting an entry which was made prior to a valid selection tentative approval, patent, deed, or confirmation to the State of Alaska pursuant to applicable law; or

(E) regarding public land entries within units of the National Wildlife Refuge System established or expanded in this Act, any such entry not properly made under applicable law, or not the subject of an application filed within the time required by applicable law, or not properly maintained thereafter under applicable law shall be adjudicated pursuant to the Act under which the entry was made.

(a)(4) Paragraph (1) of this subsection and subsection (c) of this section shall not apply to any application which was knowingly and voluntarily relinquished by the applicant.

Amendment of land description in application

(b) An applicant may amend the land description contained in his or her application if said description designates land other than that which the applicant intended to claim at the time of application and if the description as amended describes the land originally intended to be claimed. If the application is amended, this section shall operate to approve the application or to require its adjudication, as the case may be, with reference to the amended land description only: *Provided,* That the Secretary shall notify the State of Alaska and all interested parties, as shown by the records of the Department of the Interior of the intended correction of the entry's location, and any such party shall have until the one hundred and eightieth day following the effective date of this Act or sixty days following mailing of the notice, whichever is later, to file with the Department of the Interior a protest as provided in subsection (a)(3) of this section, which protest, if timely, shall be deemed filed within one hundred and eighty days of the effective date of this Act notwithstanding the actual date of filing: *Provided further,* That the Secretary may require that all applications designating land in a specific area be amended, if at all, prior to a date certain which date shall be calculated to allow for orderly adoption of a plan or survey for the specified area, and the Secretary shall mail notification of the final date for amendment to each affected applicant, and shall provide such other notice as the Secretary deems appropriate, at least sixty days prior to said date: *Provided further,* That no application may be amended for location following adoption of a final plan of survey which includes the location of the entry as described in the application or its location as desired by amendment.

Power sites and power-projects

(c) Where the land described in application (or such an application as adjusted or amended pursuant to subsection (b) or (c) of this section), was on that date withdrawn, reserved, or classified for powersite or power-project purposes, notwithstanding such withdrawal, reservation, or classification the described land shall be deemed vacant, unappropriated, and unreserved within the meaning of the Acts referred to in subsection (a)(1) of this section, and, as such, shall be subject to adjudication or approval pursuant to the terms of this section: *Provided, however,* That if the described land is included as part of a project licensed under part I of the Federal Power Act of June 10, 1920 (41 Stat. 24), as amended [16 U.S.C.A. § 791a et seq.], or is presently utilized for purposes of generating or transmitting electrical power or for any other project authorized by Act of Congress, the foregoing provision shall not apply and the application shall be adjudicated pursuant to the appropriate Act: *Provided further,* That where the applicant commenced occupancy of the land after its withdrawal or classification for powersite purposes, the entry shall be made subject to the right of reentry provided the United States by section 24 of the Federal Power Act, as amended [16 U.S.C.A. § 818]: *Provided further,* That any right of reentry reserved in a patent pursuant to this section shall expire twenty years after the effective date of this Act if at that time the land involved is not subject to a license or an application for a license under part I of the Federal Power Act, as amended, or actually utilized or being developed for a purpose authorized by that Act, as amended [16 U.S.C.A. § 791a et seq.] or other Act of Congress.

Validity of existing rights; rights acquired by actual use and national forest lands unaffected

(d) Prior to issuing a patent for an entry subject to this section, the Secretary shall identify and adjudicate any record entry or application for title to land described in the application, other than the Alaska Native Claims Settlement Act [43 U.S.C.A. § 1601 et seq.], the Alaska Statehood Act, or the Act of May 17, 1906, as amended, which entry or application claims land also described in the application, and shall determine whether such entry or application represents a valid existing right to which the application is subject. Nothing in this section shall be construed to affect rights, if any, acquired by actual use of the described land prior to its withdrawal or classification, as affecting National Forest lands.

Pub.L. 96–487, Title XIII, § 1328, Dec. 2, 1980, 94 Stat. 2489.

SUBCHAPTER VII—NATIONAL NEED MINERAL
ACTIVITY RECOMMENDATION PROCESS

§ 3231. Areas subject to national need recommendation process

The process contained in this subchapter shall apply to all public lands within Alaska except for lands within units of the National Park System and the Arctic National Wildlife Refuge.

Pub.L. 96–487, Title XV, § 1501, Dec. 2, 1980, 94 Stat. 2549.

§ 3232. Recommendations of President to Congress

Recommendation

(a) At any time after December 2, 1980, the President may transmit a recommendation to the Congress that mineral exploration, development, or extraction not permitted under this Act or other applicable law shall be permitted in a specified area of the lands referred to in section 3231 of this title. Notice of such transmittal shall be published in the Federal Register. No recommendation of the President under this section may be transmitted to the Congress before ninety days after publication in the Federal Register of notice of his intention to submit such recommendation.

Findings

(b) A recommendation may be transmitted to the Congress under subsection (a) of this section if the President finds that, based on the information available to him—

(1) there is an urgent national need for the mineral activity; and

(2) such national need outweighs the other public values of the public lands involved and the potential adverse environmental impacts which are likely to result from the activity.

Report

(c) Together with his recommendation, the President shall submit to the Congress—

(1) a report setting forth in detail the relevant factual background and the reasons for his findings and recommendation;

(2) a statement of the conditions and stipulations which would govern the activity if approved by the Congress; and

(3) in any case in which an environmental impact statement is required under the National Environmental Policy Act of 1969 [42 U.S.C.A. § 4321 et seq.], a statement which complies with the requirements of section 102(2)(C) of such Act [42 U.S.C.A. § 4332(2)(C)]. In the case of any recommendation for which an environmental impact statement is not required under section 102(2)(C) of the National Environmental Policy Act of 1969 [42 U.S.C.A. § 4332(2)(C)], the President may, if he deems it desirable, include such a statement in his transmittal to the Congress.

Approval

(d) Any recommendation under this section shall take effect only upon enactment of a joint resolution approving such recommendation within the first period of one hundred and twenty calendar days of continuous session of Congress beginning on the date after the date of receipt by the Senate and House of Representatives of such recommendation. Any recommendation of the President submitted to Congress under subsection (a) of this section shall be considered received by both Houses for purposes of this section on the first day on which both are in session occurring after such recommendation is submitted.

One-hundred-and-twenty-day computation

(e) For purposes of this section—

(1) continuity of session of Congress is broken only by an adjournment sine die; and

(2) the days on which either House is not in session because of an adjournment of more than three days to a day certain are excluded in the computation of the one-hundred-and-twenty-day calendar period.

Pub.L. 96–487, Title XV, § 1502, Dec. 2, 1980, 94 Stat. 2549.

§ 3233. Expedited Congressional review

Rulemaking

(a) This subsection is enacted by Congress—

(1) as an exercise of the rulemaking power of each House of Congress, respectively, and as such it is deemed a part of the rules of each House, respectively, but applicable only with respect to the procedure to be followed in the House in the case of resolutions described by subsection (b) of this section and it supersedes other rules only to the extent that it is inconsistent therewith; and

(2) with full recognition of the constitutional right of either House to change the rules (so far as those relate to the procedure of that House) at any time, in the same manner and to the same extent as in the case of any other rule of such House.

Resolution

(b) For purposes of this section, the term "resolution" means a joint resolution, the resolving clause of which is as follows: "That the House of Representatives and Senate approve the recommendation of the President for _____ in _____ submitted to the Congress on _____ 19__.", the first blank space therein to be filled in with appropriate activity, the second blank space therein to be filled in with the name or description of the area of land affected by the activity, and the third blank space therein to be filled with the date on which the President submits his recommendation to the House of Representatives and the Senate. Such resolution may also include material relating to the application and effect of the National Environmental Policy Act of 1969 [42 U.S.C.A. § 4321 et seq.] to the recommendation.

Referral

(c) A resolution once introduced with respect to such Presidential recommendation shall be referred to one or more committees (and all resolutions with respect to the same Presidential recommendation shall be referred to the same committee or committees) by the President of the Senate or the Speaker of the House of Representatives, as the case may be.

Other procedures

(d) Except as otherwise provided in this section the provisions of section 719f(d) of Title 15 shall apply to the consideration of the resolution.

Pub.L. 96–487, Title XV, § 1503, Dec. 2, 1980, 94 Stat. 2550.

NATIONAL PARKS OMNIBUS MANAGEMENT ACT OF 1998, TITLE II

(16 U.S.C.A. §§ 5931–5937)

SUBCHAPTER II—NATIONAL PARK SYSTEM RESOURCE INVENTORY AND MANAGEMENT

§ 5931. Purposes

The purposes of this subchapter are—

(1) to more effectively achieve the mission of the National Park Service;

(2) to enhance management and protection of national park resources by providing clear authority and direction for the conduct of scientific study in the National Park System and to use the information gathered for management purposes;

(3) to ensure appropriate documentation of resource conditions in the National Park System;

(4) to encourage others to use the National Park System for study to the benefit of park management as well as broader scientific value, where such study is consistent with sections 1, 2, 3, and 4 of this title; and

(5) to encourage the publication and dissemination of information derived from studies in the National Park System.

Pub.L. 105–391, Title II, § 201, Nov. 13, 1998, 112 Stat. 3499.

§ 5932. Research mandate

The Secretary is authorized and directed to assure that management of units of the National Park System is enhanced by the availability and utilization of a broad program of the highest quality science and information.

Pub.L. 105–391, Title II, § 202, Nov. 13, 1998, 112 Stat. 3499.

* * *

§ 5934. Inventory and monitoring program

The Secretary shall undertake a program of inventory and monitoring of National Park System resources to establish baseline information and to provide information on the long-term trends in the condition of National Park System resources. The monitoring program shall be developed in cooperation with other Federal monitoring and information collection efforts to ensure a cost-effective approach.

Pub.L. 105–391, Title II, § 204, Nov. 13, 1998, 112 Stat. 3500.

§ 5935. Availability for scientific study

In general

(a) The Secretary may solicit, receive, and consider requests from Federal or non-Federal public or private agencies, organizations, individuals, or other entities for the use of any unit of the National Park System for purposes of scientific study.

Criteria

(b) A request for use of a unit of the National Park System under subsection (a) of this section may only be approved if the Secretary determines that the proposed study—

(1) is consistent with applicable laws and National Park Service management policies; and

(2) will be conducted in a manner as to pose no threat to park resources or public enjoyment derived from those resources.

Fee waiver

(c) The Secretary may waive any park admission or recreational use fee in order to facilitate the conduct of scientific study under this section.

Negotiations

(d) The Secretary may enter into negotiations with the research community and private industry for equitable, efficient benefits-sharing arrangements.

Pub.L. 105–391, Title II, § 205, Nov. 13, 1998, 112 Stat. 3500.

§ 5936. Integration of study results into management decisions

The Secretary shall take such measures as are necessary to assure the full and proper utilization of the results of scientific study for park management decisions. In each case in which an action undertaken by the National Park Service may cause a significant adverse effect on a park resource, the administrative record shall reflect the manner in which unit resource studies have been considered. The trend in the condition of resources of the National Park System shall be a significant factor in the annual performance evaluation of each superintendent of a unit of the National Park System.

Pub.L. 105–391, Title II, § 206, Nov. 13, 1998, 112 Stat. 3500.

§ 5937. Confidentiality of information

Information concerning the nature and specific location of a National Park System resource which is endangered, threatened, rare, or commercially valuable, of mineral or paleontological objects within units of the National Park System, or of objects of cultural patrimony within units of the National Park System, may be withheld from the public in response to a request under section 552 of Title 5, unless the Secretary determines that—

(1) disclosure of the information would further the purposes of the unit of the National Park System in which the resource or object is located and would not create an unreasonable risk of harm, theft, or destruction of the resource or object, including individual organic or inorganic specimens; and

(2) disclosure is consistent with other applicable laws protecting the resource or object.

Pub.L. 105–391, Title II, § 207, Nov. 13, 1998, 112 Stat. 3501.

HEALTHY FORESTS RESTORATION ACT OF 2003

(16 U.S.C.A. §§ 6501–6591)

§ 6501. Purposes

The purposes of this chapter are—

(1) to reduce wildfire risk to communities, municipal water supplies, and other at-risk Federal land through a collaborative process of planning, prioritizing, and implementing hazardous fuel reduction projects;

(2) to authorize grant programs to improve the commercial value of forest biomass (that otherwise contributes to the risk of catastrophic fire or insect or disease infestation) for producing electric energy, useful heat, transportation fuel, and petroleum-based product substitutes, and for other commercial purposes;

(3) to enhance efforts to protect watersheds and address threats to forest and rangeland health, including catastrophic wildfire, across the landscape;

(4) to promote systematic gathering of information to address the impact of insect and disease infestations and other damaging agents on forest and rangeland health;

(5) to improve the capacity to detect insect and disease infestations at an early stage, particularly with respect to hardwood forests; and

(6) to protect, restore, and enhance forest ecosystem components—

(A) to promote the recovery of threatened and endangered species;

(B) to improve biological diversity; and

(C) to enhance productivity and carbon sequestration.

Pub.L. 108–148, § 2, Dec. 3, 2003, 117 Stat. 1888.

§ 6502. Definitions

In this chapter:

Federal land

(1) The term "Federal land" means—

(A) land of the National Forest System (as defined in section 1609(a) of this title) administered by the Secretary of Agriculture, acting through the Chief of the Forest Service; and

(B) public lands (as defined in section 1702 of Title 43), the surface of which is administered by the Secretary of the Interior, acting through the Director of the Bureau of Land Management.

Indian tribe

(2) The term "Indian tribe" has the meaning given the term in section 450b of Title 25.

Pub.L. 108–148, § 3, Dec. 3, 2003, 117 Stat. 1888.

§ 6511. Definitions

In this subchapter:

At-risk community

(1) The term "at-risk community" means an area—

(A) that is comprised of—

(i) an interface community as defined in the notice entitled "Wildland Urban Interface Communities Within the Vicinity of Federal Lands That Are at High Risk From Wildfire" issued by the Secretary of Agriculture and the Secretary of the Interior in accordance with title IV of the Department of the Interior and Related Agencies Appropriations Act, 2001 (114 Stat. 1009) (66 Fed. Reg. 753, January 4, 2001); or

(ii) a group of homes and other structures with basic infrastructure and services (such as utilities and collectively maintained transportation routes) within or adjacent to Federal land;

(B) in which conditions are conducive to a large-scale wildland fire disturbance event; and

(C) for which a significant threat to human life or property exists as a result of a wildland fire disturbance event.

Authorized hazardous fuel reduction project

(2) The term "authorized hazardous fuel reduction project" means the measures and methods described in the definition of "appropriate tools" contained in the glossary of the Implementation Plan, on Federal land described in section 6512(a) of this title and conducted under sections 6513 and 6514 of this title.

Community wildfire protection plan

(3) The term "community wildfire protection plan" means a plan for an at-risk community that—

237

(A) is developed within the context of the collaborative agreements and the guidance established by the Wildland Fire Leadership Council and agreed to by the applicable local government, local fire department, and State agency responsible for forest management, in consultation with interested parties and the Federal land management agencies managing land in the vicinity of the at-risk community;

(B) identifies and prioritizes areas for hazardous fuel reduction treatments and recommends the types and methods of treatment on Federal and non-Federal land that will protect 1 or more at-risk communities and essential infrastructure; and

(C) recommends measures to reduce structural ignitability throughout the at-risk community.

Condition class 2

(4) The term "condition class 2", with respect to an area of Federal land, means the condition class description developed by the Forest Service Rocky Mountain Research Station in the general technical report entitled "Development of Coarse–Scale Spatial Data for Wildland Fire and Fuel Management" (RMRS–87), dated April 2000 (including any subsequent revision to the report), under which—

(A) fire regimes on the land have been moderately altered from historical ranges;

(B) there exists a moderate risk of losing key ecosystem components from fire;

(C) fire frequencies have increased or decreased from historical frequencies by 1 or more return intervals, resulting in moderate changes to—

(i) the size, frequency, intensity, or severity of fires; or

(ii) landscape patterns; and

(D) vegetation attributes have been moderately altered from the historical range of the attributes.

Condition class 3

(5) The term "condition class 3", with respect to an area of Federal land, means the condition class description developed by the Rocky Mountain Research Station in the general technical report referred to in paragraph (4) (including any subsequent revision to the report), under which—

(A) fire regimes on land have been significantly altered from historical ranges;

(B) there exists a high risk of losing key ecosystem components from fire;

(C) fire frequencies have departed from historical frequencies by multiple return intervals, resulting in dramatic changes to—

(i) the size, frequency, intensity, or severity of fires; or

(ii) landscape patterns; and

(D) vegetation attributes have been significantly altered from the historical range of the attributes.

Day

(6) The term "day" means—

(A) a calendar day; or

(B) if a deadline imposed by this subchapter would expire on a nonbusiness day, the end of the next business day.

Decision document

(7) The term "decision document" means—

(A) a decision notice (as that term is used in the Forest Service Handbook);

(B) a decision record (as that term is used in the Bureau of Land Management Handbook); and

(C) a record of decision (as that term is used in applicable regulations of the Council on Environmental Quality).

Fire regime I

(8) The term "fire regime I" means an area—

(A) in which historically there have been low-severity fires with a frequency of 0 through 35 years; and

(B) that is located primarily in low elevation forests of pine, oak, or pinyon juniper.

Fire regime II

(9) The term "fire regime II" means an area—

(A) in which historically there are stand replacement severity fires with a frequency of 0 through 35 years; and

(B) That is located primarily in low-to mid-elevation rangeland, grassland, or shrubland.

Fire regime III

(10) The term "fire regime III" means an area—

(A) in which historically there are mixed severity fires with a frequency of 35 through 100 years; and

(B) that is located primarily in forests of mixed conifer, dry Douglas fir, or wet Ponderosa pine.

Implementation Plan

(11) The term "Implementation Plan" means the Implementation Plan for the Comprehensive Strategy for a Collaborative Approach for Reducing Wildland Fire Risks to Communities and the Environment, dated May 2002, developed pursuant to the conference report to accompany the

Department of the Interior and Related Agencies Appropriations Act, 2001 (House Report No. 106–64) (and subsequent revisions).

Municipal water supply system

(12) The term "municipal water supply system" means the reservoirs, canals, ditches, flumes, laterals, pipes, pipelines, and other surface facilities and systems constructed or installed for the collection, impoundment, storage, transportation, or distribution of drinking water.

Resource management plan

(13) The term "resource management plan" means—

(A) a land and resource management plan prepared for 1 or more units of land of the National Forest System described in section 6502(1)(A) of this title under section 1604 of this title; or

(B) a land use plan prepared for 1 or more units of the public land described in section 6502(1)(A) of this title under section 1712 of Title 43.

Secretary

(14) The term "Secretary" means—

(A) the Secretary of Agriculture, with respect to land of the National Forest System described in section 6502(1)(A) of this title; and

(B) the Secretary of the Interior, with respect to public lands described in section 6502(1)(B) of this title.

Threatened and endangered species habitat

(15) The term "threatened and endangered species habitat" means Federal land identified in—

(A) a determination that a species is an endangered species or a threatened species under the Endangered Species Act of 1973 (16 U.S.C. 1531 et seq.);

(B) a designation of critical habitat of the species under that Act; or

(C) a recovery plan prepared for the species under that Act.

Wildland-urban interface

(16) The term "wildland-urban interface" means—

(A) an area within or adjacent to an at-risk community that is identified in recommendations to the Secretary in a community wildfire protection plan; or

(B) in the case of any area for which a community wildfire protection plan is not in effect—

(i) an area extending 1/2-mile from the boundary of an at-risk community;

(ii) an area within 1 1/2 miles of the boundary of an at-risk community, including any land that—

(I) has a sustained steep slope that creates the potential for wildfire behavior endangering the at-risk community;

(II) has a geographic feature that aids in creating an effective fire break, such as a road or ridge top; or

(III) is in condition class 3, as documented by the Secretary in the project-specific environmental analysis; and

(iii) an area that is adjacent to an evacuation route for an at-risk community that the Secretary determines, in cooperation with the at-risk community, requires hazardous fuel reduction to provide safer evacuation from the at-risk community.

Pub.L. 108–148, Title I, § 101, Dec. 3, 2003, 117 Stat. 1889.

§ 6512. Authorized hazardous fuel reduction projects

Authorized projects

(a) As soon as practicable after December 3, 2003, the Secretary shall implement authorized hazardous fuel reduction projects, consistent with the Implementation Plan, on—

(1) Federal land in wildland-urban interface areas;

(2) condition class 3 Federal land, in such proximity to a municipal water supply system or a stream feeding such a system within a municipal watershed that a significant risk exists that a fire disturbance event would have adverse effects on the water quality of the municipal water supply or the maintenance of the system, including a risk to water quality posed by erosion following such a fire disturbance event;

(3) condition class 2 Federal land located within fire regime I, fire regime II, or fire regime III, in such proximity to a municipal water supply system or a stream feeding such a system within a municipal watershed that a significant risk exists that a fire disturbance event would have adverse effects on the water quality of the municipal water supply or the maintenance of the system, including a risk to water quality posed by erosion following such a fire disturbance event;

(4) Federal land on which windthrow or blowdown, ice storm damage, the existence of an epidemic of disease or insects, or the presence of such an epidemic on immediately adjacent land and the imminent risk it will spread, poses a significant threat to an ecosystem component, or forest or rangeland resource, on the Federal land or adjacent non-Federal land; and

(5) Federal land not covered by paragraphs (1) through (4) that contains threatened and endangered species habitat, if—

(A) natural fire regimes on that land are identified as being important for, or wildfire is identified as a threat to, an endangered species, a threatened species, or habitat of an endangered

241

species or threatened species in a species recovery plan prepared under section 1533 of this title, or a notice published in the Federal Register determining a species to be an endangered species or a threatened species or designating critical habitat;

(B) the authorized hazardous fuel reduction project will provide enhanced protection from catastrophic wildfire for the endangered species, threatened species, or habitat of the endangered species or threatened species; and

(C) the Secretary complies with any applicable guidelines specified in any management or recovery plan described in subparagraph (A).

Relation to agency plans

(b) An authorized hazardous fuel reduction project shall be conducted consistent with the resource management plan and other relevant administrative policies or decisions applicable to the Federal land covered by the project.

Acreage limitation

(c) Not more than a total of 20,000,000 acres of Federal land may be treated under authorized hazardous fuel reduction projects.

Exclusion of certain Federal land

(d) The Secretary may not conduct an authorized hazardous fuel reduction project that would occur on—

(1) a component of the National Wilderness Preservation System;

(2) Federal land on which the removal of vegetation is prohibited or restricted by Act of Congress or Presidential proclamation (including the applicable implementation plan); or

(3) a Wilderness Study Area.

Old growth stands

(e)(1) Definitions. In this subsection and subsection (f) of this section:

(A) Applicable period. The term "applicable period" means—

(i) the 2–year period beginning on December 3, 2003; or

(ii) in the case of a resource management plan that the Secretary is in the process of revising as of December 3, 2003.

(B) Covered project. The term "covered project" means an authorized hazardous fuel reduction project carried out on land described in paragraph (1), (2), (3), or (5) of subsection (a) of this section.

(C) Management direction. The term "management direction" means definitions, designations, standards, guidelines, goals, or objectives established for an old growth stand under a resource management plan developed in accordance with applicable law, including section 1604(g)(3)(B) of this title.

(D) Old growth stand. The term "old growth stand" has the meaning given the term under management direction used pursuant to paragraphs (3) and (4), based on the structure and composition characteristic of the forest type, and in accordance with applicable law, including section 1604(g)(3)(B) of this title.

(2) Project requirements. In carrying out a covered project, the Secretary shall fully maintain, or contribute toward the restoration of, the structure and composition of old growth stands according to the pre-fire suppression old growth conditions characteristic of the forest type, taking into account the contribution of the stand to landscape fire adaptation and watershed health, and retaining the large trees contributing to old growth structure.

(3) Newer management direction

(A) In general. If the management direction for an old growth stand was established on or after December 15, 1993, the Secretary shall meet the requirements of paragraph (2) in carrying out a covered project by implementing the management direction.

(B) Amendments or revisions. Any amendment or revision to management direction for which final administrative approval is granted after December 3, 2003 shall be consistent with paragraph (2) for the purpose of carrying out covered projects.

(4) Older management direction.

(A) In general. If the management direction for an old growth stand was established before December 15, 1993, the Secretary shall meet the requirements of paragraph (2) in carrying out a covered project during the applicable period by implementing the management direction.

(B) Review required. Subject to subparagraph (C), during the applicable period for management direction referred to in subparagraph (A), the Secretary shall—

(i) review the management direction for affected covered projects, taking into account any relevant scientific information made available since the adoption of the management direction; and

(ii) amend the management direction for affected covered projects to be consistent with paragraph (2), if necessary to reflect relevant scientific information the Secretary did not consider in formulating the management direction.

(C) Review not completed. If the Secretary does not complete the review of the management direction in accordance with subparagraph (B) before the end of the applicable period, the Secretary shall not carry out any portion of affected covered projects in stands that are identified as old growth stands (based on substantial supporting evidence) by any person during scoping, within the period—

(i) beginning at the close of the applicable period for the management direction governing the affected covered projects; and

(ii) ending on the earlier of—

(I) the date the Secretary completes the action required by subparagraph (B) for the management direction applicable to the affected covered projects; or

(II) the date on which the acreage limitation specified in subsection (c) of this section (as that limitation may be adjusted by a subsequent Act of Congress) is reached.

(5) Limitation to covered projects. Nothing in this subsection requires the Secretary to revise or otherwise amend a resource management plan to make the project requirements of paragraph (2) apply to an activity other than a covered project.

Large tree retention

(f)(1) In general. Except in old growth stands where the management direction is consistent with subsection (e)(2) of this section, the Secretary shall carry out a covered project in a manner that—

(A) focuses largely on small diameter trees, thinning, strategic fuel breaks, and prescribed fire to modify fire behavior, as measured by the projected reduction of uncharacteristically severe wildfire effects for the forest type (such as adverse soil impacts, tree mortality or other impacts); and

(B) maximizes the retention of large trees, as appropriate for the forest type, to the extent that the trees promote fire-resilient stands.

(2) Wildfire risk. Nothing in this subsection prevents achievement of the purposes described in section 6501(1) of this title.

Monitoring and assessing forest and rangeland health

(g)(1) In general. For each Forest Service administrative region and each Bureau of Land Management State Office, the Secretary shall—

(A) monitor the results of a representative sample of the projects authorized under this subchapter for each management unit; and

(B) not later than 5 years after December 3, 2003, and each 5 years thereafter, issue a report that includes—

(i) an evaluation of the progress towards project goals; and

(ii) recommendations for modifications to the projects and management treatments.

(2) Consistency of projects with recommendations. An authorized hazardous fuel reduction project approved following the issuance of a monitoring report shall, to the maximum extent practicable, be consistent with any applicable recommendations in the report.

(3) Similar vegetation types. The results of a monitoring report shall be made available for use (if appropriate) in an authorized hazardous fuels reduction project conducted in a similar vegetation type on land under the jurisdiction of the Secretary.

(4) Monitoring and assessments. Monitoring and assessment shall include a description of the changes in condition class, using the Fire Regime Condition Class Guidebook or successor guidance, specifically comparing end results to—

(A) pretreatment conditions;

(B) historical fire regimes; and

(C) any applicable watershed or landscape goals or objectives in the resource management plan or other relevant direction.

(5) Multiparty monitoring

(A) In general. In an area where significant interest is expressed in multiparty monitoring, the Secretary shall establish a multiparty monitoring, evaluation, and accountability process in order to assess the positive or negative ecological and social effects of authorized hazardous fuel reduction projects and projects conducted pursuant to section 6554 of this title.

(B) Diverse stakeholders. The Secretary shall include diverse stakeholders (including interested citizens and Indian tribes) in the process required under subparagraph (A).

(C) Funding. Funds to carry out this paragraph may be derived from operations funds for projects described in subparagraph (A).

(6) Collection of monitoring data. The Secretary may collect monitoring data by entering into cooperative agreements or contracts with, or providing grants to, small or micro-businesses, cooperatives, nonprofit organizations, Youth Conservation Corps work crews, or related State, local, and other non-Federal conservation corps.

(7) Tracking. For each administrative unit, the Secretary shall track acres burned, by the degree of severity, by large wildfires (as defined by the Secretary).

(8) Monitoring and maintenance of treated areas. The Secretary shall, to the maximum extent practicable, develop a process for monitoring the need for maintenance of treated areas, over time, in order to preserve the forest health benefits achieved.

Pub.L. 108–148, Title I, § 102, Dec. 3, 2003, 117 Stat. 1892.

§ 6513. Prioritization

In general

(a) In accordance with the Implementation Plan, the Secretary shall develop an annual program of work for Federal land that gives priority to authorized hazardous fuel reduction projects that provide for the protection of at-risk communities or watersheds or that implement community wildfire protection plans.

Collaboration

(b)(1) In general. The Secretary shall consider recommendations under subsection (a) of this section that are made by at-risk communities that have developed community wildfire protection plans.

(2) Exemption. The Federal Advisory Committee Act (5 U.S.C. App.) shall not apply to the planning process and recommendations concerning community wildfire protection plans.

Administration

(c)(1) In general. Federal agency involvement in developing a community wildfire protection plan, or a recommendation made in a community wildfire protection plan, shall not be considered a Federal agency action under the National Environmental Policy Act of 1969 (42 U.S.C. 4321 et seq.).

(2) Compliance. In implementing authorized hazardous fuel reduction projects on Federal land, the Secretary shall, in accordance with section 6514 of this title, comply with the National Environmental Policy Act of 1969 (42 U.S.C. 4321 et seq.).

Funding allocation

(d)(1) Federal land

(A) In general. Subject to subparagraph (B), the Secretary shall use not less than 50 percent of the funds allocated for authorized hazardous fuel reduction projects in the wildland-urban interface.

(B) Applicability and allocation. The funding allocation in subparagraph (A) shall apply at the national level. The Secretary may allocate the proportion of funds differently than is required under subparagraph (A) within individual management units as appropriate, in particular to conduct authorized hazardous fuel reduction projects on land described in section 6512(a)(4) of this title.

(C) Wildland-urban interface. In the case of an authorized hazardous fuel reduction project for which a decision notice is issued during the 1–year period beginning on December 3, 2003, the Secretary shall use existing definitions of the term "wildland-urban interface" rather than the definition of that term provided under section 6511 of this title.

(2) Non–Federal land

(A) In general. In providing financial assistance under any provision of law for hazardous fuel reduction projects on non-Federal land, the Secretary shall consider recommendations made by at-risk communities that have developed community wildfire protection plans.

(B) Priority. In allocating funding under this paragraph, the Secretary should, to the maximum extent practicable, give priority to communities that have adopted a community wildfire protection plan or have taken proactive measures to encourage willing property owners to reduce fire risk on private property.

Pub.L. 108–148, Title I, § 103, Dec. 3, 2003, 117 Stat. 1896.

§ 6514. Environmental analysis

Authorized hazardous fuel reduction projects

(a) Except as otherwise provided in this subchapter, the Secretary shall conduct authorized hazardous fuel reduction projects in accordance with—

(1) the National Environmental Policy Act of 1969 (42 U.S.C. 4331 et seq.); and

(2) other applicable laws.

Environmental assessment or environmental impact statement

(b) The Secretary shall prepare an environmental assessment or an environmental impact statement pursuant to section 102(2) of the National Environmental Policy Act of 1969 (42 U.S.C. 4332(2)) for each authorized hazardous fuel reduction project.

Consideration of alternatives

(c)(1) In general. Except as provided in subsection (d) of this section, in the environmental assessment or environmental impact statement prepared under subsection (b) of this section, the Secretary shall study, develop, and describe—

(A) the proposed agency action;

(B) the alternative of no action; and

(C) an additional action alternative, if the additional alternative—

(i) is proposed during scoping or the collaborative process under subsection (f) of this section; and

(ii) meets the purpose and need of the project, in accordance with regulations promulgated by the Council on Environmental Quality.

(2) Multiple additional alternatives. If more than 1 additional alternative is proposed under paragraph (1)(C), the Secretary shall—

(A) select which additional alternative to consider, which is a choice that is in the sole discretion of the Secretary; and

(B) provide a written record describing the reasons for the selection.

Alternative analysis process for projects in wildland-urban interface

(d)(1) Proposed agency action and 1 action alternative. For an authorized hazardous fuel reduction project that is proposed to be conducted in the wildland-urban interface, the Secretary is not required to study, develop, or describe more than the proposed agency action and 1 action alternative in the environmental assessment or environmental impact statement prepared pursuant to section 102(2) of the National Environmental Policy Act of 1969 (42 U.S.C. 4332(2)).

(2) Proposed agency action. Notwithstanding paragraph (1), but subject to paragraph (3), if an authorized hazardous fuel reduction project proposed to be conducted in the wildland-urban interface is located no further than 1 1/2 miles from the boundary of an at-risk community, the Secretary is not required to study, develop, or describe any alternative to the proposed agency action in the environmental assessment or environ-

mental impact statement prepared pursuant to section 102(2) of the National Environmental Policy Act of 1969 (42 U.S.C. 4332(2)).

(3) Proposed agency action and community wildfire protection plan alternative. In the case of an authorized hazardous fuel reduction project described in paragraph (2), if the at-risk community has adopted a community wildfire protection plan and the proposed agency action does not implement the recommendations in the plan regarding the general location and basic method of treatments, the Secretary shall evaluate the recommendations in the plan as an alternative to the proposed agency action in the environmental assessment or environmental impact statement prepared pursuant to section 102(2) of the National Environmental Policy Act of 1969 (42 U.S.C. 4332(2)).

Public notice and meeting

(e)(1) Public notice. The Secretary shall provide notice of each authorized hazardous fuel reduction project in accordance with applicable regulations and administrative guidelines.

(2) Public meeting. During the preparation stage of each authorized hazardous fuel reduction project, the Secretary shall—

(A) conduct a public meeting at an appropriate location proximate to the administrative unit of the Federal land on which the authorized hazardous fuel reduction project will be conducted; and

(B) provide advance notice of the location, date, and time of the meeting.

Public collaboration

(f) In order to encourage meaningful public participation during preparation of authorized hazardous fuel reduction projects, the Secretary shall facilitate collaboration among State and local governments and Indian tribes, and participation of interested persons, during the preparation of each authorized fuel reduction project in a manner consistent with the Implementation Plan.

Environmental analysis and public comment

(g) In accordance with section 102(2) of the National Environmental Policy Act of 1969 (42 U.S.C. 4332(2)) and the applicable regulations and administrative guidelines, the Secretary shall provide an opportunity for public comment during the preparation of any environmental assessment or environmental impact statement for an authorized hazardous fuel reduction project.

Decision document

(h) The Secretary shall sign a decision document for authorized hazardous fuel reduction projects and provide notice of the final agency actions.

Pub.L. 108–148, Title I, § 104, Dec. 3, 2003, 117 Stat. 1897.

§ 6515. Special administrative review process

Interim final regulations

(a)(1) In general. Not later than 30 days after December 3, 2003, the Secretary of Agriculture shall promulgate interim final regulations to establish a predecisional administrative review process for the period described in paragraph (2) that will serve as the sole means by which a person can seek administrative review regarding an authorized hazardous fuel reduction project on Forest Service land.

(2) Period. The predecisional administrative review process required under paragraph (1) shall occur during the period—

(A) beginning after the completion of the environmental assessment or environmental impact statement; and

(B) ending not later than the date of the issuance of the final decision approving the project.

(3) Eligibility. To be eligible to participate in the administrative review process for an authorized hazardous fuel reduction project under paragraph (1), a person shall submit to the Secretary, during scoping or the public comment period for the draft environmental analysis for the project, specific written comments that relate to the proposed action.

(4) Effective date. The interim final regulations promulgated under paragraph (1) shall take effect on the date of promulgation of the regulations.

Final regulations

(b) The Secretary shall promulgate final regulations to establish the process described in subsection (a)(1) of this section after the interim final regulations have been published and reasonable time has been provided for public comment.

Administrative review

(c)(1) In general. A person may bring a civil action challenging an authorized hazardous fuel reduction project in a Federal district court only if the person has challenged the authorized hazardous fuel reduction project by exhausting—

(A) the administrative review process established by the Secretary of Agriculture under this section; or

(B) the administrative hearings and appeals procedures established by the Department of the Interior.

(2) Issues. An issue may be considered in the judicial review of an action under section 6516 of this title only if the issue was raised in an administrative review process described in paragraph (1).

(3) Exception

(A) In general. An exception to the requirement of exhausting the administrative review process before seeking judicial review shall be available if a Federal court finds that the futility or inadequacy exception applies to a specific plaintiff or claim.

(B) Information. If an agency fails or is unable to make information timely available during the administrative review process, a court should evaluate whether the administrative review process was inadequate for claims or issues to which the information is material.

Pub.L. 108–148, Title I, § 105, Dec. 3, 2003, 117 Stat. 1899.

§ 6516. Judicial review in United States district courts

Venue

(a) Notwithstanding section 1391 of Title 28, or other applicable law, an authorized hazardous fuels reduction project conducted under this subchapter shall be subject to judicial review only in the United States district court for a district in which the Federal land to be treated under the authorized hazardous fuels reduction project is located.

Expeditious completion of judicial review

(b) In the judicial review of an action challenging an authorized hazardous fuel reduction project under subsection (a) of this section, Congress encourages a court of competent jurisdiction to expedite, to the maximum extent practicable, the proceedings in the action with the goal of rendering a final determination on jurisdiction, and (if jurisdiction exists) a final determination on the merits, as soon as practicable after the date on which a complaint or appeal is filed to initiate the action.

Injunctions

(c)(1) In general. Subject to paragraph (2), the length of any preliminary injunctive relief and stays pending appeal covering an authorized hazardous fuel reduction project carried out under this subchapter shall not exceed 60 days.

(2) Renewal

(A) In general. A court of competent jurisdiction may issue 1 or more renewals of any preliminary injunction, or stay pending appeal, granted under paragraph (1).

(B) Updates. In each renewal of an injunction in an action, the parties to the action shall present the court with updated information on the status of the authorized hazardous fuel reduction project.

(3) Balancing of short-and long-term effects. As part of its weighing the equities while considering any request for an injunction that applies to an agency action under an authorized hazardous fuel reduction project, the court reviewing the project shall balance the impact to the ecosystem likely affected by the project of—

(A) The short-and long-term effects of undertaking the agency action; against

(B) The short-and long-term effects of not undertaking the agency action.

Pub.L. 108–148, Title I, § 106, Dec. 3, 2003, 117 Stat. 1900.

§ 6517. Effect of subchapter

Other authority

(a) Nothing in this subchapter affects, or otherwise biases, the use by the Secretary of other statutory or administrative authority (including categorical exclusions adopted to implement the National Environmental Policy Act of 1969 (42 U.S.C. 4321 et seq.)) to conduct a hazardous fuel reduction project on Federal land (including Federal land identified in section 6512(d) of this title) that is not conducted using the process authorized by section 6514 of this title.

National Forest System

(b) For projects and activities of the National Forest System other than authorized hazardous fuel reduction projects, nothing in this subchapter affects, or otherwise biases, the notice, comment, and appeal procedures for projects and activities of the National Forest System contained in part 215 of title 36, Code of Federal Regulations, or the consideration or disposition of any legal action brought with respect to the procedures.

Pub.L. 108–148, Title I, § 107, Dec. 3, 2003, 117 Stat. 1900.

* * *

FEDERAL LANDS RECREATION ENHANCEMENT ACT OF 2004

(16 U.S.C.A. §§ 6801–6814)

§ 6801. Definitions

In this chapter:

Standard amenity recreation fee

(1) The term "standard amenity recreation fee" means the recreation fee authorized by section 6802(f) of this title.

Expanded amenity recreation fee

(2) The term "expanded amenity recreation fee" means the recreation fee authorized by section 6802(g) of this title.

Entrance fee

(3) The term "entrance fee" means the recreation fee authorized to be charged to enter onto lands managed by the National Park Service or the United States Fish and Wildlife Service.

Federal land management agency

(4) The term "Federal land management agency" means the National Park Service, the United States Fish and Wildlife Service, the Bureau of Land Management, the Bureau of Reclamation, or the Forest Service.

251

Federal recreational lands and waters

(5) The term "Federal recreational lands and waters" means lands or waters managed by a Federal land management agency.

National Parks and Federal Recreational Lands Pass

(6) The term "National Parks and Federal Recreational Lands Pass" means the interagency national pass authorized by section 6804 of this title.

Passholder

(7) The term "passholder" means the person who is issued a recreation pass.

Recreation fee

(8) The term "recreation fee" means an entrance fee, standard amenity recreation fee, expanded amenity recreation fee, or special recreation permit fee.

Recreation pass

(9) The term "recreation pass" means the National Parks and Federal Recreational Lands Pass or one of the other recreation passes available as authorized by section 6804 of this title.

Secretary

(10) The term "Secretary" means—

(A) the Secretary of the Interior, with respect to a Federal land management agency (other than the Forest Service); and

(B) the Secretary of Agriculture, with respect to the Forest Service.

Secretaries

(11) The term "Secretaries" means the Secretary of the Interior and the Secretary of Agriculture acting jointly.

Special account

(12) The term "special account" means the special account established in the Treasury under section 6806 of this title for a Federal land management agency.

Special recreation permit fee

(13) The term "special recreation permit fee" means the fee authorized by section 6802(h) of this title.

Pub.L. 108–447, Div. J, Title VIII, § 802, Dec. 8, 2004, 118 Stat. 3377.

§ 6802.   Recreation fee authority

Authority of Secretary

(a) Beginning in fiscal year 2005 and thereafter, the Secretary may establish, modify, charge, and collect recreation fees at Federal recreational lands and waters as provided for in this section.

Basis for recreation fees

(b) Recreation fees shall be established in a manner consistent with the following criteria:

(1) The amount of the recreation fee shall be commensurate with the benefits and services provided to the visitor.

(2) The Secretary shall consider the aggregate effect of recreation fees on recreation users and recreation service providers.

(3) The Secretary shall consider comparable fees charged elsewhere and by other public agencies and by nearby private sector operators.

(4) The Secretary shall consider the public policy or management objectives served by the recreation fee.

(5) The Secretary shall obtain input from the appropriate Recreation Resource Advisory Committee, as provided in section 6803(d) of this title.

(6) The Secretary shall consider such other factors or criteria as determined appropriate by the Secretary.

Special considerations

(c) The Secretary shall establish the minimum number of recreation fees and shall avoid the collection of multiple or layered recreation fees for similar uses, activities, or programs.

Limitations on recreation fees

(d)(1) Prohibition on fees for certain activities or services. The Secretary shall not charge any standard amenity recreation fee or expanded amenity recreation fee for Federal recreational lands and waters administered by the Bureau of Land Management, the Forest Service, or the Bureau of Reclamation under this chapter for any of the following:

(A) Solely for parking, undesignated parking, or picnicking along roads or trailsides.

(B) For general access unless specifically authorized under this section.

(C) For dispersed areas with low or no investment unless specifically authorized under this section.

(D) For persons who are driving through, walking through, boating through, horseback riding through, or hiking through Federal recreational lands and waters without using the facilities and services.

(E) For camping at undeveloped sites that do not provide a minimum number of facilities and services as described in subsection (g)(2)(A) of this section.

(F) For use of overlooks or scenic pullouts.

(G) For travel by private, noncommercial vehicle over any national parkway or any road or highway established as a part of the Federal-aid System, as defined in section 101 of Title 23, which is commonly used by the public as a means of travel between two places either or both of which are outside any unit or area at which recreation fees are charged under this chapter.

(H) For travel by private, noncommercial vehicle, boat, or aircraft over any road or highway, waterway, or airway to any land in which such person has any property right if such land is within any unit or area at which recreation fees are charged under this chapter.

(I) For any person who has a right of access for hunting or fishing privileges under a specific provision of law or treaty.

(J) For any person who is engaged in the conduct of official Federal, State, Tribal, or local government business.

(K) For special attention or extra services necessary to meet the needs of the disabled.

(2) Relation to fees for use of highways or roads. An entity that pays a special recreation permit fee or similar permit fee shall not be subject to a road cost-sharing fee or a fee for the use of highways or roads that are open to private, noncommercial use within the boundaries of any Federal recreational lands or waters, as authorized under section 537 of this title.

(3) Prohibition on fees for certain persons or places. The Secretary shall not charge an entrance fee or standard amenity recreation fee for the following:

(A) Any person under 16 years of age.

(B) Outings conducted for noncommercial educational purposes by schools or bona fide academic institutions.

(C) The U.S.S. Arizona Memorial, Independence National Historical Park, any unit of the National Park System within the District of Columbia, or Arlington House–Robert E. Lee National Memorial.

(D) The Flight 93 National Memorial.

(E) Entrance on other routes into the Great Smoky Mountains National Park or any part thereof unless fees are charged for entrance into that park on main highways and thoroughfares.

(F) Entrance on units of the National Park System containing deed restrictions on charging fees.

(G) An area or unit covered under section 203 of the Alaska National Interest Lands Conservation Act (Public Law 96–487; 16 U.S.C. 410hh–2), with the exception of Denali National Park and Preserve.

(H) A unit of the National Wildlife Refuge System created, expanded, or modified by the Alaska National Interest Lands Conservation Act (Public Law 96–487).

(I) Any person who visits a unit or area under the jurisdiction of the United States Fish and Wildlife Service and who has been issued a valid migratory bird hunting and conservation stamp issued under section 718b of this title.

(J) Any person engaged in a nonrecreational activity authorized under a valid permit issued under any other Act, including a valid grazing permit.

(4) No restriction on recreation opportunities. Nothing in this chapter shall limit the use of recreation opportunities only to areas designated for collection of recreation fees.

Entrance fee

(e)(1) Authorized sites for entrance fees. The Secretary of the Interior may charge an entrance fee for a unit of the National Park System, including a national monument administered by the National Park Service, or for a unit of the National Wildlife Refuge System.

(2) Prohibited sites. The Secretary shall not charge an entrance fee for Federal recreational lands and waters managed by the Bureau of Land Management, the Bureau of Reclamation, or the Forest Service.

Standard amenity recreation fee

(f) Except as limited by subsection (d) of this section, the Secretary may charge a standard amenity recreation fee for Federal recreational lands and waters under the jurisdiction of the Bureau of Land Management, the Bureau of Reclamation, or the Forest Service, but only at the following:

(1) A National Conservation Area.

(2) A National Volcanic Monument.

(3) A destination visitor or interpretive center that provides a broad range of interpretive services, programs, and media.

(4) An area—

(A) that provides significant opportunities for outdoor recreation;

(B) that has substantial Federal investments;

(C) where fees can be efficiently collected; and

(D) that contains all of the following amenities:

(i) Designated developed parking.

(ii) A permanent toilet facility.

(iii) A permanent trash receptacle.

(iv) Interpretive sign, exhibit, or kiosk.

(v) Picnic tables.

(vi) Security services.

Expanded amenity recreation fee

(g)(1) NPS and USFWS authority. Except as limited by subsection (d) of this section, the Secretary of the Interior may charge an expanded amenity recreation fee, either in addition to an entrance fee or by itself, at Federal recreational lands and waters under the jurisdiction of the National Park Service or the United States Fish and Wildlife Service when the Secretary of the Interior determines that the visitor uses a specific or specialized facility, equipment, or service.

(2) Other Federal land management agencies. Except as limited by subsection (d) of this section, the Secretary may charge an expanded amenity recreation fee, either in addition to a standard amenity fee or by itself, at Federal recreational lands and waters under the jurisdiction of the Forest Service, the Bureau of Land Management, or the Bureau of Reclamation, but only for the following facilities or services:

(A) Use of developed campgrounds that provide at least a majority of the following:

(i) Tent or trailer spaces.

(ii) Picnic tables.

(iii) Drinking water.

(iv) Access roads.

(v) The collection of the fee by an employee or agent of the Federal land management agency.

(vi) Reasonable visitor protection.

(vii) Refuse containers.

(viii) Toilet facilities.

(ix) Simple devices for containing a campfire.

(B) Use of highly developed boat launches with specialized facilities or services such as mechanical or hydraulic boat lifts or facilities, multi-lane paved ramps, paved parking, restrooms and other improvements such as boarding floats, loading ramps, or fish cleaning stations.

(C) Rental of cabins, boats, stock animals, lookouts, historic structures, group day-use or overnight sites, audio tour devices, portable sanitation devices, binoculars or other equipment.

(D) Use of hookups for electricity, cable, or sewer.

(E) Use of sanitary dump stations.

(F) Participation in an enhanced interpretive program or special tour.

(G) Use of reservation services.

(H) Use of transportation services.

(I) Use of areas where emergency medical or first-aid services are administered from facilities staffed by public employees or employees under a contract or reciprocal agreement with the Federal Government.

(J) Use of developed swimming sites that provide at least a majority of the following:

(i) Bathhouse with showers and flush toilets.

(ii) Refuse containers.

(iii) Picnic areas.

(iv) Paved parking.

(v) Attendants, including lifeguards.

(vi) Floats encompassing the swimming area.

(vii) Swimming deck.

Special recreation permit fee

(h) The Secretary may issue a special recreation permit, and charge a special recreation permit fee in connection with the issuance of the permit, for specialized recreation uses of Federal recreational lands and waters, such as group activities, recreation events, motorized recreational vehicle use.

Pub.L. 108–447, Div. J, Title VIII, § 803, Dec. 8, 2004, 118 Stat. 3378.

§ **6803.** Public participation

In general

(a) As required in this section, the Secretary shall provide the public with opportunities to participate in the development of or changing of a recreation fee established under this chapter.

Advance notice

(b) The Secretary shall publish a notice in the Federal Register of the establishment of a new recreation fee area for each agency 6 months before establishment. The Secretary shall publish notice of a new recreation fee or a change to an existing recreation fee established under this chapter in local newspapers and publications located near the site at which the recreation fee would be established or changed.

Public involvement

(c) Before establishing any new recreation fee area, the Secretary shall provide opportunity for public involvement by—

(1) establishing guidelines for public involvement;

(2) establishing guidelines on how agencies will demonstrate on an annual basis how they have provided information to the public on the use of recreation fee revenues; and

(3) publishing the guidelines in paragraphs (1) and (2) in the Federal Register.

Recreation Resource Advisory Committee

(d)(1) Establishment

(A) Authority to establish. Except as provided in subparagraphs (C) and (D), the Secretary or the Secretaries shall establish a Recreation Resource Advisory Committee in each State or region for Federal recreational lands and waters managed by the Forest Service or the Bureau of Land Management to perform the duties described in paragraph (2).

(B) Number of Committees. The Secretary may have as many additional Recreation Resource Advisory Committees in a State or region as the Secretary considers necessary for the effective operation of this chapter.

(C) Exception. The Secretary shall not establish a Recreation Resource Advisory Committee in a State if the Secretary determines, in consultation with the Governor of the State, that sufficient interest does not exist to ensure that participation on the Committee is balanced in terms of the points of view represented and the functions to be performed.

(D) Use of other entities. In lieu of establishing a Recreation Resource Advisory Committee under subparagraph (A), the Secretary may use a Resource Advisory Committee established pursuant to another provision of law and in accordance with that law or a recreation fee advisory board otherwise established by the Secretary to perform the duties specified in paragraph (2).

(2) Duties. In accordance with the procedures required by paragraph (9), a Recreation Resource Advisory Committee may make recommendations to the Secretary regarding a standard amenity recreation fee or an expanded amenity recreation fee, whenever the recommendations relate to public concerns in the State or region covered by the Committee regarding—

(A) the implementation of a standard amenity recreation fee or an expanded amenity recreation fee or the establishment of a specific recreation fee site;

(B) the elimination of a standard amenity recreation fee or an expanded amenity recreation fee; or

(C) the expansion or limitation of the recreation fee program.

(3) Meetings. A Recreation Resource Advisory Committee shall meet at least annually, but may, at the discretion of the Secretary, meet as often as needed to deal with citizen concerns about the recreation fee program in a timely manner.

(4) Notice of rejection. If the Secretary rejects the recommendation of a Recreation Resource Advisory Committee, the Secretary shall issue a notice that identifies the reasons for rejecting the recommendation to the Committee on Resources of the House of Representatives and the Committee on Energy and Natural Resources of the Senate not later than 30 days before the Secretary implements a decision pertaining to that recommendation.

258

(5) Composition of the Advisory Committee.

(A) Number. A Recreation Resource Advisory Committee shall be comprised of 11 members.

(B) Nominations. The Governor and the designated county official from each county in the relevant State or Region may submit a list of nominations in the categories described under subparagraph (D).

(C) Appointment. The Secretary may appoint members of the Recreation Resource Advisory Committee from the list as provided in subparagraph (B).

(D) Broad and balanced representation. In appointing the members of a Recreation Resource Advisory Committee, the Secretary shall provide for a balanced and broad representation from the recreation community that shall include the following:

(i) Five persons who represent recreation users and that include, as appropriate, persons representing the following:

(I) Winter motorized recreation, such as snowmobiling.

(II) Winter non-motorized recreation, such as snowshoeing, cross country and down hill skiing, and snowboarding.

(III) Summer motorized recreation, such as motorcycles, boaters, and off-highway vehicles.

(IV) Summer nonmotorized recreation, such as backpacking, horseback riding, mountain biking, canoeing, and rafting.

(V) Hunting and fishing.

(ii) Three persons who represent interest groups that include, as appropriate, the following:

(I) Motorized outfitters and guides.

(II) Non-motorized outfitters and guides.

(III) Local environmental groups.

(iii) Three persons, as follows:

(I) State tourism official to represent the State.

(II) A person who represents affected Indian tribes.

(III) A person who represents affected local government interests.

(6) Term

(A) Length of term. The Secretary shall appoint the members of a Recreation Resource Advisory Committee for staggered terms of 2 and 3 years beginning on the date that the members are first appointed. The Secretary may reappoint members to subsequent 2- or 3-year terms.

(B) Effect of vacancy. The Secretary shall make appointments to fill a vacancy on a Recreation Resource Advisory Committee as soon as practicable after the vacancy has occurred.

(C) Effect of unexpected vacancy. Where an unexpected vacancy occurs, the Governor and the designated county officials from each county in the relevant State shall provide the Secretary with a list of nominations in the relevant category, as described under paragraph (5)(D), not later than two months after notification of the vacancy. To the extent possible, a vacancy shall be filled in the same category and term in which the original appointment was made.

(7) Chairperson. The chairperson of a Recreation Resource Advisory Committee shall be selected by the majority vote of the members of the Committee.

(8) Quorum. Eight members shall constitute a quorum. A quorum must be present to constitute an official meeting of a Recreation Resource Advisory Committee.

(9) Approval procedures. A Recreation Resource Advisory Committee shall establish procedures for making recommendations to the Secretary. A recommendation may be submitted to the Secretary only if the recommendation is approved by a majority of the members of the Committee from each of the categories specified in paragraph (5)(D) and general public support for the recommendation is documented.

(10) Compensation. Members of the Recreation Resource Advisory Committee shall not receive any compensation.

(11) Public participation in the Recreation Resource Advisory Committee

(A) Notice of meetings. All meetings of a Recreation Resource Advisory Committee shall be announced at least one week in advance in a local newspaper of record and the Federal Register, and shall be open to the public.

(B) Records. A Recreation Resource Advisory Committee shall maintain records of the meetings of the Recreation Resource Advisory Committee and make the records available for public inspection.

(12) Federal Advisory Committee Act. A Recreation Resource Advisory Committee is subject to the provisions of the Federal Advisory Committee Act (5 U.S.C. App.).

Miscellaneous administrative provisions regarding recreation fees and recreation passes

(e)(1) Notice of entrance fees, standard amenity recreation fees, and passes. The Secretary shall post clear notice of any entrance fee, standard amenity recreation fee, and available recreation passes at appropriate locations in each unit or area of a Federal land management agency where an entrance fee or a standard amenity recreation fee is charged. The Secretary shall include such notice in publications distributed at the unit or area.

(2) Notice of recreation fee projects. To the extent practicable, the Secretary shall post clear notice of locations where work is performed using recreation fee or recreation pass revenues collected under this chapter.

Pub.L. 108–447, Div. J, Title VIII, § 804, Dec. 8, 2004, 118 Stat. 3382.

* * *

§ 6806. Special account and distribution of fees and revenues

Special account

(a) The Secretary of the Treasury shall establish a special account in the Treasury for each Federal land management agency.

Deposits

(b) Subject to subsections (c), (d), and (e) of this section, revenues collected by each Federal land management agency under this chapter shall—

(1) be deposited in its special account; and

(2) remain available for expenditure, without further appropriation, until expended.

Distribution of recreation fees and single-site agency pass revenues

(c)(1) Local distribution of funds

(A) Retention of revenues. Not less than 80 percent of the recreation fees and site-specific agency pass revenues collected at a specific unit or area of a Federal land management agency shall remain available for expenditure, without further appropriation, until expended at that unit or area.

(B) Reduction. The Secretary may reduce the percentage allocation otherwise applicable under subparagraph (A) to a unit or area of a Federal land management agency, but not below 60 percent, for a fiscal year if the Secretary determines that the revenues collected at the unit or area exceed the reasonable needs of the unit or area for which expenditures may be made for that fiscal year.

(2) Agency-wide distribution of funds. The balance of the recreation fees and site-specific agency pass revenues collected at a specific unit or area of a Federal land management and not distributed in accordance with paragraph (1) shall remain available to that Federal land management agency for expenditure on an agency-wide basis, without further appropriation, until expended.

(3) Other amounts. Other amounts collected at other locations, including recreation fees collected by other entities or for a reservation service, shall remain available, without further appropriation, until expended in accordance with guidelines established by the Secretary.

Distribution of National Parks and Federal Recreational Lands Pass revenues

(d) Revenues collected from the sale of the National Parks and Federal Recreational Lands Pass shall be deposited in the special accounts established for the Federal land management agencies in accordance with the guidelines issued under section 6804(a)(7) of this title.

Distribution of regional multientity pass revenues

(e) Revenues collected from the sale of a regional multientity pass authorized under section 6804(d) of this title shall be deposited in each participating Federal land management agency's special account in accordance with the terms of the region multientity pass agreement for the regional multientity pass.

Pub.L. 108–447, Div. J, Title VIII, § 807, Dec. 8, 2004, 118 Stat. 3388.

* * *

UNITED STATES CODE

TITLE 25 INDIANS

NATIVE AMERICAN GRAVES PROTECTION AND REPATRIATION ACT OF 1990 (NAGPRA)

(25 U.S.C.A. §§ 3001–3013)

§ 3001. Definitions

For purposes of this chapter, the term—

* * *

(2) "cultural affiliation" means that there is a relationship of shared group identity which can be reasonably traced historically or prehistorically between a present day Indian tribe or Native Hawaiian organization and an identifiable earlier group.

(3) "cultural items" means human remains and—

(A) "associated funerary objects" which shall mean objects that, as a part of the death rite or ceremony of a culture, are reasonably believed to have been placed with individual human remains either at the time of death or later, and both the human remains and associated funerary objects are presently in the possession or control of a Federal agency or museum, except that other items exclusively made for burial purposes or to contain human remains shall be considered as associated funerary objects.[1]

(B) "unassociated funerary objects" which shall mean objects that, as a part of the death rite or ceremony of a culture, are reasonably believed to have been placed with individual human remains either at the time of death or later, where the remains are not in the possession or control of the Federal agency or museum and the objects can be identified by a preponderance of the evidence as related to specific individuals or families or to known human remains or, by a preponderance of the evidence, as having been removed from a specific burial site of an individual culturally affiliated with a particular Indian tribe,

(C) "sacred objects" which shall mean specific ceremonial objects which are needed by traditional Native American religious leaders for the practice of traditional Native American religions by their present day adherents, and

(D) "cultural patrimony" which shall mean an object having ongoing historical, traditional, or cultural importance central to the Native American group or culture itself, rather than property owned by an individual Native American, and which, therefore,

---

1. So in original. The period probably should be a comma.

cannot be alienated, appropriated, or conveyed by any individual regardless of whether or not the individual is a member of the Indian tribe or Native Hawaiian organization and such object shall have been considered inalienable by such Native American group at the time the object was separated from such group.

(4) "Federal agency" means any department, agency, or instrumentality of the United States. Such term does not include the Smithsonian Institution.

(5) "Federal lands" means any land other than tribal lands which are controlled or owned by the United States, including lands selected by but not yet conveyed to Alaska Native Corporations and groups organized pursuant to the Alaska Native Claims Settlement Act of 1971 [43 U.S.C.A. § 1601 et seq.].

* * *

(7) "Indian tribe" means any tribe, band, nation, or other organized group or community of Indians, including any Alaska Native village (as defined in, or established pursuant to, the Alaska Native Claims Settlement Act [43 U.S.C.A. § 1601 et seq.]) which is recognized as eligible for the special programs and services provided by the United States to Indians because of their status as Indians.

* * *

(9) "Native American" means of, or relating to, a tribe, people, or culture that is indigenous to the United States.

* * *

(14) "Secretary" means the Secretary of the Interior.

(15) "tribal land" means—

(A) all lands within the exterior boundaries of any Indian reservation;

(B) all dependent Indian communities;[2]

(C) any lands administered for the benefit of Native Hawaiians pursuant to the Hawaiian Homes Commission Act, 1920, and section 4 of Public Law 86–3.

Pub.L. 101–601, § 2, Nov. 16, 1990, 104 Stat. 3048; Pub.L. 102–572, Title IX, § 902(b)(1), Oct. 29, 1992, 106 Stat. 4516.

§ 3002.   Ownership

Native American human remains and objects

(a) The ownership or control of Native American cultural items which are excavated or discovered on Federal or tribal lands after November 16, 1990, shall be (with priority given in the order listed)—

---

2. So in original. Probably should be followed by "and".

(1) in the case of Native American human remains and associated funerary objects, in the lineal descendants of the Native American; or

(2) in any case in which such lineal descendants cannot be ascertained, and in the case of unassociated funerary objects, sacred objects, and objects of cultural patrimony—

(A) in the Indian tribe or Native Hawaiian organization on whose tribal land such objects or remains were discovered;

(B) in the Indian tribe or Native Hawaiian organization which has the closest cultural affiliation with such remains or objects and which, upon notice, states a claim for such remains or objects; or

(C) if the cultural affiliation of the objects cannot be reasonably ascertained and if the objects were discovered on Federal land that is recognized by a final judgment of the Indian Claims Commission or the United States Court of Claims as the aboriginal land of some Indian tribe—

(1) in the Indian tribe that is recognized as aboriginally occupying the area in which the objects were discovered, if upon notice, such tribe states a claim for such remains or objects, or

(2) if it can be shown by a preponderance of the evidence that a different tribe has a stronger cultural relationship with the remains or objects than the tribe or organization specified in paragraph (1), in the Indian tribe that has the strongest demonstrated relationship, if upon notice, such tribe states a claim for such remains or objects.

Unclaimed Native American human remains and objects

(b) Native American cultural items not claimed under subsection (a) of this section shall be disposed of in accordance with regulations promulgated by the Secretary in consultation with the review committee established under section 3006 of this title, Native American groups, representatives of museums and the scientific community.

Intentional excavation and removal of Native American human remains and objects

(c) The intentional removal from or excavation of Native American cultural items from Federal or tribal lands for purposes of discovery, study, or removal of such items is permitted only if—

(1) such items are excavated or removed pursuant to a permit issued under section 470cc of Title 16 which shall be consistent with this Chapter;

(2) such items are excavated or removed after consultation with or, in the case of tribal lands, consent of the appropriate (if any) Indian tribe or Native Hawaiian organization;

(3) the ownership and right of control of the disposition of such items shall be as provided in subsections (a) and (b) of this section; and

(4) proof of consultation or consent under paragraph (2) is shown.

Inadvertent discovery of Native American remains and objects

(d)(1) Any person who knows, or has reason to know, that such person has discovered Native American cultural items on Federal or tribal lands after November 16, 1990, shall notify, in writing, the Secretary of the Department, or head of any other agency or instrumentality of the United States, having primary management authority with respect to Federal lands and the appropriate Indian tribe or Native Hawaiian organization with respect to tribal lands, if known or readily ascertainable, and, in the case of lands that have been selected by an Alaska Native Corporation or group organized pursuant to the Alaska Native Claims Settlement Act of 1971 [43 U.S.C.A. § 1601 et seq.], the appropriate corporation or group. If the discovery occurred in connection with an activity, including (but not limited to) construction, mining, logging, and agriculture, the person shall cease the activity in the area of the discovery, make a reasonable effort to protect the items discovered before resuming such activity, and provide notice under this subsection. Following the notification under this subsection, and upon certification by the Secretary of the department or the head of any agency or instrumentality of the United States or the appropriate Indian tribe or Native Hawaiian organization that notification has been received, the activity may resume after 30 days of such certification.

(d)(2) The disposition of and control over any cultural items excavated or removed under this subsection shall be determined as provided for in this section.

(d)(3) If the Secretary of the Interior consents, the responsibilities (in whole or in part) under paragraphs (1) and (2) of the Secretary of any department (other than the Department of the Interior) or the head of any other agency or instrumentality may be delegated to the Secretary with respect to any land managed by such other Secretary or agency head.

Relinquishment

(e) Nothing in this section shall prevent the governing body of an Indian tribe or Native Hawaiian organization from expressly relinquishing control over any Native American human remains, or title to or control over any funerary object, or sacred object.

Pub.L. 101–601, § 3, Nov. 16, 1990, 104 Stat. 3050.

* * *

§ 3009. Savings provision

Nothing in this chapter shall be construed to—

(1) limit the authority of any Federal agency or museum to—

* * *

(B) enter into any other agreement with the consent of the culturally affiliated tribe or organization as to the disposition of, or control over, items covered by this chapter;

* * *

(3) deny or otherwise affect access to any court;

(4) limit any procedural or substantive right which may otherwise be secured to individuals or Indian tribes or Native Hawaiian organizations; or

(5) limit the application of any State or Federal law pertaining to theft or stolen property.

Pub.L. 101–601, § 11, Nov. 16, 1990, 104 Stat. 3057.

§ 3010. Special relationship between Federal government and Indian tribes and Native Hawaiian organizations

This chapter reflects the unique relationship between the Federal Government and Indian tribes and Native Hawaiian organizations and should not be construed to establish a precedent with respect to any other individual, organization or foreign government.

Pub.L. 101–601, § 12, Nov. 16, 1990, 104 Stat. 3058.

§ 3011. Regulations

The Secretary shall promulgate regulations to carry out this chapter within 12 months of November 16, 1990.

Pub.L. 101–601, § 13, Nov. 16, 1990, 104 Stat. 3058.

* * *

§ 3013. Enforcement

The United States district courts shall have jurisdiction over any action brought by any person alleging a violation of this chapter and shall have the authority to issue such orders as may be necessary to enforce the provisions of this chapter.

Pub.L. 101–601, § 15, Nov. 16, 1990, 104 Stat. 3058.

UNITED STATES CODE

TITLE 28 JUDICIARY AND JUDICIAL PROCEDURE

QUIET TITLE ACT OF 1972

(28 U.S.C.A. § 2409a)

§ 2409a. Real property quiet title actions

(a) The United States may be named as a party defendant in a civil action under this section to adjudicate a disputed title to real property in which the United States claims an interest, other than a security interest or water rights. This section does not apply to trust or restricted Indian lands, nor does it apply to or affect actions which may be or could have been brought under sections 1346, 1347, 1491, or 2410 of this title, sections 7424, 7425, or 7426 of the Internal Revenue Code of 1954, as amended (26 U.S.C. 7424, 7425, and 7426), or section 208 of the Act of July 10, 1952 (43 U.S.C. 666).

(b) The United States shall not be disturbed in possession or control of any real property involved in any action under this section pending a final judgment or decree, the conclusion of any appeal therefrom, and sixty days; and if the final determination shall be adverse to the United States, the United States nevertheless may retain such possession or control of the real property or of any part thereof as it may elect, upon payment to the person determined to be entitled thereto of an amount which upon such election the district court in the same action shall determine to be just compensation for such possession or control.

(c) No preliminary injunction shall issue in any action brought under this section.

(d) The complaint shall set forth with particularity the nature of the right, title, or interest which the plaintiff claims in the real property, the circumstances under which it was acquired, and the right, title, or interest claimed by the United States.

(e) If the United States disclaims all interest in the real property or interest therein adverse to the plaintiff at any time prior to the actual commencement of the trial, which disclaimer is confirmed by order of the court, the jurisdiction of the district court shall cease unless it has jurisdiction of the civil action or suit on ground other than and independent of the authority conferred by section 1346(f) of this title.

(f) A civil action against the United States under this section shall be tried by the court without a jury.

(g) Any civil action under this section, except for an action brought by a State, shall be barred unless it is commenced within twelve years of the date upon which it accrued. Such action shall be deemed to have accrued on the date the plaintiff or his predecessor in interest knew or should have known of the claim of the United States.

(h) No civil action may be maintained under this section by a State with respect to defense facilities (including land) of the United States so long as the lands at issue are being used or required by the United States for national defense purposes as determined by the head of the Federal agency with jurisdiction over the lands involved, if it is determined that the State action was brought more than twelve years after the State knew or should have known of the claims of the United States. Upon cessation of such use or requirement, the State may dispute title to such lands pursuant to the provisions of this section. The decision of the head of the Federal agency is not subject to judicial review.

(i) Any civil action brought by a State under this section with respect to lands, other than tide or submerged lands, on which the United States or its lessee or right-of-way or easement grantee has made substantial improvements or substantial investments or on which the United States has conducted substantial activities pursuant to a management plan such as range improvement, timber harvest, tree planting, mineral activities, farming, wildlife habitat improvement, or other similar activities, shall be barred unless the action is commenced within twelve years after the date the State received notice of the Federal claims to the lands.

(j) If a final determination in an action brought by a State under this section involving submerged or tide lands on which the United States or its lessee or right-of-way or easement grantee has made substantial improvements or substantial investments is adverse to the United States and it is determined that the State's action was brought more than twelve years after the State received notice of the Federal claim to the lands, the State shall take title to the lands subject to any existing lease, easement, or right-of-way. Any compensation due with respect to such lease, easement, or fight-of-way shall be determined under existing law.

(k) Notice for the purposes of the accrual of an action brought by a State under this section shall be—

(1) by public communications with respect to the claimed lands which are sufficiently specific as to be reasonably calculated to put the claimant on notice of the Federal claim to the lands, or

(2) by the use, occupancy, or improvement of the claimed lands which, in the circumstances, is open and notorious.

(*l*) For purposes of this section, the term "tide or submerged lands" means "lands beneath navigable waters" as defined in section 2 of the Submerged Lands Act (43 U.S.C. 1301).

(m) Not less than one hundred and eighty days before bringing any action under this section, a State shall notify the head of the Federal agency with jurisdiction over the lands in question of the State's intention to file suit, the basis therefor, and a description of the lands included in the suit.

(n) Nothing in this section shall be construed to permit suits against the United States based upon adverse possession.

Added Pub.L. 92–562, § 3(a), Oct. 25, 1972, 86 Stat. 1176. As amended Pub.L. 99–598, Nov. 4, 1986, 100 Stat. 3351.

UNITED STATES CODE

TITLE 30 MINERAL LANDS AND MINING

MINING AND MINERALS POLICY ACT OF 1970

(30 U.S.C.A. § 21a)

§ 21a.   **National mining and minerals policy; definition of minerals; execution of policy under other authorized programs; report to Congress**

The Congress declares that it is the continuing policy of the Federal Government in the national interest to foster and encourage private enterprise in (1) the development of economically sound and stable domestic mining, minerals, metal and mineral reclamation industries, (2) the orderly and economic development of domestic mineral resources, reserves, and reclamation of metals and minerals to help assure satisfaction of industrial, security and environmental needs, (3) mining, mineral, and metallurgical research, including the use and recycling of scrap to promote the wise and efficient use of our natural and reclaimable mineral resources, and (4) the study and development of methods for the disposal, control, and reclamation of mineral waste products, and the reclamation of mined land, so as to lessen any adverse impact of mineral extraction and processing upon the physical environment that may result from mining or mineral activities.

For the purpose of this section "minerals" shall include all minerals and mineral fuels including oil, gas, coal, oil shale and uranium.

It shall be the responsibility of the Secretary of the Interior to carry out this policy when exercising his authority under such programs as may be authorized by law other than this section.

Pub.L. 91–631, § 2, Dec. 31, 1970, 84 Stat. 1876, as amended Pub.L. 104–66, Title I, § 1081(b), Dec. 21, 1995, 109 Stat. 721; renumbered § 101, Pub.L. 104–325, § 2(1), (2), Oct. 19, 1996, 110 Stat. 3994.

GENERAL MINING LAW OF 1872 (as amended)

(30 U.S.C.A. §§ 21–42)

§ 21.   **Mineral lands reserved**

In all cases lands valuable for minerals shall be reserved from sale, except as otherwise expressly directed by law.

R.S. § 2318.

§ 22. Lands open to purchase by citizens

Except as otherwise provided, all valuable mineral deposits in lands belonging to the United States, both surveyed and unsurveyed, shall be free and open to exploration and purchase, and the lands in which they are found to occupation and purchase, by citizens of the United States and those who have declared their intention to become such, under regulations prescribed by law, and according to the local customs or rules of miners in the several mining districts, so far as the same are applicable and not inconsistent with the laws of the United States.

R.S. § 2319; Feb. 25, 1920, c. 85, § 1, 41 Stat. 437.

§ 23. Length of claims on veins or lodes

Mining claims upon veins or lodes of quartz or other rock in place bearing gold, silver, cinnabar, lead, tin, copper, or other valuable deposits, located prior to May 10, 1872, shall be governed as to length along the vein or lode by the customs, regulations, and laws in force at the date of their location. A mining claim located after the 10th day of May 1872, whether located by one or more persons, may equal, but shall not exceed, one thousand five hundred feet in length along the vein or lode; but no location of a mining claim shall be made until the discovery of the vein or lode within the limits of the claim located. No claim shall extend more than three hundred feet on each side of the middle of the vein at the surface, nor shall any claim be limited by any mining regulation to less than twenty-five feet on each side of the middle of the vein at the surface, except where adverse rights existing on the 10th day of May 1872 render such limitation necessary. The end lines of each claim shall be parallel to each other.

R.S. § 2320.

* * *

§ 26. Locators' rights of possession and enjoyment

The locators of all mining locations made on any mineral vein, lode, or ledge, situated on the public domain, their heirs and assigns, where no adverse claim existed on the 10th day of May 1872 so long as they comply with the laws of the United States, and with State, territorial, and local regulations not in conflict with the laws of the United States governing their possessory title, shall have the exclusive right of possession and enjoyment of all the surface included within the lines of their locations, and of all veins, lodes, and ledges throughout their entire depth, the top or apex of which lies inside of such surface lines extended downward vertically, although such veins, lodes, or ledges may so far depart from a perpendicular in their course downward as to extend outside the vertical side lines of such surface locations. But their right of possession to such outside parts of such veins or ledges shall be confined to such portions thereof as lie between vertical planes drawn downward as above described, through the end lines of their locations, so continued in their own direction that such planes will intersect such exterior parts of such veins or ledges. Nothing in this section shall authorize the locator or possessor of a vein or lode which extends in its downward course beyond the vertical lines of his claim to enter upon the surface of a claim owned or possessed by another.

R.S. § 2322.

§ 27. Mining tunnels; right to possession of veins on line with; abandonment of right

Where a tunnel is run for the development of a vein or lode, or for the discovery of mines, the owners of such tunnel shall have the right of possession of all veins or lodes within three thousand feet from the face of such tunnel on the line thereof, not previously known to exist, discovered in such tunnel, to the same extent as if discovered from the surface; and locations on the line of such tunnel of veins or lodes not appearing on the surface, made by other parties after the commencement of the tunnel, and while the same is being prosecuted with reasonable diligence, shall be invalid; but failure to prosecute the work on the tunnel for six months shall be considered as an abandonment of the right to all undiscovered veins on the line of such tunnel.

R.S. § 2323.

§ 28. Mining district regulations by miners: location, recordation, and amount of work; marking of location on ground; records; annual labor or improvements on claims pending issue of patent; co-owner's succession in interest upon delinquency in contributing proportion of expenditures; tunnel as lode expenditure

The miners of each mining district may make regulations not in conflict with the laws of the United States, or with the laws of the State or Territory in which the district is situated, governing the location, manner of recording, amount of work necessary to hold possession of a mining claim, subject to the following requirements: The location must be distinctly marked on the ground so that its boundaries can be readily traced. All records of mining claims made after May 10, 1872, shall contain the name or names of the locators, the date of the location, and such a description of the claim or claims located by reference to some natural object or permanent monument as will identify the claim. On each claim located after the 10th day of May 1872, that is granted a waiver under section 28f of this title, and until a patent has been issued therefor, not less than $100 worth of labor shall be performed or improvements made during each year. On all claims located prior to the 10th day of May 1872, $10 worth of labor shall be performed or improvements made each year, for each one hundred feet in length along the vein until a patent has been issued therefor; but where such claims are held in common, such expenditure may be made upon any one claim; and upon a failure to comply with these conditions, the claim or mine upon which such failure occurred shall be open to relocation in the same manner as if no location of the same had ever been made, provided that the original locators, their heirs, assigns, or legal representatives, have not resumed work upon the claim after failure and before such location.

273

Upon the failure of any one of several co-owners to contribute his proportion of the expenditures required hereby, the co-owners who have performed the labor or made the improvements may, at the expiration of the year, give such delinquent co-owner personal notice in writing or notice by publication in the newspaper published nearest the claim, for at least once a week for ninety days, and if at the expiration of ninety days after such notice in writing or by publication such delinquent should fail or refuse to contribute his proportion of the expenditure required by this section, his interest in the claim shall become the property of his co-owners who have made the required expenditures. The period within which the work required to be done annually on all unpatented mineral claims located since May 10, 1872, including such claims in the Territory of Alaska, shall commence at 12 o'clock meridian on the 1st day of September succeeding the date of location of such claim.

Where a person or company has or may run a tunnel for the purposes of developing a lode or lodes, owned by said person or company, the money so expended in said tunnel shall be taken and considered as expended on said lode or lodes, whether located prior to or since May 10, 1872; and such person or company shall not be required to perform work on the surface of said lode or lodes in order to hold the same as required by this section. On all such valid claims the annual period ending December 31, 1921, shall continue to 12 o'clock meridian July 1, 1922.

R.S. § 2324; Feb. 11, 1875, c. 41, 18 Stat. 315; Jan. 22, 1880, c. 9, § 2, 21 Stat. 61; Aug. 24, 1921, c. 84, 42 Stat. 186; Aug. 23, 1958, Pub.L. 85–736, § 1, 72 Stat. 829, as amended Aug. 10, 1993, Pub.L. 103–66, Title X, § 10105(b), 107 Stat. 406.

§ 28–1. Inclusion of certain surveys in labor requirements of mining claims; conditions and restrictions

The term "labor", as used in the third sentence of section 28 of this title, shall include, without being limited to, geological, geochemical and geophysical surveys conducted by qualified experts and verified by a detailed report filed in the county office in which the claim is located which sets forth fully (a) the location of the work performed in relation to the point of discovery and boundaries of the claim, (b) the nature, extent, and cost thereof, (c) the basic findings therefrom, and (d) the name, address, and professional background of the person or persons conducting the work. Such surveys, however, may not be applied as labor for more than two consecutive years or for more than a total of five years on any one mining claim, and each such survey shall be nonrepetitive of any previous survey on the same claim.

Pub.L. 85–876, § 1, Sept. 2, 1958, 72 Stat. 1701.

§ 28–2. Same; definitions

As used in section 28–1 of this title,

(a) The term "geological surveys" means surveys on the ground for mineral deposits by the proper application of the principles and techniques of the science of geology as they relate to the search for and discovery of mineral deposits;

(b) The term "geochemical surveys" means surveys on the ground for mineral deposits by the proper application of the principles and techniques of the science of chemistry as they relate to the search for and discovery of mineral deposits;

(c) The term "geophysical surveys" means surveys on the ground for mineral deposits through the employment of generally recognized equipment and methods for measuring physical differences between rock types or discontinuities in geological formations;

(d) The term "qualified expert" means an individual qualified by education or experience to conduct geological, geochemical or geophysical surveys, as the case may be.

Pub.L. 85–876, § 2, Sept. 2, 1958, 72 Stat. 1701.

§ 28b. Annual assessment work on mining claims; temporary deferment; conditions

The performance of not less than $100 worth of labor or the making of improvements aggregating such amount, which labor or improvements are required under the provisions of section 28 of this title to be made during each year, may be deferred by the Secretary of the Interior as to any mining claim or group of claims in the United States upon the submission by the claimant of evidence satisfactory to the Secretary that such mining claim or group of claims is surrounded by lands over which a right-of-way for the performance of such assessment work has been denied or is in litigation or is in the process of acquisition under State law or that other legal impediments exist which affect the right of the claimant to enter upon the surface of such claim or group of claims or to gain access to the boundaries thereof.

June 31, 1949, c. 232, § 1, 63 Stat. 214.

§ 28c. Same; length and termination of deferment

The period for which said deferment may be granted shall end when the conditions justifying deferment have been removed: *Provided,* That the initial period shall not exceed one year but may be renewed for a further period of one year if justifiable conditions exist: *Provided further,* That the relief available under sections 28b to 28e of this title is in addition to any relief available under any other Act of Congress with respect to mining claims.

June 21, 1949, c. 232, § 2, 63 Stat. 215.

§ 28d. Same; performance of deferred work

All deferred assessment work shall be performed not later than the end of the assessment year next subsequent to the removal or cessation of the causes for deferment or the expiration of any deferments granted under sections 28b to 28e of this title and shall be in addition to the annual assessment work required by law in such year.

June 21, 1949, c. 232, § 3, 63 Stat. 215.

§ 28e. Same; recordation of deferment

Claimant shall file or record or cause to be filed or recorded in the office where the notice or certificate of location of such claim or group of claims is filed or recorded, a notice to the public of claimant's petition to the Secretary of the Interior for deferment under sections 28b to 28e of this title, and of the order or decision disposing of such petition.

June 21, 1949, c. 232, § 4, 63 Stat. 215.

§ 28f. Fee

Claim maintenance fee

(a) The holder of each unpatented mining claim, mill, or tunnel site, located pursuant to the mining laws of the United States, whether located before, on or after November 5, 2001, shall pay to the Secretary of the Interior, on or before September 1 of each year for years 2002 through 2003, a claim maintenance fee of $100 per claim or site[1] Such claim maintenance fee shall be in lieu of the assessment work requirement contained in the Mining Law of 1872 (30 U.S.C. 28 to 28e) and the related filing requirements contained in section 1744(a) and (c) of Title 43.

Time of payment

(b) The claim maintenance fee payable pursuant to subsection (a) of this section for any assessment year shall be paid before the commencement of the assessment year, except that for the initial assessment year in which the location is made, the locator shall pay the claim maintenance fee at the time the location notice is recorded with the Bureau of Land Management. The location fee imposed under section 28g of this title shall be payable not later than 90 days after the date of location.

Oil shale claims subject to claim maintenance fees under Energy Policy Act of 1992

(c) This section shall not apply to any oil shale claims for which a fee is required to be paid under section 2511(e)(2) of the Energy Policy Act of 1992 (Public Law 102–486; 106 Stat. 3111; 30 U.S.C. 242).

Waiver

(d)(1) The claim maintenance fee required under this section may be waived for a claimant who certifies in writing to the Secretary that on the date the payment was due, the claimant and all related parties—

(A) held not more than 10 mining claims, mill sites, or tunnel sites, or any combination thereof, on public lands; and

(B) have performed assessment work required under the Mining Law of 1872 (30 U.S.C. 28–28e) to maintain the mining claims held by the claimant and such related parties for the assessment year ending

---

1. So in original. A period should probably appear.

on noon of September 1 of the calendar year in which payment of the claim maintenance fee was due.

(d)(2) For purposes of paragraph (1), with respect to any claimant, the term "related party" means—

(A) the spouse and dependent children (as defined in section 152 of Title 26), of the claimant; and

(B) a person who controls, is controlled by, or is under common control with the claimant.

For purposes of this section, the term control includes actual control, legal control, and the power to exercise control, through or by common directors, officers, stockholders, a voting trust, or a holding company or investment company, or any other means.

(d)(3) If a small miner waiver application is determined to be defective for any reason, the claimant shall have a period of 60 days after receipt of written notification of the defect or defects by the Bureau of Land Management to: (A) cure such defect or defects, or (B) pay the $100 claim maintenance fee due for such period.

Pub.L. 103–66, Title X, § 10101, Aug. 10, 1993, 107 Stat. 405; Pub.L. 105–240, § 116, Sept. 25, 1998, 112 Stat. 1570; Pub.L. 105–277, Div. A, § 101(e) [Title I], Oct. 21, 1998, 112 Stat. 2681–235; Pub.L. 107–63, Title I, November 5, 2001, 115 Stat. 418.

§ 28g. Location fee

Notwithstanding any other provision of law, for every unpatented mining claim, mill or tunnel site located after August 10, 1993, and before September 30, 2003, pursuant to the Mining Laws of the United States, the locator shall, at the time the location notice is recorded with the Bureau of Land Management, pay to the Secretary of the Interior a location fee, in addition to the claim maintenance fee required by section 28f of this title, of $25.00 per claim.

Pub.L. 103–66, Title X, § 10102, Aug. 10, 1993, 107 Stat. 406; Pub.L. 105–277, Div. A, § 101(e) [Title I], Oct. 21, 1998, 112 Stat. 2681–235; Pub.L. 107–63, Title I, November 5, 2001, 115 Stat. 419.

§ 28h. Co-ownership

The co-ownership provisions of the Mining Law of 1872 (30 U.S.C. 28) shall remain in effect, except that in applying such provisions, the annual claim maintenance fee required under this Act shall, where applicable, replace applicable assessment requirements and expenditures.

Pub.L. 103–66, Title X, § 10103, Aug. 10, 1993, 107 Stat. 406.

§ 28i. Failure to pay

Failure to pay the claim maintenance fee or the location fee as required by sections 28f to 28k of this title shall conclusively constitute a forfeiture of the unpatented mining claim, mill or tunnel site by the claimant and the claim shall be deemed null and void by operation of law.

Pub.L. 103–66, Title X, § 10104, Aug. 10, 1993, 107 Stat. 406.

§ 28j. Other requirements

Federal Land Policy and Management Act requirements

(a) Nothing in sections 28f to 28k of this title shall change or modify the requirements of section 314(b) of the Federal Land Policy and Management Act of 1976 (43 U.S.C. 1744(b)), or the requirements of section 314(c) of the Federal Land Policy and Management Act of 1976 (43 U.S.C. 1744(c)) related to filings required by section 314(b), and such requirements shall remain in effect with respect to claims, and mill or tunnel sites for which fees are required to be paid under this section.

Fee adjustments

(c)(1) The Secretary of the Interior shall adjust the fees required by sections 28f to 28k of this title to reflect changes in the Consumer Price Index published by the Bureau of Labor Statistics of the Department of Labor every 5 years after August 10, 1993, or more frequently if the Secretary determines an adjustment to be reasonable.

(c)(2) The Secretary shall provide claimants notice of any adjustment made under this subsection not later than July 1 of any year in which the adjustment is made.

(c)(3) A fee adjustment under this subsection shall begin to apply the first assessment year which begins after adjustment is made.

Pub.L. 103–66, Title X, § 10105, Aug. 10, 1993, 107 Stat. 406.

§ 28k. Regulations

The Secretary of the Interior shall promulgate rules and regulations to carry out the terms and conditions of sections 28f to 28k of this title as soon as practicable after August 10, 1993.

Pub.L. 103–66, Title X, § 10106, Aug. 10, 1993, 107 Stat. 407.

§ 29. Patents; procurement procedure; filing application under oath, plat and field notes, notices, and affidavits; posting plat and notice on claim; publication and posting notice in office; certificate; adverse claims; payment per acre; objections; non-resident claimant's agent for execution of application and affidavits

A patent for any land claimed and located for valuable deposits may be obtained in the following manner: Any person, association, or corporation authorized to locate a claim under this chapter and sections 71 to 76 of this title, having claimed and located a piece of land for such purposes, who has, or have, complied with the terms of this chapter and sections 71 to 76 of this title, may file in the proper land office an application for a patent, under oath, showing such compliance, together with a plat and field notes of the claim or claims in common, made by or under the direction of the

Director of the Bureau of Land Management, showing accurately the boundaries of the claim or claims, which shall be distinctly marked by monuments on the ground, and shall post a copy of such plat, together with a notice of such application for a patent, in a conspicuous place on the land embraced in such plat previous to the filing of the application for a patent, and shall file an affidavit of at least two persons that such notice has been duly posted, and shall file a copy of the notice in such land office, and shall thereupon be entitled to a patent for the land, in the manner following: The register of the land office, upon the filing of such application, plat, field notes, notices, and affidavits, shall publish a notice that such application has been made, for the period of sixty days, in a newspaper to be by him designated as published nearest to such claim; and he shall also past such notice in his office for the same period. The claimant at the time of filing this application, or at any time thereafter, within the sixty days of publication, shall file with the register a certificate of the Director of the Bureau of Land Management that $500 worth of labor has been expended or improvements made upon the claim by himself or grantors; that the plat is correct, with such further description by such reference to natural objects or permanent monuments as shall identify the claim, and furnish an accurate description, to be incorporated in the patent. At the expiration of the sixty days of publication the claimant shall file his affidavit, showing that the plat and notice have been posted in a conspicuous place on the claim during such period of publication. If no adverse claim shall have been filed with the register of the proper land office at the expiration of the sixty days of publication, it shall be assumed that the applicant is entitled to a patent, upon the payment to the proper officer of $5 per acre, and that no adverse claim exists; and thereafter no objection from third parties to the issuance of a patent shall be heard, except it be shown that the applicant has failed to comply with the terms of this chapter and sections 71 to 76 of this title. * * *

R.S. § 2325; Jan. 22, 1880, c. 9, § 1, 21 Stat. 61; Mar. 3, 1925, c. 462, 43 Stat. 1144, 1145; 1946 Reorg. Plan No. 3, § 403, eff. July 16, 1946, 11 F.R. 7876, 60 Stat. 1100.

§ 30. Adverse claims; oath of claimants; requisites; waiver; stay of land office proceedings; judicial determination of right of possession; successful claimants' filing of judgment roll, certificate of labor, and description of claim in land office, and acreage and fee payments; issuance of patents for entire or partial claims upon certification of land office proceedings and judgment roll; alienation of patent title

Where an adverse claim is filed during the period of publication, it shall be upon oath of the person or persons making the same, and shall show the nature, boundaries, and extent of such adverse claim, and all proceedings, except the publication of notice and making and filing of the affidavit thereof, shall be stayed until the controversy shall have been settled or decided by a court of competent jurisdiction, or the adverse claim waived. It shall be the duty of the adverse claimant, within thirty days after filing his claim, to commence proceedings in a court of competent jurisdiction, to determine the question of the right of possession, and prosecute the same with reasonable diligence to final judgment; and a failure so to do shall be a waiver of his adverse claim. After such judgment shall have been rendered, the party entitled to the possession of the claim, or any portion thereof, may, without giving further notice, file a certified copy of the judgment roll with the register of the land office, together with the certificate of the Director of the Bureau of Land Management that the requisite amount of labor has been expended or improvements made thereon, and the description required in other cases, and shall pay to the register $5 per acre for his claim, together with the proper fees, whereupon the whole proceedings and the judgment roll shall be certified by the register to the Director of the Bureau of Land Management, and a patent shall issue thereon for the claim, or such portion thereof as the applicant shall appear, from the decision of the court, to rightly possess. If it appears from the decision of the court that several parties are entitled to separate and different portions of the claim, each party may pay for his portion of the claim, with the proper fees, and file the certificate and description by the Director of the Bureau of Land Management whereupon the register shall certify the proceedings and judgment roll to the Director of the Bureau of Land Management, as in the preceding case, and patents shall issue to the several parties according to their respective rights. Nothing herein contained shall be construed to prevent the alienation of the title conveyed by a patent for a mining claim to any person whatever.

R.S. § 2326; Mar. 3, 1925, c. 462, 43 Stat. 1144, 1145; 1946 Reorg. Plan No. 3, § 403, eff. July 16, 1946, 11 F.R. 7876, 60 Stat. 1100.

* * *

§ 32. Same; findings by jury; costs

If, in any action brought pursuant to section 30 of this title, title to the ground in controversy shall not be established by either party, the jury shall so find, and judgment shall be entered according to the verdict. In such case costs shall not be allowed to either party, and the claimant shall not proceed in the land office or be entitled to a patent for the ground in controversy until he shall have perfected his title.

Mar. 3, 1881, c. 140, 21 Stat. 505.

§ 33. Existing rights

All patents for mining claims upon veins or lodes issued prior to May 10, 1872, shall convey all the rights and privileges conferred by this chapter and sections 71 to 76 of this title where no adverse rights existed on the 10th day of May, 1872.

R.S. § 2328.

§ 34. Description of vein claims on surveyed and unsurveyed lands; monuments on ground to govern conflicting calls

The description of vein or lode claims upon surveyed lands shall designate the location of the claims with reference to the lines of the public survey, but need not conform therewith; but where patents have been or shall be issued for claims upon unsurveyed lands, the Director of the Bureau of Land Management in extending the public survey, shall adjust the same to the boundaries of said patented claims so as in no case to interfere with or change the true location of such claims as they are officially established upon the ground. Where patents have issued for mineral lands, those lands only shall be segregated and shall be deemed to be patented which are bounded by the lines actually marked, defined, and established upon the ground by the monuments of the official survey upon which the patent grant is based, and the Director of the Bureau of Land Management in executing subsequent patent surveys, whether upon surveyed or unsurveyed lands, shall be governed accordingly. The said monuments shall at all times constitute the highest authority as to what land is patented, and in case of any conflict between the said monuments of such patented claims and the descriptions of said claims in the patents issued therefor the monuments on the ground shall govern, and erroneous or inconsistent descriptions or calls in the patent descriptions shall give way thereto.

R.S. § 2327; Apr. 28, 1904, c. 1796, 33 Stat. 545; Mar. 3, 1925, c. 462, 43 Stat. 1144; 1946 Reorg. Plan No. 3, § 403, eff. July 16, 1946, 11 F.R. 7876, 60 Stat. 1100.

§ 35. Placer claims; entry and proceedings for patent under provisions applicable to vein or lode claims; conforming entry to legal subdivisions and surveys; limitation of claims; homestead entry of segregated agricultural land

Claims usually called "placers," including all forms of deposit, excepting veins of quartz, or other rock in place, shall be subject to entry and patent, under like circumstances and conditions, and upon similar proceedings, as are provided for vein or lode claims; but where the lands have been previously surveyed by the United States, the entry in its exterior limits shall conform to the legal subdivisions of the public lands. And where placer claims are upon surveyed lands, and conform to legal subdivisions, no further survey or plat shall be required, and all placer-mining claims located after the 10th day of May 1872, shall conform as near as practicable with the United States system of public-land surveys, and the rectangular subdivisions of such surveys, and no such location shall include more than twenty acres for each individual claimant; but where placer claims cannot be conformed to legal subdivisions, survey and plat shall be made as on unsurveyed lands; and where by the segregation of mineral land in any legal subdivision a quantity of agricultural land less than forty acres remains, such fractional portion of agricultural land may be entered by any party qualified by law, for homestead purposes.

R.S. §§ 2329, 2331; Mar. 3, 1891, c. 561, § 4, 26 Stat. 1097.

§ 36. Same; subdivisions of 10–acre tracts; maximum of placer locations; homestead claims of agricultural lands; sale of improvements

Legal subdivisions of forty acres may be subdivided into ten-acre tracts; and two or more persons, or associations of persons, having contiguous claims of any size, although such claims may be less than ten acres each, may make joint entry thereof; but no location of a placer claim, made after the 9th day of July 1870, shall exceed one hundred and sixty acres for any one person or association of persons, which location shall conform to the United States surveys; and nothing in this section contained shall defeat or impair any bona fide homestead claim upon agricultural lands, or authorize the sale of the improvements of any bona fide settler to any purchaser.

R.S. § 2330; Mar. 3, 1891, c. 561, § 4, 26 Stat. 1097.

§ 37. Same; proceedings for patent where boundaries contain vein or lode; application; statement including vein or lode; issuance of patent: acreage payments for vein or lode and placer claim; costs of proceedings; knowledge affecting construction of application and scope of patent

Where the same person, association, or corporation is in possession of a placer claim, and also a vein or lode included within the boundaries thereof, application shall be made for a patent for the placer claim, with the statement that it includes such vein or lode, and in such case a patent shall issue for the placer claim, subject to the provisions of this chapter and sections 71 to 76 of this title, including such vein or lode, upon the payment of $5 per acre for such vein or lode claim, and twenty-five feet of surface on each side thereof. The remainder of the placer claim, or any placer claim not embracing any vein or lode claim, shall be paid for at the rate of $2.50 per acre, together with all costs of proceedings; and where a vein or lode, such as is described in section 23 of this title, is known to exist within the boundaries of a placer claim, an application for a patent for such placer claim which does not include an application for the vein or lode claim shall be construed as a conclusive declaration that the claimant of the placer claim has no right of possession of the vein or lode claim; but where the existence of a vein or lode in a placer claim is not known, a patent for the placer claim shall convey all valuable mineral and other deposits within the boundaries thereof.

R.S. § 2333.

§ 38. Evidence of possession and work to establish right to patent

Where such person or association, they and their grantors, have held and worked their claims for a period equal to the time prescribed by the statute of limitations for mining claims of the State or Territory where the same may be situated, evidence of such possession and working of the claims for such period shall be sufficient to establish a right to a patent thereto under this chapter and sections 71 to 76 of this title, in the absence of any adverse claim; but nothing in this chapter and sections 71 to 76 of this title shall be deemed to impair any lien which may have attached in any way whatever to any mining claim or property thereto attached prior to the issuance of a patent.

R.S. § 2332.

§ 39. Surveyors of mining claims

The Director of the Bureau of Land Management may appoint in each land district containing mineral lands as many competent surveyors as shall apply for appointment to survey mining claims. The expenses of the survey of vein or lode claims, and the survey and subdivision of placer claims into smaller quantities than one hundred and sixty acres, together with the cost of publication of notices, shall be paid by the applicants, and they shall be at liberty to obtain the same at the most reasonable rates, and they shall also be at liberty to employ any United States deputy surveyor to make the survey. * * *

R.S. § 2334; Mar. 3, 1925, c. 462, 43 Stat. 1144, 1145; 1946 Reorg. Plan No. 3, § 403, eff. July 16, 1946, 11 F.R. 7876, 60 Stat. 1100.

* * *

§ 41. Intersecting or crossing veins

Where two or more veins intersect or cross each other, priority of title shall govern, and such prior location shall be entitled to all ore or mineral contained within the space of intersection; but the subsequent location shall have the right-of-way through the space of intersection for the purposes of the convenient working of the mine. And where two or more veins unite, the oldest or prior location shall take the vein below the point of union, including all the space of intersection.

R.S. § 2336.

§ 42. Patents for nonmineral lands: application, survey, notice, acreage limitation, payment—Vein or lode and mill site owners eligible

(a) Where nonmineral land not contiguous to the vein or lode is used or occupied by the proprietor of such vein or lode for mining or milling purposes, such nonadjacent surface ground may be embraced and included in an application for a patent for such vein or lode, and the same may be patented therewith, subject to the same preliminary requirements as to survey and notice as are applicable to veins or lodes; but no location made of such nonadjacent land shall exceed five acres, and payment for the same must be made at the same rate as fixed by this chapter and sections 71 to 76 of this title for the superficies of the lode. The owner of a quartz mill or reduction works, not owning a mine in connection therewith, may also receive a patent for his mill site, as provided in this section.

Placer claim owners eligible

(b) Where nonmineral land is needed by the proprietor of a placer claim for mining, milling, processing, beneficiation, or other operations in connection with such claim, and is used or occupied by the proprietor for such purposes, such land may be included in an application for a patent for such claim, and may be patented therewith subject to the same requirements as to survey and notice as are applicable to placers. No location made of such nonmineral land shall exceed five acres and payment for the same shall be made at the rate applicable to placer claims which do not include a vein or lode.

R.S. § 2337; Mar. 18, 1960, Pub.L. 86–390, 74 Stat. 7.

MINING—GENERAL PROVISIONS

(30 U.S.C.A. §§ 43–161)

§ 43. Conditions of sale by local legislature

As a condition of sale, in the absence of necessary legislation by Congress, the local legislature of any State or Territory may provide rules for working mines, involving easements, drainage, and other necessary means to their complete development; and those conditions shall be fully expressed in the patent.

R.S. § 2338.

* * *

§ 47. Impairment of rights or interests in certain mining property

Nothing contained in this chapter and sections 71 to 76 of this title shall be construed to impair in any way, rights or interests in mining property acquired under laws in force prior to July 9, 1870; nor to affect the provisions of the act entitled "An act granting to A. Sutro the right-of-way and other privileges to aid in the construction of a draining and exploring tunnel to the Comstock lode, in the State of Nevada", approved July 25, 1866.

R.S. § 2344.

* * *

§ 49a. Mining laws of United States extended to Alaska; exploration and mining for precious metals; regulations; conflict of laws; permits; dumping tailings; pumping from sea; reservation of roadway; title to land below line of high tide or high-water mark; transfer of title to future State

The laws of the United States relating to mining claims, mineral locations, and rights incident thereto are extended to the Territory of Alaska: * * * Any rights or privileges acquired hereunder with respect to mining operations in land, title to which is transferred to a future State upon its admission to the Union and which is situated within its boundaries, shall be terminable by such State, and the said mining operations shall be subject to the laws of such State.

June 6, 1900, c. 786, § 26, 31 Stat. 329; May 31, 1938, c. 297, 52 Stat. 588; Aug. 8, 1947, c. 514, § 1, 61 Stat. 916; Aug. 14, 1958, Pub.L. 85–662, 72 Stat. 615.

* * *

§ 50. Grants to States or corporations not to include mineral lands

No act passed at the first session of the Thirty-eighth Congress, granting lands to States or corporations to aid in the construction of roads or for other purposes, or to extend the time of grants made prior to the 30th day of January 1865 shall be so construed as to embrace mineral lands, which in all cases are reserved exclusively to the United States, unless otherwise specially provided in the act or acts making the grant.

R.S. § 2346.

§ 51. Water users' vested and accrued rights; enumeration of uses; protection of interest; rights-of-way for canals and ditches; liability for injury or damage to settlers' possession

Whenever, by priority of possession, rights to the use of water for mining, agricultural, manufacturing, or other purposes have vested and accrued, and the same are recognized and acknowledged by the local customs, laws, and the decisions of courts, the possessors and owners of such vested rights shall be maintained and protected in the same; and the right-of-way for the construction of ditches and canals for the purposes herein specified is acknowledged and confirmed; but whenever any person, in the construction of any ditch or canal, injures or damages the possession of any settler on the public domain, the party committing such injury or damage shall be liable to the party injured for such injury or damage.

R.S. § 2339.

Repeals

Provision of this section, "and the right-of-way for the construction of ditches and canals for the purposes herein specified is acknowledged and confirmed; but whenever any person, in the construction of any ditch or canal, injures or damages the possession of any settler on the public domain, the party committing such injury or damage shall be liable to the party injured for such injury or damage," was repealed by Pub.L. 94–579, Title VII, § 706(a), Oct. 21, 1976, 90 Stat. 2793, effective on and after Oct. 21, 1976, insofar as applicable to the issuance of rights-of-way over, upon, under, and through the public lands and lands in the National Forest System.

§ 52. Patents or homesteads subject to vested and accrued water rights

All patents granted, or homesteads allowed, shall be subject to any vested and accrued water rights, or rights to ditches and reservoirs used in connection with such water rights, as may have been acquired under or recognized by section 51 of this title.

R.S. § 2340; Mar. 3, 1891, c. 561, § 4, 26 Stat. 1097.

Repeals

Provision of this section, ", or rights to ditches and reservoirs used in connection with such water rights," was repealed by Pub.L. 94–579, Title VII, § 706(a), Oct. 21, 1976, 90 Stat. 2793, effective on and after Oct. 21, 1976, insofar as applicable to the issuance of rights-of-way over, upon, under, and through the public lands and lands in the National Forest System.

§ 53. Possessory actions for recovery of mining titles or for damages to such title

No possessory action between persons, in any court of the United States, for the recovery of any mining title, or for damages to any such title, shall be affected by the fact that the paramount title to the land in which such mines lie is in the United States; but each case shall be adjudged by the law of possession.

R.S. § 910.

§ 54. Liability for damages to stock raising and homestead entries by mining activities

Notwithstanding the provisions of any Act of Congress to the contrary, any person who hereafter prospects for, mines, or removes by strip or open pit mining methods, any minerals from any land included in a stock raising or other homestead entry or patent, and who had been liable under such an existing Act only for damages caused thereby to the crops or improvements of the entryman or patentee, shall also be liable for any damage that may be caused to the value of the land for grazing by such prospecting for, mining, or removal of minerals. Nothing in this section shall be considered to impair any vested right in existence on June 21, 1949.

June 21, 1949, c. 232, § 5, 63 Stat. 215.

* * *

§ 161. Entry of building-stone lands; previous law unaffected

Any person authorized to enter lands under the mining laws of the United States may enter lands that are chiefly valuable for building stone under the provisions of the law in relation to placer mineral claims. Lands reserved for the benefit of the public schools or donated to any States shall not be subject to entry under this section. Nothing contained in this section shall be construed to repeal section 471 of Title 16 relating to the establishment of national forests.

Aug. 4, 1892, c. 375, §§ 1, 3, 27 Stat. 348.

MINERAL LEASING ACT OF 1920 (as amended)

(30 U.S.C.A. §§ 181–287)

CHAPTER 3A—LEASES AND PROSPECTING PERMITS

1. GENERAL PROVISIONS

§ 181. Lands subject to disposition; persons entitled to benefits; reciprocal privileges; helium rights reserved

Deposits of coal, phosphate, sodium, potassium, oil, oil shale, gilsonite (including all vein-type solid hydrocarbons), or gas, and lands containing such deposits owned by the United States, including those in national forests, but excluding lands acquired under the Appalachian Forest Act, approved March 1, 1911 (36 Stat. 961), and those in incorporated cities, towns, and villages and in national parks and monuments, those acquired under other Acts subsequent to February 25, 1920, and lands within the naval petroleum and oil-shale reserves, except as hereinafter provided, shall be subject to disposition in the form and manner provided by this chapter to citizens of the United States, or to associations of such citizens, or to any corporation organized under the laws of the United States, or of any State or Territory thereof, or in the case of coal, oil, oil shale, or gas, to municipalities. Citizens of another country, the laws, customs, or regulations of which deny similar or like privileges to citizens or corporations of this country, shall not by stock ownership, stock holding, or stock control, own any interest in any lease acquired under the provisions of this chapter.

The term "oil" shall embrace all nongaseous hydrocarbon substances other than those substances leasable as coal, oil shale, or gilsonite (including all vein-type solid hydrocarbons).

The term "combined hydrocarbon lease" shall refer to a lease issued in a special tar sand area pursuant to section 226 of this title after November 16, 1981.

The term "special tar sand area" means (1) an area designated by the Secretary of the Interior's orders of November 20, 1980 (45 FR 76800–76801) and January 21, 1981 (46 FR 6077–6078) as containing substantial deposits of tar sand.

The United States reserves the ownership of and the right to extract helium from all gas produced from lands leased or otherwise granted under the provisions of this chapter, under such rules and regulations as shall be prescribed by the Secretary of the Interior: *Provided further,* That in the extraction of helium from gas produced from such lands it shall be so extracted as to cause no substantial delay in the delivery of gas produced from the well to the purchaser thereof.

Feb. 25, 1920, ch. 85, § 1, 41 Stat. 437; Feb. 7, 1927, ch. 66, § 5, 44 Stat. 1058; Aug. 8, 1946, ch. 916, § 1, 60 Stat. 950; Sept. 2, 1960, Pub.L. 86–705, § 7(a), 74 Stat. 790; as amended Nov. 16, 1981, Pub.L. 97–78, § 1(1), (4), 95 Stat. 1070.

§ 182. Lands disposed of with reservation of deposits of coal, and so forth

The provisions of this chapter shall also apply to all deposits of coal, phosphate, sodium, oil, oil shale, gilsonite (including all vein-type solid hydrocarbons), or gas in the lands of the United States, which lands may have been or may be disposed of under laws reserving to the United States such deposits, with the right to prospect for, mine, and remove the same, subject to such conditions as are or may hereafter be provided by such laws reserving such deposits.

Feb. 25, 1920, ch. 85, § 34, 41 Stat. 450; Sept. 2, 1960, Pub.L. 86–705, § 7(a), 74 Stat. 790; as amended Nov. 16, 1981, Pub.L. 97–78, § 1(1), 95 Stat. 1070.

§ 183. Cancellation of prospecting permits

The Secretary of the Interior shall reserve and may exercise the authority to cancel any prospecting permit upon failure by the permittee to exercise due diligence in the prosecution of the prospecting work in accordance with the terms and conditions stated in the permit, and shall insert in every such permit issued under the provisions of this chapter appropriate provisions for its cancellation by him.

Feb. 25, 1920, c. 85, § 26, 41 Stat. 448.

§ 184. Limitations on leases held, owned or controlled by persons, associations or corporations

Coal leases

(a) No person, association, or corporation, or any subsidiary, affiliate, or persons controlled by or under common control with such person, association, or corporation shall take, hold, own or control at one time, whether acquired directly from the Secretary under this chapter or otherwise, coal leases or permits on an aggregate of more than 75,000 acres in any one State and in no case greater than an aggregate of 150,000 acres in the United States: *Provided*, That any person, association, or corporation currently holding, owning, or controlling more than an aggregate of 150,-000 acres in the United States on the date of enactment of this section shall not be required on account of this section to relinquish said leases or permits: *Provided, further*, That in no case shall such person, association, or corporation be permitted to take, hold, own, or control any further Federal coal leases or permits until such time as their holdings, ownership, or control of Federal leases or permits has been reduced below an aggregate of 150,000 acres within the United States.

288

Sodium leases or permits, acreage

(b)(1) No person, association, or corporation, except as otherwise provided in this subsection, shall take, hold, own, or control at one time, whether acquired directly from the Secretary under this chapter, or otherwise, sodium leases or permits on an aggregate of more than five thousand one hundred and twenty acres in any one State.

(b)(2) The Secretary may, in his discretion, where the same is necessary in order to secure the economic mining of sodium compounds leasable under this chapter, permit a person, association, or corporation to take or hold sodium leases or permits on up to 30,720 acres in any one State.

Phosphate leases, acreage

(c) No person, association, or corporation shall take, hold, own, or control at one time, whether acquired directly from the Secretary under this chapter, or otherwise, phosphate leases or permits on an aggregate of more than twenty thousand four hundred and eighty acres in the United States.

Oil or gas leases, acreage, Alaska; options, semiannual statements

(d)(1) No person, association, or corporation, except as otherwise provided in this chapter, shall take, hold, own or control at one time, whether acquired directly from the Secretary under this chapter, or otherwise, oil or gas leases (including options for such leases or interests therein) on land held under the provisions of this chapter exceeding in the aggregate two hundred forty-six thousand and eighty acres in any one State other than Alaska[1]. *Provided, however,* That acreage held in special tar sand areas shall not be chargeable against such State limitations. In the case of the State of Alaska, the limit shall be three hundred thousand acres in the northern leasing district and three hundred thousand acres in the southern leasing district, and the boundary between said two districts shall be the left limit of the Tanana River from the border between the United States and Canada to the confluence of the Tanana and Yukon Rivers, and the left limit of the Yukon River from said confluence to its principal southern mouth.

(d)(2) No person, association, or corporation shall take, hold, own, or control at one time options to acquire interests in oil or gas leases under the provisions of this chapter which involve, in the aggregate, more than two hundred thousand acres of land in any one State other than Alaska, or, in the case of Alaska, more than two hundred thousand acres in each of its two leasing districts, as hereinbefore described. No option to acquire any interest in such an oil or gas lease shall be enforcible if entered into for a period of more than three years (which three years shall be inclusive of any renewal period if a right to renew is reserved by any party to the option) without the prior approval of the Secretary. In any case in which an option to acquire the optionor's entire interest in the whole or a part of the acreage under a lease is entered into, the acreage to which the option is

1. So in original. Probably should be followed by a colon.

applicable shall be charged both to the optionor and to the optionee, but the charge to the optionor shall cease when the option is exercised. In any case in which an option to acquire a part of the optionor's interest in the whole or a part of the acreage under a lease is entered into, the acreage to which the option is applicable shall be fully charged to the optionor and a share thereof shall also be charged to the optionee, as his interest may appear, but after the option is exercised said acreage shall be charged to the parties pro rata as their interests may appear. In any case in which an assignment is made of a part of a lessee's interest in the whole or part of the acreage under a lease or an application for a lease, the acreage shall be charged to the parties pro rata as their interests may appear. No option or renewal thereof shall be enforcible until notice thereof has been filed with the Secretary or an officer or employee of the Department of the Interior designated by him to receive the same. Each such notice shall include, in addition to any other matters prescribed by the Secretary, the names and addresses of the parties thereto, the serial number of the lease or application for a lease to which the option is applicable, and a statement of the number of acres covered thereby and of the interests and obligations of the parties thereto and shall be subscribed by all parties to the option or their duly authorized agents. An option which has not been exercised shall remain charged as hereinbefore provided until notice of its relinquishment or surrender has been filed, by either party, with the Secretary or any officer or employee of the Department of the Interior designated by him to receive the same. In addition, each holder of any such option shall file with the Secretary or an officer or employee of the Department of the Interior as aforesaid within ninety days after the 30th day of June and the 31st day of December in each year a statement showing, in addition to any other matters prescribed by the Secretary, his name, the name and address of each grantor of an option held by him, the serial number of every lease or application for a lease to which such an option is applicable, the number of acres covered by each such option, the total acreage in each State to which such options are applicable, and his interest and obligation under each such option. The failure of the holder of an option so to file shall render the option unenforcible[2] by him. The unenforcibility[3] of any option under the provisions of this paragraph shall not diminish the number of acres deemed to be held under option by any person, association, or corporation in computing the amount chargeable under the first sentence of this paragraph and shall not relieve any party thereto of any liability to cancellation, forfeiture, forced disposition, or other sanction provided by law. The Secretary may prescribe forms on which the notice and statements required by this paragraph shall be made.

Association or stockholder interests, conditions; combined interests

(e)(1) No person, association, or corporation shall take, hold, own or control at one time any interest as a member of an association or as a stockholder in a corporation holding a lease, option, or permit under the provisions of this chapter which, together with the area embraced in any

---

2. So in original. Probably should be "unenforceable".

3. So in original. Probably should be "unenforceability".

direct holding, ownership or control by him of such a lease, option, or permit or any other interest which he may have as a member of other associations or as a stockholder in other corporations holding, owning or controlling such leases, options, or permits for any kind of minerals, exceeds in the aggregate an amount equivalent to the maximum number of acres of the respective kinds of minerals allowed to any one lessee, optionee, or permittee under this chapter, except that no person shall be charged with his pro rata share of any acreage holdings of any association or corporation unless he is the beneficial owner of more than 10 per centum of the stock or other instruments of ownership or control of such association or corporation, and except that within three years after September 2, 1960 no valid option in existence prior to September 2, 1960 held by a corporation or association on September 2, 1960 shall be chargeable to any stockholder of such corporation or to a member of such association so long as said option shall be so held by such corporation or association under the provisions of this chapter.

(e)(2) No contract for development and operation of any lands leased under this chapter, whether or not coupled with an interest in such lease, and no lease held, owned, or controlled in common by two or more persons, associations, or corporations shall be deemed to create a separate association under the preceding paragraph of this subsection between or among the contracting parties or those who hold, own or control the lease in common, but the proportionate interest of each such party shall be charged against the total acreage permitted to be held, owned or controlled by such party under this chapter. The total acreage so held, owned, or controlled in common by two or more parties shall not exceed, in the aggregate, an amount equivalent to the maximum number of acres of the respective kinds of minerals allowed to any one lessee, optionee, or permittee under this chapter.

Limitations on other sections; combined interests permitted for certain purposes

(f) Nothing contained in subsection (e) of this section shall be construed (i) to limit sections 227, 228, 251 of this title or (ii), subject to the approval of the Secretary, to prevent any number of lessees under this chapter from combining their several interests so far as may be necessary for the purpose of constructing and carrying on the business of a refinery or of establishing and constructing, as a common carrier, a pipeline or railroad to be operated and used by them jointly in the transportation of oil from their several wells or from the wells of other lessees under this chapter or in the transportation of coal or (iii) to increase the acreage which may be taken, held, owned, or controlled under this section.

Forbidden interests acquired by descent, will, judgment, or decree; permissible holding period

(g) Any ownership or interest otherwise forbidden in this chapter which may be acquired by descent, will, judgment, or decree may be held for two years after its acquisition and no longer.

Cancellation, forfeiture, or disposal of interests for violation; bona fide purchasers and other valid interests; sale by Secretary; record of proceedings

(h)(1) If any interest in any lease is owned, or controlled, directly or indirectly, by means of stock or otherwise, in violation of any of the provisions of this chapter, the lease may be canceled, or the interest so owned may be forfeited, or the person so owning or controlling the interest may be compelled to dispose of the interest, in any appropriate proceeding instituted by the Attorney General. Such a proceeding shall be instituted in the United States district court for the district in which the leased property or some part thereof is located or in which the defendant may be found.

(h)(2) The right to cancel or forfeit for violation of any of the provisions of this chapter shall not apply so as to affect adversely the title or interest of a bona fide purchaser of any lease, interest in a lease, option to acquire a lease or an interest therein, or permit which lease, interest, option, or permit was acquired and is held by a qualified person, association, or corporation in conformity with those provisions, even though the holdings of the person, association, or corporation from which the lease, interest, option, or permit was acquired, or of his predecessor in title (including the original lessee of the United States) may have been canceled or forfeited or may be or may have been subject to cancellation or forfeiture for any such violation. If, in any such proceeding, an underlying lease, interest, option, or permit is canceled or forfeited to the Government and there are valid interests therein or valid options to acquire the lease or an interest therein which are not subject to cancellation, forfeiture, or compulsory disposition, the underlying lease, interest, option, or permit shall be sold by the Secretary to the highest responsible qualified bidder by competitive bidding under general regulations subject to all outstanding valid interests therein and valid options pertaining thereto. Likewise if, in any such proceeding, less than the whole interest in a lease, interest, option, or permit is canceled or forfeited to the Government, the partial interests so canceled or forfeited shall be sold by the Secretary to the highest responsible qualified bidder by competitive bidding under general regulations. If competitive bidding fails to produce a satisfactory offer the Secretary may, in either of these cases, sell the interest in question by such other method as he deems appropriate on terms not less favorable to the Government than those of the best competitive bid received.

(h)(3) The commencement and conclusion of every proceeding under this subsection shall be promptly noted on the appropriate public records of the Bureau of Land Management.

Bona fide purchasers, conditions for obtaining dismissals

(i) Effective September 21, 1959, any person, association, or corporation who is a party to any proceeding with respect to a violation of any provision of this chapter, whether initiated prior to said date or thereafter, shall have the right to be dismissed promptly as such a party upon showing that he holds and acquired as a bona fide purchaser the interest involving him as such a party without violating any provisions of this chapter. No hearing upon any such showing shall be required unless the Secretary presents prima facie evidence indicating a possible violation of this chapter on the part of the alleged bona fide purchaser.

Waiver or suspension of rights

(j) If during any such proceeding, a party thereto files with the Secretary a waiver of his rights under his lease (including particularly, where applicable, rights to drill and to assign) or if such rights are suspended by the Secretary pending a decision in the proceeding, whether initiated prior to enactment of this chapter or thereafter, payment of rentals and running of time against the term of the lease or leases involved shall be suspended as of the first day of the month following the filing of the waiver or suspension of the rights until the first day of the month following the final decision in the proceeding or the revocation of the waiver or suspension.

Unlawful trusts; forfeiture

(k) Except as otherwise provided in this chapter, if any lands or deposits subject to the provisions of this chapter shall be subleased, trusteed, possessed, or controlled by any device permanently, temporarily, directly, indirectly, tacitly, or in any manner whatsoever, so that they form a part of or are in any wise controlled by any combination in the form of an unlawful trust, with the consent of the lessee, optionee, or permittee, or form the subject of any contract or conspiracy in restraint of trade in the mining or selling of coal, phosphate, oil, oil shale, gilsonite (including all vein-type solid hydrocarbons), gas, or sodium entered into by the lessee, optionee, or permittee or any agreement or understanding, written, verbal, or otherwise, to which such lessee, optionee, or permittee shall be a party, of which his or its output is to be or become the subject, to control the price or prices thereof or of any holding of such lands by any individual, partnership, association, corporation, or control in excess of the amounts of lands provided in this chapter, the lease, option, or permit shall be forfeited by appropriate court proceedings.

Rules and regulations; notice to and consultation with Attorney General; application of antitrust laws; definitions

(*l*)(1) At each stage in the formulation and promulgation of rules and regulations concerning coal leasing pursuant to this chapter, and at each stage in the issuance, renewal, and readjustment of coal leases under this chapter, the Secretary of the Interior shall consult with and give due consideration to the views and advice of the Attorney General of the United States.

(*l*)(2) No coal lease may be issued, renewed, or readjusted under this chapter until at least thirty days after the Secretary of the Interior notifies the Attorney General of the proposed issuance, renewal, or readjustment. Such notification shall contain such information as the Attorney General may require in order to advise the Secretary of the Interior as to whether such lease would create or maintain a situation inconsistent with the antitrust laws. If the Attorney General advises the Secretary of the Interior that a lease would create or maintain such a situation, the Secretary of the Interior may not issue such lease, nor may he renew or readjust such lease for a period not to exceed one year, as the case may be, unless he thereafter conducts a public hearing on the record in accordance with subchapter II of chapter 5 of Title 5 and finds therein that such issuance, renewal, or readjustment is necessary to effectuate the purposes of this chapter, that it is consistent with the public interest, and that there are no reasonable alternatives consistent with this chapter, the antitrust laws, and the public interest.

(*l*)(3) Nothing in this chapter shall be deemed to convey to any person, association, corporation, or other business organization immunity from civil or criminal liability, or to create defenses to actions, under any antitrust law.

(*l*)(4) As used in this subsection, the term "antitrust law" means—

(A) the Act entitled "An Act to protect trade and commerce against unlawful restraints and monopolies", approved July 2, 1890 (15 U.S.C. 1 et seq.), as amended;

(B) the Act entitled "An Act to supplement existing laws against unlawful restraints and monopolies, and for other purposes", approved October 15, 1914 (15 U.S.C. 12 et seq.), as amended;

(C) the Federal Trade Commission Act (15 U.S.C. 41 et seq.), as amended;

(D) sections 73 and 74 of the Act entitled "An Act to reduce taxation, to provide revenue for the Government, and for other purposes", approved August 27, 1894 (15 U.S.C. 8 and 9), as amended; or

(E) the Act of June 19, 1936, chapter 592 (15 U.S.C. 13, 13a, 13b, and 21a).

Feb. 25, 1920, c. 85, § 27, 41 Stat. 448; Apr. 30, 1926, c. 197, 44 Stat. 373; July 3, 1930, c. 854, § 1, 46 Stat. 1007; Mar. 4, 1931, c. 506, 46 Stat. 1524; Aug. 8, 1946, c. 916, § 6, 60 Stat. 954; June 1, 1948, c. 365, 62 Stat. 285; June 3, 1948, c. 379, § 6, 62 Stat. 291; Aug. 2, 1954, c. 650, 68 Stat. 648; Aug. 13, 1957, Pub.L. 85–122, 71 Stat. 341; Aug. 21, 1958, Pub.L. 85–698, 72 Stat. 688; Sept. 21, 1959, Pub.L. 86–294, § 1, 73 Stat. 571; Mar. 18, 1960, Pub.L. 86–391, § 1(c), 74 Stat. 8; Sept. 2, 1960, Pub.L. 86–705, § 3, 74 Stat. 785; Aug. 31, 1964, Pub.L. 88–526, § 1, 78 Stat. 710; Aug. 31, 1964, Pub.L. 88–548, 78 Stat. 754; Aug. 4, 1976, Pub.L. 94–377, § § 11, 15, 90 Stat. 1090, 1091; Nov. 16, 1981, Pub.L. 97–78, § 1(2), (5), 95 Stat. 1070. As amended Apr. 28, 2000, Pub.L. 106–191, § 2, 114 Stat. 232; November 7, 2000, Pub.L. 106–463, § 3, 114 Stat. 2011.

§ 184a. Authorization of States to include in agreements for conservation of oil and gas resources lands acquired from United States

Notwithstanding the provisions of any applicable grant, deed, patent, exchange, or law of the United States, any State owning lands or interests therein acquired by it from the United States may consent to the operation or development of such lands or interests, or any part thereof, under agreements approved by the Secretary of the Interior made jointly or severally with lessees or permittees of lands or mineral deposits of the

United States or others, for the purpose of more properly conserving the oil and gas resources within such State. Such agreements may provide for the cooperative or unit operation or development of part or all of any oil or gas pool, field, or area; for the allocation of production and the sharing of proceeds from the whole or any specified part thereof regardless of the particular tract from which production is obtained or proceeds are derived; and, with the consent of the State, for the modification of the terms and provisions of State leases for lands operated and developed thereunder, including the term of years for which said leases were originally granted, to conform said leases to the terms and provisions of such agreements: *Provided,* That nothing in this section contained, nor the effectuation of it, shall be construed as in any respect waiving, determining or affecting any right, title, or interest, which otherwise may exist in the United States, and that the making of any agreement, as provided in this section, shall not be construed as an admission as to the title or ownership of the lands included.

Jan. 26, 1940, c. 14, 54 Stat. 17.

§ 185. Rights-of-way for pipelines through Federal lands

Grant of authority

(a) Rights-of-way through any Federal lands may be granted by the Secretary of the Interior or appropriate agency head for pipeline purposes for the transportation of oil, natural gas, synthetic liquid or gaseous fuels, or any refined product produced therefrom to any applicant possessing the qualifications provided in section 181 of this title in accordance with the provisions of this section.

Definitions

(b)(1) For the purposes of this section "Federal lands" means all lands owned by the United States except lands in the National Park System, lands held in trust for an Indian or Indian tribe, and lands on the Outer Continental Shelf. A right-of-way through a Federal reservation shall not be granted if the Secretary or agency head determines that it would be inconsistent with the purposes of the reservation.

(b)(2) "Secretary" means the Secretary of the Interior.

(b)(3) "Agency head" means the head of any Federal department or independent Federal office or agency, other than the Secretary of the Interior, which has jurisdiction over Federal lands.

* * *

Width limitations

(d) The width of a right-of-way shall not exceed fifty feet plus the ground occupied by the pipeline (that is, the pipe and its related facilities) unless the Secretary or agency head finds, and records the reasons for his finding, that in his judgment a wider right-of-way is necessary for operation and maintenance after construction, or to protect the environment or public safety. Related facilities include but are not limited to valves, pump stations, supporting structures, bridges, monitoring and communication devices, surge and storage tanks, terminals, roads, airstrips and campsites, and they need not necessarily be connected or contiguous to the pipe and may be the subjects of separate rights-of-way.

Temporary permits

(e) A right-of-way may be supplemented by such temporary permits for the use of Federal lands in the vicinity of the pipeline as the Secretary or agency head finds are necessary in connection with construction, operation, maintenance, or termination of the pipeline, or to protect the natural environment or public safety.

Regulatory authority

(f) Rights-of-way or permits granted or renewed pursuant to this section shall be subject to regulations promulgated in accord with the provisions of this section and shall be subject to such terms and conditions as the Secretary or agency head may prescribe regarding extent, duration, survey, location, construction, operation, maintenance, use, and termination.

* * *

Environmental protection

(h)(1) Nothing in this section shall be construed to amend, repeal, modify, or change in any way the requirements of section 102(2)(C) [42 U.S.C.A. § 4332(2)(C)] or any other provision of the National Environmental Policy Act of 1969 [42 U.S.C.A. § 4321 et seq.].

(h)(2) The Secretary or agency head, prior to granting a right-of-way or permit pursuant to this section for a new project which may have a significant impact on the environment, shall require the applicant to submit a plan of construction, operation, and rehabilitation for such right-of-way or permit which shall comply with this section. The Secretary or agency head shall issue regulations or impose stipulations which shall include, but shall not be limited to: (A) requirements for restoration, revegetation, and curtailment of erosion of the surface of the land; (B) requirements to insure that activities in connection with the right-of-way or permit will not violate applicable air and water quality standards nor related facility siting standards established by or pursuant to law; (C) requirements designed to control or prevent (i) damage to the environment (including damage to fish and wildlife habitat), (ii) damage to public or private property, and (iii) hazards to public health and safety; and (D) requirements to protect the interests of individuals living in the general area of the right-of-way or permit who rely on the fish, wildlife, and biotic resources of the area for subsistence purposes. Such regulations shall be applicable to every right-of-way or permit granted pursuant to this section, and may be made applicable by the Secretary or agency head to existing rights-of-way or permits, or rights-of-way or permits to be renewed pursuant to this section.

* * *

Public hearings

(k) The Secretary or agency head by regulation shall establish procedures, including public hearings where appropriate, to give Federal, State, and local government agencies and the public adequate notice and an opportunity to comment upon right-of-way applications filed after the date of enactment of this subsection.

* * *

Duration of grant

(n) Each right-of-way or permit granted or renewed pursuant to this section shall be limited to a reasonable term in light of all circumstances concerning the project, but in no event more than thirty years. In determining the duration of a right-of-way the Secretary or agency head shall, among other things, take into consideration the cost of the facility, its useful life, and any public purpose it serves. The Secretary or agency head shall renew any right-of-way, in accordance with the provisions of this section, so long as the project is in commercial operation and is operated and maintained in accordance with all of the provisions of this section.

Suspension or termination of right-of-way

(*o*)(1) Abandonment of a right-of-way or noncompliance with any provision of this section may be grounds for suspension or termination of the right-of-way if (A) after due notice to the holder of the right-of-way, (B) a reasonable opportunity to comply with this section, and (C) an appropriate administrative proceeding pursuant to section 554 of Title 5, the Secretary or agency head determines that any such ground exists and that suspension or termination is justified. No administrative proceeding shall be required where the right-of-way by its terms provides that it terminates on the occurrence of a fixed or agreed upon condition, event, or time.

(*o*)(2) If the Secretary or agency head determines that an immediate temporary suspension of activities within a right-of-way or permit area is necessary to protect public health or safety or the environment, he may abate such activities prior to an administrative proceeding.

(*o*)(3) Deliberate failure of the holder to use the right-of-way for the purpose for which it was granted or renewed for any continuous two-year period shall constitute a rebuttable presumption of abandonment of the right-of-way: *Provided,* That where the failure to use the right-of-way is due to circumstances not within the holder's control the Secretary or agency head is not required to commence proceedings to suspend or terminate the right-of-way.

Joint use of rights-of-way

(p) In order to minimize adverse environmental impacts and the proliferation of separate rights-of-way across Federal lands, the utilization of rights-of-way in common shall be required to the extent practical, and each right-of-way or permit shall reserve to the Secretary or agency head the right to grant additional rights-of-way or permits for compatible uses on or adjacent to rights-of-way or permit area granted pursuant to this section.

Statutes

(q) No rights-of-way for the purposes provided for in this section shall be granted or renewed across Federal lands except under and subject to the provisions, limitations, and conditions of this section. Any application for a fight-of-way filed under any other law prior to the effective date of this provision may, at the applicant's option, be considered as an application under this section. The Secretary or agency head may require the applicant to submit any additional information he deems necessary to comply with the requirements of this section.

Common carriers

(r)(1) Pipelines and related facilities authorized under this section shall be constructed, operated, and maintained as common carriers.

(r)(2)(A) The owners or operators of pipelines subject to this section shall accept, convey, transport, or purchase without discrimination all oil or gas delivered to the pipeline without regard to whether such oil or gas was produced on Federal or non-Federal lands.

(r)(2)(B) In the case of oil or gas produced from Federal lands or from the resources on the Federal lands in the vicinity of the pipeline, the Secretary may, after a full hearing with due notice thereof to the interested parties and a proper finding of facts, determine the proportionate amounts to be accepted, conveyed, transported or purchased.

(r)(3)(A) The common carrier provisions of this section shall not apply to any natural gas pipeline operated by any person subject to regulation under the Natural Gas Act [15 U.S.C.A. § 717 et seq.] or by any public utility subject to regulation by a State or municipal regulatory agency having jurisdiction to regulate the rates and charges for the sale of natural gas to consumers within the State or municipality.

(r)(3)(B) Where natural gas not subject to State regulatory or conservation laws governing its purchase by pipelines is offered for sale, each such pipeline shall purchase, without discrimination, any such natural gas produced in the vicinity of the pipeline.

(r)(4) The Government shall in express terms reserve and shall provide in every lease of oil lands under this chapter that the lessee, assignee, or beneficiary, if owner or operator of a controlling interest in any pipeline or of any company operating the pipeline which may be operated accessible to the oil derived from lands under such lease, shall at reasonable rates and without discrimination accept and convey the oil of the Government or of any citizen or company not the owner of any pipeline operating a lease or purchasing gas or oil under the provisions of this chapter.

(r)(5) Whenever the Secretary has reason to believe that any owner or operator subject to this section is not operating any oil or gas pipeline in complete accord with its obligations as a common carrier hereunder, he may request the Attorney General to prosecute an appropriate proceeding before the Secretary of Energy or Federal Energy Regulatory Commission or any appropriate State agency or the United States district court for the district in which the pipeline or any part thereof is located, to enforce such obligation or to impose any penalty provided therefor, or the Secretary may, by proceeding as provided in this section, suspend or terminate the said grant of right-of-way for noncompliance with the provisions of this section.

(r)(6) The Secretary or agency head shall require, prior to granting or renewing a right-of-way, that the applicant submit and disclose all plans, contracts, agreements, or other information or material which he deems necessary to determine whether a right-of-way shall be granted or renewed and the terms and conditions which should be included in the right-of-way. Such information may include, but is not limited to: (A) conditions for, and agreements among owners or operators, regarding the addition of pumping facilities, looping, or otherwise increasing the pipeline or terminal's throughput capacity in response to actual or anticipated increases in demand; (B) conditions for adding or abandoning intake, offtake, or storage points or facilities; and (C) minimum shipment or purchase tenders.

* * *

Existing rights-of-way

(t) The Secretary or agency head may ratify and confirm any fight-of-way or permit for an oil or gas pipeline or related facility that was granted under any provision of law before the effective date of this subsection, if it is modified by mutual agreement to comply to the extent practical with the provisions of this section. Any action taken by the Secretary or agency head pursuant to this subsection shall not be considered a major Federal action requiring a detailed statement pursuant to section 102(2)(C) [42 U.S.C.A. § 4332(2)(C)] of the National Environmental Policy Act of 1970 (Public Law 90–190; 42 U.S.C.A. § 4321).

Limitations on export

(u) Any domestically produced crude oil transported by pipeline over rights-of-way granted pursuant to this section, except such crude oil which is either exchanged in similar quantity for convenience or increased efficiency of transportation with persons or the government of an adjacent foreign state, or which is temporarily exported for convenience or increased efficiency of transportation across parts of an adjacent foreign state and reenters the United States, shall be subject to all of the limitations and licensing requirements of the Export Administration Act of 1979 (50 U.S.C.App. 2401 and following) and, in addition, before any crude oil subject to this section may be exported under the limitations and licensing requirements and penalty and enforcement provisions of the Export Administration Act of 1979 the President must make and publish an express finding that such exports will not diminish the total quantity or quality of petroleum available to the United States, and are in the national interest and are in accord with the provisions of the Export Administration Act of

1979: *Provided,* That the President shall submit reports to the Congress containing findings made under this section, and after the date of receipt of such report Congress shall have a period of sixty calendar days, thirty days of which Congress must have been in session, to consider whether exports under the terms of this section are in the national interest. If the Congress within this time period passes a concurrent resolution of disapproval stating disagreement with the President's finding concerning the national interest, further exports made pursuant to the aforementioned Presidential findings shall cease.

* * *

State standards

(v) The Secretary or agency head shall take into consideration and to the extent practical comply with State standards for right-of-way construction, operation, and maintenance.

Reports

(w)(1) The Secretary and other appropriate agency heads shall report to the Committee on Natural Resources of the United States House of Representatives and the Committee on Energy and Natural Resources of the United States Senate annually on the administration of this section and on the safety and environmental requirements imposed pursuant thereto.

(w)(2) The Secretary or agency head shall promptly notify the Committee on Natural Resources of the United States House of Representatives and the Committee on Energy and Natural Resources of the United States Senate upon receipt of an application for a right-of-way for a pipeline twenty-four inches or more in diameter, and no right-of-way for such a pipeline shall be granted until a notice of intention to grant the right-of-way, together with the Secretary's or agency head's detailed findings as to the terms and conditions he proposes to impose, has been submitted to such committees.

(w)(3) Periodically, but at least once a year, the Secretary of the Department of Transportation shall cause the examination of all pipelines and associated facilities on Federal lands and shall cause the prompt reporting of any potential leaks or safety problems.

(w)(4) Repealed. Pub.L. 104–66, Title I, § 1121(k), Dec. 21, 1995, 109 Stat. 724.

Liability

(x)(1) The Secretary or agency head shall promulgate regulations and may impose stipulations specifying the extent to which holders of rights-of-way and permits under this chapter shall be liable to the United States for damage or injury incurred by the United States in connection with the right-of-way or permit. Where the right-of-way or permit involves lands which are under the exclusive jurisdiction of the Federal Government, the Secretary or agency head shall promulgate regulations specifying the extent to which holders shall be liable to third parties for injuries incurred in connection with the right-of-way or permit.

(x)(2) The Secretary or agency head may, by regulation or stipulation, impose a standard of strict liability to govern activities taking place on a right-of-way or permit area which the Secretary or agency head determines, in his discretion, to present a foreseeable hazard or risk of danger to the United States.

(x)(3) Regulations and stipulations pursuant to this subsection shall not impose strict liability for damage or injury resulting from (A) an act of war, or (B) negligence of the United States.

(x)(4) Any regulation or stipulation imposing liability without fault shall include a maximum limitation on damages commensurate with the foreseeable risks or hazards presented. Any liability for damage or injury in excess of this amount shall be determined by ordinary rules of negligence.

(x)(5) The regulations and stipulations shall also specify the extent to which such holders shall indemnify or hold harmless the United States for liability, damage, or claims arising in connection with the right-of-way or permit.

(x)(6) Any regulation or stipulation promulgated or imposed pursuant to this section shall provide that all owners of any interest in, and all affiliates or subsidiaries of any holder of, a right-of-way or permit shall be liable to the United States in the event that a claim for damage or injury cannot be collected from the holder.

(x)(7) In any case where liability without fault is imposed pursuant to this subsection and the damages involved were caused by the negligence of a third party, the rules of subrogation shall apply in accordance with the law of the jurisdiction where the damage occurred.

Antitrust laws

(y) The grant of a right-of-way or permit pursuant to this section shall grant no immunity from the operation of the Federal antitrust laws.

Feb. 25, 1920, c. 85, § 28, 41 Stat. 449; Aug. 21, 1935, c. 599, § 1, 49 Stat. 678; Aug. 12, 1953, c. 408, 67 Stat. 557; Nov. 16, 1973, Pub.L. 93–153, Title I, § 101, 87 Stat. 576; Aug. 4, 1977, Pub.L. 95–91, Title III, §§ 301(b), 306, Title IV, § 402(a), (b), Title VII, §§ 703, 707, 91 Stat. 578, 581, 583, 584, 606, 607; July 12, 1985, Pub.L. 99–64, Title I, § 123(b), 99 Stat. 156, as amended Oct. 30, 1990, Pub.L. 101–475, § 1, 104 Stat. 1102; Nov. 2, 1994, Pub.L. 103–437, § 11(a)(1), 108 Stat. 4589; Nov. 28, 1995, Pub.L. 104–58, Title II, § 201, 109 Stat. 560; Dec. 21, 1995, Pub.L. 104–66, Title I, § 1121(k), 109 Stat. 724.

Unconstitutionality of Legislative Veto Provisions

The provisions of section 1254(c)(2) of Title 8, Aliens and Nationality, which authorize a House of Congress, by resolution, to invalidate an action of the Executive Branch, were declared unconstitutional in Immigration and Naturalization Service v. Chadha, 1983, 103 S. Ct. 2764, 462 U.S. 919, 77 L. Ed. 2d 317. See similar provisions in subsec. (u) of this section.

§ 187. Assignment or subletting of leases; relinquishment of rights under leases; conditions in leases for protection of diverse interests in operation of mines, wells, and so forth; State laws not impaired

No lease issued under the authority of this chapter shall be assigned or sublet, except with the consent of the Secretary of the Interior. The lessee may, in the discretion of the Secretary of the Interior, be permitted at any time to make written relinquishment of all rights under such a lease, and upon acceptance thereof be thereby relieved of all future obligations under said lease, and may with like consent surrender any legal subdivision of the area included within the lease. Each lease shall contain provisions for the purpose of insuring the exercise of reasonable diligence, skill, and care in the operation of said property; a provision that such rules for the safety and welfare of the miners and for the prevention of undue waste as may be prescribed by said Secretary shall be observed, including a restriction of the workday to not exceeding eight hours in any one day for underground workers except in cases of emergency; provisions prohibiting the employment of any child under the age of sixteen in any mine below the surface; provisions securing the workmen complete freedom of purchase; provision requiring the payment of wages at least twice a month in lawful money of the United States, and providing proper rules and regulations to insure the fair and just weighing or measurement of the coal mined by each miner, and such other provisions as he may deem necessary to insure the sale of the production of such leased lands to the United States and to the public at reasonable prices, for the protection of the interests of the United States, for the prevention of monopoly, and for the safeguarding of the public welfare. None of such provisions shall be in conflict with the laws of the State in which the leased property is situated.

Feb. 25, 1920, ch. 85, § 30, 41 Stat. 449; As amended Oct. 30, 1978, Pub.L. 95–554, § 5, 92 Stat. 2074.

§ 187a. Oil or gas leases; partial assignments

Notwithstanding anything to the contrary in section 187 of this title, any oil or gas lease issued under the authority of this chapter may be assigned or subleased, as to all or part of the acreage included therein, subject to final approval by the Secretary and as to either a divided or undivided interest therein, to any person or persons qualified to own a lease under this chapter, and any assignment or sublease shall take effect as of the first day of the lease month following the date of filing in the proper land office of three original executed counterparts thereof, together with any required bond and proof of the qualification under this chapter of the assignee or sublessee to take or hold such lease or interest therein. Until such approval, however, the assignor or sublessor and his surety shall continue to be responsible for the performance of any and all obligations as if no assignment or sublease had been executed. The Secretary shall disapprove the assignment or sublease only for lack of qualification of the assignee or sublessee or for lack of sufficient bond: *Provided, however,* That the Secretary may, in his discretion, disapprove an assignment of any of the following, unless the assignment constitutes the entire lease or is demonstrated to further the development of oil and gas:

(1) A separate zone or deposit under any lease.

(2) A part of a legal subdivision.

(3) Less than 640 acres outside Alaska or of less than 2,560 acres within Alaska.

Requests for approval of assignment or sublease shall be processed promptly by the Secretary. Except where the assignment or sublease is not in accordance with applicable law, the approval shall be given within 60 days of the date of receipt by the Secretary of a request for such approval. Upon approval of any assignment or sublease, the assignee or sublessee shall be bound by the terms of the lease to the same extent as if such assignee or sublessee were the original lessee, any conditions in the assignment or sublease to the contrary notwithstanding. Any partial assignment of any lease shall segregate the assigned and retained portions thereof, and as above provided, release and discharge the assignor from all obligations thereafter accruing with respect to the assigned lands; and such segregated leases shall continue in full force and effect for the primary term of the original lease, but for not less than two years after the date of discovery of oil or gas in paying quantities upon any other segregated portion of the lands originally subject to such lease. Assignments under this section may also be made of parts of leases which are in their extended term because of any provision of this chapter. Upon the segregation by an assignment of a lease issued after September 2, 1960 and held beyond its primary term by production, actual or suspended, or the payment of compensatory royalty, the segregated lease of an undeveloped, assigned, or retained part shall continue for two years, and so long thereafter as oil or gas is produced in paying quantities.

Feb. 25, 1920, c. 85, § 30A, formerly § 30a, as added Aug. 8, 1946, c. 916, § 7, 60 Stat. 955, and amended July 29, 1954, c. 644, § 1(6), 68 Stat. 585; Sept. 2, 1960, Pub.L. 86–705, § 6, 74 Stat. 790; renumbered and amended Pub.L. 100–203, Title V, § 5103, Dec. 22, 1987, 101 Stat. 1330–258.

§ 187b. Same; oil or gas leases; written relinquishment of rights; release of obligations

Notwithstanding any provision to the contrary in section 187 of this title, a lessee may at any time make and file in the appropriate land office a written relinquishment of all rights under any oil or gas lease issued under the authority of this chapter or of any legal subdivision of the area included within any such lease. Such relinquishment shall be effective as of the date of its filing, subject to the continued obligation of the lessee and his surety to make payment of all accrued rentals and royalties and to place all wells on the lands to be relinquished in condition for suspension or abandonment in accordance with the applicable lease terms and regulations; thereupon the lessee shall be released of all obligations thereafter accruing under said lease with respect to the lands relinquished, but no such relinquishment shall release such lessee, or his bond, from any liability for breach of any obligation of the lease, other than an obligation to drill, accrued at the date of the relinquishment.

Feb. 25, 1920, c. 85, § 30–, formerly § 30b, as added Aug. 8, 1946, c. 916, § 8, 60 Stat. 956, and renumbered Pub.L. 100–203, Title V, § 5103, Dec. 22, 1987, 101 Stat. 1330–258.

§ 188. Failure to comply with provisions of lease

Forfeiture

(a) Except as otherwise herein provided, any lease issued under the provisions of this chapter may be forfeited and canceled by an appropriate proceeding in the United States district court for the district in which the property, or some part thereof, is located whenever the lessee fails to comply with any of the provisions of this chapter, of the lease, or of the general regulations promulgated under this chapter and in force at the date of the lease; and the lease may provide for resort to appropriate methods for the settlement of disputes or for remedies for breach of specified conditions thereof.

Cancellation

(b) Any lease issued after August 21, 1935, under the provisions of section 226 of this title shall be subject to cancellation by the Secretary of the Interior after 30 days notice upon the failure of the lessee to comply with any of the provisions of the lease, unless or until the leasehold contains a well capable of production of oil or gas in paying quantities, or the lease is committed to an approved cooperative or unit plan or communitization agreement under section 226(m) of this title which contains a well capable of production of unitized substances in paying quantities. Such notice in advance of cancellation shall be sent the lease owner by registered letter directed to the lease owner's record post-office address, and in case such letter shall be returned as undelivered, such notice shall also be posted for a period of thirty days in the United States land office for the district in which the land covered by such lease is situated, or in the event that there is no district land office for such district, then in the post office nearest such land. Notwithstanding the provisions of this section, however, upon failure of a lessee to pay rental on or before the anniversary date of the lease, for any lease on which there is no well capable of producing oil or gas in paying quantities, the lease shall automatically terminate by operation of law: *Provided, however,* That when the time for payment falls upon any day in which the proper office for payment is not open, payment may be received the next official working day and shall be considered as timely made: *Provided,* That if the rental payment due under a lease is paid on or before the anniversary date but either (1) the amount of the payment has been or is hereafter deficient and the deficiency is nominal, as determined by the Secretary by regulation, or (2) the payment was calculated in accordance with the acreage figure stated in the lease, or in any decision affecting the lease, or made in accordance with a bill or decision which has been rendered by him and such figure, bill, or decision is found to be in error resulting in a deficiency, such lease shall not automatically terminate unless (1) a new lease had been issued prior to May 12, 1970, or (2) the lessee fails to pay the deficiency within the period prescribed in a notice of deficiency sent to him by the Secretary.

Reinstatement

(c) Where any lease has been or is hereafter terminated automatically by operation of law under this section for failure to pay on or before the anniversary date the full amount of rental due, but such rental was paid on or tendered within twenty days thereafter, and it is shown to the satisfaction of the Secretary of the Interior that such failure was either justifiable or not due to a lack of reasonable diligence on the part of the lessee, the Secretary may reinstate the lease if—

(1) a petition for reinstatement, together with the required rental, including back rental accruing from the date of termination of the lease, is filed with the Secretary; and

(2) no valid lease has been issued affecting any of the lands covered by the terminated lease prior to the filing of said petition. The Secretary shall not issue any new lease affecting any of the lands covered by such terminated lease for a reasonable period, as determined in accordance with regulations issued by him. In any case where a reinstatement of a terminated lease is granted under this subsection and the Secretary finds that the reinstatement of such lease will not afford the lessee a reasonable opportunity to continue operations under the lease, the Secretary may, at his discretion, extend the term of such lease for such period as he deems reasonable: *Provided,* That (A) such extension shall not exceed a period equivalent to the time beginning when the lessee knew or should have known of the termination and ending on the date the Secretary grants such petition; (B) such extension shall not exceed a period equal to the unexpired portion of the lease or any extension thereof remaining at the date of termination; and (C) when the reinstatement occurs after the expiration of the term or extension thereof the lease may be extended from the date the Secretary grants the petition.

* * *

Unpatented oil placer mining claims

(f) Where an unpatented oil placer mining claim validly located prior to February 24, 1920, which has been or is currently producing or is capable of producing oil and gas, has been or is hereafter deemed conclusively abandoned for failure to file timely the required instruments or copies of instruments required by section 1744 of Title 43, and it is shown to the satisfaction of the Secretary that such failure was inadvertent, justifiable, or not due to lack of reasonable diligence on the part of the owner, the Secretary may issue, for the lands covered by the abandoned unpatented oil placer mining claim, a noncompetitive oil and gas lease, consistent with the provisions of section 226(e) of this title, to be effective from the statutory date the claim was deemed conclusively abandoned. Issuance of such a lease shall be conditioned upon:

(1) a petition for issuance of a noncompetitive oil and gas lease, together with the required rental and royalty, including back rental and royalty accruing from the statutory date of abandonment of the oil placer mining claim, being filed with the Secretary—

(A) with respect to any claim deemed conclusively abandoned on or before January 12, 1983, on or before the one hundred and twentieth day after January 12, 1983, or

(B) with respect to any claim deemed conclusively abandoned after January 12, 1983, on or before the one hundred and twentieth day after final notification by the Secretary or a court of competent jurisdiction of the determination of the abandonment of the oil placer mining claim;

(2) a valid lease not having been issued affecting any of the lands covered by the abandoned oil placer mining claim prior to the filing of such petition: *Provided, however,* That after the filing of a petition for issuance of a lease under this subsection, the Secretary shall not issue any new lease affecting any of the lands covered by such abandoned oil placer mining claim for a reasonable period, as determined in accordance with regulations issued by him;

(3) a requirement in the lease for payment of rental, including back rentals accruing from the statutory date of abandonment of the oil placer mining claim, of not less than $5 per acre per year;

(4) a requirement in the lease for payment of royalty on production removed or sold from the oil placer mining claim, including all royalty on production made subsequent to the statutory date the claim was deemed conclusively abandoned, of not less than 12 1/2 percent; and

(5) compliance with the notice and reimbursement of costs provisions of paragraph (4) of subsection (e) of this section but addressed to the petition covering the conversion of an abandoned unpatented oil placer mining claim to a noncompetitive oil and gas lease.

* * *

Discretion of Secretary

(j) Where, in the judgment of the Secretary of the Interior, drilling operations were being diligently conducted on the last day of the primary term of the lease, and, except for nonpayment of rental, the lessee would have been entitled to extension of his lease, pursuant to section 226–1 of this title, the Secretary of the Interior may reinstate such lease notwithstanding the failure of the lessee to have made payment of the next year's rental, provided the conditions of subparagraphs (1) and (2) of subsection (c) of this section are satisfied.

Feb. 25, 1920, c. 85, § 31, 41 Stat. 450; Aug. 8, 1946, c. 916, § 9, 60 Stat. 956; July 29, 1954, c. 644, § 1(7), 68 Stat. 585; Oct. 15, 1962, Pub.L. 87–822, § 1, 76 Stat. 943; May 12, 1970, Pub.L. 91–245, §§ 1, 2, 84 Stat. 206; Jan. 12, 1983, Pub.L. 97–451, Title IV, § 401, 96 Stat. 2462. As amended Pub.L. 100–203, Title V, §§ 5102(d)(2), 5104, Dec. 22, 1987, 101 Stat.

1330–258, 1330–259; Pub.L. 101–567, § 1, Nov. 15, 1990, 104 Stat. 2802; Pub.L. 103–437, § 11(a)(1), Nov. 2, 1994, 108 Stat. 4589.

* * *

§ 189. Rules and regulations; boundary lines; State rights unaffected; taxation

The Secretary of the Interior is authorized to prescribe necessary and proper rules and regulations and to do any and all things necessary to carry out and accomplish the purposes of this chapter, also to fix and determine the boundary lines of any structure, or oil or gas field, for the purposes of this chapter. Nothing in this chapter shall be construed or held to affect the rights of the States or other local authority to exercise any rights which they may have, including the right to levy and collect taxes upon improvements, output of mines, or other rights, property, or assets of any lessee of the United States.

Feb. 25, 1920, c. 85, § 32, 41 Stat. 450.

* * *

§ 191. Disposition of moneys received

(a) All money received from sales, bonuses, royalties including interest charges collected under the Federal Oil and Gas Royalty Management Act of 1982 [30 U.S.C.A. § 1701 et seq.], and rentals of the public lands under the provisions of this chapter and the Geothermal Steam Act of 1970 [30 U.S.C.A. § 1001 et seq.], shall be paid into the Treasury of the United States; and, subject to the provisions of subsection (b) of this section, 50 per centum thereof shall be paid by the Secretary of the Treasury to the State other than Alaska within the boundaries of which the leased lands or deposits are or were located; said moneys paid to any of such States on or after January 1, 1976, to be used by such State and its subdivisions, as the legislature of the State may direct giving priority to those subdivisions of the State socially or economically impacted by development of minerals leased under this chapter, for (i) planning, (ii) construction and mainte-nance of public facilities, and (iii) provision of public service; and excepting those from Alaska, 40 per centum thereof shall be paid into, reserved, appropriated, as part of the reclamation fund created by the Act of Congress known as the Reclamation Act, approved June 17, 1902, and of those from Alaska, 90 per centum thereof shall be paid to the State of Alaska for disposition by the legislature thereof: *Provided*, That all moneys which may accrue to the United States under the provisions of this chapter and the Geothermal Steam Act of 1970 from lands within the naval petroleum reserves shall be deposited in the Treasury as "miscellaneous receipts", as provided by section 7433(b) of Title 10. All moneys received under the provisions of this chapter and the Geothermal Steam Act of 1970 not otherwise disposed of by this section shall be credited to miscellaneous receipts. Payments to States under this section with respect to any moneys received by the United States, shall be made not later than the last business day of the month in which such moneys are warranted by the United States Treasury to the Secretary as having been received, except for any portion of such moneys which is under challenge and placed in a suspense account pending resolution of a dispute. Such warrants shall be issued by the United States Treasury not later than 10 days after receipt of such moneys by the Treasury. Moneys placed in a suspense account which are determined to be payable to a State shall be made not later than the last business day of the month in which such dispute is resolved. Any such amount placed in a suspense account pending resolution shall bear interest until the dispute is resolved.

(b)(1) In calculating the amount to be paid to States during any fiscal year under this section or under any other provision of law requiring payment to a State of any revenues derived from the leasing of any onshore lands or interest in land owned by the United States for the production of the same types of minerals leasable under this chapter or of geothermal steam, 50 percent of the portion of the enacted appropriation of the Department of the Interior and any other agency during the preceding fiscal year allocable to the administration of all laws providing for the leasing of any onshore lands or interest in land owned by the United States for the production of the same types of minerals leasable under this chapter or of geothermal steam, and to enforcement of such laws, shall be deducted from the receipts derived under those laws in approximately equal amounts each month (subject to paragraph (4)) prior to the division and distribution of such receipts between the States and the United States.

(b)(2) The proportion of the deduction provided in paragraph (1) allocable to each State shall be determined by dividing the monies disbursed to the State during the preceding fiscal year derived from onshore mineral leasing referred to in paragraph (1) in that State by the total money disbursed to States during the preceding fiscal year from such onshore mineral leasing in all States.

(b)(3) In the event the deduction apportioned to any State under this subsection exceeds 50 percent of the Secretary of the Interior's estimate of the amounts attributable to onshore mineral leasing referred to in paragraph (1) within that State during the preceding fiscal year, the deduction from receipts received from leases in that State shall be limited to such estimated amounts and the total amount to be deducted from such onshore mineral leasing receipts shall be reduced accordingly.

(b)(4) If the amount otherwise deductible under this subsection in any month from the portion of receipts to be distributed to a State exceeds the amount payable to the State during that month, any amount exceeding the amount payable shall be carried forward and deducted from amounts payable to the State in subsequent months. If any amount remains to be carried forward at the end of the fiscal year, such amount shall not be deducted from any disbursements in any subsequent fiscal year.

(b)(5) All deductions to be made pursuant to this subsection shall be made in full during the fiscal year in which such deductions were incurred.

Feb. 25, 1920, c. 85, § 35, 41 Stat. 450; May 27, 1947, c. 83, 61 Stat. 119; Aug. 3, 1950, c. 527, 64 Stat. 402; July 10, 1957, Pub.L. 85–88, § 2, 71 Stat. 282; July 7, 1958, Pub.L. 85–508, §§ 6(k), 28(b), 72 Stat. 343, 351; Apr. 21, 1976, Pub.L. 94–273, § 6(2), 90 Stat. 377; Aug. 4, 1976, Pub.L. 94–377, § 9, 90 Stat. 1090; Sept. 28, 1976, Pub.L. 94–422, Title III, § 301, 90 Stat. 1323;

Oct. 21, 1976, Pub.L. 94–579, Title III, § 317(a), 90 Stat. 2770; Jan. 12, 1983, Pub.L. 97–451, Title I, § 104(a), 111(g), 96 Stat. 2451, 2456; as amended Dec. 22, 1987, Pub.L. 100–203, Title V, § 5109, 101 Stat. 1330–261; Sept. 22, 1988, Pub.L. 100–443, § 5(b), 102 Stat. 1768; Aug. 10, 1993, Pub.L. 103–66, Title X, § 10201, 107 Stat. 407. Oct. 30, 2000, Pub.L. 106–393, Title V, § 503, 114 Stat. 1624.

§ 192. Payment of royalties in oil or gas; sale of such oil or gas

All royalty accruing to the United States under any oil or gas lease or permit under this chapter on demand of the Secretary of the Interior shall be paid in oil or gas.

* * *

Feb. 25, 1920, c. 85, § 36, 41 Stat. 451; July 13, 1946, c. 574, 60 Stat. 533.

* * *

§ 193. Disposition of deposits of coal, and so forth

The deposits of coal, phosphate, sodium, potassium, oil, oil shale, and gas, herein referred to, in lands valuable for such minerals, including lands and deposits in Lander, Wyoming, coal entries numbered 18 to 49, inclusive, shall be subject to disposition only in the form and manner provided in this chapter, except as provided in sections 1716 and 1719 of Title 43, and except as to valid claims existent on February 25, 1920, and thereafter maintained in compliance with the laws under which initiated, which claims may be perfected under such laws, including discovery.

Feb. 25, 1920, ch. 85, § 37, 41 Stat. 451; Feb. 7, 1927, ch. 66, § 5, 44 Stat. 1058; Aug. 8, 1946, ch. 916, § 11, 60 Stat. 957; as amended Oct. 30, 1978, Pub.L. 95–554, § 4, 92 Stat. 2074.

§ 193a. Preference right of United States to purchase coal for Army and Navy; price for coal; civil actions; jurisdiction

The United States shall, at all times, have the preference right to purchase so much of the product of any mine or mines opened upon the lands sold under the provisions of this Act, as may be necessary for the use of the Army and Navy, and at such reasonable and remunerative price as may be fixed by the President; but the producers of any coal so purchased who may be dissatisfied with the price thus fixed shall have the right to prosecute suits against the United States in the United States Court of Federal Claims for the recovery of any additional sum or sums they may claim as justly due upon such purchase.

May 28, 1908, ch. 211, § 2, 35 Stat. 424; as amended Apr. 2, 1982, Pub.L. 97–164, Title I, § 160(a)(10), 96 Stat. 48; as amended Oct. 29, 1992, Pub.L. 102–572, Title IX, § 902(b)(1), 106 Stat. 4516.

2. COAL

§ 201. Leases and exploration

Division into tracts; bidding and award; negotiated sales on exercise of right-of. way permits; leases to public agencies; fair market value of leases; leases in National Forests; comprehensive land-use plans; notice of proposed lease offering

(a)(1) The Secretary of the Interior is authorized to divide any lands subject to this Chapter which have been classified for coal leasing into leasing tracts of such size as he finds appropriate and in the public interest and which will permit the mining of all coal which can be economically extracted in such tract and thereafter he shall, in his discretion, upon the request of any qualified applicant or on his own motion, from time to time, offer such lands for leasing and shall award leases thereon by competitive bidding: *Provided,* That notwithstanding the competitive bidding requirement of this section, the Secretary may, subject to such conditions which he deems appropriate, negotiate the sale at fair market value of coal the removal of which is necessary and incidental to the exercise of a right-of-way permit issued pursuant to Title V of the Federal Land Policy and Management Act of 1976 [43 U.S.C.A. § 1761 et seq.]. No less than 50 per centum of the total acreage offered for lease by the Secretary in any one year shall be leased under a system of deferred bonus payment. Upon default or cancellation of any coal lease for which bonus payments are due, any unpaid remainder of the bid shall be immediately payable to the United States. A reasonable number of leasing tracts shall be reserved and offered for lease in accordance with this section to public bodies, including Federal agencies, rural electric cooperatives, or nonprofit corporations controlled by any of such entities: *Provided,* That the coal so offered for lease shall be for use by such entity or entities in implementing a definite plan to produce energy for their own use or for sale to their members or customers (except for short-term sales to others). No bid shall be accepted which is less than the fair market value, as determined by the Secretary, of the coal subject to the lease. Prior to his determination of the fair market value of the coal subject to the lease, the Secretary shall give opportunity for and consideration to public comments on the fair market value. Nothing in this section shall be construed to require the Secretary to make public his judgment as to the fair market value of the coal to be leased, or the comments he receives thereon prior to the issuance of the lease. He is authorized, in awarding leases for coal lands improved and occupied or claimed in good faith, prior to February 25, 1920, to consider and recognize equitable rights of such occupants or claimants.

(a)(2)(A) The Secretary shall not issue a lease or leases under the terms of this Chapter to any person, association, corporation, or any subsidiary, affiliate, or persons controlled by or under common control with such person, association, or corporation, where any such entity holds a lease or leases issued by the United States to coal deposits and has held such lease or leases for a period of ten years when such entity is not, except as provided for in section 207(b) of this title, producing coal from the lease deposits in commercial quantities. In computing the ten-year period referred to in the preceding sentence, periods of time prior to August 4, 1976, shall not be counted.

(a)(2)(B) Any lease proposal which permits surface coal mining within the boundaries of a National Forest which the Secretary proposes to issue under this chapter shall be submitted to the Governor of each State within which the coal deposits subject to such lease are located. No such lease may be issued under this chapter before the expiration of the sixty-day period beginning on the date of such submission. If any Governor to whom a proposed lease was submitted under this subparagraph objects to the issuance of such lease, such lease shall not be issued before the expiration of the six-month period beginning on the date the Secretary is notified by the Governor of such objection. During such six-month period, the Governor may submit to the Secretary a statement of reasons why such lease should not be issued and the Secretary shall, on the basis of such statement, reconsider the issuance of such lease.

(a)(3)(A)(i) No lease sale shall be held unless the lands containing the coal deposits have been included in a comprehensive land-use plan and such sale is compatible with such plan. The Secretary of the Interior shall prepare such land-use plans on lands under his responsibility where such plans have not been previously prepared. The Secretary of the Interior shall inform the Secretary of Agriculture of substantial development interest in coal leasing on lands within the National Forest System. Upon receipt of such notification from the Secretary of the Interior, the Secretary of Agriculture shall prepare a comprehensive land-use plan for such areas where such plans have not been previously prepared. The plan of the Secretary of Agriculture shall take into consideration the proposed coal development in these lands: *Provided,* That where the Secretary of the Interior finds that because of non-Federal interest in the surface or because the coal resources are insufficient to justify the preparation costs of a Federal comprehensive land-use plan, the lease sale can be held if the lands containing the coal deposits have been included in either a comprehensive land-use plan prepared by the State within which the lands are located or a land use analysis prepared by the Secretary of the Interior.

(a)(3)(A)(ii) In preparing such land-use plans, the Secretary of the Interior or, in the case of lands within the National Forest System, the Secretary of Agriculture, or in the case of a finding by the Secretary of the Interior that because of non-Federal interests in the surface or insufficient Federal coal, no Federal comprehensive land-use plans can be appropriately prepared, the responsible State entity shall consult with appropriate State agencies and local governments and the general public and shall provide an opportunity for public hearing on proposed plans prior to their adoption, if requested by any person having an interest which is, or may be, adversely affected by the adoption of such plans.

(a)(3)(A)(iii) Leases covering lands the surface of which is under the jurisdiction of any Federal agency other than the Department of the Interior may be issued only upon consent of the other Federal agency and upon such conditions as it may prescribe with respect to the use and protection of the nonmineral interests in those lands.

(a)(3)(B) Each land-use plan prepared by the Secretary (or in the case of lands within the National Forest System, the Secretary of Agriculture pursuant to subparagraph (A)(i)) shall include an assessment of the amount of coal deposits in such land, identifying the amount of such coal which is recoverable by deep mining operations and the amount of such coal which is recoverable by surface mining operations.

(a)(3)(C) Prior to issuance of any coal lease, the Secretary shall consider effects which mining of the proposed lease might have on an impacted community or area, including, but not limited to, impacts on the environment, on agricultural and other economic activities, and on public services. Prior to issuance of a lease, the Secretary shall evaluate and compare the effects of recovering coal by deep mining, by surface mining, and by any other method to determine which method or methods or sequence of methods achieves the maximum economic recovery of the coal within the proposed leasing tract. This evaluation and comparison by the Secretary shall be in writing but shall not prohibit the issuance of a lease; however, no mining operating plan shall be approved which is not found to achieve the maximum economic recovery of the coal within the tract. Public hearings in the area shall be held by the Secretary prior to the lease sale.

(a)(3)(D) No lease sale shall be held until after the notice of the proposed offering or lease has been given once a week for three consecutive weeks in a newspaper of general circulation in the county in which the lands are situated in accordance with regulations prescribed by the Secretary.

(a)(3)(E) Each coal lease shall contain provisions requiring compliance with the Federal Water Pollution Control Act (33 U.S.C. 1151–1175) and the Clean Air Act [42 U.S.C.A. § 7401 et seq.].

Exploration licenses; term; rights and conditions; violations

(b)(1) The Secretary may, under such regulations as he may prescribe, issue to any person an exploration license. No person may conduct coal exploration for commercial purposes for any coal on lands subject to this chapter without such an exploration license. Each exploration license shall be for a term of not more than two years and shall be subject to a reasonable fee. An exploration license shall confer no right to a lease under this chapter. The issuance of exploration licenses shall not preclude the Secretary from issuing coal leases at such times and locations and to such persons as he deems appropriate. No exploration license will be issued for any land on which a coal lease has been issued. A separate exploration license will be required for exploration in each State. An application for an exploration license shall identify general areas and probable methods of exploration. Each exploration license shall contain such reasonable conditions as the Secretary may require, including conditions to insure the protection of the environment, and shall be subject to all applicable Federal, State, and local laws and regulations. Upon violation of any such conditions or laws the Secretary may revoke the exploration license.

(b)(2) A licensee may not cause substantial disturbance to the natural land surface. He may not remove any coal for sale but may remove a reasonable amount of coal from the lands subject to this chapter included under his license for analysis and study. A licensee must comply with all applicable rules and regulations of the Federal agency having jurisdiction over the surface of the lands subject to this chapter. Exploration licenses covering lands the surface of which is under the jurisdiction of any Federal agency other than the Department of the Interior may be issued only upon such conditions as it may prescribe with respect to the use and protection of the nonmineral interests in those lands.

(b)(3) The licensee shall furnish to the Secretary copies of all data (including, but not limited to, geological, geophysical, and core drilling analyses) obtained during such exploration. The Secretary shall maintain the confidentiality of all data so obtained until after the areas involved have been leased or until such time as he determines that making the data available to the public would not damage the competitive position of the licensee, whichever comes first.

(b)(4) Any person who willfully conducts coal exploration for commercial purposes on lands subject to this chapter without an exploration license issued hereunder shall be subject to a fine of not more than $1,000 for each day of violation. All data collected by said person on any Federal lands as a result of such violation shall be made immediately available to the Secretary, who shall make the data available to the public as soon as it is practicable. No penalty under this subsection shall be assessed unless such person is given notice and opportunity for a hearing with respect to such violation.

Feb. 25, 1920, ch. 85, § 2(a), (b), 41 Stat. 438, June 3, 1948, ch. 379, § 1, 62 Stat. 289; Sept. 9, 1959, Pub.L. 86–252, § 2, 73 Stat. 490; Aug. 31, 1964, Pub.L. 88–526, § 2(a), (b), 78 Stat. 710; Aug. 4, 1976; as amended Aug. 4, 1976, Pub.L. 94–377, §§ 2–4, 90 Stat. 1083, 1085; Oct. 30, 1978, Pub.L. 95–554, § 2, 92 Stat. 2073.

§ 202. Common carriers; limitations of lease or permit

No company or corporation operating a common-carrier railroad shall be given or hold a permit or lease under the provisions of this chapter for any coal deposits except for its own use for railroad purposes; and such limitations of use shall be expressed in all permits and leases issued to such companies or corporations; and no such company or corporation shall receive or hold under permit or lease. More than ten thousand two hundred and forty acres in the aggregate nor more than one permit or lease for each two hundred miles of its railroad lines served or to be served from such coal deposits exclusive of spurs or switches and exclusive of branch lines built to connect the leased coal with the railroad, and also exclusive of parts of the railroad operated mainly by power produced otherwise than by steam.

Nothing in this section and section 201 of this title shall preclude such a railroad of less than two hundred miles in length from securing one permit or lease thereunder but no railroad shall hold a permit or lease for lands in any State in which it does not operate main or branch lines.

Feb. 25, 1920, c. 85, § 2, 41 Stat. 438; June 13, 1944, c. 244, 58 Stat. 275; June 3, 1948, c. 379, § 1, 62 Stat. 289.

§ 202a. Consolidation of coal leases into logical mining unit

Approval by Secretary; public hearing; definition

(1) The Secretary, upon determining that maximum economic recovery of the coal deposit or deposits is served thereby, may approve the consolidation of coal leases into a logical mining unit. Such consolidation may only take place after a public hearing, if requested by any person whose interest is or may be adversely affected. A logical mining unit is an area of land in which the coal resources can be developed in an efficient, economical, and orderly manner as a unit with due regard to conservation of coal reserves and other resources. A logical mining unit may consist of one or more Federal leaseholds, and may include intervening or adjacent lands in which the United States does not own the coal resources, but all the lands in a logical mining unit must be under the effective control of a single operator, be able to be developed and operated as a single operation and be contiguous.

Mining plan; requirements

(2) After the Secretary has approved the establishment of a logical mining unit, any mining plan approved for that unit must require such diligent development, operation, and production that the reserves of the entire unit will be mined within a period established by the Secretary which shall not be more than forty years.

Conditions for approval

(3) In approving a logical mining unit, the Secretary may provide, among other things, that (i) diligent development, continuous operation, and production on any Federal lease or non-Federal land in the logical mining unit shall be construed as occurring on all Federal leases in that logical mining unit, and (ii) the rentals and royalties for all Federal leases in a logical mining unit may be combined, and advanced royalties paid for any lease within a logical mining unit may be credited against such combined royalties.

Amendment to lease

(4) The Secretary may amend the provisions of any lease included in a logical mining unit so that mining under that lease will be consistent with the requirements imposed on that logical mining unit.

Leases issued before date of enactment of this Act

(5) Leases issued before the date of enactment of this Act may be included with the consent of all lessees in such logical mining unit, and, if so included, shall be subject to the provisions of this section.

Lessee required to form unit

(6) By regulation the Secretary may require a lessee under this chapter to form a logical mining unit, and may provide for determination of participating acreage within a unit.

Required acreage

(7) No logical mining unit shall be approved by the Secretary if the total acreage (both Federal and non-Federal) of the unit would exceed twenty-five thousand acres.

Acreage limitations for coal leases not waived

(8) Nothing in this section shall be construed to waive the acreage limitations for coal leases contained in section 184(a) of this title.

Feb. 25, 1920, c. 85, § 2(d), as added Aug. 4, 1976, Pub.L. 94–377, § 5(b), 90 Stat. 1086.

* * *

§ 205. Consolidation of leases

If, in the judgment of the Secretary of the Interior, the public interest will be subserved thereby, lessees holding under lease areas not exceeding the maximum permitted under this chapter may consolidate their leases through the surrender of the original leases and the inclusion of such areas in a new lease of not to exceed two thousand five hundred and sixty acres of contiguous lands.

Feb. 25, 1920, c. 85, § 5, 41 Stat. 439.

* * *

§ 207. Conditions of lease

Term of lease; annual rentals; royalties; readjustment of conditions

(a) A coal lease shall be for a term of twenty years and for so long thereafter as coal is produced annually in commercial quantities from that lease. Any lease which is not producing in commercial quantities at the end of ten years shall be terminated. The Secretary shall by regulation prescribe annual rentals on leases. A lease shall require payment of a royalty in such amount as the Secretary shall determine of not less than 12% per centum of the value of coal as defined by regulation, except the Secretary may determine a lesser amount in the case of coal recovered by underground mining operations. The lease shall include such other terms and conditions as the Secretary shall determine. Such rentals and royalties and other terms and conditions of the lease will be subject to readjustment at the end of its primary term of twenty years and at the end of each ten-year period thereafter if the lease is extended.

Diligent development and continued operation; suspension of condition on payment of advance royalties

(b) Each lease shall be subject to the conditions of diligent development and continued operation of the mine or mines, except where operations under the lease are interrupted by strikes, the elements, or casualties not attributable to the lessee. The Secretary of the Interior, upon determining that the public interest will be served thereby, may suspend the condition of continued operation upon the payment of advance royalties.

315

Such advance royalties shall be no less than the production royalty which would otherwise be paid and shall be computed on a fixed reserve to production ratio (determined by the Secretary). The aggregate number of years during the period of any lease for which advance royalties may be accepted in lieu of the condition of continued operation shall not exceed ten. The amount of any production royalty paid for any year shall be reduced (but not below 0) by the amount of any advance royalties paid under such lease to the extent that such advance royalties have not been used to reduce production royalties for a prior year. No advance royalty paid during the initial twenty-year term of a lease shall be used to reduce a production royalty after the twentieth year of a lease. The Secretary may, upon six months' notification to the lessee cease to accept advance royalties in lieu of the requirement of continued operation. Nothing in this subsection shall be construed to affect the requirement contained in the second sentence of subsection (a) of this section relating to commencement of production at the end of ten years.

Operation and reclamation plan

(c) Prior to taking any action on a leasehold which might cause a significant disturbance of the environment, and not later than three years after a lease is issued, the lessee shall submit for the Secretary's approval an operation and reclamation plan. The Secretary shall approve or disapprove the plan or require that it be modified. Where the land involved is under the surface jurisdiction of another Federal agency, that other agency must consent to the terms of such approval.

Feb. 25, 1920, ch. 85, § 7, 41 Stat. 439; as amended Aug. 4, 1976, Pub.L. 94–377, § 6, 90 Stat. 1087.

* * *

§ 208–1. Exploratory program for evaluation of known recoverable coal resources

Authorization; purpose

(a) The Secretary is authorized and directed to conduct a comprehensive exploratory program designed to obtain sufficient data and information to evaluate the extent, location, and potential for developing the known recoverable coal resources within the coal lands subject to this chapter. This program shall be designed to obtain the resource information necessary for determining whether commercial quantities of coal are present and the geographical extent of the coal fields and for estimating the amount of such coal which is recoverable by deep mining operations and the amount of such coal which is recoverable by surface mining operations in order to provide a basis for—

(1) developing a comprehensive land use plan pursuant to section 2;

(2) improving the information regarding the value of public resources and revenues which should be expected from leasing;

(3) increasing competition among producers of coal, or products derived from the conversion of coal, by providing data and information to all potential bidders equally and equitably;

(4) providing the public with information on the nature of the coal deposits and the associated stratum and the value of the public resources being offered for sale; and

(5) providing the basis for the assessment of the amount of coal deposits in those lands subject to this chapter under subparagraph (B) of section 201(a)(3) of this title.

* * *

Implementation plan for coal lands exploration program; development and transmittal to Congress; contents

(g) Within six months after the date of enactment of this Act, the Secretary shall develop and transmit to Congress an implementation plan for the coal lands exploration program authorized by this section, including procedures for making the data and information available to the public pursuant to subsection (d) of this section, and maps and reports pursuant to subsection (f) of this section. The implementation plan shall include a projected schedule of exploratory activities and identification of the regions and areas which will be explored under the coal lands exploration program during the first five years following the enactment of this section. In addition, the implementation plan shall include estimates of the appropriations and staffing required to implement the coal lands exploration program.

* * *

Feb. 25, 1920, c. 85, § 8A, as added Aug. 4, 1976, Pub.L. 94–377, § 7, 90 Stat. 1087.

* * *

§ 209. Suspension, waiver, or reduction of rents or royalties to promote development or operation; extension of lease on suspension of operations and production

The Secretary of the Interior, for the purpose of encouraging the greatest ultimate recovery of coal, oil, gas, oil shale, gilsonite (including all vein-type solid hydrocarbons), phosphate, sodium, potassium and sulphur, and in the interest of conservation of natural resources, is authorized to waive, suspend, or reduce the rental, or minimum royalty, or reduce the royalty on an entire leasehold, or on any tract or portion thereof segregated for royalty purposes, whenever in his judgment it is necessary to do so in order to promote development, or whenever in his judgment the leases cannot be successfully operated under the terms provided therein. *Provided, however,* That in order to promote development and the maximum production of tar sand, at the request of the lessee, the Secretary shall review, prior to commencement of commercial operations, the royalty rates established in each combined hydrocarbon lease issued in special tar sand areas. For purposes of this section, the term "tar sand" means any consolidated or unconsolidated rock (other than coal, oil shale, or gilsonite) that either: (1) contains a hydrocarbonaceous material with a gas-free viscosity, at original reservoir temperature, greater than 10,000 centipoise, or (2) contains a hydrocarbonaceous material and is produced by mining or quarrying. In the event the Secretary of the Interior, in the interest of conservation, shall direct or shall assent to the suspension of operations and production under any lease granted under the terms of this chapter, any payment of acreage rental or of minimum royalty prescribed by such lease likewise shall be suspended during such period of suspension of operations and production; and the term of such lease shall be extended by adding any such suspension period thereto. The provisions of this section shall apply to all oil and gas leases issued under this chapter, including those within an approved or prescribed plan for unit or cooperative development and operation. Nothing in this section shall be construed as granting to the Secretary the authority to waive, suspend, or reduce advance royalties.

Feb. 25, 1920, ch. 85, § 39, as added Feb. 9, 1933, ch. 45, 47 Stat. 798, and amended Aug. 8, 1946, ch. 916, § 10, 60 Stat. 957; June 3, 1948, ch. 379, § 7, 62 Stat. 291; As amended Aug. 4, 1976, Pub.L. 94–377, § 14, 90 Stat. 1091; Nov. 16, 1981, Pub.L. 97–78, § 1(3), (7), 95 Stat. 1070, 1071.

4. OIL AND GAS

§ 223. Leases; amount and survey of land; term of lease; royalties and annual rental

Upon establishing to the satisfaction of the Secretary of the Interior that valuable deposits of oil or gas have been discovered within the limits of the land embraced in any permit, the permittee shall be entitled to a lease for one-fourth of the land embraced in the prospecting permit: *Provided,* That the permittee shall be granted a lease for as much as one hundred and sixty acres of said lands, if there be that number of acres within the permit. The area to be selected by the permittee, shall be in reasonably compact form and, if surveyed, to be described by the legal subdivisions of the public-land surveys; if unsurveyed, to be surveyed by the Government at the expense of the applicant for lease in accordance with rules and regulations to be prescribed by the Secretary of the Interior, and the lands leased shall be conformed to and taken in accordance with the legal subdivisions of such surveys; deposits made to cover expense of surveys shall be deemed appropriated for that purpose, and any excess deposits may be repaid to the person or persons making such deposit or their legal representatives. Such leases shall be for a term of twenty years upon a royalty of 5 per centum in amount or value of the production and the annual payment in advance of a rental of $1 per acre, the rental paid for any one year to be credited against the royalties as they accrue for that year, and shall continue in force otherwise as prescribed in section 226 of this title for leases issued prior to August 21, 1935. The permittee shall also be entitled to a preference right to a lease for the remainder of the land in his prospecting permit at a royalty of not less than 12 1/2 per centum in amount or value of the production nor more than the royalty rate prescribed by regulation in force on January 1, 1935, for secondary leases issued under this section, and under such other conditions as are fixed for oil or gas leases issued under section 226 of this title the royalty to be determined by competitive bidding or fixed by such other method as the Secretary may by regulations prescribe: *Provided further,* That the Secretary shall have the right to reject any or all bids.

Feb. 25, 1920, c. 85, § 14, 41 Stat. 442; Aug. 21, 1935, c. 599, § 1, 49 Stat. 676.

§ 224. Payments for oil or gas taken prior to application for lease

Until the permittee shall apply for lease to the one quarter of the permit area heretofore provided for he shall pay to the United States 20 per centum of the gross value of all oil or gas secured by him from the lands embraced within his permit and sold or otherwise disposed of or held by him for sale or other disposition.

Feb. 25, 1920, c. 85, § 15, 41 Stat. 442.

§ 225. Condition of lease; forfeiture for violation

All leases of lands containing oil or gas, made or issued under the provisions of this chapter, shall be subject to the condition that the lessee will, in conducting his explorations and mining operations, use all reasonable precautions to prevent waste of oil or gas developed in the land, or the entrance of water through wells drilled by him to the oil sands or oil-bearing strata, to the destruction or injury of the oil deposits. Violations of the provisions of this section shall constitute grounds for the forfeiture of the lease, to be enforced as provided in this chapter.

Feb. 25, 1920, c. 85, § 16, 41 Stat. 443; Aug. 8, 1946, c. 916, § 2, 60 Stat. 951.

§ 226. Lease of oil and gas lands

Authority of Secretary

(a) All lands subject to disposition under this chapter which are known or believed to contain oil or gas deposits may be leased by the Secretary.

Lands within known geologic structure of a producing oil or gas field; lands within special tar sand areas; competitive bidding; royalties

(b)(1)(A) All lands to be leased which are not subject to leasing under paragraphs (2) and (3) of this subsection shall be leased as provided in this paragraph to the highest responsible qualified bidder by competitive bidding under general regulations in units of not more than 2,560 acres, except in Alaska, where units shall be not more than 5,760 acres. Such units shall be as nearly compact as possible. Lease sales shall be conducted by oral bidding. Lease sales shall be held for each State where eligible lands are available at least quarterly and more frequently if the Secretary of the

Interior determines such sales are necessary. A lease shall be conditioned upon the payment of a royalty at a rate of not less than 12.5 percent in amount or value of the production removed or sold from the lease. The Secretary shall accept the highest bid from a responsible qualified bidder which is equal to or greater than the national minimum acceptable bid, without evaluation of the value of the lands proposed for lease. Leases shall be issued within 60 days following payment by the successful bidder of the remainder of the bonus bid, if any, and the annual rental for the first lease year. All bids for less than the national minimum acceptable bid shall be rejected. Lands for which no bids are received or for which the highest bid is less than the national minimum acceptable bid shall be offered promptly within 30 days for leasing under subsection (c) of this section and shall remain available for leasing for a period of 2 years after the competitive lease sale.

(b)(1)(B) The national minimum acceptable bid shall be $2 per acre for a period of 2 years from December 22, 1987. Thereafter, the Secretary may establish by regulation a higher national minimum acceptable bid for all leases based upon a finding that such action is necessary: (i) to enhance financial returns to the United States; and (ii) to promote more efficient management of oil and gas resources on Federal lands. Ninety days before the Secretary makes any change in the national minimum acceptable bid, the Secretary shall notify the Committee on Natural Resources of the United States House of Representatives and the Committee on Energy and Natural Resources of the United States Senate. The proposal or promulgation of any regulation to establish a national minimum acceptable bid shall not be considered a major Federal action subject to the requirements of section 4332(2)(C) of Title 42.

* * *

Lands subject to leasing under subsection (b); first qualified applicant

(c)(1) If the lands to be leased are not leased under subsection (b)(1) of this section or are not subject to competitive leasing under subsection (b)(2) of this section, the person first making application for the lease who is qualified to hold a lease under this chapter shall be entitled to a lease of such lands without competitive bidding, upon payment of a non-refundable application fee of at least $75. A lease under this subsection shall be conditioned upon the payment of a royalty at a rate of 12.5 percent in amount or value of the production removed or sold from the lease. Leases shall be issued within 60 days of the date on which the Secretary identifies the first responsible qualified applicant.

(c)(2)(A) Lands (i) which were posted for sale under subsection (b)(1) of this section but for which no bids were received or for which the highest bid was less than the national minimum acceptable bid and (ii) for which, at the end of the period referred to in subsection (b)(1) of this section no lease has been issued and no lease application is pending under paragraph (1) of this subsection, shall again be available for leasing only in accordance with subsection (b)(1) of this section.

(c)(2)(B) The land in any lease which is issued under paragraph (1) of this subsection or under subsection (b)(1) of this section which lease terminates, expires, is cancelled or is relinquished shall again be available for leasing only in accordance with subsection (b)(1) of this section.

Annual rentals

(d) All leases issued under this section, as amended by the Federal Onshore Oil and Gas Leasing Reform Act of 1987, shall be conditioned upon payment by the lessee of a rental of not less than $1.50 per acre per year for the first through fifth years of the lease and not less than $2 per acre per year for each year thereafter. A minimum royalty in lieu of rental of not less than the rental which otherwise would be required for that lease year shall be payable at the expiration of each lease year beginning on or after a discovery of oil or gas in paying quantities on the lands leased.

Primary terms

(e) Competitive and noncompetitive leases issued under this section shall be for a primary term of 10 years: *Provided, however,* That competitive leases issued in special tar sand areas shall also be for a primary term of ten years. Each such lease shall continue so long after its primary term as oil or gas is produced in paying quantities. Any lease issued under this section for land on which, or for which under an approved cooperative or unit plan of development or operation, actual drilling operations were commenced prior to the end of its primary term and are being diligently prosecuted at that time shall be extended for two years and so long thereafter as oil or gas is produced in paying quantities.

Notice of proposed action; posting of notice; terms and maps

(f) At least 45 days before offering lands for lease under this section, and at least 30 days before approving applications for permits to drill under the provisions of a lease or substantially modifying the terms of any lease issued under this section, the Secretary shall provide notice of the proposed action. Such notice shall be posted in the appropriate local office of the leasing and land management agencies. Such notice shall include the terms or modified lease terms and maps or a narrative description of the affected lands. Where the inclusion of maps in such notice is not practicable, maps of the affected lands shall be made available to the public for review. Such maps shall show the location of all tracts to be leased, and of all leases already issued in the general area. The requirements of this subsection are in addition to any public notice required by other law.

Regulation of surface-disturbing activities; approval of plan of operations; bond or surety; failure to comply with reclamation requirements as barring lease; opportunity to comply with requirements

(g) The Secretary of the Interior, or for National Forest lands, the Secretary of Agriculture, shall regulate all surface-disturbing activities conducted pursuant to any lease issued under this chapter, and shall determine reclamation and other actions as required in the interest of conservation of surface resources. No permit to drill on an oil and gas lease issued under this chapter may be granted without the analysis and approval by the Secretary concerned of a plan of operations covering proposed surface-disturbing activities within the lease area. The Secretary concerned shall, by rule or regulation, establish such standards as may be necessary to ensure that an adequate bond, surety, or other financial arrangement will be established prior to the commencement of surface disturbing activities on any lease, to ensure the complete and timely reclamation of the lease tract, and the restoration of any lands or surface waters adversely affected by lease operations after the abandonment or cessation of oil and gas operations on the lease. The Secretary shall not issue a lease or leases or approve the assignment of any lease or leases under the terms of this section to any person, association, corporation, or any subsidiary, affiliate, or person controlled by or under common control with such person, association, or corporation, during any period in which, as determined by the Secretary of the Interior or Secretary of Agriculture, such entity has failed or refused to comply in any material respect with the reclamation requirements and other standards established under this section for any prior lease to which such requirements and standards applied. Prior to making such determination with respect to any such entity the concerned Secretary shall provide such entity with adequate notification and an opportunity to comply with such reclamation requirements and other standards and shall consider whether any administrative or judicial appeal is pending. Once the entity has complied with the reclamation requirement or other standard concerned an oil or gas lease may be issued to such entity under this chapter.

National Forest Systems Lands

(h) The Secretary of the Interior may not issue any lease on National Forest System Lands reserved from the public domain over the objection of the Secretary of Agriculture.

Termination

(i) No lease issued under this section which is subject to termination because of cessation of production shall be terminated for this cause so long as reworking or drilling operations which were commenced on the land prior to or within sixty days after cessation of production are conducted thereon with reasonable diligence, or so long as oil or gas is produced in paying quantities as a result of such operations. No lease issued under this section shall expire because operations or production is suspended under any order, or with the consent, of the Secretary. No lease issued under this section covering lands on which there is a well capable of producing oil or gas in paying quantities shall expire because the lessee fails to produce the same unless the lessee is allowed a reasonable time, which shall be not less than sixty days after notice by registered or certified mail, within which to place such well in producing status or unless, after such status is established, production is discontinued on the leased premises without permission granted by the Secretary under the provisions of this chapter.

Drainage agreements; primary term of lease, extension; report to Congress

(j) Whenever it appears to the Secretary that lands owned by the United States are being drained of oil or gas by wells drilled on adjacent lands, he may negotiate agreements whereby the United States, or the

United States and its lessees, shall be compensated for such drainage. Such agreements shall be made with the consent of the lessees, if any, affected thereby. If such agreement is entered into, the primary term of any lease for which compensatory royalty is being paid, or any extension of such primary term, shall be extended for the period during which such compensatory royalty is paid and for a period of one year from discontinuance of such payment and so long thereafter as oil or gas is produced in paying quantities.

Mining claims; suspension of running time of lease

(k) If, during the primary term or any extended term of any lease issued under this section, a verified statement is filed by any mining claimant pursuant to subsection (c) of section 527 of this title, whether such filing occur prior to September 2, 1960 or thereafter, asserting the existence of a conflicting unpatented mining claim or claims upon which diligent work is being prosecuted as to any lands covered by the lease, the running of time under such lease shall be suspended as to the lands involved from the first day of the month following the filing of such verified statement until a final decision is rendered in the matter.

Exchange of leases; conditions

(*l*) The Secretary of the Interior shall, upon timely application therefor, issue a new lease in exchange for any lease issued for a term of twenty years, or any renewal thereof, or any lease issued prior to August 8, 1946, in exchange for a twenty-year lease, such new lease to be for a primary term of five years and so long thereafter as oil or gas is produced in paying quantities and at a royalty rate of not less than 12% per centum in amount or value of the production removed or sold from such leases, except that the royalty rate shall be 12% per centum in amount or value of the production removed or sold from said leases as to (1) such leases, or such parts of the lands subject thereto and the deposits underlying the same, as are not believed to be within the productive limits of any producing oil or gas deposit, as such productive limits are found by the Secretary to have existed on August 8, 1946; and (2) any production on a lease from an oil or gas deposit which was discovered after May 27, 1941, by a well or wells drilled within the boundaries of the lease, and which is determined by the Secretary to be a new deposit; and (3) any production on or allocated to a lease pursuant to an approved cooperative or unit plan of development or operation from an oil or gas deposit which was discovered after May 27, 1941, on land committed to such plan, and which is determined by the Secretary to be a new deposit, where such lease, or a lease for which it is exchanged, was included in such plan at the time of discovery or was included in a duly executed and filed application for the approval of such plan at the time of discovery.

Cooperative or unit plan; authority of Secretary of the Interior to alter or modify; communitization or drilling agreements; term of lease, conditions; Secretary to approve operating, drilling, or development contracts, and subsurface storage

(m) For the purpose of more properly conserving the natural resources of any oil or gas pool, field, or like area, or any part thereof (whether or not any part of said oil or gas pool, field, or like area, is then subject to any cooperative or unit plan of development or operation), lessees thereof and their representatives may unite with each other, or jointly or separately with others, in collectively adopting and operating under a cooperative or unit plan of development or operation of such pool, field, or like area, or any part thereof, whenever determined and certified by the Secretary of the Interior to be necessary or advisable in the public interest. The Secretary is thereunto authorized, in his discretion, with the consent of the holders of leases involved, to establish, alter, change, or revoke drilling, producing, rental, minimum royalty, and royalty requirements of such leases and to make such regulations with reference to such leases, with like consent on the part of the lessees, in connection with the institution and operation of any such cooperative or unit plan as he may deem necessary or proper to secure the proper protection of the public interest. The Secretary may provide that oil and gas leases hereafter issued under this chapter shall contain a provision requiring the lessee to operate under such a reasonable cooperative or unit plan, and he may prescribe such a plan under which such lessee shall operate, which shall adequately protect the rights of all parties in interest, including the United States.

Any plan authorized by the preceding paragraph which includes lands owned by the United States may, in the discretion of the Secretary, contain a provision whereby authority is vested in the Secretary of the Interior, or any such person, committee, or State or Federal officer or agency as may be designated in the plan, to alter or modify from time to time the rate of prospecting and development and the quantity and rate of production under such plan. All leases operated under any such plan approved or prescribed by the Secretary shall be excepted in determining holdings or control under the provisions of any section of this chapter.

When separate tracts cannot be independently developed and operated in conformity with an established well-spacing or development program, any lease, or a portion thereof, may be pooled with other lands, whether or not owned by the United States, under a communitization or drilling agreement providing for an apportionment of production or royalties among the separate tracts of land comprising the drilling or spacing unit when determined by the Secretary of the Interior to be in the public interest, and operations or production pursuant to such an agreement shall be deemed to be operations or production as to each such lease committed thereto.

Any lease issued for a term of twenty years, or any renewal thereof, or any portion of such lease that has become the subject of a cooperative or unit plan of development or operation of a pool, field, or like area, which plan has the approval of the Secretary of the Interior, shall continue in force until the termination of such plan. Any other lease issued under any section of this chapter which has heretofore or may hereafter be committed to any such plan that contains a general provision for allocation of oil or gas shall continue in force and effect as to the land committed so long as the lease remains subject to the plan: *Provided,* That production is had in paying quantities under the plan prior to the expiration date of the term of such lease. Any lease heretofore or hereafter committed to any such plan embracing lands that are in part within and in part outside of the area covered by any such plan shall be segregated into separate leases as to the lands committed and the lands not committed as of the effective date of unitization: *Provided, however,* That any such lease as to the nonunitized portion shall continue in force and effect for the term thereof but for not less than two years from the date of such segregation and so long thereafter as oil and gas is produced in paying quantities. The minimum royalty or discovery rental under any lease that has become subject to any cooperative or unit plan of development or operation, or other plan that contains a general provision for allocation of oil or gas, shall be payable only with respect to the lands subject to such lease to which oil or gas shall be allocated under such plan. Any lease which shall be eliminated from any such approved or prescribed plan, of from any communitization or drilling agreement authorized by this section, and any lease which shall be in effect at the termination of any such approved or prescribed plan, or at the termination of any such communitization or drilling agreement, unless relinquished, shall continue in effect for the original term thereof, but for not less than two years, and so long thereafter as oil or gas is produced in paying quantities.

The Secretary of the Interior is hereby authorized, on such conditions as he may prescribe, to approve operating, drilling, or development contracts made by one or more lessees of oil or gas leases, with one or more persons, associations, or corporations whenever, in his discretion, the conservation of natural products or the public convenience or necessity may require it or the interests of the United States may be best subserved thereby. All leases operated under such approved operating, drilling, or development contracts, and interests thereunder, shall be excepted in determining holdings or control under the provisions of this chapter.

The Secretary of the Interior, to avoid waste or to promote conservation of natural resources, may authorize the subsurface storage of oil or gas, whether or not produced from federally owned lands, in lands leased or subject to lease under this chapter. Such authorization may provide for the payment of a storage fee or rental on such stored oil or gas or, in lieu of such fee or rental, for a royalty other than that prescribed in the lease when such stored oil or gas is produced in conjunction with oil or gas not previously produced. Any lease on which storage is so authorized shall be extended at least for the period of storage and so long thereafter as oil or gas not previously produced is produced in paying quantities.

Conversion of oil and gas leases and claims on hydrocarbon resources to combined hydrocarbon leases for primary term of 10 years; application

(n)(1)(A) The owner of (1) an oil and gas lease issued prior to November 16, 1981, or (2) a valid claim to any hydrocarbon resources leasable under this section based on a mineral location made prior to January 21, 1926, and located within a special tar sand area shall be entitled to convert such lease or claim to a combined hydrocarbon lease for a primary term of ten years upon the filing of an application within two years from November 16, 1981, containing an acceptable plan of operations which assures reasonable protection of the environment and diligent development of those resources requiring enhanced recovery methods of development or mining.

325

For purposes of conversion, no claim shall be deemed invalid solely because it was located as a placer location rather than a lode location or vice versa, notwithstanding any previous adjudication on that issue.

(n)(1)(B) The Secretary shall issue final regulations to implement this section within six months of November 16, 1981. If any oil and gas lease eligible for conversion under this section would otherwise expire after November 16, 1981, and before six months following the issuance of implementing regulations, the lessee may preserve his conversion right under such lease for a period ending six months after the issuance of implementing regulations by filing with the Secretary, before the expiration of the lease, a notice of intent to file an application for conversion. Upon submission of a complete plan of operations in substantial compliance with the regulations promulgated by the Secretary for the filing of such plans, the Secretary shall suspend the running of the term of any oil and gas lease proposed for conversion until the plan is finally approved or disapproved. The Secretary shall act upon a proposed plan of operations within fifteen months of its submittal.

(n)(1)(C) When an existing oil and gas lease is converted to a combined hydrocarbon lease, the royalty shall be that provided for in the original oil and gas lease and for a converted mining claim, 12% per centum in amount or value of production removed or sold from the lease.

(n)(2) Except as provided in this section, nothing in the Combined Hydrocarbon Leasing Act of 1981 shall be construed to diminish or increase the rights of any lessee under any oil and gas lease issued prior to November 16, 1981.

Feb. 25, 1920, ch. 85, § 17, 41 Stat. 443; July 3, 1930, ch. 854, § 1, 46 Stat. 1007; Mar. 4, 1931, ch. 506, 46 Stat. 1523; Aug. 21, 1935, ch. 599, § 1, 49 Stat. 676; Aug. 8, 1946, ch. 916, § 3, 60 Stat. 951; July 29, 1954, ch. 644, § 1(1)–(3), 68 Stat. 583; June 11, 1960, Pub.L. 86–507, § 1(21), 74 Stat. 201; Sept. 2, 1960, Pub.L. 86–705, § 2, 74 Stat. 781; As amended Nov. 16, 1981, Pub.L. 97–78, § 1(6), (8), 95 Stat. 1070, 1071. As amended Pub.L. 100–208, Title V, § 5103(a)–(d)(1), Dec. 22, 1987, 101 Stat. 1330–256, 1330–257; as amended Pub.L. 102–486, Title XXV, §§ 2507(a), 2508(a), 2509, Oct. 24, 1992, 106 Stat. 3107, 3108, 3109; Pub.L. 103–437, § 11(a)(1), Nov. 2, 1994, 108 Stat. 4589; Pub.L. 104–66, Title I, § 1081(a), Dec. 21, 1995, 109 Stat. 721.

§ 226–1. Expiration and extension of noncompetitive oil or gas leases; withdrawal of lands from leasing; known and unknown geologic structure of producing fields; cooperative or unit plan leases

(a) Upon the expiration of the initial five-year term of any noncompetitive oil or gas lease which was issued prior to September 2, 1960 and which has been maintained in accordance with applicable statutory requirements and regulations, the record titleholder thereof shall be entitled to a single extension of the lease, unless then otherwise provided by law, for such lands covered by it as are not, on the expiration date of the lease, withdrawn from leasing. A withdrawal, however, shall not affect the right to an extension if actual drilling operations on such lands were commenced prior to the effective date of the withdrawal and were being diligently prosecuted on the expiration date of the lease. No withdrawal shall be effective within the meaning of this section until ninety days after notice thereof has been sent by registered or certified mail to each lessee to be affected by such withdrawal.

(b) As to lands not within the known geologic structure of a producing oil or gas field, a noncompetitive oil or gas lease to which this section is applicable shall be extended for a period of five years and so long thereafter as oil or gas is produced in paying quantities. As to lands within the known geologic structure of a producing oil or gas field, a noncompetitive lease to which this section is applicable shall be extended for a period of two years and so long thereafter as oil or gas is produced in paying quantities.

(c) Any noncompetitive oil or gas lease extended under this section shall be subject to the rules and regulations in force at the expiration of the initial five-year term of the lease. No extension shall be granted, however, unless within a period of ninety days prior to the expiration date of the lease an application therefor is filed by the record titleholder or an assignee whose assignment has been filed for approval or an operator whose operating agreement has been fried for approval.

Commencement of actual drilling

(d) Any lease issued prior to September 2, 1960 which has been maintained in accordance with applicable statutory requirements and regulations and which pertains to land on which, or for which under an approved cooperative or unit plan of development or operation, actual drilling operations were commenced prior to the end of its primary term and are being diligently prosecuted at that time shall be extended for two years and so long thereafter as oil or gas is produced in paying quantities.

Pub.L. 86–705, § 4, Sept. 2, 1960, 74 Stat. 789.

§ 226–2. Limitations for filing oil and gas contests

No action contesting a decision of the Secretary involving any oil and gas lease shall be maintained unless such action is commenced or taken within ninety days after the final decision of the Secretary relating to such matter. No such action contesting such a decision of the Secretary rendered prior to September 2, 1960 shall be maintained unless the same be commenced or taken within ninety days after September 2, 1960.

Feb. 25, 1920, c. 85, § 42, as added Sept. 2, 1960, Pub.L. 86–705, § 5, 74 Stat. 790.

§ 226–3. Lands not subject to oil and gas leasing

Prohibition

(a) The Secretary shall not issue any lease under this chapter or under the Geothermal Steam Act of 1970 on any of the following Federal lands:

(1) Lands recommended for wilderness allocation by the surface managing agency.

(2) Lands within Bureau of Land Management wilderness study areas.

(3) Lands designated by Congress as wilderness study areas, except where oil and gas leasing is specifically allowed to continue by the statute designating the study area.

(4) Lands within areas allocated for wilderness or further planning in Executive Communication 1504, Ninety–Sixth Congress (House Document numbered 96–119), unless such lands are allocated to uses other than wilderness by a land and resource management plan or have been released to uses other than wilderness by an act of Congress.

Exploration

(b) In the case of any area of National Forest or public lands subject to this section, nothing in this section shall affect any authority of the Secretary of the Interior (or for National Forest Lands reserved from the public domain, the Secretary of Agriculture) to issue permits for exploration for oil and gas, coal, oil shale, phosphate, potassium, sulphur, gilsonite or geothermal resources by means not requiring construction of roads or improvement of existing roads if such activity is conducted in a manner compatible with the preservation of the wilderness environment.

Feb. 25, 1920, c. 85, § 43, as added Dec. 22, 1987, Pub.L. 100–203, Title V, § 5112, 101 Stat. 1330–262, and amended Sept. 22, 1988, Pub.L. 100–443, § 5(c), 102 Stat. 1768.

* * *

§ 229a. Water struck while drilling for oil or gas; acquisition and disposition by Secretary of the Interior; preferential right of vicinity; revolving fund

(a) All prospecting permits and leases for oil or gas made or issued under the provisions of this chapter shall be subject to the condition that in case the permittee or lessee strikes water while drilling instead of oil or gas, the Secretary of the Interior may, when such water is of such quality and quantity as to be valuable and usable at a reasonable cost for agricultural, domestic, or other purposes, purchase the casing in the well at the reasonable value thereof to be fixed under rules and regulations to be prescribed by the Secretary.

(b) In cases where water wells producing such water have heretofore been or may hereafter be drilled upon lands embraced in any prospecting permit or lease heretofore issued under this chapter, the Secretary may in like manner purchase the casing in such wells.

(c) The Secretary may make such purchase and may lease or operate such wells for the purpose of producing water and of using the same on the public lands or of disposing of such water for beneficial use on other lands, and where such wells have heretofore been plugged or abandoned or where such wells have been drilled prior to the issuance of any permit or lease by persons not in privity with the permittee or lessee, the Secretary may develop the same for the purposes of this section: *Provided*, That owners or occupants of lands adjacent to those upon which such water wells may be developed shall have a preference right to make beneficial use of such water.

(d) The Secretary may use so much of any funds available for the plugging of wells as he may find necessary to start the program provided for by this section, and thereafter he may use the proceeds from the sale or other disposition of such water as a revolving fund for the continuation of such program, and such proceeds are hereby appropriated for such purpose.

(e) Nothing in this section shall be construed to restrict operations under any oil or gas lease or permit under any other provision of this chapter.

Feb. 25, 1920, ch. 85, § 40, as added June 16, 1934, ch. 557, 48 Stat. 977 and amended Oct. 21, 1976, Pub.L. 94–579, Title VII, § 704(a), 90 Stat. 2792.

* * *

§ 236a. Lands in naval petroleum reserves and naval oil-shale reserves; effect of other laws

Nothing in sections 185, 221, 223, 223a, and 226 of this title and this section shall be construed as affecting any lands within the borders of the naval petroleum reserves and naval oil-shale reserves or agreements concerning operations thereunder or in relation to the same, but the Secretary of the Navy is hereby authorized, with the consent of the President, to enter into agreements such as those provided for under sections 184 and 226 of this title, which agreement shall not, unless expressed therein, operate to extend the terms of any lease affected thereby.

Aug. 21, 1935, c. 599, § 3, 49 Stat. 679.

§ 236b. Existing leases within naval petroleum reserves not affected

Nothing in this act shall be construed as affecting existing leases within the borders of the naval petroleum reserves, or agreements concerning operations thereunder or in relation thereto.

Aug. 8, 1946, ch. 916, § 13, 60 Stat. 958; Aug. 10, 1956, ch. 1041, § 53, 70A Stat. 675.

* * *

5. OIL SHALE

§ 241. Leases of lands

Authorization; survey; terms, royalties and annual rentals; readjustments on renewals; rights of existing claimants; fraud of claimants

(a) The Secretary of the Interior is hereby authorized to lease to any person or corporation qualified under this chapter any deposits of oil shale and gilsonite (including all vein-type solid hydrocarbons) belonging to the United States and the surface of so much of the public lands containing such deposits, or land adjacent thereto, as may be required for the extraction and reduction of the leased minerals, under such rules and regulations, not inconsistent with this chapter, as he may prescribe. No lease hereunder shall exceed five thousand one hundred and twenty acres of land, to be described by the legal subdivisions of the public-land surveys, or if unsurveyed, to be surveyed by the United States, at the expense of the applicant, in accordance with regulations to be prescribed by the Secretary of the Interior. Leases may be for indeterminate periods, upon such conditions as may be imposed by the Secretary of the Interior, including covenants relative to methods of mining, prevention of waste, and productive development. For the privilege of mining, extracting, and disposing of the oil or other minerals covered by a lease under this section the lessee shall pay to the United States such royalties as shall be specified in the lease and an annual rental, payable at the beginning of each year, at the rate of 50 cents per acre per annum, for the lands included in the lease, the rental paid for any one year to be credited against the royalties accruing for that year; such royalties to be subject to readjustment at the end of each twenty-year period by the Secretary of the Interior. For the purpose of encouraging the production of petroleum products from shales the Secretary may, in his discretion, waive the payment of any royalty and rental during the first five years of any lease. Any person having a valid claim to such minerals under existing laws on January 1, 1919, shall, upon the relinquishment of such claim, be entitled to a lease under the provisions of this section for such area of the land relinquished as shall not exceed the maximum area authorized by this section to be leased to an individual or corporation. No claimant for a lease who has been guilty of any fraud or who had knowledge or reasonable grounds to know of any fraud, or who has not acted honestly and in good faith, shall be entitled to any of the benefits of this section. Not more than one lease shall be granted under this section to any one person, association, or corporation except that with respect to leases for native asphalt, solid and semisolid bitumen, and bituminous rock (including oil-impregnated rock or sands from which oil is recoverable only by special treatment after the deposit is mined or quarried) no person, association, or corporation shall acquire or hold more than seven thousand six hundred eighty acres in any one State without respect to the number of leases.

* * *

Multiple use principle leases; gilsonite including all vein-type solid hydrocarbons

(c) With respect to gilsonite (including all vein-type solid hydrocarbons) a lease under the multiple use principle may issue notwithstanding the existence of an outstanding lease issued under any other provision of this chapter.

Offsite leases

(d)(1) The Secretary may within the State of Colorado lease to the holder of the Federal oil shale lease known as Federal Prototype Tract C-a

330

additional lands necessary for the disposal of oil shale wastes and the materials removed from mined lands, and for the building of plants, reduction works, and other facilities connected with oil shale operations (which lease shall be referred to hereinafter as an "offsite lease"). The Secretary may only issue one offsite lease not to exceed six thousand four hundred acres. An offsite lease may not serve more than one Federal oil shale lease and may not be transferred except in conjunction with the transfer of the Federal oil shale lease that it serves.

(d)(2) The Secretary may issue one offsite lease of not more than three hundred and twenty acres to any person, association or corporation which has the right to develop oil shale on non-Federal lands. An offsite lease serving non-Federal off shale land may not serve more than one oil shale operation and may not be transferred except in conjunction with the transfer of the non-Federal oil shale land that it serves. Not more than two offsite leases may be issued under this paragraph.

(d)(3) An offsite lease shall include no rights to any mineral deposits.

(d)(4) The Secretary may issue offsite leases after consideration of the need for such lands, impacts on the environment and other resource values, and upon a determination that the public interest will be served thereby.

(d)(5) An offsite lease for lands the surface of which is under the jurisdiction of a Federal agency other than the Department of the Interior shall be issued only with the consent of that other Federal agency and shall be subject to such terms and conditions as it may prescribe.

(d)(6) An offsite lease shall be for such periods of time and shall include such lands, subject to the acreage limitations contained in this subsection, as the Secretary determines to be necessary to achieve the purposes for which the lease is issued, and shall contain such provisions as he determines are needed for protection of environmental and other resource values.

(d)(7) An offsite lease shall provide for the payment of an annual rental which shall reflect the fair market value of the rights granted and which shall be subject to such revisions as the Secretary, in his discretion, determines may be needed from time to time to continue to reflect the fair market value.

(d)(8) An offsite lease may, at the option of the lessee, include provisions for payments in any year which payments shall be credited against any portion of the annual rental for a subsequent year to the extent that such payment is payable by the Secretary of the Treasury under section 191 of this title to the State within the boundaries of which the leased lands are located. Such funds shall be paid by the Secretary of the Treasury to the appropriate State in accordance with section 191 of this title, and such funds shall be distributed by the State only to those counties, municipalities, or jurisdictional subdivisions impacted by oil shale development and/or where the lease is serves.

(d)(9) An offsite lease shall remain subject to leasing under the other provisions of this chapter where such leasing would not be incompatible with the offsite lease.

Considerations governing issuance of offsite lease

(e) In recognition of the unique character of oil shale development:

(1) In determining whether to offer or issue an offsite lease under subsection (d) of this section, the Secretary shall consult with the Governor and appropriate State, local, and tribal officials of the State where the lands to be leased are located, and of any additional State likely to be affected significantly by the social, economic, or environmental effects of development under such lease, in order to coordinate Federal and State planning processes, minimize duplication of permits, avoid delays, and anticipate and mitigate likely impacts of development.

(2) The Secretary may issue an offsite lease under this subsection after consideration of (A) the need for leasing, (B) impacts on the environment and other resource values, (C) socioeconomic factors, and (D) information from consultations with the Governors of the affected States.

(3) Before determining whether to offer an offsite lease under subsection (d) of this section, the Secretary shall seek the recommendation of the Governor of the State in which the lands to be leased are located as to whether or not to lease such lands, what alternative actions are available, and what special conditions could be added to the proposed lease to mitigate impacts. The Secretary shall accept the recommendations of the Governor if he determines that they provide for a reasonable balance between the national interest and the State's interests. The Secretary shall communicate to the Governor, in writing, and publish in the Federal Register the reasons for his determination to accept or reject such Governor's recommendations.

Feb. 25, 1920, ch. 85, § 21, 41 Stat. 445; Sept. 2, 1960, Pub.L. 86–705, § 7, 74 Stat. 790; as amended Nov. 16, 1981, Pub.L. 97–78, § 1(1), 95 Stat. 1070; Dec. 30, 1982, Pub.L. 97–394, Title III, § 318, 96 Stat. 1999.

* * *

ACQUIRED LANDS ACT OF 1947 (as amended)

(30 U.S.C.A. §§ 351–59)

§ 351. Definitions

As used in this chapter "United States" includes Alaska. "Acquired lands" or "lands acquired by the United States" include all lands heretofore or hereafter acquired by the United States to which the "mineral leasing laws" have not been extended, including such lands acquired under the provisions of the Act of March 1, 1911 (36 Stat. 961, 16 U.S.C. sec. 552). "Secretary" means the Secretary of the Interior. "Mineral leasing laws" shall mean the Act of October 20, 1914 (38 Stat. 741, 48 U.S.C. sec. 432); the Act of February 25, 1920 (41 Stat. 437, 30 U.S.C. sec. 181); the Act of April 17, 1926 (44 Stat. 301, 30 U.S.C. sec. 271); the Act of February 7, 1927 (44 Stat. 1057, 30 U.S.C. sec. 2814) and all Acts heretofore or hereafter enacted which are amendatory of or supplementary to any of the foregoing Acts. "Lease" includes "prospecting permit" unless the context otherwise requires. The term "oil" shall embrace all nongaseous hydrocarbon substances other than those leasable as coal, oil shale, or gilsonite (including all vein-type solid hydrocarbons).

Aug. 7, 1947, ch. 513, § 2, 61 Stat. 913; as amended Nov. 16, 1981, Pub.L. 97–78, § 1(9)(a), 95 Stat. 1072.

§ 352. Deposits subject to lease; consent of department heads; lands excluded

Except where lands have been acquired by the United States for the development of the mineral deposits, by foreclosure or otherwise for resale, or reported as surplus pursuant to the provisions of the Surplus Property Act of 1944, all deposits of coal, phosphate, oil, oil shale, gilsonite (including all vein-type solid hydrocarbons), gas, sodium, potassium, and sulfur which are owned or may hereafter be acquired by the United States and which are within the lands acquired by the United States (exclusive of such deposits in such acquired lands as are (a) situated within incorporated cities, towns and villages, national parks or monuments, or (b) tidelands or submerged lands) may be leased by the Secretary under the same conditions as contained in the leasing provisions of the mineral leasing laws, subject to the provisions hereof. Coal or lignite under acquired lands set apart for military or naval purposes may be leased by the Secretary, with the concurrence of the Secretary of Defense, to a governmental entity (including any corporation primarily acting as an agency or instrumentality of a State) which produces electrical energy for sale to the public if such governmental entity is located in the State in which such lands are located. The provisions of sections 271 to 276 of this title shall apply to deposits of sulfur covered by this chapter wherever situated. No mineral deposit covered by this section shall be leased except with the consent of the head of the executive department, independent establishment, or instrumentality having jurisdiction over the lands containing such deposit, or holding a mortgage or deed of trust secured by such lands which is unsatisfied of record, and subject to such conditions as that official may prescribe to insure the adequate utilization of the lands for the primary purposes for which they have been acquired or are being administered: * * *

Aug. 7, 1947, ch. 513, § 3, 61 Stat. 914; as amended Aug. 4, 1976, Pub.L. 94–377, § 12, 90 Stat. 1090; Nov. 16, 1981, Pub.L. 97–78, § 1(9)(b), 95 Stat. 1072.

* * *

§ 354. Lease of partial or future interests in deposits

Where the United States does not own all of the mineral deposits under any lands sought to be leased and which are affected by this chapter, the Secretary is authorized to lease the interest of the United States in any such mineral deposits when, in the judgment of the Secretary, the public interest will be best served thereby; subject, however, to the provisions of section 352 of this title. Where the United States does not own any interest or owns less than a full interest in the minerals that may be produced from any lands sought to be leased, and which are or will be affected by this chapter and where, under the provisions of its acquisition, the United States is to acquire all or any part of such mineral deposits in the future, the Secretary may lease any interest of the United States then owned or to be acquired in the future in the same manner as provided in the preceding sentence.

Aug. 7, 1947, c. 513, § 5, 61 Stat. 914.

* * *

§ 357. State or local government rights; taxation

Nothing contained in this chapter shall be construed to affect the rights of the State or other local authorities to exercise any right which they may have with respect to properties covered by leases issued under this chapter, including the right to levy and collect taxes upon improvements, output of mines, or other rights, property, or assets of any lessee of the United States.

Aug. 7, 1947, c. 513, § 8, 61 Stat. 915.

§ 358. Rights under prior leases; priority of pending applications; exchange of leases

Nothing in this chapter shall affect any rights acquired by any lessee of lands subject to this chapter under the law as it existed prior to August 7, 1947, and such rights shall be governed by the law in effect at the time of their acquisition; but any person qualified to hold a lease who, on August 7, 1947, had pending an application for an oil and gas lease for any lands subject to this chapter which on the date the application was filed was not situated within the known geologic structure of a producing oil or gas field, shall have a preference right over others to a lease of such lands without competitive bidding. Any person holding a lease on lands subject hereto, which lease was issued prior to August 7, 1947, shall be entitled to exchange such lease for a new lease issued under the provisions of this chapter, at any time prior to the expiration of such existing lease.

Aug. 7, 1947, c. 513, § 9, 61 Stat. 915.

§ 359. Rules and regulations

The Secretary of the Interior is authorized to prescribe such rules and regulations as are necessary and appropriate to carry out the purposes of this chapter, which rules and regulations shall be the same as those prescribed under the mineral leasing laws to the extent that they are applicable.

Aug. 7, 1947, c. 513, § 10, 61 Stat. 915.

MULTIPLE MINERAL DEVELOPMENT ACT OF 1954 (as amended)

(30 U.S.C.A. §§ 521-31)

§ 521.   Mineral leasing claims

(a) Subject to the conditions and provisions of this chapter and to any valid intervening rights acquired under the laws of the United States, any mining claim located under the mining laws of the United States subsequent to July 31, 1939, and prior to February 10, 1954, on lands of the United States, which at the time of location were—

(1) included in a permit or lease issued under the mineral leasing laws; or

(2) covered by an application or offer for a permit or lease which had been filed under the mineral leasing laws; or

(3) known to be valuable for minerals subject to disposition under the mineral leasing laws,

shall be effective to the same extent in all respects as if such lands at the time of location, and at all times thereafter, had not been so included or covered or known: *Provided, however,* That, in order to be entitled to the benefits of this chapter, the owner of any such mining claim located prior to January 1, 1953, must have posted and filed for record, within the time allowed by the provisions of sections 501 to 505 of this title, an amended notice of location as to such mining claim, stating that such notice was filed pursuant to the provisions of said sections and for the purpose of obtaining the benefits thereof: * * *

Aug. 13, 1954, c. 730, § 1 68 Stat. 708.

* * *

§ 523.   Uranium leases—Right to locate mining claims

(a) Subject to the conditions and provisions of this chapter and to any valid prior rights acquired under the laws of the United States, the owner of any pending uranium lease application or of any uranium lease shall have, for a period of one hundred and twenty days after August 13, 1954, as limited in subsection (b) of this section, the right to locate mining claims upon the lands covered by said application or lease.

* * *

Aug. 13, 1954, c. 730, § 3, 68 Stat. 709.

§ 524.   Reservation of minerals to United States

Every mining claim or millsite—

(1) heretofore located under the mining laws of the United States which shall be entitled to benefits under sections 521 to 523 of this title; or

(2) located under the mining laws of the United States after August 13, 1954, shall be subject, prior to issuance of a patent therefor, to a reservation to the United States of all Leasing Act minerals and of the right (as limited in section 526 of this title) of the United States, its lessees, permittees, and licensees to enter upon the land covered by such mining claim or millsite and to prospect for, drill for, mine, treat, store, transport, and remove Leasing Act minerals and to use so much of the surface and subsurface of such mining claim or millsite as may be necessary for such purposes, and whenever reasonably necessary, for the purpose of prospecting for, drilling for, mining, treating, storing, transporting, and removing Leasing Act minerals on and from other lands; and any patent issued for any such mining claim or millsite shall contain such reservation as to, but only as to, such lands covered thereby which at the time of the issuance of such patent were—

(a) included in a permit or lease issued under the mineral leasing laws; or

(b) covered by an application or offer for a permit or lease filed under the mineral leasing laws; or

(c) known to be valuable for minerals subject to disposition under the mineral leasing laws.

Aug. 13, 1954, c. 730, § 4, 68 Stat. 710.

§ 525.   Future location of claims on mineral lands

Subject to the conditions and provisions of this chapter, mining claims and millsites may hereafter be located under the mining laws of the United States on lands of the United States which at the time of location are—

(a) included in a permit or lease issued under the mineral leasing laws; or

(b) covered by an application or offer for a permit or lease filed under the mineral leasing laws; or

(c) known to be valuable for minerals subject to disposition under the mineral leasing laws;

to the same extent in all respects as if such lands were not so included or covered or known.

Aug. 13, 1954, c. 730, § 5, 68 Stat. 710.

§ 526.   Mining and Leasing Act operations—Multiple use

(a) Where the same lands are being utilized for mining operations and Leasing Act operations, each of such operations shall be conducted, so far as reasonably practicable, in a manner compatible with such multiple use.

Mining operations to avoid damage to mineral deposits and interference with mineral operations

(b) Any mining operations pursuant to rights under any unpatented or patented mining claim or millsite which shall be subject to a reservation to the United States of Leasing Act minerals as provided in this chapter, shall be conducted, so far as reasonably practicable, in a manner which will avoid damage to any known deposit of any Leasing Act mineral. Subject to the provisions of subsection (d) of this section, mining operations shall be so conducted as not to endanger or materially interfere with any existing surface or underground improvements, workings, or facilities which may have been made for the purpose of Leasing Act operations, or with the utilization of such improvements, workings, or facilities.

Leasing Act operations to avoid damage to mineral deposits and interference with mining operations

(c) Any Leasing Act operations on lands covered by an unpatented or patented mining claim or millsite which shall be subject to a reservation to the United States of Leasing Act minerals as provided in this chapter shall be conducted, so far as reasonably practicable, in a manner which will avoid damage to any known deposit of any mineral not so reserved from such mining claim or millsite. Subject to the provisions of subsection (d) of this section, Leasing Act operations shall be so conducted as not to endanger or materially interfere with any existing surface or underground improvements, workings, or facilities which may have been made for the purpose of mining operations, or with the utilization of such improvements, workings, or facilities.

Damage or interference permitted by court

(d) If, upon petition of either the mining operator or the Leasing Act operator, any court of competent jurisdiction shall find that a particular use in connection with one of such operations cannot be reasonably and properly conducted without endangering or materially interfering with the then existing improvements, workings, or facilities of the other of such operations or with the utilization thereof, and shall find that under the conditions and circumstances, as they then appear, the injury or damage which would result from denial of such particular use would outweigh the injury or damage which would result to such then existing improvements, workings, or facilities or from interference with the utilization thereof if that particular use were allowed, then and in such event such court may permit such use upon payment (or upon furnishing of security determined by the court to be adequate to secure payment) to the party or parties who would be thus injured or damaged, of an amount to be fixed by the court as constituting fair compensation for the then reasonably contemplated injury or damage which would result to such then existing improvements, workings, or facilities or from interference with the utilization thereof by reason of the allowance of such particular use.

Information regarding operations to be furnished on request

(e) Where the same lands are being utilized for mining operations and Leasing Act operations, then upon request of the party conducting either of said operations, the party conducting the other of said operations shall furnish to and at the expense of such requesting party copies of any information which said other party may have, as to the situs of any improvements, workings, or facilities theretofore made upon such lands, and upon like request, shall permit such requesting party, at the risk of

337

such requesting party, to have access at reasonable times to any such improvements, workings, or facilities for the purpose of surveying and checking or determining the situs thereof. If damage to or material interference with a party's improvements, workings, facilities, or with the utilization thereof shall result from such party's failure, after request, to so furnish to the requesting party such information or from denial of such access, such failure or denial shall relieve the requesting party of any liability for the damage or interference resulting by reason of such failure or denial. Failure of a party to furnish requested information or access shall not impose upon such party any liability to the requesting party other than for such costs of court and attorney's fees as may be allowed to the requesting party in enforcing by court action the obligations of this section as to the furnishing of information and access. The obligation hereunder of any party to furnish requested information shall be limited to map and survey information then available to such party with respect to the situs of improvements, workings, and facilities and the furnishing thereof shall not be deemed to constitute any representation as to the accuracy of such information.

Aug. 13, 1954, c. 730, § 6, 68 Stat. 710.

§ 527. Determination of unpatented mining claims— Filing of notice

(a) Any applicant, offeror, permittee, or lessee under the mineral leasing laws may file in the office of the Secretary of the Interior, or in such office as the Secretary may designate, a request for publication of notice of such application, offer, permit, or lease, * * *

The filing of such request for publication shall be accompanied by a certified copy of such recorded notice and an affidavit or affidavits of a person or persons over twenty-one years of age setting forth that the affiant or affronts have examined the lands involved in a reasonable effort to ascertain whether any person or persons were in actual possession of or engaged in the working of such lands or any part thereof, and, if no person or persons were found to be in actual possession of or engaged in the working of said lands or any part thereof on the date of such examination, setting forth such fact, or, if any person or persons were so found to be in actual possession or engaged in such working on the date of such examination, setting forth the name and address of each such person, unless affiant shall have been unable through reasonable inquiry to obtain information as to the name and address of any such person, in which event the affidavit shall set forth fully the nature and results of such inquiry.

* * *

Thereupon the Secretary of the Interior, or his designated representative, at the expense of the requesting person (who, prior to the commencement of publication, must furnish the agreement of the publisher to hold such requesting person alone responsible for charges of publication), shall cause notice of such application, offer, permit, or lease to be published in a newspaper having general circulation in the county in which the lands involved are situate.

* * *

Failure to file verified statement

(b) If any claimant under any unpatented mining claim heretofore located which embraces any of the lands described in any notice published in accordance with the provisions of subsection (a) of this section shall fail to file a verified statement, as above provided, within one hundred and fifty days from the date of the first publication of such notice, such failure shall be conclusively deemed, except as otherwise provided in subsection (e) of this section, (i) to constitute a waiver and relinquishment by such mining claimant of any and all right, title, and interest under such mining claim as to, but only as to, leasing Act minerals, and (ii) to constitute a consent by such mining claimant that such mining claim and any patent issued therefor, shall be subject to the reservation specified in section 524 of this title, and (iii) to preclude thereafter any assertion by such mining claimant of any right or title to or interest in any Leasing Act mineral by reason of such mining claim.

Hearings

(c) If any verified statement shall be filed by a mining claimant as provided in subsection (a) of this section, then the Secretary of the Interior or his designated representative shall fix a time and place for a hearing to determine the validity and effectiveness of the mining claimant's asserted right or interest in Leasing Act minerals, which place of hearing shall be in the county where the lands in question or parts thereof are located, unless the mining claimant agrees otherwise.

Request for copy of notice

(d) Any person claiming any right in Leasing Act minerals under or by virtue of any unpatented mining claim heretofore located and desiring to receive a copy of any notice of any application, offer, permit, or lease which may be published as above provided in subsection (a) of this section, and which may affect lands embraced in such mining claim, may cause to be filed for record in the county office of record where the notice or certificate of location of such mining claim shall have been recorded, a duly acknowledged request for a copy of any such notice.

* * *

Failure to deliver or mail copy of notice

(e) If any applicant, offeror, permittee, or lessee shall fail to comply with the requirements of subsection (a) of this section as to the personal delivery or mailing of a copy of notice to any person, the publication of such notice shall be deemed wholly ineffectual as to that person or as to the rights asserted by that person and the failure of that person to file a verified statement, as provided in such notice, shall in no manner affect, diminish, prejudice or bar any rights of that person.

Aug. 13, 1954, c. 730, § 7, 68 Stat. 711; June 11, 1960, Pub.L. 86–507, § 1(25), 74 Stat. 201.

§ 528.   Waiver and relinquishment of mineral rights

The owner or owners of any mining claim heretofore located may, at any time prior to issuance of patent therefor, waive and relinquish all rights thereunder to Leasing Act minerals. The execution and acknowledgment of such a waiver and relinquishment by such owner or owners and the recordation thereof in the office where the notice or certificate of location of such mining claim is of record shall render such mining claim thereafter subject to the reservation referred to in section 524 of this title and any patent issued therefor shall contain such a reservation, but no such waiver or relinquishment shall be deemed in any manner to constitute any concession as to the date of priority of rights under said mining claim or as to the validity thereof.

Aug. 13, 1954, c. 730, § 8, 68 Stat. 715.

* * *

§ 530.   Definitions

As used in this chapter "mineral leasing laws" shall mean the Act of October 20, 1914; the Act of February 25, 1920; the Act of April 17, 1926; the Act of February 7, 1927; and all Acts heretofore or hereafter enacted which are amendatory of or supplementary to any of the foregoing Acts; "Leasing Act minerals" shall mean all minerals which, upon August 13, 1954, are provided in the mineral leasing laws to be disposed of thereunder; "Leasing Act operations" shall mean operations conducted under a lease, permit, or license issued under the mineral leasing laws in or incidental to prospecting for, drilling for, mining, treating, storing, transporting, or removing Leasing Act minerals; "mining operations" shall mean operations under any unpatented or patented mining claim or millsite in or incidental to prospecting for, mining, treating, storing, transporting, or removing minerals other than Leasing Act minerals and any other use under any claim of right or title based upon such mining claim or millsite; "Leasing Act operator" shall mean any party who shall conduct Leasing Act operations; "mining operator" shall mean any party who shall conduct mining operations; "Atomic Energy Act" shall mean the Act of August 1, 1946 (60 Stat. 755), as amended; "Atomic Energy Commission" shall mean the United States Atomic Energy Commission established under the Atomic Energy Act or any amendments thereof; "fissionable source material" shall mean uranium, thorium, and all other materials referred to in section 5(b)(1) of the Atomic Energy Act as reserved or to be reserved to the United States; "uranium lease application" shall mean an application for a uranium lease filed with said Commission with respect to lands which would be open for entry under the mining laws except for their being lands embraced within an offer, application, permit, or lease under the mineral leasing laws or lands known to be valuable for minerals leasable under those laws; "uranium lease" shall mean a uranium mining lease issued by said Commission with respect to any such lands; and "person" shall mean any individual, corporation, partnership, or other legal entity.

Aug. 13, 1954, c. 730, § 11, 68 Stat. 716; Dec. 24, 1970, Pub.L. 91–581, § 26, 84 Stat. 1573.

* * *

COMMON VARIETIES ACT OF 1947 (as amended)

(30 U.S.C.A. §§ 601–604)

§ 601. Rules and regulations governing disposal of materials; payment; removal without charge; lands excluded

The Secretary, under such rules and regulations as he may prescribe, may dispose of mineral materials (including but not limited to common varieties of the following: sand, stone, gravel, pumice, pumicite, cinders, and clay) and vegetative materials (including but not limited to yucca, manzanita, mesquite, cactus, and timber or other forest products) on public lands of the United States, including, for the purposes of this subchapter, land described in sections 1181a to 1181j of Title 43, if the disposal of such mineral or vegetative materials (1) is not otherwise expressly authorized by law, including, but not limited to, sections 315 to 315g, 315h to 315m, 315n, 315o–1, and 1171 of Title 43, and the United States mining laws, and (2) is not expressly prohibited by laws of the United States, and (3) would not be detrimental to the public interest. Such materials may be disposed of only in accordance with the provisions of this subchapter and upon the payment of adequate compensation therefor, to be determined by the Secretary: *Provided, however,* That, to the extent not otherwise authorized by law, the Secretary is authorized in his discretion to permit any Federal, State, or Territorial agency, unit or subdivision, including municipalities, or any association or corporation not organized for profit, to take and remove, without charge, materials and resources subject to this subchapter, for use other than for commercial or industrial purposes or resale. Where the lands have been withdrawn in aid of a function of a Federal department or agency other than the department headed by the Secretary or of a State, Territory, county, municipality, water district or other local governmental subdivision or agency, the Secretary may make disposals under this subchapter only with the consent of such other Federal department or agency or of such State, Territory, or local governmental unit. Nothing in this subchapter shall be construed to apply to lands in any national park, or national monument or to any Indian lands, or lands set aside or held for the use or benefit of Indians, including lands over which jurisdiction has been transferred to the Department of the Interior by Executive order for the use of Indians. As used in this subchapter, the word "Secretary" means the Secretary of the Interior except that it means the Secretary of Agriculture where the lands involved are administered by him for national forest purposes or for the purposes of sections 1010 to 1012 of Title 7 or where withdrawn for the purpose of any other function of the Department of Agriculture.

July 31, 1947, c. 406, § 1, 61 Stat. 681; July 23, 1955, c. 375, § 1, 69 Stat. 367.

§ 602. Bidding; advertising and other notice; conditions for negotiation of contract

(a) The Secretary shall dispose of materials under this subchapter to the highest responsible qualified bidder after formal advertising and such other public notice as he deems appropriate: *Provided, however,* That the Secretary may authorize negotiation of a contract for the disposal of materials if—

(1) the contract is for the sale of less than two hundred fifty thousand beard-feet of timber; or, if

(2) the contract is for the disposal of materials to be used in connection with a public works improvement program on behalf of a Federal, State, or local governmental agency and the public exigency will not permit the delay incident to advertising; or, if

(3) the contract is for the disposal of property for which it is impracticable to obtain competition.

(b) Repealed. Pub.L. 96–470, Title I, § 102(a), Oct. 19, 1980, 94 Stat. 2237.

July 31, 1947, ch. 406, § 2, 61 Stat. 681; Sept. 25, 1962, Pub.L. 87–689, § 1, 76 Stat. 587; as amended Apr. 21, 1976, Pub.L. 94–273, § 20, 90 Stat. 379; Oct. 19, 1980, Pub.L. 96–470, Title I, § 102(a), 94 Stat. 2237.

* * *

SURFACE RESOURCES ACT OF 1955 (as amended)

(30 U.S.C.A. §§ 611–15)

§ 611. Common varieties of sand, stone, gravel, pumice, pumicite, or cinders, and petrified wood

No deposit of common varieties of sand, stone, gravel, pumice, pumicite, or cinders and no deposit of petrified wood shall be deemed a valuable mineral deposit within the meaning of the mining laws of the United States so as to give effective validity to any mining claim hereafter located under such mining laws: *Provided, however,* That nothing herein shall affect the validity of any mining location based upon discovery of some other mineral occurring in or in association with such a deposit. "Common varieties" as used in sections 601, 603, and 611 to 615 of this title does not include deposits of such materials which are valuable because the deposit has some property giving it distinct and special value and does not include so called "block pumice" which occurs in nature in pieces having one dimension of two inches or more. "Petrified wood" as used in sections 601, 603, and 611 to 615 of this title means agatized, opalized, petrified, or silicified wood, or any material formed by the replacement of wood by silica or other matter.

July 23, 1955, c. 375, § 3, 69 Stat. 368; Sept. 28, 1962, Pub.L. 87–713, § 1, 76 Stat. 652.

§ 612. Unpatented mining claims—Prospecting, mining or processing operations

(a) Any mining claim hereafter located under the mining laws of the United States shall not be used, prior to issuance of patent therefor, for any purposes other than prospecting, mining or processing operations and uses reasonably incident thereto.

Reservations in the United States to use of the surface and surface resources

(b) Rights under any mining claim hereafter located under the mining laws of the United States shall be subject, prior to issuance of patent therefor, to the right of the United States to manage and dispose of the vegetative surface resources thereof and to manage other surface resources thereof (except mineral deposits subject to location under the mining laws of the United States). Any such mining claim shall also be subject, prior to issuance of patent therefor, to the right of the United States, its permittees, and licensees, to use so much of the surface thereof as may be necessary for such purposes or for access to adjacent land: *Provided, however,* That any use of the surface of any such mining claim by the United States, its permittees or licensees, shall be such as not to endanger or materially interfere with prospecting, mining or processing operations or uses reasonably incident thereto: *Provided further,* That if at any time the locator requires more timber for his mining operations than is available to him from the claim after disposition of timber therefrom by the United States, subsequent to the location of the claim, he shall be entitled, free of charge, to be supplied with timber for such requirements from the nearest timber administered by the disposing agency which is ready for harvesting under the rules and regulations of that agency and which is substantially equivalent in kind and quantity to the timber estimated by the disposing agency to have been disposed of from the claim: *Provided further,* That nothing in sections 601, 603, and 611 to 615 of this title shall be construed as affecting or intended to affect or in any way interfere with or modify the laws of the States which lie wholly or in part westward of the ninety-eighth meridian relating to the ownership, control, appropriation, use, and distribution of ground or surface waters within any unpatented mining claim.

Severance or removal of timber

(c) Except to the extent required for the mining claimant's prospecting, mining or processing operations and uses reasonably incident thereto, or for the construction of buildings or structures in connection therewith, or to provide clearance for such operations or uses, or to the extent authorized by the United States, no claimant of any mining claim hereafter located under the mining laws of the United States shall, prior to issuance of patent therefor, sever, remove, or use any vegetative or other surface resources thereof which are subject to management or disposition by the United States under subsection (b) of this section. Any severance or removal of timber which is permitted under the exceptions of the preceding

343

sentence, other than severance or removal to provide clearance, shall be in accordance with sound principles of forest management.

July 23, 1955, c. 375, § 4, 69 Stat. 368.

§ 613. Procedure for determining title uncertainties— Notice to mining claimants; request; publication; service

(a) The head of a Federal department or agency which has the responsibility for administering surface resources of any lands belonging to the United States may file as to such lands in the office of the Secretary of the Interior, or in such office as the Secretary of the Interior may designate, a request for publication of notice to mining claimants, for determination of surface rights, which request shall contain a description of the lands covered thereby, showing the section or sections of the public land surveys which embrace the lands covered by such request, or if such lands are unsurveyed, either the section or sections which would probably embrace such lands when the public land surveys are extended to such lands or a tie by courses and distances to an approved United States mineral monument.

The filing of such request for publication shall be accompanied by an affidavit or affidavits of a person or persons over twenty-one years of age setting forth that the affiant or affiants have examined the lands involved in a reasonable effort to ascertain whether any person or persons were in actual possession of or engaged in the working of such lands or any part thereof, and, if no person or persons were found to be in actual possession of or engaged in the working of said lands or any part thereof on the date of such examination, setting forth such fact, or, if any person or persons were so found to be in actual possession or engaged in such working on the date of such examination, setting forth the name and address of each such person, unless affiant shall have been unable through reasonable inquiry to obtain information as to the name and address of any such person, in which event the affidavit shall set forth fully the nature and results of such inquiry.

The filing of such request for publication shall also be accompanied by the certificate of a title or abstract company, or of a title abstractor, or of an attorney, based upon such company's abstractor's, or attorney's examination of those instruments which are shown by the tract indexes in the county office of record as affecting the lands described in said request, setting forth the name of any person disclosed by said instruments to have an interest in said lands under any unpatented mining claim heretofore located, together with the address of such person if such address is disclosed by such instruments of record. "Tract indexes" as used herein shall mean those indexes, if any, as to surveyed lands identifying instruments as affecting a particular legal subdivision of the public land surveys, and as to unsurveyed lands identifying instruments as affecting a particular probable legal subdivision according to a projected extension of the public land surveys.

Thereupon the Secretary of the Interior, at the expense of the requesting department or agency, shall cause notice to mining claimants to be published in a newspaper having general circulation in the county in which the lands involved are situate.

Such notice shall describe the lands covered by such request, as provided heretofore, and shall notify whomever it may concern that if any person claiming or asserting under, or by virtue of, any unpatented mining claim heretofore located, rights as to such lands or any part thereof, shall fail to file in the office where such request for publication was filed (which office shall be specified in such notice) and within one hundred and fifty days from the date of the first publication of such notice (which date shall be specified in such notice), a verified statement which shall set forth, as to such unpatented mining claim—

(1) the date of location;

(2) the book and page of recordation of the notice or certificate of location;

(3) the section or sections of the public land surveys which embrace such mining claims; or if such lands are unsurveyed, either the section or sections which would probably embrace such mining claim when the public land surveys are extended to such lands or a tie by courses and distances to an approved United States mineral monument;

(4) whether such claimant is a locator or purchaser under such location; and

(5) the name and address of such claimant and names and addresses so far as known to the claimant of any other person or persons claiming any interest or interests in or under such unpatented mining claim;

such failure shall be conclusively deemed (i) to constitute a waiver and relinquishment by such mining claimant of any right, title, or interest under such mining claim contrary to or in conflict with the limitations or restrictions specified in section 612 of this title as to hereafter located unpatented mining claims, and (ii) to constitute a consent by such mining claimant that such mining claim, prior to issuance of patent therefor, shall be subject to the limitations and restrictions specified in section 612 of this title as to hereafter located unpatented mining claims, and (iii) to preclude thereafter, prior to issuance of patent, any assertion by such mining claimant of any right or title to or interest in or under such mining claim contrary to or in conflict with the limitations or restrictions specified in section 612 of this title as to hereafter located unpatented mining claims.

If such notice is published in a daily paper, it shall be published in the Wednesday issue for nine consecutive weeks, or, if in a weekly paper, in nine consecutive issues, or if in a semiweekly or triweekly paper, in the issue of the same day of each week for nine consecutive weeks.

Within fifteen days after the date of first publication of such notice, the department or agency requesting such publication (1) shall cause a copy of such notice to be personally delivered to or to be mailed by registered mail or by certified mail addressed to each person in possession or engaged in the working of the land whose name and address is shown by an affidavit filed as aforesaid, and to each person who may have filed, as to any lands described in said notice, a request for notices, as provided in subsection (d) of this section, and shall cause a copy of such notice to be mailed by registered mail or by certified mail to each person whose name and address is set forth in the title or abstract company's or title abstractor's or attorney's certificate filed as aforesaid, as having an interest in the lands described in said notice under any unpatented mining claim heretofore located, such notice to be directed to such person's address as set forth in such certificate; and (2) shall file in the office where said request for publication was filed an affidavit showing that copies have been so delivered or mailed.

Failure to file verified statement

(b) If any claimant under any unpatented mining claim heretofore located which embraces any of the lands described in any notice published in accordance with the provisions of subsection (a) of this section, shall fail to file a verified statement, as provided in such subsection (a), within one hundred and fifty days from the date of the first publication of such notice, such failure shall be conclusively deemed, except as otherwise provided in subsection (e) of this section, (i) to constitute a waiver and relinquishment by such mining claimant of any right, title, or interest under such mining claim contrary to or in conflict with the limitations or restrictions specified in section 612 of this title as to hereafter located unpatented mining claims, and (ii) to constitute a consent by such mining claimant that such mining claim, prior to issuance of patent therefor, shall be subject to the limitations and restrictions specified in section 612 of this title as to hereafter located unpatented mining claims, and (iii) to preclude thereafter, prior to issuance of patent, any assertion by such mining claimant of any right or title to or interest in or under such mining claim contrary to or in conflict with the limitations or restrictions specified in section 612 of this title as to hereafter located unpatented mining claims.

Hearings

(c) If any verified statement shall be filed by a mining claimant as provided in subsection (a) of this section, then the Secretary of Interior shall fix a time and place for a hearing to determine the validity and effectiveness of any right or title to, or interest in or under such mining claim, which the mining claimant may assert contrary to or in conflict with the limitations and restrictions specified in section 612 of this title as to hereafter located unpatented mining claims, which place of hearing shall be in the county where the lands in question or parts thereof are located, unless the mining claimant agrees otherwise. Where verified statements are filed asserting rights to an aggregate of more than twenty mining claims, any single hearing shall be limited to a maximum of twenty mining claims unless the parties affected shall otherwise stipulate and as many separate hearing shall be set as shall be necessary to comply with this provision. The procedures with respect to notice of such a hearing and the conduct thereof, and in respect to appeals shall follow the then established general procedures and rules of practice of the Department of the Interior in respect to contests or protests affecting public lands of the United States. If, pursuant to such a hearing the final decision rendered in the matter shall affirm the validity and effectiveness of any mining claimant's so asserted right or interest under the mining claim, then no subsequent proceedings under this section shall have any force or effect upon the so-affirmed right or interest of such mining claimant under such mining claim. If at any time prior to a hearing the department or agency requesting publication of notice and any person filing a verified statement pursuant to such notice shall so stipulate, then to the extent so stipulated, but only to such extent, no hearing shall be held with respect to rights asserted under that verified statement, and to the extent defined by the stipulation the rights asserted under that verified statement shall be deemed to be unaffected by that particular published notice.

* * *

July 23, 1955, c. 375, § 5, 69 Stat. 369; June 11, 1960, Pub.L. 86–507, § 1(26), 74 Stat. 201.

§ 614. Waiver of rights

The owner or owners of any unpatented mining claim heretofore located may waive and relinquish all rights thereunder which are contrary to or in conflict with the limitations or restrictions specified in section 612 of this rifle as to hereafter located unpatented mining claims. The execution and acknowledgment of such a waiver and relinquishment by such owner or owners and the recordation thereof in the office where the notice or certificate of location of such mining claim is of record shall render such mining claim thereafter and prior to issuance of patent subject to the limitations and restrictions in section 612 of this title in all respects as if said mining claim had been located after enactment of sections 601, 603, and 611 to 615 of this title, but no such waiver or relinquishment shall be deemed in any manner to constitute any concession as to the date of priority of rights under said mining claim or as to the validity thereof.

July 23, 1955, c. 375, § 6, 69 Stat. 372.

§ 615. Limitation of existing rights

Nothing in sections 601, 603, and 611 to 615 of this title shall be construed in any manner to limit or restrict or to authorize the limitation or restriction of any existing rights of any claimant under any valid mining claim heretofore located, except as such rights may be limited or restricted as a result of a proceeding pursuant to section 613 of this title, or as a result of a waiver and relinquishment pursuant to section 614 of this title; and nothing in sections 601, 603, and 611 to 615 of this title shall be construed in any manner to authorize inclusion in any patent hereafter issued under the mining laws of the United States for any mining claim heretofore or hereafter located, of any reservation, limitation, or restriction not otherwise authorized by law, or to limit or repeal any existing authority to include any reservation, limitation, or restriction in any such patent, or to limit or restrict any use of the lands covered by any patented or unpatented mining claim by the United States, its lessees, permittees, and licensees which is otherwise authorized by law.

July 23, 1955, c. 375, § 7, 69 Stat. 372.

MINING CLAIM OCCUPANCY ACT OF 1962

(30 U.S.C.A. §§ 701–09)

§ 701. Authorization to convey; acreage limitations; qualified applicants; payment; "qualified officer of the United States" defined

The Secretary of the Interior may convey to any occupant of an unpatented mining claim which is determined by the Secretary to be an invalid interest, up to and including a fee simple, in and to an area within the claim of not more than (a) five acres or (b) the acreage actually occupied by him, whichever is less. The Secretary may make a like conveyance to any occupant of an unpatented mining claim who, after notice from a qualified officer of the United States that the claim is believed to be invalid, relinquishes to the United States all right in and to such claim which he may have under the mining laws. Any conveyance authorized by this section, however, shall be made only to a qualified applicant, as that term is defined in section 702 of this title, who applies therefor within the period ending June 30, 1971, and upon payment of an amount established in accordance with section 705 of this title.

As used in this section, the term "qualified officer of the United States" means the Secretary of the Interior or an employee of the Department of the Interior so designated by him: *Provided,* That the Secretary may delegate his authority to designate qualified officers to the head of any other department or agency of the United States with respect to lands within the administrative jurisdiction of that department or agency.

Pub.L. 87–851, § 1, Oct. 23, 1962, 76 Stat. 1127; Pub.L. 90–111, § 1, Oct. 23, 1967, 81 Stat. 311.

§ 702. "Qualified applicant" defined

For the purposes of this chapter a qualified applicant is a residential occupant-owner, as of October 23, 1962, of valuable improvements in an unpatented mining claim which constitute for him a principal place of residence and which he and his predecessors in interest were in possession of for not less than seven years prior to July 23, 1962.

Pub.L. 87–851, § 2, Oct. 23, 1962, 76 Stat. 1127.

§ 703. Withdrawal of lands in aid of a governmental unit

Where the lands for which application is made under section 701 of this title have been withdrawn in aid of a function of a Federal department or agency other than the Department of the Interior, or of a State, county, municipality, water district, or other local governmental subdivision or agency, the Secretary of the Interior may convey an interest therein only with the consent of the head of the governmental unit concerned and under such terms and conditions as said head may deem necessary.

Pub.L. 87–851, § 3, Oct. 23, 1962, 76 Stat. 1127.

§ 704. Purchase of substitute lands; limitations; conditions; payment; conveyance of less than a fee

(a) If the Secretary of the Interior determines that conveyance of an interest under section 701 of this title is otherwise justified but the consent required by section 703 of this title is not given, he may, in accordance with such procedural rules and regulations as he may prescribe, grant the applicant a right to purchase, for residential use, an interest in another tract of land, five acres or less in area, from tracts made available by him for sale under this chapter (1) from the unappropriated and unreserved lands of the United States, or (2) from lands subject to classification under section 315f of Title 43. Said right shall not be granted until arrangements satisfactory to the Secretary have been made for termination of the applicant's occupancy of his unpatented mining claim and for settlement of any liability for the unauthorized use thereof which may have been incurred and shall expire five years from the date on which it was granted unless sooner exercised. The amount to be paid for the interest shall be determined in accordance with section 705 of this title.

(b) Any conveyance of less than a fee made under this chapter shall include provision for removal from the tract of any improvements or other property of the applicant at the close of the period for which the conveyance is made, or if it be an interest terminating on the death of the applicant, within one year thereafter.

Pub.L. 87–851, § 4, Oct. 23, 1962, 76 Stat. 1127.

§ 705. Purchase price of conveyed interest; installment payments

The Secretary of the Interior, prior to any conveyance under this chapter, shall determine the fair market value of the interest to be conveyed, exclusive of the value of any improvements placed on the lands involved by the applicant or his predecessors in interest. Said value shall be determined as of the date of appraisal. In establishing the purchase price to be paid by the applicant for the interest, the Secretary shall take into consideration any equities of the applicant and his predecessors in interest, including conditions of prior use and occupancy. In any event the purchase price for any interest conveyed shall not exceed its fair market value nor be less than $5 per acre. The Secretary may, in his discretion, allow payment to be made in installments.

Pub.L. 87–851, § 5, Oct. 23, 1962, 76 Stat. 1128.

§ 706. Liabilities of occupants; trespass; limitations

(a) The execution of a conveyance as authorized by section 701 of this title shall not relieve any occupant of the land conveyed of any liability, existing on the date of said conveyance, to the United States for unauthorized use of the land in and to which an interest is conveyed.

(b) Except where a mining claim embracing land applied for under this chapter by a qualified applicant was located at a time when the land included therein was withdrawn or otherwise not subject to such location, no trespass charges shall be sought or collected by the United States from any qualified applicant who has filed an application for land in the mining claim pursuant to this chapter, based upon occupancy of such claim, whether residential or otherwise, for any period preceding the final administrative determination of the invalidity of the mining claim by the Secretary of the Interior or the voluntary relinquishment of the mining claim, whichever occurs earlier. Nothing contained in this chapter shall be construed as creating any liability for trespass to the United States which would not exist in the absence of this chapter. Relief under this section shall be limited to persons who file applications for conveyances pursuant to section 701 of this title within the period ending June 30, 1971.

Pub.L. 87–851, § 6, Oct. 23, 1962, 76 Stat. 1128; Pub.L. 90–111, § 2, Oct. 23, 1967, 81 Stat. 311.

§ 707. Reservation of mineral rights

In any conveyance under this chapter the mineral interests of the United States in the lands conveyed are reserved for the term of the estate conveyed. Minerals locatable under the mining laws or disposable under sections 601 to 604 of this title, are withdrawn from all forms of entry and appropriation for the term of the estate. The underlying oil, gas and other leasable minerals of the United States are reserved for exploration and development purposes, but without the right of surface ingress and egress, and may be leased by the Secretary under the mineral leasing laws.

Pub.L. 87–851, § 7, Oct. 23, 1962, 76 Stat. 1128.

§ 708. Assignments; succession

Rights and privileges to qualify as an applicant under this chapter shall not be assignable, but may pass through devise or descent.

Pub.L. 87–851, § 8, Oct. 23, 1962, 76 Stat. 1128.

§ 709. Disposition of payments and fees

Payments of filing fees and survey costs, and the payments of the purchase price for patents in fee shall be disposed of by the Secretary of the Interior as are such fees, costs, and purchase prices in the disposition of public lands. All payments and fees for occupancy in conveyances of less than the fee, or for permits for life or shorter periods, shall be disposed of by the administering department or agency as are other receipts for the use of the lands involved.

Pub.L. 87–851, § 9, Oct. 23, 1962, 76 Stat. 1128.

* * *

FEDERAL OIL AND GAS ROYALTY MANAGEMENT ACT OF 1982

(30 U.S.C.A. §§ 1701–57)

§ 1701. Congressional statement of findings and purposes

(a) Congress finds that—

(1) the Secretary of the Interior should enforce effectively and uniformly existing regulations under the mineral leasing laws providing for the inspection of production activities on lease sites on Federal and Indian lands;

(2) the system of accounting with respect to royalties and other payments due and owing on oil and gas produced from such lease sites is archaic and inadequate;

(3) it is essential that the Secretary initiate procedures to improve methods of accounting for such royalties and payments and to provide for routine inspection of activities related to the production of oil and gas on such lease sites; and

(4) the Secretary should aggressively carry out his trust responsibility in the administration of Indian oil and gas.

(b) It is the purpose of this chapter—

(1) to clarify, reaffirm, expand, and define the responsibilities and obligations of lessees, operators, and other persons involved in transportation or sale of oil and gas from the Federal and Indian lands and the Outer Continental Shelf;

(2) to clarify, reaffirm, expand, and define the authorities and responsibilities of the Secretary of the Interior to implement and maintain a royalty management system for oil and gas leases on Federal lands, Indian lands, and the Outer Continental Shelf;

(3) to require the development of enforcement practices that ensure the prompt and proper collection and disbursement of oil and gas revenues owed to the United States and Indian lessors and those inuring to the benefit of States;

(4) to fulfill the trust responsibility of the United States for the administration of Indian oil and gas resources; and

(5) to effectively utilize the capabilities of the States and Indian tribes in developing and maintaining an efficient and effective Federal royalty management system.

Pub.L. 97–451, § 2, Jan. 12, 1983, 96 Stat. 2448.

* * *

SUBCHAPTER I—FEDERAL ROYALTY MANAGEMENT
AND ENFORCEMENT

§ 1711. Duties of Secretary

Establishment of inspection, collection, and accounting and auditing system

(a) The Secretary shall establish a comprehensive inspection, collection and fiscal and production accounting and auditing system to provide the capability to accurately determine oil and gas royalties, interest, fines, penalties, fees, deposits, and other payments owed, and to collect and account for such amounts in a timely manner.

Annual inspection of lease sites; training

(b) The Secretary shall—

(1) establish procedures to ensure that authorized and properly identified representatives of the Secretary will inspect at least once annually each lease site producing or expected to produce significant quantities of oil or gas in any year of which has a history of noncompliance with applicable provisions of law or regulations; and

(2) establish and maintain adequate programs providing for the training of all such authorized representatives in methods and techniques of inspection and accounting that will be used in the implementation of this chapter.

Audit and reconciliation of lease accounts; contracts with certified public accountants; availability of books, accounts, records, etc., related to audit

(1) The Secretary shall audit and reconcile, to the extent practicable, all current and past lease accounts for leases of oil or gas and take appropriate actions to make additional collections or refunds as warranted. The Secretary shall conduct audits and reconciliations of lease accounts in conformity with the business practices and record-keeping systems which were required of the lessee by the Secretary for the period covered by the audit. The Secretary shall give priority to auditing those lease accounts identified by a State or Indian tribe as having significant potential for underpayment. The Secretary may also audit accounts and records of selected lessees and operators.

(2) The Secretary may enter into contracts or other appropriate arrangements with independent certified public accountants to undertake audits of accounts and records of any lessee or operator relating to the lease of oil or gas. Selection of such independent certified public accountants shall be by competitive bidding in accordance with the Federal Property and Administrative Services Act of 1949 (41 U.S.C. 252), except that the Secretary may not enter into a contract or other arrangement with any independent certified public accountant to audit any lessee or operator where such lessee or operator is a primary audit client of such certified public accountant.

(3) All books, accounts, financial records, reports, files, and other papers of the Secretary, or used by the Secretary, which are reasonably necessary to facilitate the audits required under this section shall be made available to any person or governmental entity conducting audits under this chapter.

Pub.L. 97–451, Title I, § 101, Jan. 12, 1983, 96 Stat. 2449.

§ 1712. Duties of lessees, operators, and motor vehicle transporters

Liability for royalty payments

(a) In order to increase receipts and achieve effective collections of royalty and other payments, a lessee who is required to make any royalty or other payment under a lease or under the mineral leasing laws, shall make such payments in the time and manner as may be specified by the Secretary or the applicable delegated State. A lessee may designate a person to make all or part of the payments due under a lease on the lessee's behalf and shall notify the Secretary or the applicable delegated State in writing of such designation, in which event said designated person may, in its own name, pay, offset or credit monies, make adjustments, request and receive refunds and submit reports with respect to payments required by the lessee. Notwithstanding any other provision of this chapter to the contrary, a designee shall not be liable for any payment obligation under the lease. The person owning operating rights in a lease shall be primarily liable for its pro rata share of payment obligations under the lease. If the person owning the legal record title in a lease is other than the operating rights owner, the person owning the legal record title shall be secondarily liable for its pro rata share of such payment obligations under the lease.

Development of and compliance with security plan and minimum site security measures by operators; notification to Secretary of well production

(b) An operator shall—

(1) develop and comply with a site security plan designed to protect the oil or gas produced or stored on an onshore lease site from theft, which plan shall conform with such minimum standards as the Secretary may prescribe by rule, taking into account the variety of circumstances at lease sites;

(2) develop and comply with such minimum site security measures as the Secretary deems appropriate to protect oil or gas produced or stored on a lease site or on the Outer Continental Shelf from theft; and

(3) not later than the 5th business day after any well begins production anywhere on a lease site or allocated to a lease site, or resumes production in the case of a well which has been off of production for more than 90 days, notify the Secretary, in the manner prescribed by the Secretary, of the date on which such production has begun or resumed.

Possession of documentation by transporters of oil or gas by motor vehicle or pipeline

(c)(1) Any person engaged in transporting by motor vehicle any oil from any lease site, or allocated to any such lease site, shall carry, on his person, in his vehicle, or in his immediate control, documentation showing, at a minimum, the amount, origin, and intended first destination of the oil.

(c)(2) Any person engaged in transporting any oil or gas by pipeline from any lease site, or allocated to any lease site, on Federal or Indian lands shall maintain documentation showing, at a minimum, amount, origin, and intended first destination of such oil or gas.

Pub.L. 97–451, Title I, § 102, Jan. 12, 1983, 96 Stat. 2450; as amended Pub.L. 104–185, § 6(g), Aug. 13, 1996, 110 Stat. 1715.

* * *

§ 1718. Inspections

Motor vehicles on lease sites; vehicles not on lease site

(a)(1) On any lease site on Federal or Indian lands, any authorized and properly identified representative of the Secretary may stop and inspect any motor vehicle that he has probable cause to believe is carrying oil from a lease site on Federal or Indian lands or allocated to such a lease site, for the purpose of determining whether the driver of such vehicle has documentation related to such oil as required by law.

(a)(2) Any authorized and properly identified representative of the Secretary, accompanied by any appropriate law enforcement officer, or an appropriate law enforcement officer alone, may stop and inspect any motor vehicle which is not on a lease site if he has probable cause to believe the vehicle is carrying oil from a lease site on Federal or Indian lands or allocated to such a lease site. Such inspection shall be for the purpose of determining whether the driver of such vehicle has the documentation required by law.

Inspection of lease sites for compliance with mineral leasing laws and this chapter

(b) Authorized and properly identified representatives of the Secretary may without advance notice, enter upon, travel across and inspect lease sites on Federal or Indian lands and may obtain from the operator immediate access to secured facilities on such lease sites, for the purpose of making any inspection or investigation for determining whether there is compliance with the requirements of the mineral leasing laws and this chapter. The Secretary shall develop guidelines setting forth the coverage and the frequency of such inspections.

Right of Secretary to enter upon and travel across lease sites

(c) For the purpose of making any inspection or investigation under this chapter, the Secretary shall have the same right to enter upon or travel across any lease site as the lessee or operator has acquired by purchase, condemnation, or otherwise.

Pub.L. 97–451, Title I, § 108, Jan. 12, 1983, 96 Stat. 2453.

§ 1719. Civil penalties

Failure to comply with applicable law, to permit inspection, or to notify Secretary of assignment; exceptions to application of penalty

(a) Any person who—

(1) after due notice of violation or after such violation has been reported under subparagraph (A), fails or refuses to comply with any requirements of this chapter or any mineral leasing law, any rule or regulation thereunder, or the terms of any lease or permit issued thereunder; or

(2) fails to permit inspection authorized in section 1718 of this title or fails to notify the Secretary of any assignment under section 1712(a)(2) of this title

shall be liable for a penalty of up to $500 per violation for each day such violation continues, dating from the date of such notice or report. A penalty under this subsection may not be applied to any person who is otherwise liable for a violation of paragraph (1) if:

(A) the violation was discovered and reported to the Secretary or his authorized representative by the liable person and corrected within 20 days after such report or such longer time as the Secretary may agree to; or

(B) after the due notice of violation required in paragraph (1) has been given to such person by the Secretary or his authorized representative, such person has corrected the violation within 20 days of such notification or such longer time as the Secretary may agree to.

Failure to take corrective action

(b) If corrective action is not taken within 40 days or a longer period as the Secretary may agree to, after due notice or the report referred to in subsection (a)(1) of this section, such person shall be liable for a civil penalty of not more than $5,000 per violation for each day such violation continues, dating from the date of such notice or report.

Failure to make royalty payment; failure to permit lawful entry, inspection, or audit; failure to notify Secretary of well production

(c) Any person who—

(1) knowingly or willfully fails to make any royalty payment by the date as specified by statute, regulation, order or terms of the lease;

(2) fails or refuses to permit lawful entry, inspection, or audit; or

(3) knowingly or willfully fails or refuses to comply with section 1712(b)(3) of this title,

shall be liable for a penalty of up to $10,000 per violation for each day such violation continues.

False information; unauthorized removal, etc., of oil or gas; purchase, sale, etc., of stolen oil or gas

(d) Any person who—

(1) knowingly or willfully prepares, maintains, or submits false, inaccurate, or misleading reports, notices, affidavits, records, data, or other written information;

(2) knowingly or willfully takes or removes, transports, uses or diverts any oil or gas from the lease site without having valid legal authority to do so; or

(3) purchases, accepts, sells, transports, or conveys to another, any oil or gas knowing or having reason to know that such oil or gas was stolen or unlawfully removed or diverted,

shall be liable for a penalty of up to $25,000 per violation for each day such violation continues.

Hearing

(e) No penalty under this section shall be assessed until the person charged with a violation has been given the opportunity for a hearing on the record.

Deduction of penalty from sums owed by United States

(f) The amount of any penalty under this section, as finally determined may be deducted from any sums owing by the United States to the person charged.

Compromise or reduction of penalties

(g) On a case-by-case basis the Secretary may compromise or reduce civil penalties under this section.

Notice

(h) Notice under this subsection (a) of this section shall be by personal service by an authorized representative of the Secretary or by registered mail. Any person may, in the manner prescribed by the Secretary, designate a representative to receive any notice under this subsection.

Reasons on record for amount of penalty

(i) In determining the amount of such penalty, or whether it should be remitted or reduced, and in what amount, the Secretary shall state on the record the reasons for his determinations.

Review

(j) Any person who has requested a hearing in accordance with subsection (e) of this section within the time the Secretary has prescribed for such a hearing and who is aggrieved by a final order of the Secretary under this section may seek review of such order in the United States district court for the judicial district in which the violation allegedly took place. Review by the district court shall be only on the administrative record and not de novo. Such an action shall be barred unless filed within 90 days after the Secretary's final order.

Failure to pay penalty

(k) If any person fails to pay an assessment of a civil penalty under this chapter—

(1) after the order making the assessment has become a final order and if such person does not file a petition for judicial review of the order in accordance with subsection (j) of this section, or

(2) after a court in an action brought under subsection (j) of this section has entered a final judgment in favor of the Secretary,

the court shall have jurisdiction to award the amount assessed plus interest from the date of the expiration of the 90–day period referred to in subsection (j) of this section. Judgment by the court shall include an order to pay.

Non-liability for leases automatically terminated

(*l*) No person shall be liable for a civil penalty under subsection (a) or (b) of this section for failure to pay any rental for any lease automatically terminated pursuant to section 188 of this title.

Pub.L. 97–451, Title I, § 109, Jan. 12, 1983, 96 Stat. 2454.

References in Text. This chapter, referred to in subsecs. (a)(1) and (k), was in the original "this Act", meaning Pub.L. 97–451, Jan. 12, 1983, 96 Stat. 2447, known as the Federal Oil and Gas Royalty Management Act of 1982, which enacted this chapter, amended sections 188 and 191 of this title, and enacted provisions set out as notes under sections 1701, 1714, and 1752 of this title. For complete classification of this Act to the Code, see Short Title note set out under section 1701 of this title and Tables volume.

Effective Date. Section applicable to oil and gas leases issued before, on, or after Jan. 12, 1983, except that in the case of a lease issued before such date, no provision of this section or any rule or regulation prescribed under this section to alter the express and specific provisions of such lease, see section 305 of Pub.L. 97–451, set out as a note under section 1701 of this title.

Legislative History. For legislative history and purpose of Pub.L. 97–451, see 1982 U.S.C0de Cong. and Admin.News, p. 4268.

§ 1720. Criminal penalties

Any person who commits an act for which a civil penalty is provided in section 1719(d) of this title shall, upon conviction, be punished by a fine of not more than $50,000, or by imprisonment for not more than 2 years, or both.

Pub.L. 97–451, Title I, § 110, Jan. 12, 1983, 96 Stat. 2455.

UNITED STATES CODE

TITLE 42 PUBLIC HEALTH AND WELFARE

NATIONAL ENVIRONMENTAL POLICY ACT OF 1969 (as amended)

(42 U.S.C.A. §§ 4321–61)

§ 4321. Congressional declaration of purpose

The purposes of this chapter are: To declare a national policy which will encourage productive and enjoyable harmony between man and his environment; to promote efforts which will prevent or eliminate damage to the environment and biosphere and stimulate the health and welfare of man; to enrich the understanding of the ecological systems and natural resources important to the Nation; and to establish a Council on Environmental Quality.

Pub.L. 91–190, § 2, Jan. 1, 1970, 83 Stat. 852.

SUBCHAPTER I—POLICIES AND GOALS

§ 4331. Congressional declaration of national environmental policy

Creation and maintenance of conditions under which man and nature can exist in productive harmony

(a) The Congress, recognizing the profound impact of man's activity on the interrelations of all components of the natural environment, particularly the profound influences of population growth, high-density urbanization, industrial expansion, resource exploitation, and new and expanding technological advances and recognizing further the critical importance of restoring and maintaining environmental quality to the overall welfare and development of man, declares that it is the continuing policy of the Federal Government, in cooperation with State and local governments, and other concerned public and private organizations, to use all practicable means and measures, including financial and technical assistance, in a manner calculated to foster and promote the general welfare, to create and maintain conditions under which man and nature can exist in productive harmony, and fulfill the social, economic, and other requirements of present and future generations of Americans.

Continuing responsibility of Federal Government to use all practicable means to improve and coordinate Federal plans, functions, programs, and resources

(b) In order to carry out the policy set forth in this chapter, it is the continuing responsibility of the Federal Government to use all practicable means, consistent with other essential considerations of national policy, to improve and coordinate Federal plans, functions, programs, and resources to the end that the Nation may—

(1) fulfill the responsibilities of each generation as trustee of the environment for succeeding generations;

(2) assure for all Americans safe, healthful, productive, and esthetically and culturally pleasing surroundings;

(3) attain the widest range of beneficial uses of the environment without degradation, risk to health or safety, or other undesirable and unintended consequences;

(4) preserve important historic, cultural, and natural aspects of our national heritage, and maintain, wherever possible, an environment which supports diversity and variety of individual choice;

(5) achieve a balance between population and resource use which will permit high standards of living and a wide sharing of life's amenities; and

(6) enhance the quality of renewable resources and approach the maximum attainable recycling of depletable resources.

Responsibility of each person to contribute to preservation and enhancement of environment

(c) The Congress recognizes that each person should enjoy a healthful environment and that each person has a responsibility to contribute to the preservation and enhancement of the environment.

Pub.L. 91–190, Title I, § 101, Jan. 1, 1970, 83 Stat. 852.

§ 4332. Cooperation of agencies; reports; availability of information; recommendations; international and national coordination of efforts

The Congress authorizes and directs that, to the fullest extent possible: (1) the policies, regulations, and public laws of the United States shall be interpreted and administered in accordance with the policies set forth in this chapter, and (2) all agencies of the Federal Government shall—

(A) utilize a systematic, interdisciplinary approach which will insure the integrated use of the natural and social sciences and the environmental design arts in planning and in decisionmaking which may have an impact on man's environment;

(B) identify and develop methods and procedures, in consultation with the Council on Environmental Quality established by subchapter II of this chapter, which will insure that presently unquantified environmental amenities and values may be given appropriate consideration in decisionmaking along with economic and technical considerations;

(C) include in every recommendation or report on proposals for legislation and other major Federal actions significantly affecting the quality of the human environment, a detailed statement by the responsible official on—

    (i) the environmental impact of the proposed action,

    (ii) any adverse environmental effects which cannot be avoided should the proposal be implemented,

    (iii) alternatives to the proposed action,

    (iv) the relationship between local short-term uses of man's environment and the maintenance and enhancement of long-term productivity, and

    (v) any irreversible and irretrievable commitments of resources which would be involved in the proposed action should it be implemented.

Prior to making any detailed statement, the responsible Federal official shall consult with and obtain the comments of any Federal agency which has jurisdiction by law or special expertise with respect to any environmental impact involved. Copies of such statement and the comments and views of the appropriate Federal, State, and local agencies, which are authorized to develop and enforce environmental standards, shall be made available to the President, the Council on Environmental Quality and to the public as provided by section 552 of Title 5, and shall accompany the proposal through the existing agency review processes;

    (D) Any detailed statement required under subparagraph (C) after January 1, 1970, for any major Federal action funded under a program of grants to States shall not be deemed to be legally insufficient solely by reason of having been prepared by a State agency or official, if:

    (i) the State agency or official has statewide jurisdiction and has the responsibility for such action,

    (ii) the responsible Federal official furnishes guidance and participates in such preparation,

    (iii) the responsible Federal official independently evaluates such statement prior to its approval and adoption, and

    (iv) after January 1, 1976, the responsible Federal official provides early notification to, and solicits the views of, any other State or any Federal land management entity of any action or any alternative thereto which may have significant impacts upon such State or affected Federal land management entity and, if there is any disagreement on such impacts, prepares a written assessment of such impacts and views for incorporation into such detailed statement.

The procedures in this subparagraph shall not relieve the Federal official of his responsibilities for the scope, objectivity, and content of the entire statement or of any other responsibility under this chapter; and further, this subparagraph does not affect the legal sufficiency of statements prepared by State agencies with less than statewide jurisdiction.[1]

    1. So in original.

(E) study, develop, and describe appropriate alternatives to recommended courses of action in any proposal which involves unresolved conflicts concerning alternative uses of available resources;

(F) recognize the worldwide and long-range character of environmental problems and, where consistent with the foreign policy of the United States, lend appropriate support to initiatives, resolutions, and programs designed to maximize international cooperation in anticipating and preventing a decline in the quality of mankind's world environment;

(G) make available to States, counties, municipalities, institutions, and individuals, advice and information useful in restoring, maintaining, and enhancing the quality of the environment;

(H) initiate and utilize ecological information in the planning and development of resource-oriented projects; and

(I) assist the Council on Environmental Quality established by subchapter II of this chapter.

Pub.L. 91–190, Title I, § 102, Jan. 1, 1970, 83 Stat. 853; Pub.L. 94–83, Aug. 9, 1975, 89 Stat. 424.

§ 4333.   Conformity of administrative procedures to national environmental policy

All agencies of the Federal Government shall review their present statutory authority, administrative regulations, and current policies and procedures for the purpose of determining whether there are any deficiencies or inconsistencies therein which prohibit full compliance with the purposes and provisions of this chapter and shall propose to the President not later than July 1, 1971, such measures as may be necessary to bring their authority and policies into conformity with the intent, purposes, and procedures set forth in this chapter.

Pub.L. 91–190, Title I, § 103, Jan. 1, 1970, 83 Stat. 854.

* * *

UNITED STATES CODE
TITLE 43 PUBLIC LANDS

SECRETARY OF INTERIOR—DELEGATION OF AUTHORITY

(43 U.S.C.A. § 2)

§ 2.   Duties concerning public lands

The Secretary of the Interior or such officer as he may designate shall perform all executive duties appertaining to the surveying and sale of the public lands of the United States, or in anywise respecting such public lands, and, also, such as relate to private claims of land, and the issuing of patents for all grants of land under the authority of the Government.

R.S. § 453; Feb. 18, 1875, c. 80, § 1, 18 Stat. 317; 1946 Reorg. Plan No. 3, § 403, eff. July 16, 1946, 11 F.R. 7876, 60 Stat. 1100.

RESERVATION OF MINERAL RIGHTS

(43 U.S.C.A. § 299)

§ 299.   Reservation of coal and mineral rights

General provisions

(a) All entries made and patents issued under the provisions of this subchapter shall be subject to and contain a reservation to the United States of all the coal and other minerals in the lands so entered and patented, together with the right to prospect for, mine, and remove the same. The coal and other mineral deposits in such lands shall be subject to disposal by the United States in accordance with the provisions of the coal and mineral land laws in force at the time of such disposal. Any person qualified to locate and enter the coal or other mineral deposits, or having the right to mine and remove the same under the laws of the United States, shall have the right at all times to enter upon the lands entered or patented, as provided by this subchapter, for the purpose of prospecting for coal or other mineral therein, provided he shall not injure, damage, or destroy the permanent improvements of the entryman or patentee, and shall be liable to and shall compensate the entryman or patentee for all damages to the crops on such lands by reason of such prospecting. Any person who has acquired from the United States the coal or other mineral deposits in any such land, or the right to mine and remove the same, may reenter and occupy so much of the surface thereof as may be required for all purposes reasonably incident to the mining or removal of the coal or other minerals, first, upon securing the written consent or waiver of the homestead entryman or patentee; second, upon payment of the damages to crops or other tangible improvements to the owner thereof, where agree-

362

ment may be had as to the amount thereof; or, third, in lieu of either of the foregoing provisions, upon the execution of a good and sufficient bond or undertaking to the United States for the use and benefit of the entryman or owner of the land, to secure the payment of such damages to the crops or tangible improvements of the entryman or owner, as may be determined and fixed in an action brought upon the bond or undertaking in a court of competent jurisdiction against the principal and sureties thereon, such bond or undertaking to be in form and in accordance with rules and regulations prescribed by the Secretary of the Interior and to be filed with and approved by the officer designated by the Secretary of the Interior of the local land office of the district wherein the land is situate, subject to appeal to the Secretary of the Interior or such officer as he may designate: *Provided*, That all patents issued for the coal or other mineral deposits herein reserved shall contain appropriate notations declaring them to be subject to the provisions of this subchapter with reference to the disposition, occupancy, and use of the land as permitted to an entryman under this subchapter.

* * *

Dec. 29, 1916, c. 9, § 9, 39 Stat. 864; Oct. 28, 1921, c. 114, § 1, 42 Stat. 208; Mar. 3, 1925, c. 462, 43 Stat. 1145; 1946 Reorg. Plan No. 3, § 403, eff. July 16, 1946, 11 F.R. 7876, 60 Stat. 1100, as amended April 16, 1993, Pub.L. 103–23, § 1(a), (b), 107 Stat. 60, 65.

TAYLOR GRAZING ACT OF 1934 (as amended)

(43 U.S.C.A. §§ 315–315r)

§ 315. Grazing districts; establishment; restrictions; prior rights; rights-of-way; hearing and notice; hunting or fishing rights

In order to promote the highest use of the public lands pending its final disposal, the Secretary of the Interior is authorized, in his discretion, by order to establish grazing districts or additions thereto and/or to modify the boundaries thereof, of vacant, unappropriated, and unreserved lands from any part of the public domain of the United States (exclusive of Alaska), which are not in national forests, national parks and monuments, Indian reservations, revested Oregon and California Railroad grant lands, or revested Coos Bay Wagon Road grant lands, and which in his opinion are chiefly valuable for grazing and raising forage crops: *Provided,* That no lands withdrawn or reserved for any other purpose shall be included in any such district except with the approval of the head of the department having jurisdiction thereof. Nothing in this chapter shall be construed in any way to diminish, restrict, or impair any right which has been heretofore or may be hereafter initiated under existing law validly affecting the public lands, and which is maintained pursuant to such law except as otherwise expressly provided in this chapter, nor to affect any land heretofore or hereafter surveyed which, except for the provisions of this chapter, would be a part of any grant to any State, nor as limiting or restricting the power or authority of any State as to matters within its jurisdiction. Whenever any grazing district is established pursuant to this chapter, the Secretary shall grant to owners of land adjacent to such district, upon application of any such owner, such rights-of-way over the lands included in such district for stock-driving purposes as may be necessary for the convenient access by any such owner to marketing facilities or to lands not within such district owned by such person or upon which such person has stock-grazing rights. * * * Nothing in this chapter shall be construed as in any way altering or restricting the right to hunt or fish within a grazing district in accordance with the laws of the United States or of any State, or as vesting in any permittee any right whatsoever to interfere with hunting or fishing within a grazing district.

June 28, 1934, c. 865, § 1, 48 Stat. 1269; June 26, 1936, c. 842, Title I, § 1, 49 Stat. 1976; May 28, 1954, c. 243, § 2, 68 Stat. 151.

§ 315a.   Protection, administration, regulation, and improvement of districts; rules and regulations; study of erosion and flood control; offenses

The Secretary of the Interior shall make provision for the protection, administration, regulation, and improvement of such grazing districts as may be created under the authority of section 315 of this title, and he shall make such rules and regulations and establish such service, enter into such cooperative agreements, and do any and all things necessary to accomplish the purposes of this chapter and to insure the objects of such grazing districts, namely, to regulate their occupancy and use, to preserve the land and its resources from destruction or unnecessary injury, to provide for the orderly use, improvement, and development of the range; and the Secretary of the Interior is authorized to continue the study of erosion and flood control and to perform such work as may be necessary amply to protect and rehabilitate the areas subject to the provisions of this chapter, through such funds as may be made available for that purpose, and any willful violation of the provisions of this chapter or of such rules and regulations thereunder after actual notice thereof shall be punishable by a fine of not more than $500.

June 28, 1934, c. 865, § 2, 48 Stat. 1270.

§ 315b.   Grazing permits; fees; vested water rights; permits not to create right in land

The Secretary of the Interior is authorized to issue or cause to be issued permits to graze livestock on such grazing districts to such bona fide settlers, residents, and other stock owners as under his rules and regulations are entitled to participate in the use of the range, upon the payment annually of reasonable fees in each case to be fixed or determined from time to time in accordance with governing law. * * * Preference shall be given in the issuance of grazing permits to those within or near a district who are landowners engaged in the livestock business, bona fide occupants or settlers, or owners of water or water rights, as may be necessary to permit the proper use of lands, water or water rights owned, occupied, or leased by them, except that until July 1, 1935, no preference shall be given in the issuance of such permits to any such owner, occupant, or settler, whose rights were required between January 1, 1934, and December 31, 1934, both dates, inclusive, except that no permittee complying with the rules and regulations laid down by the Secretary of the Interior shall be denied the renewal of such permit, if such denial will impair the value of the grazing unit of the permittee, when such unit is pledged as security for any bona fide loan. Such permits shall be for a period of not more than ton years, subject to the preference right of the permittees to renewal in the discretion of the Secretary of the Interior, who shall specify from time to time numbers of stock and seasons of use. During periods of range depletion due to severe drought or other natural causes, or in case of a general epidemic of disease, during the life of the permit, the Secretary of the Interior is authorized, in his discretion, to remit, reduce, refund in whole or in part, or authorize postponement of payment of grazing fees for such depletion period so long as the emergency exists: *Provided further,* That nothing in this subchapter shall be construed or administered in any way to diminish or impair any right to the possession and use of water for mining, agriculture, manufacture, or other purposes which has heretofore vested or accrued under existing law validly affecting the public lands or which may be hereafter initiated or acquired and maintained in accordance with such law. So far as consistent with the purposes and provisions of this subchapter, grazing privileges recognized and acknowledged shall be adequately safeguarded, but the creation of a grazing district or the issuance of a permit pursuant to the provisions of this subchapter shall not create any right, title, interest, or estate in or to the lands.

June 28, 1934, c. 865, § 3, 48 Stat. 1270; Aug. 6, 1947, c. 507, § 1, 61 Stat. 790; as amended Oct. 21, 1976, Pub.L. 94–579, Title IV, § 401(b)(3), 90 Stat. 2773.

§ 315c. Fences, wells, reservoirs, and other improvements; construction; permits; partition fences

Fences, wells, reservoirs, and other improvements necessary to the care and management of the permitted livestock may be constructed on the public lands within such grazing districts under permit issued by the authority of the Secretary, or under such cooperative arrangement as the Secretary may approve. Permittees shall be required by the Secretary of the Interior to comply with the provisions of law of the State within which the grazing district is located with respect to the cost and maintenance of partition fences. No permit shall be issued which shall entitle the permittee to the use of such improvements constructed and owned by. a prior occupant until the applicant has paid to such prior occupant the reasonable value of such improvements to be determined under rules and regulations of the Secretary of the Interior. The decision of the Secretary in such cases is to be final and conclusive.

June 28, 1934, c. 865, § 4, 48 Stat. 1271.

§ 315d. Grazing stock for domestic purposes; use of natural resources

The Secretary of the Interior shall permit, under regulations to be prescribed by him, the free grazing within such districts of livestock kept for domestic purposes; and provided that so far as authorized by existing law or laws hereinafter enacted, nothing contained in this chapter shall prevent the use of timber, stone, gravel, clay, coal, and other deposits by miners, prospectors for mineral, bona fide settlers and residents, for firewood, fencing, buildings, mining, prospecting, and domestic purposes within areas subject to the provisions of this chapter.

June 28, 1934, c. 865, § 5, 48 Stat. 1271.

§ 315e. Rights-of-way; development of mineral resources

Nothing contained in this chapter shall restrict the acquisition, granting or use of permits or rights-of-way within grazing districts under existing law; or ingress or egress over the public lands in such districts for all proper and lawful purposes; and nothing contained in this chapter shall restrict prospecting, locating, developing, mining, entering, leasing, or patenting the mineral resources of such districts under law applicable thereto.

June 28, 1934, c. 865, § 6, 48 Stat. 1272.

§ 315f. Homestead entry within district or withdrawn lands; classification; preferences

The Secretary of the Interior is authorized, in his discretion, to examine and classify any lands withdrawn or reserved by Executive order of November 26, 1934 (numbered 6910), and amendments thereto, and Executive order of February 5, 1935 (numbered 6964), or within a grazing district, which are more valuable or suitable for the production of agricultural crops than for the production of native grasses and forage plants, or more valuable or suitable for any other use than for the use provided for under this subchapter, or proper for acquisition in satisfaction of any outstanding lien, exchange or script rights or land grant, and to open such lands to entry, selection, or location for disposal in accordance with such classification under applicable public-land laws, except that homestead entries shall not be allowed for tracts exceeding three hundred and twenty acres in area. Such lands shall not be subject to disposition, settlement, or occupation until after the same have been classified and opened to entry: *Provided,* That locations and entries under the mining laws including the Act of February 25, 1920, as amended [30 U.S.C.A. § 181 et seq.], may be made upon such withdrawn and reserved areas without regard to classification and without restrictions or limitation by any provision of this chapter. Where such lands are located within grazing districts reasonable notice shall be given by the Secretary of the Interior to any grazing permittee of such lands. The applicant, after his entry, selection, or location is allowed, shall be entitled to the possession and use of such lands: *Provided,* That upon the application of any applicant qualified to make entry, selection, or location, under the public-land laws, filed in the land office of the proper district, the Secretary of the Interior shall cause any tract to be classified, and such application, if allowed by the Secretary of the Interior, shall entitle the applicant to a preference right to enter, select, or locate such lands if opened to entry as herein provided.

June 28, 1934, c. 865, § 7, 48 Stat. 1272; June 26, 1936, c. 842, Title I, § 2, 49 Stat. 1976.

§ 315h. Cooperation with associations, land officials, and agencies engaged in conservation or propagation of wild life; local hearings on appeals; acceptance and use of contributions

The Secretary of the Interior shall provide, by suitable rules and regulations, for cooperation with local associations of stockmen, State land officials, and official State agencies engaged in conservation or propagation of wild life interested in the use of the grazing districts. The Secretary of the Interior shall provide by appropriate rules and regulations for local hearings on appeals from the decisions of the administrative officer in charge in a manner similar to the procedure in the land department. * * *

June 28, 1934, c. 865, § 9, 48 Stat. 1273; June 19, 1948, c. 548, § 2, 62 Stat. 533.

§ 315i. Disposition of moneys received; availability for improvements

Except as provided in sections 315h and 315j of this title, all moneys received under the authority of this subchapter shall be deposited in the Treasury of the United States as miscellaneous receipts, but the following proportions of the moneys so received shall be distributed as follows: (a) 12½ per centum of the moneys collected as grazing fees under section 315b of this title during any fiscal year shall be paid at the end thereof by the Secretary of the Treasury to the State in which the grazing districts producing such moneys are situated, to be expended as the State legislature of such State may prescribe for the benefit of the county or counties in which the grazing districts producing such moneys are situated: * * *

June 28, 1934, ch. 865, § 10, 48 Stat. 1273; June 26, 1936, ch. 842, Title I, § 4, 49 Stat. 1978; Aug. 6, 1947, ch. 507, § 2, 61 Stat. 790; as amended Oct. 21, 1976, Pub.L. 94–579, Title IV, § 401(b)(2), 90 Stat. 2773.

* * *

§ 315k. Cooperation with governmental departments; coordination of range administration

The Secretary of the Interior is hereby authorized to cooperate with any department of the Government in carrying out the purposes of this subchapter and in the coordination of range administration, particularly where the same stock grazes part time in a grazing district and part time in a national forest or other reservation.

June 28, 1934, c. 865, § 12, 48 Stat. 1274.

§ 315l. Lands under national-forest administration

The President of the United States is authorized to reserve by proclamation and place under national-forest administration in any State where national forests may be created or enlarged by Executive order any unappropriated public lands lying within watersheds forming a part of the national forests which, in his opinion, can best be administered in connection with existing national-forest administration units, and to place under the Interior Department administration any lands within national forests, principally valuable for grazing, which, in his opinion, can best be administered under the provisions of this chapter: *Provided,* That such reservations or transfers shall not interfere with legal rights acquired under any public-land laws so long as such rights are legally maintained. Lands placed under the national-forest administration under the authority of this chapter shall be subject to all the laws and regulations relating to national forests, and lands placed under the Interior Department administration shall be subject to all public-land laws and regulations applicable to grazing districts created under authority of this chapter. Nothing in this section shall be construed so as to limit the powers of the President (relating to reorganizations in the executive departments) granted by sections 124–132 of Title 5.

June 28, 1934, c. 865, § 13, 48 Stat. 1274.

§ 315m.   Lease of isolated or disconnected tracts for grazing; preferences

The Secretary of the Interior is further authorized, in his discretion, where vacant, unappropriated, and unreserved lands of the public domain are so situated as not to justify their inclusion in any grazing district to be established pursuant to sections 315–315g, 315h–315m, 315n, 315o and 315o–1 of this title, to lease any such lands for grazing purposes, upon such terms and conditions as the Secretary may prescribe: *Provided,* That preference shall be given to owners, homesteaders, lessees, or other lawful occupants of contiguous lands to the extent necessary to permit proper use of such contiguous lands, except, that when such isolated or disconnected tracts embrace seven hundred and sixty acres or less, the owners, homesteaders, lessees, or other lawful occupants of lands contiguous thereto or cornering thereon shall have a preference right to lease the whole of such tract, during a period of ninety days after such tract is offered for lease, upon the terms and conditions prescribed by the Secretary: *Provided further,* That when public lands are restored from a withdrawal, the Secretary may grant an appropriate preference right for a grazing lease, license, or permit to users of the land for grazing purposes under authority of the agency which had jurisdiction over the lands immediately prior to the time of their restoration.

June 28, 1934, c. 865, § 15, 48 Stat. 1275; June 26, 1936, c. 842, Title I, § 5, 49 Stat. 1978; May 28, 1954, c. 243, § 1, 68 Stat. 151.

§ 315m–1.   Lease of State, county, or privately owned lands; period of lease; rental

The Secretary of the Interior in his discretion is authorized to lease at rates to be determined by him any State, county, or privately owned lands chiefly valuable for grazing purposes and lying within the exterior boundaries of a grazing district when, in his judgment, the leasing of such lands will promote the orderly use of the district and aid in conserving the forage resources of the public lands therein: *Provided,* That no such leases shall run for a period of more than ten years and in no event shall the grazing fees paid the United States for the grazing privileges on any of the lands leased under the provisions of this section be less than the rental paid by the United States for any of such lands: *Provided further,* That nothing in this section shall be construed as authorizing the appropriation of any moneys except that moneys heretofore or hereafter appropriated for construction, purchase, and maintenance of range improvements within grazing districts, pursuant to the provisions of sections 315i and 315j of this title, may be made additionally available by Congress for the leasing of land under this section and sections 315m–2 to 315m–4 of this title.

June 23, 1938, c. 603, § 1, 52 Stat. 1033.

§ 315m–2. Same; administration of leased lands

The lands leased under sections 315m–1 to 315m–4 of this title shall be administered under the provisions of this chapter, commonly known as the Taylor Grazing Act.

June 23, 1938, c. 603, § 2, 52 Stat. 1033.

* * *

§ 315n. State police power not abridged

Nothing in this chapter shall be construed as restricting the respective States from enforcing any and all statutes enacted for police regulation, nor shall the police power of the respective States be, by this chapter, impaired or restricted, and all laws heretofore enacted by the respective States or any thereof, or that may hereafter be enacted as regards public health or public welfare, shall at all times be in full force and effect: *Provided, however,* That nothing in this section shall be construed as limiting or restricting the power and authority of the United States.

June 28, 1934, c. 865, § 16, 48 Stat. 1275.

* * *

DESERT LANDS ACT OF 1877 (as amended)

(43 U.S.C.A. §§ 321–39)

§ 321. Entry right generally; extent of right to appropriate waters

It shall be lawful for any citizen of the United States, or any person of requisite age "who may be entitled to become a citizen, and who has filed his declaration to become such" and upon payment of 25 cents per acre—to file a declaration under oath with the officer designated by the Secretary of the Interior of the land district in which any desert land is situated, that he intends to reclaim a tract of desert land not exceeding one-half section, by conducting water upon the same, within the period of three years thereafter: *Provided, however,* That the right to the use of water by the person so conducting the same, on or to any tract of desert land of three hundred and twenty acres shall depend upon bona fide prior appropriation; and such right shall not exceed the amount of water actually appropriated, and necessarily used for the purpose of irrigation and reclamation; and all surplus water over and above such actual appropriation and use, together with the water of all lakes, rivers, and other sources of water supply upon the public lands and not navigable, shall remain and be held free for the appropriation and use of the public for irrigation, mining, and manufacturing purposes subject to existing rights. Said declaration shall describe particularly said one-half section of land if surveyed, and, if unsurveyed, shall describe the same as nearly as possible without a survey. At any time within the period of three years after filing said declaration, upon making satisfactory proof to the officer designated by the Secretary of the Interior of the reclamation of said tract of land in the manner aforesaid, and upon the payment to such officer of the additional sum of $1 per acre for a tract of land not exceeding three hundred and twenty acres to any one person, a patent for the same shall be issued to him. Except as provided in section 3 of the Act of June 16, 1955, as amended, no person may make more than one entry under sections 321–323, 325 and 327–329 of this title. However, in that entry one or more tracts may be included, and the tracts so entered need not be contiguous. The aggregate acreage of desert land which may be entered by any one person under this section shall not exceed three hundred and twenty acres, and all the tracts entered by one person shall be sufficiently close to each other to be managed satisfactorily as an economic unit, as determined under rules and regulations issued by the Secretary of the Interior.

Mar. 3, 1877, c. 107, § 1, 19 Stat. 377; Aug. 30, 1890, c. 837, § 1, 26 Stat. 391; Mar. 3, 1891, c. 561, § 2, 26 Stat. 1096; Oct. 28, 1921, c. 114, § 1, 42 Stat. 208; Mar. 3, 1925, c. 462, 43 Stat. 1145; 1946 Reorg. Plan No. 3, § 403, eff. July 16, 1946, 11 F.R. 7876, 60 Stat. 1100; Aug. 14, 1958, Pub.L. 85–641, § 1, 72 Stat. 596.

§ 322. Desert lands defined; question how determined

All lands exclusive of timber lands and mineral lands which will not, without irrigation, produce some agricultural crop, shall be deemed desert lands, within the meaning of sections 321–323, 325 and 327–329 of this title, which fact shall be ascertained by proof of two or more credible witnesses under oath, whose affidavits shall be filed in the land office in which said tract of land may be situated.

The determination of what may be considered desert land shall be subject to the decision and regulation of the Secretary of the Interior or such officer as he may designate.

Mar. 3, 1877, c. 107, §§ 2, 3, 19 Stat. 377; 1946 Reorg. Plan No. 3, § 403, eff. July 16, 1946, 11 F.R. 7876, 60 Stat. 1100.

§ 323. Application to certain States

Sections 321–323, 325 and 327–329 of this title shall only apply to and take effect in the States of California, Colorado, Oregon, Nevada, Washington, Idaho, Montana, Utah, Wyoming, Arizona, New Mexico, and North and South Dakota.

Mar. 3, 1877, c. 107, §§ 3, 8, 19 Stat. 377; Mar. 3, 1891, c. 561, § 2, 26 Stat. 1096; Jan. 6, 1921, c. 12, 41 Stat. 1086.

§ 324. Assignment of entries

No assignment after March 28, 1908, of an entry made under sections 321–323, 325 and 327–329 of this title shall be allowed or recognized, except it be to an individual who is shown to be qualified to make entry under said sections of the land covered by the assigned entry, and such assignments may include all or part of an entry; but no assignment to or for the benefit of any corporation or association shall be authorized or recognized.

Mar. 28, 1908, c. 112, § 2, 35 Stat. 52.

§ 325. Resident citizenship of State as qualification for entry

Excepting in the State of Nevada, no person shall be entitled to make entry of desert lands unless he be a resident citizen of the State or Territory in which the land sought to be entered is located.

Mar. 3, 1877, c. 107, § 8, as added Mar. 3, 1891, c. 561, § 2, 26 Stat. 1096, and amended Jan. 6, 1921, c. 12, 41 Stat. 1086.

§ 326. Unsurveyed lands not subject to entry; preferential right of entry after survey

From and after March 28, 1908, the right to make entry of desert lands under the provisions of sections 321–323, 325, and 327–329 of this title, shall be restricted to surveyed public lands of the character contemplated by said sections, and no such entries of unsurveyed lands shall be allowed or made of record: *Provided, however,* That any individual qualified to make entry of desert lands under said sections who has, prior to survey, taken possession of a tract of unsurveyed desert land not exceeding in area three hundred and twenty acres in compact form, and has reclaimed or has in good faith commenced the work of reclaiming the same, shall have the preference right to make entry of such tract under said sections, in conformity with the public land surveys, within ninety days after the filing of the approved plat of survey in the district land office.

Mar. 28, 1908, c. 112, § 1, 35 Stat. 52.

§ 327. Filing irrigation plan; association of entrymen

At the time of filing the declaration required in section 321 of this title the party shall also file a map of said land, which shall exhibit a plan showing the mode of contemplated irrigation, and which plan shall be sufficient to thoroughly irrigate and reclaim said land, and prepare it to raise ordinary agricultural crops, and shall also show the source of the water to be used for irrigation and reclamation. Persons entering or proposing to enter separate sections, or fractional parts of sections, of

371

desert lands, may associate together in the construction of canals and ditches for irrigating and reclaiming all of said tracts, and may file a joint map or maps showing their plan of internal improvements.

Mar. 3, 1877, c. 107, § 4, as added Mar. 3, 1891, c. 561, § 2, 26 Stat. 1096.

§ 328.   Expenditure and cultivation requirements

No land shall be patented to any person under sections 321–323, 325 and 327–329 of this title unless he or his assignors shall have expended in the necessary irrigation, reclamation, and cultivation thereof, by means of main canals and branch ditches, and in permanent improvements upon the land, and in the purchase of water rights for the irrigation of the same, at least $3 per acre of whole tract reclaimed and patented in the manner following: Within one year after making entry for such tract of desert land as aforesaid the party so entering shall expend not less than $1 per acre for the purposes aforesaid; and he shall in like manner expend the sum of $1 per acre during the second and also during the third year thereafter, until the full sum of $3 per acre is so expended. Said party shall file during each year with the officer designated by the Secretary of the Interior proof, by the affidavits of two or more credible witnesses, that the full sum of $1 per acre has been expended in such necessary improvements during such year, and the manner in which expended, and at the expiration of the third year a map or plan showing the character and extent of such improvements. If any party who has made such application shall fail during any year to file the testimony aforesaid the lands shall revert to the United States, and the 25 cents advanced payment shall be forfeited to the United States, and the entry shall be canceled. Nothing herein contained shall prevent a claimant from making his final entry and receiving his patent at an earlier date than hereinbefore prescribed, provided that he then makes the required proof of reclamation to the aggregate extent of $3 per acre: *Provided,* That proof be further required of the cultivation of one-eighth of the land.

Mar. 3, 1877, c. 107, § 5, as added Mar. 3, 1891, c. 561, § 2, 26 Stat. 1096 and amended 1946 Reorg. Plan No. 3, § 403, eff. July 16, 1946, 11 F.R. 7876, 60 Stat. 1100.

§ 329.   Issue of patent on final proof; citizenship requirement as to patentee; limit as to amount of holding

At any time after filing the declaration, and within the period of four years thereafter, upon making satisfactory proof to the officer designated by the Secretary of the Interior of the reclamation and cultivation of said land to the extent and cost and in the manner aforesaid, and substantially in accordance with the plans herein provided for, and that he or she is a citizen of the United States, and upon payment to such officer of the additional sum of $1 per acre for said land, a patent shall issue therefor to the applicant or his assigns; but no person or association of persons shall hold by assignment or otherwise prior to the issue of patent, more than three hundred and twenty acres of such arid or desert lands, but this section shall not apply to entries made or initiated prior to March 3, 1891: *Provided, however,* That additional proofs may be required at any time within the period prescribed by law, and that the claims or entries made under sections 321–323, 325 and 327–329 of this title shall be subject to contest, as provided by the law, relating to homestead cases, for illegal inception, abandonment, or failure to comply with the requirements of law, and upon satisfactory proof thereof shall be canceled, and the lands, and moneys paid therefor, shall be forfeited to the United States.

Mar. 3, 1877, c. 107, § 7, as added Mar. 3, 1891, c. 561, § 2, 26 Stat. 1096, and amended Oct. 28, 1921, c. 114, § 1, 42 Stat. 208; Mar. 3, 1925, c. 462, 43 Stat. 1145; 1946 Reorg. Plan No. 3, § 403, eff. July 16, 1946, 11 F.R. 7876, 60 Stat. 1100.

* * *

RECLAMATION ACT OF 1902 (as amended)

(43 U.S.C.A. §§ 371–431)

§ 371. **Definitions; "Secretary," "reclamation law," "reclamation fund," "project," and "division of a project"**

When used in this section and sections 376, 377, 412, 417, 433, 462, 466, 472, 478, 493, 494, 500, 501 and 526 of this title—

(a) The word "Secretary" means the Secretary of the Interior.

(b) The words "reclamation law" mean the Act of June 17, 1902 (32 Stat. 388), and all Acts amendatory thereof or supplementary thereto.

(c) The words "reclamation fund" mean the fund provided by the reclamation law.

(d) The word "project" means a Federal irrigation project authorized by the reclamation law.

(e) The words "division of a project" mean a substantial irrigable area of a project designated as a division by order of the Secretary.

Dec. 5, 1924, c. 4, § 4, subsec. A, 43 Stat. 701.

§ 372. **Water right as appurtenant to land and extent of right**

The right to the use of water acquired under the provisions of sections 372, 373, 381, 383, 391, 392, 411, 416, 419, 421, 431,432, 434, 439, 461, 491 and 498 of this title shall be appurtenant to the land irrigated, and beneficial use shall be the basis, the measure, and the limit of the right.

June 17, 1902, c. 1093, § 8, 32 Stat. 390.

§ 373. **General authority of the Secretary of the Interior**

The Secretary of the Interior is hereby authorized to perform any and all acts and to make such rules and regulations as may be necessary and proper for the purpose of carrying out the provisions of sections 372, 373, 381, 383, 391, 392, 411, 416, 419, 421, 431, 432, 434, 439, 461, 491 and 498 of this title into full force and effect.

June 17, 1902, c. 1093, § 10, 32 Stat. 390; Aug. 13, 1914, c. 247, § 15, 38 Stat. 690.

* * *

§ 374.   Sale of lands acquired in connection with irrigation project

Whenever in the opinion of the Secretary of the Interior any lands which have been acquired under the provisions of the Act of June 17, 1902 (32 Stat. 388), commonly called the "Reclamation Act" or under the provisions of any Act amendatory thereof or supplementary thereto, for any irrigation works contemplated by the reclamation law, are not needed for the purposes for which they were acquired, said Secretary of the Interior may cause said lands, together with the improvements thereon, to be appraised by three disinterested persons, to be appointed by him, and thereafter to sell the same for not less than the appraised value at public auction to the highest bidder, after giving public notice of the time and place of sale by posting upon the land and by publication for not less than thirty days in a newspaper of general circulation in the vicinity of the land.

Upon payment of the purchase price, the Secretary of the Interior is authorized by appropriate deed to convey all the right, title, and interest of the United States of, in, and to said lands to the purchaser at said sale, subject, however, to such reservations, limitations, or conditions as said Secretary may deem proper: *Provided,* That not over one hundred and sixty acres shall be sold to any one person.

The moneys derived from the sale of such lands shall be covered into the reclamation fund and be placed to the credit of the project for which such lands had been acquired.

Feb. 2, 1911, c. 32, §§ 1–3, 36 Stat. 895.

§ 375.   Sale of land improved at expense of reclamation fund

Whenever in the opinion of the Secretary of the Interior any public lands which have been withdrawn for or in connection with construction or operation of reclamation projects under the provisions of the Act of June 17, 1902, known as the Reclamation Act and Acts amendatory thereof and supplemental thereto, which are not otherwise reserved and which have been improved by and at the expense of the reclamation fund for administration or other like purposes, are no longer needed for the purposes for which they were withdrawn and improved, the Secretary of the Interior may cause said lands, together with the improvements thereon, to be appraised by three disinterested persons to be appointed by him, and thereafter sell the same, for not less than the appraised value, at public auction to the highest bidder, after giving public notice of the time and place of sale by posting upon the land and by publication for not less than thirty days in a newspaper of general circulation in the vicinity of the land, not less than one-fifth the purchase price shall be paid at the time of sale, and the remainder in not more than four annual payments with interest at 6 per centum per annum, payable annually, on deferred payments.

Upon payment of the purchase price the Secretary of the Interior is authorized, by appropriate patent, to convey all the right, title, and interest of the United States in and to said lands to the purchaser at said sale, subject, however, to such reservations, limitations, or conditions as said Secretary may deem proper: *Provided*, That not over one hundred and sixty acres shall be sold to any one person, and if said lands are irrigable under the project in which located they shall be sold subject to compliance by the purchaser with all the terms, conditions, and limitations of the reclamation law applicable to lands of that character: *Provided*, That the accepted bidder must, prior to issuance of patent, furnish satisfactory evidence that he or she is a citizen of the United States.

The moneys derived from the sale of such lands shall be covered into the reclamation fund and be placed to the credit of the project for which such lands had been withdrawn.

May 20, 1920, c. 192, §§ 1–3, 41 Stat. 605, 606.

* * *

§ 377a. Limitation on use of funds where organizations or individuals are in arrears on contract charges

No funds appropriated to the Bureau of Reclamation for operation and maintenance in this Act or in subsequent Energy and Water Development Appropriations Acts, except those derived from advances by water users, shall hereafter be used for the particular benefits of lands (a) within the boundaries of an irrigation district, (b) of any member of a water users' organization, or (c) of any individual when such district, organization, or individual is in arrears for more than twelve months in the payment of charges due under a contract entered into with the United States pursuant to laws administered by the Bureau of Reclamation.

Pub.L. 99–141, Title II, § 200, Nov. 1, 1985, 99 Stat. 570, Oct. 2, 1992, Pub.L. 102–377, Title II, 106 Stat. 1331.

* * *

§ 383. Vested rights and State laws unaffected by certain sections [commonly known as § 8]

Nothing in sections 372, 373, 381, 383, 391, 392, 411, 416, 419, 421, 431, 432, 434, 439, 461, 491 and 498 of this title shall be construed as affecting or intended to affect or to in any way interfere with the laws of any State or Territory relating to the control, appropriation, use, or distribution of water used in irrigation, or any vested right acquired thereunder, and the Secretary of the Interior, in carrying out the provisions of such sections, shall proceed in conformity with such laws, and nothing in such sections shall in any way affect any right of any State or of the Federal Government or of any landowner, appropriator, or user of water in, to, or from any interstate stream or the waters thereof.

June 17, 1902, c. 1093, § 8, 32 Stat. 390.

* * *

§ 389. Relocation of highways, railroads, transmission lines, etc., exchange of water, water rights or electric energy

The Secretary is authorized, in connection with the construction or operation and maintenance of any project, (a) to purchase or condemn suitable lands or interests in lands for relocation of highways, roadways, railroads, telegraph, telephone, or electric transmission lines, or any other properties whatsoever, the relocation of which in the judgment of the Secretary is necessitated by said construction or operation and maintenance, and to perform any or all work involved in said relocations on said lands or interests in lands, other lands or interests in lands owned and held by the United States in connection with the construction or operation and maintenance of said project, or properties not owned by the United States; (b) to enter into contracts with the owners of said properties whereby they undertake to acquire any or all property needed for said relocation, or to perform any or all work involved in said relocations; and (c) for the purpose of effecting completely said relocations, to convey or exchange Government properties acquired or improved under (a) above, with or without improvements, or other properties owned and held by the United States in connection with the construction or operation and maintenance of said project, or to grant perpetual easements therein or thereover. Grants or conveyances hereunder shall be by instruments executed by The Secretary without regard to provisions of law governing the patenting of public lands.

The Secretary is further authorized, for the purpose of orderly and economical construction or operation and maintenance of any project, to enter into such contracts for exchange or replacement of water, water rights, or electric energy or for the adjustment of water rights, as in his judgment are necessary and in the interests of the United States and the project.

Aug. 4, 1939. c. 418, § 14, 53 Stat. 1197.

§ 390. Utilization of dams and reservoir projects for irrigation purposes; additional construction; necessity of authorization; apportionment of cost; limitation

On and after December 22, 1944, whenever the Secretary of the Army determines, upon recommendation by the Secretary of the Interior that any dam and reservoir project operated under the direction of the Secretary of the Army may be utilized for irrigation purposes, the Secretary of the Interior is authorized to construct, operate, and maintain, under the provisions of the Federal reclamation laws (Act of June 17, 1902, 32 Stat. 388, and Acts amendatory thereof or supplementary thereto), such additional works in connection therewith as he may deem necessary for irrigation purposes. Such irrigation works may be undertaken only after a report and findings thereon have been made by the Secretary of the Interior as provided in said Federal reclamation laws and after subsequent specific: authorization of the Congress by an authorization Act; and, within the limits of the water users' repayment ability such report may be predicated on the allocation to irrigation of an appropriate portion of the cost of structures and facilities used for irrigation and other purposes. Dams and reservoirs operated under the direction of the Secretary of the Army may be utilized after December 22, 1944, for irrigation purposes only in conformity with the provisions of this section, but the foregoing requirement shall not prejudice lawful uses now existing: *Provided,* That this section shall not apply to any dam or reservoir heretofore constructed in whole or in part by the Army engineers, which provides conservation storage of water for irrigation purposes. In the case of any reservoir project constructed and operated by the Corps of Engineers, the Secretary of the Army is authorized to allocate water which was allocated in the project purpose for municipal and industrial water supply and which is not under contract for delivery, for such periods as he may deem reasonable, for the interim use for irrigation purposes of such storage until such storage is required for municipal and industrial water supply. No contracts for the interim use of such storage shall be entered into which would significantly affect then-existing uses of such storage.

Dec. 22, 1944, c. 665, § 8, 58 Stat. 891. As amended Nov. 17, 1986, Pub.L. 99–662, Title IX, § 931, 100 Stat. 4196.

§ 391.   Establishment of "reclamation fund"

All moneys received from the sale and disposal of public lands in Arizona, California, Colorado, Idaho, Kansas, Montana, Nebraska, Nevada, New Mexico, North Dakota, Oklahoma, Oregon, South Dakota, Utah, Washington, and Wyoming, beginning with the fiscal year ending June 30, 1901, including the surplus of fees and commissions in excess of allowances to officers designated by the Secretary of the Interior, and excepting the 5 per centum of the proceeds of the sales of public lands in the above States set aside by law for educational and other purposes, shall be, and the same are hereby, reserved, set aside, and appropriated as a special fund in the Treasury to be known as the "reclamation fund," to be used in the examination and survey for and the construction and maintenance of irrigation works for the storage, diversion, and development of waters for the reclamation of arid and semiarid lands in the said States and Territories, and in the State of Texas, American Samoa, Guam, the Northern Mariana Islands and the Virgin Islands, and for the payment of all other expenditures provided for in this Act.

June 17, 1902, c. 1093, § 1, 32 Stat. 388; June 12, 1906, c. 3288, 34 Stat. 259, as amended Aug. 27, 1986, Pub.L. 99–396, § 17, 100 Stat. 843; Oct. 28, 1921, c. 114, § 1, 42 Stat. 208; Mar. 3, 1925, c. 462, 43 Stat. 1145; 1946 Reorg. Plan No. 3, § 403, eff. July 16, 1946, 11 F.R. 7876, 60 Stat. 1100.

§ 392. Payments into reclamation fund of moneys received from entrymen and water-right applicants

All moneys received from entrymen or applicants for water rights shall be paid into the reclamation fund.

June 17, 1902, c. 1093, § 5, 32 Stat. 389.

* * *

§ 431. Limitation as to amount of water; qualifications of applicant

No right to the use of water for land in private ownership shall be sold for a tract exceeding one hundred and sixty acres to any one landowner, and no such sale shall be made to any landowner unless he be an actual bona fide resident on such land, or occupant thereof residing in the neighborhood of said land, and no such right shall permanently attach until all payments therefor are made.

June 17, 1902, c. 1093, § 5, 32 Stat. 389.

* * *

RECLAMATION REFORM ACT OF 1982

(43 U.S.C.A. §§ 390aa–390zz–1)

§ 390aa. Congressional declaration of purpose; short title

Sections 390aa to 390zz–1 of this title shall amend and supplement the Act of June 17, 1902, and Acts supplementary thereto and amendatory thereof (43 U.S.C. 371), hereinafter referred to as "Federal reclamation law". Sections 390aa to 390zz–1 of this title may be referred to as the "Reclamation Reform Act of 1982".

Pub.L. 97–293, Title II, § 201, Oct. 12, 1982, 98 Stat. 1263.

§ 390bb. Definitions

As used in sections 390aa to 390zz–1 of this title:

(1) The term "contract" means any repayment or water service contract between the United States and a district providing for the payment of construction charges to the United States including normal operation, maintenance, and replacement costs pursuant to Federal reclamation law.

(2) The term "district" means any individual or any legal entity established under State law which has entered into a contract or is eligible to contract with the Secretary for irrigation water.

(3)(A) The term "full cost" means an annual rate as determined by the Secretary that shall amortize the expenditures for construction properly allocable to irrigation facilities in service, including all operation and maintenance deficits funded, less payments, over such periods as may be required under Federal reclamation law or applicable contract provisions, with interest on both accruing from October 12, 1982, on costs outstanding at that date, or from the date incurred in the case of costs arising subsequent to October 12, 1982: *Provided,* That operation, maintenance, and replacement charges required under Federal reclamation law, including sections 390aa to 390zz–1 of this title, shall be collected in addition to the full cost charge.

* * *

(5) The term "irrigation water" means water made available for agricultural purposes from the operation of reclamation project facilities pursuant to a contract with the Secretary.

(6) The term "landholding" means total irrigable acreage of one or more tracts of land situated in one or more districts owned or operated under a lease which is served with irrigation water pursuant to a contract with the Secretary. In determining the extent of a landholding the Secretary shall add to any landholding held directly by a qualified or limited recipient that portion of any landholding held indirectly by such qualified or limited recipient which benefits that qualified or limited recipient in proportion to that landholding.

(7) The term "limited recipient" means any legal entity established under State or Federal law benefiting more than twenty-five natural persons.

(8) The term "project" means any reclamation or irrigation project, including incidental features thereof, authorized by Federal reclamation law, or constructed by the United States pursuant to such law, or in connection with which there is a repayment or water service contract executed by the United States pursuant to such law, or any project constructed by the Secretary through the Bureau of Reclamation for the reclamation of lands.

(9) The term "qualified recipient" means an individual who is a citizen of the United States or a resident alien thereof or any legal entity established under State or Federal law which benefits twenty-five natural persons or less.

(10) The term "recordable contract" means a contract between the Secretary and a landowner in writing capable of being recorded under State law providing for the sale or disposition of lands held in excess of the ownership limitations of Federal reclamation law including sections 390aa to 390zz–1 of this title.

(11) The term "Secretary" means the Secretary of the Interior.

Pub.L. 97–293, Title II, § 202, Oct. 12, 1982, 96 Stat. 1263; Pub.L. 99–514, § 2, Oct. 22, 1986, 100 Stat. 2095.

§ 390cc. New or amended contracts

Generally

(a) The provisions of sections 390aa to 390zz–1 of this title shall be applicable to any district which—

(1) enters into a contract with the Secretary subsequent to October 12, 1982;

(2) enters into any amendment of its contract with the Secretary subsequent to October 12, 1982, which enables the district to receive supplemental or additional benefits; or

(3) which amends its contract for the purpose of conforming to the provisions of sections 390aa to 390zz–1 of this title.

Amendment of existing contracts

(b) Any district which has an existing contract with the Secretary as of October 12, 1982, which does not enter into an amendment of such contract as specified in subsection (a) of this section shall be subject to Federal reclamation law in effect immediately prior to October 12, 1982, as that law is amended or supplemented by sections 209 through 230 of this title. Within a district that does not enter into an amendment of its contract with the Secretary within four and one-half years of October 12, 1982, irrigation water may be delivered to lands leased in excess of a landholding of one hundred and sixty acres only if full cost, as defined in section 390bb(3)(A) of this title, is paid for such water as is assignable to those lands leased in excess of such landholding of one hundred and sixty acres: *Provided,* That the interest rate used in computing full cost under this subsection shall be the same as provided in section 390ee(a)(3) of this title.

Election by qualified or limited recipients in districts electing not to conform

(c) In the absence of an amendment to a contract, as specified in subsection (a) of this section, a qualified recipient or limited recipient may elect to be subject to the provisions of sections 390aa to 390zz–1 of this title by executing an irrevocable election in a form approved by the Secretary to comply with sections 390aa to 390zz–1 of this title. The district shall thereupon deliver irrigation water to and collect from such recipient, for the credit of the United States, the additional charges required by sections 390aa to 390zz–1 of this title and assignable to the recipient making the election.

Consent of non-Federal party

(d) Amendments to contracts which are not required by the provisions of sections 390aa to 390zz–1 of this title shall not be made without the consent of the non-Federal party.

Pub.L. 97–293, Title II, § 203, Oct. 12, 1982, 96 Stat. 1264.

§ 390dd. Limitation on ownership

Except as provided in section 390ii of this title irrigation water may not be delivered to—

(1) a qualified recipient for use in the irrigation of lands owned by such qualified recipient in excess of nine hundred and sixty acres of class i lands or the equivalent thereof; or

(2) a limited recipient for the use in the irrigation of lands owned by such limited recipient in excess of six hundred and forty acres of class I hinds or the equivalent thereof; whether situated in one or more districts.

Pub.L. 97–293, Title II, § 204, Oct. 12, 1982, 96 Stat. 1265.

§ 390ee. Pricing

Delivery of irrigation water at full cost

(a) Notwithstanding any other provision of law, any contract with a district entered into by the Secretary as specified in section 390cc of this title, shall provide for the delivery of irrigation water at full cost as defined in section 390bb(3) of this title to:

(1) a landholding in excess of nine hundred and sixty acres of class I lands or the equivalent thereof for a qualified recipient,

(2) a landholding in excess of three hundred and twenty acres of class I land or the equivalent thereof for a limited recipient receiving irrigation water on or before October 1, 1981; and

(3) the entire landholding of a limited recipient not receiving irrigation water on or before October 1, 1981: *Provided,* That the interest rate used in computing full cost under this paragraph shall be determined by the Secretary of the Treasury on the basis of the arithmetic average of—

(A) the computed average interest rate payable by the Treasury upon its outstanding marketable public obligations which are neither due nor callable for redemption for fifteen years from the date of issuance; and

(B) the weighted average of market yields on all interest-bearing, marketable issues sold by the Treasury during the fiscal year preceding the fiscal year in which the expenditures are made, or October 12, 1982, for expenditures made before October 12, 1982.

Delivery of irrigation water at prior terms and conditions

(b) Any contract with a district entered into by the Secretary as specified in section 390cc of this title, shall provide for the delivery of irrigation water to lands not in excess of the landholdings described in subsection (a) of this section upon terms and conditions related to pricing established by the Secretary pursuant to Federal reclamation law in effect immediately prior to October 12, 1982, or, in the case of an amended contract, upon the terms and conditions established by such contract prior to the date of its amendment. However, the portion of any price established under this subsection which relates to operation and maintenance charges shall be established pursuant to section 390hh of this title.

Delivery of irrigation water to lands under recordable contracts

(c) Notwithstanding any extension of time of any recordable contract as provided in section 390ii(e) of this title, lands under recordable contract shall be eligible to receive irrigation water at less than full cost for a period not to exceed ten years from the date such recordable contract was executed by the Secretary in the case of contracts existing prior to October 12, 1982, or five years from the date such recordable contract was executed by the Secretary in the case of contracts entered into subsequent to October 12, 1982, or the time specified in section 390rr of this title for lands described in that section: *Provided,* That in no case shall the right to receive water at less than full cost under this subsection terminate sooner than eighteen months after the date on which the Secretary again commences the processing or the approval of the disposition of such lands.

Pub.L. 97–293, Title II, § 205, Oct. 12, 1982, 96 Stat. 1265.

§ 390ff. Certification of compliance

As a condition to the receipt of irrigation water for lands in a district which has contract as specified in section 390cc of this title, each landowner and lessee within such district shall furnish the district, in a form prescribed by the Secretary, a certificate that they are in compliance with the provisions of sections 390aa to 390zz–1 of this title including a statement of the number of acres leased, the term of any lease, and a certification that the rent paid reflects the reasonable value of the irrigation water to the productivity of the land. The Secretary may require any lessee to submit to him, for his examination, a complete copy of any such lease executed by each of the parties thereto.

Pub.L. 97–293, Title II, § 206, Oct. 12, 1982, 96 Stat. 1266.

§ 390gg. Equivalency

Upon the request of any district, the ownership and pricing limitations imposed by sections 390aa to 390zz–1 of this title shall apply to the irrigable lands classified within such district by the Secretary as having class I productive potential or the equivalent thereof in larger acreage of less productive potential, as determined by the Secretary, taking into account all factors which significantly affect productivity, including but not limited to topography, soil characteristics, length of growing season, elevation, adequacy of water supply, and crop adaptability.

Pub.L. 97–293, Title II, § 207, Oct. 12, 1982, 96 Stat. 1266.

§ 390hh. Operation and maintenance charges

Price adequate to recover charges

(a) The price of irrigation water delivered by the Secretary pursuant to a contract or an amendment to a contract with a district, as specified in section 390cc of this title, shall be at least sufficient to recover all operation and maintenance charges which the district is obligated to pay to the United States.

Modification of price

(b) Whenever a district enters into a contract or requests that its contract be amended as specified in section 390cc of this title, and each

year thereafter, the Secretary shall calculate such operation and maintenance charges and shall modify the price of irrigation water delivered
under the contract as necessary to reflect any changes in such costs by
amending the district's contract accordingly.

Districts not operating from Federal funds

(c) This section shall not apply to districts which operate and maintain
project facilities and finance the operation and maintenance thereof from
non-Federal funds.

Pub.L. 97–293, Title II, § 208, Oct. 12, 1982, 96 Stat. 1267.

§ 390ii. Disposition of excess lands

Disposal of lands in excess of ownership limitations within reasonable time

(a) Irrigation water made available in the operation of reclamation
project facilities may not be delivered for use in the irrigation of lands held
in excess of the ownership limitations imposed by Federal reclamation law,
including sections 390aa to 390zz–1 of this title, unless and until the
owners thereof shall have executed a recordable contract with the Secretary, in accordance with the terms and conditions required by Federal
reclamation law, requiring the disposal of their interest in such excess
lands within a reasonable time to be established by the Secretary. In the
case of recordable contracts entered into prior to October 12, 1982, such
reasonable time shall not exceed ten years after the recordable contract is
executed by the Secretary. In the case of recordable contracts entered into
after October 12, 1982, except as provided in section 390rr of this title,
such reasonable time shall not exceed five years after the recordable
contract is executed by the Secretary.

Continued delivery of irrigation water to lands held in excess of ownership limitations

(b) Lands held in excess of the ownership limitations imposed by
Federal reclamation law, including sections 390aa to 390zz–1 of this title,
which, on October 12, 1982, are, or are capable of, receiving delivery of
irrigation water made available by the operation of existing reclamation
project facilities may receive such deliveries only—

(1) if the disposal of the owner's interest in such lands is required
by an existing recordable contract with the Secretary, or

(2) if the owners of such lands have requested that a recordable
contract be executed by the Secretary.

Amendment of existing recordable contracts

(c) Recordable contracts existing on October 12, 1982, shall be amended at the request of the landowner to conform with the ownership limitations contained in sections 390aa to 390zz–1 of this title: *Provided,* That
the time period for disposal of excess lands specified in the existing

recordable contract shall not be extended except as provided in subsection (e) of this section.

Power of attorney requirement in contracts; exercise of power by Secretary

(d) Any recordable contract covering excess lands sales shall provide that a power of attorney shall vest in the Secretary to sell any excess lands not disposed of by the owners thereof within the period of time specified in the recordable contract. In the exercise of that power, the Secretary shall sell such lands through an impartial selection process only to qualified purchasers according to such reasonable rules and regulations as the Secretary may establish: *Provided,* That the Secretary shall recover for the owner the fair market value of the land unrelated to irrigation water deliveries plus the fair market value of improvements thereon.

Extension of time for disposal of excess lands

(e) In the event that the owner of any lands in excess of the ownership limitations of Federal reclamation law has heretofore entered into a recordable contract with the Secretary for the disposition of such excess lands and has been prevented from disposing of them because the Secretary may have withheld the processing or approval of the disposition of the lands (whether he may have been compelled to do so by court order or for other reasons), the period of time for the disposal of such lands by the owner thereof pursuant to the contract shall be extended from the date on which the Secretary again commences the processing or the approval of the disposition of such lands for a period which shall be equal to the remaining period of time under the recordable contract for the disposal thereof by the owner at the time the decision of the Secretary to withhold the processing or approval of such disposition first became effective.

Eligibility of excess lands for irrigation water after disposition

(f) Excess lands which have been or may be disposed of in compliance with Federal: reclamation law, including sections 390aa to 390zz–1 of this title, shall not be considered eligible to receive irrigation water unless—

(1) they are held by nonexcess owners; and

(2) in the case of disposals made after October 12, 1982, their title is burdened by a covenant prohibiting their sale, for a period of ten years after their original disposal to comply with Federal reclamation law, including sections 390aa to 390zz–1 of this title, for values exceeding the sum of the value of newly added improvements and the value of the land as increased by market appreciation unrelated to the delivery of irrigation water. Upon expiration of the terms of such covenant, the title to such lands shall be freed of the burden of any limitations on subsequent sale values which might otherwise be imposed by the operation of section 423e of this title.

Pub.L. 97–293, Title II, § 209, Oct. 12, 1982, 96 Stat. 1267.

§ 390jj. Water conservation

Implementation of program by non-Federal recipients

(a) The Secretary shall, pursuant to his authorities under otherwise existing Federal reclamation law, encourage the full consideration and incorporation of prudent and responsible water conservation measures in the operations of non-Federal recipients of irrigation water from Federal reclamation projects, where such measures are shown to be economically feasible for such non-Federal recipients.

Requirements of plan

(b) Each district that has entered into a repayment contract or water service contract pursuant to Federal reclamation law or the Water Supply Act of 1958, as amended (43 U.S.C. 390b), shall develop a water conservation plan which shall contain definite goals, appropriate water conservation measures, and a time schedule for meeting the water conservation objectives.

Pub.L. 97–293, Title II, § 210, Oct. 12, 1982, 96 Stat. 1268.

§ 390kk. Residency not required

Notwithstanding any other provision of law, irrigation water made available from the operation of reclamation project facilities shall not be withheld from delivery to any project lands for the reason that the owners, lessees, or operators do not live on or near them.

Pub.L. 97–293, Title II, § 211, Oct. 12, 1982, 96 Stat. 1269.

§ 390ll. Corps of Engineers projects

Ownership or pricing limitations or Federal reclamation laws not applicable

(a) Notwithstanding any other provision of law, neither the ownership or pricing limitation provisions nor the other provisions of Federal reclamation law, including sections 390aa to 390zz–1 of this title, shall be applicable to lands receiving benefits from Federal water resources projects constructed by the United States Army Corps of Engineers, unless—

(1) the project has, by Federal statute, explicitly been designated, made a part of, or integrated with a Federal reclamation project; or

(2) the Secretary, pursuant to his authority under Federal reclamation law, has provided project works for the control or conveyance of an agricultural water supply for the lands involved.

Payment of construction, operation, maintenance and administrative costs allocated to conservation or irrigation storage

(b) Notwithstanding any other provision of this section to the contrary, obligations that require water users, pursuant to contracts with the Secretary, to repay the share of construction costs and to pay the share of the operation and maintenance and contract administrative costs of a Corps of Engineers project which are allocated to conservation storage or irrigation storage shall remain in effect.

Pub.L. 97–293, Title II, § 212, Oct. 12, 1982, 96 Stat. 1269.

§ 390mm.   Repayment of construction charges

Ownership and pricing limitations inapplicable when repayment obligation has been discharged

(a) The ownership and full cost pricing limitations of sections 390aa to 390zz–1 of this title and the ownership limitations provided in any other provision of Federal reclamation law shall not apply to lands in a district after the obligation of a district for the repayment of the construction costs of the project facilities used to make project water available for delivery to such lands shall have been discharged by a district (or by a person within the district pursuant to a contract existing on October 12, 1982), by payment of periodic installments throughout a specified contract term, including individual or district accelerated payments where so provided in contracts existing on October 12, 1982.

Certification of freedom from ownership and pricing limitations

(b)(1) The Secretary shall provide, upon request of any owner of a landholding for which repayment has occurred, a certificate acknowledging that the landholding is free of the ownership or full cost pricing limitation of Federal reclamation law. Such certificate shall be in a form suitable for entry in the land records of the county in which such landholding is located.

(b)(2) Any certificate issued by the Secretary prior to October 12, 1982, acknowledging that the landholding is free of the acreage limitation of Federal reclamation law is hereby ratified.

Lump sum or accelerated repayment of construction costs

(c) Nothing in sections 390aa to 390zz–1 of this title shall be construed as authorizing or permitting lump sum or accelerated repayment of construction costs, except in the case of a repayment contract which is in effect upon October 12, 1982, which provides for such lump sum or accelerated repayment by an individual or district.

Pub.L. 97–293, Title II, § 213, Oct. 12, 1982, 96 Stat. 1269.

* * *

§ 390tt.   Contract required

Irrigation water temporarily made available from reclamation facilities in excess of ordinary quantities not otherwise storable for project purposes or at times when such irrigation water would not have been available without the operations of those facilities, may be used for irrigation, municipal, or industrial purposes only to the extent covered by a contract requiring payment for the use of such irrigation water, executed in accordance with the Reclamation Project Act of 1939 [43 U.S.C.A. § 485 et seq.], or other applicable provisions of Federal reclamation law.

Pub.L. 97–293, Title II, § 220, Oct. 12, 1982, 96 Stat. 1271.

§ 390uu. Waiver of sovereign immunity

Consent is given to join the United States as a necessary party defendant in any suit to adjudicate, confirm, validate, or decree the contractual rights of a contracting entity and the United States regarding any contract executed pursuant to Federal reclamation law. The United States, when a party to any suit, shall be deemed to have waived any right to plead that it is not amenable thereto by reason of its sovereignty, and shall be subject to judgments, orders, and decrees of the court having jurisdiction, and may obtain review thereof, in the same manner and to the same extent as a private individual under like circumstances. Any suit pursuant to this section may be brought in any United States district court in the State in which the land involved is situated.

Pub.L. 97–293, Title II, § 221, Oct. 12, 1982, 96 Stat. 1271.

* * *

§ 390ww. Administrative provisions

Existing Federal reclamation law

(a) The provisions of Federal reclamation law shall remain in full force and effect, except to the extent such law is amended by, or is inconsistent with, this subchapter.

Existing statutory exemptions from ownership or pricing limitations of Federal reclamation law

(b) Nothing in this subchapter shall repeal or amend any existing statutory exemptions from the ownership or pricing limitations of Federal reclamation law.

Regulations; collection of necessary data

(c) The Secretary may prescribe regulations and shall collect all data necessary to carry out the provisions of this subchapter and other provisions of Federal reclamation law.

Pub.L. 97–293, Title II, § 224(a)–(c), (e), Oct. 12, 1982, 96 Stat. 1272; as amended Pub.L. 100–203, Title V, § 5302(a), Dec. 22, 1987, 101 Stat. 1330–268, 1330–269; Pub.L. 103–437, § 16(a)(3), Nov. 2, 1994, 108 Stat. 4594; Pub.L. 104–66, Title I, § 1081(d), Dec. 21, 1995, 109 Stat. 721.

§ 390xx. Validation of contracts entered into prior to October 1, 1981

The provisions of any contract entered into prior to October 1, 1981, by the Secretary with a district, which define project or nonproject water, or describe the delivery of project water through nonproject facilities or nonproject water through project facilities to lands within the district, are hereby authorized and validated on the part of the United States.

Pub.L. 97–293, Title II, § 225, Oct. 12, 1982, 96 Stat. 1273.

§ 390yy. Leasing requirements

Notwithstanding any other provision of Federal reclamation law, including sections 390aa to 390zz–1 of this title, lands which receive irrigation water may be leased only if the lease instrument is—

(1) written; and

(2) for a term not to exceed ten years, including any exercisable options: *Provided, however,* That leases of lands for the production of perennial crops having an average life of more than ten years may be for periods of time equal to the average life of the perennial crop but in any event not to exceed twenty-five years.

Pub.L. 97–293, Title II, § 227, Oct. 12, 1982, 96 Stat. 1273.

* * *

CAREY ACT OF 1894 (as amended)

(43 U.S.C.A. §§ 641–48)

§ 641. Grant of desert land to States authorized

To aid the public-land States in the reclamation of the desert lands therein, and the settlement, cultivation and sale thereof in small tracts to actual settlers, the Secretary of the Interior with the approval of the President is, as of August 18, 1894, authorized and empowered, upon proper application of the State to contract and agree, from time to time, with each of the States in which there may be situated desert lands as defined by the Act approved March 3, 1877, and the Act amendatory thereof, approved March 3, 1891, binding the United States to donate, grant and patent to the State free of cost for survey or price such desert lands, not exceeding one million acres in each State, as the State may cause to be irrigated, reclaimed, occupied, and not less than twenty acres of each one hundred and sixty acre tract cultivated by actual settlers, as thoroughly as is required of citizens who may enter under the said desert-land law, within ten years from the date of approval by the Secretary of the Interior of the State's application for the segregation of such lands; and if actual construction of reclamation works is not begun within three years after the segregation of the lands or within such further period not exceeding three years, as shall be allowed by the Secretary of the Interior, the said Secretary of the Interior, in his discretion, may restore such lands to the public domain; and if the State fails, within ten years from the date of such segregation, to cause the whole or any part of the lands so segregated to be so irrigated and reclaimed, the Secretary of the Interior may, in his discretion, continue said segregation for a period not exceeding five years, or may, in his discretion, restore such lands not irrigated and reclaimed to the public domain upon the expiration of the ten-year period or of any extension thereof.

Before the application of any State is allowed or any contract or agreement is executed or any segregation of any of the land from the public domain is ordered by the Secretary of the Interior, the State shall file a map of the said land proposed to be irrigated which shall exhibit a plan showing the mode of the contemplated irrigation and which plan shall be sufficient to thoroughly irrigate and reclaim said land and prepare it to raise ordinary agricultural crops and shall also show the source of the water to be used for irrigation and reclamation.

* * *

Aug. 18, 1894, ch. 301, § 4, 28 Stat. 422; Mar. 3, 1901, ch. 853, 31 Stat. 1188; Jan. 6, 1921, ch. 10, 41 Stat. 1085; As amended Oct. 21, 1976, Pub.L. 94–579, Title VII, § 704(a), 90 Stat. 2792.

* * *

§ 642. Liens for expenses of reclamation

Under any law heretofore or hereafter enacted by any State, providing, for the reclamation of arid lands, in pursuance and acceptance of the terms of the grant made in section 641 of this title, a lien or liens is hereby authorized to be created by the State to which such lands are granted and by no other authority whatever, and when created shall be valid on and against the separate legal subdivisions of land reclaimed, for the actual cost and necessary expenses of reclamation and reasonable interest thereon from the date of reclamation until disposed of to actual settlers; and when an ample supply of water is actually furnished in a substantial ditch or canal, or by artesian wells or reservoirs, to reclaim a particular tract or tracts of such lands, then patents shall issue for the same to such State without regard to settlement or cultivation: *Provided,* That in no event, in no contingency, and under no circumstances shall the United States be in any manner directly or indirectly liable for any amount of any such lien or liability, in whole or in part.

June 11, 1896, c. 420, § 1, 29 Stat. 434.

* * *

MINING LAW OF 1866

(43 U.S.C.A. § 661)

§ 661. Appropriation of waters on public lands; rights-of-way for canals and ditches

Whenever, by priority of possession, rights to the use of water for mining, agricultural, manufacturing, or other purposes, have vested and accrued, and the same are recognized and acknowledged by the local customs, laws, and the decisions of courts, the possessors and owners of such vested rights shall be maintained and protected in the same; and the right of way for the construction of ditches and canals for the purposes herein specified is acknowledged and confirmed; but whenever any person, in the construction of any ditch or canal, injures or damages the possession of any settler on the public domain, the party committing such injury or damage shall be liable to the party injured for such injury or damage.

All patents granted, or preemption or homesteads allowed, shall be subject to any vested and accrued water rights, or rights to ditches and reservoirs used in connection with such water fights, as may have been acquired under or recognized by this section.

R.S. §§ 2339, 2340.

Amendment of Section

Pub.L. 94–579, Title VII, § 706(a), Oct. 21, 1976, 90 Stat. 2793, provided that effective on and after Oct. 21, 1976, insofar as applicable to the issuance of rights-of-way over, upon, under, and through the public lands and lands in the National Forest System this section is amended to read as follows:

"Whenever, by priority of possession, rights to the use of water for mining, agricultural, manufacturing, or other purposes, have vested and accrued, and the same are recognized and acknowledged by the local customs, laws, and the decisions of courts, the possessors and owners of such vested rights shall be maintained and protected in the same.

"All patents granted, or preemption or homesteads allowed, shall be subject to any vested and accrued water rights as may have been acquired under or recognized by this section."

* * *

MCCARRAN AMENDMENT OF 1952

(43 U.S.C.A. § 666)

§ 666. Suits for adjudication of water rights—Joinder of United States as defendant; costs

(a) Consent is given to join the United States as a defendant in any suit (1) for the adjudication of rights to the use of water of a river system or other source, or (2) for the administration of such rights, where it appears that the United States is the owner of or is in the process of acquiring water rights by appropriation under State law, by purchase, by exchange, or otherwise, and the United States is a necessary party to such suit. The United States, when a party to any such suit, shall (1) be deemed to have waived any right to plead that the State laws are inapplicable or that the United States is not amenable thereto by reason of its sovereignty, and (2) shall be subject to the judgments, orders, and decrees of the court having jurisdiction, and may obtain review thereof, in the same manner and to the same extent as a private individual under like circumstances: *Provided,* That no judgment for costs shall be entered against the United States in any such suit.

Service of summons

(b) Summons or other process in any such suit shall be served upon the Attorney General or his designated representative.

Joinder in suits involving use of interstate streams by State

(c) Nothing in this section shall be construed as authorizing the joinder of the United States in any suit or controversy in the Supreme Court of the United States involving the right of States to the use of the water of any interstate stream.

July 10, 1952 c. 651, Title II, § 208(a)–(c), 66 Stat. 560.

RECTANGULAR SURVEY OF PUBLIC LANDS

(43 U.S.C.A. §§ 751–75)

§ 751. Rules of survey

First. The public lands shall be divided by north and south lines run according to the true meridian, and by others crossing them at right angles, so as to form townships of six miles square, unless where the line of an Indian reservation, or of tracts of land surveyed or patented prior to May 18, 1796, or the course of navigable rivers, may render this impracticable; and in that case this rule must be departed from no further than such particular circumstances require.

Second. The corners of the townships must be marked with progressive numbers from the beginning; each distance of a mile between such corners must be also distinctly marked with marks different from those of the corners.

Third. The township shall be subdivided into sections, containing, as nearly as may be, six hundred and forty acres each, by running parallel lines through the same from east to west and from south to north at the distance of one mile from each other, and marking corners at the distance of each half mile. The sections shall be numbered, respectively, beginning with the number one in the northeast section and proceeding west and east alternately through the township with progressive numbers, until the thirty-six be completed.

Fourth. The deputy surveyors, respectively, shall cause to be marked on a tree near each corner established in the manner described, and within the section, the number of such section, and over it the number of the township within which such section may be; and the deputy surveyors shall carefully note, in their respective field books, the names of the corner trees marked and the numbers so made.

Fifth. Where the exterior lines of the townships which may be subdivided into sections or half-sections exceed, or do not extend six miles, the excess or deficiency shall be specially noted, and added to or deducted from the western and northern ranges of sections or half-sections in such township, according as the error may be in running the lines from east to west, or from north to south; the sections and half-sections bounded on the northern and western lines of such townships shall be sold as containing only the quantity expressed in the returns and plats respectively, and all others as containing the complete legal quantity.

Sixth. All lines shall be plainly marked upon trees, and measured with chains, containing two perches of sixteen and one-half feet each, subdivided into twenty-five equal links; and the chain shall be adjusted to a standard to be kept for that purpose.

Seventh. Every surveyor shall note in his field book the true situations of all mines, salt licks, salt springs, and mill-seats which come to his knowledge; all watercourses over which the line he runs may pass; and also the quality of the lands.

Eighth. These field books shall be returned to the Secretary of the Interior or such officer as he may designate, who shall cause therefrom a description of the whole lands surveyed to be made out and transmitted to the officers who may superintend the sales. He shall also cause a fair plat to be made of the townships and fractional parts of townships contained in the lands, describing the subdivisions thereof, and the marks of the corners. This plat shall be recorded in books to be kept for that purpose; and a copy thereof shall be kept open at the office of the Secretary of the Interior or of such agency as he may designate for public information and other copies shall be sent to the places of the sale, and to the Bureau of Land Management.

Derived from Act of May 18, 1796, 1 Stat. 465; R.S. § 2395; Mar. 3, 1925, c. 462, 43 Stat. 1144; 1946 Reorg. Plan No. 3, § 403, eff. July 16, 1946, 11 F.R. 7876, 60 Stat. 1100; Apr. 29, 1950, c. 134, § 1, 64 Stat. 92.

§ 751a.   Survey system extended to Alaska

The system of public land surveys is extended to the Territory of Alaska.

Mar. 3, 1899 c. 424, § 1, 30 Stat. 1098.

* * *

§ 752.   Boundaries and contents of public lands; how ascertained

The boundaries and contents of the several sections, half-sections, and quarter-sections of the public lands shall be ascertained in conformity with the following principles:

First. All the corners marked in the surveys, returned by the Secretary of the Interior or such agency as he may designate, shall be established as the proper corners of sections, or subdivisions of sections, which they were intended to designate; and the corners of half- and quarter-sections, not marked on the surveys, shall be placed as nearly as possible equidistant from two corners which stand on the same line.

Second. The boundary lines, actually run and marked in the surveys returned by the Secretary of the Interior or such agency as he may designate, shall be established as the proper boundary lines of the sections, or subdivisions, for which they were intended, and the length of such lines, as returned, shall be held and considered as the true length thereof. And the boundary lines which have not been actually run and marked shall be ascertained, by running straight lines from the established corners to the opposite corresponding corners; but in those portions of the fractional townships where no such opposite corresponding corners have been or can be fixed, the boundary lines shall be ascertained by running from the established corners due north and south or east and west lines, as the case may be, to the water-course, Indian boundary line, or other external boundary of such fractional township.

Third. Each section or subdivision of section, the contents whereof have been returned by the Secretary of the Interior or such agency as he may designate, shall be held and considered as containing the exact quantity expressed in such return; and the half sections and quarter sections, the contents whereof shall not have been thus returned, shall be held and considered as containing the one-half or the one-fourth part, respectively, of the returned contents of the section of which they may make part.

R.S. § 2396; Mar. 3, 1925, c. 462, 43 Stat. 1144; 1946 Reorg. Plan No. 403, eff. July 16, 1946, 11 F.R. 7876, 60 Stat. 1100.

* * *

§ 766. Geological surveys, extension of public surveys, expenses of subdividing

There shall be no further geological survey by the Government, unless authorized by law. The public surveys shall extend over all mineral lands; and all subdividing of surveyed lands into lots less than one hundred and sixty acres may be done by county and local surveyors at the expense of claimants; but nothing in this section contained shall require the survey of waste or useless lands.

R.S. § 2406.

§ 770. Rectangular mode of survey, departure from

The Secretary of the Interior may, by regulation, provide that departures may be made from the system of rectangular surveys whenever it is not feasible or economical to extend the rectangular surveys in the regular manner or whenever such departure would promote the beneficial use of lands.

R.S. § 2410; Apr. 29, 1950, c. 134, § 2, 64 Stat. 93.

* * *

§ 774. Protection of surveyor by marshal

Whenever the President is satisfied that forcible opposition has been offered, or is likely to be offered, to any surveyor or deputy surveyor in the discharge of his duties in surveying the public lands, it may be lawful for the President to order the marshal of the State or district, by himself or deputy, to attend such surveyor or deputy surveyor with sufficient force to protect such officer in the execution of his duty, and to remove force should any be offered.

R.S. § 2413.

* * *

GRANTS TO STATES

(43 U.S.C.A. §§ 851–73)

§ 851. Deficiencies in grants to State by reason of settlements, etc., on designated sections generally

Where settlements with a view to preemption or homestead have been, or shall hereafter be made, before the survey of the lands in the field, which are found to have been made on sections sixteen or thirty-six, those sections shall be subject to the claims of such settlers; and if such sections or either of them have been or shall be granted, reserved, or pledged for the use of schools or colleges in the State in which they lie, other lands of equal acreage are hereby appropriated and granted, and may be selected, in accordance with the provisions of section 852 of this title, by said State, in lieu of such as may be thus taken by preemption or homestead settlers. And other lands of equal acreage are also hereby appropriated and granted and may be selected, in accordance with the provisions of section 852 of this title, by said State where sections sixteen or thirty-six are, before title could pass to the State, included within any Indian, military, or other reservation, or are, before title could pass to the State, otherwise disposed of by the United States: *Provided,* That the selection of any lands under this section in lieu of sections granted or reserved to a State shall be a waiver by the State of its right to the granted or reserved sections. And other lands of equal acreage are also appropriated and granted, and may be selected, in accordance with the provisions of section 852 of this title, by said State to compensate deficiencies for school purposes, where sections sixteen or thirty-six are fractional in quantity, or where one or both are wanting by reason of the township being fractional, or from any natural cause whatever. And it shall be the duty of the Secretary of the Interior, without awaiting the extension of the public surveys, to ascertain and determine, by protraction or otherwise, the number of townships that will be included within such Indian, military, or other reservations, and thereupon the State shall be entitled to select indemnity lands to the extent of section for section in lieu of sections therein which have been or shall be granted, reserved, or pledged; but such selections may not be made within the boundaries of said reservation: *Provided, however,* That nothing in this section contained shall prevent any State from awaiting the extinguishment of any such military, Indian, or other reservation and the restoration of the lands therein embraced to the public domain and then taking the sections sixteen and thirty-six in place therein.

R.S. § 2275; Feb. 28, 1891, c. 384, 26 Stat. 796; Aug. 27, 1958, Pub.L. 85–771, § 1, 72 Stat. 928; June 24, 1966, Pub.L. 89–470, § 1, 80 Stat. 220.

§ 852. Selections to supply deficiencies of school lands

(a) The lands appropriated by section 851 of this title shall be selected from any unappropriated, surveyed or unsurveyed public lands within the State where such losses or deficiencies occur subject to the following restrictions:

(1) No lands mineral in character may be selected by a State except to the extent that the selection is being made as indemnity for mineral lands lost to the State because of appropriation before title could pass to the State;

(2) No lands on a known geologic structure of a producing oil or gas field may be selected except to the extent that the selection is being made as indemnity for lands on such a structure lost to the State because of appropriation before title could pass to the State; and

(3) Land subject to a mineral lease or permit may be selected if none of the land subject to that lease or permit is in a producing or producible status, subject, however, to the restrictions and conditions of the preceding and following paragraphs of this subsection.

(4) If a selection is consummated as to a portion but not all of the lands subject to any mineral lease or permit, then, as to such portion and for so long only as such lease or permit or any lease issued pursuant to such permit shall remain in effect, there shall be automatically reserved to the United States the mineral or minerals for which the lease or permit was issued, together with such further rights as may be necessary for the full and complete enjoyment of all rights, privileges and benefits under or with respect to the lease or permit: *Provided, however,* That after approval of the selection the Secretary of the Interior shall determine what portion of any rents and royalties accruing thereafter which may be paid under the lease or permit is properly applicable to that portion of the land subject to the lease or permit selected by the State, the portion applicable being determined by applying to the sum of the rents and royalties the same ratio as that existing between the acreage selected by the State and the total acreage subject to the lease or permit; of the portion applicable to the selected land 90 per centum shall be paid to the State by the United States annually and 10 per centum shall be deposited in the Treasury of the United States as miscellaneous receipts.

(5) If a selection is consummated as to all of the lands subject to any mineral lease or permit or if, where the selecting State has previously acquired title to a portion of the lands subject to a mineral lease or permit, a selection is consummated as to all of the remaining lands subject to that lease or permit, then and upon condition that the United States shall retain all rents and royalties theretofore paid and that the lessee or permittee shall have and may enjoy under and with respect to that lease or permit all the rights, privileges, and benefits which he would have had or might have enjoyed had the selection not

395

been made and approved, the State shall succeed to all the rights of the United States under the lease or permit as to the mineral or minerals covered thereby, subject, however, to all obligations of the United States under and with respect to that lease or permit.

* * *

(d)(1) The term "unappropriated public lands" as used in this section shall include, without otherwise affecting the meaning thereof, lands withdrawn for coal, phosphate, nitrate, potash, oil, gas, asphaltic minerals, oil shale, sodium, and sulphur, but otherwise subject to appropriation, location, selection, entry, or purchase under the nonmineral laws of the United States; lands withdrawn by Executive Order Numbered 5327, of April 15, 1930, if otherwise available for selection; and the retained or reserved interest of the United States in lands which have been disposed of with a reservation to the United States of all minerals or any specified mineral or minerals.

(d)(2) The determination, for the purposes of this section of the mineral character of lands lost to a State shall be made as of the date of application for selection and upon the basis of the best evidence available at that time.

R.S. § 2276; Feb. 28, 1891, ch. 384, 26 Stat. 796; Aug. 27, 1958, Pub.L. 85–771, § 2, 72 Stat. 928; Sept. 14, 1960, Pub.L. 86–786, §§ 1, 2, 74 Stat. 1024; As amended June 24, 1966, Pub.L. 89–470, § 2, 80 Stat. 220.

* * *

§ 857. Grant to new States for internal improvements; acreage limitation; selections, locations and surveys of lands

There is granted, for purposes of internal improvement, to each new State admitted into the Union, after September 4, 1841, upon such admission, so much public land as, including the quantity that was granted to such State before its admission and while under a territorial government, will make five hundred thousand acres.

The selections of lands, granted in this section, shall be made within the limits of each State so admitted into the Union, in such manner as the legislatures thereof, respectively, may direct; and such lands shall be located in parcels conformably to sectional divisions and subdivisions of not less than three hundred and twenty acres in any one location, on any public land not reserved from sale by law of Congress or by proclamation of the President. The locations may be made at any time after the public lands in any such new State have been surveyed according to law.

R.S. §§ 2378, 2379.

§ 858. Grants to counties for seats of justice; erection of public buildings

There shall be granted to the several counties or parishes of each State and Territory, where there are public lands, at the minimum price for which public lands of the United States are sold, the right of preemption to one quarter section of land, in each of the counties or parishes, in trust for such counties or parishes, respectively, for the establishment of seats of justice therein; but the proceeds of the sale of each of such quarter section shall be appropriated for the purpose of erecting public buildings in the county or parish for which it is located, after deducting therefrom the amount originally paid for the same. And the seat of justice for such counties or parishes, respectively, shall be fixed previously to a sale of the adjoining lands within the county or parish for which the same is located.

R.S. § 2286.

§ 859. Fee-simple to pass in all grants

Where lands have been or may hereafter be granted by any law of Congress to any one of the several States and Territories, and where such law does not convey the fee-simple title of the lands, or require patents to be issued therefor, the list of such lands which have been or may hereafter be certified by the Secretary of the Interior or such officer as he may designate, under the seal of his office, either as originals or copies of the originals or records shall be regarded as conveying the fee-simple of all the lands embraced in such lists that are of the character contemplated by such Act of Congress, and intended to be granted thereby, but where lands embraced in such lists are not of the character embraced by such Acts of Congress, and are not intended to be granted thereby, the lists, so far as these lands are concerned, shall be perfectly null and void, and no right, title, claim, or interest shall be conveyed thereby.

R.S. § 2449; 1946 Reorg. Plan No. 3, § 403, eff. July 16, 1946, 11 F.R. 7876, 60 Stat. 1100.

* * *

RECREATION AND PUBLIC PURPOSES ACT OF 1926

(43 U.S.C.A. §§ 869 through 869–4)

§ 869. Disposal of lands for public or recreational purposes

Application; conditions; classification; restoration if not applied for

(a) The Secretary of the Interior upon application filed by a duly qualified applicant under section 869–1 of this title may, in the manner prescribed by sections 869 to 869–4 of this title, dispose of any public lands to a State, Territory, county, municipality, or other State, Territorial, or Federal instrumentality or political subdivision for any public purposes, or to a nonprofit corporation or nonprofit association for any recreational or any public purpose consistent with its articles of incorporation or other creating authority. Before the land may be disposed of under sections 869 to 869–4 of this title it must be shown to the satisfaction of the Secretary that the land is to be used for an established or definitely proposed project, that the land involved is not of national significance nor more than is reasonably necessary for the proposed use, and that for proposals of over 640 acres comprehensive land use plans and zoning regulations applicable to the area in which the public lands to be disposed of are located have been adopted by the appropriate State or local authority. The Secretary shall provide an opportunity for participation by affected citizens in disposals under sections 869 to 869-4 of this title, including public hearings or meetings where he deems it appropriate to provide public comments, and shall hold at least one public meeting on any proposed disposal of more than six hundred forty acres under sections 869 to 869-4 of this title. The Secretary may classify public lands in Alaska for disposition under sections 869 to 869-4 of this title. Lands so classified may not be appropriated under any other public land law unless the Secretary revises such classification or authorizes the disposition of an interest in the lands under other applicable law. If, within eighteen months following such classification, no application has been filed for the purpose for which the lands have been so classified, then the Secretary shall restore such lands to appropriation under the applicable public land laws.

Acreage limitations

(b) Conveyances made in any one calendar year shall be limited as follows:

(i) For recreational purposes:

(A) To any State or the State park agency or any other agency having jurisdiction over the State park system of such State designated by the Governor of that State as its sole representative for acceptance of lands under this provision, hereinafter referred to as the State, or to any political subdivision of such State, six thousand four hundred acres, and such additional acreage as may be needed for small roadside parks and rest sites of not more than ten acres each.

(B) To any nonprofit corporation or nonprofit association, six hundred and forty acres.

(C) No more than twenty-five thousand six hundred acres may be conveyed for recreational purposes under sections 869 to 869-4 of this title in any one State per calendar year. Should any State or political subdivision, however, fail to secure, in any one year, six thousand four hundred acres, not counting lands for small roadside parks and rest sites, conveyances may be made thereafter if pursuant to an application on file with the Secretary of the Interior on or before the last day of said year and to the extent that the conveyance would not have exceeded the limitations of said year.

(ii) For public purposes other than recreation:

(A) To any State or agency or instrumentality thereof, for any one program, six hundred and forty acres.

(B) To any political subdivision of a State, six hundred and forty acres.

(C) To any nonprofit corporation or nonprofit association, six hundred and forty acres.

Lands withdrawn in aid of functions of a department, agency, State, etc.; lands excepted from disposal

(c) Where the lands have been withdrawn in aid of a function of a Federal department or agency other than the Department of the Interior, or of a State. Territory, county, municipality, water district, or other local governmental subdivision or agency, the Secretary of the Interior may make disposals under sections 869 to 869–4 of this title only with the consent of such Federal department or agency, or of such State, Territory, or local governmental unit. Nothing in sections 869 to 869–4 of this title shall be construed to apply to lands in any national forest, national park, or national monument, or national wildlife refuge, or to any Indian lands or lands set aside or held for the use or benefit of Indians, including lands over which jurisdiction has been transferred to the Department of the Interior by Executive order for the use of Indians, or, except insofar as sections 869 to 869–4 of this title apply to leases of land to States and counties and to State and Federal instrumentalities and political subdivisions and to municipal corporations, to the revested Oregon and California Railroad grant lands and the reconveyed Coos Bay Wagon Road grant lands in the State of Oregon. Nor shall any disposition be made under sections 869 to 869–4 of this title for any use authorized under any other law, except for a use authorized under sections 682a to 682e of this title.

June 14, 1926, c. 578, § 1, 44 Stat. 741; June 4, 1954, c. 263, 68 Stat. 173; June 23, 1959, Pub.L. 86–66, § 2, 73 Stat. 110; Sept. 21, 1959, Pub.L. 86–292, § 1, 73 Stat. 571; Sept. 13, 1960, Pub.L. 86–755, 74 Stat. 899; as amended Oct. 21, 1976, Pub.L. 94–579, Title II, § 212(a), (b), 90 Stat. 2759.

* * *

§ 869–1. Same; sale or lease; reservation of mineral deposits; termination of lease for nonuse

The Secretary of the Interior may after due consideration as to the power value of the land, whether or not withdrawn therefor, (a) sell such land to the State, Territory, county, or other State, Territorial, or Federal instrumentality or political subdivision in which the lands are situated, or to a nearby municipal corporation in the same State or Territory, for the purpose for which the land has been classified, and conveyances of such land for historic-monument purposes or recreational purposes under this section shall be made without monetary consideration, while conveyances for any other purpose under this section shall be made at a price to be fixed by the Secretary of the Interior through appraisal or otherwise, after taking into consideration the purpose for which the lands are to be used, (b) lease such land to the State, Territory, county, or other State, Territorial, or Federal instrumentality or political subdivision in which the lands are situated, or to a nearby municipal corporation in the same State or Territory, for the purpose for which the land has been classified, at a reasonable annual rental, except that leases of such lands for recreational purposes shall be made without monetary consideration, for a period up to twenty-five years, and, at the discretion of the Secretary, with a privilege of renewal for a like period, (c) sell such land to a nonprofit corporation or nonprofit association, for the purpose for which the land has been classified, at a price to be fixed by the Secretary of the Interior through appraisal, after taking into consideration the purpose for which the lands are to be used, or (d) lease such land to a nonprofit corporation or nonprofit association at a reasonable annual rental, for a period up to twenty years, and, at the discretion of the Secretary, with a privilege of renewal for a like period. Each patent or lease so issued shall contain a reservation to the United States of all mineral deposits in the lands conveyed or leased and of the right to mine and remove the same, under applicable laws and regulations to be established by the Secretary. Each lease shall contain a provision for its termination upon a finding by the Secretary that the land has not been used by the lessee for the purpose specified in the lease for such period, not over five years, as may be specified in the lease, or that such land or any part thereof is being devoted to another use.

June 14, 1926; ch. 578, § 2, as added June 4, 1954, ch. 263, 68 Stat. 174, as amended June 20, 1966, Pub.L. 89–457, § 1, 80 Stat. 210; Oct. 21, 1976, Pub.L. 94–579, Title II, § 212(c), (d), 90 Stat. 2760.

§ 869-2. Conditions of transfer by grantee; solid waste disposal

Conditions of transfer by grantee

(a) Title to lands conveyed by the Government under sections 869 to 869–4 of this title may not be transferred by the grantee or its successor except, with the consent of the Secretary of the Interior, to a transferee which would be a qualified grantee under section 869–1(a) or 869–1(c) of this title and subject to the acreage limitation contained in section 869(b) of this title. A grantee or its successor may not change the use specified in the conveyance to another or additional use except, with the consent of the Secretary, to a use for which such grantee or its successor could obtain a conveyance under sections 869 to 869–4 of this title. If at any time after the lands are conveyed by the Government, the grantee or its successor attempts to transfer title to or control over these lands to another or the lands are devoted to a use other than that for which the lands were conveyed, without the consent of the Secretary, title to the lands shall revert to the United States.

New disposal sites

(b)(1) Notwithstanding the provisions of subsection (a) of this section, if the Secretary receives an application for conveyance of land under sections 869 to 869–4 of this title for the express purpose of solid waste disposal or for another purpose which the Secretary finds may include the disposal, placement, or release of any hazardous substance, the Secretary may convey such land subject only to the provisions of this subsection.

(b)(2) Prior to issuance of any conveyance of land under this subsection the Secretary shall investigate the land covered by an application for such conveyance to determine whether or not any hazardous substance is present on such land. Such investigation shall include a review of any available records as to the use of such land and all appropriate analysis of the soil, water and air associated with such land. No land shall be conveyed under this subsection if such investigation indicates that any hazardous substance is present on such land.

(b)(3) No application for conveyance under this subsection shall be acted on by the Secretary until the applicant has furnished evidence, satisfactory to the Secretary, that a copy of the application and information concerning the proposed use of the land covered by the application has been provided to the Environmental Protection Agency and to all other State and Federal agencies with responsibility for enforcement of State and Federal laws applicable to lands used for the disposal, placement, or release of solid waste or any hazardous substance.

(b)(4) No application for conveyance under this subsection shall be acted on by the Secretary until the applicant has given a warranty that use of the land covered by the application will be consistent with all applicable State and Federal laws, including laws dealing with the disposal, placement, or release of hazardous substances, and that the applicant will hold the United States harmless from any liability that may arise out of any violation of any such law.

(b)(5) A conveyance under this subsection shall be made to the extent that the applicant has demonstrated to the Secretary that the land covered by an application meets all applicable State and local requirements and is appropriate in character and reasonable in acreage in order to meet an existing or reasonably anticipated need for solid waste disposal or for another proposed use that the Secretary finds may include the disposal, placement, or release of any hazardous substance.

(b)(6) A conveyance under this subsection shall be subject to the following conditions:

(A) Except as otherwise provided in subparagraphs (B) and (D) of this paragraph, the document of conveyance shall provide that the lands conveyed under this subsection shall revert to the United States, unless substantially all of the lands have been used, on or before the date five years after the date of conveyance, for the purpose or purposes specified in the application, or for other use or uses authorized under subsection (a) of this section with the consent of the Secretary.

(B) In the event that at any time after such conveyance any portion of such lands has not been used for the purpose or purposes specified in the application, and the party to whom such lands were conveyed by the Secretary shall transfer ownership of such unused portion to any other party, the party to whom such lands were conveyed by the Secretary shall be liable to pay the Secretary, on behalf of the United States, the fair market value of such transferred portion as of the date of such transfer, including the value of any improvements thereon. Subject to appropriations, all amounts received by the Secretary under this subparagraph shall be retained by the

Secretary and used for the management of public lands and shall remain available until expended.

(C) Pricing for conveyances of land under this subsection shall be in accordance with the provisions of section 869–1 of this title, except that no compensation shall be required for the inclusion of only the limited reverter specified in this paragraph.

(D) Each patent issued under this subsection shall specify that no portion of the lands covered by such patent shall under any circumstances revert to the United States if such portion has been used for solid waste disposal or for any other purpose that the Secretary finds may result in the disposal, placement, or release of any hazardous substance.

(b)(7) For purposes of this section the term "hazardous substance" has the same meaning as such term has when used in the Comprehensive Environmental Response, Compensation, and Liability Act (42 U.S.C. 9601 et seq.).

Existing disposal sites

(c)(1) Upon the application or with the concurrence of any party to whom the Secretary, prior to November 10, 1988, conveyed land under sections 869 to 869–4 of this title, the Secretary may renounce the reversionary interests of the United States in such land, or portion thereof, if the Secretary finds that such land, or portion thereof, has been used for solid waste disposal or for any other purpose which the Secretary finds may result in the disposal, placement, or release of any hazardous substance, and the Secretary may rescind any portion of any patent or other instrument of conveyance inconsistent with such renunciation. After such renunciation, affected lands shall not under any circumstances revert to the United States by the operation of law, and shall cease to be subject to the provisions of subsection (a) of this section.

(c)(2) Upon the application or with the concurrence of a party to whom the Secretary, prior to November 10, 1988, leased lands pursuant to sections 869 so 869–4 of this title, the Secretary may convey in fee the lands covered by such lease or any portion thereof which have been used for solid waste disposal or for any other purpose that the Secretary finds may result in the disposal, placement, or release of any hazardous substance. Notwithstanding any other provision of sections 869 to 869–4 of this title, a patent issued pursuant to this paragraph shall not contain a reverter provision and the lands covered by such patent shall not under any circumstances revert to the United States by operation of law after the issuance of such patent and shall not be subject to the provisions of subsection (a) of this section.

June 14, 1926, c. 578, § 3, as added June 4, 1954, c. 263, 68 Stat. 175, and amended Sept. 21, 1959, Pub.L. 86–292, § 2, 73 Stat. 571. As amended Nov. 10, 1988, Pub.L. 100–648, § 2, 102 Stat. 3813.

* * *

RIGHTS–OF–WAY AND OTHER EASEMENTS IN PUBLIC LANDS

(43 U.S.C.A. §§ 931–71)

§ 931. Navigable rivers as public highways

All navigable rivers, within the territory occupied by the public lands, shall remain and be deemed public highways; and, in all cases where the opposite banks of any streams not navigable belong to different persons, the stream and the bed thereof shall become common to both.

R.S. § 2476.

§ 931a. Authority of Attorney General to grant easements and rights-of-way to States, etc.

The Attorney General, whenever he deems it advantageous to the Government and upon such terms and conditions as he deems advisable, is hereby authorized on behalf of the United States to grant to any State, or any agency or political subdivision thereof, easements in and rights-of-way over lands belonging to the United States which are under his supervision and control. Such grant may include the use of such easements or rights-of-way by public utilities to the extent authorized and under the conditions imposed by the laws of such State relating to use of public highways. Such partial, concurrent, or exclusive jurisdiction over the areas covered by such easements or rights-of-way, as the Attorney General deems necessary or desirable, is hereby ceded to such State. The Attorney General is hereby authorized to accept or secure on behalf of the United States from the State in which is situated any land conveyed in exchange for any such easement or right-of-way, such jurisdiction as he may deem necessary or desirable over the land so acquired.

May 9, 1941, c. 94, 55 Stat. 183.

§ 932. Repealed. Pub.L. 94–579, Title VII, § 706(a), Oct. 21, 1976, 90 Stat. 2793

Note

Section, R.S. § 2477, authorized rights-of-way for the construction of highways over public lands not reserved for public uses.

[Ed.: R.S. 2477 is set out in the Historical Supplement, infra.]

* * *

§ 945. Reservation in patents of right-of-way for ditches or canals

In all patents for lands taken up after August 30, 1890, under any of the land laws of the United States or on entries or claims validated by the Act of August 30, 1890, west of the one hundredth meridian, it shall be expressed that there is reserved from the lands in said patent described a right of way thereon for ditches or canals constructed by the authority of the United States.

Aug. 30, 1890, c. 837, § 1, 26 Stat. 391.

§ 945a. Compensation for rights-of-way for certain reclamation projects

Notwithstanding the existence of any reservation of right-of-way to the United States for canals under section 945 of this title, or any State statute, the Secretary of the Interior shall pay just compensation, including severance damages, to the owners of private land utilized for ditches or canals in connection with any reclamation project, or any unit or any division of a reclamation project, provided the construction of said ditches or canals commenced after January 1, 1961, and such compensation shall be paid notwithstanding the execution of any agreements or any judgments entered in any condemnation proceeding, prior to September 2, 1964.

Pub.L. 88–561, § 1, Sept. 2, 1964, 78 Stat. 808, amended Pub.L. 89–624, Oct. 4, 1966, 80 Stat. 873.

§ 945b. Jurisdiction; procedure

Jurisdiction of an action brought by the United States or the landowner for the determination of just compensation pursuant to section 945a of this title is hereby conferred on the United States district court in the district in which any such land is situated, without limitation to the amount of compensation sought by such suit. The procedure for such an action shall be governed by the Federal Rules of Civil Procedure for the condemnation of real and personal property.

Pub.L. 88–561, § 2, as added Pub.L. 89–624, Oct. 4, 1966, 80 Stat. 874.

§ 946. Right-of-way to canal ditch companies and irrigation or drainage districts for irrigation or drainage purposes and operation and maintenance of reservoirs, canals, and laterals

The right of way through the public lands and reservations of the United States is hereby granted to any canal ditch company, irrigation or drainage district formed for the purpose of irrigation or drainage, and duly organized under the laws of any State or Territory, and which shall have filed, or may hereafter file, with the Secretary of the Interior a copy of its articles of incorporation or, if not a private corporation, a copy of the law under which the same is formed and due proof of its organization under the same, to the extent of the ground occupied by the water of any reservoir and of any canals and laterals and fifty feet on each side of the marginal limits thereof, and, upon presentation of satisfactory showing by the applicant, such additional right of way as the Secretary of the Interior may deem necessary for the proper operation and maintenance of said reservoirs, canals, and laterals; also the right to take from the public lands adjacent to the line of the canal or ditch, material, earth, and stone necessary for the construction of such canal or ditch: *Provided,* That no such right of way shall be so located as to interfere with the proper occupation by the Government of any such reservation, and all maps of location shall be subject to the approval of the department of the Government having jurisdiction of such reservation; and the privilege herein granted shall not be construed to interfere with the control of water for irrigation and other purposes under authority of the respective States or Territories.

Mar. 3, 1891, c. 561, § 18, 26 Stat. 1101; Mar. 4, 1917, c. 184, § 1, 39 Stat. 1197; May 28, 1926, c. 409, 44 Stat. 668.

Repeal of Section

Section repealed by Pub.L. 94–579, Title VII, § 706(a), Oct. 21, 1976, 90 Stat. 2793, effective on and after Oct. 21, 1976, insofar as applicable to the issuance of rights-of-way over, upon, under, and through the public lands and lands in the National Forest System.

UNLAWFUL INCLOSURES ACT OF 1885 (as amended)

(43 U.S.C.A. §§ 1061–66)

§ 1061. Inclosure of or assertion of right to public lands without title

All inclosures of any public lands in any State or Territory of the United States, heretofore or to be hereafter made, erected, or constructed by any person, party, association, or corporation, to any of which land included within the inclosure the person, party, association, or corporation making or controlling the inclosure had no claim or color of title made or acquired in good faith, or an asserted right thereto by or under claim, made in good faith with a view to entry thereof at the proper land office under the general laws of the United States at the time any such inclosure was or shall be made, are hereby declared to be unlawful, and the maintenance, erection, construction, or control of any such inclosure is hereby forbidden and prohibited; and the assertion of a right to the exclusive use and occupancy of any part of the public lands of the United States in any State or any of the Territories of the United States, without claim, color of title, or asserted right as above specified as to inclosure, is likewise declared unlawful, and prohibited.

Feb. 25, 1885, c. 149, § 1, 23 Stat. 321.

§ 1062. Suits for violations of law

It shall be the duty of the United States attorney for the proper district, on affidavit filed with him by any citizen of the United States that section 1061 of this title is being violated showing a description of the land inclosed with reasonable certainty, not necessarily by metes and bounds nor by governmental subdivisions of surveyed lands, but only so that the inclosure may be identified, and the persons guilty of the violation as nearly as may be, and by description, if the name cannot on reasonable inquiry be ascertained, to institute a civil suit in the proper United States district court, or territorial district court, in the name of the United States, and against the parties named or described who shall be in charge of or controlling the inclosure complained of as defendants; and jurisdiction is also conferred on any United States district court or territorial district court having jurisdiction over the locality where the land inclosed, or any part thereof, shall be situated, to hear and determine proceedings in equity, by writ of injunction, to restrain violations of the provisions of this chapter; and it shall be sufficient to give the court jurisdiction if service of original process be had in any civil proceeding on any agent or employee having charge or control of the inclosure. In any case if the inclosure shall be found to be unlawful, the court shall make the proper order, judgment, or decree for the destruction of the inclosure, in a summary way, unless the inclosure shall be removed by the defendant within five days after the order of the court.

Feb. 25, 1885, c. 149, § 2, 23 Stat. 321; Mar. 3, 1911, c. 231, § 291, 36 Stat. 1167; June 25, 1948, c. 646, § 1, 62 Stat. 909; Nov. 8, 1964, Pub.L. 98–620, Title IV, § 402(43), 98 Stat. 3360.

§ 1063. Obstruction of settlement on or transit over public lands

No person, by force, threats, intimidation, or by any fencing or inclosing, or any other unlawful means, shall prevent or obstruct, or shall combine and confederate with others to prevent or obstruct, any person from peaceably entering upon or establishing a settlement or residence on any tract of public land subject to settlement or entry under the public land laws of the United States, or shall prevent or obstruct free passage or transit over or through the public lands: *Provided,* This section shall not be held W affect the right or title of persons, who have gone upon, improved, or occupied said lands under the land laws of the United States, claiming title thereto, in good faith.

Feb. 25, 1885, c. 149, § 3, 23 Stat. 322.

§ 1064. Violations of chapter; punishment

Any person violating any of the provisions of this chapter, whether as owner, part owner, or agent, or who shall aid, abet, counsel, advise, or assist in any violation hereof, shall be deemed guilty of a misdemeanor and fined in a sum not exceeding $1,000, or be imprisoned not exceeding one year, or both, for each offense.

Feb. 25, 1885, c. 149, § 4, 23 Stat. 322; Mar. 10, 1908, c. 75, 35 Stat. 40.

§ 1065. Summary removal of inclosures

The President is authorized to take such measures as shall be necessary to remove and destroy any unlawful inclosure of any of the public lands mentioned in this chapter, and to employ civil or military force as may be necessary for that purpose.

Feb. 25, 1885, c. 149, § 5, 23 Stat. 322.

§ 1066. Permission of Secretary to sue

Where the alleged unlawful inclosure includes less than one hundred and sixty acres of land, no suit shall be brought under the provisions of this chapter without authority from the Secretary of the Interior.

Feb. 25, 1885, c. 149, § 6, 23 Stat. 322.

COLOR OF TITLE ACT OF 1928 (as amended)

(43 U.S.C.A. §§ 1068–1068b)

§ 1068. Lands held in adverse possession; issuance of patent; reservation of minerals; conflicting claims

The Secretary of the Interior (a) shall, whenever it shall be shown to his satisfaction that a tract of public land has been held in good faith and in peaceful, adverse, possession by a claimant, his ancestors or grantors, under claim or color of title for more than twenty years, and that valuable improvements have been placed on such land or some part thereof has been reduced to cultivation, or (b) may, in his discretion, whenever it shall be shown to his satisfaction that a tract of public land has been held in good faith and in peaceful, adverse, possession by a claimant, his ancestors or grantors, under claim or color of title for the period commencing not later than January 1, 1901, to the date of application during which time they have paid taxes levied on the land by State and local governmental units, issue a patent for not to exceed one hundred and sixty acres of such land upon the payment of not less than $1.25 per acre: *Provided,* That where the area so held is in excess of one hundred and sixty acres the Secretary may determine what particular subdivisions, not exceeding one hundred and sixty acres, may be patented hereunder: *Provided, further,* That coal and all other minerals contained therein are hereby reserved to the United States; that said coal and other minerals shall be subject to sale or disposal by the United States under applicable leasing and mineral land laws, and permittees, lessees, or grantees of the United States shall have the right to enter upon said lands for the purpose of prospecting for and mining such deposits: *And provided further,* That no patent shall issue under the provisions of this chapter for any tract to which there is a conflicting claim adverse to that of the applicant, unless and until such claim shall have been finally adjudicated in favor of such applicant.

Dec. 22, 1928, c. 47, § 1, 45 Stat. 1069; July 28, 1953, c. 254, § 1, 67 Stat. 227.

§ 1068a. Appraisal

Upon the filing of an application to purchase any lands subject to the operation of this chapter, together with the required proof, the Secretary of the Interior shall cause the lands described in said application to be appraised, said appraisal to be on the basis of the value of such lands at the date of appraisal, exclusive of any increased value resulting from the development or improvement of the lands by the applicant or his predecessors in interest, and in such appraisal the Secretary shall consider and give full effect to the equities of any such applicant.

Dec. 22, 1928, c. 47, § 2, 45 Stat. 1070.

§ 1068b. Mineral reservation

If the claimant requests that the patent to be issued under this chapter not contain a mineral reservation and if he can establish to the satisfaction of the Secretary that the requirements of this chapter have been complied with by such claimant and his predecessors for the period commencing not later than January 1, 1901, to the date of application, no mineral reservation shall be made unless the lands are, at the time of issuance of the patent, within a mineral withdrawal or subject to an outstanding mineral lease.

Dec. 22, 1928, c. 47, § 3, as added July 28, 1953, c. 254, § 2, 67 Stat. 228.

LIMITATIONS OF ACTIONS—PATENTS

(43 U.S.C.A. § 1166)

§ 1166. Limitations of suits to annul patents

Suits by the United States to vacate and annul any patent shall only be brought within six years after the date of the issuance of such patents.

Mar. 3, 1891, c. 559, § 1, 26 Stat. 1093; Mar. 3, 1891, c. 561, § 8, 26 Stat. 1099.

* * *

OREGON AND CALIFORNIA RAILROAD LANDS ACT

(43 U.S.C.A. §§ 1181a–1181j)

§ 1181a. Conservation management by Department of the Interior; permanent forest production; sale of timber; subdivision

Notwithstanding any provisions in the Acts of June 9, 1916 (39 Stat. 218), and February 26, 1919 (40 Stat. 1179), as amended, such portions of the revested Oregon and California Railroad and reconveyed Coos Bay Wagon Road grant lands as are or may hereafter come under the jurisdiction of the Department of the Interior, which have heretofore or may hereafter be classified as timberlands, and power-site lands valuable for timber, shall be managed, except as provided in section 1181c of this title, for permanent forest production, and the timber thereon shall be sold, cut, and removed in conformity with the principal[1] of sustained yield for the purpose of providing a permanent source of timber supply, protecting watersheds, regulating stream flow, and contributing to the economic stability of local communities and industries, and providing recreational

---

1. So in original. Probably should be "principle".

facilties[2]: *Provided,* That nothing in this section shall be construed to interfere with the use and development of power sites as may be authorized by law.

The annual productive capacity for such lands shall be determined and declared as promptly as possible after August 28, 1937, but until such determination and declaration are made the average annual cut therefrom shall not exceed one-half billion feet board measure: *Provided,* That timber from said lands in an amount not less than one-half billion feet board measure, or not less than the annual sustained yield capacity when the same has been determined and declared, shall be sold annually, or so much thereof as can be sold at reasonable prices on a normal market.

If the Secretary of the Interior determines that such action will facilitate sustained-yield management, he may subdivide such revested lands into sustained-yield forest units, the boundary lines of which shall be so established that a forest unit will provide, insofar as practicable, a permanent source of raw materials for the support of dependent communities and local industries of the region; but until such subdivision is made the land shall be treated as a single unit in applying the principle of sustained yield: *Provided,* That before the boundary lines of such forest units are established, the Department, after published notice thereof, shall hold a hearing thereon in the vicinity of such lands open to the attendance of State and local officers, representatives of dependent industries, residents, and other persons interested in the use of such lands. Due consideration shall be given to established lumbering operations in subdividing such lands when necessary to protect the economic stability of dependent communities. Timber sales from a forest unit shall be limited to the productive capacity of such unit and the Secretary is authorized, in his discretion, to reject any bids which may interfere with the sustained-yield management plan of any unit.

Aug. 28, 1937, c. 876, Title I, § 1, 50 Stat. 874.

* * *

SECRETARY OF THE INTERIOR—POWERS

(43 U.S.C.A. § 1201)

§ 1201. Power of Secretary or designated officer

The Secretary of the Interior, or such officer as he may designate, is authorized to enforce and carry into execution, by appropriate regulations, every part of the provisions of Title 32 of the Revised Statutes not otherwise specially provided for.

R.S. § 2478; 1946 Reorg.Plan No. 3, § 403, eff. July 16, 1946, 11 F.R. 7876, 60 Stat. 1100.

* * *

---

2. So in original. Probably should be "facilities".

SUBMERGED LANDS ACT OF 1953

(43 U.S.C.A. §§ 1301–1315)

§ 1301. Definitions

When used in this subchapter and subchapter II of this chapter

(a) The term "lands beneath navigable waters" means—

(1) all lands within the boundaries of each of the respective States which are covered by nontidal waters that were navigable under the laws of the United States at the time such State became a member of the Union, or acquired sovereignty over such lands and waters thereafter, up to the ordinary high water mark as heretofore or hereafter modified by accretion, erosion, and reliction;

(2) all lands permanently or periodically covered by tidal waters up to but not above the line of mean high tide and seaward to a line three geographical miles distant from the coast line of each such State and to the boundary line of each such State where in any case such boundary as it existed at the time such State became a member of the Union, or as heretofore approved by Congress, extends seaward (or into the Gulf of Mexico) beyond three geographical miles,[1] and

(3) all filled in, made, or reclaimed lands which formerly were lands beneath navigable waters, as hereinabove defined;

(b) The term "boundaries" includes the seaward boundaries of a State or its boundaries in the Gulf of Mexico or any of the Great Lakes as they existed at the time such State became a member of the Union, or as heretofore approved by the Congress, or as extended or confirmed pursuant to section 1312 of this title but in no event shall the term "boundaries" or the term "lands beneath navigable waters" be interpreted as extending from the coast line more than three geographical miles into the Atlantic Ocean or the Pacific Ocean, or more than three marine leagues into the Gulf of Mexico, except that any boundary between a State and the United States under this subchapter or subchapter II of this chapter which has been or is hereafter fixed by coordinates under a final decree of the United States Supreme Court shall remain immobilized at the coordinates provided under such decree and shall not be ambulatory;

(c) The term "coast line" means the line of ordinary low water along that portion of the coast which is in direct contact with the open sea and the line marking the seaward limit of inland waters;

(d) The terms "grantees" and "lessees" include (without limiting the generality thereof) all political subdivisions, municipalities, public and private corporations, and other persons holding grants or leases from a State, or from its predecessor sovereign if legally validated, to lands beneath navigable waters if such grants or leases were issued in accordance with the constitution, statutes, and decisions of the courts of the State in which such lands are situated, or of its predecessor sovereign: *Provided,*

---

1. So in original. Probably should be a semicolon.

however, That nothing herein shall be construed as conferring upon said grantees or lessees any greater rights or interests other than are described herein and in their respective grants from the State, or its predecessor sovereign;

(e) The term "natural resources" includes, without limiting the generality thereof, oil, gas, and all other minerals, and fish, shrimp, oysters, clams, crabs, lobsters, sponges, kelp, and other marine animal and plant life but does not include water power, or the use of water for the production of power;

(f) The term "lands beneath navigable waters" does not include the beds of streams in lands now or heretofore constituting a part of the public lands of the United States if such streams were not meandered in connection with the public survey of such lands under the laws of the United States and if the title to the beds of such streams was lawfully patented or conveyed by the United States or any State to any person;

(g) The term "State" means any State of the Union;

(h) The term "person" includes, in addition to a natural person, an association, a State, a political subdivision of a State, or a private, public, or municipal corporation.

May 22, 1953, c. 65, Title I, § 2, 67 Stat. 29. As amended Apr. 7, 1986, Pub.L. 99–272, Title VIII, § 8005, 100 Stat. 151.

§ 1302. Resources seaward of the Continental Shelf

Nothing in this subchapter or subchapter II of this chapter shall be deemed to affect in any wise the rights of the United States to the natural resources of that portion of the subsoil and seabed of the Continental Shelf lying seaward and outside of the area of lands beneath navigable waters, as defined in section 1301 of this title, all of which natural resources appertain to the United States, and the jurisdiction and control of which by the United States is hereby confirmed.

May 22, 1953, c. 65, Title II, § 9, 67 Stat. 32.

§ 1303. Amendment, modification, or repeal of other laws

Nothing in this subchapter or subchapter II of this chapter shall be deemed to amend, modify, or repeal the Acts of July 26, 1866 (14 Stat. 251), July 9, 1870 (16 Stat. 217), March 3, 1877 (19 Stat. 377), June 17, 1902 (32 Stat. 388), and December 22, 1944 (58 Stat. 887), and Acts amendatory thereof or supplementary thereto.

May 22, 1953, c. 65, Title II, § 7, 67 Stat. 32.

§ 1311. Rights of the States

Confirmation and establishment of title and ownership of lands and resources; management, administration, leasing, development, and use

(a) It is hereby determined and declared to be in the public interest that (1) title to and ownership of the lands beneath navigable waters within the boundaries of the respective States, and the natural resources within such lands and waters, and (2) the right and power to manage, administer, lease, develop, and use the said lands and natural resources all in accordance with applicable State law be, and they are hereby, subject to the provisions hereof, recognized, confirmed, established, and vested in and assigned to the respective States or the persons who were on June 5, 1950, entitled thereto under the law of the respective States in which the land is located, and the respective grantees, lessees, or successors in interest thereof;

Release and relinquishment of title and claims of United States; payment to States of moneys paid under leases

(b)(1) The United States hereby releases and relinquishes unto said States and persons aforesaid, except as otherwise reserved herein, all right, title, and interest of the United States, if any it has, in and to all said lands, improvements, and natural resources; (2) the United States hereby releases and relinquishes all claims of the United States, if any it has, for money or damages arising out of any operations of said States or persons pursuant to State authority upon or within said lands and navigable waters; and (3) the Secretary of the Interior or the Secretary of the Navy or the Treasurer of the United States shall pay to the respective States or their grantees issuing leases covering such lands or natural resources all moneys paid thereunder to the Secretary of the Interior or to the Secretary of the Navy or to the Treasurer of the United States and subject to the control of any of them or to the control of the United States on May 22, 1953, except that portion of such moneys which (1) is required to be returned to a lessee; or (2) is deductible as provided by stipulation or agreement between the United States and any of said States;

Leases in effect on June 5, 1950

(c) The rights, powers, and titles hereby recognized, confirmed, established, and vested in and assigned to the respective States and their grantees are subject to each lease executed by a State, or its grantee, which was in force and effect on June 5, 1950, in accordance with its terms and provisions and the laws of the State issuing, or whose grantee issued, such lease, and such rights, powers, and titles are further subject to the rights herein now granted to any person holding any such lease to continue to maintain the lease, and to conduct operations thereunder, in accordance with its provisions, for the full term thereof, and any extensions, renewals, or replacements authorized therein, or heretofore authorized by the laws of the State issuing, or whose grantee issued such lease: *Provided, however,* That, if oil or gas was not being produced from such lease on and before December 11, 1950, or if the primary term of such lease has expired since December 11, 1950, then for a term from May 22, 1953 equal to the term remaining unexpired on December 11, 1950, under the provisions of such lease or any extensions, renewals, or replacements authorized therein, or heretofore authorized by the laws of the State issuing, or whose grantee issued, such lease: *Provided, however,* That within ninety days from May 22, 1953 (i) the lessee shall pay to the State or its grantee issuing such lease all rents, royalties, and other sums payable between June 5, 1950, and May 22, 1953, under such lease and the laws of the State issuing or whose grantee issued such lease, except such rents, royalties, and other sums as have been paid to the State, its grantee, the Secretary of the Interior or the Secretary of the Navy or the Treasurer of the United States and not refunded to the lessee; and (ii) the lessee shall file with the Secretary of the Interior or the Secretary of the Navy and with the State issuing or whose grantee issued such lease, instruments consenting to the payment by the Secretary of the Interior or the Secretary of the Navy or the Treasurer of the United States to the State or its grantee issuing the lease, of all rents, royalties, and other payments under the control of the Secretary of the Interior or the Secretary of the Navy or the Treasurer of the United States or the United States which have been paid, under the lease, except such rentals, royalties, and other payments as have also been paid by the lessee to the State or its grantee;

Authority and rights of the United States respecting navigation, flood control and production of power

(d) Nothing in this subchapter or subchapter I of this chapter shall affect the use, development, improvement, or control by or under the constitutional authority of the United States of said lands and waters for the purposes of navigation or flood control or the production of power, or be construed as the release or relinquishment of any rights of the United States arising under the constitutional authority of Congress to regulate or improve navigation, or to provide for flood control, or the production of power;

Ground and surface waters west of the 98th meridian

(e) Nothing in this subchapter or subchapter I of this chapter shall be construed as affecting or intended to affect or in any way interfere with or modify the laws of the States which lie wholly or in part westward of the ninety-eighth meridian, relating to the ownership and control of ground and surface waters; and the control, appropriation, use, and distribution of such waters shall continue to be in accordance with the laws of such States.

May 22, 1953, c. 65, Title II, § 3, 67 Stat. 30.

§ 1312. Seaward boundaries of States

The seaward boundary of each original coastal State is hereby approved and confirmed as a line three geographical miles distant from its coast line or, in the case of the Great Lakes, to the international boundary. Any State admitted subsequent to the formation of the Union which has not already done so may extend its seaward boundaries to a line three geographical miles distant from its coast line, or to the international boundaries of the United States in the Great Lakes or any other body of water traversed by such boundaries. Any claim heretofore or hereafter asserted either by constitutional provision, statute, or otherwise, indicating the intent of a State so to extend its boundaries is hereby approved and confirmed, without prejudice to its claim, if any it has, that its boundaries extend beyond that line. Nothing in this section is to be construed as questioning or in any manner prejudicing the existence of any State's seaward boundary beyond three geographical miles if it was so provided by its constitution or laws prior to or at the time such State became a member of the Union, or if it has been heretofore approved by Congress.

May 22, 1953, c. 65, Title II, § 4, 67 Stat. 31.

§ 1313. Exceptions from confirmation and establishment of States' title, power and rights

There is excepted from the operation of section 1311 of this title—

(a) all tracts or parcels of land together with all accretions thereto, resources therein, or improvements thereon, title to which has been lawfully and expressly acquired by the United States from any State or from any person in whom title had vested under the law of the State or of the United States, and all lands which the United States lawfully holds under the law of the State; all lands expressly retained by or ceded to the United States when the State entered the Union (otherwise than by a general retention or cession of lands underlying the marginal sea); all lands acquired by the United States by eminent domain proceedings, purchase, cession, gift, or otherwise in a proprietary capacity; all lands filled in, built up, or otherwise reclaimed by the United States for its own use; and any rights the United States has in lands presently and actually occupied by the United States under claim of right;

(b) such lands beneath navigable waters held, or any interest in which is held by the United States for the benefit of any tribe, band, or group of Indians or for individual Indians; and

(c) all structures and improvements constructed by the United States in the exercise of its navigational servitude.

May 22, 1953, c. 65, Title II, § 5, 67 Stat. 32.

§ 1314. Rights and powers retained by the United States; purchase of natural resources; condemnation of lands

(a) The United States retains all its navigational servitude and rights in and powers of regulation and control of said lands and navigable waters for the constitutional purposes of commerce, navigation, national defense, and international affairs, all of which shall be paramount to, but shall not be deemed to include, proprietary rights of ownership, or the rights of management, administration, leasing, use, and development of the lands and natural resources which are specifically recognized, confirmed, established, and vested in and assigned to the respective States and others by section 1311 of this title.

(b) In time of war or when necessary for national defense, and the Congress or the President shall so prescribe, the United States shall have the right of first refusal to purchase at the prevailing market price, all or any portion of the said natural resources, or to acquire and use any portion of said lands by proceeding in accordance with due process of law and paying just compensation therefor.

May 22, 1953, c. 65, Title II, § 6, 67 Stat. 32.

§ 1315. Rights acquired under laws of the United States unaffected

Nothing contained in this subchapter or subchapter I of this chapter shall affect such rights, if any, as may have been acquired under any law of the United States by any person in lands subject to this subchapter or subchapter I of this chapter and such rights, if any, shall be governed by the law in effect at the time they may have been acquired: *Provided, however,* That nothing contained in this subchapter or subchapter I of this chapter is intended or shall be construed as a finding, interpretation, or construction by the Congress that the law under which such rights may be claimed in fact or in law applies to the lands subject to this subchapter or subchapter I of this chapter, or authorizes or compels the granting of such rights in such lands, and that the determination of the applicability or effect of such law shall be unaffected by anything contained in this subchapter or subchapter I of this chapter.

May 22, 1953, c. 65, Title II, § 8, 67 Stat. 32.

OUTER CONTINENTAL SHELF LANDS ACT OF 1953 (as amended)

(43 U.S.C.A. §§ 1331–1356)

§ 1331. Definitions

When used in this subchapter—

(a) The term "outer Continental Shelf" means all submerged lands lying seaward and outside of the area of lands beneath navigable waters as defined in section 1301 of this title, and of which the subsoil and seabed appertain to the United States and are subject to its jurisdiction and control;

(b) The term "Secretary" means the Secretary of the Interior, except that with respect to functions under this subchapter transferred to, or vested in, the Secretary of Energy or the Federal Energy Regulatory Commission by or pursuant to the Department of Energy Organization Act (42 U.S.C. 7101 et seq.), the term "Secretary" means the Secretary of Energy, or the Federal Energy Regulatory Commission, as the case may be;

(c) The term "lease" means any form of authorization which is issued under section 1337 of this title or maintained under section 1335 of this title and which authorizes exploration for, and development and production of, minerals;

(d) The term "person" includes, in addition to a natural person, an association, a State, a political subdivision of a State, or a private, public, or municipal corporation;

(e) The term "coastal zone" means the coastal waters (including the lands therein and thereunder) and the adjacent shorelands (including the waters therein and thereunder), strongly influenced by each other and in proximity to the shorelines of the several coastal States, and includes islands, transition and intertidal areas, salt marshes, wetlands, and beaches, which zone extends seaward to the outer limit of the United States territorial sea and extends inland from the shorelines to the extent necessary to control shorelands, the uses of which have a direct and significant impact on the coastal waters, and the inward boundaries of which may be identified by the several coastal States, pursuant to the authority of section 1454(b)(1) of Title 16;

(f) The term "affected State" means, with respect to any program, plan, lease[1] sale, or other activity, proposed, conducted, or approved pursuant to the provisions of this subchapter, any State—

(1) the laws of which are declared, pursuant to section 1333(a)(2) of this title, to be the law of the United States for the portion of the outer Continental Shelf on which such activity is, or is proposed to be, conducted;

(2) which is, or is proposed to be, directly connected by transportation facilities to any artificial island or structure referred to in section 1333(a)(1) of this title;

(3) which is receiving, or in accordnace[2] with the proposed activity will receive, oil for processing, refining, or transshipment which was extracted from the outer Continental Shelf and transported directly to such State by means of vessels or by a combination of means including vessels;

(4) which is designated by the Secretary as a State in which there is a substantial probability of significant impact on or damage to the coastal, marine, or human environment, or a State in which there will be significant changes in the social, governmental, or economic infrastructure, resulting from the exploration, development, and production of oil and gas anywhere on the outer Continental Shelf; or

(5) in which the Secretary finds that because of such activity there is, or will be, a significant risk of serious damage, due to factors such as prevailing winds and currents, to the marine or coastal environment in the event of any oilspill, blowout, or release of oil or gas from vessels, pipelines, or other transshipment facilities;

(g) The term "marine environment" means the physical, atmospheric, and biological components, conditions, and factors which interactively determine the productivity, state, condition, and quality of the marine ecosystem, including the waters of the high seas, the contiguous zone, transitional and intertidal areas, salt marshes, and wetlands within the coastal zone and on the outer Continental Shelf;

(h) The term "coastal environment" means the physical atmospheric, and biological components, conditions, and factors which interactively determine the productivity, state, condition, and quality of the terrestrial ecosystem from the shoreline inward to the boundaries of the coastal zone;

---

1. So in original.

2. So in original. Probably should be "accordance".

416

(i) The term "human environment" means the physical, social, and economic components, conditions, and factors which interactively determine the state, condition, and quality of living conditions, employment, and health of those affected, directly or indirectly, by activities occurring on the outer Continental Shelf;

(j) The term "Governor" means the Governor of a State, or the person or entity designated by, or pursuant to, State law to exercise the powers granted to such Governor pursuant to this subchapter;

(k) The term "exploration" means the process of searching for minerals, including (1) geophysical surveys where magnetic, gravity, seismic, or other systems are used to detect or imply the presence of such minerals, and (2) any drilling, whether on or off known geological structures, including the drilling of a well in which a discovery of oil or natural gas in paying quantities is made and the drilling of any additional delineation well after such discovery which is needed to delineate any reservoir and to enable the lessee to determine whether to proceed with development and production;

(*l*) The term "development" means those activities which take place following discovery of minerals in paying quantities, including geophysical activity, drilling, platform construction, and operation of all onshore support facilities, and which are for the purpose of ultimately producing the minerals discovered;

(m) The term "production" means those activities which take place after the successful completion of any means for the removal of minerals, including such removal, field operations, transfer of minerals to shore, operation monitoring, maintenance, and work-over drilling;

* * *

(o) The term "fair market value" means the value of any mineral (1) computed at a unit price equivalent to the average unit price at which such mineral was sold pursuant to a lease during the period for which any royalty or net profit share is accrued or reserved to the United States pursuant to such lease, or (2) if there were no such sales, or if the Secretary finds that there were an insufficient number of such sales to equitably determine such value, computed at the average unit price at which such mineral was sold pursuant to other leases in the same region of the outer Continental Shelf during such period, or (3) if there were no sales of such mineral from such region during such period, or if the Secretary finds that there are an insufficient number of such sales to equitably determine such value, at an appropriate price determined by the Secretary;

(p) The term "major Federal action" means any action or proposal by the Secretary which is subject to the provisions of section 4332(2)(C) of Title 42; and

(q) The term "minerals" includes oil, gas, sulphur, geopressured-geothermal and associated resources, and all other minerals which are authorized by an Act of Congress to be produced from "public lands" as defined in section 1702 of this title.

Aug. 7, 1953, c. 345, § 2, 67 Stat. 462; Sept. 18, 1978, Pub.L. 95–372, Title II, § 201, 92 Stat. 632.

§ 1332. Congressional declaration of policy

It is hereby declared to be the policy of the United States that—

(1) the subsoil and seabed of the outer Continental Shelf appertain to the United States and are subject to its jurisdiction, control, and power of disposition as provided in this subchapter;

(2) this subchapter shall be construed in such a manner that the character of the waters above the outer Continental Shelf as high seas and the right to navigation and fishing therein shall not be affected;

(3) the outer Continental Shelf is a vital national resource reserve held by the Federal Government for the public, which should be made available for expeditious and orderly development, subject to environmental safeguards, in a manner which is consistent with the maintenance of competition and other national needs;

(4) since exploration, development, and production of the minerals of the outer Continental Shelf will have significant impacts on coastal and non-coastal areas of the coastal States, and on other affected States, and, in recognition of the national interest in the effective management of the marine, coastal, and human environments—

(A) such States and their affected local governments may require assistance in protecting their coastal zones and other affected areas from any temporary or permanent adverse effects of such impacts;

(B) the distribution of a portion of the receipts from the leasing of mineral resources of the outer Continental Shelf adjacent to State lands, as provided under section 1337(g) of this title, will provide affected coastal States and localities with funds which may be used for the mitigation of adverse economic and environmental effects related to the development of such resources; and

(C) such States, and through such States, affected local governments, are entitled to an opportunity to participate, to the extent consistent with the national interest, in the policy and planning decisions made by the Federal Government relating to exploration for, and development and production of, minerals of the outer Continental Shelf.[1]

(5) the rights and responsibilities of all States and, where appropriate, local governments, to preserve and protect their marine, human, and coastal environments through such means as regulation of land, air, and water uses, of safety, and of related development and activity should be considered and recognized; and

(6) operations in the outer Continental Shelf should be conducted in a safe manner by well-trained personnel using technology, precautions, and techniques sufficient to prevent or minimize the likelihood of blowouts, loss of well control, fires, spillages, physical obstruction to other users of the

---

1. So in original. The period probably should be a semicolon.

waters or subsoil and seabed, or other occurrences which may cause damage to the environment or to property, or endanger life or health.

Aug. 7, 1953, c. 345, § 3, 67 Stat. 462; Sept. 18, 1978, Pub.L. 95–372, Title II, § 202, 92 Stat. 634; as amended Apr. 7, 1986, Pub.L. 99–272, Title VIII, § 8002, 100 Stat. 148.

§ 1333. Laws and regulations governing lands

Constitution and United States laws; laws of adjacent States; publication of projected State lines; international boundary disputes; restriction on State taxation and jurisdiction

(a)(1) The Constitution and laws and civil and political jurisdiction of the United States are extended to the subsoil and seabed of the outer Continental Shelf and to all artificial islands, and all installations and other devices permanently or temporarily attached to the seabed, which may be erected thereon for the purpose of exploring for, developing, or producing resources therefrom, or any such installation or other device (other than a ship or vessel) for the purpose of transporting such resources, to the same extent as if the outer Continental Shelf were an area of exclusive Federal jurisdiction located within a State: *Provided, however*, That mineral leases on the outer Continental Shelf shall be maintained or issued only under the provisions of this subchapter.

(a)(2)(A) To the extent that they are applicable and not inconsistent with this subchapter or with other Federal laws and regulations of the Secretary now in effect or hereafter adopted, the civil and criminal laws of each adjacent State, now in effect or hereafter adopted, amended, or repealed are declared to be the law of the United States for that portion of the subsoil and seabed of the outer Continental Shelf, and artificial islands and fixed structures erected thereon, which would be within the area of the State if its boundaries were extended seaward to the outer margin of the outer Continental Shelf, and the President shall determine and publish in the Federal Register such projected lines extending seaward and defining each such area. All of such applicable laws shall be administered and enforced by the appropriate officers and courts of the United States. State taxation laws shall not apply to the outer Continental Shelf.

(a)(2)(B) Within one year after September 18, 1978, the President shall establish procedures for setting[1] any outstanding international boundary dispute respecting the outer Continental Shelf.

(a)(3) The provisions of this section for adoption of State law as the law of the United States shall never be interpreted as a basis for claiming any interest in or jurisdiction on behalf of any State for any purpose over the seabed and subsoil of the outer Continental Shelf, or the property and natural resources thereof or the revenues therefrom.

* * *

---

1. So in original. Probably should be "settling".

Provisions as nonexclusive

(f) The specific application by this section of certain provisions of law to the subsoil and seabed of the outer Continental Shelf and the artificial islands, installations, and other devices referred to in subsection (a) of this section or to acts or offenses occurring or committed thereon shall not give rise to any inference that the application to such islands and structures, acts, or offenses of any other provision of law is not intended.

Aug. 7, 1953, c. 345, § 4, 67 Stat. 462; Jan. 3, 1975, Pub.L. 93–627, § 19(f), 88 Stat. 2146; Sept. 18, 1978, Pub.L. 95–372, Title II, § 203, 92 Stat. 635; Sept. 28, 1984, Pub.L. 98–426, § 27(d)(2), 98 Stat. 1654.

§ 1334. Administration of leasing

Rules and regulations; amendment; cooperation with State agencies; subject matter and scope of regulations

(a) The Secretary shall administer the provisions of this subchapter relating to the leasing of the outer Continental Shelf, and shall prescribe such rules and regulations as may be necessary to carry out such provisions. The Secretary may at any time prescribe and amend such rules and regulations as he determines to be necessary and proper in order to provide for the prevention of waste and conservation of the natural resources of the outer Continental Shelf, and the protection of correlative rights therein, and, notwithstanding any other provisions herein, such rules and regulations shall, as of their effective date, apply to all operations conducted under a lease issued or maintained under the provisions of this subchapter. In the enforcement of safety, environmental, and conservation laws and regulations, the Secretary shall cooperate with the relevant departments and agencies of the Federal Government and of the affected States. In the formulation and promulgation of regulations, the Secretary shall request and give due consideration to the views of the Attorney General with respect to matters which may affect competition. In considering any regulations and in preparing any such views, the Attorney General shall consult with the Federal Trade Commission. The regulations prescribed by the Secretary under this subsection shall include, but not be limited to, provisions—

(a)(1) for the suspension or temporary prohibition of any operation or activity, including production, pursuant to any lease or permit (A) at the request of a lessee, in the national interest, to facilitate proper development of a lease or to allow for the construction or negotiation for use of transportation facilities, or (B) if there is a threat of serious, irreparable, or immediate harm or damage to life (including fish and other aquatic life), to property, to any mineral deposits (in areas leased or not leased), or to the marine, coastal, or human environment, and for the extension of any permit or lease affected by suspension or prohibition under clause (A) or (B) by a period equivalent to the period of such suspension or prohibition, except that no permit or lease shall be so extended when such suspension or prohibition is the result of gross negligence or willful violation of such lease or permit, or of regulations issued with respect to such lease or permit;

(a)(2) with respect to cancellation of any lease or permit—

(A) that such cancellation may occur at any time, if the Secretary determines, after a hearing, that—

(i) continued activity pursuant to such lease or permit would probably cause serious harm or damage to life (including fish and other aquatic life), to property, to any mineral (in areas leased or not leased), to the national security or defense, or to the marine, coastal, or human environment;

(ii) the threat of harm or damage will not disappear or decrease to an acceptable extent within a reasonable period of time; and

(iii) the advantages of cancellation outweigh the advantages of continuing such lease or permit in force;

(B) that such cancellation shall not occur unless and until operations under such lease or permit shall have been under suspension, or temporary prohibition, by the Secretary, with due extension of any lease or permit term continuously for a period of five years, or for a lesser period upon request of the lessee;

(C) that such cancellation shall entitle the lessee to receive such compensation as he shows to the Secretary as being equal to the lesser of (i) the fair value of the canceled rights as of the date of cancellation, taking account of both anticipated revenues from the lease and anticipated costs, including costs of compliance with all applicable regulations and operating orders, liability for clean-up costs or damages, or both, in the case of an oilspill, and all other costs reasonably anticipated on the lease, or (ii) the excess, if any, over the lessee's revenues, from the lease (plus interest thereon from the date of receipt to date of reimbursement) of all consideration paid for the lease and all direct expenditures made by the lessee after the date of issuance of such lease and in connection with exploration or development, or both, pursuant to the lease (plus interest on such consideration and such expenditures from date of payment to date of reimbursement), except that (I) with respect to leases issued before September 18, 1978, such compensation shall be equal to the amount specified in clause (i) of this subparagraph; and (II) in the case of joint leases which are canceled due to the failure of one or more partners to exercise due diligence, the innocent parties shall have the right to seek damages for such loss from the responsible party or parties and the right to acquire the interests of the negligent party or parties and be issued the lease in question;

(a)(3) for the assignment or relinquishment of a lease;

(a)(4) for unitization, pooling, and drilling agreements;

(a)(5) for the subsurface storage of oil and gas other than by the Federal Government;

(a)(6) for drilling or easements necessary for exploration, development, and production;

(a)(7) for the prompt and efficient exploration and development of a lease area; and

(a)(8) for compliance with the national ambient air quality standards pursuant to the Clean Air Act (42 U.S.C. 7401 et seq.), to the extent that activities authorized under this subchapter significantly affect the air quality of any State.

Compliance with regulations as condition for issuance, continuation, assignment, or other transfer of leases

(b) The issuance and continuance in effect of any lease, or of any assignment or other transfer of any lease, under the provisions of this subchapter shall be conditioned upon compliance with regulations issued under this subchapter.

Cancellation of nonproducing lease

(c) Whenever the owner of a nonproducing lease fails to comply with any of the provisions of this subchapter, or of the lease, or of the regulations issued under this subchapter, such lease may be canceled by the Secretary, subject to the right of judicial review as provided in this subchapter, if such default continues for the period of thirty days after mailing of notice by registered letter to the lease owner at his record post office address.

Cancellation of producing lease

(d) Whenever the owner of any producing lease fails to comply with any of the provisions of this subchapter, of the lease, or of the regulations issued under this subchapter, such lease may be forfeited and canceled by an appropriate proceeding in any United States district court having jurisdiction under the provisions of this subchapter.

Pipeline rights-of-way; forfeiture of grant

(e) Rights-of-way through the submerged lands of the outer Continental Shelf, whether or not such lands are included in a lease maintained or issued pursuant to this subchapter, may be granted by the Secretary for pipeline purposes for the transportation of oil, natural gas, sulphur, or other minerals, or under such regulations and upon such conditions as may be prescribed by the Secretary, or where appropriate the Secretary of Transportation, including (as provided in section 1347(b) of this title) assuring maximum environmental protection by utilization of the best available and safest technologies, including the safest practices for pipeline burial and upon the express condition that oil or gas pipelines shall transport or purchase without discrimination, oil or natural gas produced from submerged lands or outer Continental Shelf lands in the vicinity of the pipelines in such proportionate amounts as the Federal Energy Regulatory Commission, in consultation with the Secretary of Energy, may, after a full hearing with due notice thereof to the interested parties, determine

422

to be reasonable, taking into account, among other things, conservation and the prevention of waste. Failure to comply with the provisions of this section or the regulations and conditions prescribed under this section shall be grounds for forfeiture of the grant in an appropriate judicial proceeding instituted by the United States in any United States district court having jurisdiction under the provisions of this subchapter.

* * *

Federal action affecting outer Continental Shelf; notification; recommended changes

(h) The head of any Federal department or agency who takes any action which has a direct and significant effect on the outer Continental Shelf or its development shall promptly notify the Secretary of such action and the Secretary shall thereafter notify the Governor of any affected State and the Secretary may thereafter recommend such changes in such action as are considered appropriate.

Flaring of natural gas

(i) After September 18, 1978, no holder of any oil and gas lease issued or maintained pursuant to this subchapter shall be permitted to flare natural gas from any well unless the Secretary finds that there is no practicable way to complete production of such gas, or that such flaring is necessary to alleviate a temporary emergency situation or to conduct testing or work-over operations.

Cooperative development of common hydrocarbon-bearing areas

(g)(1) Findings

(A)[3] The Congress of the United States finds that the unrestrained competitive production of hydrocarbons from a common hydrocarbon-bearing geological area underlying the Federal and State boundary may result in a number of harmful national effects, including—

(i) the drilling of unnecessary wells, the installation of unnecessary facilities and other imprudent operating practices that result in economic waste, environmental damage, and damage to life and property;

(ii) the physical waste of hydrocarbons and an unnecessary reduction in the amounts of hydrocarbons that can be produced from certain hydrocarbon-bearing areas; and

(iii) the loss of correlative rights which can result in the reduced value of national hydrocarbon resources and disorders in the leasing of Federal and State resources.

(g)(2) Prevention of harmful effects

The Secretary shall prevent, through the cooperative development of an area, the harmful effects of unrestrained competitive production

3. So in original. No subpar. (B) was enacted.

of hydrocarbons from a common hydrocarbon-bearing area underlying the Federal and State boundary.

Aug. 7, 1953, c. 345, § 5, 67 Stat. 464; Sept. 18, 1978, Pub.L. 95–372, Title II, § 204, 92 Stat. 636; as amended Aug. 18, 1990, Pub.L. 101–380, Title VI, § 6004(a), 104 Stat. 558.

§ 1337. Grant of leases by Secretary

Oil and gas leases; award to highest responsible qualified bidder; method of bidding; royalty relief; Congressional consideration of bidding system; notice

(a)(1) The Secretary is authorized to grant to the highest responsible qualified bidder or bidders by competitive bidding, under regulations promulgated in advance, any oil and gas lease on submerged lands of the outer Continental Shelf which are not covered by leases meeting the requirements of subsection (a) of section 1335 of this title. Such regulations may provide for the deposit of cash bids in an interest-bearing account until the Secretary announces his decision on whether to accept the bids, with the interest earned thereon to be paid to the Treasury as to bids that are accepted and to the unsuccessful bidders as to bids that are rejected. The bidding shall be by sealed bid and, at the discretion of the Secretary, on the basis of—

(A) cash bonus bid with a royalty at not less than 12 1/2 per centum fixed by the Secretary in amount or value of the production saved, removed, or sold;

(B) variable royalty bid based on a per centum in amount or value of the production saved, removed, or sold, with either a fixed work commitment based on dollar amount for exploration or a fixed cash bonus as determined by the Secretary, or both;

(C) cash bonus bid, or work commitment bid based on a dollar amount for exploration with a fixed cash bonus, and a diminishing or sliding royalty based on such formulae as the Secretary shall determine as equitable to encourage continued production from the lease area as resources diminish, but not less than 12 1/2 per centum at the beginning of the lease period in amount or value of the production saved, removed, or sold;

(D) cash bonus bid with a fixed share of the net profits of no less than 30 per centum to be derived from the production of oil and gas from the lease area;

(E) fixed cash bonus with the net profit share reserved as the bid variable;

(F) cash bonus bid with a royalty at no less than 12 1/2 per centum fixed by the Secretary in amount or value of the production saved, removed, or sold and a fixed per centum share of net profits of no less than 30 per centum to be derived from the production of oil and gas from the lease area;

(G) work commitment bid based on a dollar amount for exploration with a fixed cash bonus and a fixed royalty in amount or value of the production saved, removed, or sold;

(H) cash bonus bid with royalty at no less than 12 and 1/2 per centum fixed by the Secretary in amount or value of production saved, removed, or sold, and with suspension of royalties for a period, volume, or value of production determined by the Secretary, which suspensions may vary based on the price of production from the lease; or

(I) subject to the requirements of paragraph (4) of this subsection, any modification of bidding systems authorized in subparagraphs (A) through (G), or any other systems of bid variables, terms, and conditions which the Secretary determines to be useful to accomplish the purposes and policies of this subchapter, except that no such bidding system or modification shall have more than one bid variable.

(a)(2) The Secretary may, in his discretion, defer any part of the payment of the cash bonus, as authorized in paragraph (1) of this subsection, according to a schedule announced at the time of the announcement of the lease sale, but such payment shall be made in total no later than five years after the date of the lease sale.

* * *

Terms and provisions of oil and gas leases

(b) An oil and gas lease issued pursuant to this section shall—

(b)(1) be for a tract consisting of a compact area not exceeding five thousand seven hundred and sixty acres, as the Secretary may determine, unless the Secretary finds that a larger area is necessary to comprise a reasonable economic production unit;

(b)(2) be for an initial period of—

(A) five years; or

(B) not to exceed ten years where the Secretary finds that such longer period is necessary to encourage exploration and development in areas because of unusually deep water or other unusually adverse conditions,

and as long after such initial period as oil or gas is produced from the area in paying quantities, or drilling or well reworking operations as approved by the Secretary are conducted thereon;

(b)(3) require the payment of amount or value as determined by one of the bidding systems set forth in subsection (a) of this section;

(b)(4) entitle the lessee to explore, develop, and produce the oil and gas contained within the lease area, conditioned upon due diligence requirements and the approval of the development and production plan required by this subchapter;

(b)(5) provide for suspension or cancellation of the lease during the initial lease term or thereafter pursuant to section 1334 of this title;

(b)(6) contain such rental and other provisions as the Secretary may prescribe at the time of offering the area for lease; and (b)(7) provide a requirement that the lessee offer 20 per centum of the crude oil, condensate, and natural gas liquids produced on such lease, at the market value and point of delivery applicable to Federal royalty oil, to small or independent refiners as defined in the Emergency Petroleum Allocation Act of 1973 [15 U.S.C.A. § 751 et seq.].

* * *

Due diligence

(d) No bid for a lease may be submitted if the Secretary finds, after notice and hearing, that the bidder is not meeting due diligence requirements on other leases.

* * *

Other mineral leases; award to highest bidder; terms and conditions; agreements for use of resources for shore protection, beach or coastal wetlands restoration, or other projects

(k)(1) The Secretary is authorized to grant to the qualified persons offering the highest cash bonuses on a basis of competitive bidding leases of any mineral other than oil, gas, and sulphur in any area of the outer Continental Shelf not then under lease for such mineral upon such royalty, rental, and other terms and conditions as the Secretary may prescribe at the time of offering the area for lease.

(k)(2)(A) Notwithstanding paragraph (1), the Secretary may negotiate with any person an agreement for the use of Outer Continental Shelf sand, gravel and shell resources—

(i) for use in a program of, or project for, shore protection, beach restoration, or coastal wetlands restoration undertaken by a Federal, State, or local government agency; or

(ii) for use in a construction project, other than a project described in clause (i), that is funded in whole or in part by or authorized by the Federal Government.

(B) In carrying out a negotiation under this paragraph, the Secretary may assess a fee based on an assessment of the value of the resources and the public interest served by promoting development of the resources. No fee shall be assessed directly or indirectly under this subparagraph against a Federal, State, or local government agency.

(C) The Secretary may, through this paragraph and in consultation with the Secretary of Commerce, seek to facilitate projects in the coastal zone, as such term is defined in section 1453 of Title 16, that promote the policy set forth in section 1452 of Title 16.

(D) Any Federal agency which proposes to make use of sand, gravel and shell resources subject to the provisions of this subchapter shall enter into a Memorandum of Agreement with the Secretary concerning the potential use of those resources. The Secretary shall notify the Committee on Merchant Marine and Fisheries and the Committee on Natural Resources of the House of Representatives and the Committee on Energy and Natural Resources of the Senate on any proposed project for the use of those resources prior to the use of those resources.

Publication of notices of sale and terms of bidding

(*l*) Notice of sale of leases, and the terms of bidding, authorized by this section shall be published at least thirty days before the date of sale in accordance with rules and regulations promulgated by the Secretary.

Disposition of revenues

(m) All moneys paid to the Secretary for or under leases granted pursuant to this section shall be deposited in the Treasury in accordance with section 1338 of this title.

Issuance of lease as nonprejudicial to ultimate settlement or adjudication of controversies

(n) The issuance of any lease by the Secretary pursuant to this subchapter, or the making of any interim arrangements by the Secretary pursuant to section 1336 of this title shall not prejudice the ultimate settlement or adjudication of the question as to whether or not the area involved is in the outer Continental Shelf.

Cancellation of leases for fraud

(o) The Secretary may cancel any lease obtained by fraud or misrepresentation.

Aug. 7, 1953, c. 345, § 8, 67 Stat. 468; Sept. 18, 1978, Pub.L. 95–372, Title II, § 205(a), (b), 92 Stat. 640, 644; as amended Apr. 7, 1986, Pub.L. 99–272, Title VIII, § 8003, 100 Stat. 148; Dec. 22, 1987, Pub.L. 100–202, § 101(g)[Title I], 101 Stat. 1329–225; Oct. 31, 1994, Pub.L. 103–426, § 1(a), 108 Stat. 4371; Nov. 28, 1995, Pub.L. 104–58, Title III, §§ 302, 303, 109 Stat. 563, 565; Nov. 10, 1998, Pub.L. 105–362, Title IX, § 901(k), 112 Stat. 3290; Aug. 17, 1999, Pub.L. 106–53, Title II, § 215(b)(1), 113 Stat. 292.

§ 1341. Reservation of lands and rights

Withdrawal of unleased lands by President

(a) The President of the United States may, from time to time, withdraw from disposition any of the unleased lands of the outer Continental Shelf.

First refusal of mineral purchases

(b) In time of war, or when the President shall so prescribe, the United States shall have the right of first refusal to purchase at the market price all or any portion of any mineral produced from the outer Continental Shelf.

National security clause

(c) All leases issued under this subchapter, and leases, the maintenance and operation of which are authorized under this subchapter, shall contain or be construed to contain a provision whereby authority is vested in the Secretary, upon a recommendation of the Secretary of Defense, during a state of war or national emergency declared by the Congress or the President of the United States after August 7, 1953, to suspend operations under any lease; and all such leases shall contain or be construed to contain provisions for the payment of just compensation to the lessee whose operations are thus suspended.

National defense areas; suspension of operations; extension of leases

(d) The United States reserves and retains the right to designate by and through the Secretary of Defense, with the approval of the President, as areas restricted from exploration and operation that part of the outer Continental Shelf needed for national defense; and so long as such designation remains in effect no exploration or operations may be conducted on any part of the surface of such area except with the concurrence of the Secretary of Defense; and if operations or production under any lease theretofore issued on lands within any such restricted area shall be suspended, any payment of rentals, minimum royalty, and royalty prescribed by such lease likewise shall be suspended during such period of suspension of operation and production, and the term of such lease shall be extended by adding thereto any such suspension period, and the United States shall be liable to the lessee for such compensation as is required to be paid under the Constitution of the United States.

* * *

Aug. 7, 1953, c. 345, § 12, 67 Stat. 469.

§ 1344. Outer Continental Shelf leasing program

Schedule of proposed oil and gas lease sales

(a) The Secretary, pursuant to procedures set forth in subsections (c) and (d) of this section, shall prepare and periodically revise, and maintain an oil and gas leasing program to implement the policies of this subchapter. The leasing program shall consist of a schedule of proposed lease sales indicating, as precisely as possible, the size, timing, and location of leasing activity which he determines will best meet national energy needs for the five-year period following its approval or reapproval. Such leasing program shall be prepared and maintained in a manner consistent with the following principles:

(a)(1) Management of the outer Continental Shelf shall be conducted in a manner which considers economic, social, and environmental values of the renewable and nonrenewable resources contained in the outer Continental Shelf, and the potential impact of oil and gas exploration on other resource values of the outer Continental Shelf and the marine, coastal, and human environments.

(a)(2) Timing and location of exploration, development, and production of oil and gas among the oil-and gas-bearing physiographic regions of the outer Continental Shelf shall be based on a consideration of—

(A) existing information concerning the geographical, geological, and ecological characteristics of such regions;

(B) an equitable sharing of developmental benefits and environmental risks among the various regions;

(C) the location of such regions with respect to, and the relative needs of, regional and national energy markets;

(D) the location of such regions with respect to other uses of the sea and seabed, including fisheries, navigation, existing or proposed sealanes, potential sites of deepwater ports, and other anticipated uses of the resources and space of the outer Continental Shelf;

(E) the interest of potential oil and gas producers in the development of oil and gas resources as indicated by exploration or nomination;

(F) laws, goals, and policies of affected States which have been specifically identified by the Governors of such States as relevant matters for the Secretary's consideration;

(G) the relative environmental sensitivity and marine productivity of different areas of the outer Continental Shelf; and

(H) relevant environmental and predictive information for different areas of the outer Continental Shelf.

(a)(3) The Secretary shall select the timing and location of leasing, to the maximum extent practicable, so as to obtain a proper balance between the potential for environmental damage, the potential for the discovery of oil and gas, and the potential for adverse impact on the coastal zone.

(a)(4) Leasing activities shall be conducted to assure receipt of fair market value for the lands leased and the rights conveyed by the Federal Government.

* * *

Aug. 7, 1953, c. 345, § 18, as added Sept. 18, 1978, Pub.L. 95–372, Title II, § 208, 92 Stat. 649.

§ 1345. Coordination and consultation with affected State and local governments

Recommendations regarding size, time, or location of proposed lease sales

(a) Any Governor of any affected State or the executive of any affected local government in such State may submit recommendations to the Secretary regarding the size, timing, or location of a proposed lease sale or with respect to a proposed development and production plan. Prior to submitting recommendations to the Secretary, the executive of any affected local government in any affected State must forward his recommendations to the Governor of such State.

Time for submission of recommendations

(b) Such recommendations shall be submitted within sixty days after notice of such proposed lease sale or after receipt of such development and production plan.

Acceptance or rejection of recommendations

(c) The Secretary shall accept recommendations of the Governor and may accept recommendations of the executive of any affected local government if he determines, after having provided the opportunity for consultation, that they provide for a reasonable balance between the national interest and the well-being of the citizens of the affected State. For purposes of this subsection, a determination of the national interest shall be based on the desirability of obtaining oil and gas supplies in a balanced manner and on the findings, purposes, and policies of this subchapter. The Secretary shall communicate to the Governor, in writing, the reasons for his determination to accept or reject such Governor's recommendations, or to implement any alternative means identified in consultation with the Governor to provide for a reasonable balance between the national interest and the well-being of the citizens of the affected State.

Finality of acceptance or rejection of recommendations

(d) The Secretary's determination that recommendations provide, or do not provide, for a reasonable balance between the national interest and the well-being of the citizens of the affected State shall be final and shall not, alone, be a basis for invalidation of a proposed lease sale or a proposed development and production plan in any suit or judicial review pursuant to section 1349 of this title, unless found to be arbitrary or capricious.

Cooperative agreements

(e) The Secretary is authorized to enter into cooperative agreements with affected States for purposes which are consistent with this subchapter and other applicable Federal law. Such agreements may include, but need not be limited to, the sharing of information (in accordance with the provisions of section 1352 of this title), the joint utilization of available expertise, the facilitating of permitting procedures, joint planning and review, and the formation of joint surveillance and monitoring arrangements to carry out applicable Federal and State laws, regulations, and stipulations relevant to outer Continental Shelf operations both onshore and offshore.

Aug. 7, 1953, c. 345, § 19, as added Sept. 18, 1978, Pub.L. 95–372, Title II, § 208, 92 Stat. 652.

§ 1346. Environmental studies

Information for assessment and management of impacts on environment; time for study; impacts on marine biota from pollution or large spills

(a)(1) The Secretary shall conduct a study of any area or region included in any oil and gas lease sale or other lease in order to establish information needed for assessment and management of environmental impacts on the human, marine, and coastal environments of the outer Continental Shelf and the coastal areas which may be affected by oil and gas or other mineral development in such area or region.

(a)(2) Each study required by paragraph (1) of this subsection shall be commenced not later than six months after September 18, 1978, with respect to any area or region where a lease sale has been held or announced by publication of a notice of proposed lease sale before September 18, 1978, and not later than six months prior to the holding of a lease sale with respect to any area or region where no lease sale has been held or scheduled before September 18, 1978. In the case of an agreement under section 1337(k)(2) of this title, each study required by paragraph (1) of this subsection shall be commenced not later than 6 months prior to commencing negotiations for such agreement or the entering into the memorandum of agreement as the case may be. The Secretary may utilize information collected in any study prior to September 18, 1978.

(a)(3) In addition to developing environmental information, any study of an area or region, to the extent practicable, shall be designed to predict impacts on the marine biota which may result from chronic low level pollution or large spills associated with outer Continental Shelf production, from the introduction of drill cuttings and drilling muds in the area, and from the laying of pipe to serve the offshore production area, and the impacts of development offshore on the affected and coastal areas.

Additional studies subsequent to leasing and development of area

(b) Subsequent to the leasing and developing of any area or region, the Secretary shall conduct such additional studies to establish environmental information as he deems necessary and shall monitor the human, marine, and coastal environments of such area or region in a manner designed to provide time-series and data trend information which can be used for comparison with any previously collected data for the purpose of identifying any significant changes in the quality and productivity of such environments, for establishing trends in the areas studied and monitored, and for designing experiments to identify the causes of such changes.

Procedural regulations for conduct of studies; cooperation with affected States; utilization of information from Federal, State and local governments and agencies

(c) The Secretary shall, by regulation, establish procedures for carrying out his duties under this section, and shall plan and carry out such duties in full cooperation with affected States. To the extent that other Federal agencies have prepared environmental impact statements, are conducting studies, or are monitoring the affected human, marine, or coastal environment, the Secretary may utilize the information derived therefrom in lieu of directly conducting such activities. The Secretary may also utilize information obtained from any State or local government, or from any person, for the purposes of this section. For the purpose of carrying out his responsibilities under this section, the Secretary may by agreement utilize, with or without reimbursement, the services, personnel, or facilities of any Federal, State, or local government agency.

Consideration of relevant environmental information in developing regulations, lease conditions and operating orders

(d) The Secretary shall consider available relevant environmental information in making decisions (including those relating to exploration plans, drilling permits, and development and production plans), in developing appropriate regulations and lease conditions, and in issuing operating orders.

Assessment of cumulative effects of activities on environment; submission to Congress

(e) As soon as practicable after the end of every 3 fiscal years, the Secretary shall submit to the Congress and make available to the general public an assessment of the cumulative effect of activities conducted under this subchapter on the human, marine, and coastal environments.

* * *

Aug. 7, 1953, c. 345, § 20, as added Sept. 18, 1978, Pub.L. 95–372, Title II, § 208, 92 Stat. 653; as amended Oct. 31, 1994, Pub.L. 103–426, § 1(b), 108 Stat. 4371; Dec. 21, 1995, Pub.L. 104–66, Title I, § 1082(b), 109 Stat. 722.

§ 1349. Citizens suits, jurisdiction and judicial review

Persons who may bring actions; persons against whom action may be brought; time of action; intervention by Attorney General; costs and fees; security

(a)(1) Except as provided in this section, any person having a valid legal interest which is or may be adversely affected may commence a civil action on his own behalf to compel compliance with this subchapter against any person, including the United States, and any other government instrumentality or agency (to the extent permitted by the eleventh amendment to the Constitution) for any alleged violation of any provision of this subchapter or any regulation promulgated under this subchapter, or of the terms of any permit or lease issued by the Secretary under this subchapter.

(a)(2) Except as provided in paragraph (3) of this subsection, no action may be commenced under subsection (a)(1) of this section—

(A) prior to sixty days after the plaintiff has given notice of the alleged violation, in writing under oath, to the Secretary and any other appropriate Federal official, to the State in which the violation allegedly occurred or is occurring, and to any alleged violator; or

(B) if the Attorney General has commenced and is diligently prosecuting a civil action in a court of the United States or a State with respect to such matter, but in any such action in a court of the United States any person having a legal interest which is or may be adversely affected may intervene as a matter of right.

(a)(3) An action may be brought under this subsection immediately after notification of the alleged violation in any case in which the alleged violation constitutes an imminent threat to the public health or safety or would immediately affect a legal interest of the plaintiff.

(a)(4) In any action commenced pursuant to this section, the Attorney General, upon the request of the Secretary or any other appropriate Federal official, may intervene as a matter of right.

(a)(5) A court, in issuing any final order in any action brought pursuant to subsection (a)(1) or subsection (c) of this section, may award costs of litigation, including reasonable attorney and expert witness fees, to any party, whenever such court determines such award is appropriate. The court may, if a temporary restraining order or preliminary injunction is sought, require the filing of a bond or equivalent security in a sufficient amount to compensate for any loss or damage suffered, in accordance with the Federal Rules of Civil Procedure.

(a)(6) Except as provided in subsection (c) of this section, all suits challenging actions or decisions allegedly in violation of, or seeking enforcement of, the provisions of this subchapter, or any regulation promulgated under this subchapter, or the terms of any permit or lease issued by the Secretary under this subchapter, shall be undertaken in accordance with the procedures described in this subsection. Nothing in this section shall restrict any right which any person or class of persons may have under any other Act or common law to seek appropriate relief.

* * *

Aug. 7, 1953, c. 345, § 23, added Sept. 18, 1978, Pub.L. 95–372, Title II, § 208, 92 Stat. 657, and amended Nov. 8, 1984, Pub.L. 98–620, Title IV, § 402(44), 98 Stat. 3360.

* * *

SECRETARY OF THE INTERIOR—DUTIES

§ 1457. Duties of Secretary

The Secretary of the Interior is charged with the supervision of public business relating to the following subjects and agencies:

1. Alaska Railroad.

2. Alaska Road Commission.

3. Bounty-lands.

4. Bureau of Land Management.

5. United States Bureau of Mines.

6. Bureau of Reclamation.

7. Division of Territories and Island Possessions.

8. Fish and Wildlife Service.

9. United States Geological Survey.

10. Indians.

11. National Park Service.

12. Petroleum conservation.

13. Public lands, including mines.

R.S. § 441; Mar. 3, 1879, c. 182, 20 Stat. 394; Jan. 12, 1895, c. 23, 28 Stat. 601; June 17, 1902, c. 1093, 32 Stat. 388; Feb. 14, 1903, c. 552, § 4, 32 Stat. 826; Mar. 4, 1911, c. 285, § 1, 36 Stat. 1422; July 1, 1916, c. 209, § 1, 39 Stat. 309; Aug. 25, 1916, c. 408, 39 Stat. 535; Ex. Ord. No. 3861, eff. June 8, 1923; Ex. Ord. No. 4175, eff. Mar. 17, 1925; Ex. Ord. No. 5398, eff. July 21, 1930; June 30, 1932, ch. 320, § 1, 47 Stat. 446; Ex. Ord. No. 6611, eff. Feb. 22, 1934; Ex. Ord. No. 6726, eff. May 29, 1934; June 28, 1934, c. 865, § 1, 48 Stat. 1269; 1939 Reorg. Plan No. I, § 201, eff. July 1, 1939, 4 F.R. 2728, 53 Stat. 1424; 1939 Reorg. Plan No. II, § 4(e), (f), eff. July 1, 1939, 4 F.R. 2731, 53 Stat. 1433; 1940 Reorg. Plan No. III, § 3, eff. June 30, 1940, 5 F.R. 2108, 54 Stat. 1232; 1940 Reorg. Plan No. IV, § 11, eff. June 30, 1940, 5 F.R. 2422, 54 Stat. 1236; 1946 Reorg. Plan No. 3, § 403(a), eff. July 16, 1946, 11 F.R. 7876, 60 Stat. 1100; June 17, 1957, Pub.L. 85–56, Title XXII, § 2201(1), 71 Stat. 157; as amended May 18, 1992, Pub.L. 102–285, § 10, 106 Stat. 171.

FEDERAL LAND POLICY AND MANAGEMENT ACT OF 1976 (as amended)

(43 U.S.C.A. §§ 1701–84)

SUBCHAPTER I—GENERAL PROVISIONS

§ 1701. Congressional declaration of policy

(a) The Congress declares that it is the policy of the United States that—

(1) the public lands be retained in Federal ownership, unless as a result of the land use planning procedure provided for in this Act, it is determined that disposal of a particular parcel will serve the national interest;

(2) the national interest will be best realized if the public lands and their resources are periodically and systematically inventoried and their present and future use is projected through a land use planning process coordinated with other Federal and State planning efforts;

(3) public lands not previously designated for any specific use and all existing classifications of public lands that were effected by executive action or statute before October 21, 1976, be reviewed in accordance with the provisions of this Act;

(4) the Congress exercise its constitutional authority to withdraw or otherwise designate or dedicate Federal lands for specified purposes and that Congress delineate the extent to which the Executive may withdraw lands without legislative action;

(5) in administering public land statutes and exercising discretionary authority granted by them, the Secretary be required to establish comprehensive rules and regulations after considering the views of the general public; and to structure adjudication procedures to assure

adequate third party participation, objective administrative review of initial decisions, and expeditious decisionmaking;

(6) judicial review of public land adjudication decisions be provided by law;

(7) goals and objectives be established by law as guidelines for public land use planning, and that management be on the basis of multiple use and sustained yield unless otherwise specified by law;

(8) the public lands be managed in a manner that will protect the quality of scientific, scenic, historical, ecological, environmental, air and atmospheric, water resource, and archeological values; that, where appropriate, will preserve and protect certain public lands in their natural condition; that will provide food and habitat for fish and wildlife and domestic animals; and that will provide for outdoor recreation and human occupancy and use;

(9) the United States receive fair market value of the use of the public lands and their resources unless otherwise provided for by statute;

(10) uniform procedures for any disposal of public land, acquisition of non-Federal land for public purposes, and the exchange of such lands be established by statute, requiring each disposal, acquisition, and exchange to be consistent with the prescribed mission of the department or agency involved, and reserving to the Congress review of disposals in excess of a specified acreage;

(11) regulations and plans for the protection of public land areas of critical environmental concern be promptly developed;

(12) the public lands be managed in a manner which recognizes the Nation's need for domestic sources of minerals, food, timber, and fiber from the public lands including implementation of the Mining and Minerals Policy Act of 1970 (84 Stat. 1876, 30 U.S.C. 21a) as it pertains to the public lands; and

(13) the Federal Government should, on a basis equitable to both the Federal and local taxpayer, provide for payments to compensate States and local governments for burdens created as a result of the immunity of Federal lands from State and local taxation.

(b) The policies of this Act shall become effective only as specific statutory authority for their implementation is enacted by this Act or by subsequent legislation and shall then be construed as supplemental to and not in derogation of the purposes for which public lands are administered under other provisions of law.

Pub.L. 94–579, Title I, § 102, Oct. 21, 1976, 90 Stat. 2744.

[Uncodified Savings Provisions of Federal Land Policy & Management Act]

Section 701 of Pub.L. 94–579, 90 Stat. 2786–87, provided that:

"(a) Nothing in this Act or in any amendment made by this Act, shall be construed as terminating any valid lease, permit, patent, right-of-way, or other land use right or authorization existing on the date of approval of this Act [Oct. 21, 1976].

"(b) Notwithstanding any provision of this Act, in the event of conflict with or inconsistency between this Act and the Acts of August 28, 1937 (50 Stat. 874; 43 U.S.C. 1181a–1181j) [sections 1181a to 1181j of this title], and May 24, 1939 (53 Stat. 753), insofar as they relate to management of timber resources, and disposition of revenues from lands and resources, the latter Acts shall prevail.

"(c) All withdrawals, reservations, classifications, and designations in effect as of the date of approval of this Act [Oct. 21, 1976] shall remain in full force and effect until modified under the provisions of this Act or other applicable law.

"(d) Nothing in this Act, or in any amendments made by this Act, shall be construed as permitting any person to place, or allow to be placed, spent oil shale, overburden, or byproducts from the recovery of other minerals found with oil shale, on any Federal land other than Federal land which has been leased for the recovery of shale oil under the Act of February 25, 1920 (41 Stat. 437, as amended; 30 U.S.C. 181 et seq.) [section 181 et seq. of Title 30].

"(e) Nothing in this Act shall be construed as modifying, revoking, or changing any provision of the Alaska Native Claims Settlement Act (85 Stat. 688, as amended; 43 U.S.C. 1601 et seq.) [section 1601 et seq. of this title].

"(f) Nothing in this Act shall be deemed to repeal any existing law by implication.

"(g) Nothing in this Act shall be construed as limiting or restricting the power and authority of the United States or—

"(1) as affecting in any way any law governing appropriation or use of, or Federal right to, water on public lands;

"(2) as expanding or diminishing Federal or State jurisdiction, responsibility, interests, or rights in water resources development or control;

"(3) as displacing, superseding, limiting, or modifying any interstate compact or the jurisdiction or responsibility of any legally established joint or common agency of two or more States or of two or more States and the Federal Government;

"(4) as superseding, modifying, or repealing, except as specifically set forth in this Act, existing laws applicable to the various Federal agencies which are authorized to develop or participate in the development of water resources or to exercise licensing or regulatory functions in relation thereto;

"(5) as modifying the terms of any interstate compact;

"(6) as a limitation upon any State criminal statute or upon the police power of the respective States, or as derogating the authority of a local police officer in the performance of his duties, or as depriving any State or political subdivision thereof of any right it may have to exercise civil and criminal jurisdiction on the national resource lands; or as amending, limiting, or infringing the existing laws providing grants of lands to the States.

"(h) All actions by the Secretary concerned under this Act shall be subject to valid existing rights.

"(i) The adequacy of reports required by this Act to be submitted to the Congress or its committees shall not be subject to judicial review.

"(j) Nothing in this Act shall be construed as affecting the distribution of livestock grazing revenues to local governments under the Granger–Thye Act (64 Stat. 85, 16 U.S.C. 580h), under the Act of May 23, 1908 (35 Stat. 260, as amended; 16 U.S.C. 500), under the Act of March 4, 1913 (37 Stat. 843, as amended; 16 U.S.C. 501), and under the Act of June 20, 1910 (36 Stat. 557)."

Severability of Provisions

Section 707 of Pub.L. 94–579, 90 Stat. 2794, provided that: "If any provision of this Act or the application thereof is held invalid, the remainder of the Act and, the application thereof shall not be affected thereby."

[End of Uncodified Disclaimers]

§ 1702. Definitions

Without altering in any way the meaning of the following terms as used in any other statute, whether or not such statute is referred to in, or amended by, this Act, as used in this Act—

(a) The term "areas of critical environmental concern" means areas within the public lands where special management attention is required (when such areas are developed or used or where no development is required) to protect and prevent irreparable damage to important historic, cultural, or scenic values, fish and wildlife resources or other natural systems or processes, or to protect life and safety from natural hazards.

(b) The term "holder" means any State or local governmental entity, individual, partnership, corporation, association, or other business entity receiving or using a right-of-way under subchapter V of this chapter.

(c) The term "multiple use" means the management of the public lands and their various resource values so that they are utilized in the combination that will best meet the present and future needs of the American people; making the most judicious use of the land for some or all of these resources or related services over areas large enough to provide sufficient latitude for periodic adjustments in use to conform to changing needs and conditions; the use of some land for less than all of the resources; a combination of balanced and diverse resource uses that takes into account the long-term needs of future generations for renewable and nonrenewable resources, including, but not limited to, recreation, range, timber, minerals, watershed, wildlife and fish, and natural scenic, scientific and historical values; and harmonious and coordinated management of the various resources without permanent impairment of the productivity of the land and the quality of the environment with consideration being given to the relative values of the resources and not necessarily to the combination of uses that will give the greatest economic return or the greatest unit output.

(d) The term "public involvement" means the opportunity for participation by affected citizens in rulemaking, decisionmaking, and planning with respect to the public lands, including public meetings or hearings held at locations near the affected lands, or advisory mechanisms, or such other procedures as may be necessary to provide public comment in a particular instance.

(e) The term "public lands" means any land and interest in land owned by the United States within the several States and administered by the Secretary of the Interior through the Bureau of Land Management, without regard to how the United States acquired ownership, except—

(1) lands located on the Outer Continental Shelf; and

(2) lands held for the benefit of Indians, Aleuts, and Eskimos.

(f) The term "right-of-way" includes an easement, lease, permit, or license to occupy, use, or traverse public lands granted for the purpose listed in subchapter V of this chapter.

(g) The term "Secretary", unless specifically designated otherwise, means the Secretary of the Interior.

(h) The term "sustained yield" means the achievement and maintenance in perpetuity of a high-level annual or regular periodic output of the various renewable resources of the public lands consistent with multiple use.

(i) The term "wilderness" as used in section 1782 of this title shall have the same meaning as it does in section 1131(c) of Title 16.

(j) The term "withdrawal" means withholding an area of Federal land from settlement, sale, location, or entry, under some or all of the general land laws, for the purpose of limiting activities under those laws in order to maintain other public values in the area or reserving the area for a particular public purpose or program; or transferring jurisdiction over an area of Federal land, other than "property" governed by the Federal Property and Administrative Services Act, as amended (40 U.S.C. 472) from one department, bureau or agency to another department, bureau or agency.

(k) An "allotment management plan" means a document prepared in consultation with the lessees or permittees involved, which applies to livestock operations on the public lands or on lands within National Forests in the eleven contiguous Western States and which:

(1) prescribes the manner in, and extent to, which livestock operations will be conducted in order to meet the multiple-use, sustained-yield, economic and other needs and objectives as determined for the lands by the Secretary concerned; and

(2) describes the type, location, ownership, and general specifications for the range improvements to be installed and maintained on the lands to meet the livestock grazing and other objectives of land management; and

(3) contains such other provisions relating to livestock grazing and other objectives found by the Secretary concerned to be consistent with the provisions of this Act and other applicable law.

(*l*) The term "principal or major uses" includes, and is limited to, domestic livestock grazing, fish and wildlife development and utilization, mineral exploration and production, rights-of-way, outdoor recreation, and timber production.

(m) The term "department" means a unit of the executive branch of the Federal Government which is headed by a member of the President's Cabinet and the term "agency" means a unit of the executive branch of the Federal Government which is not under the jurisdiction of a head of a department.

(n) The term "Bureau" means the Bureau of Land Management.

(*o*) The term "eleven contiguous Western States" means the States of Arizona, California, Colorado, Idaho, Montana, Nevada, New Mexico, Oregon, Utah, Washington, and Wyoming.

(p) The term "grazing permit and lease" means any document authorizing use of public lands or lands in National Forests in the eleven contiguous Western States for the purpose of grazing domestic livestock.

Pub.L. 94–579, Title I, § 103, Oct. 21, 1976, 90 Stat. 2745.

SUBCHAPTER II—LAND USE PLANNING AND LAND ACQUISITION AND DISPOSITION

§ 1711. Continuing inventory and identification of public lands; preparation and maintenance

(a) The Secretary shall prepare and maintain on a continuing basis an inventory of all public lands and their resource and other values (including, but not limited to, outdoor recreation and scenic values), giving priority to areas of critical environmental concern. This inventory shall be kept current so as to reflect changes in conditions and to identify new and emerging resource and other values. The preparation and maintenance of such inventory or the identification of such areas shall not, of itself, change or prevent change of the management or use of public lands.

(b) As funds and manpower are made available, the Secretary shall ascertain the boundaries of the public lands; provide means of public identification thereof including, where appropriate, signs and maps; and provide State and local governments with data from the inventory for the purpose of planning and regulating the uses of non-Federal lands in proximity of such public lands.

Pub.L. 94–579, Title II, § 201, Oct. 21, 1976, 90 Stat. 2747.

§ 1712. Land use plans

Development, maintenance, and revision by Secretary

(a) The Secretary shall, with public involvement and consistent with the terms and conditions of this Act, develop, maintain, and, when appropriate, revise land use plans which provide by tracts or areas for the use of the public lands. Land use plans shall be developed for the public lands regardless of whether such lands previously have been classified, withdrawn, set aside, or otherwise designated for one or more uses.

Coordination of plans for National Forest System lands with Indian land use planning and management programs for purposes of development and revision

(b) In the development and revision of land use plans, the Secretary of Agriculture shall coordinate land use plans for lands in the National Forest System with the land use planning and management programs of and for Indian tribes by, among other things, considering the policies of approved tribal land resource management programs.

Criteria for development and revision

(c) In the development and revision of land use plans, the Secretary shall—

(1) use and observe the principles of multiple use and sustained yield set forth in this and other applicable law;

(2) use a systematic interdisciplinary approach to achieve integrated consideration of physical, biological, economic, and other sciences;

(3) give priority to the designation and protection of areas of critical environmental concern;

(4) rely, to the extent it is available, on the inventory of the public lands, their resources, and other values;

(5) consider present and potential uses of the public lands;

(6) consider the relative scarcity of the values involved and the availability of alternative means (including recycling) and sites for realization of those values;

(7) weigh long-term benefits to the public against short-term benefits;

(8) provide for compliance with applicable pollution control laws, including State and Federal air, water, noise, or other pollution standards or implementation plans; and

(9) to the extent consistent with the laws governing the administration of the public lands, coordinate the land use inventory, planning, and management activities of or for such lands with the land use planning and management programs of other Federal departments and agencies and of the States and local governments within which the lands are located, including, but not limited to, the statewide outdoor recreation plans developed under the Act of September 3, 1964 (78

Stat. 897), as amended [16 U.S.C.A. § 460l–4 et seq.], and of or for Indian tribes by, among other things, considering the policies of approved State and tribal land resource management programs. In implementing this directive, the Secretary shall, to the extent he finds practical, keep apprised of State, local and tribal land use plans; assure that consideration is given to those State, local and tribal plans that are germane in the development of land use plans for public lands; assist in resolving, to the extent practical, inconsistencies between Federal and non-Federal Government plans, and shall provide for meaningful public involvement of State and local government officials, both elected and appointed, in the development of land use programs, land use regulations, and land use decisions for public lands, including early public notice of proposed decisions which may have a significant impact on non-Federal lands. Such officials in each State are authorized to furnish advice to the Secretary with respect to the development and revision of land use plans, land use guidelines, land use rules, and land use regulations for the public lands within such State and with respect to such other land use matters as may be referred to them by him. Land use plans of the Secretary under this section shall be consistent with State and local plans to the maximum extent he finds consistent with Federal law and the purposes of this Act.

Review and inclusion of classified public lands; review of existing land use plans; modification and termination of classifications

(d) Any classification of public lands or any land use plan in effect on October 21, 1976, is subject to review in the land use planning process conducted under this section, and all public lands, regardless of classification, are subject to inclusion in any land use plan developed pursuant to this section. The Secretary may modify or terminate any such classification consistent with such land use plans.

Management decisions for implementation of developed or revised plans

(e) The Secretary may issue management decisions to implement land use plans developed or revised under this section in accordance with the following:

(1) Such decisions, including but not limited to exclusions (that is, total elimination) of one or more of the principal or major uses made by a management decision shall remain subject to reconsideration, modification, and termination through revision by the Secretary or his delegate, under the provisions of this section, of the land use plan involved.

(2) Any management decision or action pursuant to a management decision that excludes (that is, totally eliminates) one or more of the principal or major uses for two or more years with respect to a tract of land of one hundred thousand acres or more shall be reported by the Secretary to the House of Representatives and the Senate. If within ninety days from the giving of such notice (exclusive of days on which either House has adjourned for more than three consecutive

days), the Congress adopts a concurrent resolution of nonapproval of the management decision or action, then the management decision or action shall be promptly terminated by the Secretary. * * *

(3) Withdrawals made pursuant to section 1714 of this title may be used in carrying out management decisions, but public lands shall be removed from or restored to the operation of the Mining Law of 1872, as amended (R.S. 2318–2352; 30 U.S.C. 21 et seq.) or transferred to another department, bureau, or agency only by withdrawal action pursuant to section 1714 of this title or other action pursuant to applicable law: *Provided,* That nothing in this section shall prevent a wholly owned Government corporation from acquiring and holding rights as a citizen under the Mining Law of 1872.

Procedures applicable to formulation of plans and programs for public land management

(f) The Secretary shall allow an opportunity for public involvement and by regulation shall establish procedures, including public hearings where appropriate, to give Federal, State, and local governments and the public, adequate notice and opportunity to comment upon and participate in the formulation of plans and programs relating to the management of the public lands.

Pub.L. 94–579, Title II, § 202, Oct. 21, 1976, 90 Stat. 2747.

§ 1713. Sales of public land tracts

Criteria for disposal; excepted lands

(a) A tract of the public lands (except land in units of the National Wilderness Preservation System, National Wild and Scenic Rivers Systems, and National System of Trails) may be sold under this Act where, as a result of land use planning required under section 1712 of this title, the Secretary determines that the sale of such tract meets the following disposal criteria:

(1) such tract because of its location or other characteristics is difficult and uneconomic to manage as part of the public lands, and is not suitable for management by another Federal department or agency; or

(2) such tract was acquired for a specific purpose and the tract is no longer required for that or any other Federal purpose; or

(3) disposal of such tract will serve important public objectives, including but not limited to, expansion of communities and economic development, which cannot be achieved prudently or feasibly on land other than public land and which outweigh other public objectives and values, including, but not limited to, recreation and scenic values, which would be served by maintaining such tract in Federal ownership.

Conveyance of land of agricultural value and desert in character

(b) Where the Secretary determines that land to be conveyed under clause (3) of subsection (a) of this section is of agricultural value and is desert in character, such land shall be conveyed either under the sale authority of this section or in accordance with other existing law.

Congressional approval procedures applicable to tracts in excess of two thousand five hundred acres

(c) Where a tract of the public lands in excess of two thousand five hundred acres has been designated for sale, such sale may be made only after the end of the ninety days (not counting days on which the House of Representatives or the Senate has adjourned for more than three consecutive days) beginning on the day the Secretary has submitted notice of such designation to the Senate and the House of Representatives, and then only if the Congress has not adopted a concurrent resolution stating that such House does not approve of such designation. * * *

Sale price

(d) Sales of public lands shall be made at a price not less than their fair market value as determined by the Secretary.

Maximum size of tracts

(e) The Secretary shall determine and establish the size of tracts of public lands to be sold on the basis of the land use capabilities and development requirements of the lands; and, where any such tract which is judged by the Secretary to be chiefly valuable for agriculture is sold, its size shall be no larger than necessary to support a family-sized farm.

Competitive bidding requirements

(f) Sales of public lands under this section shall be conducted under competitive bidding procedures to be established by the Secretary. However, where the Secretary determines it necessary and proper in order (1) to assure equitable distribution among purchasers of lands, or (2) to recognize equitable considerations or public policies, including but not limited to, a preference to users, he may sell those lands with modified competitive bidding or without competitive bidding. In recognizing public policies, the Secretary shall give consideration to the following potential purchasers:

(1) the State in which the land is located;

(2) the local government entities in such State which are in the vicinity of the land;

(3) adjoining landowners;

(4) individuals; and

(5) any other person.

Acceptance or rejection of offers to purchase

(g) The Secretary shall accept or reject, in writing, any offer to purchase made through competitive bidding at his invitation no later than thirty days after the receipt of such offer or, in the case of a tract in excess of two thousand five hundred acres, at the end of thirty days after the end of the ninety-day period provided in subsection (c) of this section, whichever is later, unless the offeror waives his right to a decision within such thirty-day period. Prior to the expiration of such periods the Secretary may refuse to accept any offer or may withdraw any land or interest in land from sale under this section when he determines that consummation of the sale would not be consistent with this Act or other applicable law.

Pub.L. 94–579, Title II, § 203, Oct. 21, 1976, 90 Stat. 2750.

Unconstitutionality of Legislative Veto Provisions

The provisions of section 1254(c)(2) of Title 8, Aliens and Nationality, which authorize a House of Congress, by resolution, to invalidate an action of the Executive Branch, were declared unconstitutional in Immigration and Naturalization Service v. Chadha, 1983, 103 S. Ct. 2764, 462 U.S. 919, 77 L. Ed. 2d 317. See similar provisions in subsec. (c) of this section.

§ 1714. Withdrawals of lands

Authorization and limitation; delegation of authority

(a) On and after the effective date of this Act the Secretary is authorized to make, modify, extend, or revoke withdrawals but only in accordance with the provisions and limitations of this section. The Secretary may delegate this withdrawal authority only to individuals in the Office of the Secretary who have been appointed by the President, by and with the advice and consent of the Senate.

Application and procedure B applicable subsequent to submission of application

(b)(1) Within thirty days of receipt of an application for withdrawal, and whenever he proposes a withdrawal on his own motion, the Secretary shall publish a notice in the Federal Register stating that the application has been submitted for filing or the proposal has been made and the extent to which the land is to be segregated while the application is being considered by the Secretary. Upon publication of such notice the land shall be segregated from the operation of the public land laws to the extent specified in the notice. The segregative effect of the application shall terminate upon (a) rejection of the application by the Secretary, (b) withdrawal of lands by the Secretary, or (c) the expiration of two years from the date of the notice.

(b)(2) The publication provisions of this subsection are not applicable to withdrawals under subsection (e) hereof.

Congressional approval procedures applicable to withdrawals aggregating five thousand acres or more

(c)(1) On and after October 21, 1976, a withdrawal aggregating five thousand acres or more may be made (or such a withdrawal or any other withdrawal involving in the aggregate five thousand acres or more which terminates after such date of approval may be extended) only for a period of not more than twenty years by the Secretary on his own motion or upon request by a department or agency head. The Secretary shall notify both Houses of Congress of such a withdrawal no later than its effective date and the withdrawal shall terminate and become ineffective at the end of ninety days (not counting days on which the Senate or the House of Representatives has adjourned for more than three consecutive days) beginning on the day notice of such withdrawal has been submitted to the Senate and the House of Representatives, if the Congress has adopted a concurrent resolution stating that such House does not approve the withdrawal. If the committee to which a resolution has been referred during the said ninety day period, has not reported it at the end of thirty calendar days after its referral, it shall be in order to either discharge the committee from further consideration of such resolution or to discharge the committee from consideration of any other resolution with respect to the Presidential recommendation. A motion to discharge may be made only by an individual favoring the resolution, shall be highly privileged (except that it may not be made after the committee has reported such a resolution), and debate thereon shall be limited to not more than one hour, to be divided equally between those favoring and those opposing the resolution. An amendment to the motion shall not be in order, and it shall not be in order to move to reconsider the vote by which the motion was agreed to or disagreed to. If the motion to discharge is agreed to or disagreed to, the motion may not be made with respect to any other resolution with respect to the same Presidential recommendation. When the committee has reprinted, or has been discharged from further consideration of a resolution, it shall at any time thereafter be in order (even though a previous motion to the same effect has been disagreed to) to move to proceed to the consideration of the resolution. The motion shall be highly privileged and shall not be debatable. An amendment to the motion shall not be in order, and it shall not be in order to move to reconsider the vote by which the motion was agreed to or disagreed to.

(c)(2) With the notices required by subsection (c)(1) of this section and within three months after filing the notice under subsection (e) of this section, the Secretary shall furnish to the committees—

(1) a clear explanation of the proposed use of the land involved which led to the withdrawal;

(2) an inventory and evaluation of the current natural resource uses and values of the site and adjacent public and nonpublic land and how it appears they will be affected by the proposed use, including particularly aspects of use that might cause degradation of the environment, and also the economic impact of the change in use on individuals, local communities, and the Nation;

(3) an identification of present users of the land involved, and how they will be affected by the proposed use;

(4) an analysis of the manner in which existing and potential resource uses are incompatible with or in conflict with the proposed use, together with a statement of the provisions to be made for

continuation or termination of existing uses, including an economic analysis of such continuation or termination;

(5) an analysis of the manner in which such lands will be used in relation to the specific requirements for the proposed use;

(6) a statement as to whether any suitable alternative sites are available (including cost estimates) for the proposed use or for uses such a withdrawal would displace;

(7) a statement of the consultation which has been or will be had with other Federal departments and agencies, with regional, State, and local government bodies, and with other appropriate individuals and groups;

(8) a statement indicating the effect of the proposed uses, if any, on State and local government interests and the regional economy;

(9) a statement of the expected length of time needed for the withdrawal;

(10) the time and place of hearings and of other public involvement concerning such withdrawal;

(11) the place where the records on the withdrawal can be examined by interested parties; and

(12) a report prepared by a qualified mining engineer, engineering geologist, or geologist which shall include but not be limited to information on: general geology, known mineral deposits, past and present mineral production, mining claims, mineral leases, evaluation of future mineral potential, present and potential market demands.

Withdrawals aggregating less than five thousand acres; procedure applicable

(d) A withdrawal aggregating less than five thousand acres may be made under this subsection by the Secretary on his own motion or upon request by a department or an agency head—

(1) for such period of time as he deems desirable for a resource use; or

(2) for a period of not more than twenty years for any other use, including but not limited to use for administrative sites, location of facilities, and other proprietary purposes; or

(3) for a period of not more than five years to preserve such tract for a specific use then under consideration by the Congress.

Emergency withdrawals; procedure applicable; duration

(e) When the Secretary determines, or when the Committee on Natural Resources of the House of Representatives or the Committee on Energy and Natural Resources of the Senate notifies the Secretary, that an emergency situation exists and that extraordinary measures must be taken to preserve values that would otherwise be lost, the Secretary notwithstanding the provisions of subsections (c)(1) and (d) of this section, shall immediately make a withdrawal and file notice of such emergency withdrawal with both of those Committees. Such emergency withdrawal shall be effective when made but shall last only for a period not to exceed three years and may not be extended except under the provisions of subsection (c)(1) or (d), whichever is applicable, and (b)(1) of this section. The information required in subsection (c)(2) of this subsection shall be furnished the committees within three months after filing such notice.

Review of existing withdrawals and extensions; procedure applicable to extensions; duration

(f) All withdrawals and extensions thereof, whether made prior to or after October 21, 1976, having a specific period shall be reviewed by the Secretary toward the end of the withdrawal period and may be extended or further extended only upon compliance with the provisions of subsection (c)(1) or (d) of this section, whichever is applicable, and only if the Secretary determines that the purpose for which the withdrawal was first made requires the extension, and then only for a period no longer than the length of the original withdrawal period. The Secretary shall report on such review and extensions to the Committee on Natural Resources of the House of Representatives and the Committee on Energy and Natural Resources of the Senate.

Processing and adjudication of existing applications

(g) All applications for withdrawal pending on October 21, 1976 shall be processed and adjudicated to conclusion within fifteen years of October 21, 1976, in accordance with the provisions of this section. The segregative effect of any application not so processed shall terminate on that date.

Public hearing required for new withdrawals

(h) All new withdrawals made by the Secretary under this section (except an emergency withdrawal made under subsection (e) of this section) shall be promulgated after an opportunity for a public hearing.

Consent for withdrawal of lands under administration of department or agency other than Department of the Interior

(i) In the case of lands under the administration of any department or agency other than the Department of the Interior, the Secretary shall make, modify, and revoke withdrawals only with the consent of the head of the department or agency concerned, except when the provisions of subsection (e) of this section apply.

Applicability of other Federal laws withdrawing lands as limiting authority

(j) The Secretary shall not make, modify, or revoke any withdrawal created by Act of Congress; make a withdrawal which can be made only by Act of Congress; modify or revoke any withdrawal creating national monuments under the Act of June 8, 1906 (34 Stat. 225; 16 U.S.C. 431–433); or modify, or revoke any withdrawal which added lands to the National Wildlife Refuge System prior to October 21, 1976, or which thereafter adds lands to that System under the terms of this Act. Nothing in this Act is intended to modify or change any provision of the Act of February 27, 1976 (90 Stat. 199; 16 U.S.C. 668dd(a)).

* * *

Review of existing withdrawals in certain States; procedure applicable for determination of future status of lands; authorization of appropriations

(*l*)(1) The Secretary shall, within fifteen years of October 21, 1976, review withdrawals existing on October 21, 1976, in the States of Arizona, California, Colorado, Idaho, Montana, Nevada, New Mexico, Oregon, Utah, Washington, and Wyoming of (1) all Federal lands other than withdrawals of the public lands administered by the Bureau of Land Management and of lands which, on October 21, 1976, were part of Indian reservations and other Indian holdings, the National Forest System, the National Park System, the National Wildlife Refuge System, other lands administered by the Fish and Wildlife Service or the Secretary through the Fish and Wildlife Service, the National Wild and Scenic Rivers System, and the National System of Trails; and (2) all public lands administered by the Bureau of Land Management and of lands in the National Forest System (except those in wilderness areas, and those areas formally identified as primitive or natural areas or designated as national recreation areas) which closed the lands to appropriation under the Mining Law of 1872 (17 Stat. 91, as amended; 30 U.S.C. 22 et seq.) or to leasing under the Mineral Leasing Act of 1920 (41 Stat. 437, as amended; 30 U.S.C. 181 et seq.).

(*l*)(2) In the review required by paragraph (1) of this subsection, the Secretary shall determine whether, and for how long, the continuation of the existing withdrawal of the lands would be, in his judgment, consistent with the statutory objectives of the programs for which the lands were dedicated and of the other relevant programs. The Secretary shall report his recommendations to the President, together with statements of concurrence or nonconcurrence submitted by the heads of the departments or agencies which administer the lands. The President shall transmit this report to the President of the Senate and the Speaker of the House of Representatives, together with his recommendations for action by the Secretary, or for legislation. The Secretary may act to terminate withdrawals other than those made by Act of the Congress in accordance with the recommendations of the President unless before the end of ninety days (not counting days on which the Senate and the House of Representatives has adjourned for more than three consecutive days) beginning on the day the report of the President has been submitted to the Senate and the House of Representatives the Congress has adopted a concurrent resolution indicating otherwise. If the committee to which a resolution has been referred during the said ninety day period, has not reported it at the end of thirty calendar days after its referral, it shall be in order to either discharge the committee from further consideration of such resolution or to discharge the committee from consideration of any other resolution with respect to the Presidential recommendation. A motion to discharge may be made only by an individual favoring the resolution, shall be highly privileged (except that it may not be made after the committee has reported such a resolution), and debate thereon shall be limited to not more than one hour, to be divided equally between those favoring and those opposing the resolution. An amendment to the motion shall not be in order, and it shall not be in order to move to reconsider the vote by which the motion was agreed to or disagreed to. If the motion to discharge is agreed to or disagreed to, the motion may not be made with respect to any other resolution with respect to the same Presidential recommendation. When the committee has reprinted, or has been discharged from further consideration of a resolution, it shall at any time thereafter be in order (even though a previous motion to the same effect has been disagreed to) to move to proceed to the consideration of the resolution. The motion shall be highly privileged and shall not be debatable. An amendment to the motion shall not be in order, and it shall not be in order to move to reconsider the vote by which the motion was agreed to or disagreed to.

* * *

Pub.L. 94–579, Title II, § 204, Oct. 21, 1976, 90 Stat. 2751, as amended Pub.L. 103–437, § 16(d)(1), Nov. 2, 1994, 108 Stat. 4594.

Unconstitutionality of Legislative Veto Provisions

The provisions of section 1254(c)(2) of Title 8, Aliens and Nationality, which authorize a House of Congress, by resolution, to invalidate an action of the Executive Branch, were declared unconstitutional in Immigration and Naturalization Service v. Chadha, 1983, 103 S. Ct. 2764, 462 U.S. 919, 77 L. Ed. 2d 317. See similar provisions in this section.

§ 1715. Acquisition of public lands and access over non-Federal lands to National Forest System units

Authorization and limitations on authority of Secretary of Interior and Secretary of Agriculture

(a) Notwithstanding any other provisions of law, the Secretary, with respect to the public lands and the Secretary of Agriculture, with respect to the acquisition of access over non-Federal lands to units of the National Forest System, are authorized to acquire pursuant to this Act by purchase, exchange, donation, or eminent domain, lands or interests therein: *Provided,* That with respect to the public lands, the Secretary may exercise the power of eminent domain only if necessary to secure access to public lands, and then only if the lands so acquired are confined to as narrow a corridor as is necessary to serve such purpose. Nothing in this subsection shall be construed as expanding or limiting the authority of the Secretary of Agriculture to acquire land by eminent domain within the boundaries of units of the National Forest System.

Conformity to departmental policies and land-use plan of acquisitions

(b) Acquisitions pursuant to this section shall be consistent with the mission of the department involved and with applicable departmental land-use plans.

Status of lands and interests in lands upon acquisition by Secretary of the Interior; transfers to Secretary of Agriculture of lands and interests in lands acquired within National Forest System boundaries

(c) Except as provided in subsection (e), lands and interests in lands acquired by the Secretary pursuant to this section or section 1716 of this title shall, upon acceptance of title, become public lands and, for the administration of public land laws not repealed by this Act, shall remain public lands. If such acquired lands or interests in lands are located within the exterior boundaries of a grazing district established pursuant to section 315 of this title, they shall become a part of that district. Lands and interests in lands acquired pursuant to this section which are within boundaries of the National Forest System may be transferred to the Secretary of Agriculture and shall then become National Forest System lands and subject to all the laws, rules, and regulations applicable thereto.

Status of lands and interests in lands upon acquisition by Secretary of Agriculture

(d) Lands and interests in lands acquired by the Secretary of Agriculture pursuant to this section shall, upon acceptance of title, become National Forest System lands subject to all the laws, rules, and regulations applicable thereto.

Status and administration of lands acquired in exchange for lands revested in or reconveyed to United States

(e) Lands acquired by the Secretary pursuant to this section or section 1716 of this title in exchange for lands which were revested in the United States pursuant to the provisions of the Act of June 9, 1916 (39 Stat. 218) or reconveyed to the United States pursuant to the provisions of the Act of February 26, 1919 (40 Stat. 1179), shall be considered for all purposes to have the same status as, and shall be administered in accordance with the same provisions of law applicable to, the revested or reconveyed lands exchanged for the lands acquired by the Secretary.

Pub.L. 94–579, Title II, § 205, Oct. 21, 1976, 90 Stat. 2755. As amended Pub.L. 99–632, § 5, Nov. 7, 1986, 100 Stat. 3521.

§ 1716. Exchanges of public lands or interests therein within the National Forest System

Authorization and limitations on authority of Secretary of the Interior and Secretary of Agriculture

(a) A tract of public land or interests therein may be disposed of by exchange by the Secretary under this Act and a tract of land or interests therein within the National Forest System may be disposed of by exchange by the Secretary of Agriculture under applicable law where the Secretary concerned determines that the public interest will be well served by making that exchange: *Provided,* That when considering public interest the Secretary concerned shall give full consideration to better Federal land management and the needs of State and local people, including needs for lands for the economy, community expansion, recreation areas, food, fiber, minerals, and fish and wildlife and the Secretary concerned finds that the values and the objectives which Federal lands or interests to be conveyed may serve if retained in Federal ownership are not more than the values of the non-Federal lands or interests and the public objectives they could serve if acquired.

Implementation requirements; cash equalization waiver

(b) In exercising the exchange authority granted by subsection (a) of this section or by section 1715(a) of this title, the Secretary concerned may accept title to any non-Federal land or interests therein in exchange for such land, or interests therein which he finds proper for transfer out of Federal ownership and which are located in the same State as the non-Federal land or interest to be acquired. For the purposes of this subsection, unsurveyed school sections which, upon survey by the Secretary, would become State lands, shall be considered as "non-Federal lands". The values of the lands exchanged by the Secretary under this Act and by the Secretary of Agriculture under applicable law relating to lands within the National Forest System either shall be equal, or if they are not equal, the values shall be equalized by the payment of money to the grantor or to the Secretary concerned as the circumstances require so long as payment does not exceed 25 per centum of the total value of the lands or interests transferred out of Federal ownership. The Secretary concerned and the other party or parties involved in the exchange may mutually agree to waive the requirement for the payment of money to equalize values where the Secretary concerned determines that the exchange will be expedited thereby and that the public interest will be better served by such a waiver of cash equalization payments and where the amount to be waived is no more than 3 per centum of the value of the lands being transferred out of Federal ownership or $15,000, whichever is less, except that the Secretary of Agriculture shall not agree to waive any such requirement for payment of money to the United States. The Secretary concerned shall try to reduce the amount of the payment of money to as small an amount as possible.

Status of lands acquired upon exchange by Secretary of the Interior

(c) Lands acquired by the Secretary by exchange under this section which are within the boundaries of any unit of the National Forest System, National Park System, National Wildlife Refuge System, National Wild and Scenic Rivers System, National Trails System, National Wilderness Preservation System, or any other system established by Act of Congress, or the boundaries of the California Desert Conservation Area, or the boundaries of any national conservation area or national recreation area established by Act of Congress, upon acceptance of title by the United States shall immediately be reserved for and become a part of the unit or area within which they are located, without further action by the Secretary, and shall thereafter be managed in accordance with all laws, rules, and regulations applicable to such unit or area.

Appraisal of land; submission to arbitrator; determination to proceed or withdraw from exchange; use of other valuation process; suspension of deadlines

(d)(1) No later than ninety days after entering into an agreement to initiate an exchange of land or interests therein pursuant to this Act or other applicable law, the Secretary concerned and other party or parties involved in the exchange shall arrange for appraisal (to be completed within a time frame and under such terms as are negotiated by the parties) of the lands or interests therein involved in the exchange in accordance with subsection (f) of this section.

(d)(2) If within one hundred and eighty days after the submission of an appraisal or appraisals for review and approval by the Secretary concerned, the Secretary concerned and the other party or parties involved cannot agree to accept the findings of an appraisal or appraisals, the appraisal or appraisals shall be submitted to an arbitrator appointed by the Secretary from a list of arbitrators submitted to him by the American Arbitration Association for arbitration to be conducted in accordance with the real estate valuation arbitration rules of the American Arbitration Association. Such arbitration shall be binding for a period of not to exceed two years on the Secretary concerned and the other party or parties involved in the exchange insofar as concerns the value of the lands which were the subject of the appraisal or appraisals.

(d)(3) Within thirty days after the completion of the arbitration, the Secretary concerned and the other party or parties involved in the exchange shall determine whether to proceed with the exchange, modify the exchange to reflect the findings of the arbitration or any other factors, or to withdraw from the exchange. A decision to withdraw from the exchange may be made by either the Secretary concerned or the other party or parties involved.

(d)(4) Instead of submitting the appraisal to an arbitrator, as provided in paragraph (2) of this section, the Secretary concerned and the other party or parties involved in an exchange may mutually agree to employ a process of bargaining or some other process to determine the values of the properties involved in the exchange.

(d)(5) The Secretary concerned and the other party or parties involved in an exchange may mutually agree to suspend or modify any of the deadlines contained in this subsection.

Simultaneous issue of patents or titles

(e) Unless mutually agreed otherwise by the Secretary concerned and the other party or parties involved in an exchange pursuant to this Act or other applicable law, all patents or titles to be issued for land or interests therein to be acquired by the Federal Government and lands or interest therein to be transferred out of Federal ownership shall be issued simultaneously after the Secretary concerned has taken any necessary steps to assure that the United States will receive acceptable title.

New rules and regulations; appraisal rules and regulations; "costs and other responsibilities or requirements" defined

(f)(1) Within one year after August 20, 1988, the Secretaries of the Interior and Agriculture shall promulgate new and comprehensive rules and regulations governing exchanges of land and interests therein pursuant to this Act and other applicable law. Such rules and regulations shall fully reflect the changes in law made by subsections (d) through (i) of this section and shall include provisions pertaining to appraisals of lands and interests therein involved in such exchanges.

(f)(2) The provisions of the rules and regulations issued pursuant to paragraph (1) of this subsection governing appraisals shall reflect nationally recognized appraisal standards, including, to the extent appropriate, the Uniform Appraisal Standards for Federal Land Acquisitions: *Provided, however,* That the provisions of such rules and regulations shall—

(A) ensure that the same nationally approved appraisal standards are used in appraising lands or interest therein being acquired by the Federal Government and appraising lands or interests therein being transferred out of Federal ownership; and

(B) with respect to costs or other responsibilities or requirements associated with land exchanges—

(i) recognize that the parties involved in an exchange may mutually agree that one party (or parties) will assume, without compensation, all or part of certain costs or other responsibilities or requirements ordinarily borne by the other party or parties; and

(ii) also permit the Secretary concerned, where such Secretary determines it is in the public interest and it is in the best interest of consummating an exchange pursuant to this Act or other applicable law, and upon mutual agreement of the parties, to make adjustments to the relative values involved in an exchange transaction in order to compensate a party or parties to the exchange for assuming costs or other responsibilities or requirements which would ordinarily be borne by the other party or parties.

As used in this subparagraph, the term "costs or other responsibilities or requirements" shall include, but not be limited to, costs or other requirements associated with land surveys and appraisals, mineral examinations, title searches, archeological surveys and salvage, removal of encumbrances, arbitration pursuant to subsection (d) of this section, curing deficiencies preventing highest and best use, and other costs to comply with laws, regulations and policies applicable to exchange transactions, or which are necessary to bring the Federal or non-Federal lands or interests involved in the exchange to their highest and best use for the appraisal and exchange purposes. Prior to making any adjustments pursuant to this subparagraph, the Secretary concerned shall be satisfied that the amount of such adjustment is reasonable and accurately reflects the approximate value of any costs or services provided or any responsibilities or requirements assumed.

Exchanges to proceed under existing laws and regulations pending new rules and regulations

(g) Until such time as new and comprehensive rules and regulations governing exchange of land and interests therein are promulgated pursuant to subsection (f) of this section, land exchanges may proceed in accordance with existing laws and regulations, and nothing in the Act shall be construed to require any delay in, or otherwise hinder, the processing and consummation of land exchanges pending the promulgation of such new and comprehensive rules and regulations. Where the Secretary concerned and the party or parties involved in an exchange have agreed to initiate an exchange of land or interests therein prior to August 20, 1988, subsections (d) through (i) of this section shall not apply to such exchanges unless the Secretary concerned and the party or parties involved in the exchange mutually agree otherwise.

Exchange of lands or interests of approximately equal value; conditions; "approximately equal value" defined

(h)(1) Notwithstanding the provisions of this Act and other applicable laws which require that exchanges of land or interests therein be for equal value, where the Secretary concerned determines it is in the public interest and that the consummation of a particular exchange will be expedited thereby, the Secretary concerned may exchange lands or interests therein which are of approximately equal value in cases where—

(A) the combined value of the lands or interests therein to be transferred from Federal ownership by the Secretary concerned in such exchange is not more than $150,000; and

(B) the Secretary concerned finds in accordance with the regulations to be promulgated pursuant to subsection (f) of this section that a determination of approximately equal value can be made without formal appraisals, as based on a statement of value made by a qualified appraiser and approved by an authorized officer; and

(C) the definition of and procedure for determining "approximately equal value" has been set forth in regulations by the Secretary concerned and the Secretary concerned documents how such determination was made in the case of the particular exchange involved.

(h)(2) As used in this subsection, the term "approximately equal value" shall have the same meaning with respect to lands managed by the Secretary of Agriculture as it does in the Act of January 22, 1983 (commonly known as the "Small Tracts Act").

Segregation from appropriation under mining and public land laws

(i)(1) Upon receipt of an offer to exchange lands or interests in lands pursuant to this Act or other applicable laws, at the request of the head of the department or agency having jurisdiction over the lands involved, the Secretary of the Interior may temporarily segregate the Federal lands under consideration for exchange from appropriation under the mining laws. Such temporary segregation may only be made for a period of not to exceed five years. Upon a decision not to proceed with the exchange or upon deletion of any particular parcel from the exchange offer, the Federal lands involved or deleted shall be promptly restored to their former status under the mining laws. Any segregation pursuant to this paragraph shall be subject to valid existing rights as of the date of such segregation.

(i)(2) All non-Federal lands which are acquired by the United States through exchange pursuant to this Act or pursuant to other law applicable to lands managed by the Secretary of Agriculture shall be automatically segregated from appropriation under the public land law, including the mining laws, for ninety days after acceptance of title by the United States. Such segregation shall be subject to valid existing rights as of the date of such acceptance of title. At the end of such ninety day period, such segregation shall end and such lands shall be open to operation of the public land laws and to entry, location, and patent under the mining laws except to the extent otherwise provided by this Act or other applicable law, or appropriate actions pursuant thereto.

Pub.L. 94–579, Title II, § 206, Oct. 21, 1976, 90 Stat. 2756. As amended Pub.L. 100–409, §§ 3, 9, Aug. 20, 1988, 102 Stat. 1087, 1092.

§ 1717. Qualifications of conveyees

No tract of land may be disposed of under this Act, whether by sale, exchange, or donation, to any person who is not a citizen of the United States, or in the case of a corporation, is not subject to the laws of any State or of the United States.

Pub.L. 94–579, Title II, § 207, Oct. 21, 1976, 90 Stat. 2757.

§ 1718. Documents of conveyance; terms, covenants, etc.

The Secretary shall issue all patents or other documents of conveyance after any disposal authorized by this Act. The Secretary shall insert in any such patent or other document of conveyance he issues, except in the case of land exchanges, for which the provisions of subsection 1716(b) of this title shall apply, such terms, covenants, conditions, and reservations as he deems necessary to insure proper land use and protection of the public interest: *Provided,* That a conveyance of lands by the Secretary, subject to such terms, covenants, conditions, and reservations, shall not exempt the grantee from compliance with applicable Federal or State law or State land use plans: *Provided further,* That the Secretary shall not make conveyances of public lands containing terms and conditions which would, at the time of the conveyance, constitute a violation of any law or regulation pursuant to State and local land use plans, or programs.

Pub.L. 94–579, Title II, § 208, Oct. 21, 1976, 90 Stat. 2757.

§ 1719. Mineral interests; reservation and conveyance requirements and procedures

(a) All conveyances of title issued by the Secretary, except those involving land exchanges provided for in section 1716 of this title, shall reserve to the United States all minerals in the lands, together with the right to prospect for, mine, and remove the minerals under applicable law and such regulations as the Secretary may prescribe, except that if the Secretary makes the findings specified in subsection (b) of this section, the minerals may then be conveyed together with the surface to the prospective surface owner as provided in subsection (b) of this section.

(b)(1) The Secretary, after consultation with the appropriate department or agency head, may convey mineral interests owned by the United States where the surface is or will be in non-Federal ownership, regardless of which Federal entity may have administered the surface, if he finds (1) that there are no known mineral values in the land, or (2) that the reservation of the mineral rights in the United States is interfering with or precluding appropriate non-mineral development of the land and that such development is a more beneficial use of the land than mineral development.

(b)(2) Conveyance of mineral interests pursuant to this section shall be made only to the existing or proposed record owner of the surface, upon payment of administrative costs and the fair market value of the interests being conveyed.

* * *

Pub.L. 94–579, Title II, § 209, Oct. 21, 1976, 90 Stat. 2757.

§ 1720. Coordination by Secretary of the Interior with State and local governments

At least sixty days prior to offering for sale or otherwise conveying public lands under this Act, the Secretary shall notify the Governor of the State within which such lands are located and the head of the governing body of any political subdivision of the State having zoning or other land use regulatory jurisdiction in the geographical area within which such lands are located, in order to afford the appropriate body the opportunity to zone or otherwise regulate, or change or amend existing zoning or other regulations concerning the use of such lands prior to such conveyance. The Secretary shall also promptly notify such public officials of the issuance of the patent or other document of conveyance for such lands.

Pub.L. 94–579, Title II, § 210, Oct. 21, 1976, 90 Stat. 2758.

§ 1721. Conveyances of public lands to States, local governments, etc.

Unsurveyed islands; authorization and limitations on authority

(a) The Secretary is hereby authorized to convey to States or their political subdivisions under the Recreation and Public Purposes Act (44 Stat. 741 as amended; 43 U.S.C.A. § 869 et seq.), as amended, but without regard to the acreage limitations contained therein, unsurveyed islands determined by the Secretary to be public lands of the United States. The conveyance of any such island may be made without survey: *Provided, however,* That such island may be surveyed at the request of the applicant State or its political subdivision if such State or subdivision donates money or services to the Secretary for such survey, the Secretary accepts such money or services, and such services are conducted pursuant to criteria established by the Director of the Bureau of Land Management. Any such island so surveyed shall not be conveyed without approval of such survey by the Secretary prior to the conveyance.

Omitted lands; authorization and limitations on authority

(b)(1) The Secretary is authorized to convey to States and their political subdivisions under sections 869 to 869–4 of this title, but without regard to the acreage limitations contained therein, lands other than islands determined by him after survey to be public lands of the United States erroneously or fraudulently omitted from the original surveys (hereinafter referred to as "omitted lands"). Any such conveyance shall not be made without a survey: *Provided,* That the prospective recipient may donate money or services to the Secretary for the surveying necessary prior to conveyance if the Secretary accepts such money or services, such services are conducted pursuant to criteria established by the Director of the Bureau of Land Management, and such survey is approved by the Secretary prior to the conveyance.

(b)(2) The Secretary is authorized to convey to the occupant of any omitted lands which, after survey, are found to have been occupied and developed for a five-year period prior to January 1, 1975, if the Secretary determines that such conveyance is in the public interest and will serve objectives which outweigh all public objectives and values which would be served by retaining such lands in Federal ownership. Conveyance under this subparagraph shall be made at not less than the fair market value of the land, as determined by the Secretary, and upon payment in addition of administrative costs, including the cost of making the survey, the cost of appraisal, and the cost of making the conveyance.

Conformity with land use plans and programs and coordination with State and local governments of conveyances

(c)(1) No conveyance shall be made pursuant to this section until the relevant State government, local government, and areawide planning agency designated pursuant to section 204 of the Demonstration Cities and Metropolitan Development Act of 1966 and/or title IV of the Intergovernmental Cooperation Act of 1968 have notified the Secretary as to the consistency of such conveyance with applicable State and local government land use plans and programs.

(c)(2) The provisions of section 1720 of this title shall be applicable to all conveyances under this section.

Applicability of other statutory requirements for authorized use of conveyed lands

(d) The final sentence of section 869(c) of this title shall not be applicable to conveyances under this section.

Limitations on uses of conveyed lands

(e) No conveyance pursuant to this section shall be used as the basis for determining the baseline between Federal and State ownership, the boundary of any State for purposes of determining the extent of a State's submerged lands or the line of demarcation of Federal jurisdiction, or any similar or related purpose.

Applicability to lands within National Forest System, National Park System, National Wildlife Refuge System, and National Wild and Scenic Rivers System

(f) The provisions of this section shall not apply to any lands within the National Forest System, defined in section 1601 of Title 16, the National Park System, the National Wildlife Refuge System, and the National Wild and Scenic Rivers System.

Applicability to other statutory provisions authorizing sale of specific omitted lands

(g) Nothing in this section shall supersede the provisions of sections 1068 to 1068b of this title, and the Act of May 31, 1962, or any other Act authorizing the sale of specific omitted lands.

Pub.L. 94–579, Title II, § 211, Oct. 21, 1976, 90 Stat. 2758.

§ 1722. Sale of public lands subject to unintentional trespass

Preference right of contiguous landowners; offering price

(a) Notwithstanding the provisions of the Act of September 26, 1968 (82 Stat. 870; 43 U.S.C. 1431–1435), hereinafter called the "1968 Act", with respect to applications under the 1968 Act which were pending before the Secretary as of the effective date of this subsection and which he approves for sale under the criteria prescribed by the 1968 Act, he shall give the right of first refusal to those having a preference right under section 2 of the 1968 Act [43 U.S.C.A. § 1432]. The Secretary shall offer such lands to such preference right holders at their fair market value (exclusive of any values added to the land by such holders and their predecessors in interest) as determined by the Secretary as of September 26, 1973.

Procedures applicable

(b) Within three years after October 21, 1976, the Secretary shall notify the filers of applications subject to paragraph (a) of this section whether he will offer them the lands applied for and at what price; that is, their fair market value as of September 26, 1973, excluding any value added to the lands by the applicants or their predecessors in interest. He will also notify the President of the Senate and the Speaker of the House of Representatives of the lands which he has determined not to sell pursuant to paragraph (a) of this section and the reasons therefor. With respect to such lands which the Secretary determined not to sell, he shall take no other action to convey those lands or interests in them before the end of ninety days (not counting days on which the House of Representatives or the Senate has adjourned for more than three consecutive days) beginning on the date the Secretary has submitted such notice to the Senate and House of Representatives. If, during that ninety-day period, the Congress adopts a concurrent resolution stating the length of time such suspension of action should continue, he shall continue such suspension for the specified time period. If the committee to which a resolution has been referred during the said ninety-day period, has not reported it at the end of thirty calendar days after its referral, it shall be in order to either discharge the committee from further consideration of such resolution or to discharge the committee from consideration of any other resolution with respect to the suspension of action. A motion to discharge may be made only by an individual favoring the resolution, shall be highly privileged (except that it may not be made after the committee has reported such a resolution), and debate thereon shall be limited to not more than one hour, to be divided equally between those favoring and those opposing the resolution. An amendment to the motion shall not be in order, and it shall not be in order to move to reconsider the vote by which the motion was agreed to or disagreed to. If the motion to discharge is agreed to or disagreed to, the motion may not be made with respect to any other resolution with respect to the same suspension of action. When the committee has reprinted, or has been discharged from further consideration of a resolution, it shall at any time thereafter be in order (even though a previous motion to the same effect has been disagreed to) to move to proceed to the consideration of the resolution. The motion shall be highly privileged and shall not be debatable. An amendment to the motion shall not be in order, and it shall not be in order to move to reconsider the vote by which the motion was agreed to or disagreed to.

Time for processing of applications and sales

(c) Within five years after October 21, 1976, the Secretary shall complete the processing of all applications filed under the 1968 Act and hold sales covering all lands which he has determined to sell thereunder.

Pub.L. 94–579, Title II, § 214, Oct. 21, 1976, 90 Stat. 2760.

* * *

SUBCHAPTER III—ADMINISTRATION

§ 1731. Bureau of Land Management

Director; appointment, qualifications, functions, and duties

(a) The Bureau of Land Management established by Reorganization Plan Numbered 3, of 1946 shall have as its head a Director. Appointments to the position of Director shall hereafter be made by the President, by and with the advice and consent of the Senate. The Director of the Bureau shall have a broad background and substantial experience in public land and natural resource management. He shall carry out such functions and shall perform such duties as the Secretary may prescribe with respect to the management of lands and resources under his jurisdiction according to the applicable provisions of this Act and any other applicable law.

Statutory transfer of functions, powers and duties relating to administration of laws

(b) Subject to the discretion granted to him by Reorganization Plan Numbered 3 of 1950, the Secretary shall carry out through the Bureau all functions, powers, and duties vested in him and relating to the administration of laws which, on October 21, 1976, were carried out by him through the Bureau of Land Management established by section 403 of Reorganization Plan Numbered 3 of 1946. The Bureau shall administer such laws according to the provisions thereof existing as of October 21, 1976, as modified by the provisions of this Act or by subsequent law.

* * *

Existing regulations relating to administration of laws

(d) Nothing in this section shall affect any regulation of the Secretary with respect to the administration of laws administered by him through the Bureau on October 21, 1976.

Pub.L. 94–579, Title III,§ 301, Oct. 21, 1976, 90 Stat. 2762.

§ 1732.   Management of use, occupancy, and development of public lands

Multiple use and sustained yield requirements applicable; exception

(a) The Secretary shall manage the public lands under principles of multiple use and sustained yield, in accordance with the land use plans developed by him under section 1712 of this title when they are available, except that where a tract of such public land has been dedicated to specific uses according to any other provisions of law it shall be managed in accordance with such law.

Easements, permits, etc., for utilization through habitation, cultivation, and development of small trade or manufacturing concerns; applicable statutory requirements

(b) In managing the public lands, the Secretary shall, subject to this Act and other applicable law and under such terms and conditions as are consistent with such law, regulate, through easements, permits, leases, licenses, published rules, or other instruments as the Secretary deems appropriate, the use, occupancy, and development of the public lands, including, but not limited to, long-term leases to permit individuals to utilize public lands for habitation, cultivation, and the development of small trade or manufacturing concerns: *Provided,* That unless otherwise provided for by law, the Secretary may permit Federal departments and agencies to use, occupy, and develop public lands only through rights-of-way under section 1767 of this title, withdrawals under section 1714 of this title, and, where the proposed use and development are similar or closely related to the programs of the Secretary for the public lands involved, cooperative agreements under section 1737(b) of this title: *Provided further,* That nothing in this Act shall be construed as authorizing the Secretary concerned to require Federal permits to hunt and fish on public lands or on lands in the National Forest System and adjacent waters or as enlarging or diminishing the responsibility and authority of the States for management of fish and resident wildlife. However, the Secretary concerned may designate areas of public land and of lands in the National Forest System where, and establish periods when, no hunting or fishing will be permitted for reasons of public safety, administration, or compliance with provisions of applicable law. Except in emergencies, any regulations of the Secretary concerned relating to hunting and fishing pursuant to this section shall be put into effect only after consultation with the appropriate State fish and game department. Nothing in this Act shall modify or change any provision of Federal law relating to migratory birds or to endangered or threatened species. Except as provided in sections 1744, 1781(f), and 1782 of this title and in the last sentence of this paragraph, no provision of this section or any other section of this Act shall in any way amend the Mining Law of 1872 or impair the rights of any locators or claims under that Act, including, but not limited to, rights of ingress and egress. In managing the public lands the Secretary shall, by regulation or otherwise, take any action necessary to prevent unnecessary or undue degradation of the lands.

Revocation or suspension provision in instrument authorizing use, occupancy or development; violation of provision; procedure applicable

(c) The Secretary shall insert in any instrument providing for the use, occupancy, or development of the public lands a provision authorizing revocation or suspension, after notice and hearing, of such instrument upon a final administrative finding of a violation of any term or condition of the instrument, including, but not limited to, terms and conditions requiring compliance with regulations under Acts applicable to the public lands and compliance with applicable State or Federal air or water quality standard or implementation plan: *Provided,* That such violation occurred on public lands covered by such instrument and occurred in connection with the exercise of rights and privileges granted by it: *Provided further,* That the Secretary shall terminate any such suspension no later than the date upon which he determines the cause of said violation has been rectified: *Provided further,* That the Secretary may order an immediate temporary suspension prior to a hearing or final administrative finding if he determines that such a suspension is necessary to protect health or safety or the environment: *Provided further,* That, where other applicable law contains specific provisions for suspension, revocation, or cancellation of a permit, license, or other authorization to use, occupy, or develop the public lands, the specific provisions of such law shall prevail.

Authorization to utilize certain public lands in Alaska for military purposes

(d)(1) The Secretary of the Interior, after consultation with the Governor of Alaska, may issue to the Secretary of Defense or to the Secretary of a military department within the Department of Defense or to the Commandant of the Coast Guard a nonrenewable general authorization to utilize public lands in Alaska (other than within a conservation system unit or the Steese National Conservation Area or the White Mountains National Recreation Area) for purposes of military maneuvering, military training, or equipment testing not involving artillery firing, aerial or other gunnery, or other use of live ammunition or ordnance.

(d)(2) Use of public lands pursuant to a general authorization under this subsection shall be limited to areas where such use would not be inconsistent with the plans prepared pursuant to section 1712 of this title. Each such use shall be subject to a requirement that the using department shall be responsible for any necessary cleanup and decontamination of the lands used, and to such other terms and conditions (including but not limited to restrictions on use of off-road or all-terrain vehicles) as the Secretary of the Interior may require to—

(A) minimize adverse impacts on the natural, environmental, scientific, cultural, and other resources and values (including fish and wildlife habitat) of the public lands involved; and

(B) minimize the period and method of such use and the interference with or restrictions on other uses of the public lands involved.

(d)(3)(A) A general authorization issued pursuant to this subsection shall not be for a term of more than three years and shall be revoked in whole or in part, as the Secretary of the Interior finds necessary, prior to the end of such term upon a determination by the Secretary of the Interior that there has been a failure to comply with its terms and conditions or that activities pursuant to such an authorization have had or might have a significant adverse impact on the resources or values of the affected lands.

(d)(3)(B) Each specific use of a particular area of public lands pursuant to a general authorization under this subsection shall be subject to specific authorization by the Secretary and to appropriate terms and conditions, including such as are described in paragraph (2) of this subsection.

(d)(4) Issuance of a general authorization pursuant to this subsection shall be subject to the provisions of section 1712(f) of this title, section 3120 of Title 16, and all other applicable provisions of law. The Secretary of a military department (or the commandant of the Coast Guard) requesting such authorization shall reimburse the Secretary of the Interior for the costs of implementing this paragraph. An authorization pursuant to this subsection shall not authorize the construction of permanent structures or facilities on the public lands.

(d)(5) To the extent that public safety may require closure to public use of any portion of the public lands covered by an authorization issued pursuant to this subsection, the Secretary of the military department concerned or the Commandant of the Coast Guard shall take appropriate steps to notify the public concerning such closure and to provide appropriate warnings of risks to public safety.

(d)(6) For purposes of this subsection, the term "conservation system unit" has the same meaning as specified in section 3102 of Title 16.

Pub.L. 94–579, Title III,§ 302, Oct. 21, 1976, 90 Stat. 2762. As amended Pub.L. 100–586, Nov. 3, 1988, 102 Stat. 2980.

§ 1733. Enforcement authority

Regulations for implementation of management, use, and protection requirements; violations; criminal penalties

(a) The Secretary shall issue regulations necessary to implement the provisions of this Act with respect to the management, use, and protection of the public lands, including the property located thereon. Any person who knowingly and willfully violates any such regulation which is lawfully issued pursuant to this Act shall be fined no more than $1,000 or imprisoned no more than twelve months, or both. Any person charged with a violation of such regulation may be tried and sentenced by any United States magistrate judge designated for that purpose by the court by which he was appointed, in the same manner and subject to the same conditions and limitations as provided for in section 3401 of Title 18.

Civil actions by Attorney General for violations of regulations; nature of relief; jurisdiction

(b) At the request of the Secretary, the Attorney General may institute a civil action in any United States district court for an injunction or other appropriate order to prevent any person from utilizing public lands in violation of regulations issued by the Secretary under this Act.

Contracts for enforcement of Federal laws and regulations by local law enforcement officials; procedure applicable; contract requirements and implementation

(c)(1) When the Secretary determines that assistance is necessary in enforcing Federal laws and regulations relating to the public lands or their resources he shall offer a contract to appropriate local officials having law enforcement authority within their respective jurisdictions with the view of achieving maximum feasible reliance upon local law enforcement officials in enforcing such laws and regulations. The Secretary shall negotiate on reasonable terms with such officials who have authority to enter into such contracts to enforce such Federal laws and regulations. In the performance of their duties under such contracts such officials and their agents are authorized to carry firearms; execute and serve any warrant or other process issued by a court or officer of competent jurisdiction; make arrests without warrant or process for a misdemeanor he has reasonable grounds to believe is being committed in his presence or view, or for a felony if he has reasonable grounds to believe that the person to be arrested has committed or is committing such felony; search without warrant or process any person, place, or conveyance according to any Federal law or rule of law; and seize without warrant or process any evidentiary item as provided by Federal law. The Secretary shall provide such law enforcement training as he deems necessary in order to carry out the contracted for responsibilities. While exercising the powers and authorities provided by such contract pursuant to this section, such law enforcement officials and their agents shall have all the immunities of Federal law enforcement officials.

(c)(2) The Secretary may authorize Federal personnel or appropriate local officials to carry out his law enforcement responsibilities with respect to the public lands and their resources. Such designated personnel shall receive the training and have the responsibilities and authority provided for in paragraph (1) of this subsection.

Cooperation with regulatory and law enforcement officials of any State or political subdivision in enforcement of laws or ordinances

(d) In connection with the administration and regulation of the use and occupancy of the public lands, the Secretary is authorized to cooperate with the regulatory and law enforcement officials of any State or political subdivision thereof in the enforcement of the laws or ordinances of such State or subdivision. Such cooperation may include reimbursement to a State or its subdivision for expenditures incurred by it in connection with activities which assist in the administration and regulation of use and occupancy of the public lands.

Uniformed desert ranger force in California Desert Conservation Area; establishment; enforcement of Federal laws and regulations

(e) In connection with the administration and regulation of the use and occupancy of the public lands, the Secretary is authorized to cooperate with the regulatory and law enforcement officials of any State or political subdivision thereof in the enforcement of the laws or ordinances of such State or subdivision. Such cooperation may include reimbursement to a State or its subdivision for expenditures incurred by it in connection with activities which assist in the administration and regulation of use and occupancy of the public lands.

Applicability of other Federal enforcement provisions

(f) Nothing in this Act shall be construed as reducing or limiting the enforcement authority vested in the Secretary by any other statute.

Unlawful activities

(g) The use, occupancy, or development of any portion of the public lands contrary to any regulation of the Secretary or other responsible authority, or contrary to any order issued pursuant to any such regulation, is unlawful and prohibited.

Pub.L. 94–579, Title III, § 303, Oct. 21, 1976, 90 Stat. 2763, as amended 101–650, Title III, § 321, Dec. 1, 1990, 104 Stat. 5117.

§ 1734.   Fees, charges, and commissions

Authority to establish and modify

(a) Notwithstanding any other provision of law, the Secretary may establish reasonable filing and service fees and reasonable charges, and commissions with respect to applications and other documents relating to the public lands and may change and abolish such fees, charges, and commissions.

* * *

Pub.L. 94–579, Title III, § 304, Oct. 21, 1976, 90 Stat. 2765.

§ **1734a.** Availability of excess fees

In fiscal year 1997 and thereafter, all fees, excluding mining claim fees, in excess of the fiscal year 1996 collections established by the Secretary of the Interior under the authority of section 1734 of this title for processing, recording, or documenting authorizations to use public lands or public land natural resources (including cultural, historical, and mineral) and for providing specific services to public land users, and which are not presently being covered into any Bureau of Land Management appropriation accounts, and not otherwise dedicated by law for a specific distribution, shall be made immediately available for program operations in this account and remain available until expended.

Pub.L. 104–208, Div. A, Title I, § 101(d) [Title I], Sept. 30, 1996, 110 Stat. 3009–182.

§ **1735.** Forfeitures and deposits

Credit to separate account in Treasury; appropriation and availability

(a) Any moneys received by the United States as a result of the forfeiture of a bond or other security by a resource developer or purchaser or permittee who does not fulfill the requirements of his contract or permit or does not comply with the regulations of the Secretary; or as a result of a compromise or settlement of any claim whether sounding in tort or in contract involving present or potential damage to the public lands shall be credited to a separate account in the Treasury and are hereby authorized to be appropriated and made available, until expended as the Secretary may direct, to cover the cost to the United States of any improvement, protection, or rehabilitation work on those public lands which has been rendered necessary by the action which has led to the forfeiture, compromise, or settlement.

* * *

Pub.L. 94–579, Title III, § 305, Oct. 21, 1976, 90 Stat. 2765.

* * *

§ **1739.** Advisory councils

Establishment; membership; operation

(a) The Secretary shall establish advisory councils of not less than ten and not more than fifteen members appointed by him from among persons who are representative of the various major citizens' interests concerning the problems relating to land use planning or the management of the public lands located within the area for which an advisory council is established. At least one member of each council shall be an elected official of general purpose government serving the people of such area. To the extent practicable there shall be no overlap or duplication of such councils. Appointments shall be made in accordance with rules prescribed by the Secretary. The establishment and operation of an advisory council established under this section shall conform to the requirements of the Federal Advisory Committee Act (86 Stat. 770).

* * *

Functions

(d) An advisory council may furnish advice to the Secretary with respect to the land use planning, classification, retention, management, and disposal of the public lands within the area for which the advisory council is established and such other matters as may be referred to it by the Secretary.

Public participation; procedures applicable

(e) In exercising his authorities under this Act, the Secretary, by regulation, shall establish procedures, including public hearings where appropriate, to give the Federal, State, and local governments and the public adequate notice and an opportunity to comment upon the formulation of standards and criteria for, and to participate in, the preparation and execution of plans and programs for, and the management of, the public lands.

Pub.L. 94–579, Title Ill, § 309, Oct. 21, 1976, 90 Stat. 2767, amended Pub.L. 95–514, § 13, Oct. 25, 1978, 92 Stat. 1808.

§ 1740. Rules and regulations

The Secretary with respect to the public lands shall promulgate rules and regulations to carry out the purposes of this Act and of other laws applicable to the public lands, and the Secretary of Agriculture, with respect to lands within the National Forest System, shall promulgate rules and regulations to carry out the purposes of this Act. The promulgation of such rules and regulations shall be governed by the provisions of chapter 5 of Title 5, without regard to section 553(a)(2). Prior to the promulgation of such rules and regulations, such lands shall be administered under existing rules and regulations concerning such lands to the extent practical.

Pub.L. 94–579, Title III,§ 310, Oct. 21, 1976, 90 Stat. 2767.

* * *

§ 1744. Recordation of mining claims

Filing requirements

(a) The owner of an unpatented lode or placer mining claim located prior to October 21, 1976, shall, within the three-year period following October 21, 1976, and prior to December 31 of each year thereafter, file the instruments required by paragraphs (1) and (2) of this subsection. The owner of an unpatented lode or placer mining claim located after October 21, 1976 shall, prior to December 31 of each year following the calendar year in which the said claim was located, file the instruments required by paragraphs (1) and (2) of this subsection:

(1) File for record in the office where the location notice or certificate is recorded either a notice of intention to hold the mining claim (including but not limited to such notices as are provided by law to be filed when there has been a suspension or deferment of annual assessment work), an affidavit of assessment work performed thereon, on[1] a detailed report provided by section 28–1 of Title 30, relating thereto.

(2) File in the office of the Bureau designated by the Secretary a copy of the official record of the instrument filed or recorded pursuant to paragraph (1) of this subsection, including a description of the location of the mining claim sufficient to locate the claimed lands on the ground.

Additional filing requirements

(b) The owner of an unpatented lode or placer mining claim or mill or tunnel site located prior to October 21, 1976 shall, within the three-year period following October 21, 1976, file in the office of the Bureau designated by the Secretary a copy of the official record of the notice of location or certificate of location, including a description of the location of the mining claim or mill or tunnel site sufficient to locate the claimed lands on the ground. The owner of an unpatented lode or placer mining claim or mill or tunnel site located after October 21, 1976 shall, within ninety days after the date of location of such claim, file in the office of the Bureau designated by the Secretary a copy of the official record of the notice of location or certificate of location, including a description of the location of the mining claim or mill or tunnel site sufficient to locate the claimed lands on the ground.

Failure to file as constituting abandonment; defective or untimely filing

(c) The failure to file such instruments as required by subsections (a) and (b) of this section shall be deemed conclusively to constitute an abandonment of the mining claim or mill or tunnel site by the owner; but it shall not be considered a failure to file if the instrument is defective or not timely filed for record under other Federal laws permitting filing or recording thereof, or if the instrument is filed for record by or on behalf of some but not all of the owners of the mining claim or mill or tunnel site.

Validity of claims, waiver of assessment, etc., as unaffected

(d) Such recordation or application by itself shall not render valid any claim which would not be otherwise valid under applicable law. Nothing in this section shall be construed as a waiver of the assessment and other requirements of such law.

Pub.L. 94–579, Title III, § 314, Oct. 21, 1976, 90 Stat. 2769.

1. So in original. Probably should be "or".

§ **1745.** Disclaimer of interest in lands

Issuance of recordable document; criteria

(a) After consulting with any affected Federal agency, the Secretary is authorized to issue a document of disclaimer of interest or interests in any lands in any form suitable for recordation, where the disclaimer will help remove a cloud on the title of such lands and where he determines (1) a record interest of the United States in lands has terminated by operation of law or is otherwise invalid; or (2) the lands lying between the meander line shown on a plat of survey approved by the Bureau or its predecessors and the actual shoreline of a body of water are not lands of the United States; or (3) accreted, relicted, or avulsed lands are not lands of the United States.

Procedures applicable

(b) No document or disclaimer shall be issued pursuant to this section unless the applicant therefor has filed with the Secretary an application in writing and notice of such application setting forth the grounds supporting such application has been published in the Federal Register at least ninety days preceding the issuance of such disclaimer and until the applicant therefor has paid to the Secretary the administrative costs of issuing the disclaimer as determined by the Secretary. All receipts shall be deposited to the then-current appropriation from which expended.

Construction as quit-claim deed from United States

(c) Issuance of a document of disclaimer by the Secretary pursuant to the provisions of this section and regulations promulgated hereunder shall have the same effect as a quit-claim deed from the United States.

Pub.L. 94–579, Title Ill, § 315, Oct. 21, 1976, 90 Stat. 2770.

* * *

§ **1747.** Loans to States and political subdivisions; purposes; amounts; allocation; terms and conditions; interest rate; security; limitations; forbearance for benefit of borrowers; recordkeeping requirements; discrimination prohibited; deposit of receipts

(1) The Secretary is authorized to make loans to States and their political subdivisions in order to relieve social or economic impacts occasioned by the development of minerals leased in such States pursuant to the Act of February 25, 1920, as amended [30 U.S.C.A. § 181 et seq.]. Such loans shall be confined to the uses specified for the 50 per centum of mineral leasing revenues to be received by such States and subdivisions pursuant to section 35 of such Act [30 U.S.C.A. § 191].

(2) The total amount of loans outstanding pursuant to this section for any State and political subdivisions thereof in any year shall be not more than the anticipated mineral leasing revenues to be received by that State

pursuant to section 35 of the Act of February 25, 1920, as amended [30 U.S.C.A. § 191], for the ten years following.

* * *

Pub.L. 94–579, Title III,§ 317(c), Oct. 21, 1976, 90 Stat. 2771; Pub.L. 95–352, § 1(f), Aug. 20, 1978, 92 Stat. 515.

* * *

SUBCHAPTER IV—RANGE MANAGEMENT

§ 1751. Grazing fees; feasibility study; contents; submission of report; annual distribution and use of range betterment funds; nature of distributions

(a) The Secretary of Agriculture and the Secretary of the Interior shall jointly cause to be conducted a study to determine the value of grazing on the lands under their jurisdiction in the eleven Western States with a view to establishing a fee to be charged for domestic livestock grazing on such lands which is equitable to the United States and to the holders of grazing permits and leases on such lands. In making such study, the Secretaries shall take into consideration the costs of production normally associated with domestic livestock grazing in the eleven Western States, differences in forage values, and such other factors as may relate to the reasonableness of such fees. The Secretaries shall report the result of such study to the Congress not later than one year from and after October 21, 1976, together with recommendations to implement a reasonable grazing fee schedule based upon such study. If the report required herein has not been submitted to the Congress within one year after October 21, 1976, the grazing fee charge then in effect shall not be altered and shall remain the same until such report has been submitted to the Congress. Neither Secretary shall increase the grazing fee in the 1977 grazing year.

(b)(1) Congress finds that a substantial amount of the Federal range lands is deteriorating in quality, and that installation of additional range improvements could arrest much of the continuing deterioration and could lead to substantial betterment of forage conditions with resulting benefits to wildlife, watershed protection, and livestock production. Congress therefore directs that 50 per centum or $10,000,000 per annum, whichever is greater of all moneys received by the United States as fees for grazing domestic livestock on public lands (other than from ceded Indian lands) under the Taylor Grazing Act (48 Stat. 1269; 43 U.S.C. 315 et seq.) and the Act of August 28, 1937 (50 Stat. 874; 43 U.S.C. 1181d), and on lands in National Forests in the sixteen contiguous Western States under the provisions of this section shall be credited to a separate account in the Treasury, one-half of which is authorized to be appropriated and made available for use in the district, region, or national forest from which such moneys were derived, as the respective Secretary may direct after consultation with district, regional, or national forest user representatives, for the purpose of on-the-ground range rehabilitation, protection, and improvements on such lands, and the remaining one-half shall be used for on-the-ground range rehabilitation, protection, and improvements as the Secretary concerned directs. Any funds so appropriated shall be in addition to any other appropriations made to the respective Secretary for planning and administration of the range betterment program and for other range management. Such rehabilitation, protection, and improvements shall include all forms of range land betterment including, but not limited to, seeding and reseeding, fence construction, weed control, water development, and fish and wildlife habitat enhancement as the respective Secretary may direct after consultation with user representatives. The annual distribution and use of range betterment funds authorized by this paragraph shall not be considered a major Federal action requiring a detailed statement pursuant to section 4332(c) of Title 42.

(b)(2) All distributions of moneys made under subsection (b)(1) of this section shall be in addition to distributions made under section 10 of the Taylor Grazing Act [43 U.S.C.A. § 315i] and shall not apply to distribution of moneys made under section 11 of that Act [43 U.S.C.A. § 315j]. The remaining moneys received by the United States as fees for grazing domestic livestock on the public lands shall be deposited in the Treasury as miscellaneous receipts.

Pub.L. 94–579, Title IV, § 401(a), (b)(1), (2), Oct. 21, 1976, 90 Stat. 2772; Pub.L. 95–514, § 6(b), Oct. 25, 1978, 92 Stat. 1806.

§ 1752. Grazing leases and permits

Terms and conditions

(a) Except as provided in subsection (b) of this section, permits and leases for domestic livestock grazing on public lands issued by the Secretary under the Act of June 28, 1934 (48 Stat. 1269, as amended; 43 U.S.C.A. § 315 et seq.) or the Act of August 28, 1937 (50 Stat. 874, as amended; 43 U.S.C.A. §§ 1181a–1181j), or by the Secretary of Agriculture, with respect to lands within National Forests in the sixteen contiguous Western States, shall be for a term of ten years subject to such terms and conditions the Secretary concerned deems appropriate and consistent with the governing law, including, but not limited to, the authority of the Secretary concerned to cancel, suspend, or modify a grazing permit or lease, in whole or in part, pursuant to the terms and conditions thereof, or to cancel or suspend a grazing permit or lease for any violation of a grazing regulation or of any term or condition of such grazing permit or lease.

Terms of lesser duration

(b) Permits or leases may be issued by the Secretary concerned for a period shorter than ten years where the Secretary concerned determines that—

(1) the land is pending disposal; or

(2) the land will be devoted to a public purpose prior to the end of ten years; or

(3) it will be in the best interest of sound land management to specify a shorter term: *Provided,* That the absence from an allotment management plan of details the Secretary concerned would like to include but which are undeveloped shall not be the basis for establishing a term shorter than ten years: *Provided further,* That the absence

470

of completed land use plans or court ordered environmental statements shall not be the sole basis for establishing a term shorter than ten years unless the Secretary determines on a case-by-case basis that the information to be contained in such land use plan or court ordered environmental impact statement is necessary to determine whether a shorter term should be established for any of the reasons set forth in items (1) through (3) of this subsection.

First priority for renewal of expiring permit or lease

(c) So long as (1) the lands for which the permit or lease is issued remain available for domestic livestock grazing in accordance with land use plans prepared pursuant to section 1712 of this title or section 1604 of Title 16, (2) the permittee or lessee is in compliance with the rules and regulations issued and the terms and conditions in the permit or lease specified by the Secretary concerned, and (3) the permittee or lessee accepts the terms and conditions to be included by the Secretary concerned in the new permit or lease, the holder of the expiring permit or lease shall be given first priority for receipt of the new permit or lease.

Allotment management plan requirements

(d) All permits and leases for domestic livestock grazing issued pursuant to this section may incorporate an allotment management plan developed by the Secretary concerned. However, nothing in this subsection shall be construed to supersede any requirement for completion of court ordered environmental impact statements prior to development and incorporation of allotment management plans. If the Secretary concerned elects to develop an allotment management plan for a given area, he shall do so in careful and considered consultation, cooperation and coordination with the lessees, permittees, and landowners involved, the district grazing advisory boards established pursuant to section 1753 of this title, and any State or States having lands within the area to be covered by such allotment management plan. Allotment management plans shall be tailored to the specific range condition of the area to be covered by such plan, and shall be reviewed on a periodic basis to determine whether they have been effective in improving the range condition of the lands involved or whether such lands can be better managed under the provisions of subsection (e) of this section. The Secretary concerned may revise or terminate such plans or develop new plans from time to time after such review and careful and considered consultation, cooperation and coordination with the parties involved. As used in this subsection, the terms "court ordered environmental impact statement" and "range condition" shall be defined as in the "Public Rangelands Improvement Act of 1978 [43 U.S.C.A. § 1901 et seq.]."

Omission of allotment management plan requirements and incorporation of appropriate terms and conditions; reexamination of range conditions

(e) In all cases where the Secretary concerned has not completed an allotment management plan or determines that an allotment management plan is not necessary for management of livestock operations and will not be prepared, the Secretary concerned shall incorporate in grazing permits and leases such terms and conditions as he deems appropriate for management of the permitted or leased lands pursuant to applicable law. The Secretary concerned shall also specify therein the numbers of animals to be grazed and the seasons of use and that he may reexamine the condition of the range at any time and, if he finds on re-examination that the condition of the range requires adjustment in the amount or other aspect of grazing use, that the permittee or lessee shall adjust his use to the extent the Secretary concerned deems necessary. Such readjustment shall be put into full force and effect on the date specified by the Secretary concerned.

Allotment management plan applicability to non-Federal lands; appeal rights

(f) Allotment management plans shall not refer to livestock operations or range improvements on non-Federal lands except where the non-Federal lands are intermingled with, or, with the consent of the permittee or lessee involved, associated with, the Federal lands subject to the plan. The Secretary concerned under appropriate regulations shall grant to lessees and permittees the right of appeal from decisions which specify the terms and conditions of allotment management plans. The preceding sentence of this subsection shall not be construed as limiting any other right of appeal from decisions of such officials.

Cancellation of permit or lease; determination of reasonable compensation; notice

(g) Whenever a permit or lease for grazing domestic livestock is canceled in whole or in part, in order to devote the lands covered by the permit or lease to another public purpose, including disposal, the permittee or lessee shall receive from the United States a reasonable compensation for the adjusted value, to be determined by the Secretary concerned, of his interest in authorized permanent improvements placed or constructed by the permittee or lessee on lands covered by such permit or lease, but not to exceed the fair market value of the terminated portion of the permittee's or lessee's interest therein. Except in cases of emergency, no permit or lease shall be canceled under this subsection without two years' prior notification.

Applicability of provisions to rights, etc., in or to public lands or lands in National Forests

(h) Nothing in this Act shall be construed as modifying in any way law existing on October 21, 1976, with respect to the creation of right, title, interest or estate in or to public lands or lands in National Forests by issuance of grazing permits and leases.

Pub.L. 94–579, Title IV, § 402, Oct. 21, 1976, 90 Stat. 2773, amended Pub.L. 95–514, §§ 7, 8, Oct. 25, 1978, 92 Stat. 1807.

§ 1753. Grazing advisory boards

Establishment; maintenance

(a) For each Bureau district office and National Forest headquarters office in the sixteen contiguous Western States having jurisdiction over more than five hundred thousand acres of lands subject to commercial livestock grazing (hereinafter in this section referred to as "office"), the Secretary and the Secretary of Agriculture, upon the petition of a simple majority of the livestock lessees and permittees under the jurisdiction of such office, shall establish and maintain at least one grazing advisory board of not more than fifteen advisers.

Functions

(b) The function of grazing advisory boards established pursuant to this section shall be to offer advice and make recommendations to the head of the office involved concerning the development of allotment management plans and the utilization of range-betterment funds.

Appointment and terms of members

(c) The number of advisers on each board and the number of years an adviser may serve shall be determined by the Secretary concerned in his discretion. Each board shall consist of livestock representatives who shall be lessees or permittees in the area administered by the office concerned and shall be chosen by the lessees and permittees in the area through an election prescribed by the Secretary concerned.

Meetings

(d) Each grazing advisory board shall meet at least once annually.

Federal Advisory Committee Act applicability

(e) Except as may be otherwise provided by this section, the provisions of the Federal Advisory Committee Act (86 Stat. 770) shall apply to grazing advisory boards.

Expiration date

(f) The provisions of this section shall expire December 31, 1985.

Pub.L. 94–579, Title IV, § 403, Oct. 21, 1976, 90 Stat. 2775, amended Pub.L. 95–514, § 10, Oct. 25, 1978, 92 Stat. 1808.

SUBCHAPTER V—RIGHTS–OF–WAY

§ 1761. Grant, issue, or renewal of rights-of-way; authorized purposes; procedures applicable

Authorized purposes

(a) The Secretary, with respect to the public lands (including public lands, as defined in section 1702(e) of this title, which are reserved from entry pursuant to section 24 of the Federal Power Act [16 U.S.C.A. § 818]) and, the Secretary of Agriculture, with respect to lands within the National Forest System (except in each case land designated as wilderness), are authorized to grant, issue, or renew rights-of-way over, upon, under, or through such lands for—

473

(1) reservoirs, canals, ditches, flumes, laterals, pipes, pipelines, tunnels, and other facilities and systems for the impoundment, storage, transportation, or distribution of water;

(2) pipelines and other systems for the transportation or distribution of liquids and gases, other than water and other than oil, natural gas, synthetic liquid or gaseous fuels, or any refined product produced therefrom, and for storage and terminal facilities in connection therewith;

(3) pipelines, slurry and emulsion systems, and conveyor belts for transportation and distribution of solid materials, and facilities for the storage of such materials in connection therewith;

(4) systems for generation, transmission, and distribution of electric energy, except that the applicant shall also comply with all applicable requirements of the Federal Energy Regulatory Commission under the Federal Power Act, including part 1 thereof (41 Stat. 1063, 16 U.S.C. 791a–825r);

(5) systems for transmission or reception of radio, television, telephone, telegraph, and other electronic signals, and other means of communication;

(6) roads, trails, highways, railroads, canals, tunnels, tramways, airways, livestock driveways, or other means of transportation except where such facilities are constructed and maintained in connection with commercial recreation facilities on lands in the National Forest System; or

(7) such other necessary transportation or other systems or facilities which are in the public interest and which require rights-of-way over, upon, under, or through such lands.

Procedures applicable; administration

(b)(1) The Secretary concerned shall require, prior to granting, issuing, or renewing a right-of-way, that the applicant submit and disclose those plans, contracts, agreements, or other information reasonably related to the use, or intended use, of the right-of-way, including its effect on competition, which he deems necessary to a determination, in accordance with the provisions of this Act, as to whether a right-of-way shall be granted, issued, or renewed and the terms and conditions which should be included in the right-of-way.

(b)(2) If the applicant is a partnership, corporation, association, or other business entity, the Secretary concerned, prior to granting a right-to-way pursuant to this subchapter, shall require the applicant to disclose the identity of the participants in the entity, when he deems it necessary to a determination, in accordance with the provisions of this subchapter, as to whether a right-of-way shall be granted, issued, or renewed and the terms and conditions which should be included in the right-of-way. Such disclosures shall include, where applicable: (A) the name and address of each partner; (B) the name and address of each shareholder owning 3 per centum or more of the shares, together with the number and percentage of any class of voting shares of the entity which such shareholder is authorized to vote; and (C) the name and address of each affiliate of the entity together with, in the case of an affiliate controlled by the entity, the number of shares and the percentage of any class of voting stock of that affiliate owned, directly or indirectly, by that entity, and, in the case of an affiliate which controls that entity, the number of shares and the percentage of any class of voting stock of that entity owned, directly or indirectly, by the affiliate.

(b)(3) The Secretary of Agriculture shall have the authority to administer all rights-of-way granted or issued under authority of previous Acts with respect to lands under the jurisdiction of the Secretary of Agriculture, including rights-of-way granted or issued pursuant to authority given to the Secretary of the Interior by such previous Acts.

Permanent easement for water systems; issuance, preconditions, etc.

(c)(1) Upon receipt of a written application pursuant to paragraph (2) of this subsection from an applicant meeting the requirements of this subsection, the Secretary of Agriculture shall issue a permanent easement, without a requirement for reimbursement, for a water system as described in subsection (a)(1) of this section, traversing Federal lands within the National Forest System ("National Forest Lands"), constructed and in operation or placed into operation prior to October 21, 1976, if—

(A) the traversed National Forest lands are in a State where the appropriation doctrine governs the ownership of water rights;

(B) at the time of submission of the application the water system is used solely for agricultural irrigation or livestock watering purposes;

(C) the use served by the water system is not located solely on Federal lands;

(D) the originally constructed facilities comprising such system have been in substantially continuous operation without abandonment;

(E) the applicant has a valid existing right, established under applicable State law, for water to be conveyed by the water system;

(F) a recordable survey and other information concerning the location and characteristics of the system as necessary for proper management of National Forest lands is provided to the Secretary of Agriculture by the applicant for the easement; and

(G) the applicant submits such application on or before December 31, 1996.

(c)(2)(A) Nothing in this subsection shall be construed as affecting any grants made by any previous Act. To the extent any such previous grant of right-of-way is a valid existing right, it shall remain in full force and effect unless an owner thereof notifies the Secretary of Agriculture that such owner elects to have a water system on such right-of-way governed by the provisions of this subsection and submits a written application for issuance of an easement pursuant to this subsection, in which case upon the issuance of an easement pursuant to this subsection such previous grant shall be deemed to have been relinquished and shall terminate.

(c)(2)(B) Easements issued under the authority of this subsection shall be fully transferable with all existing conditions and without the imposition of fees or new conditions or stipulations at the time of transfer. The holder shall notify the Secretary of Agriculture within sixty days of any address change of the holder or change in ownership of the facilities.

(c)(2)(C) Easements issued under the authority of this subsection shall include all changes or modifications to the original facilities in existence as of October 21, 1976, the date of enactment of this Act.

(c)(2)(D) Any future extension or enlargement of facilities after October 21, 1976, shall require the issuance of a separate authorization, not authorized under this subsection.

(c)(3)(A) Except as otherwise provided in this subsection, the Secretary of Agriculture may terminate or suspend an easement issued pursuant to this subsection in accordance with the procedural and other provisions of section 1766 of this title. An easement issued pursuant to this subsection shall terminate if the water system for which such easement was issued is used for any purpose other than agricultural irrigation or livestock watering use. For purposes of subparagraph (D) of paragraph (1) of this subsection, non-use of a water system for agricultural irrigation or livestock watering purposes for any continuous five-year period shall constitute a rebuttable presumption of abandonment of the facilities comprising such system.

(c)(3)(B) Nothing in this subsection shall be deemed to be an assertion by the United States of any right or claim with regard to the reservation, acquisition, or use of water. Nothing in this subsection shall be deemed to confer on the Secretary of Agriculture any power or authority to regulate or control in any manner the appropriation, diversion, or use of water for any purpose (nor to diminish any such power or authority of such Secretary under applicable law) or to require the conveyance or transfer to the United States of any right or claim to the appropriation, diversion, or use of water.

(c)(3)(C) Except as otherwise provided in this subsection, all rights-of-way issued pursuant to this subsection are subject to all conditions and requirements of this Act.

(c)(3)(D) In the event a right-of-way issued pursuant to this subsection is allowed to deteriorate to the point of threatening persons or property and the holder of the right-of-way, after consultation with the Secretary of Agriculture, refuses to perform the repair and maintenance necessary to remove the threat to persons or property, the Secretary shall have the right to undertake such repair and maintenance on the right-of-way and to assess the holder for the costs of such repair and maintenance, regardless of whether the Secretary had required the holder to furnish a bond or other security pursuant to subsection (i) of this section.

Rights-of-way on certain Federal lands

(d) With respect to any project or portion thereof that was licensed pursuant to, or granted an exemption from, part I of the Federal Power Act

[16 U.S.C.A. §§ 791a et seq.] which is located on lands subject to a reservation under section 24 of the Federal Power Act [16 U.S.C.A. § 818] and which did not receive a permit, right-of-way or other approval under this section prior to October 24, 1992, no such permit, right-of-way, or other approval shall be required for continued operation, including continued operation pursuant to section 15 of the Federal Power Act [16 U.S.C.A. § 808], of such project unless the Commission determines that such project involves the use of any additional public lands or National Forest lands not subject to such reservation.

As amended Pub.L. 99–545, § 1(b), (c), Oct. 27, 1986, 100 Stat. 3047, 3048. Pub.L. 94–579, Title V, § 501, Oct. 21, 1976, 90 Stat. 2776, as amended Pub.L. 99–545, § 1(b), (c), Oct. 27, 1986, 100 Stat. 3047, 3048; Pub.L. 102–486, Title XXIV, § 2401, Oct. 24, 1992, 106 Stat. 3096.

§ 1762. Roads

Authority to acquire, construct, and maintain; financing arrangements

(a) The Secretary, with respect to the public lands, is authorized to provide for the acquisition, construction, and maintenance of roads within and near the public lands in locations and according to specifications which will permit maximum economy in harvesting timber from such lands tributary to such roads and at the same time meet the requirements for protection, development, and management of such lands for utilization of the other resources thereof. Financing of such roads may be accomplished (1) by the Secretary utilizing appropriated funds, (2) by requirements on purchasers of timber and other products from the public lands, including provisions for amortization of road costs in contracts, (3) by cooperative financing with other public agencies and with private agencies or persons, or (4) by a combination of these methods: *Provided,* That, where roads of a higher standard than that needed in the harvesting and removal of the timber and other products covered by the particular sale are to be constructed, the purchaser of timber and other products from public lands shall not, except when the provisions of the second proviso of this subsection apply, be required to bear that part of the costs necessary to meet such higher standard, and the Secretary is authorized to make such arrangements to this end as may be appropriate: *Provided further,* That when timber is offered with the condition that the purchaser thereof will build a road or roads in accordance with standards specified in the offer, the purchaser of the timber will be responsible for paying the full costs of construction of such roads.

Recordation of copies of affected instruments

(b) Copies of all instruments affecting permanent interests in land executed pursuant to this section shall be recorded in each county where the lands are located.

Maintenance or reconstruction of facilities by users

(c) The Secretary may require the user or users of a road, trail, land, or other facility administered by him through the Bureau, including purchasers of Government timber and other products, to maintain such facilities in a satisfactory condition commensurate with the particular use requirements of each. Such maintenance to be borne by each user shall be proportionate to total use. The Secretary may also require the user or users of such a facility to reconstruct the same when such reconstruction is determined to be necessary to accommodate such use. * * *

Fund for user fees for delayed payment to grantor

(d) Whenever the agreement under which the United States has obtained for the use of, or in connection with, the public lands a right-of-way or easement for a road or an existing road or the right to use an existing road provides for delayed payments to the Government's grantor, any fees or other collections received by the Secretary for the use of the road may be placed in a fund to be available for making payments to the grantor.

Pub.L. 94–579, Title V, § 502, Oct. 21, 1976, 90 Stat. 2777.

§ 1763. Right-of-way corridors; criteria and procedures applicable for designation

In order to minimize adverse environmental impacts and the proliferation of separate rights-of-way, the utilization of rights-of-way in common shall be required to the extent practical, and each right-of-way or permit shall reserve to the Secretary concerned the right to grant additional rights-of-way or permits for compatible uses on or adjacent to rights-of-way granted pursuant to this Act. In designating right-of-way corridors and in determining whether to require that rights-of-way be confined to them, the Secretary concerned shall take into consideration national and State land use policies, environmental quality, economic efficiency, national security, safety, and good engineering and technological practices. The Secretary concerned shall issue regulations containing the criteria and procedures he will use in designating such corridors. Any existing transportation and utility corridors may be designated as transportation and utility corridors pursuant to this subsection without further review.

Pub.L. 94–579, Title V, § 503, Oct. 21, 1976, 90 Stat. 2778.

§ 1764. General requirements

Boundary specifications; criteria; temporary use of additional lands

(a) The Secretary concerned shall specify the boundaries of each right-of-way as precisely as is practical. Each right-of-way shall be limited to the ground which the Secretary concerned determines (1) will be occupied by facilities which constitute the project for which the right-of-way is granted, issued, or renewed, (2) to be necessary for the operation or maintenance of the project, (3) to be necessary to protect the public safety, and (4) will do no unnecessary damage to the environment. The Secretary concerned may authorize the temporary use of such additional lands as he determines to be reasonably necessary for the construction, operation, maintenance, or termination of the project or a portion thereof, or for access thereto.

Terms and conditions of right-of-way or permit

(b) Each right-of-way or permit granted, issued, or renewed pursuant to this section shall be limited to a reasonable term in light of all circumstances concerning the project. In determining the duration of a right-of-way the Secretary concerned shall, among other things, take into consideration the cost of the facility, its useful life, and any public purpose it serves. The right-of-way shall specify whether it is or is not renewable and the terms and conditions applicable to the renewal.

Applicability of regulations or stipulations

(c) Rights-of-way shall be granted, issued, or renewed pursuant to this subchapter under such regulations or stipulations, consistent with the provisions of this subchapter or any other applicable law, and shall also be subject to such terms and conditions as the Secretary concerned may prescribe regarding extent, duration, survey, location, construction, maintenance, transfer or assignment, and termination.

Submission of plan of construction, operation, and rehabilitation by new project applicants; plan requirements

(d) The Secretary concerned prior to granting or issuing a right-of-way pursuant to this subchapter for a new project which may have a significant impact on the environment, shall require the applicant to submit a plan of construction, operation, and rehabilitation for such right-of-way which shall comply with stipulations or with regulations issued by that Secretary, including the terms and conditions required under section 1765 of this title.

Regulatory requirements for terms and conditions; revision and applicability of regulations

(e) The Secretary concerned shall issue regulations with respect to the terms and conditions that will be included in rights-of-way pursuant to section 1765 of this title. Such regulations shall be regularly revised as needed. Such regulations shall be applicable to every right-of-way granted or issued pursuant to this subchapter and to any subsequent renewal thereof, and may be applicable to rights-of-way not granted or issued, but renewed pursuant to this subchapter.

Removal or use of mineral and vegetative materials

(f) Mineral and vegetative materials, including timber, within or without a right-of-way, may be used or disposed of in connection with construction or other purposes only if authorization to remove or use such materials has been obtained pursuant to applicable laws or for emergency repair work necessary for those rights-of-way authorized under section 1761(c) of this title.

Rental payments; amount, waiver, etc.

(g) The holder of a right-of-way shall pay in advance the fair market value thereof, as determined by the Secretary granting, issuing, or renewing such right-of-way. The Secretary concerned may require either annual payment or a payment covering more than one year at a time except that private individuals may make at their option either annual payments or payments covering more than one year if the annual fee is greater than one hundred dollars. The Secretary concerned may waive rentals where a right-of-way is granted, issued or renewed in consideration of a right-of-way conveyed to the United States in connection with a cooperative cost share program between the United States and the holder. The Secretary concerned may, by regulation or prior to promulgation of such regulations, as a condition of a right-of-way, require an applicant for or holder of a right-of-way to reimburse the United States for all reasonable administrative and other costs incurred in processing an application for such right-of-way and in inspection and monitoring of construction, operation, and termination of the facility pursuant to such right-of-way: *Provided, however*, That the Secretary concerned need not secure reimbursement in any situation where there is in existence a cooperative cost share right-of-way program between the United States and the holder of a right-of-way. Rights-of-way may be granted, issued, or renewed to a Federal, State, or local government or any agency or instrumentality thereof, to nonprofit associations or nonprofit corporations which are not themselves controlled or owned by profitmaking corporations or business enterprises, or to a holder where he provides without or at reduced charges a valuable benefit to the public or to the programs of the Secretary concerned, or to a holder in connection with the authorized use or occupancy of Federal land for which the United States is already receiving compensation for such lesser charge, including free use as the Secretary concerned finds equitable and in the public interest. Such rights-of-way issued at less than fair market value are not assignable except with the approval of the Secretary issuing the right-of-way. The moneys received for reimbursement of reasonable costs shall be deposited with the Treasury in a special account and are hereby authorized to be appropriated and made available until expended. Rights-of-way shall be granted, issued, or renewed, without rental fees, for electric or telephone facilities eligible for financing pursuant to the Rural Electrification Act of 1936, as amended [7 U.S.C.A. § 901 et seq.], determined without regard to any application requirement under that Act, or any extensions from such facilities: *Provided*, That nothing in this sentence shall be construed to affect the authority of the Secretary granting, issuing, or renewing the right-of-way to require reimbursement of reasonable administrative and other costs pursuant to the second sentence of this subsection.

Liability for damage or injury incurred by United States for use and occupancy of rights-of-way; indemnification of United States; no-fault liability; amount of damages

(h)(1) The Secretary concerned shall promulgate regulations specifying the extent to which holders of rights-of-way under this subchapter shall be liable to the United States for damage or injury incurred by the United States caused by the use and occupancy of the rights-of-way. The regulations shall also specify the extent to which such holders shall indemnify or hold harmless the United States for liabilities, damages, or claims caused by their use and occupancy of the rights-of-way.

(h)(2) Any regulation or stipulation imposing liability without fault shall include a maximum limitation on damages commensurate with the foreseeable risks or hazards presented. Any liability for damage or injury in excess of this amount shall be determined by ordinary rules of negligence.

Bond or security requirements

(i) Where he deems it appropriate, the Secretary concerned may require a holder of a right-of-way to furnish a bond, or other security, satisfactory to him to secure all or any of the obligations imposed by the terms and conditions of the right-of-way or by any rule or regulation of the Secretary concerned.

Criteria for grant, issue, or renewal of right-of-way

(j) The Secretary concerned shall grant, issue, or renew a right-of-way under this subchapter only when he is satisfied that the applicant has the technical and financial capability to construct the project for which the right-of-way is requested, and in accord with the requirements of this subchapter.

Pub.L. 94–579, Title V, § 504, Oct. 21, 1976, 90 Stat. 2778; Pub.L. 98–300, May 25, 1984, 98 Stat. 215. As amended Pub.L. 99–545, § 2, Oct. 27, 1986, 100 Stat. 3049; Pub.L. 104–333, Div. I, Title X, § 1032(a), Nov. 12, 1996, 110 Stat. 4239.

§ 1765. Terms and conditions

Each right-of-way shall contain—

(a) terms and conditions which will (i) carry out the purposes of this Act and rules and regulations issued thereunder; (ii) minimize damage to scenic and esthetic values and fish and wildlife habitat and otherwise protect the environment; (iii) require compliance with applicable air and water quality standards established by or pursuant to applicable Federal or State law; and (iv) require compliance with State standards for public health and safety, environmental protection, and siting, construction, operation, and maintenance of or for rights-of-way for similar purposes if those standards are more stringent than applicable Federal standards; and

(b) such terms and conditions as the Secretary concerned deems necessary to (i) protect Federal property and economic interests; (ii) manage efficiently the lands which are subject to the right-of-way or adjacent thereto and protect the other lawful users of the lands adjacent to or traversed by such right-of-way; (iii) protect lives and property; (iv) protect the interests of individuals living in the general area traversed by the right-of-way who rely on the fish, wildlife, and other biotic resources of the area for subsistence purposes; (v) require location of the right-of-way along a route that will cause least damage to the environment, taking into consideration feasibility and other relevant factors; and (vi) otherwise protect the public interest in the lands traversed by the right-of-way or adjacent thereto.

Pub.L. 94–579, Title V, § 505, Oct. 21, 1976, 90 Stat. 2780.

§ 1766. Suspension or termination; grounds; procedures applicable

Abandonment of a right-of-way or noncompliance with any provision of this subchapter, condition of the right-of-way, or applicable rule or regulation of the Secretary concerned may be grounds for suspension or termination of the right-of-way if, after due notice to the holder of the right-of-way and, with respect to easements, an appropriate administrative proceeding pursuant to section 554 of Title 5, the Secretary concerned determines that any such ground exists and that suspension or termination is justified. No administrative proceeding shall be required where the right-of-way by its terms provides that it terminates on the occurrence of a fixed or agreed-upon condition, event, or time. If the Secretary concerned determines that an immediate temporary suspension of activities within a right-of-way for violation of its terms and conditions is necessary to protect public health or safety or the environment, he may abate such activities prior to an administrative proceeding. Prior to commencing any proceeding to suspend or terminate a right-of-way the Secretary concerned shall give written notice to the holder of the grounds for such action and shall give the holder a reasonable time to resume use of the right-of-way or to comply with this subchapter, condition, rule, or regulation as the case may be. Failure of the holder of the right-of-way to use the right-of-way for the purpose for which it was granted, issued, or renewed, for any continuous five-year period, shall constitute a rebuttable presumption of abandonment of the right-of-way, except that where the failure of the holder to use the right-of-way for the purpose for which it was granted, issued, or renewed for any continuous five-year period is due to circumstances not within the holder's control, the Secretary concerned is not required to commence proceedings to suspend or terminate the right-of-way.

Pub.L. 94–579, Title V, § 506, Oct. 21, 1976, 90 Stat. 2780.

* * *

§ 1768. Conveyance of lands covered by right-of-way; terms and conditions

If under applicable law the Secretary concerned decides to transfer out of Federal ownership any lands covered in whole or in part by a right-of-way, including a right-of-way granted under the Act of November 16, 1973 (87 Stat. 576; 30 U.S.C. 185), the lands may be conveyed subject to the right-of-way; however, if the Secretary concerned determines that retention of Federal control over the right-of-way is necessary to assure that the purposes of this subchapter will be carried out, the terms and conditions of the right-of-way complied with, or the lands protected, he shall (a) reserve to the United States that portion of the lands which lies within the boundaries of the right-of-way, or (b) convey the lands, including that portion within the boundaries of the right-of-way, subject to the right-of-way and reserving to the United States the right to enforce all or any of the terms and conditions of the right-of-way, including the right to renew it or extend it upon its termination and to collect rents.

Pub.L. 94–579, Title V, § 508, Oct. 21, 1976, 90 Stat. 2781.

§ 1769. Existing right-of-way or right-of-use unaffected; exception; fights-of-way for railroad and appurtenant communication facilities; applicability of existing terms and conditions

(a) Nothing in this subchapter shall have the effect of terminating any right-of-way or right-of-use heretofore issued, granted, or permitted. However, with the consent of the holder thereof, the Secretary concerned may cancel such a right-of-way or right-of-use and in its stead issue a right-of-way pursuant to the provisions of this subchapter.

(b) When the Secretary concerned issues a right-of-way under this subchapter for a railroad and appurtenant communication facilities in connection with a realinement[1] of a railroad on lands under his jurisdiction by virtue of a right-of-way granted by the United States, he may, when he considers it to be in the public interest and the lands involved are not within an incorporated community and are of approximately equal value, notwithstanding the provisions of this subchapter, provide in the new right-of-way the same terms and conditions as applied to the portion of the existing right-of-way relinquished to the United States with respect to the payment of annual rental, duration of the right-of-way, and the nature of the interest in lands granted. The Secretary concerned or his delegate shall take final action upon all applications for the grant, issue, or renewal of rights-of-way under subsection (b) of this section no later than six months after receipt from the applicant of all information required from the applicant by this subchapter.

Pub.L. 94–579, Title V, § 509, Oct. 21, 1976, 90 Stat. 2781.

§ 1770. Applicability of provisions to other Federal laws

Right of way

(a) Effective on and after October 21, 1976, no right-of-way for the purposes listed in this subchapter shall be granted, issued, or renewed over, upon, under, or through such lands except under and subject to the provisions, limitations, and conditions of this subchapter: *Provided,* That nothing in this subchapter shall be construed as affecting or modifying the provisions of the Act of October 13, 1964 and in the event of conflict with, or inconsistency between, this subchapter and the Act of October 13, 1964, the latter shall prevail: *Provided further,* That nothing in this Act should be construed as making it mandatory that, with respect to forest roads, the Secretary of Agriculture limit rights-of-way grants or their term of years or require disclosure pursuant to section 1761(b) of this title or impose any other condition contemplated by this Act that is contrary to present practices of that Secretary under the Act of October 13, 1964. Any pending application for a right-of-way under any other law on the effective date of this section shall be considered as an application under this subchapter. The Secretary concerned may require the applicant to submit any addition-

---

1. So in original. Probably should be "realignment".

al information he deems necessary to comply with the requirements of this subchapter.

* * *

Pub.L. 94–579, Title V, § 510, Oct. 21, 1976, 90 Stat. 2782.

* * *

SUBCHAPTER VI—DESIGNATED MANAGEMENT AREAS

§ 1781.   California Desert Conservation Area

Congressional findings

(a) The Congress finds that—

(1) the California desert contains historical, scenic, archeological, environmental, biological, cultural, scientific, educational, recreational, and economic resources that are uniquely located adjacent to an area of large population;

(2) the California desert environment is a total ecosystem that is extremely fragile, easily scarred, and slowly healed;

(3) the California desert environment and its resources, including certain rare and endangered species of wildlife, plants, and fishes, and numerous archeological and historic sites, are seriously threatened by air pollution, inadequate Federal management authority, and pressures of increased use, particularly recreational use, which are certain to intensify because of the rapidly growing population of southern California;

(4) the use of all California desert resources can and should be provided for in a multiple use and sustained yield management plan to conserve these resources for future generations, and to provide present and future use and enjoyment, particularly outdoor recreation uses, including the use, where appropriate, of off-road recreational vehicles;

(5) the Secretary has initiated a comprehensive planning process and established an interim management program for the public lands in the California desert; and

(6) to insure further study of the relationship of man and the California desert environment, preserve the unique and irreplaceable resources, including archeological values, and conserve the use of the economic resources of the California desert, the public must be provided more opportunity to participate in such planning and management, and additional management authority must be provided to the Secretary to facilitate effective implementation of such planning and management.

Statement of purpose

(b) It is the purpose of this section to provide for the immediate and future protection and administration of the public lands in the California desert within the framework of a program of multiple use and sustained yield, and the maintenance of environmental quality.

* * *

Preparation and implementation of comprehensive long-range plan for management, use, etc.

(d) The Secretary, in accordance with section 1712 of this title, shall prepare and implement a comprehensive, long-range plan for the management, use, development, and protection of the public lands within the California Desert Conservation Area. Such plan shall take into account the principles of multiple use and sustained yield in providing for resource use and development, including, but not limited to, maintenance of environmental quality, rights-of-way, and mineral development. Such plan shall be completed and implementation thereof initiated on or before September 30, 1980.

* * *

Applicability of mining laws

(f) Subject to valid existing rights, nothing in this Act shall affect the applicability of the United States mining laws on the public lands within the California Desert Conservation Area, except that all mining claims located on public lands within the California Desert Conservation Area shall be subject to such reasonable regulations as the Secretary may prescribe to effectuate the purposes of this section. Any patent issued on any such mining claim shall recite this limitation and continue to be subject to such regulations. Such regulations shall provide for such measures as may be reasonable to protect the scenic, scientific, and environmental values of the public lands of the California Desert Conservation Area against undue impairment, and to assure against pollution of the streams and waters within the California Desert Conservation Area.

Pub.L. 94–579, Title VI, § 601, Oct. 21, 1976, 90 Stat. 2782.

§ 1782. Bureau of Land Management Wilderness Study

Lands subject to review and designation as wilderness

(a) Within fifteen years after October 21, 1976, the Secretary shall review those roadless areas of five thousand acres or more and roadless islands of the public lands, identified during the inventory required by section 1711(a) of this title as having wilderness characteristics described in the Wilderness Act of September 3, 1964 (78 Stat. 890; 16 U.S.C. 1131 et seq.) and shall from time to time report to the President his recommendation as to the suitability or nonsuitability of each such area or island for preservation as wilderness: *Provided,* That prior to any recommendations for the designation of an area as wilderness the Secretary shall cause mineral surveys to be conducted by the United States Geological Survey and the United States Bureau of Mines to determine the mineral values, if any, that may be present in such areas: *Provided further,* That the Secretary shall report to the President by July 1, 1980, his recommendations on those areas which the Secretary has prior to November 1, 1975, formally identified as natural or primitive areas. The review required by this subsection shall be conducted in accordance with the procedure specified in section 3(d) of the Wilderness Act [16 U.S.C.A. § 1132(d)].

Presidential recommendation for designation as wilderness

(b) The President shall advise the President of the Senate and the Speaker of the House of Representatives of his recommendations with respect to designation as wilderness of each such area, together with a map thereof and a definition of its boundaries. Such advice by the President shall be given within two years of the receipt of each report from the Secretary. A recommendation of the President for designation as wilderness shall become effective only if so provided by an Act of Congress.

Status of lands during period of review and determination

(c) During the period of review of such areas and until Congress has determined otherwise, the Secretary shall continue to manage such lands according to his authority under this Act and other applicable law in a manner so as not to impair the suitability of such areas for preservation as wilderness, subject, however, to the continuation of existing mining and grazing uses and mineral leasing in the manner and degree in which the same was being conducted on October 21, 1976: *Provided*, That, in managing the public lands the Secretary shall by regulation or otherwise take any action required to prevent unnecessary or undue degradation of the lands and their resources or to afford environmental protection. Unless previously withdrawn from appropriation under the mining laws, such lands shall continue to be subject to such appropriation during the period of review unless withdrawn by the Secretary under the procedures of section 1714 of this title for reasons other than preservation of their wilderness character. Once an area has been designated for preservation as wilderness, the provisions of the Wilderness Act [16 U.S.C.A. § 1131 et seq.] which apply to national forest wilderness areas shall apply with respect to the administration and use of such designated area, including mineral surveys required by section 4(d)(2) of the Wilderness Act [16 U.S.C.A. § 1133(d)(2)], and mineral development, access, exchange of lands, and ingress and egress for mining claimants and occupants.

Pub.L. 94–579, Title VI, § 603, Oct. 21, 1976, 90 Stat. 2785; as amended Pub.L. 102–154, Title I, Nov. 13, 1991, 105 Stat. 1000; Pub.L. 102–285, § 10, May 18, 1992, 106 Stat. 171.

* * *

§ 1784. Lands in Alaska; designation as wilderness; management by Bureau of Land Management pending congressional action

Notwithstanding any other provision of law, section 1782 of this title shall not apply to any lands in Alaska. However, in carrying out his duties under sections 1711 and 1712 of this title and other applicable laws, the Secretary may identify areas in Alaska which he determines are suitable as wilderness and may, from time to time, make recommendations to the Congress for inclusion of any such areas in the National Wilderness Preservation System, pursuant to the provisions of the Wilderness Act [16 U.S.C.A. § 1131 et seq.]. In the absence of congressional action relating to any such recommendation of the Secretary, the Bureau of Land Management shall manage all such areas which are within its jurisdiction in accordance with the applicable land use plans and applicable provisions of law.

Pub.L. 96–487, Title XIII, § 1320, Dec. 2, 1980, 94 Stat. 2487.

PUBLIC RANGELANDS IMPROVEMENT ACT OF 1978

(43 U.S.C.A. §§ 1901–08)

§ 1901. Congressional findings and declaration of policy

(a) The Congress finds and declares that—

(1) vast segments of the public rangelands are producing less than their potential for livestock, wildlife habitat, recreation, forage, and water and soil conservation benefits, and for that reason are in an unsatisfactory condition;

(2) such rangelands will remain in an unsatisfactory condition and some areas may decline further under present levels of, and funding for, management;

(3) unsatisfactory conditions on public rangelands present a high risk of soil loss, desertification, and a resultant underproductivity for large acreages of the public lands; contribute significantly to unacceptable levels of siltation and salinity in major western watersheds including the Colorado River; negatively impact the quality and availability of scarce western water supplies; threaten important and frequently critical fish and wildlife habitat; prevent expansion of the forage resource and resulting benefits to livestock and wildlife production; increase surface runoff and flood danger; reduce the value of such lands for recreational and esthetic purposes; and may ultimately lead to unpredictable and undesirable long-term local and regional climatic and economic changes;

(4) the above-mentioned conditions can be addressed and corrected by an intensive public rangelands maintenance, management, and improvement program involving significant increases in levels of rangeland management and improvement funding for multiple-use values;

(5) to prevent economic disruption and harm to the western livestock industry, it is in the public interest to charge a fee for livestock grazing permits and leases on the public lands which is based on a formula reflecting annual changes in the costs of production;

* * *

(b) The Congress therefore hereby establishes and reaffirms a national policy and commitment to:

(1) inventory and identify current public rangelands conditions and trends as a part of the inventory process required by section 1711(a) of this title;

(2) manage, maintain and improve the condition of the public rangelands so that they become as productive as feasible for all rangeland values in accordance with management objectives and the land use planning process established pursuant to section 1712 of this title;

(3) charge a fee for public grazing use which is equitable and reflects the concerns addressed in paragraph (a)(5) above;

* * *

(c) The policies of this chapter shall become effective only as specific statutory authority for their implementation is enacted by this chapter or by subsequent legislation, and shall be construed as supplemental to and not in derogation of the purposes for which public rangelands are administered under other provisions of law.

Pub.L. 95–514, § 2, Oct. 25, 1978, 92 Stat. 1803.

§ 1902. Definitions

As used in this chapter—

(a) The terms "rangelands" or "public rangelands" means lands administered by the Secretary of the Interior through the Bureau of Land Management or the Secretary of Agriculture through the Forest Service in the sixteen contiguous Western States on which there is domestic livestock grazing or which the Secretary concerned determines may be suitable for domestic livestock grazing.

(b) The term "allotment management plan" is the same as defined in section 1702(k) of this title, except that as used in this Chapter such term applies to the sixteen contiguous Western States.

(c) The term "grazing permit and lease" means any document authorizing use of public lands or lands in national forests in the sixteen contiguous Western States for the purpose of grazing domestic livestock.

(d) The term "range condition" means the quality of the land reflected in its ability in specific vegetative areas to support various levels of productivity in accordance with range management objectives and the land use planning process, and relates to soil quality, forage values (whether seasonal or year-round), wildlife habitat, watershed and plant communities, the present state of vegetation of a range site in relation to the potential plant community for that site, and the relative degree to which the kinds, proportions, and amounts of vegetation in a plant community resemble that of the desired community for that site.

(e) The term "native vegetation" means those plant species, communities, or vegetative associations which are endemic to a given area and which would normally be identified with a healthy and productive range condition occurring as a result of the natural vegetative process of the area.

(f) The term "range improvement" means any activity or program on or relating to rangelands which is designed to improve production of forage; change vegetative composition; control patterns of use; provide water; stabilize soil and water conditions; and provide habitat for livestock and wildlife. The term includes, but is not limited to, structures, treatment projects, and use of mechanical means to accomplish the desired results.

(g) The term "court ordered environmental impact statement" means any environmental statements which are required to be prepared by the Secretary of the Interior pursuant to the final judgment or subsequent modification thereof as set forth on June 18, 1975, in the matter of Natural Resources Defense Council against Andrus.

(h) The term "Secretary" unless specifically designated otherwise, means the Secretary of the Interior.

(i) The term "sixteen contiguous Western States" means the States of Arizona, California, Colorado, Idaho, Kansas, Montana, Nebraska, Nevada, New Mexico, North Dakota, Oklahoma, Oregon, South Dakota, Utah, Washington, and Wyoming.

Pub.L. 95–514, § 3, Oct. 25, 1978, 92 Stat. 1804.

§ 1903. Rangelands inventory and management; public availability

(a) Following enactment of this chapter, the Secretary of the Interior and the Secretary of Agriculture shall update, develop (where necessary) and maintain on a continuing basis thereafter, an inventory of range conditions and record of trends of range conditions on the public rangelands, and shall categorize or identify such lands on the basis of the range conditions and trends thereof as they deem appropriate. Such inventories shall be conducted and maintained by the Secretary as a part of the inventory process required by section 201(a) of the Federal Land Policy and Management Act (43 U.S.C. 1711), and by the Secretary of Agriculture in accordance with section 1603 of Title 16; shall be kept current on a regular basis so as to reflect changes in range conditions; and shall be available to the public.

(b) The Secretary shall manage the public rangelands in accordance with the Taylor Grazing Act (43 U.S.C. 315–315(*o*)), the Federal Land Policy and Management Act of 1976 (43 U.S.C. 1701–1782), and other applicable law consistent with the public rangelands improvement program pursuant to this chapter. Except where the land use planning process required pursuant to section 202 of the Federal Land Policy and Management Act (43 U.S.C. 1712) determines otherwise or the Secretary determines, and sets forth his reasons for this determination, that grazing uses should be discontinued (either temporarily or permanently) on certain lands, the goal of such management shall be to improve the range conditions of the public rangelands so that they become as productive as feasible in accordance with the rangeland management objectives established through the land use planning process, and consistent with the values and objectives listed in sections 1901(a) and (b)(2) of this title.

Pub.L. 95–514, § 4, Oct. 25, 1978, 92 Stat. 1805.

§ 1904. Range improvement funding

Authorization of additional appropriations

(a) In order to accomplish the purposes of this chapter, there are hereby authorized to be appropriated the sum of an additional $15,000,000 annually in fiscal years 1980 through 1982; for fiscal years 1983 through 1986 an amount no less than the amount authorized for 1982; and for fiscal years 1987 through 1999 an amount not less than $5,000,000 annually more than the amount authorized for fiscal year 1986. Such funds shall be in addition to any range, wildlife, and soil and water management moneys which have been requested by the Secretary under the provisions of section 1748 of this title, and in addition to the moneys which are available for range improvements under section 1751 of this title.

Availability of unappropriated funds for subsequent fiscal years

(b) Any amounts authorized by this section not appropriated in one or more fiscal years shall be available for appropriation in any subsequent years.

Fund limitations for prescribed uses; distribution, consultation and coordination; public hearings and meetings; interested parties; priority of cooperative agreements with range users

(c) No less than 80 per centum of such funds provided herein shall be used for on-the-ground range rehabilitation, maintenance and the construction of range improvements (including project layout, project design, and project supervision). No more than 15 per centum of such funds provided herein shall be used to hire and train such experienced and qualified personnel as are necessary to implement on-the-ground supervision and enforcement of the land use plans required pursuant to section 1712 of this title and such allotment management plans as may be developed. Such funds shall be distributed as the Secretary deems advisable after careful and considered consultation and coordination, including public hearings and meetings where appropriate, with the district grazing advisory beards established pursuant to section 1753 of this title, and the advisory councils established pursuant to section 1739 of this title, range user representatives, and other interested parties. To the maximum extent practicable, and where economically sound, the Secretary shall give priority to entering into cooperative agreements with range users (or user groups) for the installation and maintenance of on-the-ground range improvements.

Environmental assessment record and environmental impact statement requirements

(d) Prior to the use of any funds authorized by this section the Secretary shall cause to have prepared an environmental assessment record on each range improvement project. Thereafter, improvement projects may be constructed unless the Secretary determines that the project will have a significant impact on the quality of human environment, necessitating an environmental impact statement pursuant to the National Environmental Policy Act [42 U.S.C.A. § 4321 et seq.] prior to the expenditure of funds.

Pub.L. 95–514, § 5, Oct. 25, 1978, 92 Stat. 1805.

§ 1905. Grazing fees: economic value of use of land; fair market value components; annual percentage change limitation

For the grazing years 1979 through 1985, the Secretaries of Agriculture and Interior shall charge the fee for domestic livestock grazing on the public rangelands which Congress finds represents the economic value of the use of the land to the user, and under which Congress finds fair market value for public grazing equals the $1.23 base established by the 1966 Western Livestock Grazing Survey multiplied by the result of the Forage Value Index (computed annually from data supplied by the Economic Research Service) added to the Combined Index (Beef Cattle Price Index minus the Price Paid Index) and divided by 100: *Provided,* That the annual increase or decrease in such fee for any given year shall be limited to not more than plus or minus 25 per centum of the previous year's fee.

Pub.L. 95–514, § 6(a), Oct. 25, 1978, 92 Stat. 1806.

EXECUTIVE ORDER NO. 12548

Feb. 14, 1986, 51 F.R. 5985

DETERMINATION OF GRAZING FEES AND CONTINUATION OF EXISTING ADMINISTRATIVE RULES, PRACTICES, POLICIES AND REGULATIONS

By the authority vested in me as of the United States of America, and in President by the Constitution and laws order to provide for establishment of appropriate fees for the grazing of domestic livestock on public rangelands, it is ordered as follows:

Section 1. Determination of Fees. The Secretaries of Agriculture and the Interior are directed to exercise their authority, to the extent permitted by law under the various statutes they administer, to establish fees for domestic livestock grazing on the public range-lands which annually equals the $1.23 base established by the 1966 Western Livestock Grazing Survey multiplied by the result of the Forage Value Index (computed annually from data supplied by the Statistical Reporting Service) added to the Combined Index (Beef Cattle Price Index minus the Prices Paid Index) and divided by 100; *provided,* that the annual increase or decrease in such fee for any given year shall be limited to

not more than plus or minus 25 percent of the previous year's fee, and *provided further,* that the fee shall not be less than $1.35 per animal unit month.

Sec. 2. Definitions. As used in this Order, the term:

(a) "Public rangelands" has the same meaning as in the Public Rangelands Improvement Act of 1978 (Public Law 95–514);

(b) "Forage Value Index" means the weighted average estimate of the annual rental charge per head per month for pasturing cattle on private rangelands in the 11 Western States (Montana, Idaho, Wyoming, Colorado, New Mexico, Arizona, Utah, Nevada, Washington, Oregon, and California) (computed by the Statistical Reporting Service from the June Enumerative Survey) divided by $3.85 and multiplied by 100;

(c) "Beef Cattle Price Index" means the weighted average annual selling price for beef cattle (excluding calves) in the 11 Western States (Montana, Idaho, Wyoming, Colorado, New Mexico, Arizona, Utah, Nevada, Washington, Oregon, and California) for November through October (computed by the Statistical Reporting Service) divided by $22.04 per hundred weight and multiplied by 100; and

(d) "Prices Paid Index" means the following selected components from the Statistical Reporting Service's Annual National Index of Prices Paid by Farmers for Goods and Services adjusted by the weights indicated in parentheses to reflect livestock production costs in the Western States: 1. Fuels and Energy (14.5); 2. Farm and Motor Supplies (12.0); 3. Autos and Trucks (4.5); 4. Tractors and Self-Propelled Machinery (4.5); 5. Other Machinery (12.0); 6. Building and Fencing Materials (14.5); 7. Interest (6.0); 8. Farm Wage Rates (14.0); 9. Farm Services (18.0).

Sec. 3. Any and all existing rules, practices, policies, and regulations relating to the administration of the formula for grazing fees in section 8(a) of the Public Rangelands Improvement Act of 1978 [this section] shall continue in full force and effect.

Sec. 4. This Order shall be effective immediately.

RONALD REAGAN

THE WHITE HOUSE.

§ 1906. Authority for cooperative agreements and payments effective as provided in appropriations

Notwithstanding any other provision of this chapter, authority to enter into cooperative agreements and to make payments under this chapter shall be effective only to the extent or in such amounts as are provided in advance in appropriation Acts.

Pub.L. 95–514, § 9, Oct. 25, 1978, 92 Stat. 1807.

§ 1907. National Grassland exemptions

All National Grasslands are exempted from the provisions of this chapter.

Pub.L. 95–514, § 11, Oct. 25, 1978, 92 Stat. 1808.

§ 1908. Experimental stewardship program

Scope of program

(a) The Secretaries of Interior and Agriculture are hereby authorized and directed to develop and implement, on an experimental basis on selected areas of the public rangelands which are representative of the broad spectrum of range conditions, trends, and forage values, a program which provides incentives to, or rewards for, the holders of grazing permits and leases whose stewardship results in an improvement of the range condition of lands under permit or lease. Such program shall explore innovative grazing management policies and systems which might provide incentives to improve range conditions. These may include, but need not be limited to—

(1) cooperative range management projects designed to foster a greater degree of cooperation and coordination between the Federal and State agencies charged with the management of the rangelands and with local private range users,

(2) the payment of up to 50 per centum of the amount due the Federal Government from grazing permittees in the form of range improvement work,

(3) such other incentives as he may deem appropriate.

Report to Congress

(b) No later than December 31, 1985, the Secretaries shall report to the Congress the results of such experimental program, their evaluation of the fee established in section 1905 of this title and other grazing fee options, and their recommendations to implement a grazing fee schedule for the 1986 and subsequent grazing years.

Pub.L. 95–514, § 12, Oct. 25, 1978, 92 Stat. 1808.

ABANDONED SHIPWRECKS ACT OF 1987

(43 U.S.C.A. §§ 2101–2106)

§ 2101. Congressional statement of findings

The Congress finds that—

(a) States have the responsibility for management of a broad range of living and nonliving resources in State waters and submerged lands; and

(b) included in the range of resources are certain abandoned shipwrecks, which have been deserted and to which the owner has relinquished ownership rights with no retention.

Pub.L. 100–298, § 2, Apr. 28, 1988, 102 Stat. 432.

§ 2102. Definitions

For purposes of this chapter—

(a) the term "embedded" means firmly affixed in the submerged lands or in coralline formations such that the use of tools of excavation is required in order to move the bottom sediments to gain access to the shipwreck, its cargo, and any part thereof;

(b) the term "National Register" means the National Register of Historic Places maintained by the Secretary of the Interior under section 470a of Title 16;

(c) the terms "public lands", "Indian lands", and "Indian tribe" have the same meaning given the terms in the Archaeological Resource[1] Protection Act of 1979 (16 U.S.C. 470aa–470ll);

(d) the term "shipwreck" means a vessel or wreck, its cargo, and other contents;

(e) the term "State" means a State of the United States, the District of Columbia, Puerto Rico, Guam, the Virgin Islands, American Samoa, and the Northern Mariana Islands; and

(f) the term "submerged lands" means the lands—

---

1. So in original. Probably should be "Resources".

(1) that are "lands beneath navigable waters," as defined in section 1301 of this title;

(2) of Puerto Rico, as described in section 749 of Title 48;

(3) of Guam, the Virgin Islands and American Samoa, as described in section 1705 of Title 48; and

(4) of the Commonwealth of the Northern Mariana Islands, as described in section 801 of Public Law 94–241.

Pub.L. 100–298, § 3, Apr. 28, 1988, 102 Stat. 432.

§ 2103.   Rights of access

Access rights

(a) In order to—

(1) clarify that State waters and shipwrecks offer recreational and educational opportunities to sport divers and other interested groups, as well as irreplaceable State resources for tourism, biological sanctuaries, and historical research; and

(2) provide that reasonable access by the public to such abandoned shipwrecks be permitted by the State holding title to such shipwrecks pursuant to section 2105 of this title,

it is the declared policy of the Congress that States carry out their responsibilities under this chapter to develop appropriate and consistent policies so as to—

(A) protect natural resources and habitat areas;

(B) guarantee recreational exploration of shipwreck sites; and

(C) allow for appropriate public and private sector recovery of shipwrecks consistent with the protection of historical values and environmental integrity of the shipwrecks and the sites.

Parks and protected areas

(b) In managing the resources subject to the provisions of this chapter, States are encouraged to create underwater parks or areas to provide additional protection for such resources. Funds available to States from grants from the Historic Preservation Fund shall be available, in accordance with the provisions of title I of the National Historic Preservation Act, for the study, interpretation, protection, and preservation of historic shipwrecks and properties.

Pub.L. 100–298, § 4, Apr. 28, 1988, 102 Stat. 433.

§ 2104.   Preparation of guidelines

Purposes of guidelines; publication in Federal Register

(a) In order to encourage the development of underwater parks and the administrative cooperation necessary for the comprehensive management of underwater resources related to historic shipwrecks, the Secretary of the Interior, acting through the Director of the National Park Service, shall within nine months after April 28, 1988, prepare and publish guide-lines in the Federal Register which shall seek to:

(1) maximize the enhancement of cultural resources;

(2) foster a partnership among sport divers, fishermen, archeolo-gists, salvors, and other interests to manage shipwreck resources of the States and the United States;

(3) facilitate access and utilization by recreational interests;

(4) recognize the interests of individuals and groups engaged in shipwreck discovery and salvage.

Consultation

(b) Such guidelines shall be developed after consultation with appro-priate public and private sector interests (including the Secretary of Commerce, the Advisory Council on Historic Preservation, sport divers, State Historic Preservation Officers, professional dive operators, salvors, archeologists, historic preservationists, and fishermen).

Use of guidelines in developing legislation and regulations

(c) Such guidelines shall be available to assist States and the appropri-ate Federal agencies in developing legislation and regulations to carry out their responsibilities under this chapter.

Pub.L. 100–298, § 5, Apr. 28, 1988, 102 Stat. 433.

§ 2105. Rights of ownership

United States title

(a) The United States asserts title to any abandoned shipwreck that is—

(1) embedded in submerged lands of a State;

(2) embedded in coralline formations protected by a State on submerged lands of a State; or

(3) on submerged lands of a State and is included in or deter-mined eligible for inclusion in the National Register.

Notice of shipwreck location; eligibility determination for inclusion in National Register of Historic Places

(b) The public shall be given adequate notice of the location of any shipwreck to which title is asserted under this section. The Secretary of the Interior, after consultation with the appropriate State Historic Preserva-tion Officer, shall make a written determination that an abandoned ship-wreck meets the criteria for eligibility for inclusion in the National Regis-ter of Historic Places under clause[1](a)(3) of this section.

---

1. So in original. Probably should be "subsection".

Transfer of title to States

(c) The title of the United States to any abandoned shipwreck asserted under subsection (a) of this section is transferred to the State in or on whose submerged lands the shipwreck is located.

Exception

(d) Any abandoned shipwreck in or on the public lands of the United States is the property of the United States Government. Any abandoned shipwreck in or on any Indian lands is the property of the Indian tribe owning such lands.

Reservation of rights

(e) This section does not affect any right reserved by the United States or by any State (including any right reserved with respect to Indian lands) under—

(1) section 1311, 1313, or 1314 of this title; or

(2) section 414 or 415 of Title 33.

Pub.L. 100–298, § 6, Apr. 28, 1988, 102 Stat. 433.

§ 2106. Relationship to other laws

Law of salvage and law of finds

(a) The law of salvage and the law of finds shall not apply to abandoned shipwrecks to which section 2105 of this title applies.

Laws of United States

(b) This chapter shall not change the laws of the United States relating to shipwrecks, other than those to which this chapter applies.

Effective date

(c) This chapter shall not affect any legal proceeding brought prior to April 28, 1988.

Pub.L. 100–298, § 7, Apr. 28, 1988, 102 Stat. 434.

FEDERAL LAND TRANSACTION FACILITATION ACT OF 2000

(43 U.S.C.A. §§ 2301–2306)

§ 2301. Findings

Congress finds that—

(1) the Bureau of Land Management has authority under the Federal Land Policy and Management Act of 1976 (*43 U.S.C. 1701* et seq.) to sell land identified for disposal under its land use planning;

(2) the Bureau of Land Management has authority under that Act to exchange Federal land for non-Federal land if the exchange would be in the public interest;

(3) through land use planning under that Act, the Bureau of Land Management has identified certain tracts of public land for disposal;

(4) the Federal land management agencies of the Departments of the Interior and Agriculture have authority under existing law to acquire land consistent with the mission of each agency;

(5) the sale or exchange of land identified for disposal and the acquisition of certain non-Federal land from willing landowners would—

    (A) allow for the reconfiguration of land ownership patterns to better facilitate resource management;

    (B) contribute to administrative efficiency within Federal land management units; and

    (C) allow for increased effectiveness of the allocation of fiscal and human resources within the Federal land management agencies;

(6) a more expeditious process for disposal and acquisition of land, established to facilitate a more effective configuration of land ownership patterns, would benefit the public interest;

(7) many private individuals own land within the boundaries of Federal land management units and desire to sell the land to the Federal Government;

(8) such land lies within national parks, national monuments, national wildlife refuges, national forests, and other areas designated for special management;

(9) Federal land management agencies are facing increased workloads from rapidly growing public demand for the use of public land, making it difficult for Federal managers to address problems created by the existence of inholdings in many areas;

(10) in many cases, inholders and the Federal Government would mutually benefit from Federal acquisition of the land on a priority basis;

(11) proceeds generated from the disposal of public land may be properly dedicated to the acquisition of inholdings and other land that will improve the resource management ability of the Federal land management agencies and adjoining landowners;

(12) using proceeds generated from the disposal of public land to purchase inholdings and other such land from willing sellers would enhance the ability of the Federal land management agencies to—

    (A) work cooperatively with private landowners and State and local governments; and

    (B) promote consolidation of the ownership of public and private land in a manner that would allow for better overall resource management;

(13) in certain locations, the sale of public land that has been identified for disposal is the best way for the public to receive fair market value for the land; and

(14) to allow for the least disruption of existing land and resource management programs, the Bureau of Land Management may use non-Federal entities to prepare appraisal documents for agency review and approval consistent with applicable provisions of the Uniform Standards for Federal Land Acquisition.

Pub.L. 106–248, Title II, § 202, July 25, 2000, 114 Stat. 613.

§ 2302.   Definitions

In this chapter:

(1) Exceptional resource

The term "exceptional resource" means a resource of scientific, natural, historic, cultural, or recreational value that has been documented by a Federal, State, or local governmental authority, and for which there is a compelling need for conservation and protection under the jurisdiction of a Federal agency in order to maintain the resource for the benefit of the public.

(2) Federally designated area

The term "federally designated area" means land in Alaska and the eleven contiguous Western States (as defined in section 1702(*o*) of this title) that on July 25, 2000, was within the boundary of—

(A) a national monument, area of critical environmental concern, national conservation area, national riparian conservation area, national recreation area, national scenic area, research natural area, national outstanding natural area, or a national natural landmark managed by the Bureau of Land Management;

(B) a unit of the National Park System;

(C) a unit of the National Wildlife Refuge System;

(D) an area of the National Forest System designated for special management by an Act of Congress; or

(E) an area within which the Secretary or the Secretary of Agriculture is otherwise authorized by law to acquire lands or interests therein that is designated as—

(i) wilderness under the Wilderness Act (16 U.S.C. 1131 et seq.);

(ii) a wilderness study area;

(iii) a component of the Wild and Scenic Rivers System under the Wild and Scenic Rivers Act (16 U.S.C. 1271 et seq.); or

(iv) a component of the National Trails System under the National Trails System Act (16 U.S.C. 1241 et seq.).

(3) Inholding

The term "inholding" means any right, title, or interest, held by a non-Federal entity, in or to a tract of land that lies within the boundary of a federally designated area.

(4) Public land

The term "public land" means public lands (as defined in section 1702 of this title).

(5) Secretary

The term "Secretary" means the Secretary of the Interior.

Pub.L. 106–248, Title II, § 203, July 25, 2000, 114 Stat. 614.

§ 2303. Identification of inholdings

In general

(a) The Secretary and the Secretary of Agriculture shall establish a procedure to—

(1) identify, by State, inholdings for which the landowner has indicated a desire to sell the land or interest therein to the United States; and

(2) prioritize the acquisition of inholdings in accordance with section 2305(c)(3) of this title.

Public notice

(b) As soon as practicable after July 25, 2000, and periodically thereafter, the Secretary and the Secretary of Agriculture shall provide public notice of the procedures referred to in subsection (a) of this section, including any information necessary for the consideration of an inholding under section 2305 of this title. Such notice shall include publication in the Federal Register and by such other means as the Secretary and the Secretary of Agriculture determine to be appropriate.

Identification

(c) An inholding—

(1) shall be considered for identification under this section only if the Secretary or the Secretary of Agriculture receive notification of a desire to sell from the landowner in response to public notice given under subsection (b) of this section; and

(2) shall be deemed to have been established as of the later of—

(A) the earlier of—

(i) the date on which the land was withdrawn from the public domain; or

(ii) the date on which the land was established or designated for special management; or

(B) the date on which the inholding was acquired by the current owner.

No obligation to convey or acquire

(d) The identification of an inholding under this section creates no obligation on the part of a landowner to convey the inholding or any obligation on the part of the United States to acquire the inholding.

Pub.L. 106–248, Title II, § 204, July 25, 2000, 114 Stat. 615.

§ 2304.   Disposal of public land

In general

(a) The Secretary shall establish a program, using funds made available under section 2305 of this title, to complete appraisals and satisfy other legal requirements for the sale or exchange of public land identified for disposal under approved land use plans (as in effect on July 25, 2000) under section 1712 of this title.

Sale of public land

(b)(1) In general

The sale of public land so identified shall be conducted in accordance with sections 1713 and 1719 of this title.

(b)(2) Exceptions to competitive bidding requirements

The exceptions to competitive bidding requirements under section 1713(f) of this title shall apply to this section in cases in which the Secretary determines it to be necessary.

Report in public land statistics

(c) The Secretary shall provide in the annual publication of Public Land Statistics, a report of activities under this section.

Termination of authority

(d) The authority provided under this section shall terminate 10 years after July 25, 2000.

Pub.L. 106–248, Title II, § 205, July 25, 2000, 114 Stat. 615.

§ 2305.   Federal Land Disposal Account

Deposit of proceeds

(a) Notwithstanding any other law (except a law that specifically provides for a proportion of the proceeds to be distributed to any trust funds of any States), the gross proceeds of the sale or exchange of public land under this chapter shall be deposited in a separate account in the Treasury of the United States to be known as the "Federal Land Disposal Account".

Availability

(b) Amounts in the Federal Land Disposal Account shall be available to the Secretary and the Secretary of Agriculture, without further Act of appropriation, to carry out this chapter.

Use of the Federal Land Disposal Account

(c)(1) In general

Funds in the Federal Land Disposal Account shall be expended in accordance with this subsection.

(c)(2) Fund allocation

(A) Purchase of land

Except as authorized under subparagraph (C), funds shall be used to purchase lands or interests therein that are otherwise authorized by law to be acquired, and that are—

(i) inholdings; and

(ii) adjacent to federally designated areas and contain exceptional resources.

(B) Inholdings

Not less than 80 percent of the funds allocated for the purchase of land within each State shall be used to acquire inholdings identified under section 2303 of this title.

(C) Administrative and other expenses

An amount not to exceed 20 percent of the funds deposited in the Federal Land Disposal Account may be used by the Secretary for administrative and other expenses necessary to carry out the land disposal program under section 2304 of this title.

(D) Same State purchases

Of the amounts not used under subparagraph (C), not less than 80 percent shall be expended within the State in which the funds were generated. Any remaining funds may be expended in any other State.

(c)(3) Priority

The Secretary and the Secretary of Agriculture shall develop a procedure for prioritizing the acquisition of inholdings and non-Federal lands with exceptional resources as provided in paragraph (2). Such procedure shall consider—

(A) the date the inholding was established (as provided in section 2303(c) of this title);

(B) the extent to which acquisition of the land or interest therein will facilitate management efficiency; and

(C) such other criteria as the Secretary and the Secretary of Agriculture deem appropriate.

(c)(4) Basis of sale

Any land acquired under this section shall be—

(A) from a willing seller;

(B) contingent on the conveyance of title acceptable to the Secretary, or the Secretary of Agriculture in the case of an acquisition of National Forest System land, using title standards of the Attorney General;

(C) at a price not to exceed fair market value consistent with applicable provisions of the Uniform Appraisal Standards for Federal Land Acquisitions; and

(D) managed as part of the unit within which it is contained.

Contaminated sites and sites difficult and uneconomic to manage

(d) Funds in the Federal Land Disposal Account shall not be used to purchase land or an interest in land that, as determined by the Secretary or the Secretary of Agriculture—

(1) contains a hazardous substance or is otherwise contaminated; or

(2) because of the location or other characteristics of the land, would be difficult or uneconomic to manage as Federal land.

Land and Water Conservation Fund Act

(e) Funds made available under this section shall be supplemental to any funds appropriated under the Land and Water Conservation Fund Act (16 U.S.C. 460l–4 et seq.).

Termination

(f) On termination of activities under section 2304 of this title—

(1) the Federal Land Disposal Account shall be terminated; and

(2) any remaining balance in the account shall become available for appropriation under section 3 of the Land and Water Conservation Fund Act (16 U.S.C. 460l–6).

Pub.L. 106–248, Title II, § 206, July 25, 2000, 114 Stat. 616.

§ 2306.   Special provisions

In general

(a) Nothing in this chapter provides an exemption from any limitation on the acquisition of land or interest in land under any Federal law in effect on July 25, 2000.

Other law

(b) This chapter shall not apply to land eligible for sale under—

(1) Public Law 96–568 (commonly known as the "Santini–Burton Act") (94 Stat. 3381); or

(2) the Southern Nevada Public Land Management Act of 1998 (112 Stat. 2343).

Exchanges

(c) Nothing in this chapter precludes, preempts, or limits the authority to exchange land under authorities providing for the exchange of Federal lands, including but not limited to—

(1) the Federal Land Policy and Management Act of 1976 (43 U.S.C. 1701 et seq.); or

(2) the Federal Land Exchange Facilitation Act of 1988 (102 Stat. 1086) or the amendments made by that Act.

No new right or benefit

(d) Nothing in this chapter creates a right or benefit, substantive or procedural, enforceable at law or in equity by a party against the United States, its agencies, its officers, or any other person.

Pub.L. 106–248, Title II, § 207, July 25, 2000, 114 Stat. 617.

HISTORICAL SUPPLEMENT

NORTHWEST ORDINANCE OF 1787

(1 Stat. 51)

An Act to provide for the Government of the
Territory Northwest of the river Ohio.

It is hereby ordained and declared, by the authority aforesaid, That the
following articles shall be considered as articles of compact between the
original States, and the people and States in the said territory, and forever
remain unalterable, unless by common consent, to wit:

ART. I. No person, demeaning himself in a peaceable and orderly
manner, shall ever be molested on account of his mode of worship or
religious sentiments, in the said territory.

ART II. The inhabitants of the said territory, shall always be entitled to
the benefits of the writ of habeas corpus, and of the trial by jury; of a
proportionate representation of the people in the legislature, and of judicial
proceedings according to the course of the common law. All persons shall
be bailable, unless for capital offenses, where the proof shall be evident, or
the presumption great. All fines shall be moderate; and no cruel or unusual
punishments shall be inflicted. No man shall be deprived of his liberty or
property, but by the judgment of his peers, or the law of the land, and
should the public exigencies make it necessary, for the common preservation, to take any person's property, or to demand his particular services,
full compensation shall be made for the same. And in the just preservation
of rights and property, it is understood and declared, that no law ought
ever to be made, or have force in the said territory, that shall in any
manner whatever interfere with, or affect private contracts or engage-
ments, bona fide, and without fraud previously formed.

ART. III. Religion, morality, and knowledge, being necessary to good
government and the happiness of mankind, schools and the means of
education shall forever be encouraged. The utmost good faith shall always
be observed towards the Indians; their land and property shall never be
taken from them without their consent; and in their property, rights and
liberty, they never shall be invaded or disturbed, unless in just and lawful
wars authorized by Congress; but laws founded in justice and humanity
shall from time to time be made, for preventing wrongs being done to
them, and for preserving peace and friendship with them.

ART. IV. The said territory, and the States which may be formed
therein, shall forever remain a part of this confederacy of the United States
of America, subject to the articles of confederation, and to such alterations
therein, as shall be constitutionally made; and to all the acts and ordinances of the United States in Congress assembled, conformable thereto.
The inhabitants and settlers in the said territory, shall be subject to pay a
part of the federal debts, contracted or to be contracted, and a proportional
part of the expenses of government, to be apportioned on them by Con-

gress, according to the same common rule and measure, by which apportionments thereof shall be made on the other States; and the taxes for paying their proportion, shall be laid and levied by the authority and direction of the legislatures of the district or districts or new States, as in the original States, within the time agreed upon by the United States in Congress assembled. The legislatures of those districts or new States, shall never interfere with the primary disposal of the soil by the United States in Congress assembled, nor with any regulations Congress may find necessary for securing the title in such soil to the bona fide purchasers. No tax shall be imposed on land the property of the United States; and in no case shall non-resident proprietors be taxed higher than residents. The navigable waters leading into the Mississippi and St. Lawrence, and the carrying places between the same, shall be common highways, and forever free, as well to the inhabitants of the said territory, as to the citizens of the United States, and those of any other States that may be admitted into the confederacy, without any tax, impost, or duty therefor.

ART. V. There shall be formed in the said territory, not less than three, nor more than five States; and the boundaries of the States, as soon as Virginia shall alter her act of cession, and consent to the same, shall become fixed and established as follows, to wit: The western State in the said territory, shall be bounded by the Mississippi, the Ohio and Wabash rivers; a direct line drawn from the Wabash and Post Vincents due north to the territorial line between the United States and Canada; and by the said territorial line to the Lake of the Woods and Mississippi. The middle State shall be bounded by the said direct line, the Wabash from Post Vincents to the Ohio; by the Ohio, by a direct line drawn due north from the mouth of the Great Miami, to the said territorial line, and by the said territorial line. The eastern State shall be bounded by the last mentioned direct line, the Ohio, Pennsylvania, and the said territorial line: Provided however, and it is further understood and declared, that the boundaries of these three States shall be subject so far to be altered, that if Congress shall hereafter find it expedient, they shall have authority to form one or two States in that part of the said territory which lies north of an east and west line drawn through the southerly bend or extreme of lake Michigan. And whenever any of the said States shall have sixty thousand free inhabitants therein, such State shall be admitted, by its delegates, into the Congress of the United States, on an equal footing with the original States, in all respects whatever; and shall be at liberty to form a permanent constitution and State government: Provided the constitution and government so to be formed, shall be republican, and in conformity to the principles contained in these articles; and so far as it can be consistent with the general interest of the confederacy, such admission shall be allowed at an earlier period, and when there may be a loss number of free inhabitants in the State than sixty thousand.

ART. VI. There shall be neither slavery nor involuntary servitude in the said territory, otherwise than in punishment of crimes, whereof the party shall have been duly convicted: Provided always, that any person escaping into the same, from whom labour or service is lawfully claimed in any one of the original States, such fugitive may be lawfully reclaimed, and conveyed to the person claiming his or her labour or service as aforesaid.

Done by the United States in Congress assembled, the thirteenth day of July, in the year of our Lord one thousand seven hundred and eighty-seven, and of their sovereignty and independence the twelfth.

PREEMPTION ACT OF 1841

(5 Stat. 453; R.S. 2257–88)

(Repealed 1891)

SEC. 2257. All lands belonging to the United States, to which the Indian title has been or may hereafter be extinguished, shall be subject to the right of preemption, under the conditions, restrictions, and stipulations provided by law.

SEC. 2258. The following classes of lands, unless otherwise specially provided for by law, shall not be subject to the rights of preemption, to wit:

First. Lands included in any reservation by any treaty, law, or proclamation of the President, for any purpose.

Second. Lands included within the limits of any incorporated town, is selected as the site of a city or town.

Third. Lands actually settled and occupied for purposes of trade and business and not for agriculture.

Fourth. Lands on which are situated any known salines or mines.

SEC. 2259. Every person, being the head of a family, or widow, or single person, over the age of twenty-one years, and a citizen of the United States, or having filed a declaration of intention to become such, as required by the naturalization laws, who has made, or hereafter makes, a settlement in person on the public lands subject to preemption, and who inhabits and improves the same, and who has erected or shall erect a dwelling thereon, is authorized to enter with the register of the landshare for the district in which such land lies, by legal subdivisions, any number of acres not exceeding one hundred and sixty, or a quarter-section of land, to include the residence of such claimant, upon paying to the United States the minimum price of such land.

SEC. 2260. The following classes of persons, unless otherwise specially provided for by law, shall not acquire any right of preemption under the provisions of the preceding section, to wit:

First. No person who is the proprietor of three hundred and twenty acres of land in any State or Territory.

Second. No person who quits or abandons his residence on his own land to reside on the public lands in the same State or Territory.

SEC. 2261. No person shall be entitled to more than one pre-emptive right by virtue of the provisions of section twenty-two hundred and fifty-nine: nor where a party has filed his declaration of intention to claim the benefits of such provisions, for one tract of land, shall he file, at any future time, a second declaration for another tract.

SEC. 2262. Before any person claiming the benefit of this chapter is allowed to enter lands, he shall make oath before the receiver or register of the land-district in which the land is situated that he has never had the benefit of any right of preemption under section twenty-two hundred and fifty-nine; that he is not the owner of three hundred and twenty acres of land in any State or Territory; that he has not settled upon and improved such land to sell the same on speculation, but in good faith to appropriate it to his own exclusive use; and that he has not directly or indirectly, made any agreement or contract, in any way or manner, with any person whatsoever, by which the title which he might acquire from the Government of the United States should inure in whole or in part to the benefit of any person except himself; and if any person taking such oath swears falsely in the premises, he shall forfeit the money which he may have paid for such land, and all right and title to the same; and any grant or conveyance which he may have made, except in the hands of bona-fide purchasers, for a valuable consideration, shall be null and void, except as provided in section twenty-two hundred and eighty-eight. And it shall be the duty of the officer administering such oath to file a certificate thereof in the public land-office of such district, and to transmit a duplicate copy to the General Land–Office, either of which shall be good and sufficient evidence that such oath was administered according to law.

SEC. 2263. Prior to any entries being made under and by virtue of the provisions of section twenty-two hundred and fifty-nine, proof of the settlement and improvement thereby required shall be made to the satisfaction of the register and receiver of the land-district in which such lands lie, agreeably to such rules as may be prescribed by the Secretary of the Interior; and all assignments and transfers of the right hereby secured, prior to the issuing of the patent, shall be null and void.

* * *

SEC. 2275. Where settlements, with a view to preemption, have been made before the survey of the lands in the field, which are found to have been made on sections sixteen or thirty-six, those sections shall be subject to the preemption claim of such settler; and if they, or either of them, have been or shall be reserved or pledged for the use of schools or colleges in the State or Territory in which the lands lie, other lands of like quantity are appropriated in lieu of such as may be patented by pre-emptors; and other lands are also appropriated to compensate deficiencies for school purposes, where sections sixteen or thirty-six are fractional in quantity, or where one or both are wanting by reason of the township being fractional, or from any natural cause whatever.

* * *

SEC. 2279. No person shall have the right of pre-emption to more than one hundred and sixty acres along the line of railroads within the limits granted by any act of Congress.

* * *

SEC. 2281. All settlers on public lands which have been or may be withdrawn from market in consequence of proposed railroads, and who had settled thereon prior to such withdrawal, shall be entitled to pre-emption at the ordinary minimum to the lands settled on and cultivated by them; but they shall file the proper notices of their claims and make proof and payment as in other cases.

* * *

HOMESTEAD ACT OF 1862 (as amended)

(43 U.S.C.A. §§ 161–284)

(Repealed 1976)

GENERAL PROVISIONS

§ 161. Entry of unappropriated public lands

Every person who is the head of a family, or who has arrived at the age of twenty-one years, and is a citizen of the United States, or who has filed his declaration of intention to become such, as required by the naturalization laws, shall be entitled to enter one-quarter section, or a less quantity, of unappropriated public lands, to be located in a body in conformity to the legal subdivisions of the public lands; but no person who is the proprietor of more than one hundred and sixty acres of land in any State or Territory, shall acquire any right under the homestead law. And every person owning and residing on land may, under the provisions of this section, enter other land lying contiguous to his land, which shall not, with the land so already owned and occupied, exceed in the aggregate one hundred and sixty acres.

R.S. § 2289; Mar. 3. 1891, c. 561, § 5, 26 Stat. 1097.

§ 162. Application for entry; affidavit

Any person applying to enter land under section 161 of this title shall first make and subscribe before the proper officer and file in the proper land office an affidavit that he or she is the head of a family, or is over twenty-one years of age, and that such application is honestly and in good faith made for the purpose of actual settlement and cultivation, and not for the benefit of any other person, persons, or corporation, and that he or she will faithfully and honestly endeavor to comply with all the requirements of law as to settlement, residence, and cultivation necessary to acquire title to the land applied for; that he or she is not acting as agent of any person, corporation, or syndicate in making such entry, nor in collusion with any person, corporation, or syndicate to give them the benefit of the land entered, or any part thereof, or the timber thereon; that he or she does not apply to enter the same for the purpose of speculation, but in good faith to obtain a home for himself, or herself, and that he or she has not directly or indirectly made, and will not make, any agreement or contract in any way or manner, with any person or persons, corporation, or syndicate whatsoever, by which the title which he or she might acquire from the Government of the United States should inure, in whole or in part, to the benefit of any person, except himself, or herself, and upon filing such affidavit with the officer designated by the Secretary of the Interior on payment of $5 when the entry is of not more than eighty acres, and on payment of $10 when the entry is for more than eighty acres, he or she shall thereupon be permitted to enter the amount of land specified.

R.S. § 2290; Mar. 3, 1891, c. 561, § 5, 26 Stat. 1097; Oct. 28, 1921, c. 114, § 1, 42 Stat. 208; Mar. 3, 1925, c. 462, 43 Stat. 1145; 1946 Reorg.Plan No. 3, § 403, eff. July 16, 1946, 11 F.R. 7876, 60 Stat. 1100.

* * *

§ **164.** Certificate or patent; issuance

No certificate shall be given or patent issued therefor until the expiration of three years from the date of such entry; and if at the expiration of such time, or at any time within two years thereafter, the person making such entry, or if he be dead his widow, or in case of her death his heirs or devisee, or in case of a widow making such entry her heirs or devisee, in case of her death, proves by himself and by two credible witnesses that he, she, or they have a habitable house upon the land and have actually resided upon and cultivated the same for the term of three years succeeding the time of filing the affidavit and makes affidavit that no part of such land has been alienated, except as provided in section 174 of this title, and that he, she, or they will bear true allegiance to the Government of the United States, then in such case he, she, or they, if at that time citizens of the United States, shall be entitled to a patent, as in other cases provided by law: *Provided,* That upon filing in the local land office notice of the beginning of such absence the entryman shall be entitled to a continuous leave of absence from the land for a period not exceeding five months in each year after establishing residence, and upon the termination of such absence the entryman shall file a notice of such termination in the local land office, but in case of commutation the fourteen months' actual residence required by law must be shown, and the person commuting must be at the time a citizen of the United States: *Provided further,* That when the person making entry dies before the offer of final proof those succeeding to the entry must show that the entryman had complied with the law in all respects to the date of his death, and that they have since complied with the law in all respects, as would have been required of the entryman had he lived, excepting that they are relieved from any requirement of residence upon the land: *Provided further,* That the entryman shall, in order to comply with the requirements of cultivation herein provided for, cultivate not less than one-sixteenth of the area of his entry, beginning with the second year of the entry, and not less than one-eighth, beginning with the third year of the entry and until final proof, except that in the case of entries under section 218(f) of this title, double the area of cultivation herein provided shall be required, but the Secretary of the Interior may, upon a satisfactory showing, under rules and regulations prescribed by him, reduce the required area of cultivation: * * *

R.S. § 2291; June 6, 1912, c. 153, 37 Stat. 123.

* * *

§ 173. Commutation after fourteen months

All commutations of homestead entries shall be allowed after the expiration of fourteen months from date of settlement. Nothing in sections 161–164, 169, 171, 173, 175, 183, 184, 191, 201, 211, 239, 254, 255, 271, 272, 274, 277 and 278 of this title shall be so construed as to prevent any person who shall avail himself of the benefits of section 161 of this title from paying the minimum price for the quantity of land so entered at any time after the expiration of fourteen calendar months from the date of such entry, and obtaining a patent therefor, upon making proof of settlement and of residence and cultivation for such period of fourteen months.

R.S. § 2301; Mar. 3, 1891, c. 561, § 6, 26 Stat. 1098; June 3, 1896, c. 312, § 2, 29 Stat. 197.

* * *

LANDS SUBJECT TO ENTRY

§ 201. Mineral lands

Mineral lands shall not be liable to entry and settlement under the provisions of sections 161–164, 169, 171, 173, 175, 183, 184, 191, 201, 211, 239, 254, 255, 271, 272, 274, 277 and 278 of this title.

R.S. § 2302.

* * *

LIMITATION AS TO AMOUNT AND ADDITIONAL AND ENLARGED ENTRIES

§ 211. Limitation of amount of homestead entry

Except as otherwise provided, no person shall be permitted to acquire title to more than one-quarter section under the provisions of sections 161–164, 169, 171, 173, 175, 183, 184, 191, 201, 211, 239, 254, 255, 271, 272, 274, 277 and 278 of this title.

R.S. § 2298.

§ 212. Limitation of aggregate amount of entries

No person who shall enter upon any of the public lands with a view to occupation, entry, or settlement under any of the land laws shall be permitted to acquire title to more than three hundred and twenty acres in the aggregate, except as otherwise provided, under all of said laws, but this limitation shall not operate to curtail the right of any person who has before August 30, 1890, made entry or settlement on the public lands, or whose occupation, entry, or settlement is validated by Act of August 30, 1890 (chapter 837, 26 Statutes 391).

The above provisions of this section shall be construed to include in the maximum amount of lands the title to which is permitted to be acquired by one person only agricultural lands and not to include lands entered or sought to be entered under mineral land laws.

Aug. 30, 1890, c. 837, § 1, 26 Stat. 391; Mar. 3, 1891, c. 561, § 17, 26 Stat. 1101.

FINAL PROOF GENERALLY

§ 251. Notice of intention to make final proof

Before final proof shall be submitted by any person claiming to enter agricultural lands under the laws providing for pre-emption or homestead entries, such person shall file with the officer designated by the Secretary of the Interior of the proper land office a notice of his or her intention to make such proof, stating therein the description of lands to be entered, and the names of the witnesses by whom the necessary facts will be established. Upon the filing of such notice, the officer shall publish a notice, that such application has been made once a week for the period of thirty days, in a newspaper to be by him designated as published nearest to such land, and he shall also post such notice in some conspicuous place in his office for the same period. Such notice shall contain the names of the witnesses as stated in the application. At the expiration of said period of thirty days, the claimant shall be entitled to make proof in the manner provided by law. The Secretary of the Interior shall make all necessary rules for giving effect to the foregoing provisions.

Mar. 3, 1879, c. 192, 20 Stat. 472; 1946 Reorg. Plan No. 3, § 403, eff. July 16, 1946, 11 F.R. 7876, 60 Stat. 1100.

* * *

§ 254. Officers before whom affidavits or proofs may be made; perjury; fees

* * *

The fees for entries and for final proofs when made before any other officer than the Secretary of the Interior shall be as follows:

For each affidavit, 25 cents.

For each deposition of claimant or witness, when not prepared by the officer, 25 cents.

For each deposition of claimant or witness prepared by the officer, $1.

Any officer demanding or receiving a greater sum for such service shall be guilty of misdemeanor and upon conviction shall be punished for each offense by a fine not exceeding $100.

R.S. § 2294; May 26, 1890, c. 355, 26 Stat. 121; Mar. 3, 1893, c. 208, 27 Stat. 593; Mar. 11, 1902, c. 182, 32 Stat. 63; Mar. 4, 1904, c. 394, 33 Stat. 59; Oct. 28, 1921, c. 114, § 1, 42 Stat. 208; Feb. 23, 1923, c. 105, 42 Stat. 1281; Mar. 3, 1925, c. 462, 43 Stat. 1145; 1946 Reorg. Plan No. 3, § 403, eff. July 16, 1946, 11 F.R. 7876, 60 Stat. 1100.

REVISED STATUTE 2477 OF 1866

(Repealed 1976)

The right of way for the construction of highways over public lands, not reserved for public uses, is hereby granted.

R.S. § 2477; July 26, 1866, c. 262, § 8, 14 Stat. 251, 253.

YELLOWSTONE PARK ACT OF 1872

(17 Stat. 32)

(Currently Codified at 30 U.S.C.A. §§ 21, 22)

An Act to set apart a certain Tract of Land lying near the Head-waters of the Yellowstone River as a public Park

Be it enacted by the Senate and House of Representatives of the United States of America in Congress assembled, That the tract of land in the Territories of Montana and Wyoming, lying near the head-waters of the Yellowstone river, and described as follows, to wit, commencing at the junction of Gardiner's river with the Yellowstone river, and running east to the meridian passing ten miles to the eastward of the most eastern point of Yellowstone lake; thence south along said meridian to the parallel of latitude passing ten miles south of the most southern point of Yellowstone lake; thence west along said parallel to the meridian passing fifteen miles west of the most western point of Madison lake; thence north along said meridian to the latitude of the junction of the Yellowstone and Gardiner's rivers; thence east to the place of beginning, is hereby reserved and withdrawn from settlement, occupancy, or sale under the laws of the United States, and dedicated and set apart as a public park or pleasuring-ground for the benefit and enjoyment of the people; and all persons who shall locate or settle upon or occupy the same, or any part thereof, except as hereinafter provided, shall be considered trespassers and removed there-from.

Sec. 2. That said public park shall be under the exclusive control of the Secretary of the Interior, whose duty it shall be, as soon as practicable, to make and publish such rules and regulations as he may deem necessary or proper for the care and management of the same. Such regulations shall provide for the preservation, from injury or spoliation, of all timber, mineral deposits, natural curiosities, or wonders within said park, and their retention in their natural condition. The secretary may in his discretion, grant leases for building purposes for terms not exceeding ten years, of small parcels of ground, at such places in said park as shall require the erection of buildings for the accommodation of visitors; all of the proceeds of said leases, and all other revenues that may be derived from any source connected with said park, to be expended under his direction in the management of the same, and the construction of roads and bridle-paths therein. He shall provide against the wanton destruction of the fish and game found within said park, and against their capture or destruction for the purposes of merchandise or profit. He shall also cause all persons trespassing upon the same after the passage of this act to be removed therefrom, and generally shall be authorized to take all such measures as shall be necessary or proper to fully carry out the objects and purposes of this act.

Approved, March 1, 1872.

FOREST RESERVATION ACT OF 1891

(16 U.S.C.A. § 471)

(Repealed 1976)

Section 24 of the Act of March 3, 1891, 26 Stat. 1103, formerly codified at 16 U.S.C.A. 471, repealed by Pub.L. 94–579, 90 Stat. 2791 (1976).

Sec. 24. That the President of the United States may, from time to time, set apart and reserve, in any State or Territory having public land bearing forests, in any part of the public lands wholly or in part covered with timber or undergrowth, whether of commercial value or not, as public reservations, and the President shall, by public proclamation, declare the establishment of such reservations and the limits thereof.

FOREST SERVICE ORGANIC ACT OF 1897
(Timber Sale Provisions Only)

(16 U.S.C.A. § 476)

(Repealed 1976)

§ 476.   Sale of timber

For the purpose of preserving the living and growing timber and promoting the younger growth on national forests, the Secretary of Agriculture, under such rules and regulations as he shall prescribe, may cause to be designated and appraised so much of the dead, matured, or large growth of trees found upon such national forests as may be compatible with the utilization of the forests thereon, and may sell the same for not less than the appraised value in such quantities to each purchaser as he shall prescribe, to be used in the State or Territory in which such timber reservation may be situated, respectively, but not for export therefrom. Before such sale shall take place notice thereof shall be given by the said Secretary of Agriculture for not less than thirty days, by publication in one or more newspapers of general circulation, as he may deem necessary, in the State or Territory where such reservation exists. In cases of unusual emergency the Secretary of Agriculture may, in the exercise of his discretion, permit the purchase of timber and cord wood in advance of advertisement of sale at rates of value approved by him and subject to payment of the full amount of the highest bid resulting from the usual advertisement of sale. He may, in his discretion, sell without advertisement, in quantities to suit applicants, at a fair appraisement, timber and cord wood and other forest products not exceeding $2,000 in appraised value. In cases in which advertisement is had and no satisfactory bid is received, or in cases in which the bidder fails to complete the purchase, the timber may be sold, without further advertisement, at private sale, in the discretion of the Secretary of Agriculture, at not less than the appraised valuation, in quantities to suit purchasers. Payments for such timber to be made to the receiver of the local land office of the district wherein said timber may be sold, under such rules and regulations as the Secretary of Agriculture may prescribe; and the moneys arising therefrom shall be accounted for by the receiver of such land office to the Secretary of Agriculture, in a separate account, and shall be covered into the Treasury. Such timber, before being sold, shall be marked and designated, and shall be cut and removed under the supervision of some person appointed for that purpose by the Secretary of Agriculture not interested in the purchase or removal of such timber nor in the employment of the purchaser thereof. Such supervisor shall make report in writing to the Secretary of Agriculture and to the receiver in the land office in which such reservation shall be located of his doings in the premises.

June 4, 1897, c. 2, § 1, 30 Stat. 35; June 6, 1900, c. 804, 31 Stat. 661; Feb. 1, 1905, c. 288, § 1, 33 Stat. 628; June 30, 1906, c. 3913, 34 Stat. 684; Mar. 3, 1925, c. 457, § 3, 43 Stat. 1132; May 27, 1952, c. 337, 66 Stat. 95.

PICKETT ACT OF 1910

(43 U.S.C.A. §§ 141–42)

(Repealed 1976)

§ 141. Withdrawal and reservation of lands for water-power sites or other purposes

The President may, at any time in his discretion, temporarily withdraw from settlement, location, sale, or entry any of the public lands of the United States, including Alaska, and reserve the same for water-power sites, irrigation, classification of lands, or other public purposes to be specified in the orders of withdrawals, and such withdrawals or reservations shall remain in force until revoked by him or by an Act of Congress.

June 25, 1910, c. 421, § 1, 36 Stat. 847.

§ 142. Rights of occupants or claimants of oil or gas bearing lands; exceptions to withdrawals

All lands withdrawn under the provisions of this section and section 141 of this title shall at all times be open to exploration, discovery, occupation, and purchase under the mining laws of the United States, so far as the same apply to metalliferous minerals: *Provided,* That the rights of any person who, at the date of any order of withdrawal, is a bona fide occupant or claimant of oil-or gas-bearing lands and who, at such date, is in the diligent prosecution of work leading to the discovery of oil or gas, shall not be affected or impaired by such order so long as such occupant or claimant shall continue in diligent prosecution of said work * * *.

[Ed.: Other provisions of § 142 were not repealed in 1976.]

STOCK–RAISING HOMESTEAD ACT OF 1916

(43 U.S.C.A. §§ 291–302)

(Repealed 1976, Except § 299)

STOCK–RAISING HOMESTEAD

§ 291. Entry on unappropriated, unreserved lands; authorization; area; naval petroleum reserves and naval oil state reserves excepted

From and after December 29, 1916, it shall be lawful for any person qualified to make entry under the homestead laws of the United States to make a stock-raising homestead entry for not exceeding six hundred and forty acres of unappropriated, unreserved public lands in reasonably compact form: *Provided, however,* That the land so entered shall thereto-fore have been designated by the Secretary of the Interior as "stock-raising lands": *Provided further,* That for the purposes of this section lands withdrawn or reserved solely as valuable for oil or gas shall not be deemed to be appropriated or reserved: *Provided further,* That the provisions of this section shall not apply to naval petroleum reserves and naval oil-shale reserves: *And provided further,* That should said lands be within the limits of the geological structure of a producing oil or gas field entry can only be allowed, in the discretion of the Secretary of the Interior, in the absence of objection after due notice by the lessee or permittee, and any patent therefor shall contain a reservation to the United States of all minerals in said lands and the right to prospect for, mine, and remove the same.

Dec. 29, 1916, c. 9, § 1, 39 Stat. 862; Feb. 28, 1931, c. 328, 46 Stat. 1454; June 9, 1933, c. 53, 48 Stat. 119.

§ 292. Designation of lands subject to entry; applications

The Secretary of the Interior is authorized, on application or otherwise, to designate as stock-raising lands subject to entry under sections 291–301 of this title lands the surface of which is, in his opinion, chiefly valuable for grazing and raising forage crops, do not contain merchantable timber, are not susceptible of irrigation from any known source of water supply, and are of such character that six hundred and forty acres are reasonably required for the support of a family * * *.

Dec. 29, 1916, c. 9, § 2, 39 Stat. 862; Oct. 28, 1921, c. 114, § 1, 42 Stat. 208; June 6, 1924, c. 274, 43 Stat. 469; Mar. 3, 1925, c. 462, 43 Stat. 1145; 1946 Reorg. Plan No. 3, § 403, eff. July 16, 1946, 11 F.R. 7876, 60 Stat. 1100.

§ 293. Persons entitled to make entry; effect of entries

Any qualified homestead entryman may make entry under the homestead laws of lands so designated by the Secretary of the Interior, according to legal subdivisions, in areas not exceeding six hundred and forty acres,

515

and in compact form so far as may be subject to the provisions of sections 291–301 of this title, and secure title thereto by compliance with the terms of the homestead laws: *Provided,* That a former homestead entry of land of the character described in section 292 of this title shall not be a bar to the entry of a tract within a radius of twenty miles from such former entry under the provisions of sections 291–301 of this title, which, together with the former entry, shall not exceed six hundred and forty acres, subject to the requirements of law as to residence and improvements, except that no residence shall be required on such additional entry if the entryman owns and is residing on his former entry: *Provided further,* That the entryman shall be required to enter all contiguous areas of the character described in sections 291–301 of this title open to entry prior to the entry of any noncontiguous land: *And provided further,* That instead of cultivation as required by the homestead laws the entryman shall be required to make permanent improvements upon the land entered before final proof is submitted tending to increase the value of the same for stock-raising purposes of the value of not less than $1.25 per acre, and at least one-half of such improvements shall be placed upon the land within three years after the date of entry thereof.

Dec. 29, 1916, c. 9, § 3, 39 Stat. 863; Oct. 25, 1918, c. 195, 40 Stat. 1016.

§ 294.   Additional entries; amount

Any homestead entryman of lands of the character described in sections 291–301 of this title, who has not submitted final proof upon his existing entry shall have the right to enter, subject to the provisions of said sections such amount of lands designated for entry under the provisions of said sections within a radius of twenty miles from said existing entry, as shall not, together with the amount embraced in his original entry, exceed six hundred and forty acres, and residence upon the original entry shall be credited on both entries, but improvements must be made on the additional entry equal to $1.25 for each acre thereof: *Provided,* That the entryman shall be required to enter all contiguous areas of the character described in said sections open to entry prior to the entry of any noncontiguous land.

Dec. 29, 1916, c. 9, § 4, 39 Stat. 863; Sept. 29, 1919, c. 63, 41 Stat. 287.

* * *

§ 297.   Commutation

The commutation provisions of the homestead laws shall not apply to any entries made under sections 291–301 of this title.

Dec. 29, 1916, c. 9, § 7, 39 Stat. 864.

* * *

§ 299.   Reservation of coal and mineral rights

All entries made and patents issued under the provisions of sections 291–301 of this title shall be subject to and contain a reservation to the United States of all the coal and other minerals in the lands so entered and patented, together with the right to prospect for, mine, and remove the same. The coal and other mineral deposits in such lands shall be subject to